International Review of
RESEARCH IN
MENTAL RETARDATION

Handbook of Assessment
in Persons with
Intellectual Disability

VOLUME 34

International Review of
RESEARCH IN MENTAL RETARDATION

EDITED BY

LARAINE MASTERS GLIDDEN

DEPARTMENT OF PSYCHOLOGY
ST. MARY'S COLLEGE OF MARYLAND
ST. MARY'S CITY, MARYLAND

Handbook of Assessment in Persons with Intellectual Disability

A Volume in

International Review of
RESEARCH IN MENTAL RETARDATION

VOLUME 34

EDITED BY

Johnny L. Matson

LOUISIANA STATE UNIVERSITY
DEPARTMENT OF PSYCHOLOGY
BATON ROUGE, LOUISIANA

ELSEVIER

AMSTERDAM • BOSTON • HEIDELBERG • LONDON
NEW YORK • OXFORD • PARIS • SAN DIEGO
SAN FRANCISCO • SINGAPORE • SYDNEY • TOKYO
Academic Press is an imprint of Elsevier

Academic Press is an imprint of Elsevier
84 Theobald's Road, London WC1X 8RR, UK
Radarweg 29, PO Box 211, 1000 AE Amsterdam, The Netherlands
Linacre House, Jordan Hill, Oxford OX2 8DP, UK
30 Corporate Drive, Suite 400, Burlington, MA 01803, USA
525 B Street, Suite 1900, San Diego, CA 92101-4495, USA

First edition 2007

ISBN: 978-0-12-366235-4
ISSN: 0074-7750

For information on all Academic Press publications
visit our website at books.elsevier.com

Pinted and bound in USA
07 08 09 10 11 10 9 8 7 6 5 4 3 2 1

Contents

Adaptive Behavior Scales

Dennis R. Dixon

Educational Assessment

Mark F. O'Reilly, Bonnie O'Reilly, Jeff Sigafoos, Giulio Lancioni, Vanessa Green, and Wendy Machalicek

Autism and Pervasive Developmental Disorders

Bart M. Sevin, Cheryl L. Knight, and Scott A. Braud

Psychopathology: Depression, Anxiety, and Related Disorders

Peter Sturmey

Psychotropic Medication Effect and Side Effects

Erik A. Mayville

Memory Disorders

Heather Anne Stewart and Holly Garcie-Merritt

Assessment of Self-Injurious and Aggressive Behavior

Johannes Rojahn, Theodore A. Hoch, Katie Whittaker, and Melissa L. González

Social Skills

Jonathan Wilkins and Johnny L. Matson

Self-Care Skills

Rebecca L. Mandal, Brandi Smiroldo, and Joann Haynes-Powell

Feeding Disorders

David E. Kuhn, Peter A. Girolami, and Charles S. Gulotta

Pain Assessment

Frank Andrasik and Carla Rime

Contributors

Numbers in parentheses indicate the pages on which the authors' contributions begin.

Frank Andrasik (415), *Department of Psychology, University of West Florida, Pensacola, Florida*

Rowland P. Barrett (27), *Emma Pendleton Bradley Hospital, Department of Psychiatry and Human Behavior, The Warren Alpert Medical School of Brown University, Providence, Rhode Island*

Jacqueline Beckett (27), *Emma Pendleton Bradley Hospital, Department of Psychiatry and Human Behavior, The Warren Alpert Medical School of Brown University, Providence, Rhode Island*

Scott A. Braud (163), *University Center for Excellence in Autism, Human Development Center, Louisiana State University Health Sciences Center, New Orleans, Louisiana*

Dennis R. Dixon (99), *Department of Behavioral Psychology, Kennedy Krieger Institute, Johns Hopkins University School of Medicine, Baltimore, Maryland*

Holly Garcie-Merritt (253), *Department of Psychology, Louisiana State University, Baton Rouge, Louisiana*

Peter A. Girolami (387), *Department of Behavioral Psychology, Kennedy Krieger Institute, Johns Hopkins Medical School, Baltimore, Maryland*

Melissa L. González (281), *Department of Psychology, Louisiana State University, Louisiana*

Vanessa Green (141), *Department of Education, University of Tasmania, Hobart, Tasmania, Australia*

Charles S. Gulotta (387), *Department of Behavioral Psychology, Kennedy Krieger Institute, Johns Hopkins Medical School, Baltimore, Maryland*

Joann Haynes-Powell (365), *Hammond Developmental Center, Hammond, Lousiana*

Theodore A. Hoch (281), *Northern Virginia Training Center and George Mason University, Virginia*

Cheryl L. Knight (163), *University Center for Excellence in Autism, Human Development Center, Louisiana State University Health Sciences Center, New Orleans, Louisiana*

David E. Kuhn (387), *Department of Behavioral Psychology, Kennedy Krieger Institute, Johns Hopkins Medical School, Baltimore, Maryland*

Giulio Lancioni (141), *Department of Psychology, University of Bari, Bari, Italy*

Wendy Machalicek (141), *Department of Special Education, The University of Texas at Austin, Austin, Texas*

Rebecca L. Mandal (365), *Resource Center for Psychiatric and Behavioral Supports, Hammond, Louisiana*

Johnny L. Matson (321), *Department of Psychology, Louisiana State University, Baton Rouge, Louisiana*

R. Matthew Reese (1), *Developmental Disabilities Center, The University of Kansas Medical Center, Kansas City, Kansas*

Erik A. Mayville (227), *Institute for Educational Planning, Connecticut Center for Child Development, Milford, Connecticut*

Bonnie O'Reilly (141), *Gullett Elementary School, Austin Independent School District, Austin, Texas*

Mark F. O'Reilly (141), *Department of Special Education, The University of Texas at Austin, Austin, Texas*

Carla Rime (415), *Department of Psychology, University of West Florida, Pensacola, Florida*

Johannes Rojahn (281), *Center for Behavioral and Cognitive Development, Department of Psychology, George Mason University, Virginia*

Stephen R. Schroeder (1), *Schiefelbusch Institute for Life Span Studies, The University of Kansas, Lawrence, Kansas*

Bart M. Sevin (163), *University Center for Excellence in Autism, Human Development Center, Louisiana State University Health Sciences Center, New Orleans, Louisiana*

Jeff Sigafoos (141), *Department of Education, University of Tasmania, Hobart, Tasmania, Australia*

Brandi Smiroldo (365), *Hammond Developmental Center, Hammond, Louisiana*

Heather Anne Stewart (253), *Department of Psychology, Louisiana State University, Baton Rouge, Louisiana*

Peter Sturmey (197), *Department of Psychology, Queens College and the Graduate Center, City University of New York, New York*

Barbara Tylenda (27), *Emma Pendleton Bradley Hospital, Department of Psychiatry and Human Behavior, The Warren Alpert Medical School of Brown University, Providence, Rhode Island*

Katie Whittaker (281), *Center for Behavioral and Cognitive Development, Department of Psychology, George Mason University, Virginia*

Jonathan Wilkins (321), *Department of Psychology, Louisiana State University, Baton Rouge, Louisiana*

Foreword

This volume, *Handbook of Assessment in Persons with Intellectual Disability*, guest edited by Johnny L. Matson, is the seventh special theme volume of the *International Review of Research in Mental Retardation* series since 2000, the year of publication of the first theme volume on *Autism*. This attention to assessment is extremely timely as a result of recent developments in the field of intellectual and other developmental disabilities. In one instance, changes in the definition of mental retardation (Luckasson et al., 1992, 2002) have led to a reexamination of assessment instruments and methods. Indeed, in two editions of a foundational volume, *What is Mental Retardation*? edited by Harvey Switzky and Stephen Greenspan (2003, 2007), scientists and clinicians have questioned and responded to basic issues regarding the essence of mental retardation.

In another instance, public policy with regard to life and death decisions has made definition and assessment a central and controversial topic. Debates about whether individuals with mental retardation who have been convicted of homicide in the first degree should be subject to the death penalty are being heard in courtrooms across the country. Frequently, these debates center on issues of assessment—reliability, validity, changes as a result of developmental level, and assessment challenges posed by individuals with disabilities of various sorts.

Thus, this volume is important both from a scientific and a practical perspective. Its editor, known internationally for his work on assessment, behavior modification, and dual diagnosis, has assembled an impressive array of contributors who have addressed assessment methods and outcomes across an exceedingly broad spectrum of persons with intellectual and other developmental disabilities. This volume will be invaluable for scientists who rely on accurate assessment to explore a variety of hypotheses. It will be essential, also, for clinicians who must perform accurate assessment in order to recommend and/or provide services to individuals with intellectual and other developmental disabilities. I am pleased that it is being published as a volume in the *International Review*, and I take this opportunity to thank Dr. Matson and the other contributors who have done a substantial service to the field.

LARAINE MASTERS GLIDDEN
SERIES EDITOR

REFERENCES

Luckasson, R., Coulter, D. L., Polloway, E. A., Reiss, S., Schalock, R. L., Snell, M. E., et al. (1992). *Mental retardation: Definition, classification and systems of supports* (9th ed.). Washington, DC: American Association on Mental Retardation.

Luckasson, R., Schalock, R. L., Spitalnik, D. M., Spreat, S., Tassé, M., Snell, M. E., et al. (2002). *Mental retardation: Definition, classification and systems of supports* (10th ed.). Washington, DC: American Association on Mental Retardation: [E-book]. Available at http://www.disabilitybooksonline.com.

Switzky, H. N., and Greenspan, S. (Eds.) (2003). *What is mental retardation? Ideas for an evolving disability.* Washington, DC: American Association on Mental Retardation.

Switzky, H. N., and Greenspan, S. (Eds.) (2006). *What is mental retardation? Ideas for an evolving disability in the 21st century* (revised and updated edition). Washington, DC: American Association on Mental Retardation.

Preface

The field of intellectual disability (ID) has seen tremendous growth in the last two decades. Since the publication of the first iteration of this volume in 1983 [Matson, J. L. & Breuning, S. (1983). Assessing the Mentally Retarded. New York: Grune and Stratton], the preferred term used to describe persons with this developmental disability has changed from mental retardation to ID. Furthermore, the number of journals devoted to the publication of research on the topic has increased dramatically. Some of these are *Mental Health Aspects of Developmental Disability*, *Journal of Intellectual Disabilities*, *Journal of Developmental and Physical Disabilities*, *The Italian Addition*, *American Journal on Mental Retardation*, *Journal of Mental Health Research in Intellectual Disabilities*, *Journal of Applied Research in Intellectual Disabilities*, as well as related journals on developmental disability, which have a major overlap with ID such as *Research in Autism Spectrum Disorders*, *Autism*, and *Focus on Autism*. A similar explosion in information has not before been seen in the history of the helping professions with respect to etiology, assessment, and treatment of ID.

Assessment research has developed dramatically, both in the number of methods available and in the refinement of existing scales. In the last two decades, every adaptive scale and IQ test has been revised and renormed. Assessment of mental health and challenging behaviors in persons with ID is being conducted with an increasing array of measuring instruments and methodologies. There is certainly much to discuss and evaluate. Having said this, considerable misinformation is available, as well as substantial "holes" in the literature. Researchers, even when publishing in scholarly journals, are sometimes unaware of sizeable amounts of the existing literature. The rapid growth of the field makes this both understandable and to some degree unavoidable.

The purpose of the present volume is to help bridge this developing information gap by providing an overview of selected topics in the assessment of persons with ID. Some of these have become staples of the field such as self-care skills and psychopathology, while others are important topics which have only recently begun to be addressed such as the identification of pain. This latter issue is crucial, and is becoming even more important as many more people with severe ID and very serious, and painful, medical conditions are able to live longer lives.

The purpose then of the present volume is to provide a scholarly overview of some of the major developments in the assessment of persons with ID. Its value is enriched immeasurably by the noted scholars who have graciously agreed to contribute chapters to this volume. Professionals in university or clinical settings and graduate students in training should be particularly interested in this volume. It again has been my pleasure to work with Elsevier and with many of the contributors who have been friends and teachers to me over the years. I hope the reader finds as much pleasure in reading the volume as it provided me in its preparation.

Johnny L. Matson

Historical Overview of Assessment in Intellectual Disability

STEPHEN R. SCHROEDER

SCHIEFELBUSCH INSTITUTE FOR LIFE SPAN STUDIES, THE UNIVERSITY OF KANSAS, LAWRENCE, KANSAS

R. MATTHEW REESE

DEVELOPMENTAL DISABILITIES CENTER, THE UNIVERSITY OF KANSAS MEDICAL CENTER, KANSAS CITY, KANSAS

I. INTRODUCTION

The history of the assessment of people with intellectual disabilities (ID) is like the unfolding of an evolutionary tree. It goes back to the roots of modern day research and practice as well as to the roots of many social policies. In some cases, it has been a life-and-death matter, as in the Supreme Court case of Atkins v. Virginia (2002), which ruled against capital punishment for people with ID. This controversial case continues, however (Perske, 2006). The development of IQ tests grew out of the need in the early 1900s to differentiate people with ID, in order to predict school success better. Out of this work emerged a new definition of intelligence, the idea of general intelligence ("g") as well as the concept of intelligence consisting of several primary abilities.

IQ tests were also misused to set immigration quotas for different nationalities, to justify the eugenics movement, and to promote sterilization. Out of these abuses grew the need in the 1930s and 1940s to assess adaptive behavior skills, in order to broaden the concept of intelligence of people with ID to reflect its social aspects more accurately.

As the awakening of the community and personal empowerment movements emerged in the 1950s, the need to assess personality characteristics, psychopathology, and behavior problems, which were impeding social independence and community integration, became more important to assess carefully.

INTERNATIONAL REVIEW OF RESEARCH IN MENTAL RETARDATION, Vol. 34
0074-7750/07 $35.00

DOI: 10.1016/S0074-7750(07)34001-9

The Manual of Terminology and Classification in Mental Retardation was developed by the American Association on Mental Deficiency (Heber, 1959) to standardize the criteria for inclusion and to promote research on the topic. It has been revised, updated, and renamed 10 times, and the association is undergoing another name change from mental retardation to intellectual disability, to reflect the themes of the times. The current definition of ID (Luckasson et al., 1992) was more an advocacy-based than a research-based definition assessing 10 areas of life-functioning supports needed in addition to IQ. It was used mostly to classify the population for purposes of entitlement (MacMillan, Gresham, & Siperstein, 1993) rather than as a prescription for programming. The 2002 revision (Luckasson et al., 2002) reduced the areas of life-functioning supports needed from 10 to 5, and a new "supports intensity scale" has been developed (Thompson et al., 2004) to assess them.

As federal entitlements to services for people with ID grew, so the need for standardized measures on work performance, social skills, language development, quality of life (QOL), family adaptation, psychopathology, and efficacy of psychopharmacology developed in the latter half of the twentieth century. At first, these measures were an extension of instruments standardized on the nondisabled population; but, as the research accumulated, it became clear that tests standardized on specialized subpopulations with ID were the most valid and reliable.

Another movement which greatly affected assessment of people with ID during this period was the advancement of the field of applied behavior analysis (ABA) in the 1960s. As an alternative to psychometric norm-referenced tests, ABA assessment relied totally on *in vivo* functional assessment in the context of the target environment, identifying stimuli and consequences that influenced behaviors, and modifying them directly (Baer, Wolf, & Risley, 1968). Single-subject designs were espoused rather than group designs. Functional assessments were later standardized more by Iwata, Dorsey, Slifer, Bauman, and Richman (1982) by collecting data in a standard analogue setting, using standard stimuli and reinforcement contingencies, to analyze and predict what would work in the *in vivo* situation. This technique called functional analysis (FA) and its variants have become very popular in the last 24 years in the United States, especially for addressing behavior problems of people with ID.

Matson in his handbook *Assessing the Mentally Retarded* (Matson & Bruening, 1983) was one of the first to address the assessment of ID formally as a field in itself. As the current volume shows, this field has grown tremendously in the last 23 years into a more mature discipline with a wide variety of specialized assessment instruments available for research and practice which have superceded their earlier progenitors. There really is no excuse to use these older instruments any more, although we still see some of them in the literature, especially used by researchers outside the field. This current overview chronicles the evolution of the movement for assessing people with ID.

II. ASSESSMENT OF ID, INTELLIGENCE, AND SCHOOL PERFORMANCE

Depictions of mental retardation can be found in early civilizations 4500 years ago (Berkson, 2004). Rosen, Clark, and Kivitz (1976) give one of the best general recent histories of ID from the Greeks up to the 1970s. Early concepts of people with ID varied from subjects of scorn to pity, and then to viewing them as fools in the middle ages. Luther and Calvin denounced them as "filled with Satan." Some of these attitudes still persist today. In some third-world countries people with ID are still seen as a punishment from God, and they are kept in seclusion.

Assessment of people with ID did not become an issue until the nineteenth century when humanitarian institutions and training programs began springing up. From descriptions of the living conditions of these places in Massachusetts by Dix (1843), it is apparent that little distinction was made between the mentally ill, criminals, the poor, and people with ID. All needed to be segregated from society. Being labeled as "mentally deficient" was no small matter to an individual.

The first systematic descriptions of people with ID as a separate population in need of training were by Itard in 1838 and Seguin in 1842 (Rosen et al., 1976). Training schools followed quickly in Europe and in the United States. When Seguin moved to the United States, these institutions quickly sprang up in Massachusetts, Ohio, Connecticut, Pennsylvania, Kentucky, New York, Iowa, Minnesota, Indiana, California, Michigan, and Nebraska by the 1880s. Like Itard and Seguin, physicians ran all of these facilities. They were not trained in psychological or behavioral assessment methodology. They simply guessed at their residents' retardation levels. As might be expected, there was very little reliability among their assessments. According to Wolfensberger (1969), their first efforts were "to make the deviant undeviant" (1850–1880), followed by "sheltering the deviant from society" (1870–1890), and then "protection of society from the deviant" (1880–1900).

The above circumstances led to Binet's work on a standardized measure of "inferior states of intelligence" for diagnostic purposes (Binet & Simon, 1905). In 1904, the French Minister of Public Instruction charged a commission to study the measures to be taken to ensure the "benefits of instruction to defective children." Binet wrote a scathing review of existing classification systems and then published his own test in 1906, to differentiate normal from "feebleminded" children age 3–12 years. It was not designed to predict future intellectual development, as his successors used it. Binet and Simon introduced the concept of "mental age" in their 1908 revision. Goddard translated this scale into English in 1910. Terman's (1916) revision became the Stanford–Binet scale, using the IQ as an intelligence quotient still in use today.

Goddard (1913) published an influential paper on the results of giving the Binet scales to the residents of his institution (Vineland Training School), all of whom scored low on the test. This led to pessimism among all of the medically oriented institutions and led to a more custodial treatment approach, that is the self-contained colony or total institution. Negative attitudes toward people with ID soon began to reappear and a dark age for people with ID again emerged.

IQ tests were given widely, not just in schools, but for a variety of reasons. The Army General Classification Test was a group IQ test adapted from the Stanford–Binet scales in 1917 when the United States entered near the end of the World War I, to classify army recruits for different jobs and to exclude people who were unfit for military service.

Inspired by nineteenth century hereditarians like Francis Galton, father of the eugenics movement, several of its proponents like Terman, Goddard, and Yerkes (who was then a colonel in the Army) proposed use of IQ tests to set immigration quotas for different races, as an argument for sterilization, and as justification for other discriminatory practices of the existing social order (Kamin, 1974). An example of their rhetoric follows from Terman (1916, 1917): "Children in this group should be segregated in special classes.... They cannot master abstractions, but they can often be made efficient workers.... There is no possibility at present of convincing society that they should be allowed to reproduce... They constitute a grave problem because of their unusually prolific breeding. If we would preserve our state for a class of people worthy to possess it, we must prevent, as far as possible, the propagation of mental degenerates... the increasing spawn of degeneracy."

Thus began the debate over heritability of intelligence, which rages to this day (see Eysenck & Kamin, 1981 for an excellent summary of the arguments). On one side were Terman, Eysenck, Jensen (Jensen, 1969), and others who believed that 80% of intelligence was inherited; on the other were Kamin and others who disputed the data, some of which was fabricated (e.g., Cyril Burt's twin studies). Their view was that environment, for example caregiving environment, socioeconomic status, and occupation of the parents also played a large role in determining IQ. This debate gave rise to the development of the culture-free test movement and to several court cases concerning the use of IQ tests in school placement (Larry P. v. Riles, 1972).

There were bright spots, however (PCMR, 1977). Goddard's successor at Vineland, Stanley Porteus, developed the Porteus Maze Test, which is often considered a culture-free intelligence test. Porteus' successor, Edgar Doll (1934), began development of the *Vineland Scale of Social Maturity* (Doll, 1935), the first widely used standardized adaptive behavior scale for people with ID. *The Training School Bulletin* was a progressive journal of theory and practice in ID for many years. The field of special education had its beginnings in the 1930s. The National Association of Retarded Children, a strong parent advocacy group, also began in the 1940s, and today, renamed the ARC-US, it is the major advocacy organization for people with ID in the United States.

Although there were early textbooks, for example Tredgold (1937), research on the experimental psychology of "mental deficiency," as it was then called, began in earnest after the World War II in the 1940s (see Routh & Schroeder, 2003 for a review). The *American Journal on Mental Deficiency* had been in existence since 1895. Ellis published his *Handbook of Mental Deficiency: Theory and Research* in 1963 (Ellis, 1963). It was one of the first handbooks on ID devoted solely to reviews of research and theory, and it served as the main handbook for many years. It is now in its third edition. Since then, many other handbooks and annual series have been published on a wide variety of topics in ID.

Research on educational assessment also began to appear in the 1960s (PCMR, 1977). The federal funding for research in mental retardation received a huge boost in the 1960s during John F. Kennedy's presidency. The National Institute for Child Health and Human Development (NICHD) and the Bureau of Education for the Handicapped (BEH) were founded in 1963 and in 1968, respectively. Advocacy for special education received a great impetus from the Education of All Handicapped Act of 1975. This law (since 1997 called the Individuals with Disabilities Education Act or IDEA) guarantees every school-aged child a free and appropriate education in the least restrictive environment possible. For most children this means the public schools, which must be accessible and accommodative of their disabilities. Thus their right to education is extended to the school system. Any school receiving Federal and State funds must comply with these rules or face losing its Federal and State funding.

These and other federal agencies promoted basic and applied research on the fundamental processes underlying assessments of people with ID. Experimental scales and test batteries based solely on theoretical models of ability substructures, for example Clausen (1966), however, had limited success. Psychometrically standardized tests based on "g," for example Stanford–Binet test, or on primary abilities, for example Wechsler Intelligence Scales (Wechsler, 1955), and behavioral assessment technology, for example FA, have prevailed up to the present.

III. ASSESSMENT OF PERSONALITY AND PSYCHOPATHOLOGY IN ID

Research on people with ID in the 1950s and 1960s was almost exclusively on borderline and mild mental retardation. The IQ cutoff point was not lowered from 90 to 70 by the American Association on Mental Retardation (AAMR) manual until 1973 (Grossman, 1973). The focus was on basic learning, memory, motor, attention, and perceptual skills in an attempt to show that people with ID were basically different from people with normal IQs. Zigler (1969) proposed that this difference was mainly developmental for higher functioning people and not a fundamental difference, but one of motivation. Thus the developmental versus difference controversy (see Zigler & Balla, 1982 for a summary) was born, and it preoccupied much of the research of that period.

It was also noticed that the variability of responsiveness was greater in people with ID than in typically developing people. This was attributed to "outer-directedness," "rigidity" (Zigler, 1966) and lack of motivation (Baumeister & Kellas, 1968).

The interest in personality structure of people with ID came mostly from researchers at Yale University headed by Zigler and his colleagues, Sarason and Masland. Masland, Sarason, and Gladwin (1958) published one of the early textbooks on "mental subnormality," which took an interdisciplinary approach to biological, psychological, and cultural factors in ID. This type of research is still being carried on by their students. Psychotherapeutic approaches to psychopathology predominated in this school of thought (Sternlicht, 1966).

Behavioral approaches to psychopathology began with people with severe and profound ID. Bijou (1966) and colleagues at the University of Washington, Lovaas at UCLA and his students (Lovaas, Freitag, Gold, & Kassorla, 1965), Spradlin and colleagues at the University of Kansas (Girardeau & Spradlin, 1964), and Sidman and colleagues at the Shriver Center in Boston (Sidman & Stoddard, 1966), as well as other behaviorists across the United States began dealing with basic skills such as daily living skills, learning skills, and behavior problems like aggression and self-injurious behavior. Two important societies were formed in the late 1960s: the Association for Behavior Therapy (AABT) and the Association for Behavior Analysis. The former was broader and more eclectic, while the latter was strictly behavior analytic, focusing on single-subject assessment and intervention; but both were behavioral and opposed to the psychodynamic zeitgeist.

Epidemiological research on populations related to ID also gave this work a boost. An early study by Heber (1961) put the prevalence of mental retardation in the United States at 3%, a very significant number. A very well-conducted total population study of the Isle of Wight by Rutter, Tizard, and Whitmore (1970) confirmed these findings and also showed that mental illness occurred about five times as often among people with ID. Even though people with severe genetic and biological handicaps were excluded from this study, it received a great deal of attention from the research community, and it is still cited as the most definitive work on the topic today.

So the stage was set for investigating psychopathology among people with ID as a respectable field of inquiry, and it exploded in the 1970s and 1980s. Menolascino (1970) published a compendium on psychiatric approaches to mental retardation. He coined the term "dual diagnosis" to designate people who have both mental retardation and mental illness simultaneously. A small number of pioneering child psychiatrists made people with ID their primary population of professional interest.

Many other handbooks followed in the next two decades which were devoted to all aspects of psychopathology in ID. At first, attempts were made to use instruments that had been validated on the typically developing population, for example the Conners Teachers Questionnaire (Conners, 1969), but these often had limited validity for the more moderately and severely retarded population.

In the 1980s, a second generation of new instruments for specifically assessing psychopathology in people with ID were developed and validated. Screening instruments like the Reiss Screen (Reiss, 1988) and fuller scales like the psychopathology instrument for mentally retarded adults (Matson, 1988) and the Diagnostic Assessment of the Severely Handicapped (Matson, Gardner, Coe, & Sovner, 1991) were general multifactorial validated assessment instruments that are still used widely for the diagnosis of mental illness among people with ID. By 1990, Aman (1991) was able to review 45 such instruments that had at least some validation research supporting their use. They ranged from self-report scales to interviews, ratings, checklists, and behavior frequency measures. In the past 15 years many new general multifactorial assessment scales have developed which are covered in Chapters 5–9 of this volume.

With the increased interest in genetics and in behavioral phenotypes (Dykens, 1995; Dykens, Hodapp, & Finacune, 2000), a new third generation of assessment instruments has developed, in order to be sensitive and specific to the behavioral idiosyncrasies of different genetic disorders. Item-independent scales have been developed, in order to assess many overlapping symptoms and their possible relationships to gene-brain behavior relationships. A good example is the battery of tests for repetitive movement disorders, for example tics, dyskinesias, compulsions, stereotypies, and self-injury developed by Bodfish and colleagues (Bodfish & Lewis, 2002; Lewis & Bodfish, 1998) or the Behavior Problem Inventory developed by

Rojahn, Matson, Lott, Esbensen, and Smalls (2001). These instruments reflect the growth of specific interests in a variety of diverse psychiatric and behavioral problems in ID which are burgeoning in the field today. Indeed the *Journal of Intellectual Disability Research*, a leading international research journal published in England, now has an entire section devoted exclusively to mental health in ID.

IV. ASSESSMENT OF PSYCHOPHARMACOLOGY IN ID

In the 150-year history of research on the psychopharmacology in ID (see Schroeder et al., 1998 for a historical review), the discovery of the antipsychotic drugs in the 1950s caused a sea change in the field. These drugs, originally designed to treat schizophrenia and affective disorders, were used extensively on a trial-and-error basis with people with ID who had no formal diagnosis of mental illness. This practice led to their excessive use and abuse, as pointed out in a critical review by Sprague and Werry (1971). Their classic paper set the standards for acceptable research on the psychopharmacology of ID: (1) double-blind, (2) placebo-control, (3) multiple standardized doses, (4) reliable evaluation of dependent variables, (5) random assignment of participants, (6) appropriate statistical analysis. These standards, though rarely met due to limitations, the ID population to consent and to their high-risk nature, are still the gold standard.

Since 1971, the use of psychotropic medications has decreased over the years (Valdovinos, Schroeder, & Kim, 2003). Although they are still used extensively, there are now state regulations governing their use, monitoring, periodic review, drug holidays, reporting of adverse drug reactions, and so on. These critical reforms all came about only with the development of appropriate assessment instruments standardized on the ID population. We will summarize these trends briefly below. A fuller treatment is in Chapter 8.

As in other domains, early research studies on psychopharmacology in ID used psychiatric rating scales developed for the mentally ill, for example the Clinical Global Impressions Scale (Guy, 1976), and others which had questionable validity in the ID population. Some of them had no validation at all or they were insensitive to drug effects (Schroeder, Rojahn, & Reese, 1997). The National Institute of Mental Health (NIMH) held a series of workshops in 1983–1985 with researchers who were using these instruments, to discuss their use and to make recommendations. These 70 + scales were published in two issues (Vol. 21, Nos. 2, 4) of the *Psychopharmacology Bulletin* in 1985. The results led to use of more standard instruments and procedures. The most powerful drug-sensitive and widely used rating scale of aberrant behavior in ID is the Aberrant Behavior Checklist (Aman, Singh, Stewart, & Field, 1985). Aman's (1991) review commissioned by NIMH has already been mentioned.

Since the 1990s, more drug-sensitive instruments have been published, for example Lewis and Bodfish (1998), repetitive movement disorders test battery previously mentioned. Some interesting findings have emerged from studies using these instruments: (1) there has been inconsistent use of terminology for movement disorders across disciplines (Bodfish & Lewis, 2002); (2) while the rating scales might have good internal consistency, they often correlated poorly across different scales, and not at all with the direct behavioral observations (Schroeder et al., 1997); (3) the use of traditional side effects scales and measures of adverse drug effects were inadequate for the ID population, and new side effects scales, such as the DISCUS and MOSES, needed to be devised for this population (see Kalachnik, 1999 for an excellent review); (4) it was rarely the case that a person had only one psychiatric diagnosis. Multiple diagnoses were the rule rather than the exception in this population (Valdovinos et al., 2003). Together these results were the source of a great deal of variability in the data that needs to be addressed in the future by a multimodal approach to appropriate behavioral observation sampling procedures (Thompson, Felce, & Symons, 2000), more specific and sensitive psychometric scales (Bodfish & Lewis, 2002), and more precise diagnoses to justify a more targeted neurobiological rationale for using medication when it is necessary (Schroeder et al., 1998).

V. ASSESSMENT OF BEHAVIOR PROBLEMS AND SKILLS DEFICITS IN ID

As Baumeister, Todd, and Sevin (1993), Aman, Sarphare, and Burrow (1995), and Valdovinos et al. (2003) point out, the most frequently used psychotropic medications used for *behavior problems* among people with ID are the antipsychotics prescribed for behavior control of aggression, self-injury, and property destruction. This has been the case since the 1950s, even though these are not recognized psychiatric diagnoses in DSM IV (APA, 1994). The DSM has been slow to acknowledge over the years the prevalence and severity of some of the behavior problems that occur among people with ID. Traditionally these problems have been addressed by the behavioral research community. Matson (1986) called for a merging of these two systems of assessment, but it has not as yet happened.

The vast majority of research on assessment and intervention with behavior problems in ID is published in behavioral journals like the *Journal of Applied Behavior Analysis* (JABA), *Research in Developmental Disabilities*

(RIDD), and, to a lesser extent, in multidisciplinary journals such as *American Journal on Mental Retardation* (AJMR) and *Journal of Autism and Developmental Disorders* (JADD). Very little is published in primarily medical journals. The assessments used in these studies are primarily behavioral analyses, such as FA. This result is probably because they do not fit neatly into psychiatric classification schemes which were not designed for people with ID. Although some psychiatric scales are being developed which are applicable to the ID population, existing trends are not expected to change much in the future. The Aberrant Behavior Checklist (Aman et al., 1985) and more specialized scales, like the Behavior Problems Inventory (Rojahn et al., 2001), are likely to continue as the prevailing instruments used to assess behavior problems in ID.

Social skills assessments took on importance with the publication of the *Vineland Scales of Social Maturity* (Doll, 1965). Later the adaptive behavior scales (Nihira, Foster, Shellhaas, & Leland, 1975) became popular and became a formal part of the AAMR definition of mental retardation until the latest revised definition (Luckasson et al., 1992, 2002). Concerns with socially adaptive behaviors were becoming of increasing interest as people with mental retardation were leaving institutions for community living, but the above scales were not particularly helpful for prescriptive programming because they emphasized mostly negative behaviors and not their positive alternatives.

Since behaviorists were doing most of this type of social skills training, they naturally turned to a task analysis, functional assessment, and direct teaching of the behaviors. One of the first examples of such a program was the Mimosa Project at Parsons State Hospital and Training Center in Kansas (Girardeau & Spradlin, 1964) where, using tokens as rewards, they taught severely retarded adolescent girls self-care skills, as well as proper social graces, for example sitting, eye contact, voice modulation, fashionable dressing, ironing, shopping in the community, and other social skills. Birnbrauer and Lawler (1964) reported on a similar program in an educational setting with severely and profoundly retarded children.

Ayllon and Michael (1959) were among the first to propose the systematic application of behavioral principles toward management using a token economy. Ayllon and Azrin (1968) published a comprehensive analysis of the token economy system. This very heuristic book was an immediate success, and many replications occurred in institutions across the United States. Indeed we were working at an institution at the time in which we ran nine different token economies involving over 600 residents, adapted to their different levels of functioning. It had its own store, its own federal reserve system, to adjust the value of the token, and so on. It became so successful that the state learned about it, felt it was a true economic system, audited it, and shut it down because they could not account for it in their accounting system. Other token systems were also shut down elsewhere, especially in prison systems, by the federal government at the urging of Senator Sam Ervin, then Chair of the Senate Judiciary Committee, of Watergate fame, because they were considered to restrict residents' constitutional right to consent to rehabilitation.

Nevertheless, other research on social skills training continued apace. It was found that a wide range of social skills could be taught, for example conversational skills, assertiveness skills, employment-related social skills, dating skills, and social problem solving skills. In almost all of these cases, the assessments were behavioral demonstration of the competency rather than a psychometric test. Since most of the programs were nested in a "treatment package," controversies developed over which parts of the package were the essential ingredients. This was difficult research to do because it was labor-intensive and often it required a large number of subjects. Since the ID population is very heterogeneous, this was often impossible. Other problems were lack of generalization and maintenance across settings and difficulty with people with more severe and profound ID. Most packages developed booster retraining and training-the-trainer strategies, to offset these difficulties.

VI. ASSESSMENT OF SPEECH, LANGUAGE, AND COMMUNICATION IN ID

Language and communication are an integral part of ID, as evidenced by the existence of language components on almost every IQ test. In the 1950s and 1960s, the field of speech, language, and hearing, however, was mainly focused on speech articulation and speech impairments. Norm-referenced tests, like the Illinois Test of Psycholinguistic Abilities (Kirk & McCarthy, 1961), were used to prescribe rather nonspecific "psychoeducational" language therapy programs in the schools. Some textbooks essentially recommended abandoning language training among people with ID.

The first systematic research program to study the communication of people with mental retardation began at the University of Kansas in its Bureau of Child Research and Parsons Research Center in the 1950s under the direction of Richard Schiefelbusch and Joseph Spradlin.

Saunders, Spradlin, and Sherman (2006) give a concise history of the Language and Communication Program at the University of Kansas. The following section relies heavily on their historical account. From the beginning, Kansas researchers participating in this effort assumed that the speech and communication of children and adults with mental retardation could be improved by the systematic application of behavioral principles.

Congruent with that assumption, some of the earliest experiments were directed toward changing specific aspects of speech. In the light of the enormous progress that has occurred during the years since 1960s concerning the development of speech and communication, the aims of many of the earliest studies may seem trivial. When the studies were conducted, however, they were significant and attempts to demonstrate that, for example, the rate of vocalizations of children with mental retardation could be modified through the systematic application of consequences (Horowitz, 1963) or that these children's vocal behavior was affected by the persons with whom they interacted. The first language sampling assessment instrument was the Parsons Language Sample (Spradlin, 1963).

In the late 1950s and early 1960s, many prominent researchers in the United States did not believe that the speech and language development of children with mental retardation could be enhanced or modified in any meaningful way via environmental means. Chomsky (1959), for example, had published his criticisms of Skinner's book (Skinner, 1957) and had proposed his theory that generative grammar was innate. Statements by Chomsky and other psycholinguists about the innateness of language led Kansas researchers to initiate a series of studies which demonstrated that many of the aspects of grammar, whether thought to be innate or not, could still be taught through the systematic application of sound behavior principles (Baer & Guess, 1973; Guess, Sailor, Rutherford, & Baer, 1968; Schumaker & Sherman, 1970).

While these early studies were aimed at demonstrating that generative aspects of spoken language could be taught, there was also a recognition of the substantial importance of receptive language. Because hearing is typically critical to such understanding and because there were not good ways of evaluating the hearing of children with severe mental retardation, project researchers at that time conducted a series of studies aimed at perfecting procedures for evaluating the hearing of such children. This research led to a set of procedures that could be used to evaluate such children with audiometric procedures previously applicable only to persons who understood and followed verbal directions (Fulton & Spradlin, 1971, 1972, 1974a,b; Lloyd, Spradlin, & Reid, 1968). Parsons researchers also began a systematic study of the development of generative receptive language. Once again they demonstrated that generative receptive language could be developed with many children, to at least a limited extent, by the systematic application of behavioral principles (Baer & Guess, 1971; Striefel & Wetherby, 1973; Striefel, Wetherby, & Karlan, 1976). These early successes in demonstrating that some children with severe mental retardation could be taught many aspects of generative language led to subsequent attempts to develop a comprehensive program for language and communication training for children with severe and profound mental retardation (Guess, Sailor, & Baer, 1978).

In spite of the fact that specific aspects of productive and receptive language could be taught to children with severe and profound mental retardation, many problems were apparent. First, not all such children seemed to profit from such training and, second, even those children who demonstrated considerable language competency within teaching situations often failed to exhibit their newly acquired skills in their daily environments. The inability to teach some children to use speech led researchers (Carrier, 1974) to develop a symbol system for children who did not learn via the speech mode. Later symbol systems for communication, for example the PECs system (Bondy & Frost, 1994), are now used widely by nonverbal communicators with ID.

The failure of children who had been taught specific language skills to use these skills in their daily environments also led Kansas researchers to begin to look carefully at those environments. Observation of the children in their daily environments (at that time these were typically institutional environments) led to the conclusion that they frequently did not have sufficient opportunities to use their newly developed skills. These observations led to a number of developments. One development was that investigators began to carefully observe the interaction of persons with mental retardation and their caretakers in their natural (i.e. noninstitutional) environments (Hart & Risley, 1980). The results of these efforts to observe children and their caregivers led a major effort within another research program by Hart and Risley. In this research, Hart and Risley examined the communicative interactions of young children in their home environments who were just beginning to develop language. This research resulted in the publication of a seminal monograph by Hart and Risley (1995), that examines the development of language by children with Down syndrome in comparison to that of typically developing children.

The observation that the systematic teaching of language failed to generalize led Stokes and Baer (1977) to develop a model of the procedures used to facilitate generalization. They proposed this in a classic paper which has served as a basis for both the experimental clinical analysis of generalization problems and tactics for nearly three decades.

In the mid-1970s Kansas researchers began to develop assessment and intervention procedures to be used in the children's natural environments to aid them to acquire and use new skills (Hart & Risley, 1975; Schumaker & Sherman, 1978). Hart and Risley (1975) developed an incidental teaching technique that encouraged children to request objects in their play environments. Pla-Check assessment systems for sampling behaviors in naturalistic settings were developed in this program. Halle and his colleagues (Halle, Baer, & Spradlin, 1981; Halle, Marshall, & Spradlin, 1979) demonstrated that if one introduced a delay between the time that a child made a nonspeech request and then prompted speaking by presenting a spoken model, the person would often begin requesting with speech after a few such occasions.

Others have now replicated these "incidental teaching" and "delayed prompt" techniques to the point that the uses of such procedures are standard practices in the fields of early intervention, special education, and speech-language pathology.

Research of the Kansas group has extended these studies to learning spelling and reading (Saunders, O'Donnell, Vaidya, & Williams, 2003) and pragmatics (Brady, McLean, McLean, & Johnston, 1995; McLean, McLean, Brady, & Etter, 1991) among people with severe retardation, and to communication with switch interfaces among the nonambulatory profoundly retarded (Saunders, Timler, et al., 2003). So Terman's (1916) previously cited generalizations about no abstraction among people with ID were slightly inaccurate.

Research on speech, language, communication, and psycholinguistics has exploded since the 1980s. Several large handbook series are available. The first was a 20-volume series published by University Park Press with Schiefelbusch and colleagues as editors. The second was a 12-volume series published by Paul Brookes Publishing Co. with Steven Warren, Joe Reichle, and Marc Fey as series editors, which continues today. While the above behavioral research has used primarily the mastery of the specific language abilities as their assessment measures (Sundberg, 1983), the field has developed a wide array of valid and reliable measures of language development (Warren & Yoder, 1997). Standard computerized methods for analysis of language samples are now available (Evans, 1996). For an excellent book on the assessment of language relevant to ID, see Cole, Dale, and Thal (1996).

VII. WORK-RELATED ASSESSMENT IN ID

With the deinstitutionalization and community integration movements in the 1970s came a renewed emphasis on assessing and developing work-related behaviors in ID, in order to foster productivity and independence. The federal Rehabilitation Services Administration (RSA) had been established after the World War II, to help wounded veterans' rehabilitation and reentry into the nation's work force. This large federal agency developed a network of branches in every state, which determined eligibility, did rehabilitation counseling, and monitored of clients' progress regularly. Eventually these services were extended to people with mental illness, as well as to people with ID, in the Rehabilitation Act of 1973.

RSA was not set up well for people with ID, and initially there was a great deal of resistance accommodating the new population. Assessments were again norm-referenced aptitude tests, like the Purdue Pegboard Test

(Tiffen, 1968) and the Kuder Preference Record (1934), scales which had little or no relevance or predictive validity for people with ID (for a good review, see Menchetti, Rusch, & Owens, 1983).

As the consumer empowerment movement gained strength in the 1980s during the Reagan Administration, The Office of Special Education (OSE) and the RSA were merged into the Office of Special Education and Rehabilitation Services (OSERS) in 1985. The first director was a parent advocate of a child with Down syndrome, Madelaine Will. The National Institute for Disabilities Research and Rehabilitation (NIDRR) was established within OSERS, with David Gray, a quadriplegic and a strong advocate, as its first director. The newly formed Rehabilitation Research and Training Centers in NIDRR stressed consumer control, self-determination, and empowerment which relied heavily on structured interviews of people with ID as their assessment tools.

Since that time a host of work-related programs for people with ID, in addition to other disabilities, have developed. A large attempt was made to move people with ID from sheltered employment into competitive employment in the community. Out of this impetus grew the supported employment movement (Rusch, 1990; Wehman, 1981; Wehman & Moon, 1988). The old work sample and vocational testing methods were largely discarded, and mastery of performance skills on the job became the main set of assessment criteria.

Supported employment has been a successful program, but it has not totally replaced sheltered employment facilities. Only a small percentage of people with ID in supported employment work full time or receive a competitive wage today. It was found that the main reason for their failure in supported employment was not so much the quality of their work, as their lack of social skills in the work place, lack of responsibility, and other factors such as their health, the economy, or intolerance of their fellow workers and managers (Lagomarcino, 1990). Recent programs have focused on training work-related social skills or self-employment (Chadsey-Rusch, 1990; Griffin & Hammis, 2003; Luecking, Fabian, & Tilson, 2004; Martin, Mithaug, Oliphant, Husch, & Frazier, 2002).

The Americans with Disabilities Act (ADA) was passed in 1990 in the G.H.W. Bush administration. It had many far-reaching provisions, one of which was that it prohibited discrimination based on one's disability. It required employers to make reasonable accommodations adapted to a person's disability, so that now even people with severe ID had a legal right to work. A large body of case law governing the ADA has developed over the past 15 years, but much of it has been gutted during the past 6 years by the Supreme Court during the G.W. Bush administration (Stowe, Turnbull, & Sublet, 2006). Total US public spending for ID has decreased since 2002 (Braddock & Hemp, 2006).

VIII. ASSESSMENT OF QUALITY OF LIFE AND FAMILY ADAPTATION IN ID

The study of QOL in ID arose from the civil rights and deinstitutionalization movements of the 1960s (Schalock & Verdugo, 2002). The principle of "normalization" (Wolfensberger, 1972) became very popular. As court cases, for example Haldeman v. Pennhurst (1977), developed which held that institutionalization deprived people with ID of their constitutional rights to a normal QOL, the need to define operationally what "quality of life" meant became important. The first QOL assessment scale in ID with empirical validation was by Schalock and Keith (1993). It was similar to QOL scales developed in the health field and in the field of aging. It covered eight domains: emotional well-being, interpersonal relations, material well-being, personal development, physical well-being, self-determination, social inclusion, and civil rights. Each of these domains has become a subfield of extensive research in ID which has spread to the international arena (Schalock et al., 2005). According to Schalock et al. (2005), QOL has become a "sensitizing notion, social construct, and overarching theme for planning, delivering, and evaluating individualized services and supports." Assessment research on QOL continues to grow rapidly, especially in the United States and Europe.

Another research initiative that emerged with the community movement in ID in the 1980s is *adaptation to having a person with ID in the family* (see Stoneman, 1997 for an excellent overview). The areas of study were, family stress models (McCubbin & Patterson, 1983), buffers and coping with stress (Turnbull et al., 1993), family systems theory, social roles (Stoneman, Brody, Davis, & Crapps, 1989), and ethnographic approaches (Gallimore, Weisner, Kaufman, & Bernheimer, 1989), models of grief, resilience, hardiness, and empowerment (Turnbull & Turnbull, 2001). Much of the assessment in these areas is qualitative or ethnographic in nature; but there are also many quantitative direct observational studies of social interactions, as well as informant questionnaires, ratings scales, and so on. Family studies in ID have become a very large area of research in the last 20 years and they promise to be even larger in the future, as people with ID increasingly come to live in the community.

IX. INTERDISCIPLINARY TEAM ASSESSMENT IN ID

The assessments described above have become tools of interdisciplinary teams. Interdisciplinary teams have a long history and have been used in medicine, education, and rehabilitation since the 1920s (Rokusek, 1995). Interdisciplinary teams did not start to gain momentum until rehabilitation centers were established during World War II. Professionals recognized that a number of specialities were needed to adequately assess and treat disabled veterans and return them to society. For individuals with mental retardation and other developmental disabilities, interdisciplinary teams gained prominence in the 1950s and 1960s. People with mental retardation frequently had multiple problems in such areas as medical, dental, language, motor, social, and cognitive development. Those diverse issues required a team to understand and coordinate treatment among providers.

In the 1960s, President Kennedy established a commission on mental retardation. The commission came to the conclusion that there needed to be more services for people with mental retardation in the United States and services needed to be provided in an interdisciplinary fashion. The commission recommended that centers be established for the interdisciplinary training of professionals who would eventually work with people with mental retardation. University Affiliated Facilities and Programs were developed in the United States to meet the need of training professionals to work in collaborative teams. Mandates for collaborative interdisciplinary teams became a part of educational law in 1975 with Public Law 94–142, Education of All Handicapped Act and subsequently the IDEA. Both University Affiliated Programs (now University Centers of Excellent in Developmental Disabilities) and IDEA continue today with emphasis on interdisciplinary assessment and coordinated education and treatment (Garner, 2000; Rainforth, York, & Macdonald, 1992; Thayer & Kropf, 1995).

Presently, interdisciplinary teams who support individuals with mental retardation to function in their home community are made up of a more diverse range of participants than therapeutic professionals such as doctors, social workers OTs, PTs, speech and language pathologists, and psychologists. Parents have always been important team members but more recently, teams may represent a broad membership base and include clergy, policemen, transportation specialists, and city planners. The goals of teams are to improve not only specific functional skills such as speech, social skills, and adaptive abilities but also a person's QOL including relationships with nondisabled people, and the ability to function as valued citizens in self-determined leisure and employment settings. Many person-centered planning teams include friends, neighbors, community members, and so on who meet on a periodic basis to move the person with mental retardation forward in improving his/her valued lifestyle (Kincaid, 1996).

X. SUMMARY AND FUTURE DIRECTIONS

The above brief overview attests to the growth and development of the field of assessment in ID over the last century. The future promises even more prolific expansion of existing domains as well as development of new ones. Some trends are as follows:

1. The development of more specialized assessment instruments tailored to subpopulations in ID, for example behavioral phenotypes such as autism, Williams syndrome, and Down syndrome. Attempts to develop general test batteries have not been satisfactory because of unique characteristics of each phenotype. New phenotypes as yet to be discovered lead to the possibility of hundreds of different genetic syndromes in need of careful behavioral characterization.
2. The possibility of multimodal assessment using concomitant psychophysiological and neuroimaging assessment has been demonstrated to great advantage in the field of learning disabilities and should be considered in ID. Although used in some psychopathological and psychopharmacological research in ID, the multimodal approach has not gained widespread popularity in the rest of the field.
3. Social validity assessments, although recommended for the past 25 years (Kazdin & Matson, 1981), have also not been used widely. In the future, they are likely to be required more frequently, in order to even gain access to research populations in ID.
4. Interdisciplinary assessment is increasingly becoming recognized as an important part of assessing people with mental retardation. Although it is expensive, its wise and efficient use may save money in the long run because of its emphasis on prevention of disabling conditions.

The importance of defining and characterizing populations of people with ID cannot be overemphasized. Improving our assessments has allowed us to delineate subgroups empirically and thereby to sharpen the hunt for new genetic syndromes and to relate them to brain function and behavior. Some day in the near future, there may be cures for some forms of ID with gene therapy and organ repair with stem cells. Behavioral and psychometric assessments have an integral role to play in these hopes and aspirations.

ACKNOWLEDGMENTS

We wish to acknowledge MCH Project No. MCJ 944 and the Social Security Administration for partial support in preparation of this manuscript. We thank Michael Wehmeyer for a critical reading of the manuscript.

REFERENCES

Aman, M. G. (1991). *Assessing psychopathology and behavior problems in persons with mental retardation: A review of available instruments*. Rockville, MD: US Department of Health and Human Services.

Aman, M. G., Sarphare, G., & Burrow, W. H. (1995). Psychotropic drugs in group homes: Prevalence and relation to demographic/psychiatric variables. *American Journal on Mental Retardation, 99,* 500–509.

Aman, M. G., Singh, N. N., Stewart, A., & Field, C. J. (1985). The aberrant behavior checklist: A behavior rating scale for the assessment of treatment effects. *American Journal of Mental Deficiency, 89,* 485–491.

American Psychiatric Association (1994). *Diagnostic and statistical manual of mental disorders 4th edition (DSM IV).* Washington, DC: American Psychiatric Press.

Ayllon, T., & Azrin, N. H. (1968). *The token economy.* New York: Appleton Century Crofts.

Ayllon, T., & Michael, J. L. (1959). The psychiatric nurse as a behavioral engineer. *Journal of the Experimental Analysis of Behavior, 3,* 123–142.

Baer, D. M., & Guess, D. (1971). Receptive training of adjectival inflections in mental retardates. *Journal of Applied Behavior Analysis, 4,* 129–139.

Baer, D. M., & Guess, D. (1973). Teaching productive noun suffixes to severely retarded children. *American Journal of Mental Deficiency, 77,* 498–505.

Baer, D. M., Wolf, M. M., & Risley, T. R. (1968). Some current dimensions of applied behavior analysis. *Journal of Applied Behavior Analysis, 1,* 91–97.

Baumeister, A. A., & Kellas, G. (1968). Reaction time and mental retardation. In N. R. Ellis (Ed.), *International review of research in mental retardation* (Vol. 3, pp. 163–193). New York: Academic Press.

Baumeister, A. A., Todd, M. E., & Sevin, J. A. (1993). Efficacy and specificity of pharmacological therapies for behavioral disorders of persons with mental retardation. *Clinical Neuropharmacology, 16,* 271–294.

Berkson, G. (2004). Intellectual and physical disabilities in prehistory and early civilization. *Mental Retardation, 42,* 195–208.

Bijou, S. W. (1966). Functional analysis of retarded development. In N. R. Ellis (Ed.), *International review of research in mental retardation* (Vol. 1, pp. 1–19). New York: Academic Press.

Binet, A., & Simon, T. (1905). Upon the necessity of establishing a scientific diagnosis of inferior states of intelligence. In A. Binet & T. Simon (Eds.) (1916). *The development of intelligence in children* (pp. 9–36). Baltimore: Williams & Wilkins.

Birnbrauer, J. S., & Lawler, J. (1964). Token reinforcement for learning. *Mental Retardation, 2,* 275–279.

Bodfish, J. W., & Lewis, M. H. (2002). Self-injury and comorbid behaviors in developmental, neurological, psychiatric, and genetic disorders. In S. R. Schroeder, M. L. Oster-Granite, & T. Thompson (Eds.), *Self-injurious behavior: Gene-brain-behavior relationships* (pp. 23–39). Washington, DC: American Psychological Association Books.

Bondy, A., & Frost, L. (1994). The delaware autistic program. In S. Harris & J. S. Handleman (Eds.), *Preschool education programs for children with autism* (pp. 37–54). Austin, TX: Pro-Ed.

Braddock, D., & Hemp, R. (2006). Growth for US public spending for intellectual/developmental disabilities slowed down 2002–2004. *Mental Retardation, 44,* 77–80.

Brady, N. C., McLean, J. E., McLean, L. K., & Johnston, S. (1995). Initiation and repair of intentional communication acts by adults with severe to profound cognitive disabilities. *Journal of Speech and Hearing Research, 38,* 1334–1348.

Carrier, J. (1974). Application of functional analysis and a nonspeech response mode to teaching language. *American Speech and Hearing Monograph No. 18*, Washington, DC.

Chadsey-Rusch, J. (1990). Teaching social skills on the job. In F. R. Rusch (Ed.), *Supported employment: Models, methods and issues* (pp. 161–180). Sycamore, IL: Sycamore Publishing Co.

Chomsky, N. (1959). A review of B. F. Skinner's verbal behavior. *Language, 35,* 26–58.

Clausen, J. (1966). *Ability structure and subgroups in mental retardation*. London: MacMillan and Co. LTD.

Cole, K. N., Dale, P. S., & Thal, D. J. (1996). *Assessment of communication and language*. Baltimore, MD: Paul Brookes Publishing Co.

Conners, C. K. (1969). A teacher rating scale for use in drug studies with children. *American Journal of Psychiatry, 126,* 884–888.

Daryl Renard Atkins v. Virginia (2002). No. 00–8452.

Dix, D. (1843). Memorial to the Legislature of Massachusetts, 1843. In M. Rosen, G. R. Clark, & M. S. Kivitz (Eds.), *The history of mental retardation: Collected papers* (Vol. 1, pp. 3–30). Baltimore, MD: University Park Press.

Doll, E. A. (1934). Social adjustment of the mental subnormal. *Journal of Educational Research, 6,* 51–60.

Doll, E. A. (1935). A genetic scale of social maturity. *American Journal of Orthopsychiatry, 5,* 180–188.

Doll, E. A. (1965). *Vineland Scale of Social Maturity*. Minneapolis, MN: American Guidance Service.

Dykens, E. M. (1995). Measuring behavioral phenotypes: Provocations from the "new genetics." *American Journal on Mental Retardation, 99,* 522–532.

Dykens, E. M., Hodapp, R. M., & Finacune, B. M. (2000). *Genetics and mental retardation syndromes: A new look at behavior and interventions*. Baltimore, MD: Paul Brookes Publishing co.

Ellis, N. R. (Ed.) (1963). *Handbook of mental deficiency*. (1st ed.). Hillsdale, NJ: Lawrence Erlbaum Associates.

Evans, J. L. (1996). Plotting the complexities of language sample analysis. In K. N. Cole, P. S. Dale, & D. J. Thal (Eds.), *Assessment of communication and language* (pp. 207–256). Baltimore, MD: Paul Brookes Publishing Co.

Eysenck, H. J., & Kamin, L. (1981). *The intelligence controversy*. New York, NY: John Wiley & Sons.

Fulton, R. T., & Spradlin, J. E. (1971). Operant audiometry with severely retarded children. *Audiology, 10,* 203–211.

Fulton, R. T., & Spradlin, J. E. (1972). SISI procedures with the severely retarded. *Journal of Speech and Hearing Research, 15,* 217–224.

Fulton, R. T., & Spradlin, J. E. (1974a). Puretone threshold measurement. In R. T. Fulton (Ed.), *Auditory stimulus-response control* (pp. 37–52). Baltimore, MD: University Park Press.

Fulton, R. T., & Spradlin, J. E. (1974b). The short increment sensitivity index (SISI). In R. T. Fulton (Ed.), *Auditory stimulus-response control* (pp. 53–64). Baltimore, MD: University Park Press.

Gallimore, R., Weisner, T. S., Kaufman, S. Z., & Bernheimer, L. P. (1989). The social construction of ecological niches: Family accommodation of developmentally delayed children. *American Journal on Mental Retardation, 94,* 216–230.

Garner, H. (2000). *Helping others through teamwork: A handbook for professionals*. Washington, DC: CWLA Press.

Girardeau, F. L., & Spradlin, J. E. (1964). Token rewards in a cottage program. *Mental Retardation, 2,* 345–352.

Goddard, H. H. (1913). The improvability of feeble-minded children. *Journal of Psychoasthenics, 17,* 121–131.

Griffin, C., & Hammis, D. (2003). *Making self-employment work for people with disabilities*. Baltimore, MD: Paul Brookes Publishing Co.

Grossman, H. J. (Ed.) (1973). *Manual of terminology and classification in mental retardation*. Washington, DC: American Association on Mental Deficiency.

Guess, D., Sailor, W., & Baer, D. M. (1978). Children with limited language. In R. L. Schiefelbusch (Ed.), *Language intervention strategies* (pp. 101–143). Baltimore, MD: University Park Press.

Guess, D., Sailor, W., Rutherford, G., & Baer, D. M. (1968). An experimental analysis of linguistic development: The productive use of the plural morpheme. *Journal of Applied Behavior Analysis, 1,* 297–306.

Guy, W. (1976). *ECDEU Assessment manual for psychopharmacology (revised).* US Department of Health education, and welfare Publication (ADM), 76–338. Rockville, MD: National Institute of Mental Health.

Haldeman v. Pennhurst State School and Hospital (1977). 446 F. Supp. 1295 (E.D. Pa.).

Halle, J. W., Baer, D. M., & Spradlin, J. E. (1981). Teachers' generalized use of delay as a stimulus control procedure to increase language use in handicapped children. *Journal of Applied Behavior Analysis, 14,* 398–409.

Halle, J. W., Marshall, A., & Spradlin, J. (1979). Time delay: A technique to increase language use and facilitate generalization in retarded children. *Journal of Applied Behavior analysis, 12,* 431–439.

Hart, B., & Risley, T. R. (1980). *In vivo* language intervention: Unanticipated generalization effects. *Journal of Applied Behavior Analysis, 13,* 407–432.

Hart, B., & Risley, T. R. (1975). Incidental teaching of language in the preschool. *Journal of Applied Behavior Analysis, 8,* 411–420.

Hart, B. M., & Risley, T. (1995). *Meaningful differences in the everyday experience of young American children.* Baltimore, MD: Paul H. Brookes.

Heber, R. (1959). A manual of terminology and classification in mental retardation. *American Journal of Mental Deficiency, 64* (Monograph Supplement No. 2) ix, 111.

Heber, R. (1961). *Epidemiology of mental retardation.* Springfield, IL: Charles C. Thomas, Publisher.

Horowitz, F. D. (1963). Partial and continuous reinforcement of vocal responses using candy, vocal, and smiling reinforcers among retardates: Part 1. *Journal of Speech and Hearing Disorders: Monograph Supplement No, 10,* 55–69.

Iwata, B. A., Dorsey, M. F., Slifer, K. J., Bauman, K., & Richman, G. S. (1982). Toward a functional analysis of self-injury. *Analysis and Intervention in Developmental Disabilities, 2,* 3–20.

Jensen, A. R. (1969). How much can we boost IQ and scholastic achievement? *Harvard Educational Review, 39,* 1–123.

Kalachnik, J. E. (1999). Measuring side effects of psychopharmacologic medication in individuals with mental retardation. *Mental Retardation and Developmental Disabilities Research Reviews, 5,* 348–359.

Kamin, L. J. (1974). *The science and politics of IQ.* Potomac, MD: Erlbaum.

Kazdin, A. E., & Matson, J. L. (1981). Social validation in mental retardation. *Applied Research in Mental Retardation, 1,* 39–53.

Kincaid, D. (1996). Person-centered planning. In L. K. Koegel, R. L. Koegel, & G. Dunlap (Eds.), *Positive behavior supports: Including people with difficult behaviors in the community* (pp. 425–438). Baltimore MD: Paul H Brookes.

Kirk, S., & McCarthy, J. (1961). Illinois Test of Psycholinguistic Abilities- an approach to differential diagnosis. *American Journal of Mental Deficiency, 66,* 339–412.

Kuder, G. F. (1934). *Kuder preference record: Vocational.* Chicago, IL: Science Research Associates, Inc.

Lagomarcino, T. R. (1990). Job separation issues in supported employment. In F. R. Rusch (Ed.), *Supported employment: Models, methods, and issues* (pp. 301–316). Sycamore, IL: Sycamore Publishing Co.

Larry P. v. Riles, 343 Supp. 1306(N.D. Cal.1972).

Lewis, M. H., & Bodfish, J. W. (1998). Repetitive behavior disorders in autism. Special Issue: "Autism". *Mental Retardation Development Disabilities Research Review, 4,* 80–89.

Lloyd, L. L., Spradlin, J. E., & Reid, M. J. (1968). An operant audiometric procedure for difficult-to-test patients. *Journal of Speech and Hearing Disorders, 33,* 236–245.

Lovaas, O. I., Freitag, G., Gold, V., & Kassorla, I. (1965). Experimental studies in childhood schizophrenia: Analysis of self-destructive behavior. *Journal of Experimental Child Psychology, 2,* 67–84.

Luckasson, R., Coulter, D. L., Polloway, E. A., Reese, S., Schalock, R. L., & Snell, M. E., et al. (1992). *Mental retardation: Definition, classification, and systems of supports* (9th ed.). Washington, DC: American Association on Mental Retardation.

Luckasson, R., Borthwick-Duffy, S., Buntinx, W. H. E., Coulter, D. L., Craig, E. M., & Reeve, A., et al. (2002). *Mental retardation: Definition, classification, and systems of supports* (10th ed.). Washington, DC: American Association on Mental Retardation.

Luecking, R. G., Fabian, E. S., & Tilson, G. R. (2004). *Working relationships*. Baltimore, MD: Paul Brookes Publishing Co.

MacMillan, D. L., Gresham, F. M., & Siperstein, G. N. (1993). Conceptual and psychometric concerns about the 1992 definition of mental retardation. *American Journal on Mental Retardation, 98,* 325–335.

Martin, J. E., Mithaug, D. E., Oliphant, M., Husch, J. V., & Frazier, E. S. (2002). *Self-directed employment*. Baltimore, MD: Paul Brookes Publishing Co.

Masland, R. L., Sarason, S. B., & Gladwin, T. (1958). *Mental subnormality*. New York, NY: Basic Books.

Matson, J. L. (1986). Self-injury and its relationship to diagnostic schemes in psychopathology. *Applied Research in Mental Retardation, 7,* 223–228.

Matson, J. L. (1988). *The psychopathology instrument for mentally retarded adults (PIMRA)*. Oak Park, IL: International Diagnostic Systems.

Matson, J. L., Gardner, W. I., Coe, D. A., & Sovner, R. (1991). A scale for evaluating emotional disorders in severely and profoundly mentally retarded persons. *British Journal of Psychiatry, 159,* 404–409.

Matson, J. L. & Bruening, S. E. (Eds.) (1983). *Assessing the mentally retarded.* New York, NY: Grune & Stratton.

McCubbin, H. I., & Patterson, J. (1983). The family stress process: The double ABCX model of adjustment and adaptation. In H. I. McCubbin, M. B. Sussman, & J. M. Patterson (Eds.), *Social stress and the family: Advances and developments in family stress theory and research* (pp. 7–37). New York, NY: Halworth.

McLean, J. E., McLean, L. K. S., Brady, N. C., & Etter, R. (1991). Communication profiles of two types of gesture using nonverbal persons with severe to profound mental retardation. *Journal of Speech and Hearing Research, 34,* 294–308.

Menchetti, B., Rusch, F. R., & Owens, S. D. (1983). Vocational training. In J. L. Matson & S. E. Bruening (Eds.), *Assessing the mentally retarded* (pp. 247–284). New York, NY: Grune & Stratton.

Menolascino, F. J. (Ed.) (1970). *Psychiatric approaches to mental retardation* New York, NY: Basic Books.

Nihira, K., Foster, R., Shellhaas, M., & Leland, H. (1975). *AAMD Adaptive behavior scale manual (revised edition)*. Washington, DC: American Association on Mental Deficiency.

Perske, R. (2006). Strange shift in the case of Daryl Atkins. *Mental Retardation, 43,* 454–455.

President's Committee on Mental Retardation (1977). *MR 76: Century of decision: Past and present*. Washington, DC: US Government Printing Office. Stock No. 040–000–00385–1.

Rainforth, B., York, J., & Macdonald, C. (1992). *Collaborative teams for students with severe disabilities*. Baltimore, MD: Paul H Brookes Publishing Company.

Reiss, S. (1988). *Test manual for the reiss screen for maladaptive behavior*. Oak Park, IL: International Diagnostic Systems.

Rojahn, J., Matson, J. L., Lott, D., Esbensen, A. J., & Smalls, Y. (2001). The Behavior Problem Inventory: An instrument for the assessment of self-injury, stereotyped behavior and aggression/destruction in individuals with developmental disabilities. *Journal of Autism and Developmental Disorders, 31,* 577–588.

Rokusek, C. (1995). An introduction to the concept of interdisciplinary practice. In B. A. Thayer & N. Kropf (Eds.), *Developmental disabilities: A handbook of interdisciplinary practice* (pp. 1–12). Cambridge, MD: Brookline Books.

Rosen, M., Clark, G. R., & Kivitz, M. S. (Eds.) (1976). *The history of mental retardation: Collected papers* (Vols. 1 & 2). Baltimore, MD: University Park Press.

Routh, D. K., & Schroeder, S. R. (2003). A history of psychological theory and research in mental retardation since World War. In L. Masters-Glidden (Ed.), *International review of research in mental retardation* (Vol. 26, pp. 1–59). New York, NY: Academic Press.

Rusch, F. R. (Ed.) (1990). *Supported employment: Models, methods, and issues.* Sycamore, IL: Sycamore Publishing Co.

Rutter, M., Tizard, J., & Whitmore, K. (1970). *Education, health, and behavior.* New York, NY: John Wiley & Sons.

Saunders, K. J., O'Donnell, J., Vaidya, M., & Williams, D. C. (2003). Recombinative generalization of within-syllable units in nonreading adults with mental retardation. *Journal of Applied Behavior Analysis, 36,* 95–99.

Saunders, M. D., Timler, G., Cullinen, T. B., Pilkey, S., Questad, K. A., & Saunders, R. R. (2003). Evidence of contingency awareness in people with profound multiple impairments: Response duration versus response rate indicators. *Research in Developmental Disabilities, 24,* 231–245.

Saunders, R. R., Spradlin, J. E., & Sherman, J. A. (2006). Communication of people with mental retardation program project. In R. L. Schiefelbusch & S. R. Schroeder (Eds.), *Doing science and doing good: A history of the bureau of child research and the schiefelbusch institute for life span studies 1921–2006* (Book II, Ch. 7). Baltimore, MD: Paul Brooks Publishing Co.

Schalock, R. L., & Keith, K. D. (1993). *Quality of life questionnaire.* Worthington, OH: IDS Publishers.

Schalock, R. L., & Verdugo, M. A. (2002). *Handbook on quality of life for human service practitioners.* Washington, DC: American Association on Mental Retardation.

Schalock, R. L., Verdugo, M. A., Jenaro, C., Wang, M., Wehmeyer, M., Jiancheng, X., et al. (2005). Cross-cultural study of quality of life indicators. *American Journal on Mental Retardation, 110,* 298–311.

Schroeder, S. R., Rojahn, J., & Reese, R. M. (1997). Reliability and validity of instruments for assessing psychotropic medication effects on self-injurious behavior in mental retardation. *Journal of Autism and Developmental Disorders, 27,* 89–102.

Schroeder, S. R., Bouras, N., Ellis, C. R., Reid, A., Sandman, C., Werry, J. S., & Wisniewski, H. (1998). Past research on psychopharmacology of people with mental retardation and developmental disabilities. In S. Reiss & M. G. Aman (Eds.), *Psychotropic medication and developmental disabilities: The international consensus handbook.* Columbus, OH: The Ohio State University.

Schumaker, J., & Sherman, J. A. (1970). Training generative verb usage by imitation and reinforcement procedures. *Journal of Applied Behavior Analysis, 3,* 273–287.

Schumaker, J. B., & Sherman, J. A. (1978). Parent as intervention agent. In R. L. Schiefelbusch (Ed.), *Language intervention strategies* (pp. 237–315). Baltimore, MD: University Park Press.

Sidman, M., & Stoddard, L. T. (1966). Programming perception and learning for retarded children. In N. R. Ellis (Ed.), *International review of research in mental retardation* (Vol. 2, pp. 152–208). New York, NY: Academic Press.

Skinner, B. F. (1957). *Verbal behavior*. New York, NY: Appleton-Century-Crofts.

Spradlin, J. E. (1963). Assessment of speech and language of retarded children: The parsons language sample. In R. L. Schiefelbusch (Ed.), *Language studies of mentally retarded children. Journal of Speech and Hearing Disorders Monograph 10,* 8–31.

Sprague, R. L., & Werry, J. S. (1971). Methodology of psychopharmacological studies with the retarded. In N. R. Ellis (Ed.), *International review of research in mental retardation* (Vol. 5, pp. 148–220). New York, NY: Academic Press.

Sternlicht, M. (1966). Psychotherapeutic procedures with the retarded. In N. R. Ellis (Ed.), *International review of research in mental retardation* (Vol. 2, pp. 279–354). New York, NY: Academic Press.

Stokes, T. F., & Baer, D. M. (1977). An implicit technology of generalization. *Journal of Applied Behavior Analysis, 10,* 349–367.

Stoneman, Z. (1997). Mental retardation and family adaptation. In W. E. Maclean (Ed.), *Ellis' handbook of mental deficiency, psychological theory and research* (pp. 405–438). Hillsdale, NJ: Lawrence Erlbaum Associates.

Stoneman, Z., Brody, G. H., Davis, C. H., & Crapps, J. M. (1989). Role relations between mentally retarded children and their older siblings: Observations in three in-home contexts. *Research in Developmental Disabilities, 10,* 61–76.

Stowe, M. J., Turnbull, H. R., & Sublet, C. (2006). The supreme court, "Our Town," and disability policy: Boardrooms and bedrooms, courtrooms and cloakrooms. *Mental Retardation, 44,* 83–99.

Striefel, S., & Wetherby, B. (1973). Instruction-following behavior of a retarded child and its controlling stimuli. *Journal of Applied Behavior Analysis, 6,* 663–670.

Striefel, S., Wetherby, B., & Karlan, G. R. (1976). Establishing generative verb-noun instruction-following skills in retarded children. *Journal of Experimental Child Psychology, 22,* 247–260.

Sundberg, M. L. (1983). Language. In J. L. Matson & S. E. Bruening (Eds.), *Assessing the mentally retarded* (pp. 285–310). New York, NY: Grune & Stratton.

Terman, L. M. (1916). *The measurement of intelligence*. Boston, MA: Houghton-Mifflin.

Terman, L. M. (1917). Feeble-minded children in the schools of California. *Schools and Society, 5,* 161–165.

Thayer, B. A. & Kropf, N. (Eds.) (1995). *Developmental disabilities: A Handbook of Interdisciplinary Practice.* Cambridge, MD: Brookline Books.

Thompson, T., Felce, D., & Symons, F. (2000). *Behavioral observation*. Baltimore, MD: Paul Brookes Publishing Co.

Thompson, J. R., Bryant, B., Campbell, E. M., Craig, E. M., Hughes, C., & Rotholz, D. A., et al. (2004). *Supports Intensity scale (SIS)*. Washington, DC: American Association on Mental Retardation.

Tiffen, J. (1968). *Purdue Pegboard.* Chicago, IL: Science Research Associates.

Tredgold, A. J. (1937). *Mental deficiency*. New York, NY: Wood.

Turnbull, A. P., Patterson, J. M., Behr, S. K., Murphy, D. L., Marquis, J., & Blue-Bannig, M. (1993). *Cognitive coping, families, and disability*. Baltimore, MD: Paul Brookes Publishing Co.

Turnbull, A. P., & Turnbull, H. R. (2001). *Families, professionals, and exceptionality* (4th ed.). Columbus, OH: Merrill Prentice-Hall.

Valdovinos, M., Schroeder, S. R., & Kim, G. (2003). Prevalence and correlates of psychotropic medication use among adults with developmental disabilities: 1970–2000. In L. M. Glidden (Ed.), *International Review of Research in Mental Retardation* (Vol. 26, pp. 175–220). New York, NY: Academic Press.

Warren, S. F., & Yoder, P. J. (1997). Communication, language, and mental retardation. In W. E. MacLean (Ed.), *Ellis' handbook of mental deficiency, psychological theory, and research* (3rd ed., pp. 379–404). Lawrence Erlbaum Associates: Hillsdale, NJ.

Wechsler, D. (1955). *Wechsler adult intelligence scale*. San Antonio, TX: The Psychological Corporation.

Wehman, P. (1981). *Competitive employment*. Baltimore, MD: Paul Brookes Publishing Co.

Wehman, P. & Moon, M. S. (Eds.) (1988). *Vocational rehabilitation and supported employment*. Baltimore, MD: Paul Brookes Publishing Co.

Wolfensberger, W. (1969). The origin and nature of our institutional models. In R. Kugel & W. Wolfensberger (Eds.), *Changing patterns on residential services for the mentally retarded* (pp. 59–171). Washington, DC: President's Committee on Mental Retardation.

Wolfensberger, W. (1972). *Normalization: The principle of normalization in human services*. Toronto: National Institute on Mental Retardation.

Zigler, E. (1966). Research on the personality structure in the retardate. In N. R. Ellis (Ed.), *International review of research in mental retardation* (Vol. 1, pp. 77–108). New York, NY: Academic Press.

Zigler, E. (1969). Developmental vs. difference theories of mental retardation and the problem of motivation. *American Journal of Mental Deficiency, 73,* 536–556.

Zigler, E., & Balla, D. (1982). *Mental retardation: The developmental vs. difference controversy*. Hillsdale, NJ: Lawrence Erlbaum Associates, publishers.

Assessing Mental Retardation Using Standardized Intelligence Tests

BARBARA TYLENDA, JACQUELINE BECKETT, AND ROWLAND P. BARRETT

EMMA PENDLETON BRADLEY HOSPITAL, DEPARTMENT OF PSYCHIATRY AND HUMAN BEHAVIOR, THE WARREN ALPERT MEDICAL SCHOOL OF BROWN UNIVERSITY, PROVIDENCE, RHODE ISLAND

I. ASSESSING MENTAL RETARDATION USING STANDARDIZED INTELLIGENCE TESTS

Mental retardation is a categorization for a heterogeneous group of individuals with deficits in cognitive and adaptive functioning manifest prior to their 18th birthday. It is not a medical disorder, although it may be coded in a medical classification of diseases. Further, despite its inclusion in all the editions of the American Psychiatric Association's *Diagnostic and Statistical Manual of Mental Disorders* (American Psychiatric Association, 1952, 1968, 1980, 1987, 1994, 2000), mental retardation is not a mental disorder. Rather, it is a deviation in development that can increase the risk of mental disorder (Sachs & Barrett, 2000). In general, the definition and categorization of mental retardation refers to a level of behavioral performance without reference to etiology (Sattler, 1992).

Mental retardation has been recognized perhaps longer than anything else we currently study in psychiatry and psychology. Qualitative descriptions of persons manifesting what we now describe as mental retardation can be found in historical records that date as far back as to the Egyptian period in 1500 BC and to the Babylonian Law Codes some 1000 years earlier (Tylenda, Hooper, & Barrett, 1987). Even before the concept of intelligence could be measured, mental retardation had been viewed as a disorder marked by deficits in intellectual ability. An early formal definition of mental retardation includes the one by Tredgold (1908): "A state of mental defect from birth, or from an early age, due to incomplete cerebral development, in consequence

INTERNATIONAL REVIEW OF RESEARCH IN MENTAL RETARDATION, Vol. 34
0074-7750/07 $35.00

DOI: 10.1016/S0074-7750(07)34002-0

of which the person affected is unable to perform his duties as a member of society in the position of life to which he was born" (p. 2). In addition, even earlier in the nineteenth century, criteria were applied to classify individuals with mental retardation by their level of "severity." Two terms were coined in 1877 to describe different levels of intellectual functioning based on decreasing language and speech abilities: imbecility and idiocy (Field & Sanchez, 1999).

However, it was not until the development of the Binet-Simon intelligence test at the beginning of the twentieth century that mental retardation's definition took on a clear, quantifiable component (i.e., intelligence as measured by IQ) with a classification system based on numerical scores and subcategories. From this period forward, intelligence, as measured by IQ, has predominated as the primary criterion for diagnosing mental retardation. Thus, the administration of a standardized intelligence test has come to play a key role in the diagnostic process. Indeed, until 1959, scores on these measures were the sole criteria by which an individual was first diagnosed and classified by category with regard to presence and level of impairment of mental retardation. In 1959, the American Association on Mental Deficiency's (AAMD) fifth definition (Heber, 1959) introduced the additional criterion of deficits in areas of adaptive behavior.

Today, individually administered intelligence tests continue to play a key role in the diagnosis of mental retardation. A deficit score on an individually administered intelligence test is the first of three criteria an individual must meet to be diagnosed as mentally retarded (deficit performance in adaptive functioning and manifest before age 18 are the other two current criteria). Consequently, measures of intelligence play a crucial role in the assessment of children and adolescents with mental retardation. This chapter will provide an overview of the various standardized intelligence tests used with children throughout the developmental period of birth through age 18 in the process of reaching the diagnosis of mental retardation. It also will provide guidelines specific to this evaluation process of young individuals with mental retardation. Finally, the oftentimes complicated nature of these young individuals' profiles will be reviewed; examples of psychological reports for various clinical cases will be shared.

II. DEFINITIONS OF MENTAL RETARDATION

While there has been debate over the definition and classification of mental retardation for several decades, the debate has focused primarily on issues related to epidemiological research, specifically, conceptual approaches and key elements for case identification (Leonard & Wen, 2002). Two internationally recognized and widely adopted definitions for mental retardation are provided by the American Association on Mental Retardation (AAMR, 2002) and the American Psychiatric Association (2000). These definitions are currently considered the "gold standard" with regard to definition and classification. They are regularly used by professionals when assessing for mental retardation in children and youth.

A. AAMR Definition

The AAMR (2002) defines mental retardation as "... a disability characterized by significant limitations both in intellectual functioning and in adaptive behavior as expressed in conceptual, social, and practical adaptive skills. This disability originates before age 18" (p. 8). According to the AAMR (2002), the intellectual criterion requires an IQ of $\sim$2 or more standard deviations (SD) below the mean, or an IQ of 70 or below. With regard to adaptive behavior criterion, the AAMR (2002) manual provides specific scores on adaptive behavior measures for a diagnosis of mental retardation. In this area, the individual must have scores of at least 2 SD below the mean on either (1) one of the following three types of adaptive behavior (i.e., conceptual, social, or practical) or (2) a total score on a standardized measure that includes an assessment of conceptual, social, and practical skills.

B. American Psychiatric Association Definition

The American Psychiatric Association's (2000) *Diagnostic and Statistical Manual of Mental Disorders, Fourth Edition, Text Revision* (*DSM-IV-TR*) defines mental retardation as "... significantly sub-average general intellectual functioning (Criterion A) that is accompanied by significant limitations in adaptive functioning in at least two of the following areas: communication, self-care, home living, social/interpersonal skills, use of community resources, self-direction, functional academic skills, work, leisure, health, and safety (Criterion B). The onset of mental retardation must occur before age 18 years" (p. 41). Consistent with the AAMR (2002) definition, criteria for significantly subaverage intellectual functioning generally is considered to be an IQ 2 or more SD below the population mean, usually an IQ of 70 or below. However, *DSM-IV-TR* (2000) states that an IQ of 75 or below may constitute the criterion in some settings.

C. Individually Administered Intelligence Test

The AAMR (2002) definition and the *DSM-IV-TR* (2000) definition both state that significant subaverage intellectual functioning must be based on results of an appropriately standardized, individually administered intelligence test. Consequently, group administered IQ testing which was frequently used until the early 1960s in school settings is no longer an acceptable standard of evaluation.

III. LEVELS OF MENTAL RETARDATION

The AAMR (2002) definition no longer includes a classification system based on degrees of severity of mental retardation. This came about from the AAMR's (2002) more recent position of incorporating measured intelligence only in the initial diagnosis.

In contrast, the American Psychiatric Association in its *DSM-IV-TR* (2000) continues to distinguish four categories of mental retardation based on degrees of severity. These include: mild mental retardation, moderate mental retardation, severe mental retardation, and profound mental retardation. The *DSM-IV-TR* (2000) specifies IQ ranges for each of the four categories. The IQ ranges overlap each other, typically by five points. They are as follows:

Mild mental retardation: IQ = 50–55 to ~70
Moderate mental retardation: IQ = 35–40 to 50–55
Severe mental retardation: IQ = 20–25 to 35–40
Profound mental retardation: IQ less than or = 20–25

This overlap in range is a result of the difference in the statistical properties of the measures used to determine intellectual functioning. Remember, for the purposes of diagnosis, subaverage intellectual functioning is defined as an IQ of 2 or more SD below the established mean IQ for the test employed. For example, with the −2 SD criterion being used, then the IQ just below the −2 SD point is 69 for the Wechsler tests (Wechsler, 1997, 2003a,b), the Stanford-Binet V (Roid, 2003b), and the Leiter International Performance Scale-Revised (Roid & Miller, 1997) but 67 on the Bayley Scale of Infant and Toddler Development (Bayley, 2005), the McCarthy Scales of Children's Abilities (McCarthy, 1972), and the original Leiter International Performance Scale (Leiter, 1948). The cutoff points vary because the former tests have a SD of 15, whereas the latter tests have a SD of 16. Other cutoff points for categories of mental retardation may be appropriate for other instruments, depending on the SD of the test; however, the −2 SD criteria always is used. Table I shows the classification system of mental retardation based on measured intelligence when various intelligence tests are employed. Adaptive functioning (discussed in Dixon, this volume) consistent with the level of mental retardation also is important in the final classification of the individual.

TABLE I
RANGE OF IQ SCORES AND ASSOCIATED CLASSIFICATION OF MENTAL RETARDATION

	Range of IQ scores	
Classification	IQ Test SD = 15	IQ Test SD = 16
Mild	69–55	67–52
Moderate	54–40	51–36
Severe	39–25	35–20
Profound	24 and below	19 and below

Given that measures of intelligence play a crucial role in the assessment of children and youth with mental retardation, such categorization of mental retardation also may have some bearing on the standardized intelligence test(s) an examiner will choose for the evaluation process. For example, while the Wechsler intelligence tests are frequently used in the assessment of mental retardation in children and adolescents, the lowest Full Scale IQ (FSIQ) obtainable on a Wechsler test is a 40. Consequently, the Wechsler cannot adequately measure IQs below 40. This issue will be discussed in greater depth later in this chapter.

A. Mild Mental Retardation

Individuals in the mild range of mental retardation comprise ~85% of all persons diagnosed with mental retardation (American Psychiatric Association, 2000). The IQ scores for these individuals fall in the range of 50–55 to 70. Comparable limitations in adaptive behavior also are present. Etiologically, this group is frequently referred to as being in the familial (or psychosocial) group of retardation. Individuals in this group predominantly are those who fall in the lower portion of the normal distribution of intelligence. The reasons for their relatively weak intellectual functioning are difficult to decipher; however, they are likely secondary to one of a variety of causes or some combination of them. This may include: (1) below-average heredity; (2) normal polygenic variation, that is the combined action of many genes; (3) subclinical brain damage yet to be diagnosed; (4) significantly below-average environment, that is low early stimulation, caretaker distress, low socioeconomic status (SES), poverty, and so on. These individuals also typically have one or more family members who also have diminished cognitive and adaptive functioning (particularly in the school setting). Seldom present are neurological or apparent physical abnormalities.

Individuals in this range of functioning often are not identified as having mental retardation until they enter school (Grossman, 1983). Parents of these children, however, frequently report that their child displayed delays in acquisition of developmental speech and motor milestones. Children with mild mental retardation may have a history of referral for speech and occupational therapy services in early childhood. Once identified as having mental retardation, these children become eligible for special education services to aid acquisition of academic, vocational, and life skills. Beyond the school-age years, individuals with mild mental retardation often live and work independently without coming to the attention of the professional service community. This integration may be secondary to the fact that intellectual limitations are more obvious in school settings than in many employment settings and community experiences. Further, this also may be a result of a gradual accumulation of adaptive skills and problem solving abilities acquired during the formative years of formal education and special education services. In general, prevalence estimates support that rates of mental retardation are much higher for young children than adults (Larson et al., 2001). This is not inconsistent with the position that many adults with mild mental retardation may integrate into society with comparatively little difficulty when compared to those individuals whose intellectual development was more seriously impaired.

B. Moderate, Severe, and Profound Mental Retardation

Individuals in the moderate, severe, and profound ranges of mental retardation, together, make up the remaining 15% of all individuals diagnosed with mental retardation (American Psychiatric Association, 2000). The IQ scores of this group falls into the IQ range of more than 3 SD below the established mean IQ for the test employed. Generally, this translates to 35–40 to 50–55, 20–25 to 35 to 40, and less than or equal to 20–25, respectively. For each level, comparable limitations with regard to adaptive functioning also are present. Etiologically, these three levels of mental retardation are jointly referred to as the organic (or biological) group. The etiology of the organic group appears to be principally associated with: (1) a genetic component linked to single gene effects [e.g., phenylketonuria (PKU)], (2) chromosomal abnormalities (e.g., Down's syndrome), and (3) brain damage (e.g., microcephaly). With regard to the latter, such brain damage may be severe and diffuse (generalized encephalopathy) in nature. Neuroanatomical malformations of the brain also may be present. There is a high probability that the origination of the damage is during the prenatal period.

1. MODERATE MENTAL RETARDATION

Individuals with moderate mental retardation usually are first identified during infancy or early childhood. Typically, they present for an interdisciplinary evaluation to a Child Development Center or an Early Intervention Program secondary to displaying delays in attaining developmental milestones. This may include motor, speech, social, or cognitive delays. With the support of special education services, individuals in this category may acquire academic skills similar to a second- to fourth-grade student, usually by the period of late adolescence. Individuals with moderate mental retardation may succeed very well in roles as semiskilled or unskilled workers. However, support and/or assistance in most areas of daily living typically are required.

2. SEVERE MENTAL RETARDATION

Individuals with severe mental retardation are commonly identified in infancy as they manifest obvious delays in acquiring motor and language skills. Physical abnormalities are not unusual. While individuals with severe mental retardation acquire some basic self-help skills, they cannot function independently and require daily support and supervision throughout their entire lives.

3. PROFOUND MENTAL RETARDATION

Individuals with profound mental retardation are typically identified at birth or soon thereafter. Early identification is usually secondary to their apparent physical abnormalities and/or compromise. Delays in development and basic skill acquisition are readily apparent beginning in infancy. Physical compromise and/or abnormalities may hinder or preclude the ability to ambulate or speak. Others will have to take on responsibility for all basic care and activities of daily living for individuals with profound mental retardation. This level of care will be lifelong.

IV. STANDARDIZED INTELLIGENCE (IQ) TESTING

A. What Intelligence Tests Measure

Standardized intelligence tests are ability tests. Ability refers to current level of knowledge or skill in a particular area. Young children are often evaluated to determine the progress of their development. A measure may assess ability in motor, language, social, or cognitive skills. Intelligence tests are ability tests in that they assess overall intellectual functioning. They provide information about the individual's repertoire of cognitive skills and knowledge at a given point in time.

Standardized intelligence tests do not measure capacity or potential, per se. As aptitude is the potential to learn or develop proficiency in some area, provided that certain conditions or training prevail, intelligence tests are not considered to be aptitude tests. However, aptitude tests also measure learned abilities. An aptitude test can measure the results of both general and incidental learning, and can predict future learning. Intelligence tests, therefore, also can be viewed as aptitude tests (in the broader sense) because they assess capacity for new learning and problem solving.

A standardized intelligence test meets criteria as such when a standard has been set from the results achieved by using the test with individuals who are representative of the population. For those readers interested in detailed description and debate on: (1) theories of intelligence, (2) veracity of intelligence as a construct, (3) measurement and change of intelligence, and (4) pros and cons of testing intelligence, the reader is referred to Sattler (1992) and Locurto (1991). In general, it is best to keep in mind that intelligence tests do not measure innate intelligence or capability. IQs are only estimates of ability. These scores are only a part of the spectrum of an individual's abilities. IQ scores do change, and IQ scores obtained from different tests may not be interchangeable.

B. Why IQ Tests Are Administered and What IQ Tests Can Reveal

An intelligence test can be administered for a variety of reasons. Completion of such testing can provide information for the purposes of: (1) measurement, (2) diagnosis, and (3) educational or occupational programming. An evaluation that includes an intelligence test may be administered to measure a child's current developmental level or cognitive abilities. It also may be conducted to ascertain a particular diagnosis for an individual. Further, an evaluation that includes an intelligence test may be carried out to gain information about: (1) groups of children, (2) degree of success of an educational or training program, or (3) level of success of a treatment. Finally, intelligence testing may be administered in effort to set up a treatment protocol for either an individual or a program/facility.

C. Stability and Change in IQ Scores for Mentally Retarded Children

The IQ obtained from standardized intelligence tests is very helpful in work with children who are mentally retarded. While correlations between Developmental Quotients obtained on infant tests and IQs obtained later in childhood tend to be very low for those with average or superior intelligence, for children with developmental disabilities, correlations tend to be substantial between IQs obtained in infancy and those obtained later in childhood. For children with developmental disabilities (including those diagnosed as mentally retarded), correlations range from .50 to .97. (Broman & Nichols, 1975; Brooks-Gunn & Lewis, 1983; Fishler, Graliker, & Koch, 1965; Fishman & Palkes, 1974; Illingworth & Birch, 1959; Keogh & Kopp, 1978; Knobloch & Pasamanick, 1960; VanderVeer & Schweid, 1974; Werner, Honzik, & Smith, 1968). For example, infants with serious developmental handicaps (e.g., Down's syndrome) who have below-average scores on infant tests during their first 20 months of life, are likely to obtain low IQ scores at later periods of development. Seventy-three percent of infants with moderate to profound mental retardation, as assessed by the Bayley Scales, were still classified as severely mentally retarded 1–3 years after the initial evaluation (Brooks-Gunn & Lewis, 1983). Generally, infants who score in mentally retarded ranges on developmental scales during the first year of life have a high probability of obtaining scores in the mentally retarded range during their school years. Infants with developmental quotients of 25 or less are likely to remain severely impacted.

However, these findings are not an endorsement of diagnosing mental retardation via a single test score in infancy. On the contrary, infants who are found to be slow at an early age can make gains rapidly at later developmental periods. Consequently, repeat evaluations should be conducted on such a child at later ages for verification of cognitive status as well as for review and modification of educational programming and treatment protocols currently in place. Some very young children with low IQs have suffered from stimulus deprivation, that is their environments have been so nonstimulating that it prevents them from developing normally. These children who then demonstrate continued decreases in IQ scores during the preschool years tend to be those whose homes or environments continue to manifest minimal stimulation (Dennis & Najarian, 1973), inconsistent routines, and either a very severe or a very inconsistent discipline regime. In contrast, children previously identified with low IQs who then demonstrate subsequent increases in IQs during the preschool years tend to be those whose homes or environments have undergone modification and present with structure, consistency, and age-appropriate stimulation, in which attention and encouragement are given in a clear manner (Dennis & Najarian, 1973; Sattler, 1992). In general, the consequences of unfavorable environments, although quite serious, can be remedied to some degree by improving the levels of attention, stimulation, and nurturance in the environments of affected children (Dennis & Najarian, 1973). The earlier this occurs, the better the developmental outcome for the child (Dennis & Najarian, 1973).

V. DIFFERENTIATING CHILDREN WITH MENTAL RETARDATION FROM CHILDREN WITH OTHER HANDICAPS

It is possible that young children, particularly those of preschool age, who are referred for a first-time developmental/cognitive evaluation for clarification of a diagnosis of mental retardation, are actually manifesting either (1) a diagnosis other than mental retardation or (2) one or more additional diagnoses concomitant with the diagnosis of mental retardation. Consequently, an evaluator who will be specializing in the evaluation and diagnosis of mental retardation should be well-versed in the presenting features and profiles for a range of other disorders and problems frequently diagnosed in the preschool population. Table II lists a range of disorders and problems in which an evaluator should be well-versed.

To aid in the process of diagnostic clarification, the evaluator may be well-served to conduct a first-time cognitive evaluation as part of an interdisciplinary evaluation (e.g., such as those frequently completed in a Child Development Center). Having the benefit of shared information and findings from other disciplines may aid differential diagnosis and appropriate, integrated recommendations. If an interdisciplinary evaluation is not possible, the evaluator should, at minimum, have access to a variety of informational materials prior to evaluating the child. These should include: (1) medical, social, and developmental histories; (2) developmental-pediatric evaluation; (3) vision and hearing evaluations; (4) speech and language evaluations; and (5) motor (occupational therapy and physical therapy) evaluation.

A. Distinguishing Between Mental Retardation and Developmental Delay

When mental retardation is suspected in an infant or a preschool-age child, the nondiagnostic condition of developmental delay should be considered as an alternative. The diagnosis of mental retardation should be made only in cases that clearly support significantly subaverage intellectual functioning and significant deficits in adaptive behavior.

Fotheringhan (1983) has outlined three reasons for distinguishing between mental retardation and developmental delay during these early years of infancy, toddler, and preschool years. First, while a child may meet diagnostic criteria for mental retardation, intelligence measures primarily reflect developmental progress. Thus, repeated assessments over time are necessary to check for changes in the rate of development and ascertain a clear diagnosis. Second, other conditions may mimic mental retardation. For example, an aphasia or cerebral palsy may limit a child's ability to communicate and, therefore, negatively impact the assessment of a child's intellectual

TABLE II

LIST OF DISORDERS AND PROBLEMS TO CONSIDER WHEN A CHILD IS REFERRED FOR A DIAGNOSTIC EVALUATION TO "RULE-IN/RULE-OUT" MENTAL RETARDATION

When conducting an assessment with a child for a possible diagnosis of mental retardation, the evaluator needs to consider the following range of disorders or problems as possible alternative or additional diagnoses/conditions:
(1) Developmental delay
(2) The "Umbrella of Neurological Impairment" which includes:
(A) Autism
(B) Pervasive developmental disorder, not otherwise specified
(C) Rett's syndrome
(D) Childhood disintegrative disorder
(E) High-functioning autism
(F) Asperger's disorder
(G) Neurological inefficiency/nonverbal learning disability
(H) Attention deficit disorder
(3) Developmental language disorder
(4) Hearing impairment
(5) Visual impairment
(6) Cerebral palsy
(7) Motor coordination disorder
(8) Regulatory disorders
(9) Attachment disorder
(10) Elective mutism
(11) Psychosocial deprivation
(12) Other psychiatric conditions
(13) Some form of a behavioral disorder
(14) Dyadic problem between caretaker and child
(15) Challenging temperament and/or inconsistency of temperament between caretaker and child

performance. Third, environmental circumstances also may negatively impact a child's test performance which, if modified, might significantly increase a child's functioning (e.g., increasing adaptive functioning beyond the range of mental retardation). Thus, as noted earlier in this section, the evaluator must be alert to the interrelatedness of developmental functioning at this age level and possible alternative roots and causes of developmental delay.

When a child demonstrates impaired cognitive and adaptive functioning and a diagnosis of mental retardation cannot be reliably made, a tentative condition of developmental delay may be appropriate. This alerts the involved parties to a variety of possibilities that can include: (1) the current cognitive deficit is ambiguous, (2) the cognitive deficit may be transitory in nature, (3) the deficits in adaptive behavior are not significant enough to warrant a diagnosis of mental retardation, or (4) the deficits in adaptive behavior may be temporary or secondary to another disorder that can resolve with intervention (e.g., lack of opportunity). Thus, it is not unusual for a very young child, where there is question of a diagnosis of mental retardation, to have such a diagnosis deferred. Typically, the child in question should be reevaluated at regular intervals to assess for rate of developmental progress and possible changes in the developmental profile.

VI. CHOOSING AN INTELLIGENCE TEST FOR AN INDIVIDUAL SUSPECTED OF HAVING MENTAL RETARDATION

Determining the test to be used for a particular child or adolescent should be based on a careful review of the referral question and any known characteristics of the individual being evaluated. Important information to consider when choosing an assessment tool includes: (1) the child's language proficiency (in English and/or another language), (2) developmental level, (3) known physical and/or cognitive limitations, and (4) prior tests used and their results.

All tests of cognitive ability are not alike. It is not enough to gain familiarity with one assessment measure and consistently use it in making a determination of mental retardation. Intelligence tests may be normed on different populations, may have higher or lower levels of reliability and validity, may be based on different conceptual models of intelligence, and may assess intelligence using different modalities (verbal, visual, kinesthetic, and so on). Particularly, in the case of individuals with known or suspected cognitive impairments, these factors will need to be taken into account when choosing a diagnostic measure. The choice of test should be made such that an individual's performance on a given measure is maximized. For example, a child with motor impairment may appear to demonstrate "processing speed deficits" or deficits in "spatial reasoning" if assessed using a motor-dependent test. The newer tests of intelligence take into account difficulties such as these, to some degree, by offering alternative ways of measuring different abilities. However, the prudent examiner may find that, in some cases, choosing a different assessment tool (or multiple assessment tools) will provide more accurate information for a given individual. In general, the prudent examiner will choose a measurement instrument based on the data presented, not on a particular bias. For this reason, the examiner who will be regularly assessing children and adolescents for diagnostic clarification of mental retardation will find it necessary to become familiar with a variety of intelligence assessment tools. Many of these assessment instruments are not part of the typical graduate assessment course experience and, therefore, competency in administration and interpretation will require additional training and practice on the part of the examining psychologist.

Due to their well-established psychometric properties, as well as their clinical and diagnostic utility, some standardized intelligence tests have become favorites of many in the assessment community. For example, the Wechsler Scales and the Stanford-Binet are often the tests of first choice for examiners of individuals having or suspected of having mental retardation. In addition to their wide use and acceptance by many psychologists, the courts, educational institutions, and social service agencies often may refuse to accept test results from alternate measures of intelligence. In such cases, it becomes the responsibility of the reporting evaluator to educate such agencies on these alternate measures (specifically, with regard to comparable psychometric properties as well as diagnostic and clinical utility) and when these alternate measures are deemed more appropriate in the assessment of a given individual.

Finally, it should be noted that the many tests presented in this chapter are generally considered to be language-based measures of intelligence. When a language-based disability is suspected, steps should be taken to obtain a language-free measure of intelligence. Such language-free measures will be discussed in a subsequent section of this chapter. However, if a child has never had a formal language or intelligence evaluation, it may be appropriate to use a traditional, language-based measure in order to establish functioning level, particularly if language competence is part of the referral question. If the assessment reveals evidence of a language-based disability, the presentation of the IQ score(s) should be made with the caveat that the test scores may have been attenuated by language functioning. In such cases, a language-free measure (e.g., Leiter International Performance Scale-Revised, 1997) will be necessary in making the overall determination of mental retardation.

VII. INTELLIGENCE TESTS EMPLOYED FOR ASSESSING MENTAL RETARDATION

The actual exercise of conducting a formal cognitive evaluation on a toddler, child, or adolescent who presents with mental retardation can be a challenging task. Indeed, consistently, it is a more challenging task compared to carrying out the same procedure with same-age typical peers. However, in these authors' professional experience, it is never an impossible task—no child is untestable. Even when the task is the evaluation of a child with severe or profound mental retardation, some cognitive scores can be deciphered. One does not have to rely solely on informal assessment procedures and functional assessment procedures. Cognitive measures can be ascertained.

A key component to success in this process lies in choosing an appropriate standardized measure(s) of intelligence. More often than not, the intelligence test chosen will be from among the "gold standard" tests normed for that child's particular age group (Exhibit 2.1). However, in some cases, it will entail using multiple standardized measures of intelligence normed for that child's particular age group, an older version of a "gold standard" test, or a combination of these two scenarios (Exhibit 2.2). In some extreme cases (such as for older children who present with severe or profound mental retardation), it will entail using a "gold standard" test normed for a younger age group (Exhibit 2.3). In this latter case, the child's actual performance and associated total raw score will need to be cross-matched to the mean IQ on that particular test to ascertain an approximate developmental age.

In recent years, an increasing number of new, standardized measures of intelligence have appeared on the market. The evaluator who typically provides formal assessment of children presenting with mental retardation would be remiss not to stay abreast of these new instruments and to evaluate how such instruments compare with older, more established measures. However, despite these newer tests being introduced, there are a handful of standardized IQ instruments that continue to be robust measures for evaluating children presenting with mental retardation. These include the following standardized instruments.

EXHIBIT 2.1

Assessment Case Illustration #1

Traditional Assessment for Diagnosis of Mental Retardation: Use of a Single, Age-Appropriate Intelligence Test

PSYCHOLOGICAL EVALUATION

Name: Ian H.
Date of birth: 4-7-96
Chronological age: 9 years, 11 months
Chronological grade: Special education
Date of admission: 12-5-05
Dates of assessment: 3-17-06 and 3-24-06

REASON FOR REFERRAL

Ian is a 9 year, 11-month-old male who was referred for a psychological evaluation by Dr. R., Seton Hospital Developmental Disabilities Program (DDP) Psychiatrist. Specifically, testing was requested to determine current levels of cognitive and adaptive behavior functioning to aid future educational placement and programming.

BACKGROUND INFORMATION

Ian was admitted to the Seton Hospital DDP on 12-5-05 due to a significant increase in aggressive and self-injurious behavior at home and school. This is Ian's fourth inpatient admission to Seton Hospital since January 2002. Ian's parents expressed concern that they felt increasingly unable to keep Ian and their other children safe in their home. They have reported that Ian's behavioral dysregulation appears to be seasonally related, but that he requires intensive supervision and structure even during times when he is functioning at his best. On current admission, Ian received multiple psychiatric diagnoses: Bipolar II Disorder, Attention Deficit Hyperactivity Disorder, Chronic Motor Tic Disorder, Post Traumatic Stress Disorder, and Mild Mental Retardation. In addition, Ian received medical diagnoses of obesity and seizure disorder.

Prior to his admission to Seton Hospital in December, Ian resided with his adoptive family, the H.'s, which includes his adoptive mother, father, one brother, and two sisters. Ian has lived with the H.'s since he was 2 years old, when he was brought into the family as a foster child subsequent to removal from his biological mother's home. He reportedly lived with his biological mother from the age of $1\frac{1}{2}$ to 2 years of age. While living with his biological mother, Ian reportedly sustained multiple abuse-related injuries, including a head trauma and multiple burn wounds. From birth to $1\frac{1}{2}$ years of age, Ian lived with a foster family that was suspected of providing less than adequate care. Ian was initially removed from his biological mother at birth, when it was determined that he was born addicted to cocaine.

Ian's early developmental history is reportedly significant for the presence of severe abuse as well as speech and motor difficulties. Ian's medical history is significant for perinatal cocaine addiction, closed head trauma, and a seizure disorder.

Ian's developmental history is significant for the presence of severe behavioral and emotional dysregulation. He has displayed aggression toward self, peers, school staff, and his family. In addition, hc has a history of obsessive-compulsive behaviors and sensory sensitivities.

Although the H.'s have been stressed with Ian's increasing difficulties, they have provided a loving home environment for him and are highly invested in his care. Since becoming a member of the H. family, Ian has received intensive special education and supportive services. In addition, the family has utilized intensive in-home and outpatient services in an attempt to meet Ian's needs. Prior to inpatient admission, Ian was receiving one-to-one special education services at school. Ian's behavioral escalations reportedly precipitated removal from his most recent special education setting.

CURRENT MEDICATIONS

Lithium, 600 mg, bedtime
Abilify, 10 mg, 8 a.m.
Tenex, 1 mg, 8 a.m., 2 p.m.; 2 mg, bedtime
Adderall, 7.5 mg, 8 a.m., 12 noon
Zonagram, 100 mg, bedtime
Lamictal, 75 mg, 8 a.m., bedtime

PROCEDURES USED

Wechsler Intelligence Scale for Children, Fourth Edition (WISC-IV)
Vineland Adaptive Behavior Scales, Second Edition (parent informant)
Behavioral observations
Parent interview
Chart review

CLINICAL FINDINGS AND IMPRESSIONS

Behavioral Observations

Ian was evaluated over the course of two sessions, each session lasting approximately one hour in length. This examination took place in a quiet, distraction-free environment. In order to obtain Ian's best performance, he was provided verbal reinforcement and a sticker chart. Ian exerted good effort on all test items presented. He appropriately increased effort and response time when presented with more difficult task items. He worked diligently even when presented with task items which appeared to be outside of his ability level. Ian's behavior across sessions was generally consistent and will be summarized as a unified narrative.

Ian presented as an appropriately dressed, well-groomed boy with dark brown hair and light brown skin. He was of average height and above average weight for a boy his age. He was friendly with the examiner on meeting but stated that he did not want to go to testing. However, he quickly changed his mind when he was reminded of opportunities for reinforcement for behaving appropriately. Transition to the testing site was unremarkable. Ian engaged in appropriate small talk on the way to the testing room, and did not need redirection at any time while walking from one building to another.

Throughout the examination, Ian appeared to be relatively focused and organized. He did not appear to need frequent reminders of attention or redirection while engaged in assessment tasks. He remained seated and did not appear overly fidgety or restless. Ian's focus and attention did seem to decrease as item difficulty increased. However, Ian demonstrated appropriate effort throughout the evaluation, even on items that appeared to be outside of his ability range.

Ian seemed to respond well to and develop rapport easily with the examiner. Although he generally appeared affectively flat, he did participate in spontaneous verbal exchanges with the examiner, and seemed socially interested. Eye contact was socially appropriate during conversation. However, during testing, Ian used eye contact extensively as an attempt to determine how well he was performing.

Ian's responses to task items gave the impression of dependency. He could become upset when help was not offered on task items. Consistent with this, he tended to be highly assurance seeking. He would frequently look up and make eye contact to determine if his responses were correct, and would become visibly agitated when he was not given indication as to whether his response was right or wrong.

Ian's verbal behavior was not significantly atypical. Amount and content of speech were relatively impoverished, but appeared congruent with his developmental level and cognitive ability. During the evaluation, he made appropriate small talk and was responsive to verbal queries.

Ian's gross motor behavior was generally unremarkable. Fine motor tasks appeared difficult for him. He held his pencil in an immature grasp and needed to be reminded to hold his paper when writing.

Given the consistency of Ian's behavior and performance across two sessions, it can be reasonably concluded that this evaluation accurately reflects Ian's current functioning and abilities when provided with one-to-one attention and a distraction-free environment.

Test Findings

Ian's intellectual functioning, as assessed by the WISC-IV, falls in the Intellectually Deficit range. He obtained a Full Scale IQ (FSIQ) score of 48 (mean = 100; SD = 15) which is over 3 SD below the mean functioning level for children in Ian's age range. The chances are 95 of 100 that Ian's actual FSIQ is between 42 and 54. In addition to his FSIQ, Ian obtained a Verbal Comprehension Index (VCI) of 63, a Perceptual Reasoning Index (PRI) of 53, a Working Memory Index (WMI) of 59, and a Processing Speed Index (PSI) of 53. These scores are all considered to be in the Intellectually Deficient range of functioning. Ian's specific WISC-IV subscale scores are summarized below (where mean = 10 and SD = 3):

Verbal Comprehension		**Perceptual Reasoning**	
Similarities	5	Block Design	1[a]
Vocabulary	3	Picture Concept	3
Comprehension	3	Matrix Reasoning	3
		Picture Completion	3
Working Memory		**Processing Speed**	
Digit Span	2	Coding	2
Letter-Number Sequence	4	Symbol Search	1

[a]This score is based on a raw score of 0.

This deficit profile was further confirmed by results of the Vineland Adaptive Behavior Scales, a caretaker response inventory assessing adaptive behavior skills domestically and in the community. For individuals in Ian's age range, the Vineland measures the ability to perform daily living activities required for personal and social sufficiency in the areas of communication, daily living skills, and socialization. When comparing Ian's adaptive behavior skills with same-aged peers in the general population, he is functioning $\sim 2\frac{1}{2}$ to 3 SD below the mean. Current standard scores and age equivalent scores are summarized below (where mean = 100 and SD = 15):

Domain	Standard score	Age equivalent
Communication	67	–
Receptive	–	2 years, 6 months
Expressive	–	4 years, 10 months
Written	–	7 years, 1 month
Daily Living Skills	63	–
Personal	–	4 years, 10 months
Domestic	–	4 years, 7 months
Community	–	5 years, 5 months
Socialization	61	–
Interpersonal relationships	–	3 years, 7 months
Play and leisure time	–	2 years, 9 months
Coping skills	–	2 years, 1 month
Adaptive Behavior Composite	62	–

Ian's domain scores are relatively consistent across domains. He does demonstrate a small (albeit, statistically insignificant) relative strength with regard to community-based skills and written expression. However, Ian's scores in all domains reflect significant weakness when compared to his same-aged peers in the general population.

SUMMARY

Ian is a 9 year, 11-month-old male who is currently an inpatient on the Seton Hospital DDP. He was admitted to the DDP as a result of a significant increase in aggressive and self-injurious behavior. He was referred for a psychological evaluation to assess current cognitive and adaptive behavior functioning.

Results of this evaluation reveal cognitive functioning to be in the Intellectually Deficient range, with a FSIQ score = 48 (more than 3 SD below the mean), and adaptive behavior functioning to be in the low range of functioning ($\sim 2\frac{1}{2}$ SD below the mean). Taken together, findings indicate that Ian currently meets eligibility criteria for a diagnosis of Mental Retardation (Mild to Moderate) given significant subaverage cognitive and adaptive behavior functioning.

Behavioral observations obtained throughout the course of this evaluation suggest that Ian tends to lack confidence in his ability to perform basic tasks independently, even those within his demonstrated ability level. Although he appears to demonstrate appropriate effort on tasks, he requires a high degree of assurance in his performance. He responds well to nonconfrontational expectation of compliance.

RECOMMENDATIONS

Given his current behavioral, cognitive, and social-emotional functioning, Ian will continue to require receiving intensive support, supervision, and monitoring. In addition, Ian will continue to require receiving intensive special education, psychiatric, and supportive services. Due to ongoing evidence of seizure activity, it is further recommended that Ian continue to receive ongoing support and monitoring of his neurological status. Specific recommendations based on the results of this assessment are provided below.

Behavioral Expectations

Ian appears to respond well to nonconfrontational expectations of compliance. He will generally comply with a task demand if given enough time to respond to a first request and if he is not engaged in a power struggle. However, once Ian appears highly disorganized and dysregulated, he may not be able to respond to verbal commands. This is likely to occur in highly stimulating environments.

Academic Functioning

Ian will benefit from instructional materials that are tailored to his current level of cognitive functioning. Ian will specifically benefit from being allowed to work independently on task items that are well within his range of functioning (independence level) in order for him to achieve some degree of confidence in his performance. Items that are presented at his instructional level (slightly above independence level) should be presented in a one-to-one instructional setting. For items presented at Ian's instructional level, cognitive modeling is imperative. Specifically, using mistakes as instructional tools should be modeled explicitly (and reinforced). In addition, Ian's need for constant assurance should be monitored and slowly (carefully) extinguished.

Emotional Lability/Obsessive Compulsive Symptoms

Ian will benefit from being provided with low-stimulation environments to decrease emotional lability. He may benefit from being explicitly taught basic (developmentally appropriate) cognitive-behavioral and self-regulation strategies for dealing with emotionally overwhelming situations. For example, Ian may benefit from the use of an overlearned visual or auditory cue, which may assist him in de-escalating and returning to baseline functioning. Teaching of the cue should be paired with relaxation training and de-escalating strategies. Ian also may respond well to exposure and response-prevention strategies for his obsessive-compulsive symptoms.

Peer Modeling

Ian may benefit from being provided with appropriate peer models for his behavior. As Ian reportedly tends to mimic chosen peers in his environment, the provision of appropriate peer models may be an efficient way for him to internalize a schema of appropriate behavioral functioning.

It was a pleasure to evaluate Ian. If any questions or concerns arise regarding this report, please feel free to contact me at 800-555-1212.

EXHIBIT 2.2

Assessment Case Illustration #2

Assessment for Diagnosis of Mental Retardation Versus a Language Disorder: Use of Multiple Intelligence Tests (Verbal and Nonverbal Instruments)

PSYCHOLOGICAL EVALUATION

Name: Matthew B.
Date of birth: 11-18-98
Chronological age: 6 years, 6 months
Chronological grade: Kindergarten
Dates of assessment: 5-23-05 and 6-7-05

REASON FOR REFERRAL

Matthew is a 6 year, 6 month old Caucasian male referred to the DDP Outpatient Clinic of Seton Hospital for a comprehensive psychological evaluation. He was referred by his parents to determine his current level of functioning and to assist in educational programming. Mr. and Mrs. B. were interested in obtaining a second opinion following a comprehensive evaluation conducted by the Bridgewater School Department.

BACKGROUND INFORMATION

The following information was obtained via parent questionnaire data, parent interview, and a thorough review of Matthew's educational and medical records. Matthew was the product of a 42-week uncomplicated pregnancy and normal vaginal delivery. Neonatal development was complicated by some respiratory problems and an undescended testicle. Matthew also experienced an apnea episode at $\sim$2 weeks of age which required a brief hospitalization. He was discharged home with an apnea monitor and subsequently had a few additional episodes. At 9 months of age, Matthew underwent surgery for a hernia repair.

By 9 months of age, Matthew's development was characterized by global delays in cognitive, motor, and physical domains. He was reported to fall within the 5th percentile for stature. At 11 months of age, Matthew was enrolled in Early Intervention services where he remained until age three. He was provided with speech therapy, physical therapy, and educational services. Matthew also underwent chromosomal analyses and an EEG, both of which were within normal limits.

In February 2001, at 27 months of age, Matthew underwent a multidisciplinary evaluation by the Infant Team at Cushing Children's Hospital. Presenting concerns included delays in language and motor development, and physical growth and size. Matthew also was exhibiting head-banging behavior at that time. Psychological assessment via the Bayley Scales of Infant Development (Second Edition) revealed an age equivalent score of 16 months. Adaptive behavior skills were roughly within the 16-month range as well. Results of a physical therapy assessment indicated that Matthew's fine and gross motor skills, feeding skills, and dressing skills all clustered at the 15- to 17-month level.

In July 2001, Matthew was evaluated by Dr. J. of the Clinical Genetics Program at Cushing Children's Hospital. Dr. J.'s impression was that Matthew was not exhibiting a degenerative neurological disorder or a specific genetic disorder. Dr. J. further stated that it was highly unlikely that Matthew's apnea was the cause of his subsequent problems. Rather, Matthew's developmental delays and apnea were considered to be symptoms of a nervous system that, from birth, was not working as it should. Though no specific etiology could be identified, it was suggested that Matthew's problems were likely a result of atypical early brain development. However, there is no family history of neurological or developmental problems. It was anticipated at that time that Matthew would continue to exhibit a slow but steady developmental progression.

In January 2004, Matthew was evaluated by neurologist, Dr. R. Primary problems included impulsivity, inattention, and developmental delays. A trial of Ritalin was implemented ~2 months later. Ritalin was discontinued in January 2005 for an unspecified reason.

Matthew underwent a triennial evaluation (November 2004) by the Bridgewater School Department. On the Wechsler Preschool and Primary Scale of Intelligence, Third Edition (WPPSI-III), Matthew earned a Verbal Scale IQ score of 58, a Performance Scale IQ score of 48, and a FSIQ score of 48. Age equivalents for adaptive behavior skills, based on parent report on the Vineland Adaptive Behavior Scales, were as follows: Communication = 2 years, 9 months; Daily Living Skills = 4 years, 9 months; and Socialization = 2 years, 9 months. Results of a Speech and

Language evaluation indicated an age equivalent of 2 years, 11 months for receptive language skills and 2 years, 6 months for expressive language skills. Developmental play assessment and classroom observations revealed that Matthew was somewhat slow and lethargic and his pencil grasp was somewhat weak. He also was observed to have a warm disposition, he smiled frequently, and he was able to follow directions well. It was concluded that Matthew exhibits even delays in all developmental domains and that he is functioning in the "mentally deficient" range. It was indicated that he benefits from a multimodal approach to learning and he works best when given a visual model.

While Matthew's parents were not dissatisfied with the results of the school evaluations, they requested the present evaluation to confirm the status of Matthew's functioning and obtain suggestions for his educational planning.

PROCEDURES USED

Leiter International Performance Scale
McCarthy Scales of Children's Abilities
Vineland Adaptive Behavior Scales (parent informants)
Structured play/free play
Parent–child interactions
Clinical interview
Behavioral observations
Chart review

CURRENT MEDICATIONS

Matthew was not taking any medications at the time of this evaluation.

CLINICAL FINDINGS AND IMPRESSIONS

Behavioral Observations

Matthew was evaluated over two separate sessions. Behavioral presentation was consistent across sessions. Consequently, results from these two meetings will be collapsed and reported as one integrated observation period.

For his initial session, Matthew was accompanied to the evaluation room by both of his parents. He appeared somewhat short in stature for his chronological age, but generally well-nourished and well-developed. His general presentation was quite neat and he exhibited some adult-like posturing (e.g., hands on his hips when making an emphatic comment). Matthew clearly exhibited a positive attachment to his parents. On his parents' initial departure from the evaluation room, Matthew exhibited intense distress.

He cried and made several pleas for his parents to remain in the room. He remained in a state of distress for ~5 min after his parents left and he sought the examiner for comfort, sitting in her lap and cuddling for a period of time. After he was calm, he persistently made statements referring to his parents' whereabouts. For example, he repeatedly stated, "Mom and Dad are downstairs," or "Mom and Dad are waiting for me." Matthew eventually was able to engage with the examiner around some fun puzzle tasks before formal testing began. Once he became more comfortable, he engaged easily with the examiner and appeared to enjoy the interpersonal interaction. He often sought eye contact and he made frequent attempts to access adult attention. Matthew coordinated verbal and nonverbal communication quite well during his interactions with the examiner.

Matthew's language skills were significantly impaired, in both receptive and expressive domains. His articulation also was quite poor which negatively impacted listener comprehension. Matthew, at times, appeared frustrated by his language impairments and he occasionally exhibited mild physical aggression (e.g., hitting the table) subsequent to communication difficulties. Matthew's nonverbal communication, on the other hand, appeared quite well-developed. Indeed, Matthew may rely on his nonverbal communication skills as a means of compensating for his limited verbal skills. Overall, Matthew communicates via a combination of modalities including verbal expression, gestures, occasional sign language, and modeling behavior he wishes another to perform.

Matthew's behavior during formal testing was characterized by inattention, distractibility, and frequent protests in response to task demands. He required excessive external structure. Matthew was often unable to attempt tasks presented to him unless the task was broken down into multiple and simple steps. When such structure was not provided, he was increasingly distractible, impulsive, and unable to complete his work. Throughout testing, Matthew frequently exhibited brief spurts of upper body tension and shaking, particularly in his hands and arms. These episodes lasted only for a few seconds and appeared to function as discharges of energy to relieve stress. When demands became too great or when Matthew was uninterested in a task, he protested by placing test materials in his mouth, knocking over test items, or hitting the table with his hands. Such behaviors appeared more like that of a three-year-old than a six-year-old. Matthew was best able to perform when given only one, simple task at a time, provided with substantial structure, and allowed frequent breaks.

Matthew's affect was generally bright throughout the evaluation. He exhibited a range of affect and his emotional expressions were consistent with the situation at hand. His overall mood appeared quite happy.

Matthew's play behavior was characterized by a strong need to be in charge. He was able to respond to the examiner's overtures during play but he much preferred directing the play interaction. If his lead was not followed, he persisted with his directive behavior. However, he did not protest if a firm limit was set. Indeed, Matthew was quite positively responsive to calm but firm limit-setting. Matthew engaged in several play sequences around the theme of "feeding" a baby doll and "burping" a baby doll. He sought engagement with the examiner during these sequences but he was mostly interested in having the examiner observe him, as opposed to being involved with him in this activity. Matthew later engaged in a playful "telephone" game with the examiner but, again, he insisted on directing this interaction.

Clinical interview with Matthew's parents revealed that Matthew's behavior during this evaluation was generally consistent with his behavior at home, in school, and in the community. Consequently, results of this evaluation appear to be an accurate representation of Matthew's current functioning and abilities.

Test Findings

Given Matthew's significant language impairment, assessment of intellectual functioning via more traditional measures (e.g., Wechsler Scales) appeared inappropriate in that such tests rely heavily on receptive and expressive language and, as a result, might underestimate Matthew's current functioning as well as provide little qualitative information about his strengths and preferred modes of learning/problem solving. The Leiter International Performance Scale, a standardized nonverbal measure of intelligence for individuals 3 years to 18 years of age, appeared more appropriate in that its major use is in the assessment of individuals with hearing, speech, or other types of language handicaps. On this nonverbal test of intellectual functioning, Matthew was able to pass all of the subtests up to the 3-year level, three of the four subtests at a 4-year level, all of the subtests at a 5-year level, and two of the four subtests at a 6-year level. He failed all subtests at the 7- and 8-year levels. This performance resulted in a mental age of 4 years, 7 months and an IQ score of 70 (where the mean score = 100 and SD = 16). This places his overall cognitive functioning at the very low end of the borderline range (mild mental retardation equals an IQ score of 67 or less).

Generally, Matthew's performance was best on tasks that required simple matching of objects or color sorting. He was able to make simple associations between related objects but, for the most part, he was unable to perform tasks that required abstract reasoning or the ability to think conceptually. Matthew's academic skills are probably at, or below, the kindergarten level, currently. Matthew evidenced low frustration tolerance and limited ability to persevere when faced with tasks that challenged his skill level. His inattention further interfered with his performance. Consequently, Matthew appears to be a child who requires considerable external structure, guidance, and encouragement in order to learn new skills or perform successfully in an academic setting.

Matthew's cognitive abilities also were evaluated via the McCarthy Scales of Children's Abilities (normed for children ages $2\frac{1}{2}$ years through $8\frac{1}{2}$ years). The McCarthy is comparable to other standardized intelligence tests having a mean of 100 and a SD of 16. The McCarthy is frequently used for the assessment of young children with learning problems or other exceptional conditions. The McCarthy provides a General Cognitive Index (GCI) which is generally comparable to the FSIQ score on other standardized intelligence tests (such as a Wechsler). Also, like a Wechsler, the McCarthy relies heavily on receptive and expressive language skill development, either in conveying the task to be completed or in the actual completion of the task. However, unlike a Wechsler which assesses intellectual functioning across two domains (verbal and nonverbal [performance]), the McCarthy measures intellectual functioning across five dimensions: verbal ability; nonverbal reasoning; number aptitude; short-term memory; and coordination.

Given Matthew's already noted weaknesses within the verbal domain and marked discrepant scores between his earlier cognitive evaluation (on the Wechsler, a highly verbally based standardized intelligence test) and current cognitive evaluation (on the Leiter, a standardized nonverbal intelligence test), the McCarthy was administered to: (1) assess the reliability of his earlier Wechsler IQ score; (2) assess the impact of language on his performance; and (3) aid in clarifying, more specifically, areas of relative strength and weakness, if possible.

On the McCarthy, Matthew's cognitive functioning fell in the moderate range of mental retardation, obtaining a GCI of <50. This score was commensurate with his November 2004 WPPSI-III FSIQ score of 48. Specific domain scale index scores and age equivalent scores were as follows:

Scale	Index score (where mean score = 50)	Age equivalent (years)
Verbal (V)	<22	3
Perceptual performance (P)	<22	4
Quantitative (Q)	<22	3½
Memory (Mem)	<22	3
Motor (Mot)	<22	3½

Again, it appears that when language is a mediating variable to task completion, Matthew's performance is worse. Overall age equivalent scores clustered between the 3- and 4-year level. Interestingly, when Matthew was asked to perform a task and was given a verbal instruction that was paired with a tangible object which he could manipulate to produce a response, his performance frequently was significantly better [see specific subscale age equivalent scores below marked with an asterisk (*)]. Indeed, such tasks were more in keeping with the format of the Leiter, and produced age equivalent scores in the 4- to 6-year range.

McCarthy subscales	Age equivalent (years)
Block building	2½
Puzzle solving*	4
Pictorial memory	2½
Word knowledge, I & II	2½
Number questions	4
Tapping sequence	3½
Right–left orientation*	5
Leg coordination	3
Arm coordination, I, II & III	3½
Imitative action	3½
Draw-a-design	3
Draw-a-child	4
Numerical memory, I	2½
Numerical memory, II	3½
Verbal fluency	4
Counting and sorting*	4
Opposite analogies	3
Conceptual grouping*	6

The above deficit profile was further confirmed by results of the Vineland Adaptive Behavior Scales (VABS), a caretaker report inventory assessing adaptive behavior skills domestically and in the community. When comparing Matthew's adaptive behavior skills with same-aged peers in the general population, he is functioning ~2–3 SD below the mean. Current standard scores and age equivalent scores are summarized below.

Domain	Standard score (where mean score = 100)	Age equivalent
Communication	49	2 years, 3 months
Daily Living Skills	64	4 years, 3 months
Socialization	69	3 years, 8 months
Motor skills	–	3 years, 10 months
Adaptive Behavior Composite	56	3 years, 6 months

Clearly, scores in all domains reflect significant weaknesses when compared to his same-aged peers and are comparable to scores in the mild to moderate range of mental retardation. Consistent with behavioral observations and results of the McCarthy Scales of Children's Abilities, Matthew's greatest weakness is in the area of communication. It is emphasized that Matthew's language deficits exceed the extent of his intellectual deficits, suggesting the presence of a language disorder distinct from, and in addition to the mental retardation. Matthew's language impairments may further account for some of his deficits in socialization. Indeed, it may be that as Matthew makes gains with regard to communication skills, his socialization skills will similarly improve.

FORMULATION

Matthew is an adorable and engaging $6\frac{1}{2}$ year old boy who presents with a history of global developmental delays. Given Matthew's long history of developmental delay and continued even developmental progression, combined with the results of the present evaluation, together indicate that a diagnosis of cognitive compromise is in order. However, the question arises whether Matthew's cognitive functioning level is in the borderline range, the mild range of mental retardation, or the moderate range of mental retardation. It is clear that Matthew exhibited significantly better performance on a nonverbal test of intelligence (Leiter IQ score = 70) than he did on a administered (November 2004) verbally based test of intelligence (WPPSI-III FSIQ score = 48) and current verbally based test of intelligence (McCarthy GCI score = <50). The 20- to 22-point difference between these two scores cannot be accounted for by measurement error alone. Rather, it suggests that Matthew's language impairments interfere with his performance on verbally based intelligence tests. Consequently, results of the WPPSI-III and McCarthy are likely to be an underestimation of Matthew's true intellectual abilities. Furthermore, it is probable that Matthew's language impairments interfere with his development of age appropriate adaptive behaviors such as social skills and daily living skills. Thus, in addition to cognitive functioning likely being in the mild range of mental retardation to borderline range, Matthew clearly appears to be manifesting a significant language disorder which cannot be subsumed under his diagnosis of cognitive compromise. Indeed, until rigorous programming for speech and language skill development is put into place for Matthew, it is difficult to ascertain whether cognitive level is actually in the borderline range or mild range of mental retardation. Consequently, it is imperative that the primary focus of Matthew's educational programming be the development of communication skills to foster optimum adaptive behavior skills and cognitive functioning.

With regard to the etiology of Matthew's developmental delays, no known etiology can be identified. However, based on a review of Matthew's medical and developmental histories, it appears that Matthew is a child whose delays may have resulted from problems in early brain development. Matthew's developmental progression has been a slow but steady one and it is likely that this upward trend will continue through his childhood years. However, it is possible that as educational demands increase and academic material becomes increasingly more abstract in nature, Matthew's progression may slow down and eventually plateau. It is impossible to predict the exact rate of growth or the point at which his skill development will level off, especially given that speech and language issues still need to be addressed. What is most important is that Matthew continues to receive intensive educational services with behavioral programming in place at home and at school to assist with his development of adaptive behavior skills.

RECOMMENDATIONS

1. Matthew will continue to require an intensive, language-based, special education program. A one-to-one format will likely be necessary for most of his educational experiences in order to maximize his academic gains. Placement in a classroom staffed by individuals with expertise in behavior management will be critical. Matthew requires considerable structure and external support in order to focus on academic material and complete tasks presented to him. Furthermore, it is strongly recommended that Matthew be considered for an extended school year program. It is probable that without educational services during the summer months, Matthew may show a regression in academic achievement.

2. Given Matthew's language impairments, it is imperative that a comprehensive, updated speech and language evaluation be conducted. Based on Matthew's performance during this testing, a primary goal of his educational program appears to be the development of a total communication system, one that incorporates multiple communication modalities. It appears important that all verbal instructions for Matthew be accompanied by visual cues and materials to manipulate, where possible. Additionally, providing Matthew with opportunities to observe other children perform a behavior/task before he is expected to act will be helpful. Use of a picture schedule also may be useful for communication purposes and to assist Matthew with following classroom routines.

3. Continuation of speech and language therapy services is clearly indicated. The updated speech and language evaluation can more clearly pinpoint the level of services needed. Further, development of sign language skills may be necessary at this time. Particular emphasis may need to be on

involving Matthew's parents in the process so Matthew may continue to practice sign language at home.

4. Though Matthew requires special education services, it will be important to provide him with as many opportunities as possible for integration with typically developing peers in order to facilitate his development of social skills. As Matthew often learns best by observing, providing him with opportunities to interact with typically developing peers may facilitate his ability to model age-appropriate social behavior.

5. Mr. and Mrs. B. may wish to consider family therapy to address behavioral management concerns, identify appropriate expectations for Matthew, and obtain support in parenting a child with special needs. It will be important to focus on Matthew's development of independent behaviors and daily living skills. Development of a specific behavior program also may be a goal of therapy. Mr. and Mrs. B. were provided with a list of local agencies which provide these specific types of outpatient family services.

6. Continuation of occupational and physical therapy services is strongly recommended in order to address Matthew's fine and gross motor skill development.

7. Should Matthew's attention problems increase and interfere with his academic achievement, Mr. and Mrs. B. may wish to consider a psychiatric medication consultation. This service could be provided through the DDP Outpatient Clinic here at Seton Hospital.

It was a pleasure to evaluate Matthew. Should any questions or concerns arise regarding this report, please feel free to contact me at 800-555-1212.

EXHIBIT 2.3

Assessment Case Illustration #3

Assessment for Diagnosis of Mental Retardation When the Individual's Cognitive Functioning Level Is Too Low for the Appropriate Age-Normed Intelligence Test: Use of an Intelligence Test Normed for a Younger Chronological Age Group

PSYCHOLOGICAL EVALUATION

Name: Charles V.
Date of birth: 8-8-95
Chronological age: 9 years, 0 months
Chronological grade: Special Education
Date of admission: 3-27-04
Dates of assessment: 8-25-04 and 8-28-04

BACKGROUND INFORMATION AND REASON FOR REFERRAL

Charles is a 9 year, 0 month old Caucasian male who is currently an inpatient on the DDP at Seton Hospital. He has been an inpatient since 3-27-04 with his hospitalization secondary to aggressive and self-injurious behaviors along with sleep disturbance. Charles lives with his parents in Troy Hills, New Jersey. He has been serviced for special education services through his local school system since his preschool years. Charles has a long history of receptive and expressive language disorders, phonological impairment, and behavioral dysregulation (in the form of hitting, hair-pulling, and running away). Prior diagnoses include: Organic Mental Disorder, Not Otherwise Specified; Developmental Disorder, Not Otherwise Specified.

Ring Chromosome 22 Syndrome (a genetic abnormality associated with mental retardation, distinct facial features, seizure disorders, and aggressive behaviors). Other diagnoses in the long record at various points in Charles' history have included: Autistic Disorder; Profound Mental Retardation; Diffuse Neurological Abnormalities Secondary to Chromosomal Abnormality; Pervasive Developmental Disorder, Not Otherwise Specified; Developmental Articulation Disorder; Developmental Expressive Language Disorder; and Developmental Coordination Disorder. A comprehensive review of Charles' prenatal, natal, medical, developmental, and family histories already has been documented in his medical record. Consequently, it will not be reviewed again here. The reader is referred to that document for details. As part of his inpatient hospitalization, a comprehensive psychological evaluation was requested. Specific request was for evaluation of cognitive, social-emotional, adaptive behavior, and behavioral functioning as well as recommendations for continued educational programming and services.

PROCEDURES USED

Leiter International Performance Scale (attempted)
Bayley Scales of Infant Development (Second Edition)
Vineland Adaptive Behavior Scales (staff informants)
Structured play/free play
Behavioral observations (evaluation room and classroom)
Clinical interview
Chart review

CLINICAL FINDINGS AND IMPRESSIONS

Behavioral Observations

Charles was accompanied to this evaluation session by his milieu therapist, Kristen, who remained for the entirety of this evaluation session. Kristen aided in administration of test items, task compliance, and behavioral programming. Physically, Charles presented as an attractive, Caucasian boy of thin build. Most notable in his physical presentation were his pale skin, long thin fingers, and very long eye lashes. Charles willingly accompanied the examiner to the testing room from his classroom. However, once in the unfamiliar setting of the examiner's office, he became visibly anxious, demonstrated by slight crying and increased nervous vocalizations. Initially, Charles did not explore this new environment with purpose. Rather, he appeared to wander aimlessly in the room responding to the physical properties of the room, that is if he hit a wall or piece of furniture, he simply redirected himself. He showed no interest at this initial point in any materials laid out in the room. Generally, with assistance and ongoing redirection, he appeared to calm down and accepted sitting in a chair at the examination table.

Throughout formal testing, Charles required ongoing support to remain seated, to attend to task instructions, and to comply with task demands. Attention span was quite limited and ongoing redirection was constantly required. When uninterested in, or too greatly challenged by a task, Charles demonstrated vocal and physical protests (e.g., bouncing in chair, attempting to leave chair, and throwing objects across the table). Charles was most attentive to test items and play materials that made noise; he was particularly responsive and soothed by melodic music. Indeed, for the most part, Charles' engagement with the environment appeared to be at the sensory-motor level. Interactions with task/play materials were at the simple cause-effect level. Frequent mouthing of objects was also an avenue of discovery regarding material properties present. At no point did Charles engage in parallel or cooperative play. There were no instances of symbolic use of play materials.

Overall, Charles' gross and fine motor development appeared impaired for chronological age. His gait was wide-based and awkward. Balance also appeared immature. He did demonstrate a good pincer grasp and a clear left-hand preference. He employed an immature, full hand grasp of oversized writing utensils. Facial muscle/motor movement was weak, resulting in moderate drool. This, also, likely contributes to his immature vocalizations.

Language development was severely impaired. Receptive language appeared stronger than expressive abilities as Charles was able to understand and respond to simple verbal instructions and commands. Expressive language appeared limited to single syllable vowel-consonant combinations. However, it should be noted that Charles' ability to listen and respond decreased significantly as his attention faded.

For the most part, Charles displayed a quite limited range of affect. Displeasure in the form of crying and whining was most pronounced as was pleasure in the form of very brief interest and attention. He did not demonstrate aggression toward others. He did, however, engage in bilateral head banging on four or five separate occasions, each time interrupted successfully with the use of a protective helmet. Such behavior consistently emerged subsequent to a demand being placed on him.

Charles' sensory responsiveness appeared within normal limits across all five senses.

In general, Charles was an active young boy who required one-to-one supervision and constant redirection to stay in his seat and on-task. He was willful but was unable to independently modulate his behavior and affect. Clinical interview with milieu therapist and classroom teacher indicated that Charles' performance during this evaluation was consistent with his behavior in the classroom and in milieu. Consequently, results of this evaluation appear to be an accurate representation of Charles' current functioning and abilities.

Test Findings

Despite Charles' chronological age of 9 years, 0 months, he was unable to complete standardized, cognitive instruments geared for his age level (i.e., WISC-III or Leiter International Performance Scale). Consequently, the Bayley Scales of Infant Development (Second Edition) was employed although this test was not standardized on children in Charles' age range. Its provision of multiple items at or below Charles' functional level allowed for a more accurate assessment of his relative strengths and weaknesses.

On the Bayley Scales of Infant Development (Second Edition), Charles achieved a basal score of 23–25 months, a ceiling score of 23–25 months, a Mental Developmental Index (MDI) of less than 50 (where mean score = 100), and an estimated mental age equivalent of 19–20 months. That is to say, Charles' current cognitive/developmental functioning is in the significantly deficit range, and his overall functioning more closely approximates that of a 19- to 20-month old rather than a 9 year, 0 month old. Item failures and, hence, developmental deficits were principally tied to his expressive language deficits, motor deficits, and marked inattention/distractibility.

As noted in the behavioral observations section, Charles' learning style was primarily tactile exploration, sensory stimulation, motor imitation, and simple cause-effect relationships. It is anticipated that slow developmental progression will ensue with the continued ongoing benefit of intensive behavioral modification and intensive interdisciplinary intervention services.

The above deficit profile was further confirmed by caretaker responses on the Vineland Adaptive Behavior Scales, a caretaker report inventory assessing adaptive behavior skills domestically and in the community. When comparing Charles' adaptive behavior functioning with children his age in the general population, he is functioning $\sim 3\frac{2}{3}$ to 5 SD below the mean. Generally, it would appear that Charles' weak Socialization Skills and Daily Living Skills are negatively impacted by language and motor deficits. Overall standard and age equivalent scores are summarized below.

Domain	Standard score (where mean score = 100)	Age equivalent
Communication	27	1 year, 2 months
Daily Living Skills	<20	1 year, 9 months
Socialization	45	1 year, 5 months
Motor Skills	–	1 year, 10 months
Adaptive Behavior Composite	28	1 year, $6\frac{1}{2}$ months

Given the past record diagnoses of Pervasive Developmental Disorder, Not Otherwise Specified (2000) and Autistic Disorder (2004), the Childhood Autism Rating Scale (CARS) was completed. The CARS is an empirical rating system which quantifies the presence/absence and degree of behavior on 15 different dimensions which are characteristic of the autistic syndrome. Scoring results on the CARS indicate that Charles is not affected by the autistic syndrome. Rather, his noted areas of difficulty were consistent with a mental retardation profile in the severe to profound range. Specifically, this included: an even, flat cognitive profile, language impairment, motor difficulties, inattention, high activity level, and some self-injurious behavior, with relatively intact sensory responses and relatively good social relatedness.

SUMMARY

Taken together, Charles is a 9 year, 0 month old male presenting with Ring 22 Chromosome Disorder. His overall profile reveals multihandicaps which appear to root in constitutional underpinnings. He presents significant weakness in all developmental domains, functioning like a toddler (of~19–20 months of age). His language, motor, and attention deficits result in a cognitive and adaptive behavior profile in the mentally retarded range (severe to profound). Slow, even developmental progression is anticipated with continued intensive behavioral modification programs, one-to-one specialty intervention services (Occupational Therapy, Physical Therapy, and Speech and Language) as well as educational programming (with emphasis on functional life skills) and the assignment of a sole aide to Charles with expertise in behavior modification.

RECOMMENDATIONS

These findings should be incorporated with other specialty evaluation findings (i.e., Occupational Therapy, Physical Therapy, Speech and Language, and Education). Integrated recommendations should be generated and documented in Charles' IEP. However, for purposes of this evaluation, the following recommendations are most strongly offered:

1. Given Charles' substantial problems with attending and instructional control, and limited generalized imitative ability, it appears imperative at this time, in order to maximize learning capacity, that the majority of his educational experiences should be in the context of one-to-one dyadic experiences with an aide solely assigned to Charles.
2. Charles continues to require intensive, highly structured, behaviorally oriented, special education services and these services should continue in full force during a summer school program.
3. In addition, continued intensive services from speech and language, occupational therapy, and physical therapy should be in place for Charles.
4. The curriculum should emphasize the development of attending, communication, social interaction skills, and teacher-pleasing behaviors. Particular emphasis should be on the development of social imagination and play skills and the development of a functional communication system. In addition, emphasis should be placed on the development of "survival skills" necessary for successful communication and social performance in the next least restrictive environment.
5. Teaching should be based on a combined developmental/behavioral model using systematic instructional procedures. Specifically, this will imply targeting of skills to be acquired, positive consequences for learning, a clearly structured scope and sequence of lessons across all instructional domains, consistent and regular evaluation of progress on IEP objectives on a daily or weekly basis, and the use of various specific teaching procedures (i.e., discrete trial learning, task analytic teaching, and incidental teaching) for instruction. Finally, the use of individual motivation systems to establish and maintain appropriate academic behavior as well as socialization and communication skills will be a very important part of Charles' school program.
6. Programming for the generalization of skills learned at school and at home must be a formal and structured process. Charles necessarily will not automatically generalize skills learned in one situation or with one person to new situations or other people. As such, it will be necessary to teach formally toward the generalization of skills taught in school, to home and to the community.
7. If not already done, Charles should be referred to the Department of Mental Retardation (DMR) for initiation of DMR services and coordination.
8. Mr. and Mrs. V. have provided a loving, creative, and committed environment for raising Charles. Given the day-to-day challenges of living with and raising a child with mental retardation and behavioral difficulties, Mr. and Mrs. V. may wish to participate with the local DMR support group for ongoing information and support about Charles' needs and the needs of families such as their own.

9. Finally, Charles should be comprehensively reevaluated in *one* year to ensure appropriate school programming and any necessary modification in treatment interventions.

It was a pleasure to evaluate Charles. If any questions or concerns arise regarding this report, please feel free to contact me at 800-555-1212.

VIII. VERBAL INTELLIGENCE TESTS FREQUENTLY USED TO ASSESS FOR MENTAL RETARDATION

A. Bayley Scales of Infant Development, Second Edition

The Bayley Scales of Infant Development, Second Edition (BSID-II) (Bayley, 1993) is the first revision to the original Bayley Scales of Infant Development (BSID) (Bayley, 1969). The BSID-II and its predecessor have long been the "gold standard" of psychometric excellence among infant and preschool tests. It is a well-developed, standardized measure of infant, toddler, and preschool development, and it provides valuable information about patterns of early mental development. The BSID-II has excellent reliability and validity. It is normed for children from 1 month to 42 months of age.

The BSID-II consists of three scales: Mental Scale, Motor Scale, and Behavior Rating Scale (BRS). The Mental Scale includes 178 items arranged by incremental months that assess the full range of early cognitive skills. These include: habituation, sustained attention, memory, manipulation of objects, shape discrimination, imitation, generalization, classification, reasoning, comprehension, problem solving, early number concepts, prewriting skills, visual perception, perceptual motor integration, vocalization, language, naming objects, and social skills. The Motor Scale includes 111 items arranged by incremental months that assess the full range of control of the gross and fine muscle groups. These include the child's muscle tone, dynamic and static balance, prewalking, prewriting, sensory integration skills, and perceptual motor development. The BRS is a Likert-type 5-point rating scale that measures the qualitative aspects of the child's test session behavior. The dimensions of behavior assessed include: motor quality, attention/arousal, emotional regulation, orientation, motivation, and engagement with people.

Administration of the BSID-II requires considerable practice and experience. While the test examiner must adhere to the standardized item administration directions, the test is designed to be flexible in order to obtain the child's optimal performance. Test items consist of child-friendly, playful activities with durable, engaging materials. In addition, some item administrations allow the caregiver to aid the examiner in eliciting the optimal response from the child. For children under 1 year of age, testing will take

~30 min for the Mental and Motor Scales. For children older than 1 year of age, testing time will range from 45 to 60 min to administer both scales. For a child with notable developmental delay or mental retardation, testing time may be somewhat longer, as short breaks in the testing session may be necessary. If testing takes place over two sessions, it is recommended that the sessions be no more than one week apart.

Two standard scores are obtained: a Mental Developmental Index (MDI), obtained from the Mental Scale, and a Psychomotor Developmental Index (PDI), obtained from the Motor Scale. These two standard scores are converted from raw scores; each standard score has a mean of 100 and a SD of 15. Scaled scores range from 50 to 150. Qualitative classifications of MDI and PDI score ranges are as follows: accelerated performance (115 and above), within normal limits (85–114), mildly delayed performance (70–84), and significantly delayed performance (69 and below). Typically, the MDI is the score used to determine if a child is presenting with a developmental delay or cognitive deficit. The test also incorporates facet scores to identify developmental strengths and weaknesses in the domains of cognitive, language, social, and motor performance.

At nearly every age, the full range of scores is available. At the 1-month age level, a raw score of 0 converts to an index scale score of 56 on the Mental Scale and an index scale score 54 on the Motor Scale. Conversely, at the 42-month age level, a raw score of 178 converts to an index scale score of 126 on the Mental Scale and an index scale score of 125 on the Motor Scale. Even at this most extreme age, the available index score range is greater than $1\frac{1}{2}$ SD above the mean, which allows a sufficient ceiling to discriminate among all but the most extreme high ability in $3\frac{1}{2}$-year olds (Bayley, 1993).

In addition, for each 1-month interval, the raw score corresponding to an index score of 100 represents the median performance for that particular age. Consequently, the examiner can derive an approximate developmental age equivalent (mental as well as motor) from a raw score even for a child who does not fall within the BSID-II's age norms. This is particularly helpful when an examiner needs to assess an older child or adolescent whose developmental functioning is quite low and who cannot be assessed on other standardized cognitive measures that meet age norms for the examinee's chronological age. An example of the BSID-II being used in the evaluation of an older teen with developmental challenges, along with the format for reporting BSID-II scores, and a qualitative description of performance on the use of this test, in this particular situation, are described in Exhibit 2.3.

It should be noted that the BSID-II has specified age item sets (22) for the Mental Scale and the Motor Scale, and basal and ceiling rules for these two scales that differ from the original BSID. As a result, there has been some controversy surrounding the BSID-II regarding whether to begin with the age item set corresponding to the child's chronological age or corrected chronological age (in the case of premature infants) or at lower age item sets for children suspected on having developmental delays. If the examiner employs correction to determine the age item set to begin test administration or if a younger age item set is employed because of developmental problems, the child's sum raw scores and associated scale scores tend to be somewhat lower than if the chronological age set were used to begin testing. This is because the child is not automatically given credit for passing the lower age item sets. Nevertheless, an accurate portrayal of strengths and weaknesses in the child's developmental profile can be ascertained. Oftentimes, this information can be quite valuable with regard to diagnostic clarification as well as developing an outline for educational programming and/or intervention services.

The BRS was scaled with a percentile rank by age metric rather than a standard score. The rationale for this was that the primary purpose of the BRS was to determine whether the child's behavior fell within "normal limits," was "questionable," or "nonoptimal." For this purpose, a percentile rank scoring system was deemed to be more appropriate.

B. Bayley Scales of Infant and Toddler Development, Third Edition

The Bayley Scales of Infant and Toddler Development, Third Edition (BSID-III) (Bayley, 2005) is the third iteration of the original BSID (Bayley, 1969), and has been released to the market.

The BSID-III very closely resembles the BSID-II with some structural additions and publisher-reported improvements. For the most part, the cognitive, language, and motor scales of the BSID-III remain unchanged from the BSID-II (although some minor modification in some test materials and test items has been made). Noted additions to the BSID-III include: a social-emotional subtest, an adaptive behavior subtest, growth scores and growth charts, a screening test, a structured caregiver report, and a scoring assistant. The test publisher's reported improvements in the BSID-III over the previous edition of the test include: easier administration, extended floor and ceiling, additional clinical validity studies, new norms, simplified scoring rules, and option for increased caretaker input. To date, there are no outside published reviews completed on this newest revision of the Bayley. Consequently, as of this writing, it is difficult to make comparisons between the BSID-II and BSID-III with regard to test administration, scoring, and interpretation, and draw conclusions with regard to preferential clinical utility, particularly as it relates to assessment for mental retardation in the very young.

C. Differential Ability Scales

The Differential Ability Scales (DAS) (Elliot, 1990) is an individually administered battery of cognitive and achievement tests for children between the ages of 2 years, 6 months and 17 years, 11 months. For the purposes of this chapter, discussion will be limited solely to the cognitive tests. Similar to other tests of cognitive ability, the DAS provides a composite measure of conceptual and reasoning abilities that can be used to determine whether a child qualifies for a diagnosis of mental retardation. In addition, the DAS provides information on specific cognitive and developmental strengths and weaknesses for the purpose of refined diagnosis and treatment planning.

The DAS score that is used to determine eligibility for a diagnosis of mental retardation is the General Composite Ability, or GCA score. The makers of the DAS provide a detailed description in their manual of why they do not use the term IQ, which relates to ongoing controversy surrounding the concept of intelligence. Regardless of this, the GCA has a high degree of concurrent validity with other major tests of cognitive ability, such as the Wechsler series, and, therefore, may be considered to be an appropriate tool in establishing a diagnosis of mental retardation. Similar to most other measures of cognitive ability, the DAS GCA has a mean of 100 and a SD of 15. The GCA is the highest of three levels of measurement in the DAS. Directly beneath the GCA are cluster scores for various domains of functioning, followed by individual subtest scores.

The DAS is different than some other measures of cognitive ability in that subset scores are not given equal weight in the determination of the overall composite measure (GCA) of abilities. Only subtests that load highly on *g* are included, where *g* is defined as "the general ability of an individual to perform complex mental processing that involves conceptualization and the transformation of information" (Elliot, 1990, p. 12). Other subtests are included in the battery in order to provide important diagnostic and treatment information. For example, memory subtests included in the battery were found to provide useful diagnostic information while not loading highly on *g*.

The authors of the DAS used exploratory factor analysis in order to determine the most appropriate way to conceptualize ability at different age levels. This resulted in a developmental differentiation in the number of cluster scores that are identified at different age levels. Between the ages of 2 years, 6 months and 3 years, 5 months, exploratory factor analyses revealed a single factor model; thus, the DAS provides only the GCA score at this level. Between the ages of 3 years, 6 months and 5 years, 11 months, exploratory factor analyses revealed a two-factor structure. At this age range, the DAS provides the Verbal Ability and Nonverbal Ability Clusters. For school aged children, ages 6 years, 0 months to 17 years, 11 months, the DAS provides three cluster level scores: Verbal Ability, Nonverbal Reasoning Ability, and Spatial Ability. The examiner's manual provides factor analytic support for the division of the nonverbal ability factor into Nonverbal Reasoning Ability and Spatial Ability. Conceptually, this distinction is reflective of the difference between visual-spatial tasks which measure spatial ability alone and those in which verbal mediation may be used to assist in reasoning. This distinction may have implications when testing a child suspected of language problems.

The examiner's manual of the DAS provides a detailed description of each of its subtests. The authors provide two age-level divisions of core subtests: the Preschool Core and the School-Age Core. The Preschool Core consists of Block Building, Verbal Comprehension, Picture Similarities, Naming Vocabulary, Pattern Construction, Early Number Concepts, and Copying. The School-Age Core consists of Recall of Designs, Word Definitions, Pattern Construction, Matrices, Similarities, and Sequential and Quantitative Reasoning. In addition to the core subtests, Diagnostic Subtests are included: Matching Letter-Like Forms, Recall of Digits, Recall of Objects—Immediate and Delayed, Recognition of Pictures, and Speed of Information Processing. The examiner's manual provides detailed information about each of these subtests and respective age ranges, as well as a list of factors which might contribute to lower scores on a particular test (e.g., attention ability, compulsivity).

The DAS is a well-standardized measure of cognitive ability in children and adolescents. In addition to excellent standardization, the DAS has good validity and reliability. Statistically and theoretically sound methods were used in creating GCA scores such that only subtests with high *g* loading are included, while subtests that do not load highly on *g* were still included for the purpose of refined diagnosis and treatment planning. Furthermore, it has been these authors' experience that children, especially younger children, seem to be highly engaged by the materials of the DAS. As a consequence of this and other attributes, the DAS may sometimes seem easier to administer than some other cognitive tests, particularly to lower functioning children.

The DAS manual provides information on a small sample of children ($n = 25$) previously and independently identified as being "educable mentally retarded" (Elliot, 1990, p. 257). Similar to the performance of children with mental retardation on other tests of cognitive ability, children with mental retardation obtained generally depressed scores. These children obtained a mean GCA score of 59.4, a mean Verbal Ability score of 63.8, a mean Nonverbal Reasoning Ability score of 63.4, and a Spatial Ability score of 65.8. Scores on Diagnostic Subtests were similarly uniformly depressed.

The DAS manual does not provide information on the performance of children who are considered to be in the severe to profound ranges of mental retardation. Furthermore, the DAS was not standardized on children functioning below this level. The appropriate lower limit of the standard GCA norms is 45, corresponding to the moderate range of mental retardation. However, unlike many tests of cognitive ability, the DAS does provide a means to obtain GCA scores for children who are functioning below this lower limit. To do this, the test developers extrapolated a downward extension of the GCA age curve generated from the standardization of scores of higher functioning children. Using this method, the DAS is able to provide GCA scores for children that extend as low as 25. It is important to note that these scores are unlikely to be as accurate, reliable, or valid as true standardized scores. However, they do provide an approximate means of discriminating between ability levels for children performing in the lowest range of cognitive functioning. This is critical for treatment planning and tracking cognitive ability over time.

D. McCarthy Scales of Children's Abilities

The McCarthy Scales of Children's Abilities (McCarthy, 1972) is an individually administered test of cognitive abilities for young children, ages $2\frac{1}{2}$ to $8\frac{1}{2}$ years. It is a well-standardized and psychometrically sound instrument (Sattler, 1992). The McCarthy provides a general level of intellectual functioning and an assessment of a child's cognitive functioning in five areas: verbal ability (to understand, process, and express verbal information), nonverbal reasoning ability (visual-motor coordination and nonverbal practical reasoning abilities), number aptitude (understanding of numbers, number concepts, and counting), short-term memory (auditory and visual), and motor functioning (fine and gross motor, and hand dominance).

Specifically, the McCarthy contains the following five scales: Verbal Scale, Perceptual Performance Scale, Quantitative Scale, Memory Scale, and Motor Scale. The McCarthy comprises 18 different tests which cluster into the five scales. There are five verbal tests, seven perceptual performance tests, three quantitative tests, four memory tests, and five motor tests. Six of the tests fall into two of the five scales. For example, drawing various geometric shapes is considered both a motor task and a perceptual performance task.

The various test items involve puzzles, toy-like materials, and game-like tasks. Most children and examiners find the procedures extremely enjoyable. Tests are arranged in an order which facilitates obtaining a child's optimum functioning. Test rapport is facilitated by having several nonverbal tasks precede initial items requiring verbalization on the part of the child. Further, these initial verbalizations are of a one-word nature which helps most children overcome any initial anxiety associated with talking to an unfamiliar person. In addition, the test has incorporated into it a "built-in" break from possible fatigue. Halfway through the test, the child is asked to participate in a variety of gross motor task items (e.g., beanbag throw, ball bouncing, skipping). While these items are part of the Motor Scale, they also provide a break from table work which can become tedious for some children.

The 18 tests are administered one after the other, most starting at the basic level and then working up to a child's best functioning within each test. Testing usually stops on a particular test when the child has made several consecutive errors (which the manual identifies for each test). The McCarthy allows the examiner to model successful performance on some of the perceptual performance tasks, as well as to complete some of the tasks that the child has been unable to complete. These procedures are in place to help minimize potential anxiety and frustration, and add to the test's attractiveness for children.

All test items are scored according to standard procedures described in the testing manual. The manual is laid out well, and is clear to follow. Typical testing time ranges from 45 to 60 min.

Once all the tests have been administered, standard scores for the five scales can be calculated. Each of the five scales has a mean of 50 and a SD of 10. In addition, an overall General Cognitive Index (GCI) score is derived which is based on the sum of the Verbal Scale score, the Perceptual Performance Scale score, and the Quantitative Scale score. The GCI has a mean of 100 and a SD of 16. Specifically, the functional definition of the GCI is an estimate of the child's ability to integrate accumulated knowledge and adapt that knowledge in order to perform the tasks on the scales (Sattler, 1992). Although McCarthy deliberately avoided calling the GCI an IQ score, the GCI resembles an IQ, conceptually and statistically (McCarthy, 1972). Specifically, the descriptive classifications associated with the GCI are almost the same as those used for IQ on thc various Wechsler scales. Further, the availability of mental ages for the GCI can serve as indications of mental competence.

Nevertheless, it has been reported that psychometrically the GCI and IQ scores are not the same. Specifically, with regard to concurrent validity, differences were reported between the McCarthy and the Stanford-Binet Form L-M (Terman & Merrill, 1960), Wechsler Intelligence Scale for Children-Revised (WISC-R) (Wechsler, 1974), and Wechsler Preschool and Primary Scale of Intelligence (WPPSI) (Wechsler, 1967) IQs for samples of gifted preschool children (Gerken, Hancock, & Wade, 1978), children with mental retardation (Levenson & Zino, 1979), children with learning-disabilities (Goh & Youngquist, 1979), and preschool children (Phillips, Pasewark, & Tindall, 1978), respectively. For gifted preschoolers, the means differed by 10 points with the mean GCI being significantly lower than the IQ derived using the Stanford-Binet: Form L-M. For children with mental retardation, McCarthy GCIs were, on the average, 20 points lower than the Stanford-Binet: Form L-M IQs (44 vs 64). For children with learning-disabilities, GCIs were, on average, lower than WISC-R IQs by 8–15 points.

Finally, for preschoolers, the mean McCarthy GCI was significantly lower than the mean WPPSI verbal, performance, and full-scale IQs. Thus, as GCI scores appears to be generally lower than IQs of some earlier editions of frequently used cognitive tests, one should exercise caution when reporting the McCarthy GCI as it does not appear to be interchangeable with IQ. Further, as the test is over 35 years old, there is inflation of GCI and scale scores over the years, consistent with the "Flynn effect" (1984, 1987, 1998, 2005, 2006).

Historically, the McCarthy has been a preferred instrument among professionals for evaluating cognitive functioning in young children, particularly for children in the $2\frac{1}{2}$ to 4 year range. Prior to their first revisions, the original Bayley Scales of Infant Development (BSID) (Bayley, 1969) was only standardized for infants and toddlers in the 2 month through 30 month range, and the original WPPSI (Wechsler, 1967) was only standardized for children in the 4 to $6\frac{1}{2}$ year range. The WPPSI's companion WISC-R (Wechsler, 1974) covered the age range of 6 years to 16 years, 11 months; thus the WISC-R overlapped with the WPPSI in the age range of 6 years to 6 years, 7 months. Consequently, during that time period, professionals frequently turned to the McCarthy as a preferred cognitive assessment for evaluating young children in the toddler and preschool age since it covered this $2\frac{1}{2}$ to 4 year age range gap. It also was appealing as the instrument made use of highly attractive materials and most young children (and examiners) found the test procedures quite enjoyable. Further, some evaluators actually preferred the McCarthy for evaluating children in this entire $2\frac{1}{2}$ to $8\frac{1}{2}$ age range since it alleviated switching across three instruments (i.e., McCarthy, WPPSI, and WISC-R) when conducting multiple reevaluations of the same child across the $2\frac{1}{2}$ to $8\frac{1}{2}$ year age period.

When the WPPSI was first revised in 1989 and became the WPPSI-R (Wechsler, 1989), its age range was expanded by decreasing its lower and upper age limits; it then covered the age range of 3 years to 7 years, 3 months. When the BSID was first revised in 1993 and became the BSID-II (Bayley, 1993), its age range also was expanded by increasing its upper age limit; it then covered the age range of 2–42 months. Thus, these first revisions of these well-known tests created a seamless continuity in age coverage for evaluating the cognitive functioning of children ages 2 months to 7 years, 3 months.

Since that time, there appears to have become less reliance on the McCarthy as a preferred cognitive instrument. However, clearly this appears more a result of being "squeezed out" by other well-known measures rather than any formal displeasure with the test. Indeed, as the McCarthy enables production of a profile of functioning with age equivalents, many examiners continue to rely on the McCarthy as a cognitive measure in a variety of situations. These include: when examinees are not responsive or only partially responsive to other well-known instruments; when trying to "tease out" specific questions regarding aspects of cognitive functioning; when trying to decipher possible interfering variables in the cognitive functioning of some children with mental retardation or dual-diagnosis; or when an initial cognitive evaluation is required but formal recording of an IQ should be deferred (e.g., when deprivation is suspected in an older child, and this child has never been formally evaluated nor received any support services or educational programming). An example of the McCarthy being used in consort with another cognitive instrument, along with the format for reporting McCarthy scores and qualitative description of performance on this test are described in Exhibit 2.2.

E. Stanford-Binet Intelligence Scales, Fifth Edition

The Stanford-Binet Intelligence Scales, Fifth Edition (SB5) (Roid, 2003a) is the latest version of one of the classic and most respected instruments designed to assess intelligence. The original version of the Stanford-Binet scales was created almost 100 years ago. The SB5 was published after a 7-year project. It is the long-awaited update of its predecessor, the Stanford-Binet Intelligence Scales, Fourth Edition (SB4) (Thorndike, Hagen, & Sattler, 1986), which was met with some disappointment by evaluators when it was introduced. The dissatisfaction with the SB4 was largely secondary to appearance and structural changes from its predecessors (including use of a point scale for all subtests rather than use of developmental age levels, and an increase in the number of subtests, to name just a few) which made it less useful in the evaluation of the very young, the developmentally disabled, and the mentally retarded (together, a large population market on which previous editions of the Stanford-Binet scales had been used).

Overall, the SB4 more closely resembled Wechsler scales in appearance, structure, and data output than previous editions of the Stanford-Binet scales. As a result, since the SB4 came to the market in 1986, use of the Stanford-Binet appeared to wane. The SB5 revived many of the classic features considered strengths in pre-SB4 editions, including toys for young children, functional age levels, and expanded ranges of scores for low- and high-functioning examinees. Consequently, with the introduction of the SB5, there appears to be renewed enthusiasm for this well-established instrument, and a resurgence of use by evaluators. Indeed, these authors consider the SB5 to be a preferred instrument for assessing individuals who display very high (gifted) or very low (mental retardation) levels of functioning. In particular, the SB5 is an ideal choice for assessing the lower limits of mental retardation as the SB5 measures IQ down to 10 and up to 225 (via an innovative Extended IQ).

The SB5 is a comprehensive, norm-referenced, and individually administered test of intelligence and cognitive abilities. The SB5 is normed for use with individuals 2 years to 89 years, 9 months. This generous age range allows for instrument continuity across a wide age span, useful for within subject test–retest comparisons as well as between subject test comparisons. As previously noted, a typical use of the SB5 includes diagnosing developmental disabilities, mental retardation, and other exceptionalities in children, adolescents, adults, and elderly adults.

The SB5 is based on the Cattell-Horn-Carroll (CHC) theory of cognitive functioning that has been investigated empirically over several decades (D'Amato, Fletcher-Janzen, & Reynolds, 2005). The SB5 produces a FSIQ, two domain scores [Nonverbal IQ (NVIQ) and Verbal IQ (VIQ)], and five factor indexes (Fluid Reasoning, Knowledge, Quantitative Reasoning, Visual-Spatial Processing, and Working Memory). These five factors of the SB5 were selected based on research on school achievement and on expert ratings based on the importance of these factors in the assessment of reasoning, especially in giftedness assessment. Further, the memory factor was shifted from an emphasis on short-term memory only, as in the SB4, to an emphasis on Working Memory. Overall, the SB5 is based on a hierarchical cognitive model (*g* model) with five factors emphasizing reasoning abilities that can be administered within a 45- to 75-min period.

Each of the five factors is considered using both verbal and nonverbal measures. The SB5 is the first intellectual battery to do this. Thus, the SB5 has 10 subtests, including two special routing subtests. These 10 subtests are: *Nonverbal* Fluid Reasoning: Object Series/Matrices (a routing subtest); *Nonverbal* Knowledge: Procedural Knowledge and Picture Absurdities; *Nonverbal* Quantitative Reasoning: Nonverbal Quantitative Reasoning Items; *Nonverbal* Visual-Spatial Reasoning: Form Board and Form Patterns; *Nonverbal* Working Memory: Delayed Response and Block Span; *Verbal* Fluid Reasoning: Early Reasoning items, Verbal Absurdities, and Verbal Analogies; *Verbal* Knowledge: Vocabulary (a routing subtest); *Verbal* Quantitative Reasoning: Verbal Quantitative Reasoning items; *Verbal* Visual-Spatial Reasoning: Position and Direction items; and *Verbal* Working Memory: Memory for Sentences and Last Word.

The mean of the composite score (FSIQ), two domain scores (NVIQ and VIQ), and five factor index scores is 100 with a SD of 15 (unlike previous editions which had a mean of 100 and a SD of 16). The FSIQ is the global measure of cognitive ability. The FSIQ is obtained via the administration of the 10 subtests. The NVIQ is obtained via administration of the five nonverbal subtests. Similarly, the VIQ is obtained via administration of the five verbal subtests. Ten profile scores, called scaled scores, also can be derived from each of the five nonverbal and five verbal subtests. The scaled scores range from 1 to 19 with a mean of 10 and a SD of 3. The evaluator also can use the two routing subtests (Object Series/Matrices and Vocabulary) together and produce a reliable estimated ability score called the Abbreviated Battery IQ.

In addition to these scores, the SB5 provides percentile ranks, confidence intervals, age equivalents, and Change-Sensitive Scores (CSS). The CSS are based on item-response theory and provides a means to identify a client's change in scores over a period of time.

Although advanced test user qualifications are a prerequisite for test administration, for those so trained, the SB5 is relatively easy to administer and straightforward to score. Examiner directions are printed clearly on the examiner's pages of three easel item books. Item Book 1 contains the routing subtests, Item Book 2 contains the nonverbal levels, and Item Book 3 contains the verbal levels. The SB5 record form is designed in a format similar to that of other intelligence batteries, and is straightforward to negotiate. A plastic tray for toys and manipulative pieces is provided in the SB5 kit to facilitate the flow of materials during test administration.

The examiner begins the standard test administration by giving the two routing subtests in Item Book 1: *Nonverbal* Fluid Reasoning—Object Series/Matrices, and *Verbal* Knowledge—Vocabulary. Estimates of an individual's ability on the nonverbal and verbal domains are obtained from the raw scores on each of these two routing tests. These scores then tailor the remaining assessment to the individual's functioning ability. The examiner uses simple conversion tables to determine on which functional levels (ranging from easy to hard, Levels 1 through 6) of the nonverbal and verbal scales to begin and continue testing.

The examiner continues on in Item Book 2 and then Item Book 3, in the standard order of administration. The SB5 makes use of testlets, a brief set of three to six items that are placed within each of the functional levels of Item Book 2 and Item Book 3. Within each testlet, items are organized by levels of increasing difficulty. The mixture of tasks (easy to challenging) within each testlet appears to promote greater interest and attention of the examinee during the testing process than the traditional point-scale format of other tests. Each functional level has four testlets. There are six nonverbal functional levels (labeled Levels 1–6) and five verbal functional levels (labeled Levels 2–6).

This two-stage testing procedure (with routing subtests administered first followed by functional level sections next) provides very precise estimates of cognitive ability in a relatively short period of time. On average, the SB5 can take 15–75 min to administer, depending on which scales are given. Most of the items on the SB5 are not timed and time bonuses are not allowed. The estimated time to acquire a FSIQ is 45–75 min. If necessary, when evaluating challenging individuals, administration of the complete test can be divided into sections (e.g., routing subtests, nonverbal book, and verbal book) and administered on separate occasions. The SB5 also allows accommodation for severe disabilities, and provides scoring procedures that do not require comparison to age-group peers.

The Abbreviated Battery IQ takes only 15–20 min to administer as this only consists of the two routing subtests. Further, the examiner may choose to administer only the VIQ (based on the five Verbal subtests) or the NVIQ (based on the five Nonverbal subtests). Each group of these subtests takes ~30 min to complete. Finally, the Nonverbal IQ can be used for assessing individuals with autism, communication disorders, hearing impairments, limited English-language skill, and other considerations where an individual's verbal ability is deemed to be limited.

The psychometric properties of the SB5 are considered to be quite sound. Extensive reliability, validity, and fairness studies were conducted as part of the impressive SB5 standardization process. High marks from reviewers have been given to the instrument in all areas. In addition, subjects were tested from officially documented groups, including individuals with mental retardation, learning disabilities, attentional deficits, and speech or hearing impairments. Expected results for these groups were found using the SB5 (Roid, 2003b).

The SB5 provides the option for computerized scoring which provides an extended score report and a brief, narrative summary report. This computerized scoring program is purchased separately from the test kit.

F. The Wechsler Scales

Currently, the Wechsler scales are the most widely used individually administered tests of intelligence in the United States (Kaufman & Lichtenberger, 1999; Prifitera, Saklofske, Weiss, & Rolfhus, 2005). The Wechsler intelligence tests include the Wechsler Preschool and Primary Scale of Intelligence, Third Edition (WPPSI-III) (Wechsler, 2003a), the Wechsler Intelligence Scale for Children, Fourth Edition (WISC-IV) (Wechsler 2003b), and the Wechsler Adult Intelligence Scale, Third Edition (WAIS-III) (Wechsler, 1997). All of the Wechsler tests have been well standardized and possess excellent reliability and validity. The Wechsler scales are often the first choice among examiners who receive a referral for an individual having or suspected of having mental retardation.

The first Wechsler test, the Wechsler-Bellevue (WB) (Wechsler, 1939), was created by David Wechsler at Bellevue Hospital. The WB represented an improvement over many earlier tests of intelligence in its much greater ease of administration and interpretation. In addition, the WB was grouped into Verbal and Performance subtests, which ultimately led to new eras in testing, such as Clinical Profile Analysis and later, Psychometric Profile Analysis (Flanagan & Kaufman, 2004). The Wechsler scales have undergone a number of iterations since the WB. However, the underlying structure of the tests changed little until the most recent versions. These most recent versions are reflective of advances in intelligence theories that have been evolving over the past half-century (Kamphaus, 2005).

G. Wechsler Preschool and Primary Scale of Intelligence, Third Edition (WPPSI-III)

The WPPSI-III is an appropriate measure of intelligence for children ages 2 years, 6 months to 7 years, 3 months and is often the first test considered in the determination of intellectual functioning in a preschool child. This test is the third iteration of preschool tests of intelligence from the Wechsler series. Similar to previous tests, the WPPSI-III provides a general measure of intelligence, the FSIQ, which is appropriate for use in determining a diagnosis of mental retardation. The WPPSI-III also provides several composite scores which may provide useful information in diagnosis and treatment.

For children between the ages of 4 years, 0 months and 7 years, 3 months, the WPPSI-III provides a FSIQ, Verbal IQ (VIQ), Performance IQ (PIQ), and Processing Speed Quotient (PSQ). For children 2 years, 6 months through 7 years, 3 months, the WPPSI-III also provides useful measures of single-word receptive and expressive vocabulary which form a General Language Composite (GLC). See Table III for a brief description of each of the Wechsler subtests.

Detailed information on scoring and interpretation of the WPPSI-III is provided in the manual as well as in alternative sources (Lichtenberger & Kaufman, 2004). Like other Wechsler IQ tests, the WPPSI-III provides three types of scores: raw, scaled, and standard. The raw score is simply the sum total of points earned on a subtest. This raw score is converted into a scaled score, which is a norm-referenced score with a mean of 10 and a SD of 3, generally ranging from 1 to 19 (Lichtenberger & Kaufman, 2004). Standard scores are then derived from the scaled scores and have a mean of 100 and a SD of 15.

For a child between the ages of 6 years, 0 months and 7 years, 3 months, the clinician has the choice of using either the WPPSI-III or WISC-IV, as both of these tests can be used in this age range. Generally speaking, the WPPSI-III would be used for children suspected of having impaired cognitive functioning, while the WISC-IV would be reserved for a child who is suspected of having average to above average intelligence. It should be noted that the WPPSI-III is not generally considered to be an appropriate IQ measure for children suspected of functioning in the severe to profound

TABLE III
WECHSLER SUBTEST DESCRIPTIONS

Subtest	Measures
Similarities[a,b,c]	Abstract verbal reasoning, long-term retrieval
Vocabulary[a,b,c]	Expressive vocabulary, long-term retrieval
Comprehension[a,b,c]	Verbal comprehension, social judgment, long-term retrieval, verbal reasoning
Information[a,b,c]	Long-term retrieval, acquired knowledge
Word Reasoning[a,b,c]	Abstract verbal reasoning, long-term retrieval
Block Design[a,b,c]	Visual-spatial analytic and synthetic reasoning, fine motor ability, speed of mental processing
Picture Concepts[a,b]	Visual inductive reasoning
Matrix Reasoning[a,b]	Visual-spatial reasoning ability, perceptual organization
Digit Span[b,c]	Short-term auditory working memory, attention, concentration
Letter-Number Sequencing[a,b,c]	Short-term auditory working memory, attention, concentration, verbal comprehension
Arithmetic[b,c]	Short-term auditory working memory, attention, concentration, numerical reasoning, long-term retrieval
Coding/Digit Symbol Coding[a,b,c]	Visual-perception, speed of mental processing, fine motor coordination, visual-motor processing speed, attention, concentration, short-term visual recall
Symbol Search[a,b,c]	Visual-perceptual discrimination, speed of mental processing, visual-motor processing speed, attention, concentration, short-term visual recall
Cancellation[b]	Attention to detail, sustained attention, vigilance, visual perceptual ability, perceptual organization

[a]WPPSI-III.
[b]WISC-IV.
[c]WAIS-III.

ranges of mental retardation, as it cannot provide information regarding strengths and weaknesses in this range of functioning. A review of a child's adaptive behavior ratings along with the medical and developmental histories will be helpful in determining whether the WPPSI-III is appropriate.

Furthermore, at early ages, it may be difficult to obtain a valid IQ for children functioning in the moderate range of mental retardation, due to the potential for a high number of raw scores of zero which would invalidate the measure. It is important to remember that although raw scores of zero can be validly converted to scaled scores, valid IQs can only be obtained if a child has earned a specific number of nonzero subtest raw scores (Wechsler, 2003a). The specific number of nonzero subtests required for obtaining IQ and index scores is provided in the test manual.

The WPPSI-III manual also provides detailed information on prorating scores and providing test substitutions. This information is provided in the event that a subtest is spoiled or a child is unable to complete a subtest due to a particular handicap, as long as the handicap is not related to the construct being measured. For example, if a child had a fine motor impairment, a test that is not fine motor dependent could be substituted for a test such as Block Design, which requires a degree of fine motor facility. Or, if a fire drill were held in the middle of the administration of the Coding subtest, thus spoiling the score, an overall prorated score could be obtained. Alternatively, the examiner could opt to substitute the Symbol Search subtest for Coding. The manual provides detailed information on the number of subtests that must be valid in order to prorate for each age range, as well as valid test substitutions. Test substitutions, whenever possible, should be decided on prior to test administration, to lower the possibility (or temptation) of substituting or prorating tests simply because a child performed better on one test than on another.

The publishers of the WPPSI-III provided data from clinical studies on children with mental retardation in order to improve the clinical use and interpretation of test scores in this population. Consistent with studies on the Wechsler Intelligence Scale for Children, Third Edition (WISC-III) (Wechsler, 1991) and WISC-IV (Wechsler, 2003b), scores obtained in the clinical sample of individuals with mental retardation were generally equally attenuated on the WPPSI-III, showing no consistent pattern of peaks or troughs in score profiles. VIQ and PIQ also showed little intra-individual discrepancy (Wechsler, 2003a). However, children in the mild and moderate mental retardation range consistently demonstrated a nonsignificant relative strength in Similarities. The mean FSIQ for children with mild mental retardation in the clinical sample provided in the WPPSI-III manual was 62.1; for moderate mental retardation it was 53.1 (Wechsler, 2003a).

H. Wechsler Intelligence Scale for Children, Fourth Edition (WISC-IV)

The WISC-IV is the fourth iteration of the Wechsler Intelligence Scale for Children (WISC) (Wechsler, 1949). It was designed to measure the intellectual functioning of children and adolescents from 6 to 16 years of age. Like other Wechsler tests, the WISC-IV is appropriate for assessing intelligence in individuals in the moderate range of mental retardation and above; it was not designed to provide an accurate estimation of functioning in individuals in the severe and profound ranges of mental retardation and, therefore, should not be used.

The WISC-IV is composed of 15 subtests, 10 of which make up the clinical core, and 5 of which compose the supplemental tests. The supplemental tests are used to provide additional clinical information, as well as to substitute for spoiled tests, or tests that may be compromised by a child's handicapping condition (e.g., poor fine motor ability). As in all Wechsler tests, items are arranged in order of increasing ability level. Different starting points are generally designated according to a child's age and estimated ability level, with stopping points usually occurring when a child has failed a certain number of tests items or reached a designated time limit; this varies depending on the type of test given. Test administration times vary between children, particularly within the mental retardation population.

The WISC-IV provides a general measure of intelligence, the FSIQ and four index scores: Verbal Comprehension (VCI); Perceptual Reasoning (PRI); Working Memory (WMI); and Processing Speed (PSI). The VCI is composed of subtests measuring a variety of different constructs within the verbal domain, including verbal reasoning, expressive vocabulary, verbal comprehension, and long-term memory. The PRI includes subtests measuring various aspects of visual-spatial reasoning ability, and includes both fine motor dependent and motor independent measures. The WMI includes measures of short-term auditory working memory. The PSI provides measures of speed of mental processing which are generally considered to be fine motor dependent. The manual provides detailed information on scoring and interpretation, as well as specific rules for prorated scores and substitutions. See Table III for a brief description of each of the subtests.

Like the WPPSI-III, the WISC-IV was standardized on a large, representative sample of the population, and has established excellent reliability and validity (Wechsler, 2003b). Included in the manual are mean scores for individuals within the mentally retarded range of intellectual functioning. On the WISC-IV, children with mild mental retardation received a mean FSIQ score of 60.5, while children with moderate mental retardation received a mean FSIQ score of 46.4. Children with mental retardation demonstrated a generally uniform depression in index scores, with no evidence of statistically significant differences between them.

I. Wechsler Adult Intelligence Scale, Third Edition (WAIS-III)

The WAIS-III (Wechsler, 1997) represents the latest edition of the Wechsler Adult Intelligence Scale, a measure that originated in 1939 with the Wechsler-Bellevue Intelligence Scale—Form 1 (Sattler, 2001). The WAIS-III is an appropriate measure to use when assessing the intelligence of individuals from 16 to 89 years of age. The FSIQ scores on the WAIS-III range from 45 to 155. Thus, this test is appropriate for measuring IQ in individuals in the moderately mentally retarded and higher ranges of functioning. It should be noted that the WISC-IV and the WAIS-III overlap at age 16. In general, when testing an individual suspected of having mental retardation, the most valid score will be obtained by using the test that is standardized on the younger population, as it will likely be able to provide more items that would be mastered by an individual in the lower ranges of cognitive ability.

Items on the WAIS-III are arranged in order of increasing ability level. Unlike the WPPSI-III and WISC-IV, however, there are no age-related start points. Instead, general start points are given, with reverse rules provided in the event that the examinee does not establish basal levels of performance after the start point. The stop points are arranged similarly to other Wechsler tests, in that they generally occur after the examinee has failed a specified number of items or reached a designated time limit. Test administration times vary, and estimates given in the manual are not likely to be congruent to those seen in individuals with mental retardation. In some cases, these individuals will take significantly less time than average, due to reaching test ceilings quickly. In other cases, examinees will take a significantly greater amount of time, due to difficulties with processing speed, attention, motor ability, fatigue, and other factors.

Similar to the other newer tests in the Wechsler series, the WAIS-III was revised from previous versions to provide better alignment with current theories of intelligence (Zhu, Weiss, Prifitera, & Coalson, 2004), including a greater emphasis on abstract and fluid reasoning, and better alignment with factor analytic studies suggesting the need for an expansion of the traditional VIQ/PIQ division (Psychological Corporation, 2002a). The WAIS-III consists of 14 subtests, 11 of which are required in order to obtain the FSIQ. In addition to the FSIQ, a VIQ and PIQ are obtainable. The WAIS-IV also provides four index scores, aligned with factor analytic findings: VCI; Perceptual Organization (POI); WMI; and PSI. These index scores are analogous to VIQ, PIQ, WMI, and PSQ of the WPPSI-III, respectively. Relative to the VIQ, the VCI is considered to be a more refined measure of verbal comprehension ability, due to the fact that measures of working memory are now a part of a separate domain (WMI). POI is likewise considered to be a more refined measure of visual-spatial and perceptual reasoning than PIQ, as processing speed measures have been teased out and factored into the PSI score (Psychological Corporation, 2002a).

A large body of empirical data supporting the reliability and validity of the Wechsler scales has been collected. The technical manual provides extensive information relating to this quality of the WAIS-III. In support of representation, the manual reports that the WAIS-III was standardized on a sample matched to 1995 census data with regard to race, ethnicity, SES, gender, educational attainment, and geographic region. In addition, the WAIS-III was reportedly divided into 13 age groups for standardization, allowing individuals to be compared to their age-matched peers from the lowest to the highest age range, representing an improvement from the WAIS-R (Psychological Corporation, 2002a).

The WAIS-III manual additionally provides information regarding the performance of individuals with mental retardation (Psychological Corporation, 2002a). Consistent with previous studies of adults with mental retardation, individuals in the study sample with mental retardation obtained relatively flat and uniformly depressed subtest, index, and IQ score profiles. The sample of individuals with mild mental retardation obtained a mean FSIQ score of 58.3, a mean VIQ score of 60.1, and a mean PIQ score of 64.0. Mean index scores in this sample were as follows: VCI = 63.4; POI = 66.8; and PSI = 63.3. For individuals with moderate mental retardation, the mean FSIQ score was 50.9, while the mean VIQ and PIQ scores were 54.7 and 55.3, respectively. Mean index scores for individuals with moderate mental retardation were as follows: VCI = 56.8; POI = 58.9; and PSI = 57.8. (WMI scores were not obtained, as individuals were not given the Letter-Number Sequencing subtest, a necessary component of this index score.) The lowest mean scores were found in Arithmetic in both populations, and both populations scored relatively poorly on Symbol Search. However, unlike what has been found in studies with children with mental retardation, the adults in the sample provided did not receive a relatively higher PSI score.

IX. NONVERBAL INTELLIGENCE TESTS FREQUENTLY USED TO ASSESS FOR MENTAL RETARDATION

A. Leiter International Performance Scale

The Leiter International Performance Scale (Leiter, 1948) is the original, preeminent, individually administered, nonverbal, standardized intelligence test. Despite some test limitations reported by Sattler (1992), it has been the preferred nonverbal instrument used in the field until a revision of this scale, the Leiter International Performance Scale-Revised (Leiter-R) (Roid & Miller, 1997) came to the market. However, this original instrument continues to have merit (particularly in evaluating for mental retardation in some children and adolescents) and be worthy of discussion despite the general statement of Ethical Standard 9.08 in the American Psychological Association's Ethics Code (American Psychological Association, 2002) regarding use of obsolete tests.

The original Leiter and the Leiter-R are quite different instruments with regard to test materials and the mechanics by which the examinee completes tasks. While the Leiter-R requires the examinee to engage in a sequence of different tasks using multiple materials (stimulus easels, picture cards, manipulates, and printed material), the original Leiter requires the examinee to complete one repetitive task: match blocks with corresponding characteristic strips positioned in a sturdy wooden frame. While the difficulty of the task increases at subsequent levels and various categories of constructs are measured, the actual task remains the same.

Oftentimes, for examinees whose cognitive functioning is in the very low end or who present with a dual-diagnosis (e.g., mental retardation and autism), such repetition of task actually is an asset as the examinee quickly learns what is expected in terms of performance. In this regard, we have repeatedly experienced in our clinical practice that, for examinees such as these, frustration with the Leiter-R can ensue because of the change in task; and that our examinees require repeated "learning" periods or sometimes just give up. Yet, these same examinees persist in an uninterrupted fashion on the original Leiter. Thus, we have retained the original Leiter in our inventory of standardized IQ test materials, and encourage evaluators to consider this instrument if the Leiter-R proves less than successful.

The original Leiter International Performance Scale (Leiter, 1948) is a nonverbal test of intelligence for individuals, 2–18 years of age. It has been most frequently used to evaluate the non-English speaking or culturally disadvantaged, and those with hearing or speech deficits, other types of language handicaps, motor deficits (including cerebral palsy), or reading problems. It also has proved quite useful in the evaluation of individuals with autism and/or mental retardation. A history of the evolution of this instrument (including preparatory work, revisions, and adaptations) can be found in Gabel, Oster, and Butnik (1986) and Sattler (1992).

The original Leiter requires an examinee to match blocks with corresponding strips positioned on a slotted, wooden frame. There are 54 standardized subtests divided into three trays of blocks and strips. Tray 1 covers years 2 through 7, Tray 2 covers years 8 through 12, and Tray 3 covers years 13 through 17. This Binet-type years-scale has four subtests at each year level from year 2 through year 16, and six tests at year 17. The categories measured are: Concretistics (matching of specific relationships), Symbolic Transformations (judging relationships between two events), Quantitative Discriminations, Spatial Imagery, Genus Matching, Progressive Discriminations, and Immediate Recall.

Instructions to the examinee are given in pantomime by either pointing to the materials in a specific fashion or completing a portion of the subtest to demonstrate the problem-solving strategy. Examinees are started at a level considerably below their chronological age which allows opportunity to understand the general problem-solving expectation of this scale. There are no time limits to this scale except on three separate subtests.

The basal score is based on the highest year level the subject passes all four subtests. The ceiling score is obtained once the examinee has *no* tests passed at two sequential year levels. Administration time is typically identified as ~30–45 min. We have found administration time to be longer with individuals who are functioning in the lower end of mental retardation or who present with a dual-diagnosis (e.g., mental retardation and autism). With these examinees, it may be fruitful to administer this test over two or more sessions (to control for fatigue and/or loss of attention).

The original Leiter makes use of the concept of mental age (MA). The MA on the Leiter is used to obtain an IQ by the ratio method ($IQ = MA/CA \times 100$) (mean = 100, SD = 16). It was later recommended that a constant of five points be added to this IQ equation because the original norms appeared to underestimate children's intelligence (Leiter, 1959). A thorough review of the *General Instructions for the Leiter International Performance Scale* (Leiter, 1969) is vital as there are some scoring peculiarities to this instrument: a scoring adjustment is made to the examinee's mental age, and there is an additional scoring caveat once the examinee reaches chronological age 13.

The format for reporting Leiter scores and qualitative description of performance on this test is described in Exhibit 2.2.

B. Leiter International Performance Scale-Revised

The Leiter International Performance Scale-Revised (Leiter-R) (Roid & Miller, 1997) is the long-awaited update to the Leiter International Performance Scale (Leiter, 1948). This individually administered, nonverbal, standardized intelligence test assesses the cognitive functioning for individuals 2 years, 0 months to 20 years, 11 months. Like the original Leiter, the Leiter-R was developed to be used with individuals who could not be reliably and validly assessed with traditional intelligence tests. Specifically, these individuals include those with communication disorders, hearing impairments, motor impairments, cognitive delay, traumatic brain injury, attention-deficit disorder, types of learning disabilities, and English as a second language.

The Leiter-R emphasizes fluid intelligence. Thus, the test developers stress that the derived IQ is not significantly influenced by the level and quality of the individual's educational, social, and family experience. The Leiter-R measures the IQ range of 30–170. Thus, it would be an appropriate tool for assessing those individuals falling in the mild to severe range of mental retardation.

The Leiter-R consists of 20 subtests organized into four domains: Reasoning, Visualization, Memory, and Attention. The 10 Reasoning and Visualization subtests assess visualization, reasoning, and spatial ability. Together, these subtests make up the Visualization and Reasoning (VR)

Battery from which an individual's intellectual ability is derived. Despite changes in test format, a considerable number of items from the original Leiter were retained in the Leiter-R and reformatted within the VR Battery.

The 10 Attention and Memory subtests are new. They assess nonverbal attention and memory functioning. Together, these subtests make up the Attention and Memory (AM) Battery. The AM Battery can add clinically useful information, particularly for individuals who present with attention deficit disorders, learning disabilities, and traumatic brain injury.

The examiner has the option of administering just the VR Battery which will provide an estimate of global nonverbal intellectual level. Thus, it is from this score that a cognitive deficit could be determined, and, in conjunction with deficit scores in adaptive functioning, a diagnosis of mental retardation could be made. The examiner also has the option of administering the VR and AM Batteries together. This may provide information regarding an interfering role of cognitive-processing deficits in memory or attention on the accurate evaluation of global intellectual ability. For example, if a child with an attention dificit disorder is highly distractible or presents with severe sequential-memory deficits, the AM Battery could provide evidence to "rule out" an incorrect diagnosis of borderline intelligence or deficit cognitive functioning.

In addition to a traditional composite IQ (with a mean of 100 and SD of 15), the Leiter-R provides subtest scale scores (with a mean of 10 and SD of 3), percentile scores, and age equivalence scores. The latter scores can be easily understood by parents and others with whom the test results will be shared.

The Leiter-R also has four rating scales (Examiner, Parent, Self, and Teacher), which offers multidimensional behavioral observation information about the individual. In addition, the Leiter-R provides Growth Scores useful in the assessment of individuals with severe handicaps. Specifically, these scores enable professionals who reevaluate the cognitive development of children and adolescents with severe mental retardation to measure the small, but important, improvement in their cognitive skills. Thus, the progression of improvement across time can be ascertained (regardless of age-based scores), as well as ascertaining the likely efficacy of current educational and treatment programs and areas where modification(s) in programming need to take place.

For the Leiter-R, the test developers reduced the physical weight of the original Leiter kit and provided improved hygienic testing materials. The original Leiter wooden blocks have been replaced by colorful, laminate playing cards, and foam rubber manipulatives. Test materials also include three flip-card stimulus easel books that include examiner directions and printed materials.

Neither the examiner nor examinee is required to speak. The examinee does not need to read or write, either. The Leiter-R requires an examinee to place the cards and manipulatives into "slots" in the "frame" which is molded into the easel base of each stimulus book. Alhough the number of subtests varies by age of the child, administration of the combined set of subtests from the VR and AM Batteries can be completed in about 90 min, or less, for most children. As with the original Leiter, we have found that shorter, multiple testing sessions may be more beneficial than one continuous test administration with children and adolescents who present with severe cognitive impairment.

The national standardization of this updated instrument was carefully constructed and included typical children and adolescents as well as nine clinical subgroups of atypical children and adolescents (including 123 children diagnosed with mental retardation). The Leiter-R mean composite full IQ for individuals in the cognitive delay (mental retardation) clinical subgroup was 62.7 and 55.4 for the 2–5 age group and 6–20 age group, respectively. Reliability and validity are extensively described in the test manual. The Leiter-R correlates .85 with the WISC-III FSIQ and .85 with the original Leiter IQ Scale.

In addition to being a measure which can provide ability estimates sensitive to small increments of improvement in cognitive ability, the Leiter-R can be a useful, nonverbal alternative for early identification of cognitive delays (2 years, 0 months up to 5 years). It also can be a useful, nonverbal alternative for the assessment of cognitive functioning in individuals with severe mental retardation when a professional team is charged with planning for transitional services from school to postschool activities (typically outlined when a child is between 14 and 16 years).

X. SPECIAL CONSIDERATIONS IN TEST ADMINISTRATION FOR CHILDREN WITH MENTAL RETARDATION

Cognitive testing is a skill that requires advanced training and supervised practice (Sattler, 2001). This is especially true with regard to assessing children. In order to obtain an optimal performance from a child, the examiner must possess flexibility, creativity, patience, attentiveness, and above all, a tremendous affinity for children. Children with mental retardation may present even greater challenges to the test administrator, presenting with specific deficits that may reduce the likelihood of obtaining an individual's maximum performance level. In order to obtain the most accurate assessment of a child's functioning level, the examiner must be extremely vigilant and aware of these factors. This generally requires a great deal of skill and preparation on the part of the examiner. In particular, it is helpful to become familiar with some common problems and solutions associated with assessing these children. These difficulties include problems with attention and focus, regulation of mood, fatigue, motivation, anxiety, rapport, and communication ability.

Children with mental retardation may present with significant difficulties in attention and focus (Kamphaus, 2005) which can easily be mistaken for a lack of ability. For most children, a distraction-free environment is important; however, for children with cognitive deficits, it is even more critical. Environmental factors that must be addressed include temperature, lighting, aromas, sounds, and visual stimuli. A child's physiological state, such as whether he or she is hungry or needs to use the restroom, also may present as significant distracters to children with cognitive impairments. Moreover, children with cognitive impairments will be less likely to alert the examiner to their state, requiring the examiner to be vigilant to subtle behavioral changes. In attempting to obtain the maximum performance with regard to a child's attention, it is important to provide multiple breaks, give allowable cues for attention and focus, and provide frequent feedback to the child (in the form of "I like how hard you're trying."). Finally, if a child regularly takes a prescription medicine to assist with attention, this medicine should be used during an assessment of cognitive ability.

Signs of fatigue may manifest in a number of different ways. Traditional signs of fatigue in children with mental retardation may include the obvious, such as yawning, slurring of speech, drooping of eyelids, slowed motor movements, resting of the head in the hands, putting the head down, or becoming irritable. However, children with mental retardation also may demonstrate fatigue by becoming suddenly oppositional, requesting to leave or to go to the bathroom, starting to cry, becoming restless, or resorting to significantly more "I don't know" answers or nonresponses. At times, cognitive overload can be related to the specific cognitive demands of a subtest. For example, a child with language difficulties may appear exhausted when responding to an open-ended verbal query, but may "perk up" after moving on to something more visual, such as a matrix-reasoning test. In this case, simply switching to a different test modality can help to ameliorate fatiguing. However, individuals with slow processing speed or limited working memory capacity, often consistently demonstrate fatigue as the cognitive load of the tasks increase, regardless of the ability being taxed. A child's cognitive and communication limitations will require the examiner to be much more vigilant to the child's level of fatigue. Rarely will a child with cognitive limitations express the need for a break, yet a lack of appropriate accommodation could result in a "shut down," in which the child no longer is able to function at his or her full capacity. For this reason, the examiner should maintain an awareness of the child's cues that he or she is having difficulty, providing breaks or preferred activities when possible. Often, it may be helpful to allow the child to have a small amount of a drink, a snack, or a walk down the hall. If the fatigue is particularly intractable, it may be necessary to administer the test in multiple sessions. It also is important to remember that, for some individuals, the provision of lunch or an alternate activity may add to, rather than reduce, the fatigue experienced (Lezak, Howieson, & Loring, 2004). It is, therefore, helpful to consult with individuals who are most familiar with the child to determine what may work best.

Relatively low degrees of intrinsic motivation to complete task items often are noted in children with mental retardation. Compared to typical children, they may require a greater degree of verbal reinforcement and other methods of external motivation. Studies have shown that children with mental retardation perform better when provided with primary or token reinforcers during test administration (Johnson, Bradley-Johnson, McCarthy, & Jamie, 1984). Giving stickers, pencils, or small pieces of cookies or crackers as a reward for staying on task and working hard is an effective practice. However, it is important that reinforcement is provided in a manner that does not break the standardized protocol of the test being administered. Obviously, reinforcement should be given for effort, not correctness. Furthermore, it is critical to obtain the approval of the child's parents or caregiver when providing such reinforcers. This is particularly true with food, as children with mental retardation may have food restrictions due to allergies, metabolic issues, difficulties with chewing and swallowing, and/or cultural/religious beliefs.

Communication problems and anxiety may negatively affect test performance in cognitive assessments (Lezak et al., 2004). In individuals with mental retardation, it may be particularly challenging to establish rapport and decrease anxiety. Many children with mental retardation present with speech and language delays, and may not always find comfort in soothing words (Spruill, Oakland, & Harrison, 2005). They also may become confused and frustrated by the verbal messages presented to them. Such children often use alternative means of negotiating and understanding their environment. For example, they may read a person's face and tone before they listen to the words spoken. For this reason, children with mental retardation may become particularly anxious when working with an examiner who tends to remain vacant and expressionless during test administration. Individuals with cognitive deficits may tend to interpret this behavior as an indication that they have done something wrong (Lezak et al., 2004). Therefore, the examiner must endeavor to communicate messages of warmth, positive regard, reinforcement, comfort, patience, and a sense of fun through their body language and affect. In addition, young children, who may be wary of strangers, may need a transition object available to help them adjust to the setting. For very young children or children who are particularly anxious, having the parent in the testing room may be the only means of ensuring an optimal performance. In this case, the parent always should be behind the child so that the child is not distracted and does not look to the parent for testing cues. The parent also should be instructed not to help or encourage the child.

It is important to remember that a determination of mental retardation requires a measure of a child's optimal performance, not simply the performance that the child happens to bring in on a given day (Spruill et al., 2005). As it is rarely a simple matter, the skillful examiner will employ careful observation, a thorough review of preliminary data, and the artistry that comes with experience, in order to obtain the most accurate measure of intelligence for each and every child. For more information on best practice in assessment, see Sattler (2001); Lezak et al. (2004); Lichtenberger and Kaufman (2004); Prifitera, Saklofske, and Weiss (2005); and Kamphaus (2005).

A. Test-Specific Considerations

Specific tests of intellectual functioning also may present unique challenges in test interpretation when assessing individuals with mental retardation. A few of these challenges are reviewed below.

1. THE WECHSLER SCALES

Overall, the Wechsler scales provide rigorously researched, reliable, and valid measures of an individual's intellectual functioning. Moreover, the Wechsler tests have been the preferred tests of intellectual functioning in children since the 1960's, and there are no tests that are more universally accepted and approved for the purpose of establishing mental retardation in children (Prifitera Saklofska, Weiss, & Rolfhus, 2005). However, despite improvements from previous versions, the instructions on the Wechsler scales still appear to rely heavily on language. This may be a particular challenge for young children with cognitive impairments, who often show delays in speech and language. In addition, the paucity of manipulatives on the WPPSI-III may make it a bit less appealing to young children than some other measures in current use. Finally, it is important to remember that the Wechsler scales were not designed to test children functioning below the moderate levels of mental retardation (Psychological Corporation, 2002a,b, 2003). In cases where a much lower ability level is suspected, alternate measures should be considered.

When using a Wechsler test, one practice that should be taken into account is that of using alternate starting points. When testing individuals suspected of having significantly subaverage ability, it may be advisable to begin at start points that are more reflective of the individual's suspected developmental age. Thus, the examinee will be more likely to feel successful on the first item presented. Doing so may help to improve rapport and compliance, and decrease anxiety and fatigue. On the WAIS-III, age-related start points are not given; rather, all individuals begin at the same point and then reverse if they do not obtain the requisite number of basal items correct. On this test, it may be helpful to begin at the easiest subtest item provided, rather than working backward. This is particularly relevant if it is known that an individual will not be able to pass the start item. It is important to note, however, that this practice does have some drawbacks. If, for example, the examinee achieves a basal level of performance after the start point, this practice will have increased the number of items required prior to achieving a ceiling, which may contribute to the examinee's fatigue and frustration. As always, it is important to review all relevant data prior to beginning the assessment, in order to determine the most effective strategy in a given situation.

A concern that arises with the newer Wechsler scales is the inclusion of processing speed measures in the calculation of the FSIQ (Madle, 2005). While the processing speed factor may indeed provide clinical utility, the inclusion of this time-dependent measure may lead to attenuated IQ scores in children with fine motor difficulties, attention deficits, seizure disorders, anxiety, depression, and/or those taking certain medications. Therefore, it is important, as always, to carefully scrutinize the child's score in relation to all other data presented (Sattler, 2001). It should be noted that it is *not* common for a typical child with mental retardation to present with a PSI that is significantly lower than other index scores. The opposite trend is generally the case, wherein the PSI tends to be slightly higher than both the VCI and PRI in children (but not adults) with mental retardation (Psychological Corporation, 2002a; Spruill et al., 2005; Wechsler, 2003b; Zhu et al., 2004). In the event that an attenuated score is suspected, the Wechsler scales provide alternative means of obtaining a cognitive ability score, such as through a General Abilities Index (GAI), or through prorating of scores (Prifitera, Saklofske, & Weiss, 2005; Psychological Corporation, 2002a,b, 2003).

2. THE DAS

The DAS is a well-standardized measure of cognitive ability in children and adolescents. However, one drawback of the DAS relates to the developmental model employed in test creation. While this model provides highly useful information in treatment planning and diagnostic decision making, and may be argued to be a more appropriate way to measure ability, it can cause problems for longitudinal comparison. The problem is that once a child reaches a certain age, constructs such as verbal ability are not measured using the same tasks on the DAS. Consequently, it may be difficult to gauge a child's growth in a specific area of development. Although the DAS developers contend that the different subtests used at different age ranges assess similar constructs, there are subtle differences that may be particularly relevant in different children. For example, at different age ranges, abilities unrelated to the construct being tested are taxed unequally in subtests that are purported to measure the same thing. For some children, this will result in age-related score differences that may be misinterpreted as a loss or gain in skill. This is a particular problem when working with children suspected of following an atypical developmental trajectory. Therefore, as with all tests, examiners must be mindful of such contributing factors prior to making interpretations of a child's score.

XI. THE FLYNN EFFECT: IQ SCORES AND MENTAL RETARDATION DIAGNOSES

Given the content of this chapter, these authors would be remiss in not reporting on the Flynn effect. The Flynn effect is a phenomenon uncovered, via massive data analyses, by James R. Flynn, a political scientist at the University of Otago in New Zealand, and reported on in a series of papers (Flynn, 1984, 1987, 1998, 2005, 2006). Using IQ test data from 20 nations in the developed world, Flynn discovered there have been IQ gains ranging from 5 to 25 points in a single generation (Flynn, 1984, 1987, 1998). The effect is stronger on tests which measure fluid intelligence (intelligence needed for on-the-spot reasoning, abstraction, and problem solving) than on tests of crystallized intelligence (intelligence centered on accumulated knowledge such as vocabulary, arithmetic, and general information). For example, the effect has been most dramatic on data analyses using the Ravens Progressive Matrices, a test of fluid intelligence. On the Ravens, the Flynn effect has been a gain of 21 points in 30 years (around .7 point gain per year). The effect has been less dramatic but still impressive on data analyses using the Wechsler scales and the Stanford-Binet series, IQ tests which measure crystallized and fluid intelligence. On these tests, the Flynn effect has been a gain of 14.31 points within 45 years (around .3 point gain per year).

Further, when reviewing Wechsler VIQs and Wechsler PIQs, Flynn discovered a 10- to 20-point increase in the Wechsler PIQs (which are more heavily loaded on fluid abilities) and a 9-point increase in the Wechsler VIQs (which are more heavily loaded on crystallized abilities) (Flynn, 1984, 1987). In these same studies, when comparing the WISC with the WISC-R, he found that individuals tested on the WISC-R had to answer more questions correctly, or had to answer harder questions, to obtain the same score as on the WISC. At a later point, Flynn (1998) estimated the mean difference in FSIQ scores between the WISC-R and the WISC-III to be 5.3 points (Flynn, 1998). From a practical perspective, this means that someone who received a score of 105 on the WISC-R would, on the average, receive a score of 100 on the WISC-III.

Initially, Flynn limited his test data analyses to the average range of the IQ distribution. As a result, for some time, less was known about the effect's impact on those individuals who score well above the mean (those in the gifted range of intelligence) and well below the mean (those in the range of mental retardation and borderline intellectual functioning). A few studies have noted a decline in IQ scores among children classified as mentally retarded once the WISC-III replaced the WISC-R. Specifically, the mean WISC-R FSIQ in samples of mentally retarded children ranged 5–9 points greater than the mean WISC-III FSIQ (Bolen, Aichinger, Hall, & Webster, 1995; Slate & Saarnio, 1995; Vance, Maddux, Fuller, & Awadh, 1996). Further, a widely cited study by Kanaya, Scullin, and Ceci (2003) also provided support that the Flynn effect is impacting IQ scores in the mentally retarded and borderline ranges. Analyses showed that the IQ gains from the WISC-R to the WISC-III were actually very close to Flynn's (1998) estimate of a 5.3-point difference; the Flynn effect fell between 5 and 6 IQ points in the mild mentally retarded and borderline ranges, almost exactly the same magnitude that Flynn found in the middle of the IQ distribution. Flynn (2005) has stated that there is overwhelming evidence that the IQ gains are at least as great for individuals' test scores in the low levels (i.e., 55–70 IQ) as they are with individuals' test scores in the average range.

Overall, the findings indicate that as time passes and IQ tests get older, people perform increasingly better on an IQ test, raising the mean IQ by several points within a matter of years. Once a test is renormed, which typically happens every 15–20 years, the mean is reset to 100, making the test harder and "hiding" the previous gains in IQ scores. Because the Flynn effect takes effect immediately on the introduction of a new IQ test, the norms are most valid at the times the norms are released.

Although there is no consensus among professionals as to why these gains are occurring or what the gains actually mean (with possible explanations including genetics, SES, higher education levels, increased problem solving ability, and increased test sophistication), all are in agreement that the gains occur and that they hold significant theoretical and practical importance. In this regard, Neisser (1998) has provided a review of these areas of importance.

Specifically, with regard to the mentally retarded population, the Flynn effect raises particular concerns in a number of areas. First, Kanaya et al. (2003) point out that because of the systematic increase in IQ seen over the past 80 years (the Flynn effect), there is reason to believe that many students are diagnosed as mentally retarded based on the year in which they are tested and test norms used rather than on their cognitive ability. As the norms age on various IQ tests, fewer children are diagnosed as mentally retarded (in the mild range) as more children's IQs rise above the 70-point cutoff.

With the introduction of new norms on various IQ tests, suddenly more children again score below the 70-point cutoff. Consequently, in some cases, the same child could be diagnosed as mentally retarded or not mentally retarded at various points in development. Thus, irrespective of the child's actual cognitive ability, the child's eligibility for special education programming could be impacted, resulting in spotty or inconsistent supports and services.

Second, Kanaya et al. (2003) indicate that some school systems and psychologists, for a variety of reasons, continue to use older tests rather than replacing them immediately with newly normed tests. Further, even within the same school district, multiple psychologists may provide evaluation services to a district. As a result, different children may be tested on different versions (norms) of the same test in the same school year. Unfortunately, in this latter case, these IQ test scores are still compared with one another, regardless of the fact that different norms were used, and diagnoses are assigned accordingly. Consequently, two children in the same classroom with the same cognitive ability could be diagnosed differently simply because different test norms were used for each child.

Overall, Kanaya et al. (2003) indicate that the times to be particularly cautious are when a test is either at the beginning or at the end of its norming cycle, with a test being least valid when administered at the end of its cycle. Needless to say, evaluators always have needed to exercise care when relying on an IQ to diagnose mental retardation. Knowledge of the Flynn effect and awareness that the effect impacts the lower end of the IQ distribution as well as the average range of the IQ distribution dictates that evaluators who assess for presence of mental retardation seriously consider the Flynn effect in the diagnostic process. Currently, methods to control for the Flynn effect have yet to be formally considered and debated in the literature. To date, Greenspan (2006) has advocated the necessity for evaluators to adjust IQs down with each subsequent year in the norming cycle of a standardized test to control for the Flynn effect. Flynn (2005) and Greenspan (2006) have offered possible formulae to do so.

In addition, some consideration might be given to introducing more formal time limits by which evaluators must begin using the newest edition of a test once the new version has been formally introduced to the marketplace. However, adherence to such regulations likely would be difficult to enforce given the reported budgetary constraints of many school systems and mental health agencies. Further, this could provide test publishers impetus to encourage premature and unnecessary test revisions. Finally, such a rigid stance in this matter could prohibit the sometimes necessary, continued use of older editions of some instruments in particular clinical case situations (e.g., use of the original Leiter as described earlier in this chapter).

XII. REPORTING FINDINGS FROM STANDARDIZED INTELLIGENCE TESTS

Whether formal evaluation reveals that an individual is mentally retarded, is manifesting dual diagnoses, or is presenting with another disability altogether, psychologists need to exercise great care in writing a formal report. The skill of constructing a well-written psychological evaluation based on test findings and other supportive information goes beyond the scope of this chapter. Indeed, such is worthy of a formal chapter on its own. However, some comments can be made here.

First, because the diagnosis of mental retardation has significant effects on the child or adolescent's life, the psychologist must be careful and accurate in reporting test findings. Further, the psychologist must be thorough in presenting all required data consistent with the definitional criteria for making a diagnosis of mental retardation. As described at the beginning of this chapter, the diagnosis of mental retardation should never be made solely on the standardized intelligence test score alone. At minimum, the report should include the documentation of significantly low performance on a nationally standardized measure of intelligence and below-average levels of adaptive behavior in a variety of settings. A thorough, professional assessment also should include multiple sources of test information, comprehensive behavioral observations in school, home, and/or other settings, input from caregivers, developmental, medical, and social histories, and other reliable sources of evidence.

With regard to the standardized IQ, itself, psychologists should be cautious when interpreting a low IQ that may reflect conditions other than low intellectual ability. Low scores can be attributed to a variety of other factors, alone or in combination. This issue was extensively reviewed in Section XI of this chapter. Psychologists also must rule out potential competing hypotheses concerning the child or adolescent's test performance, and indicate their concerns in the report, before concluding the child or adolescent is manifesting mental retardation.

However, even if the psychologist provides all this information, a weak or less than adequate report can still result. Indeed, we have seen our share of poor report writing. While the majority of psychologists provide the "required" information, many psychologists report each test instrument's scores and data as separate *and* disparate entities, without ever integrating the information into a cohesive, meaningful whole. This leaves the psychologist at risk for not addressing sometimes contradictory information in an evaluation (e.g., poor visual-motor integration skill on one test and adequate visual-motor integration performance on another instrument).

A strong psychological test report should first review test scores and interpret this information clearly. However, a strong report also should integrate test data in a cohesive fashion which, in turn, should provide the foundation for a seamless clinical case formulation. In other words, the psychologist should "paint a portrait" of the child or adolescent that can be visualized (i.e., comprehended) by all who read the report. The psychologist is challenged to not only describe the child or adolescent's precise levels of performance but also explain why the child or adolescent obtained a particular profile, and what the child or adolescent will need to aid further positive progression and development. Good report writing is as much an art as it is a science.

In addition, if the psychologist is clear that the diagnosis is mental retardation, they should not be fearful to use the term "mental retardation" in the written document or during the face-to-face feedback with the parents, caretakers, and/or school system. In the long run, it does not serve any party well to skirt the issue. However, it is the responsibility of the psychologist to clearly define what mental retardation is and what it is not (along with any other diagnosis being reported) as the parents, caretakers, and teachers may have an incorrect understanding of the diagnostic term(s).

Recommendations contained in the report should be clear and thorough. They should be driven by what the child or adolescent needs rather than any institution's budgetary restrictions. The report should be constructed in such a fashion so it is readable by parties with varied levels of education and familiarity with the tests administered. Finally, the report should be written respectfully in all aspects as this document will become part of the child or adolescent's formal record, will follow the child or adolescent for many years to come, and may be the foundation for subsequent evaluations, recommendations, and treatment services with this individual. If information about the child or adolescent's family situation is included in the formal report, the psychologist always should be truthful but simultaneously should demonstrate respect for the family and exercise discretion in how familial details are stated. The parameters of confidentiality must be followed and general respect for the family must be maintained.

XIII. SUMMARY

Mental retardation is a categorization for a heterogeneous group of individuals with concurrent deficits in intellectual and adaptive functioning manifest prior to their 18th birthday. The diagnosis is made regardless of etiology. Mental retardation is neither a mental disorder nor a medical disorder. Rather, it is a deviation in development that may increase the risk of mental disorder and may be accompanied by medical issues. The combination of developmental, medical, and psychiatric factors makes treatment of this population complicated. Accurate assessment of cognitive and adaptive functioning is required to maximize the potential for success of the comprehensive intervention protocols typically employed in the treatment of individuals with mental retardation.

This chapter examines a variety of intelligence tests that may be used in the assessment and diagnosis of mental retardation, including the Bayley Scales of Infant Development, Second Edition, the Bayley Scales of Infant and Toddler Development, Third Edition, the DAS, the McCarthy Scales of Children's Abilities, the WPPSI-III, the WISC-IV, and the WAIS-III, as well as, the Stanford-Binet Intelligence Scales, Fifth Edition (SB5), the original Leiter International Performance Scale, and the Leiter International Performance Scale-Revised. The history, conceptual bases, method of test construction, psychometric properties, testing procedures, scoring protocols, and examiner qualifications, as well as, indications and contraindications for the use of each test is reviewed in detail.

Measures of intelligence play a crucial role in the assessment, diagnosis, and treatment of children and adolescents with mental retardation. Intelligence tests may be administered for a variety of reasons. However, the identification of an individual's relative cognitive strengths and weaknesses are among the most pertinent with respect to customizing educational and occupational programming. Therefore, it is not good clinical practice to become familiar only with a single standardized test of intelligence and make determinations based solely on its findings. Different tests emphasize various elements of the construct of intelligence. Best practice standards require psychologists to become thoroughly familiar with a wide variety of intelligence tests in order to ensure that the proper test is selected and that the findings will be valid and applicable to the individual being assessed. Awareness of the range of available tests also allows for the option of using multiple assessment tools to derive the most accurate information regarding an individual's cognitive and adaptive ability. This approach further increases the probability that test results will be accurate and contribute to the development of a successful educational program, occupational training program, or treatment protocol.

There are no shortcuts to competency in terms of test selection, administration, scoring, interpretation, and report writing. Adequate training, practice, and clinical supervision are the mainstays of competency standards for intelligence testing when confronted with the complex task of differentially diagnosing mental retardation from a host of similarly appearing developmental disorders and learning disabilities. Psychologists must be aware of the many extraneous variables that may influence the test performance of individuals with mental retardation, particularly in terms of communication skill deficits and the presence of comorbid psychiatric disorder. The inability to self-report fatigue or illness due to issues of language proficiency is a constant threat to a valid assessment. So, too, are the variables of attentional and motivational deficits as well as poor self-regulation of mood and behavior, where the test performance of individuals with mental retardation are 2–6 times more likely to be adversely affected, depending on the severity of the intellectual impairment (i.e., mild vs profound mental retardation).

As a final note, it is important for psychologists to be aware of the Flynn effect and its relevance to the diagnosis of mental retardation. Understanding of the Flynn effect is particularly relevant when a psychologist has been asked to testify as an expert witness for the Court and make a differential diagnosis of mental retardation as opposed to a learning disability or psychiatric disorder. Nowhere will a psychologist's competency involving intelligence testing be more transparent than when it involves educating a community of fellow professionals (e.g., judges, lawyers, psychiatrists, and social workers) as to the many facts involved in the determination of intelligence.

REFERENCES

American Association on Mental Retardation (AAMR) (2002). *Mental retardation: Definition, classification, and systems of support* (10th ed.). Washington, DC: Author.

American Psychiatric Association (1952). *Diagnostic and statistical manual of mental disorders* (1st ed.). Washington, DC: Author.

American Psychiatric Association (1968). *Diagnostic and statistical manual of mental disorders* (2nd ed.). Washington, DC: Author.

American Psychiatric Association (1980). *Diagnostic and statistical manual of mental disorders* (3rd ed.). Washington, DC: Author.

American Psychiatric Association (1987). *Diagnostic and statistical manual of mental disorders* (3rd ed., revised). Washington, DC: Author.

American Psychiatric Association (1994). *Diagnostic and statistical manual of mental disorders* (4th ed.). Washington, DC: Author.

American Psychiatric Association (2000). *Diagnostic and statistical manual of mental disorders* (4th ed., text revision). Washington, DC: Author.

American Psychological Association (2002). Ethical principles of psychologists and code of conduct. *American Psychologist, 57,* 1060–1073.

Bayley, N. (1969). *Bayley Scales of Infant Development: Birth to two years.* San Antonio, TX: The Psychological Corporation.

Bayley, N. (1993). *Bayley Scales of Infant Development* (2nd ed.). San Antonio, TX: The Psychological Corporation.

Bayley, N. (2005). *Bayley Scales of Infant and Toddler Development.* San Antonio, TX: The Psychological Corporation.

Bolen, L. M., Aichinger, K. S., Hall, C. W., & Webster, R. E. (1995). A comparison of the performance of cognitively disabled children on the WISC-R and WISC-III. *Journal of Clinical Psychology, 51,* 89–94.

Broman, S. H., & Nichols, P. L. (1975, September). *Early mental development, social class, and school-age IQ.* Paper presented at the meeting of the American Psychological Association, Chicago.

Brooks-Gunn, J., & Lewis, M. (1983). Screening and diagnosing handicapped infants. *Topics in Early Childhood Special Education, 3,* 14–28.

D'Amato, R. C., Fletcher-Janzen, E., & Reynolds, C. R. (Eds.) (2005). *The handbook of school neuropsychology.* Hoboken, NJ: John Wiley and Sons.

Dennis, W., & Najarian, P. (1973). How reversible are the effects? In S. J. Hutt & C. Hull (Eds.), *Early human development* (pp. 274–288). London: Oxford University Press.

Elliot, C. D. (1990). *Differential Ability Scales.* San Antonio, TX: The Psychological Corporation.

Field, M. A., & Sanchez, V. A. (1999). *Equal treatment for people with mental retardation: Having and raising children.* Cambridge, MA: Harvard University Press.

Fishler, K., Graliker, B. V., & Koch, R. (1965). The predictability of intelligence with Gesell Developmental Scales in mentally retarded infants and young children. *American Journal of Mental Deficiency, 69,* 515–525.

Fishman, M. A., & Palkes, H. S. (1974). The validity of psychometric testing in children with congenital malformation of the central nervous system. *Developmental Medicine and Child Neurology, 16,* 180–185.

Flanagan, D. P., & Kaufman, A. S. (2004). *Essentials of WISC-IV assessment.* Hoboken, NJ: John Wiley & Sons.

Flynn, J. R. (1984). The mean IQ of Americans: Massive gains 1932 to 1978. *Psychological Bulletin, 95,* 29–51.

Flynn, J. R. (1987). Massive IQ gains in 14 nations: What IQ tests really measure. *Psychological Bulletin, 101,* 171–191.

Flynn, J. R. (1998). WAIS-III and WISC-III IQ gains in the United States from 1972 to 1995: How to compensate for obsolete norms. *Perceptual and Motor Skills, 86,* 1231–1239.

Flynn, J. R. (2005). *Tethering the elephant: Capital cases, IQ and the Flynn effect.* Unpublished manuscript. Dunedin, New Zealand: University of Otego.

Flynn, J. R. (2006). The Flynn effect: Rethinking intelligence and what affects it. In C. Flores-Mendoza & R. Colom (Eds.), *Introduction to the psychology of individual differences.* Porto Alegrel: ArtMeds (English translation from the Portuguese is available fromjim. flynn@stonebow.otago.ac.nz).

Fotheringhan, J. B. (1983). Mental retardation and developmental delay. In K. P. Paget & B. A. Bracken (Eds.), *The psycho-educational assessment of preschool children* (pp. 207–223). New York, NY: Grune & Stratton.

Gabel, S., Oster, G. D., & Butnik, S. M. (1986). *Understanding psychological testing in children.* New York, NY: Plenum Medical Book Company.

Gerken, K. C., Hancock, K. A., & Wade, T. H. (1978). A comparison of the Stanford-Binet intelligence scale and the McCarthy Scales of Children's Abilities with preschool children. *Psychology in the Schools, 15,* 468–472.

Goh, D. S., & Youngquist, J. A. (1979). A comparison of the McCarthy Scales of Children's Abilities and the WISC-R. *Journal of Learning Disabilities, 12,* 344–348.

Greenspan, S. (2006). Issues in the use of the "Flynn effect" to adjust IQ scores when diagnosing MR. *Psychology in Mental Retardation and Developmental Disabilities, 31*(3), 3–7.

Grossman, H. J. (1983). *Classification in mental retardation.* Washington, DC: American Association on Mental Deficiency.

Heber, R. (1959). *A manual on terminology and classification in mental retardation* (revised ed.). Washington, DC: American Association on Mental Deficiency.

Illingworth, R. S., & Birch, L. B. (1959). The diagnosis of mental retardation in infancy: A follow-up study. *Archives of Disease in Childhood, 34,* 269–273.

Johnson, C. M., Bradley-Johnson, S., McCarthy, R., & Jamie, M. (1984). Token reinforcement during WICS-R administration II. Effects on mildly retarded, black students. *Applied research in mental retardation, 5,* 43–53.

Kamphaus, R. W. (2005). *Clinical assessment of child and adolescent intelligence* (2nd ed.). New York, NY: Springer.

Kanaya, T., Scullin, M. H., & Ceci, S. J. (2003). The Flynn effect and US policies: The impact of rising IQ scores on American society via mental retardation diagnoses. *American Psychologist, 58,* 778–790.

Kaufman, A. S., & Lichtenberger, E. O. (1999). *Essentials of WAIS-III assessment.* New York, NY: John Wiley & Sons.

Keogh, B. K., & Kopp, C. B. (1978). From assessment to intervention: An elusive bridge. In F. D. Minifie & L. L. Lloyd (Eds.), *Communicative and cognitive abilities—early behavioral assessment* (pp. 523–547). Baltimore, MD: University Park Press.

Knobloch, H., & Pasamanick, B. (1960). Environmental factors affecting human development before and after birth. *Pediatrics, 26,* 210–218.

Larson, S. A., Lakin, K. C., Anderson, L., Kwak, N., Lee, J. H., & Anderson, D. (2001). Prevalence of mental retardation and developmental disabilities: Estimates from the 1994/1995 National Health Interview Survey Disability supplements. *American Journal on Mental Retardation, l06*(3), 231–252.

Leiter, R. G. (1948). *Leiter International Performance Scale.* Chicago, IL: Stoelting.

Leiter, R. G. (1959). Part I of the manual for the 1948 revision of the Leiter International Performance Scale: Evidence of the reliability and validity of the Leiter tests. *Psychological Service Center Journal, 11,* 1–72.

Leiter, R. G. (1969). *General instructions for the Leiter International Performance Scale.* Chicago, IL: Stoelting.

Leonard, H., & Wen, X. (2002). The epidemiology of mental retardation: Challenges and opportunities in the new millennium. *Mental Retardation and Developmental Disabilities Research Reviews, 8,* 117–134.

Levenson, R. L., Jr., & Zino, T. C. (1979). II. Assessment of cognitive deficiency with the McCarthy scales and Stanford Binet: A correlational analysis. *Perceptual and Motor Skills, 48,* 291–295.

Lezak, M. D., Howieson, D. B., & Loring, D. W. (Eds.) (2004). *Neuropsychological Assessment* (4th ed.). New York, NY: Oxford University Press.

Lichtenberger, E. O., & Kaufman, A. S. (2004). *Essentials of WPPSI-III assessment.* Hoboken, NJ: John Wiley & Sons.

Locurto, C. M. (1991). *Sense and nonsense about IQ: The case for uniqueness.* New York, NY: Praeger Publishers.

Madle, R. A. (2005). Test review of Wechsler Preschool and Primary Scale of Intelligence. In R. A. Spies & B. S. Blake (Eds.), *The sixteenth mental measurement yearbook* (3rd ed., pp. 1115–1118). Lincoln, NE: University of Nebraska Press.

McCarthy, D. A. (1972). *Manual for the McCarthy Scales of Children's Abilities.* San Antonio, TX: The Psychological Corporation.

Neisser, U. (Ed.) (1998). *The rising curve: Long-term gains in IQ and related measures.* Washington, DC: American Psychological Association.

Phillips, B. L., Pasewark, R. A., & Tindall, R. C. (1978). Relationship among McCarthy Scales of Children's Abilities, WPPSI, and Columbia Mental Maturity Scale. *Psychology in the Schools, 15,* 352–356.

Prifitera, A., Saklofske, D. H., & Weiss, L. G. (Eds.) (2005). *WISC-IV Clinical use and interpretation. Scientist practitioner perspectives.* Burlington, MA: Elsevier Academic Press.

Prifitera, A., Saklofske, D. H., Weiss, L. G., & Rolfhus, E. (2005). The WISC-IV in the clinical assessment context. In A. Prifitera, D. H. Saklofske, & L. G. Weiss (Eds.), *WISC-IV Clinical use and interpretation. Scientist practitioner perspectives* (pp. 3–28). Burlington, MA: Elsevier Academic Press.

Psychological Corporation (2002a). *WAIS-III WMS-III technical and interpretive manual.* San Antonio, TX: Author.

Psychological Corporation (2002b). *WPPSI-III technical and interpretive manual.* San Antonio, TX: Author.

Psychological Corporation (2003). *WISC-IV technical and interpretive manual.* San Antonio, TX: Author.

Roid, G. H. (2003a). *Stanford-Binet Intelligence Scales,* Fifth Edition. Itasca, IL: Riverside Publishing.

Roid, G. H. (2003b). *Stanford-Binet Intelligence Scales,* Fifth Edition. *Interpretive manual,* Fifth Edition. Itasca, IL: Riverside Publishing.

Roid, G. H., & Miller, L. J. (1997). *Leiter International Performance Scale—Revised: Examiner's manual.* Wood Dale, IL: Stoelting Co.

Sachs, H. T., & Barrett, R. P. (2000). Psychopathology in individuals with mental retardation. In A. J. Sameroff, M. Lewis, & S. M. Miller (Eds.), *Handbook of developmental psychopathology* (2nd ed., pp. 657–670). New York, NY: Kluwer Academics/Plenum Publishers.

Sattler, J. M. (1992). *Assessment of children: Revised and updated* (3rd ed.). San Diego, CA: Jerome M. Sattler, Publisher, Inc.

Sattler, J. M. (2001). *Assessment of children: Cognitive applications* (4th ed.). San Diego, CA: Jerome M. Sattler, Publisher, Inc.

Slate, J. R., & Saarnio, D. A. (1995). Differences between WISC-III and WISC-R IQs: A preliminary investigation. *Journal of Psychoeducational Assessment, 13,* 340–346.

Spruill, J., Oakland, T., & Harrison, P. (2005). Assessment of mental retardation. In A. Priitera, D. H. Saklofske, & L. G. Weiss (Eds.), *WISC-IV Clinical use and interpretation: Scientist practitioner perspectives* (pp. 299–331). Burlington, MA: Elsevier Academic Press.

Terman, L. M., & Merrill, M. A. (1960). *Stanford-Binet Intelligence Scale.* Boston, MA: Houghton Mifflin.

Thorndike, R. L., Hagen, E. P., & Sattler, J. M. (1986). *The Stanford-Binet Intelligence Scale—Fourth Edition: Guide for administering and scoring.* Itasca, IL: Riverside Publishing.

Tredgold, A. F. (1908). *Mental deficiency.* London: Baillere, Tindall, & Fox.

Tylenda, B., Hooper, S. R., & Barrett, R. P. (1987). Developmental learning disorders. In C. L. Frame & J. L. Matson (Eds.), *Handbook of assessment in child pychopathology: Applied issues in differential diagnosis and treatment evaluation* (pp. 187–217). New York, NY: Plenum Press.

Vance, H., Maddux, C. D., Fuller, G. B., & Awadh, A. M. (1996). A longitudinal comparison of WISC-III and WISC-R scores of special education students. *Psychology in the Schools, 33,* 113–118.

VanderVeer, B., & Schweid, E. (1974). Infant assessment: Stability of mental functioning in young retarded children. *American Journal of Mental Deficiency, 79,* 1–4.

Wechsler, D. (1939). *The measurement of adult intelligence.* Baltimore, MD: Williams & Wilkins.

Wechsler, D. (1949). *Manual for the Wechsler Intelligence Scale for Children.* San Antonio, TX: The Psychological Corporation.

Wechsler, D. (1967). *Manual for the Wechsler Preschool and Primary Scale of Intelligence.* San Antonio, TX: The Psychological Corporation.

Wechsler, D. (1974). *Manual for the Wechsler Intelligence Scale for Children-Revised.* San Antonio, TX: The Psychological Corporation.

Wechsler, D. (1989). *Wechsler Preschool and Primary Scale of Intelligence-Revised.* San Antonio, TX: The Psychological Corporation.

Wechsler, D. (1991). *Wechsler Intelligence Scale for Children* (3rd ed.). San Antonio, TX: The Psychological Corporation.

Wechsler, D. (1997). *Wechsler Adult Intelligence Scale* (3rd ed.). San Antonio, TX: The Psychological Corporation.

Wechsler, D. (2003a). *Wechsler Preschool and Primary Scale of Intelligence* (3rd ed.). San Antonio, TX: The Psychological Corporation.

Wechsler, D. (2003b). *Wechsler Intelligence Scale for Children* (4th ed.). San Antonio, TX: The Psychological Corporation.

Werner, E. E., Honzik, M. P., & Smith, R. S. (1968). Prediction of intelligence and achievement at ten years from twenty months pediatric and psychological examinations. *Child Development, 39,* 1063–1075.

Zhu, Z., Weiss, L. G., Prifitera, A., & Coalson, D. (2004). The Wechsler Intelligence Scales for Children and Adults. In M. Hersen (Chief Ed.), G. Goldstein, & S. R. Beers (Vol. Ed.), *Comprehensive handbook of psychological assessment: Vol. 1. Intellectual and neuropsychological assessment* (pp. 51–75). Hoboken, NJ: John Wiley & Sons.

Adaptive Behavior Scales

DENNIS R. DIXON

DEPARTMENT OF BEHAVIORAL PSYCHOLOGY, KENNEDY KRIEGER INSTITUTE, JOHNS HOPKINS UNIVERSITY SCHOOL OF MEDICINE BALTIMORE, MARYLAND 21205

I. HISTORY AND DEFINITION

Helping persons with intellectual disability (ID) reach their maximum level of independence is one of the most important endeavors for professionals who serve these persons. Adaptive skills are key to a person's level of independence. Indeed, training adaptive skills is among the most important goals for increasing the independence of persons with ID (Matson, Carlisle, & Bamburg, 1998). However, developing adaptive supports and training should not be done blindly, but should be based on careful assessment of an individual's profile of adaptive strengths and weaknesses.

Adaptive behavior assessment serves three broad goals (Luckasson et al., 2002). These include diagnosis, classification, and planning supports. While professionals are increasingly turning their efforts to planning supports, historically the primary reason for conducting adaptive behavior assessments remains that of diagnosis or classification. Nonetheless, the importance of adaptive behavior in regards to planning supports should not be overlooked.

The degree to which an individual can successfully perform the routine activities encompassed by the construct of adaptive behavior, and do so on a consistent basis, will have a large impact on decisions concerning what is the least restrictive environment (Pollingue, 1987). Further, adaptive skills development is often the primary factor determining the level of supervision needed (Liss et al., 2001). Heller, Miller, and Hsieh (2002) found that adaptive behavior skills were higher in those residents who moved to community settings than those who stayed in nursing homes. These individuals had higher adaptive skills both before and after community placement, indicating that not only were adaptive skills improved by community integration but they were also indicative of which individuals would move from institutional

INTERNATIONAL REVIEW OF RESEARCH IN MENTAL RETARDATION, Vol. 34
0074-7750/07 $35.00

DOI: 10.1016/S0074-7750(07)34003-2

to community settings. The importance of these classification decisions and the impact they have on the lives of the individuals that they concern necessitate that practitioners ensure that their decisions are based on valid and reliable measurement.

All discussions of adaptive behavior and its measurement come back to the definition of ID. This is because the construct of adaptive behavior is at the heart of any attempt to adequately define the condition. As Greenspan, Switzky, and Granfield (1996) contend, this construct was defined and methods of measurement were developed as efforts to return the definition of ID to how individuals behave in everyday life and for the diagnosis to not be so heavily weighted by how they perform on measures of academic intelligence.

ID is a classification that is used to determine eligibility for services. Throughout the past 100 years, researchers and policy makers have struggled with the basic problem that is common to all decisions regarding eligibility for services; that is, to include those in need of assistance and exclude those who are not. On one hand, the definition of ID must be broad enough not to exclude any individuals who should be included (type 2 error). Yet also, the definition should not be so broad as to include individuals who do not need additional support (type 1 error). The construct of adaptive behavior has emerged as a result of these efforts to balance these two types of errors (Greenspan et al., 1996).

According to the *Diagnostic and Statistical Manual of Mental Disorders,* Fourth Edition Text Revision (DSM-IV-TR) published by the American Psychiatric Association (2000), adaptive functioning refers to "how effectively individuals cope with common life demands and how well they meet the standards of personal independence expected of someone in their particular age group, sociocultural background, and community setting." The DSM-IV lists four levels of ID: mild, moderate, severe, and profound. While significant limitations in adaptive functioning are a diagnostic requirement, the actual measurement of adaptive functioning is discussed only briefly. Further, the DSM-IV's levels of ID are based solely on an individual's intellectual functioning. This method is particularly striking in light of the DSM-IV's own statement that "impairments in adaptive functioning, rather than low IQ, are usually the presenting symptoms in individuals with Mental Retardation" (p 42). In response to this inconsistency, some authors suggest that even though the DSM-IV indicates the use of well-standardized assessment scales to assess adaptive functioning, than having no standardized score or cutoff points that establish what "significant limitation in adaptive behavior" are, implies a general mistrust of the comprehensiveness and reliability of adaptive assessment measures (Reschly, Myers, & Hartel, 2002). However, these same limitations apply to measures of intelligence as well, and indeed are akin to all norm-referenced assessment tools.

Perhaps one explanation for why adaptive behavior has not been a more prominent component of the diagnosis of ID, as presented in the DSM-IV-TR (2000), is the assumption that low IQ scores are sufficient to predict low adaptive behavior. For example, Accardo and Capute (1998) state "with IQ's below 50, the adaptive impairment almost could be assumed." While this observation has merit (Liss et al., 2001), it also has the tendency to minimize the utility of adaptive behavior assessment and neglects the other applications of adaptive behavior assessments apart from merely classifying individuals.

Other definitions of ID have put a greater weight on an adaptive behavior component. The most widely cited definition of adaptive behavior is that put forth by the American Association on Mental Retardation (AAMR). Most recently, the AAMR has stated "adaptive behavior is the collection of conceptual, social, and practical skills that have been learned by people in order to function in their everyday lives" (Luckasson et al., 2002). That is, adaptive behavior is not merely one's ability to perform acts of daily living. It is a much broader concept that includes ones ability to apply intelligence to everyday settings and situations (Greenspan et al., 1996).

The American Association on Mental Deficiency (since then changed to AAMR) formally added adaptive behavior to the definition of ID in 1959 (Heber, 1959). By adding adaptive limitations to the definition of ID, the AAMD attempted to correct the over reliance on IQ scores that had developed as well as to reduce the number of individuals without significant impairment in everyday tasks who were being classified as evincing ID based solely on a low-standardized IQ test score (Luckasson et al., 2002). Nonetheless, the use of standardized assessment measures of adaptive behavior were not required until 1973, as social and legal pressures increased to require valid and objective measurements to be used when determining a diagnosis of ID.

The 1992 definition of ID by the AAMR made significant changes in the overall diagnosis and classification of ID. One of the most notable changes that came with the 1992 definition of ID was in regards to the assessment of adaptive behavior. A shift was made from assessing adaptive behavior in general to assessing adaptive skills across 10 categories. However, at the time of the publication of the 1992 definition, there were no standardized ways to assess all of these 10 areas, and there was little agreement regarding the necessity or adequacy of these 10 skill areas. Indeed, Luckasson et al. (2002) list the changes regarding adaptive skills assessment as one of the primary reasons for a general lack of adoption of the 1992 definition. Due to a lack of empirical support for the 10 skill areas, the 2002 definition altered the focus to three broad areas of adaptive behavior composed of the 10 skill areas.

The current AAMR definition puts equal importance on both intelligence and adaptive skills. Further, with the 1992 definition, a paradigm shift was made in that persons are no longer classified according to their intellectual functioning but rather, according to the level of support needed. This shift was further refined with the changes in the 2002 definition. A key theme throughout the diagnostic manual is the assessment of both limitations and strengths. Comprehensive adaptive behavior scales serve this purpose well.

II. STRUCTURE OF ADAPTIVE BEHAVIOR

Adequate assessment of adaptive behavior depends on our understanding of the underlying construct. Nonetheless, there is little consensus concerning the overall structure of adaptive behavior. An understanding of the structure of adaptive behavior will change the way in which it is measured and handled by practitioners.

Much debate has been over the issue of whether or not an adaptive behavior is a unified or multivariate construct. To explore this question, many studies have been conducted examining the factor structure of adaptive behavior. The most comprehensive review is provided by Thompson, McGrew, and Bruininks (1999) who concluded that adaptive behavior as it is currently measured is a multidimensional construct consisting of five domains. Thompson et al. (1999) further noted that the number of factors found was related to the level at which the data were analyzed, with analyses conducted at the item level finding more factors than analyses conducted at the subscale level.

The five domains found by Thompson et al. (1999) were: (1) personal independence, (2) responsibility, (3) cognitive/academic, (4) vocational/community, and (5) physical/development. The first three factors were the most commonly found in their review of factor studies. Regarding the five domains found in their review, Thompson et al. note, "no single adaptive-maladaptive behavior assessment instrument completely measures the entire range of adaptive and maladaptive behavior dimensions."

In spite of these findings that support a multivariate model of adaptive behavior, researchers and clinicians persist in using a unified adaptive behavior score for decision making (Lerman, Apgar, & Jordan, 2005). This is likely due to practical concerns of meeting institutional standards or for simplicity of research design rather than a belief that adaptive behavior is best described as a unified construct. Further, this tendency may simply be the result of the most popular assessment scales providing a comprehensive score that clinicians may assume is the best representation of the adaptive behavior construct.

III. REVIEW OF SCALES

A multitude of assessment scales have been constructed. However, while scales abound, research using adaptive assessment scales has primarily been limited to three: the Vineland Adaptive Behavior Scales, the AAMR

Adaptive Behavior Scales, and the Scales of Independent Behavior. These scales have been through multiple revisions and have been the topic of considerable amounts of research.

A. The Vineland Adaptive Behavior Scales

The Vineland Adaptive Behavior Scales (VABS) is a revision of the Vineland Social Maturity Scale (Doll, 1965). The VABS is among the most widely used scales (Balboni, Pedrabissi, Molteni, & Villa, 2001). In a survey of national service centers, Luiselli et al. (2001) found that the VABS was the most widely used assessment scale in persons with autism. The VABS has three versions: a survey form, expanded form, and a classroom edition (Sparrow, Balla, & Cicchetti, 1984). The survey form and expanded form are both versions of the interview edition.

Sparrow et al. (1984) note that the VABS may be used whenever an assessment of a person's daily functioning is required. Three broad areas are given in which the VABS may be used: diagnostic evaluations, program planning, and research. Diagnostic evaluations are listed as the most likely use of the VABS. In regards to program planning, Matson, Mayville, and Laud (2003) note that the VABS is useful for determining skill level for training; however, they recommend using more narrow-band measures such as the SPSS or MESSIER to provide more detailed information regarding social functioning or other particular domains of adaptive behavior.

In a recent discussion of the VABS, Beail (2003) noted a number of advantages and disadvantages. The advantages listed include coverage of the major domains of adaptive behavior, standardization, impressive psychometrics, and brevity (Beail, 2003). The majority of the disadvantages were due to the "age" of the scale, resulting in outdated norms or norms that are no longer reflective of the target population. Beail noted that the second edition of the VABS had the potential to address many of these shortcomings.

The Vineland Adaptive Behavior Scales, Second Edition (VABS-II; Sparrow, Cicchetti, & Balla, 2005) builds off of the foundation of the previous Vineland scales. Due to its recent publication, the scale has not been available for researchers to evaluate. However, Sparrow et al. (2005) list a number of changes in the second edition that were made as an effort to improve measurement in very young children and adults.

Many of the changes listed by Sparrow et al. (2005) appear to improve the utility of the VABS to measure adaptive behavior in persons with developmental disabilities, particularly for individuals with autism. Among these changes are the addition of items to measure the development of spoken language, the ability to maintain or initiate conversation, to understand and use nonverbal communication, and the ability to maintain social relationships. Further, items were added that address social naïveté, gullibility, and the ability to avoid victimization, all areas that are of particular concern when measuring adaptive skills in persons with mild ID (Sparrow et al., 2005). A further improvement regarding item content for persons with developmental disabilities is an increase in the number of items addressing independent living skills. This is most likely the result of the increasing awareness of the usefulness of adaptive behavior scales for planning supports for individuals with developmental disabilities to live in the least restrictive environment (Sparrow et al., 2005). The VABS-II appears to have improved significantly on the VABS in its ability to provide useful information for individuals with ID.

B. AAMR Adaptive Behavior Scales

The AAMR Adaptive Behavior Scales (ABS) is the second edition of the AAMD Adaptive Behavior Scale and consists of two versions: School and Community (ABS-S:2; Lambert, Nihira, & Leland, 1993) and the Residential and Community version (ABS-R:2; Nihira, Leland, & Lambert, 1993). There are two parts to the ABS. Part one addresses adaptive skills and personal independence. Part two addresses maladaptive behavior. Items are designed to measure an individual's typical performance of adaptive skills.

The ABS-S:2 was standardized on both children with developmental disabilities and those with typical development. Norms are provided for individuals aged 3–21 years. The ABS-S:2 is designed for identifying children who are significantly impaired in adaptive behavior relative to their peers, determining an individual's strengths and weaknesses, measuring training outcomes, and research.

The primary use of the ABS-R:2 is for determining an individual's profile of adaptive strengths and weaknesses. The ABS-R:2 provides norms for individuals with ID and is intended to be used with individuals through 79 years of age. However, norms are not available for typically developing adults. Thus, while the ABS-R:2 is reported useful for planning supports, this version should not be used to determine if an individual warrants a diagnosis of ID (Luckasson et al., 2002).

C. Scales of Independent Behavior—Revised

The Scales of Independent Behavior—Revised (SIB-R) is a structured interview that measures both adaptive and problem behaviors (Bruininks, Woodcock, Weatherman, & Hill, 1996). The test is designed to measure adaptive functioning across a variety of domains. A number of intended uses are noted in the manual including identifying areas for training, determining eligibility for services, planning programs and services, monitoring individualized training programs, program evaluation, clinical assessment/diagnosis, and classification for research (Bruininks et al., 1996). The SIB-R is a revision of the original scale that was published in 1984. Both scales have been extensively researched and have a significant foundation on strong psychometric properties.

The SIB-R is composed of two major components, the adaptive behavior component measuring broad independence and the behavior problems component. The adaptive behavior component contains four areas of independent behavior that include social interaction and communication skills, personal living skills, community living skills, and motor skills. The problem behavior component is made up of three categories of problem behavior: internalized, externalized, and asocial.

The SIB-R varies from other assessment scales of this nature in the flexibility that it allows in its administration. While the standard format of the SIB-R is as a structured interview, a checklist-administration procedure is available. As a checklist, a knowledgeable informant may complete the SIB-R independently or a single respondent may complete checklists for multiple individuals at the same time during the course of a single interview.

The Inventory for Client and Agency Planning (ICAP; Bruininks, Hill, Weatherman, & Woodcock, 1986) is a 16-page booklet that is completed by a teacher or care person who is familiar with the individual being assessed. The adaptive behavior subscale of the ICAP was constructed from 77 items taken from the original SIB. The ICAP is designed to be completed in a relatively short amount of time (15 min). The ICAP provides a wide range of information about the individual and it is not limited solely to measuring adaptive behavior. The majority of studies using the ICAP have focused on the effects of community integration.

A number of well-developed adaptive assessment scales are available. The choice of which adaptive scale to use should be determined by the intended purpose of the assessment. Frequency of use of a scale does not imply that it is the most appropriate for all occasions. While this review focused on the most commonly used scales (VABS, ABS, and SIB/ICAP), a number of other assessment scales have been developed, such as the Battelle Developmental Inventory, that also meet good psychometric standards (Reschly et al., 2002). Not every scale possesses the same attributes such as administration format, age appropriateness of item content, or cultural relevance of items. Professionals must carefully consider their selection to ensure that the chosen scale serves the intended purpose well.

IV. PSYCHOMETRIC CONCERNS

Issues of reliability and validity are common concerns for all assessment scales and are requisites for acceptance and utility (American Educational Research Association, 1999). Researchers and clinicians should not assume that a scale, by default, possesses adequate reliability and validity. The scales discussed above have demonstrated adequate reliability and validity, and present data supporting their use within their respective manuals. It is not necessary to discuss these basic requirements as they are discussed more thoroughly elsewhere (e.g., Anastasi & Urbina, 1997; Spreat, 1999). However, there are a number of concerns that are particularly relevant to adaptive behavior scales that warrant discussion.

A. Basal and Ceiling Effects

Basal and ceiling rules are used as a means to shorten the time required to administer a scale. These rules are typically used by scales administered in an interview format that present items in an assumed developmental order. By establishing a basal, it is assumed that the individual usually performs all of the previous items that precede this basal level. Likewise, the tester assumes that the individual does not or cannot perform the items following the ceiling. Basals and ceilings are set once the interviewer obtains a certain number of items endorsed as present (basal) or endorsed as not present (ceiling).

When determining the ceiling, scales in which ceiling scores are established rapidly may underestimate an individual's adaptive behavior skills if their skills have developed atypically. For example, persons with physical impairments may show limitations on tasks requiring fine motor control and thus score poorly on items concerning closing fasteners on clothing. Yet, if snaps replaced buttons, dressing independently is no longer a task that requires assistance but one that can be done independently (Pollingue, 1987). For such an individual, an early ceiling would have indicated a higher level of overall dependence than is necessary. Flexibility in establishing ceiling scores is needed.

One change made in the administration of the VABS-II from the VABS was a change in the basal and ceiling rules (Sparrow et al., 2005). The VABS required full endorsement on seven consecutive items to establish a basal and scores of zero on seven consecutive items to establish a ceiling. The basal and ceiling rules were relaxed for the VABS-II, requiring four consecutive items to establish a basal or a ceiling. While this shortens the administration time, it may negatively impact those individuals who demonstrate atypical development within the same domain.

B. Item Sampling and Age Appropriateness

Adaptive scales are often used to evaluate children for developmental delay. As a result many scales have the highest item density relating to early development. This allows for a good degree of sensitivity within this range. However, the construct as it applies to adults with ID is not as well represented. Thus, the age appropriateness of the items within a scale must be considered. A developmental perspective of adaptive assessment is essential in that what is expected by society and what is considered normal or a necessary level of independence is tied to an individual's age (Dykens, 1995; Horn & Fuchs, 1987). While referencing an individual's score to normative data representing the individual's age addresses this concern, it is also necessary that the actual items on the scale are both developmentally appropriate and age appropriate. Thus, while an adult with profound ID may have adaptive skills equivalent to 12 months of age, the same behaviors (e.g., items) should not be used to establish the adaptive behavior at the 12-month old level as would be used for a typically developing infant. For example, reaching for a caregiver may be an expected behavior for a12-month old typically developing infant but would not be appropriate to expect from an adult who is functioning at the same developmental level nor would it be a behavior warranting training.

C. Indirect Assessments and Informant Validity/Reliability

Due to limitations with communication skills or the impracticality of direct observations, the majority of scales designed for use with persons with ID rely on informant report. As a result, the utility of these assessment tools are dependent on the degree to which informants are able to respond reliably and validly concerning adaptive behavior. Most assessment scales have addressed this concern by reporting the reliability of responses among different informants. While indirect assessment does have significant limitations, it allows for examination across multiple settings and more importantly, allows for the assessment of typical performance rather than optimal performance as would be seen if the individual were asked to perform a task for the sake of assessment (Dykens, 1995).

Adaptive behavior is relative and dynamic, not absolute and static (Horn & Fuchs, 1987). For this reason, consideration of place and time are important when assessing adaptive behavior. Different skills are needed for different situations. Adaptive assessment needs to be broad and assess skills across multiple settings (Dykens, 1995). However, the same informant may not always know or be able to report well on the adaptive behavior of the individual as they function outside of the context in which they know them (Szatmari, Archer, Fisman, & Streiner, 1994; Voelker, Shore, Hakim-Larson, & Bruner, 1997). Discrepancies among informants, while a concern for reliability, may in fact simply reflect the way in which the individual varies in adaptive behavior across multiple contexts. Practitioners must use careful clinical judgment and good investigation skills when dealing with such findings.

D. Special Populations

The adaptive skills of various subgroups of persons with ID have been examined frequently. The majority of these studies have focused on persons with autism or pervasive developmental disabilities. Researchers have consistently found that individuals with autism score lower on verbal expression skills than persons matched for age or intellectual level (Paul et al., 2004; Stone, Ousley, Hepburn, Hogan, & Brown, 1999). Further, individuals with autism show a different profile of adaptive skills than persons with PDD-NOS (Njardvik, Matson, & Cherry, 1999; Paul et al., 2004). Hatton et al. (2003) found that those children without autistic behavior performed better across all domains of adaptive behavior but particularly within socialization skills when compared to individuals with fragile X. In contrast to the adaptive profile observed in autism, children with Williams syndrome showed relatively high social skills but lower daily living skills and motor skills (Mervis, Klein-Tasman, & Mastin, 2001).

Carter et al. (1998) offer supplementary norms on the VABS for individuals with autism. These norms are helpful in that they provide a more accurate description of the particular strengths and weaknesses for individuals with autism. However, it should be noted that when adaptive behavior assessments are used to determine diagnosis, the question is how an individual performs relative to the general population, not simply to other persons with a similar diagnosis.

E. Cultural Considerations

Cultural considerations when assessing adaptive behaviors are essential in that adaptive behavior is defined in relation to social norms and expectations (Horn & Fuchs, 1987). For a scale to be useful it must also be culturally sensitive (Dykens, 1995). While most comprehensive scales are designed to assess adaptive behaviors that are culturally universal, this is an assumption that has been rarely tested. Craig and Tassé (1999) discuss a number of factors related to adaptive behavior expectations that may change relative to an individual's culture. Among these factors are age, gender, family structure, and attitudes toward disabilities.

The age at which children are expected to perform specific tasks may vary based on the culture in which the child lives. Further, the tasks expected of a child may also vary. Learning to read may be an important skill for a child developing within western culture. However, this skill may not be as applicable within other cultures and thus not fit the definition of adaptive behavior when measured outside of the usual context. Likewise, differences in gender expectations are common. Skills in one domain may be required of females but not of males and vice versa. Every assessment scale is a product of the culture in which it was made. Understanding the cultural expectations for an individual's age and gender is essential when attempting to measure adaptive behavior outside of the culture in which the assessment scale was developed.

A vast majority of studies on the adaptive behavior of individuals with ID have been done within the context of western culture, particularly within the United States. However, numerous translations of adaptive scales have been conducted. For example, both the SIB-R and the VABS have been published in Spanish language versions. Likewise, Tombokan-Runtukahu and Nitko (1992) have developed a translation of the VABS and presented preliminary evaluations of the psychometric properties. Further research evaluating cross-cultural differences is needed. Not only are accurate linguistic translations necessary but also accurate cultural translations are of concern. Research addressing these differences should lead to a better understanding regarding which skills are truly universal and which are culturally defined (Craig & Tassé, 1999).

V. REVIEW OF PUBLISHED STUDIES

The past 30 years have seen a tremendous increase in the prominence of adaptive behavior as a consideration in the diagnosis of ID. As a result, many researchers developed assessment scales to measure this construct (Spreat, 1999). However, little is known concerning which adaptive behavior scales are used by researchers and practitioners. In a survey of National Service Centers, Luiselli et al. (2001) found that the VABS was the most commonly used assessment measure. However, the study was limited to those measures used in the education and treatment of individuals with autism. The present review is intended to provide information concerning which adaptive scales have been reported in studies on persons with ID over the past 10 years.

A. Literature Search

A search was made for all studies, which reported the use of an adaptive behavior scale, that were published in four journals specializing in research on persons with ID. The journals included in this search were the *American Journal on Mental Retardation, Journal of Autism and Developmental Disorders, Journal of Intellectual Disability Research,* and *Research in Developmental Disabilities*. All studies published in the selected journals from 1996 through 2005 were reviewed for the inclusion of an adaptive scale. Adaptive behavior was defined according to the AAMR definition (Luckasson et al., 2002) as "the collection of conceptual, social, and practical skills that have been learned by people in order to function in their everyday lives." Thus while scales such as the Behavior Problems Inventory (Rojahn, 1986) or the Aberrant Behavior Checklist (Aman, Singh, Stewart, & Field, 1985) are useful tools for measuring maladaptive or problem behaviors, they were not included in this review. Further, scales focusing solely on one aspect of adaptive behavior such as social skills (e.g. MESSIER; Matson, 1995) were also excluded.

The search identified 271 studies that reported using an adaptive behavior scale. These search procedures may not have resulted in an exhaustive review. However, the results should be representative of current trends and practices.

B. Results

The review identified 271 studies that included the use of an adaptive behavior scale. From the 271 studies, it is clear that numerous assessment scales have been used. However, the identified studies primarily reported the use of three scales: VABS ($n = 177$), ABS ($n = 61$), and SIB/ICAP ($n = 15$). Table I displays a breakdown of the identified studies in relation to the assessment used and the population studied.

The VABS was reported in 177 studies and was the most frequently included adaptive behavior scale. Of particular note is that in studies focusing on autism, the VABS was used almost exclusively. These findings are commensurate with those by Luiselli et al. (2001) who found the VABS to be the most widely used measure by practitioners for persons with autism. The current results indicate that researchers on autism, in addition to practitioners, also employ the VABS as the primary means to assess adaptive behavior.

The VABS was used for a number of purposes in the identified studies. The most frequently reported use was as a general measure of adaptive behavior. In these studies, VABS scores were often contrasted to other measures or participant factors such as residential placement, autism diagnosis, or cognitive abilities. The second most common use of the VABS was to determine an individual's level of ID for purposes of group classification or simply to describe the characteristics of the study participants. However, few studies reported using the VABS as a measure of maladaptive behavior.

Sixty-one of the identified studies reported use of the ABS. As was found regarding the VABS, the primary purpose cited for including the ABS was for a general measure of adaptive behavior. In contrast to the VABS though, a much larger portion of the studies including the ABS cited measuring maladaptive or challenging behavior as a primary reason for inclusion.

As noted previously, the residential and community version of the ABS does not contain norms that represent both persons with and without ID and thus, this version is not appropriate for diagnosing ID (Luckasson et al., 2002).

TABLE I
Review of Studies that Used an Adaptive Behavior Scale

Study	Participants	Adaptive Scale
Baranek et al. (2005)	43 children with Fragile X syndrome, autism, dev delay, or typical development	VABS
Berument et al. (2005)	51 individuals with autism or Down syndrome	VABS
de Bildt et al. (2005)	1059 children with ID	VABS
de Bildt, Kraijer, Sytema, & Minderaa (2005)	826 children and adolescents with ID	VABS
de Bildt, Sytema, Kraijer, Sparrow, & Minderaa (2005)	186 children with ID	VABS
Billstedt, Gillbert, & Gillberg (2005)	108 adults with autism	VABS
Burt et al. (2005)	130 individuals with Down syndrome	SIB
Chadwick, Cuddy, Kusel, & Taylor (2005)	82 children with ID or autism	VABS
Dunn & Bates (2005)	36 individuals with autism or typical development	VABS
Edgin & Pennington (2005)	58 children with Asperger syndrome, autism, or typical development	SIB
Emerson, Robertson, & Wood (2005)	615 with ID	ABS
Emerson (2005)	1542 adults with ID	LDCS
Fine et al. (2005)	98 children with autism, PDD	VABS
Gena, Couloura, & Kymissis (2005)	3 children with autism	VABS
Gross (2005)	83 children with autism, ID, developmental delay, or typical development	VABS
Harries, Guscia, Kirby, Nettelbeck, & Taplin (2005)	80 individuals with ID	ICAP; ABS
Hassall, Rose, & McDonald (2005)	46 children with ID	VABS
Hastings, Kovshoff et al. (2005)	48 children with autism	VABS
Hastings, Beck, Daley, & Hill (2005)	338 children with ID	VABS
Howard, Sparkman, Cohen, Green, & Stanislaw (2005)	61 children with autism, PDD	VABS
Keen (2005)	6 children with autism	SIB
Kishore, Nizamie, & Nizamie (2005)	60 individuals with ID	VABS
Klin, Pauls, Schultz, & Volkmar (2005)	65 individuals with Asperger syndrome	VABS
Lecavalier (2005)	284 children with ID or typical development	SIB
Matson, Dixon, Matson, & Logan (2005)	618 adults with ID	VABS
Moss et al. (2005)	8 children with Cornelia de Lange	VABS
Oliver, Hall, & Murphy (2005)	16 children with ID or autism	VABS
Oliver, Holland, Hall, & Crayton (2005)	52 individuals with Down syndrome	VABS
O'Reilly, Sigafoos, Lancioni, Edrisinha, & Andrews (2005)	1 adolescent with autism	VABS

(*continued*)

TABLE I (*Continued*)

Study	Participants	Adaptive Scale
Paul et al. (2005)	30 males with autism	VABS
Paul, Augustyn, Klin, & Volkmar (2005)	27 individuals with autism	VABS
Perry & Felce (2005a)	154 individuals with ID	ABS
Perry & Felce (2005b)	154 individuals with ID	ABS
Perry, Condillac, Freeman, Dunn-Geier, & Belair (2005)	274 children with autism, PDD, ID, or developmentally delayed	VABS
Robertson et al. (2005)	25 adults with ID	ABS
Romski, Sevcik, Adamson, & Bakeman (2005)	33 individuals with ID	ABS
Sallows & Graupner (2005)	24 children with autism	VABS
Spreat, Conroy, & Fullerton (2005)	348 adults with ID	DDQAQ
Stephens, Collins, & Dodder (2005)	2760 adults with ID	DDQAQ
Veltman et al. (2005)	1 female with PDD	VABS
Werner, Dawson, Munson, & Osterling (2005)	145 children with autism, developmental delay, or typical development	VABS
Williams, Wishart, Pitcairn, & Willis (2005)	126 children with ID or Down syndrome	VABS
Yalon-Chamovitz & Greenspan (2005)	50 adults with ID	VABS
Zwaigenbaum, Sonnenberg, Heshka, Eastwood, & Xu (2005)	1 girl with PDD	VABS
Basquill, Nezu, Nezu, & Klein (2004)	45 individuals with ID	ABS
Beck, Daley, Hastings, & Stevenson (2004)	33 children with ID	VABS
de Bildt et al. (2004)	184 children with ID	VABS
Bradley, Summers, Wood, & Bryson (2004)	24 individuals with autism or ID	VABS
Eaves & Ho (2004)	49 children with autism or PDD	VABS
Graff & Green (2004)	3 children with ID and autism	VABS
Hatton et al. (2004)	560 adults with ID	ABS
Kishore, Nizamie, Nizamie, & Jahan (2004)	60 individuals with ID	VABS
Lecavalier, Aman, Hammer, Stoica, & Matthews (2004)	330 children with autism	Nisonger
LeGoff (2004)	47 children with autism, Asperger, or PDD	VABS
Miller, Fee, & Netterville (2004)	48 children with ID	VABS
Owen et al. (2004)	93 adults with ID	SABS
Ozonoff et al. (2004)	149 individuals with autism or typical development	VABS
Paul et al. (2004)	40 individuals with autism or PDD	VABS
Prasher, Farooq, & Holder (2004)	150 adults with Down syndrome	ABS; ABDQ
Pruchno & McMullen (2004)	831 individuals with ID	ABS
Rellini, Tortolani, Trillo, Carbone, & Montecchi (2004)	65 children with autism, Asperger, or PDD	VABS
Robertson et al. (2004)	50 individuals with ID	ABS

(*continued*)

TABLE I (*Continued*)

Study	Participants	Adaptive Scale
Silverman et al. (2004)	273 adults with ID	ABS
Wallace, Schluter, & Webb (2004)	168 adults with ID	ABS
Wetherby et al. (2004)	54 children with autism, developmental delay, or typical development	VABS
Young & Ashman (2004)	100 adults with ID	ABS
Zigman et al. (2004)	148 Down syndrome with ID	ABS
Baghdadli, Pascal, Grisi, & Aussilloux (2003)	222 children with autism	VABS
de Bildt et al. (2003)	1059 individuals with ID	VABS
Bosseler & Massaro (2003)	14 children with autism	VABS
Buhrow & Bradley-Johnson (2003)	60 children with ID or typical development	BDI/VABS/ ABS
Cohen (2003)	84 children with autism	PDDBI/ VABS
Cohen, Schmidt-Lackner, Romanczyk, & Sudhalter (2003)	311 children with autism, PDD, CDD, or Asperger syndrome	PDDBI
Dube, McIlvane, Mazzitelli, & McNamara (2003)	13 individuals with ID, autism, PDD	ABS
Fidler (2003)	36 children with ID or Down syndrome	VABS
Guralnick, Hammond, & Connor (2003)	72 individuals with and without DD	VABS
Guralnick, Neville, Connor, & Hammond (2003)	74 children with ID	VABS
Hall, Thorns, & Oliver (2003)	8 individuals with developmental disabilities	VABS
Hatton et al. (2003)	70 children with Fragile X	VABS
Kay et al. (2003)	85 adults with Down syndrome	VABS
Kottorp, Bernspang, & Fisher (2003)	1724 individuals with ID	ADL
Lam, Giles, & Lavander (2003)	47 individuals with ID	VABS; ABS
Lancioni et al. (2003)	3 adults with ID	VABS
Mansell, Beadle-Brown, MacDonald, & Ashman (2003)	303 individuals with ID	ABS
Mount, Charman, Hastings, Reilly, & Cass (2003)	29 females with Rett syndrome or ID	VABS
Nachshen, Woodford, & Minnes (2003)	106 individuals with Down syndrome, autism, or fragile X	VABS
Niccols, Atkinson, & Pepler (2003)	41 children with Down syndrome	VABS
Oliver, Murphy, Hall, Arron, & Leggett (2003)	88 individuals with DD	VABS
Orsmond, Seltzer, Kraus, Hong (2003)	193 adults with ID	SIB
Ricci & Hodapp (2003)	50 individuals with Down syndrome or ID	VABS
Rogers, Hepburn, & Wehner (2003)	102 individuals with autism, fragile X, developmental delay, or typical development	VABS

(*continued*)

TABLE I (*Continued*)

Study	Participants	Adaptive Scale
Ross & Greer (2003)	5 children with autism	VABS
Saloviita, Itälinna & Leinonen (2003)	120 children with ID	ICAP
Schwartz & Rabinovitz (2003)	93 individuals with ID	ICAP
Simpson (2003)	2 adults with ID	ABS
Starr, Szatmari, Bryson, & Zwaigenbaum (2003)	58 children with autism or Asperger syndrome	VABS
Thompson & Bolton (2003)	1 adolescent male with Angelman syndrome	VABS
Tsatsanis et al. (2003)	26 children with autism	VABS
Urv, Zigman, & Silverman (2003)	529 adults with ID or Down syndrome	ABS
Van Bourgondien, Reichle, & Schopler (2003)	32 individuals with autism	VABS
Weiss, Diamond, Demark, & Lovald (2003)	97 individuals with ID	ABS
Bibby, Eikeseth, Martin, Mudford, & Reeves (2002)	66 children with autism	VABS
Copeland, Hughes, Agran, Wehmeyer, & Fowler (2002)	4 adolescents with ID	VABS
Dekker, Nunn, & Koot (2002)	1057 children with ID	VABS
Duker, van Driel, & van de Bercken (2002)	77 individuals with Down syndrome or PWS	VABS
Duvdevany (2002)	31 individuals with ID	ABS
Einam & Cuskelly (2002)	50 children with ID or typical development	ABS
Fisch, Simensen, & Schroer (2002)	36 children with autism or Fragile X	VABS
Gonzalez-Gordon, Salvador-Carulla, Romero, Gonzalez-Saiz, & Romero (2002)	80 individuals with ID	ICAP
Grigorenko et al. (2002)	80 children with developmental delays	VABS
Grissom & Borkowski (2002)	54 siblings of individuals with ID	ABS
Gross (2002)	55 children with autism, ID, developmental delay, or typical development	VABS
Gunter, Ghaziuddin, & Ellis (2002)	16 individuals with Asperger syndrome or typical development	VABS
Guralnick (2002)	64 children with ID or Down syndrome	VABS
Hallam et al. (2002)	500 individuals with ID	ABS
Kravits, Kamps, Kemmerer, & Potucek (2002)	1 girl with autism	VABS
Mansell, Ashman, Macdonald, & Beadle-Brown (2002)	495 individuals with ID	ABS
Mansell, Elliott, Beadle-Brown, Ashman, & Macdonald (2002)	49 adults with ID	BDS

(*continued*)

TABLE I (*Continued*)

Study	Participants	Adaptive Scale
McCarron. Gill, Lawlor, & Beagly (2002)	30 individuals with Down syndrome	ABS; DLSQ
McCarthy & Boyd (2002)	80 individuals with ID	ABS
McIntyre, Blacher, & Baker (2002)	103 adults with ID	VABS
Oliver, Demetriades, & Hall (2002)	3 individuals with Angelman syndrome	VABS
Panerai, Ferrante, & Zingale (2002)	16 individuals with autism or ID	VABS
Richards, Williams, & Follette (2002)	30 adults with ID	VABS
Rousey, Wild, & Blacher (2002)	64 children with ID	ABS
Smith, Felce, Ahmed et al. (2002)	56 individuals with ID	ABS
Smith, Felce, Jones, & Lowe (2002)	106 adults with ID	ABS
South et al. (2002)	119 children with autism	VABS
Spreat & Conroy (2002)	177 individuals with ID	DDQAQ
Stancliffe, Hayden, Larson, & Lakin (2002)	148 individuals with ID	ICAP
Wallace, Webb, & Schluter (2002)	168 individuals with ID	ABS
Zigman, Schupf, Urv, Zigman, & Silverman (2002)	646 adults with ID	ABS
Bailey, Hatton, Tassone, Skinner, & Taylor (2001)	53 males with fragile X	BDI
Balboni, Pedrabissi, Molteni, & Villa (2001)	226 individuals with ID	VABS
Belser & Sudhalter (2001)	30 individuals with fragile X, autism, or ID	VABS
Cooper & Browder (2001)	8 adults with ID	VABS
Duker, Averink, & Melein (2001)	8 children with ID	VABS
Eikeseth & Jahr (2001)	7 children with autism or typical development	VABS
Emerson et al. (2001)	270 individuals with ID	ABS
Hall, Oliver, & Murphy (2001)	16 children with ID	VABS
Hatton et al. (2001)	814 adults with ID	ABS
Jones et al. (2001)	106 individuals with ID	ABS
Liss et al. (2001)	123 children with ID or autism	VABS
McCarthy & Boyd (2001)	52 individuals with Down syndrome	ABS
Mervis, Klein-Tasman, & Mastin (2001)	41 children with Williams syndrome	VABS
Miltiades & Pruchno (2001)	305 individuals with ID	ABS
O'Reilly & Lancioni (2001)	1 boy with Williams syndrome	VABS
Roberts, Mirrett, & Burchinal (2001)	39 boys with Fragile X syndrome	BDI
Skinner, Correa, Skinner, & Bailey (2001)	250 children with ID	VABS
Sudhalter & Belser (2001)	30 individuals with Fragile X, autism, or ID	VABS
Taubman et al. (2001)	8 children with ID	VABS
Temple, Jozsvai, Konstantareas, & Hewitt (2001)	35 adults with Down syndrome	ABS
Zarcone et al. (2001)	20 individuals with ID	Nisonger

(*continued*)

TABLE I (*Continued*)

Study	Participants	Adaptive Scale
Bailey, Hatton, Mesibov, Ament, & Skinner (2000)	31 boys with Fragile X syndrome	BDI; VABS
Chadwick, Piroth, Walker, Bernard, & Taylor (2000)	139 children with ID	VABS
Charlop-Christy, Le, & Freeman (2000)	5 children with autism	VABS
Emerson et al. (2000)	500 adults with ID	ABS
Felce et al. (2000)	19 adults with ID	ABS
Fitzgerald et al. (2000)	5 individuals with PKU	VABS
Gillham, Carter, Volkmar, & Sparrow (2000)	95 individuals with autism, PDD, or developmental delay.	VABS
Keogh, Garnier, Bernheimer, & Gallimore (2000)	80 children with developmental delays	VABS
Laushey & Heflin (2000)	2 children with autism	VABS
Liss, Fein, Bullard, & Robins (2000)	85 individuals with autism, PDD, or typical development	VABS
Mudford et al. (2000)	16 children with autism	VABS
Oliver, Crayton, Holland, & Hall (2000)	49 adults with Down syndrome	VABS
Robertson et al. (2000)	500 individuals with ID	ABS
Smith, Groen, & Wynn (2000)	28 children with autism or PDD	VABS
Stancliffe, Abery, & Smith (2000)	74 adults with ID	ICAP
Verri, Uggetti, Vallero, Ceroni, & Federico (2000)	1 adult male with ID	ABI
Weber, Egelhoff, McKellop, & Franz (2000)	29 individuals with tuberous sclerosis	VABS
Werner, Dawson, Osterling, & Dinno (2000)	30 individuals with autism or typical development	VABS
Zwaigenbaum et al. (2000)	2 boys with autism	VABS
Assumpcao, Santos, Rosario, & Mercadante (1999)	3 individuals with autism	VABS
Baranek (1999)	32 children with autism, developmental delay, or typical development	VABS
Coe et al. (1999)	88 children with Down syndrome or typical development	VABS
Cosgrave, Tyrrell, McCarron, Gill, & Lawlor (1999)	128 individuals with Down syndrome	ABS; DLSQ
Dacey, Nelson, & Stoeckel (1999)	40 adults with ID	VABS
Duker (1999)	126 individuals with ID	VABS
El-Ghoroury & Romanczyk (1999)	9 children with autism	VABS
Freeman, Del'Homme, Guthrie, & Zhang (1999)	210 children with autism	VABS
Hannah & Midlarsky (1999)	100 siblings on individuals with ID	DNS
Hardan & Sahl (1999)	233 individuals with ID	VABS
Hughes et al. (1999)	24 children with ID or typical development	VABS
Jones et al. (1999)	19 adults with ID	ABS

(*continued*)

TABLE I (*Continued*)

Study	Participants	Adaptive Scale
Klin et al. (1999)	102 children with developmental delay	VABS
Lancioni, Van den Hof, Furniss, O'Reilly, & Cunha (1999)	4 adults with ID	VABS
Matson, Rush, Hamilton, Anderson, Bamburg, & Baglio (1999)	57 adults with ID	VABS
Matson, Bielecki, Mayville, Smalls, Bamburg, & Baglio, (1999)	185 adults with ID	VABS
McDermott, Martin, Weinrich, & Kelly (1999)	252 women with ID	VABS
Murphy, Hall, Oliver, & Kissi-Debra (1999)	614 children with developmental delay, autism, or typical development	VABS
Njardvik, Matson, & Cherry (1999)	36 adults with ID	VABS
Rogers et al. (1999)	194 children with autism	VABS
Romski, Sevcik, & Adamson (1999)	13 children with ID	VABS
Sicotte & Stemberger (1999)	28 children with PDD	VABS
Stella, Mundy, & Tuchman (1999)	90 children with autism or PDD	VABS
Stone, Ousley, Hepburn, Hogan, & Brown (1999)	60 individuals with autism or developmental delay	VABS
Wall & Gast (1999)	12 adolescents with ID	VABS
Walsh & Shenouda (1999)	284 individuals with ID	ABS
Zarcone, Crosland, Fisher, Worsdell, & Herman (1999)	5 children with ID	VABS
Ashaye, Fernando, Kohen, Mathew, & Orrell (1998)	144 adults with ID	DAS
Bacon, Fein, Morris, Waterhouse, & Allen (1998)	193 individuals with autism, develpomental delay, ID, and typical development	VABS
Bailey, Mesibov et al. (1998)	57 boys with Fragile X syndrome	BDI
Bailey, Hatton, & Skinner (1998)	46 boys with Fragile X syndrome	BDI
Beardsmore, Dorman, Cooper, & Webb (1998)	23 adults with Prader–Willi syndrome	ABS
Burt et al. (1998)	70 adults with Down syndrome	VABS
Carter et al. (1998)	684 individuals with autism	VABS
Chung (1998)	1 adolescent female with ID	VABS
Clare, Garnier, & Gallimore (1998)	103 children with developmental delay	VABS
Clarke, Boer et al. (1998)	6 individuals with Prader–Willi syndrome	VABS
Dawson, Matson, & Cherry (1998)	36 adults with autism, PDD, or ID	VABS
Dawson, Meltzoff, Osterling, Rinaldi, & Brown (1998)	59 individuals with autism, Down syndrome, or typical development	VABS
Dykens & Smith (1998)	105 children and adolescents with Smith–Magenis syndrome or Prader–Willi syndrome	VABS

(*continued*)

TABLE I (*Continued*)

Study	Participants	Adaptive Scale
Espie et al. (1998)	28 individuals with ID	VABS
Heller, Factor, Hsieh, & Hahn (1998)	232 individuals with ID	ICAP
Heller, Miller, & Factor (1998)	249 individuals with ID	ICAP
Jacobson (1998)	45810 adults, 95% with ID	DDP
Jenkins, Rose, & Jones (1998)	63 individuals with ID	ABS
Koegel, Camarata, Koegel, Ben-Tall, & Smith (1998)	5 children with autism	VABS
Koegel, Camarata, Valdez-Menchaca, & Koegel (1998)	3 children with autism	VABS
Lancioni, O'Reilly, Campodonico, & Mantini (1998a)	4 adults with ID	VABS
Lancioni, O'Reilly, Campodonico, & Mantini (1998b)	3 women with ID	VABS
Levitas & Reid (1998)	13 individuals with Rubinstein–Taybi syndrome	VABS
Linuma, Minami, Cho, Kajii, & Pachi (1998)	130 individuals with ID or typical development	VABS
Lowe, Felce, Perry, Baxter, & Jones (1998)	41 adults with ID	VABS
Matson Carlisle, & Bamburg (1998)	892 individuals with ID	VABS
Mazzocco, Baumgardner, Freund, & Reiss (1998)	17 girls with Fragile X syndrome or Turner syndrome	VABS
Moss et al. (1998)	201 individuals with ID	ABS
Prasher, Chung, & Haque (1998)	128 adults with Down syndrome	ABS
Prosser et al. (1998)	68 individuals with ID	ABS
Rose, Jones, & Fletcher (1998)	24 adults with ID	ABS
Spreat, Conroy, & Rice (1998)	40 individuals with ID	DDQAQ
Stancliffe & Hayden (1998)	71 individuals with ID	ICAP
Stancliffe & Lakin (1998)	187 individuals with ID	ICAP
Turk & Cornish (1998)	42 boys with Fragile X, Down syndrome, or typical development	VABS
Udwin, Howlin, Davies, & Mannion (1998)	70 adults with Williams syndrome	VABS
Van Bourgondien, Reichle, Campbell, & Mesibov (1998)	52 adults with autism	VABS
Zappella, Gillberg, & Ehlers (1998)	30 individuals with autism	VABS
Borthwick-Duffy, Lane, & Widaman (1997)	67 children with ID	CDER
Boutin et al. (1997)	67 individuals with autism or ID	VABS
Dykens, Finucane, & Gayley (1997)	10 individuals with Smith–Magenis syndrome	VABS
Field et al. (1997)	22 children with autism	VABS
Horrigan & Barnhill (1997)	11 male individuals with autism	VABS
Jenkins, Rose, & Lovell (1997)	39 individuals with ID	ABS
Konstantareas & Lunsky (1997)	31 individuals with autism or developmental delay	DP-II
Lord et al. (1997)	319 individuals with autism	VABS

(*continued*)

TABLE I (*Continued*)

Study	Participants	Adaptive Scale
Matson & Smiroldo (1997)	22 adults with ID	VABS
Moss & Patel (1997)	101 adults with ID	ABS
Pogson (1997)	1 adult male with ID	VABS
Prasher, Chowdhury, Rowe, & Bain (1997)	100 adults with Down syndrome	ABS
Schupf et al. (1997)	344 women with Down syndrome or ID	ABS
Seal & Bonvillian (1997)	14 adolescents with autism	VABS
Smith, Eikeseth, Klevstrand, & Lovaas (1997)	21 children with ID and PDD	VABS
VanMeter, Fein, Morris, Waterhouse, & Allen (1997)	children with autism, ID, or typical development	VABS
Brinton & Fujiki (1996)	44 individuals with ID	OMFAQ
Brooke, Collacott, & Bhaumik (1996)	1 individual with ID	VABS
Cameron, Luiselli, Littleton, & Ferrelli (1996)	1 adolescent female with ID	VABS
Carpentieri & Morgan (1996)	40 children with autism or ID	VABS
Dykens et al. (1996)	29 individuals with Fragile X syndrome	VABS
Ghaziuddin & Gerstein (1996)	17 individuals with Asperger syndrome	VABS
Koegel, Bimbela, & Schreibman (1996)	17 children with autism	VABS
Lowe, Felce, & Blackman (1996)	51 individuals with ID	ABS
Luscre & Center (1996)	3 children with autism	VABS
Maaskant et al. (1996)	1602 adults with ID	ADL
Prasher & Hall (1996)	201 adults with Down syndrome	ABS
Simon, Rosen, & Ponpipom (1996)	86 individuals with ID	VABS
Smith & Van Houten (1996)	15 children with developmental delays or typical development	VABS
Turner, Realon, Irvin, & Robinson (1996)	3 individuals with ID	VABS
Waterhouse et al. (1996)	194 children with autism or PDD	VABS; MRCHBS
Williams (1996)	25 individuals with ID	VABS
Wilson, Seaman, & Nettlebeck (1996)	60 individuals with ID	ABS
Zanolli, Daggett, & Adams (1996)	2 boys with autism	VABS

ABS—Adaptive Behavior Scale; ABDQ—Adaptive Behavior Dementia Questionnaire; ADL—Activities of Daily Living; BDI—Battelle Development Inventory; BDS—Behavior Development Survey; CDER—Child Development Evaluation Report; DAS—Disability Assessment Schedule; DDP—Developmental Disabilities Profile; DDQAQ—Developmental Disabilities Quality Assurance Questionnaire; DLSQ—Daily Living Skills Questionnaire; DNS—Disability Needs Scale; DP-II—Developmental Profile II; ICAP—Inventory for Client and Agency Planning; LDCS—Learning Disability Casemix Scale; MRCHBS—Medical Research Council Handicaps, Behavior, and Skills Schedule; OMFAQ—Oars Multidimensional Functioning Assessment Questionnaire; PDDBI—PDD Behavior Inventory; VABS—Vineland Adaptive Behavior Scales; SIB—Scales of Independent Behavior.

However, the School and Community version does possess appropriate norms for the diagnosis of ID. Researchers should be careful to note which version of the ABS they employ as their normative samples differ significantly. This was often not done within the text of the article but was implied from the citation (e.g., Grissom & Borkowski, 2002; Romski, Sevcik, Adamson, & Bakeman, 2005).

The SIB/ICAP was reported in 15 of the identified studies. The primary purpose cited for inclusion was to measure general adaptive behavior or "everyday functioning." One asset of the SIB-R is that it may be completed as a checklist directly by the informant. However, only three of the identified studies administered the SIB in a checklist format.

The form of the SIB/ICAP used varied among studies with researchers more frequently choosing to include the ICAP rather than the SIB-R. Considering the breadth of information gathered by the ICAP and the shortened administration for adaptive behavior assessment, it is understandable that researchers would choose this version, particularly if adaptive behavior assessment was not central to their research question. However, the shorter administration time comes at the cost of less specific and descriptive information that the full version of the SIB-R provides.

The primary purpose cited for including any of these adaptive behavior scales was to provide a measure of general adaptive behavior. However, the terms that researchers used to describe how the scores were interpreted or what the scores represented were variable among studies. For example, researches cited "overall developmental maturity" (Baranek et al., 2005), "functional and communication abilities" (Paul et al., 2005), "level of intellectual disability" (Hastings, Beck, Daley, & Hill, 2005), or "developmental quotient" (Oliver, Hall, & Murphy, 2005) as purposes for administering the VABS. Much of this variability is surely due to the fact that these scales have multiple uses or that only one aspect of the scale was relevant to the respective study (e.g., social skills in Klin, Pauls, Schultz, & Volkmar, 2005). However, the numerous definitions of what the scales were used to measure as cited in the identified studies also suggests that there still remains a significant amount of uncertainty or disagreement regarding the construct of adaptive behavior.

Researchers are increasingly using adaptive scales not simply for diagnostic purposes within research studies but also to evaluate differences in adaptive behaviors within groups of individuals. As noted previously, much of this work has focused on persons with autism. However, it is evident from examining Table I that many other diagnostic groups have been evaluated. This is encouraging in that it signifies that researchers have moved beyond simply evaluating intellectual differences among diagnostic categories and are now examining differences among adaptive skills (e.g. Hatton et al., 2003).

The VABS, ABS, and SIB/ICAP each list planning supports as one of their primary uses. Nonetheless, of the identified studies that used adaptive behavior scales over the past 10 years, only a few reported having used an adaptive scale to perform this task. Further research examining the utility of adaptive behavior scales to inform treatment planning is needed. Specifically regarding which test characteristics are the most useful for support planning and lead to helping the person with ID reach their maximum level of independence.

VI. CONCLUSION

Adaptive behavior scales play an important role in helping practitioners diagnose, plan supports, or determine an individual's level of independence. Much research has been conducted to develop specific scales as well as examine the underlying construct that these scales are designed to measure. While much progress has been made in this regard, a significant amount of confusion or disagreement still appears to remain regarding the nature of this construct and the most appropriate way to measure it.

The construct of adaptive behavior is fundamental to any definition of ID. Current definitions of ID (e.g., DSM-IV; AAMR) include adaptive behavior as a component, but place adaptive behavior at different levels of prominence. In the DSM-IV, adaptive behavior is a diagnostic requirement but the measurement of the construct is only briefly discussed, whereas the AAMR definition puts a greater weight on the adaptive behavior component and specifically requires the use of assessment scales standardized on both persons with and without disabilities (Luckasson et al., 2002).

While debate may still continue, it is reasonable to conclude that adaptive behavior is a multidimensional construct (Thompson et al., 1999). However, the most widely used adaptive behavior scales continue to provide a unified composite score in addition to individual domain scores. While many researchers continue to report a general adaptive score, the trend has become to evaluate differences or measure change on the more specific domain scores (Paul et al., 2004).

There are a number of unique concerns regarding the psychometric properties of tests when applied to persons with ID. First, practitioners need to consider the manner in which ceiling and basal scores are established. Scales in which ceiling scores are established rapidly may underestimate an individual's abilities in that domain if the skills have developed in an atypical order. Likewise, establishing a basal too early may overestimate their skills. It may not be safe to assume that the person is able to perform a skill unless it is truly foundational to abilities that have been assessed. A second consideration when applying adaptive behavior scales to individuals with ID is the age appropriateness of the items. The items queried for persons in the severe and profound range of ID are often rather age inappropriate and better suited to measuring an infant's development rather than how well an adult with ID functions within their everyday life. A third concern is in regards to how well the scale represents the culture in which the behavior is to be measured. Adaptive behavior is often defined in relation to social norms and expectations (Horn & Fuchs, 1987). However, a vast majority of studies exploring adaptive behavior have been conducted within western culture (Craig & Tassé, 1999). More research evaluating adaptive behaviors on individuals from other cultural backgrounds is needed.

A myriad of adaptive scales have been published (Spreat, 1999), results of this review found that researchers over the past 10 years have primarily used three adaptive behavior scales. The scales identified most frequently were the VABS, the ABS, and the SIB/ICAP. Researchers have mainly used these scales to measure participants' general level of adaptive behavior. These scales were less frequently used to establish a diagnosis of ID, as most authors cited previous diagnoses that the individuals had received through clinical services.

It is unclear from this chapter the extent to which adaptive behavior scales are used by clinicians to develop individual supports for persons with ID. However, the dearth of research studies reporting the use of adaptive behavior scales to serve this purpose is cause for concern. First, while the test authors report the utility of these scales to serve this purpose, little evidence is available to indicate how well these scales perform this task. Indeed, little is known regarding what information provided by adaptive behavior scales is relevant to the task of maximizing independence.

REFERENCES

Accardo, P. J., & Capute, A. J. (1998). Mental retardations. *Mental Retardation and Developmental Disabilities Research Reviews, 4,* 2–5.

Aman, M. G., Singh, N. N., Stewart, A. W., & Field, C. J. (1985). The Aberrant Behavior Checklist: A behavior rating scale for the assessment of treatment effects. *American Journal of Mental Deficiency, 89,* 485–491.

American Educational Research Association (1999). Standards for education and psychological testing. Washington DC: Author.

American Psychiatric Association (2000). Diagnostic and statistical manual of mental disorders (4th ed., text rev.). Washington, DC: Author.

Anastasi, A., & Urbina, S. (1997). Psychological Testing (7th ed.). Upper Saddle River, NJ: Prentice Hall.

Ashaye, O., Fernando, L., Kohen, D., Mathew, G., & Orrell, M. (1998). A five-year follow-up study of older long-stay clients with intellectual disability using the Disability Assessment Schedule. *Journal of Intellectual Disability Research, 42,* 131–136.

Assumpcao, F., Santos, R. C. S., Rosario, M., & Mercadante, M. (1999). Autism and Aarskog syndrome. *Journal of Autism and Developmental Disorders, 29,* 179–181.

Bacon, A. L., Fein, D., Morris, R., Waterhouse, L., & Allen, D. (1998). The responses of autistic children to the distress of others. *Journal of Autism and Developmental Disorders, 28,* 129–142.

Baghdadli, A., Pascal, C., Grisi, S., & Aussilloux, C. (2003). Risk factors for self-injurious behaviours among 222 young children with autistic disorders. *Journal of Intellectual Disability Research, 47,* 622–627.

Bailey, D. B. Jr., Hatton, D. D., Mesibov, G., Ament, N., & Skinner, M. (2000). Early development, temperament, and functional impairment in autism and Fragile X syndrome. *Journal of Autism and Developmental Disorders, 30,* 49–59.

Bailey, D. B. Jr., Hatton, D. D., & Skinner, M. (1998). Early development trajectories of males with Fragile X syndrome. *American Journal on Mental Retardation, 103,* 29–39.

Bailey, D. B. Jr., Hatton, D. D., Tassone, F., Skinner, M., & Taylor, A. K. (2001). Variability in FMRP and early development in males with Fragile X syndrome. *American Journal on Mental Retardation, 106,* 16–27.

Bailey, D. B. Jr., Mesibov, G. B., Hatton, D. D., Clark, R. D., Roberts, J. E., & Mayhew, L. (1998). Autistic behavior in young boys with Fragile X syndrome. *Journal of Autism and Developmental Disorders, 28,* 499–508.

Balboni, G., Pedrabissi, L., Molteni, M., & Villa, S. (2001). Discriminant validity of the Vineland Scales: Score profiles of individuals with mental retardation and a specific disorder. *American Journal on Mental Retardation, 106,* 162–172.

Baranek, G. T. (1999). Autism during infancy: A retrospective video analysis of sensory-motor and social behaviors at 9–12 months of age. *Journal of Autism and Developmental Disorders, 29,* 213–242.

Baranek, G. T., Danko, C. D., Skinner, M. L., Bailey, D. B. Jr., Hatton, D. D., Roberts, J. E., et al. (2005). Video analysis of sensory-motor features in infants with Fragile X syndrome at 9–12 months of age. *Journal of Autism and Developmental Disorders, 35,* 645–656.

Basquill, M. F., Nezu, C. M., Nezu, A. M., & Klein, T. L. (2004). Aggression-related hostility bias and social problem-solving deficits in adult males with mental retardation. *American Journal on Mental Retardation, 109,* 255–263.

Beail, N. (2003). Utility of the Vineland Adaptive Behavior Scales in diagnosis and research with adults who have mental retardation. *Mental Retardation, 41,* 286–289.

Beardsmore, A., Dorman, T., Cooper, S. A., & Webb, T. (1998). Affective psychosis and Prader-Willi syndrome. *Journal of Intellectual Disability Research, 42,* 463–471.

Beck, A., Daley, D., Hastings, R. P., & Stevenson, J. (2004). Mothers' expressed emotion towards children with and without intellectual disabilities. *Journal of Intellectual Disability Research, 48,* 628–638.

Belser, R. C., & Sudhalter, V. (2001). Conversational characteristics of children with Fragile X syndrome: Repetitive speech. *American Journal on Mental Retardation, 106,* 28–38.

Berument, S. K., Starr, E., Pickles, A., Tomlins, M., Papanikolauous, K., Lord, C., et al. (2005). Pre-linguistic Autism Diagnostic Observation Schedule adapted for older individuals with severe to profound mental retardation: A pilot study*Journal of Autism and Developmental Disorders, 35,* 821–829.

Bibby, P., Eikeseth, S., Martin, N. T., Mudford, O. C., & Reeves, D. (2002). Progress and outcomes for children with autism receiving parent-managed intensive interventions. *Research in Developmental Disabilities, 23,* 81–104.

Billstedt, E., Gillbert, C., & Gillberg, C. (2005). Autism after Adolescence: Population-based 13- to 22-year follow-up study of 120 individuals with autism diagnosed in childhood. *Journal of Autism and Developmental Disorders, 35,* 351–360.

Borthwick-Duffy, S. A., Lane, K. L., & Widaman, K. F. (1997). Measuring problem behaviors in children with mental retardation: Dimensions and predictors. *Research in Developmental Disabilities, 18,* 415–433.

Bosseler, A., & Massaro, D. W. (2003). Development and evaluation of a computer-animated tutor for vocabulary and language learning in children with autism. *Journal of Autism and Developmental Disorders, 33,* 653–672.

Boutin, P., Maziade, M., Merette, C., Mondor, M., Bedard, C., & Thivierge, J. (1997). Family history of cognitive disabilities in first-degree relatives of autistic and mentally retarded children. *Journal of Autism and Developmental Disorders, 27,* 165–176.

Bradley, E. A., Summers, J. A., Wood, H. L., & Bryson, S. E. (2004). Comparing rates of psychiatric and behavior disorders in adolescents and young adults with severe intellectual disability with and without autism. *Journal of Autism and Developmental Disorders, 34,* 151–161.

Brinton, B., & Fujiki, M. (1996). Responses to requests for clarification by older and young adults with mental retardation. *Research in Developmental Disabilities, 24,* 335–347.

Brooke, S., Collacott, R. A., & Bhaumik, S. (1996). Monosymptomatic hypochondriacal psychosis in a man with learning disabilities. *Journal of Intellectual Disability Research, 40,* 71–74.

Bruininks, R., Hill, B., Weatherman, R., & Woodcock, R. (1986). Examiner's manual: ICAP Inventory for Client and Agency Planning. Chicago: Riverside.

Bruininks, R. H., Wookcock, R. W., Weatherman, R. F., & Hill, B. K. (1996). Scales of Independent Behavior-Revised. Itasca, IL: Riverside.

Buhrow, M., & Bradley-Johnson, S. (2003). Visual preferences of students with profound mental retardation and healthy, full-term infants. *Research in Developmental Disabilities, 24,* 83–94.

Burt, D. B., Loveland, K. A., Primeaux-Hart, S., Chen, Y., Philips, N. B., Cleveland, L. A., et al. (1998). Dementia in adults with Down syndrome: Diagnostic challenges*American Journal on Mental Retardation, 103,* 130–145.

Burt, D. B., Primeaux-Hart, S., Loveland, K. A., Cleveland, L. A., Lewis, K. R., Lesser, J., et al. (2005). Aging in adults with intellectual disabilities. *American Journal on Mental Retardation, 110,* 268–284.

Cameron, M. I., Luiselli, J. K., Littleton, R. F. Jr., & Ferrelli, L. (1996). Component analysis and stimulus control assessment of a behavior deceleration treatment package. *Research in Developmental Disabilities, 17,* 203–215.

Carpentieri, S., & Morgan, S. B. (1996). Adaptive and intellectual functioning in autistic and nonautistic retarded children. *Journal of Autism and Developmental Disorders, 26,* 611–620.

Carter, A. S., Volkmar, F. R., Sparrow, S. S., Wang, J. J., Lord, C., Dawson, G., et al. (1998). The Vineland Adaptive Behavior Scales: Supplementary norms for individuals with autism. *Journal of Autism and Developmental Disorders, 28,* 287–302.

Chadwick, O., Cuddy, M., Kusel, Y., & Taylor, E. (2005). Handicaps and the development of skills between childhood and early adolescence in young people with severe intellectual disabilities. *Journal of Intellectual Disability Research, 49,* 877–888.

Chadwick, O., Piroth, N., Walker, J., Bernard, S., & Taylor, E. (2000). Factors affecting the risk of behaviour problems in children with severe intellectual disability. *Journal of Intellectual Disability Research, 44,* 108–123.

Charlop-Christy, M. H., Le, L., & Freeman, K. A. (2000). A comparison of video modeling with *in vivo* modeling for teaching children with autism. *Journal of Autism and Developmental Disorders, 30,* 537–552.

Chung, B. I. (1998). Treatment of echolalia in a girl with Rubinstein-Taybi syndrome: Functional assessment of minimizing chances to provoke echolalia. *Journal of Autism and Developmental Disorders, 28,* 573–578.

Clare, L., Garnier, H., & Gallimore, R. (1998). Parents' developmental expectations and child characteristics: Longitudinal study of children with developmental delays and their families. *American Journal on Mental Retardation, 103,* 117–129.

Clarke, D., Boer, H., Webb, T., Scott, P., Frazer, S., Vogels, A., et al. (1998). Prader-Willi syndrome and psychotic symptoms: I. Case descriptions and genetic studies. *Journal of Intellectual Disability Research, 42,* 440–450.

Coe, D. A., Matson, J. L., Russell, D. W., Slifer, K. J., Capone, G. T., Baglio, C., & Stallings, S. (1999). Behavior problems of children with Down syndrome and life events. *Journal of Autism and Developmental Disorders, 29,* 149–156.

Cohen, I. L. (2003). Criterion-related validity of the PDD Behavior Inventory. *Journal of Autism and Developmental Disorders, 33,* 47–53.

Cohen, I. L., Schmidt-Lackner, S., Romanczyk, R., & Sudhalter, V. (2003). The PDD Behavior Inventory: A rating scale for assessing response to intervention in children with Pervasive Developmental Disorder. *Journal of Autism and Developmental Disorders, 33,* 31–45.

Cooper, K. J., & Browder, D. M. (2001). Preparing staff to enhance active participation of adults with severe disabilities by offering choice and prompting performance during a community purchasing activity. *Research in Developmental Disabilities, 22,* 1–20.

Copeland, S. R., Hughes, C., Agran, M., Wehmeyer, M. L., & Fowler, S. E. (2002). An intervention package to support high school students with mental retardation in general education classrooms. *American Journal on Mental Retardation, 107,* 32–45.

Cosgrave, M. P., Tyrrell, J., McCarron, M., Gill, M., & Lawlor, B. A. (1999). Determinants of aggression, and adaptive and maladaptive behaviour in older people with Down's syndrome with and without dementia. *Journal of Intellectual Disability Research, 43,* 393–399.

Craig, E., & Tassé, M. J. (1999). Cultural and demographic group comparisons of adaptive behavior. In R. L. Schalock (Ed.), Adaptive Behavior and Its Measurement: Implications for the Field of Mental Retardation. Washington, DC: AAMR.

Dacey, C. M., Nelson, W. M. III, & Stoeckel, J. (1999). Reliability, criterion-related validity and qualitative comments of the Fourth Edition of the Stanford-Binet Intelligence Scale with a young adult population with intellectual disability. *Journal of Intellectual Disability Research, 43,* 179–184.

Dawson, G., Meltzoff, A. N., Osterling, J., Rinaldi, J., & Brown, E. (1998). Children with autism fail to orient to naturally occurring social stimuli. *Journal of Autism and Developmental Disorders, 28,* 479–485.

Dawson, J. E., Matson, J. L., & Cherry, K. E. (1998). An analysis of maladaptive behaviors in persons with autism, PDD-NOS, and mental retardation. *Research in Developmental Disabilities, 19,* 439–448.

de Bildt, A., Kraijer, D., Sytema, S., & Minderaa, R. (2005). The psychometric properties of the Vineland Adaptive Behavior Scales in children and adolescents with mental retardation. *Journal of Autism and Developmental Disorders, 35,* 53–62.

de Bildt, A., Serra, M., Luteijn, E., Kraijer, D., Sytema, D., & Minderaa, R. (2005). Social skills in children with intellectual disabilities with and without autism. *Journal of Intellectual Disability Research, 49,* 317–328.

de Bildt, A., Sytema, S., Ketelaars, C., Kraijer, D., Mulder, E., Volkmar, F., et al. (2004). Interrelationship between Autism Diagnostic Observation Schedule-Generic (ADOS-G), Autism Diagnostic Interview-Revised (ADI-R), and the Diagnostic and Statistical Manual of Mental Disorders (DSM-IV-TR) classification in children and adolescents with mental retardation. *Journal of Autism and Developmental Disorders, 34,* 129–137.

de Bildt, A., Sytema, S., Ketelaars, C., Kraijer, D., Volkmar, F., & Minderaa, R. (2003). Measuring Pervasive Developmental Disorders in children and adolescents with mental retardation: A comparison of two screening instruments used in a study of the total mentally retarded population from a designated area. *Journal of Autism and Developmental Disorders, 33,* 595–605.

de Bildt, A., Sytema, S., Kraijer, D., Sparrow, S., & Minderaa, R. (2005). Adaptive functioning and behaviour problems in relation to level of education in children and adolescents with intellectual disability. *Journal of Intellectual Disability Research, 49,* 672–681.

Dekker, M. C., Nunn, R., & Koot, H. M. (2002). Psychometric properties of the revised Developmental Behaviour Checklist scales in Dutch children with intellectual disability. *Journal of Intellectual Disability Research, 46,* 61–75.

Doll, E. A. (1965). Vineland Social Maturity Scale. Circle Pines, MN: American Guidance Service, Inc.

Dube, W. V., McIlvane, W. J., Mazzitelli, K., & McNamara, B. (2003). Reinforcer rate effects and behavioral momentum in individuals with developmental disabilities. *American Journal on Mental Retardation, 108,* 134–143.

Duker, P. C. (1999). The Verbal Behavior Assessment Scale (VerBAS): Construct validity, reliability, and internal consistency. *Research in Developmental Disabilities, 20,* 347–353.

Duker, P. C., Averink, M., & Melein, L. (2001). Response restriction as a method to establish diurnal bladder control. *American Journal on Mental Retardation, 106,* 209–215.

Duker, P. C., van Driel, S., & van de Bercken, J. (2002). Communication profiles of individuals with Down's syndrome, Angelman syndrome and pervasive developmental disorder. *Journal of Intellectual Disability Research, 46,* 35–40.

Dunn, M. A., & Bates, J. C. (2005). Developmental change in neutral processing of words by children with autism. *Journal of Autism and Developmental Disorders, 35,* 361–376.

Duvdevany, I. (2002). Self-concept and adaptive behaviour of people with intellectual disability in integrated and segregated recreation activities. *Journal of Intellectual Disability Research, 46,* 419–429.

Dykens, E. M. (1995). Adaptive behavior in males with fragile X syndrome. *Mental Retardation and Developmental Disabilities Research Reviews, 1,* 281–285.

Dykens, E. M., Finucane, B. M., & Gayley, C. (1997). Cognitive and behavioral profiles in persons with Smith-Magenis syndrome. *Journal of Autism and Developmental Disorders, 27,* 203–211.

Dykens, E., Ort, S., Cohen, I., Finucane, B., Spiridigliozzi, G., Lachiewicz, A., et al. (1996). Trajectories and profiles of adaptive behavior in males with Fragile X syndrome: Multicenter studies. *Journal of Autism and Developmental Disorders, 26,* 287–301.

Dykens, E. M., & Smith, A. C. M. (1998). Distinctiveness and correlates of maladaptive behavior in children and adolescents with Smith-Magenis syndrome. *Journal of Intellectual Disability Research, 42,* 481–489.

Eaves, L. C., & Ho, H. H. (2004). The very early identification of autism: Outcome to age 4½–5. *Journal of Autism and Developmental Disorders, 34,* 367–378.

Edgin, J. O., & Pennington, B. F. (2005). Spatial cognition in Autism Spectrum Disorders: Superior, impaired, or just intact? *Journal of Autism and Developmental Disorders, 35,* 729–745.

Eikeseth, S., & Jahr, E. (2001). The UCLA reading and writing program: An evaluation of the beginning stages. *Research in Developmental Disabilities, 22,* 289–307.

Einam, M., & Cuskelly, M. (2002). Paid employment of mothers and fathers of an adult child with multiple disabilities. *Journal of Intellectual Disability Research, 46,* 158–167.

El-Ghoroury, N. H., & Romanczyk, R. G. (1999). Play interactions of family members towards children with autism. *Journal of Autism and Developmental Disorders, 29,* 249–258.

Emerson, E. (2005). Underweight, obesity and exercise among adults with intellectual disabilities in supported accommodation in Northern England. *Journal of Intellectual Disability Research, 49,* 134–143.

Emerson, E., Robertson, J., Gregory, N., Hatton, C., Kessissoglou, S., Hallam, A., et al. (2001). Quality and costs of supported living residences and group homes in the United Kingdom. *American Journal on Mental Retardation, 106,* 401–414.

Emerson, E., Robertson, J., Gregory, N., Hatton, C., Kessissoglou, S., Hallam, A., et al. (2000). Quality and costs of community-based residential supports, village communities, and residential campuses in the United Kingdom. *American Journal on Mental Retardation, 105,* 81–102.

Emerson, E., Robertson, J., & Wood, J. (2005). Emotional and behavioural needs of children and adolescents with intellectual disabilities in an urban conurbation. *Journal of Intellectual Disability Research, 49,* 16–24.

Espie, C. A., Paul, A., McFie, J., Amos, P., Hamilton, D., McColl, J. H., et al. (1998). Sleep studies of adults with severe or profound mental retardation and epilepsy. *American Journal on Mental Retardation, 103,* 47–59.

Felce, D., Bowley, C., Baxter, H., Jones, E., Lowe, K., & Emerson, E. (2000). The effectiveness of staff support: Evaluating Active Support training using a conditional probability approach. *Research in Developmental Disabilities, 21,* 243–255.

Fidler, D. J. (2003). Parental vocalizations and perceived immaturity in Down syndrome. *American Journal on Mental Retardation, 108,* 425–434.

Field, T., Lasko, D., Mundy, P., Henteleff, T., Kabat, S., Talpins, S., et al. (1997). Autistic children's attentiveness and responsivity improve after touch therapy. *Journal of Autism and Developmental Disorders, 27,* 333–338.

Fine, S. E., Weissman, A., Gerdes, M., Pinto-Martin, J., Zackai, E. H., McDonald-McGinn, D. M., et al. (2005). Autism Spectrum Disorders and symptoms in children with molecularly confirmed 22q11.2 deletion syndrome. *Journal of Autism and Developmental Disorders, 35,* 461–470.

Fisch, G. S., Simensen, J., & Schroer, R. J. (2002). Longitudinal changes in cognitive and adaptive behavior scores in children and adolescents with the Fragile X mutation or autism. *Journal of Autism and Developmental Disorders, 32,* 107–114.

Fitzgerald, B., Morgan, J., Keene, N., Rollinson, R., Hodgson, A., & Dalrymple-Smith, J. (2000). An investigation into diet treatment for adults with previously untreated phenylketonuria and severe intellectual disability. *Journal of Intellectual Disability Research, 44,* 53–59.

Freeman, B. J., Del'Homme, M., Guthrie, D., & Zhang, F. (1999). Vineland Adaptive Behavior Scale scores as a function of age and initial IQ in 210 autistic children. *Journal of Autism and Developmental Disorders, 29,* 379–384.

Gena, A., Couloura, S., & Kymissis, E. (2005). Modifying the affective behavior of preschoolers with autism using *in-vivo* or video modeling and reinforcement contingencies. *Journal of Autism and Developmental Disorders, 35,* 545–556.

Gillham, J. E., Carter, A. S., Volkmar, F. R., & Sparrow, S. S. (2000). Toward a developmental operational definition of autism. *Journal of Autism and Developmental Disorders, 30,* 269–278.

Ghaziuddin, M., & Gerstein, L. (1996). Pedantic speaking style differentiates Asperger syndrome from high-functioning autism. *Journal of Autism and Developmental Disorders, 26,* 585–595.

Gonzalez-Gordon, R. G., Salvador-Carulla, L., Romero, C., Gonzalez-Saiz, F., & Romero, D. (2002). Feasibility, reliability and validity of the Spanish version of Psychiatric Assessment Schedule for Adults with Developmental Disability: A structured psychiatric interview for intellectual disability. *Journal of Intellectual Disability Research, 46,* 209–217.

Graff, R. B., & Green, G. (2004). Two methods for teaching simple visual discriminations to learners with severe disabilities. *Research in Developmental Disabilities, 25,* 295–307.

Greenspan, S., Switzky, H. N., & Granfield, J. M. (1996). Everyday intelligence and adaptive behavior: A theoretical framework. In J. W. Jacobson & J. A. Mulick (Eds.), Manual of Diagnosis and Professional Practice in Mental Retardation (pp. 127–136). Washington, DC: American Psychological Association.

Grigorenko, E. L., Klin, A., Pauls, D. L., Senft, R., Hooper, C., & Volkmar, F. (2002). A descriptive study of hyperlexia in a clinically referred sample of children with developmental delays. *Journal of Autism and Developmental Disorders, 32,* 3–12.

Grissom, M. O., & Borkowski, J. G. (2002). Self-efficacy in adolescents who have siblings with or without disabilities. *American Journal on Mental Retardation, 107,* 79–90.

Gross, T. F. (2002). Perception of human and nonhuman facial age by developmentally disabled children. *Journal of Autism and Developmental Disorders, 32,* 169–179.

Gross, T. F. (2005). Global local precedence in the perception of facial age and emotional expression by children with autism and other developmental disabilities. *Journal of Autism and Developmental Disorders, 35,* 773–785.

Gunter, H. L., Ghaziuddin, M., & Ellis, H. D. (2002). Asperger syndrome: Tests of right hemisphere functioning and interhemispheric communication. *Journal of Autism and Developmental Disorders, 32,* 263–281.

Guralnick, M. J. (2002). Involvement with peers: comparisons between young children with and without Down's syndrome. *Journal of Intellectual Disability Research, 46,* 379–393.

Guralnick, M. J., Hammond, M. A., & Connor, R. T. (2003). Subtypes of nonsocial play: Comparisons between young children with and without developmental delays. *American Journal on Mental Retardation, 108,* 347–362.

Guralnick, M. J., Neville, B., Connor, R. T., & Hammond, M. A. (2003). Family factors associated with the peer social competence of young children with mild delays. *American Journal on Mental Retardation, 108,* 272–287.

Hall, S., Oliver, C., & Murphy, G. (2001). Early development of self-injurious behavior: An empirical study. *American Journal on Mental Retardation, 106,* 189–199.

Hall, S., Thorns, T., & Oliver, C. (2003). Structural and environmental characteristics of stereotyped behaviors. *American Journal on Mental Retardation, 108,* 391–402.

Hallam, A., Knapp, M., Järbrink, K., Netten, A., Emerson, E., Robertson, J., et al. (2002). Costs of village community, residential campus and dispersed housing provision for people with intellectual disability. *Journal of Intellectual Disability Research, 46,* 394–404.

Hannah, M. E., & Midlarsky, E. (1999). Competence and adjustment of siblings of children with mental retardation. *American Journal on Mental Retardation, 104,* 22–37.

Hardan, A., & Sahl, R. (1999). Suicidal behavior in children and adolescents with developmental disorders. *Research in Developmental Disabilities, 20,* 287–296.

Harries, J., Guscia, R., Kirby, N., Nettelbeck, T., & Taplin, J. (2005). Support needs and adaptive behaviors. *American Journal on Mental Retardation, 110,* 393–404.

Hassall, R., Rose, J., & McDonald, J. (2005). Parenting stress in mothers of children with an intellectual disability: The effects of parental cognitions in relation to child characteristics and family support. *Journal of Intellectual Disability Research, 49,* 405–418.

Hastings, R. P., Beck, A., Daley, D., & Hill, C. (2005). Symptoms of ADHD and their correlates in children with intellectual disabilities. *Research in Developmental Disabilities, 26,* 456–468.

Hastings, R. P., Kovshoff, H., Ward, N. J., degli Espinosa, F., Brown, T., & Remington, B. (2005). Systems analysis of stress and positive perceptions in mothers and fathers of pre-school children with autism. *Journal of Autism and Developmental Disorders, 35,* 635–644.

Hatton, C., Emerson, E., Robertson, J., Gregory, N., Kessissoglou, S., Perry, J., et al. (2001). The adaptive behavior scale-residential and community (part I): Towards the development of a short form. *Research in Developmental Disabilities, 22,* 273–288.

Hatton, C., Emerson, E., Robertson, J., Gregory, N., Kessissoglou, S., & Walsh, P. N. (2004). The Resident Choice Scale: A measure to assess opportunities for self-determination in residential settings. *Journal of Intellectual Disability Research, 48,* 103–113.

Hatton, D. D., Wheeler, A. C., Skinner, M. L., Bailey, D. B., Sullivan, K. M., Roberts, J. E., et al. (2003). Adaptive behavior in children with fragile X syndrome. *American Journal on Mental Retardation, 108,* 373–390.

Heber, R. (1959). A manual on terminology and classification in mental retardation. *American Journal on Mental Deficiency (monograph suppl.), 64*(2), 1–111.

Heller, T., Factor, A. R., Hsieh, K., & Hahn, J. E. (1998). Impact of age and transitions out of nursing homes for adults with developmental disabilities. *American Journal on Mental Retardation, 103,* 236–248.

Heller, T., Miller, A. B., & Factor, A. (1998). Environmental characteristics of nursing homes and community-based settings, and the well-being of adults with intellectual disability. *Journal of Intellectual Disability Research, 42,* 418–428.

Heller, T., Miller, A. B., & Hsieh, K. (2002). Eight-year follow-up of the impact of environmental characteristics on well-being of adults with developmental disabilities. *Mental Retardation, 40,* 366–378.

Horn, E., & Fuchs, D. (1987). Using adaptive behavior in assessment and intervention: An overview. *The Journal of Special Education, 21,* 11–26.

Horrigan, J. P., & Barnhill, L. J. (1997). Risperidone and explosive aggressive autism. *Journal of Autism and Developmental Disorders, 27,* 313–323.

Howard, J. S., Sparkman, C. R., Cohen, H. G., Green, G., & Stanislaw, H. (2005). A comparison of intensive behavior analytic and eclectic treatments for young children with autism. *Research in Developmental Disabilities, 26,* 359–383.

Hughes, C., Rodi, M. S., Lorden, S. W., Pitkin, S. E., Derer, K. R., Hwang, B., et al. (1999). Social interactions of high school students with mental retardation and their general education peers. *American Journal on Mental Retardation, 104,* 533–544.

Jacobson, J. W. (1998). Psychological services utilization: Relationship to severity of behaviour problems in intellectual disability services. *Journal of Intellectual Disability Research, 42,* 307–315.

Jenkins, R., Rose, J., & Jones, T. (1998). The Checklist of Challenging Behaviour and its relationship with the Psychopathology Inventory for Mentally Retarded Adults. *Journal of Intellectual Disability Research, 42,* 273–278.

Jenkins, R., Rose, J., & Lovell, C. (1997). Psychological well-being of staff working with people who have challenging behaviour. *Journal of Intellectual Disability Research, 41,* 502–511.

Jones, E., Felce, D., Lowe, K., Bowley, C., Pagler, J., Gallagher, B., et al. (2001). Evaluation of the dissemination of active support training in staffed community residences. *American Journal on Mental Retardation, 106,* 344–358.

Jones, E., Perry, J., Lowe, K., Felce, D., Toogood, S., Dunstan, F., et al. (1999). Opportunity and the promotion of activity among adults with severe intellectual disability living in community residences: The impact of staff training in active support. *Journal of Intellectual Disability Research, 43,* 164–178.

Kay, D. W. K., Tyrer, S. P., Margallo-Lana, M. L., Moore, P. B., Fletcher, R., Berney, T. P., et al. (2003). Preliminary evaluation of a scale to assess cognitive function in adults with Down's syndrome: The Prudhoe Cognitive Function Test. *Journal of Intellectual Disability Research, 47,* 155–168.

Keen, D. (2005). The use of non-verbal repair strategies by children with autism. *Research in Developmental Disabilities, 26,* 243–254.

Keogh, B. K., Garnier, H. E., Bernheimer, L. P., & Gallimore, R. (2000). Models of child-family interactions for children with developmental delays: Child-driven or transactional? *American Journal on Mental Retardation, 105,* 32–46.

Kishore, M. T., Nizamie, A., Nizamie, S. H., & Jahan, M. (2004). Psychiatric diagnosis in persons with intellectual disability in India. *Journal of Intellectual Disability Research, 48,* 19–24.

Kishore, M. T., Nizamie, S. H., & Nizamie, A. (2005). The behavioural profile of psychiatric disorders in persons with intellectual disability. *Journal of Intellectual Disability Research, 49,* 852–857.

Klin, A., Pauls, D., Schultz, R., & Volkmar, F. (2005). Three diagnostic approaches to Asperger syndrome: Implications for research. *Journal of Autism and Developmental Disorders, 35,* 221–234.

Klin, A., Sparrow, S. S., de Bildt, A., Cicchetti, D. V., Cohen, D. J., & Volkmar, F. R. (1999). A normed study of face recognition in autism and related disorders. *Journal of Autism and Developmental Disorders, 29,* 499–508.

Koegel, L. K., Camarata, S. M., Valdez-Menchaca, M., & Koegel, R. L. (1998). Setting generalization of question-asking by children with autism. *American Journal on Mental Retardation, 102,* 346–357.

Koegel, R. L., Bimbela, A., & Schreibman, L. (1996). Collateral effects of parent training on family interactions. *Journal of Autism and Developmental Disorders, 26,* 347–359.

Koegel, R. L., Camarata, S., Koegel, L. K., Ben-Tall, A., & Smith, A. (1998). Increasing speech intelligibility in children with autism. *Journal of Autism and Developmental Disorders, 28,* 241–251.

Konstantareas, M. M., & Lunsky, Y. J. (1997). Sociosexual knowledge, experience, attitudes, and interests of individuals with autistic disorder and developmental delay. *Journal of Autism and Developmental Disorders, 27,* 397–413.

Kottorp, A., Bernspang, B., & Fisher, A. G. (2003). Validity of a performance assessment of activities of daily living for people with developmental disabilities. *Journal of Intellectual Disability Research, 47,* 597–605.

Kravits, T. R., Kamps, D. M., Kemmerer, K., & Potucek, J. (2002). Increasing communication skills for an elementary-aged student with autism using the Picture Exchange Communication System. *Journal of Autism and Developmental Disorders, 32,* 225–230.

Lam, D., Giles, A., & Lavander, A. (2003). Carers' expressed emotion, appraisal of behavioural problems and stress in children attending schools for learning disabilities. *Journal of Intellectual Disability Research, 47,* 456–463.

Lambert, N., Nihira, K., & Leland, H. (1993). AAMR Adaptive Behavior Scale – School and Community. Austin, TX: Pro-Ed.

Lancioni, G. E., O'Reilly, M. F., Campdonico, F., & Mantini, M. (1998a). Mobility versus sedentariness in task arrangements for people with multiple disabilities: An assessment of preferences. *Research in Developmental Disabilities, 19,* 465–475.

Lancioni, G. E., O'Reilly, M. F., Campdonico, F., & Mantini, M. (1998b). Task variation versus task repetition for people with profound developmental disabilities: An assessment of preferences. *Research in Developmental Disabilities, 19,* 189–199.

Lancioni, G. E., Singh, N. N., O'Reilly, M. F., Oliva, D., Campodonico, F., & Groeneweg, J. (2003). Assessing the effects of automatically delivered stimulation on the use of simple exercise tools by students with multiple disabilities. *Research in Developmental Disabilities, 24,* 475–483.

Lancioni, G. E., Van den Hof, E., Furniss, F., O'Reilly, M. F., & Cunha, B. (1999). Evaluation of a computer-aided system providing pictorial task instructions and prompts to people with severe intellectual disability. *Journal of Intellectual Disability Research, 43,* 61–66.

Laushey, K. M., & Heflin, L. J. (2000). Enhancing social skills of kindergarten children with autism through the training of multiple peers as tutors. *Journal of Autism and Developmental Disorders, 30,* 183–193.

Lecavalier, L. (2005). An evaluation of the Gilliam Autism Rating Scale. *Journal of Autism and Developmental Disorders, 35,* 795–805.

Lecavalier, L., Aman, M. G., Hammer, D., Stoica, W., & Mathews, G. L. (2004). Factor analysis of the Nisonger Child Behavior Rating Form in children with Autism Spectrum Disorders. *Journal of Autism and Developmental Disorders, 34,* 709–721.

LeGoff, D. B. (2004). Use of LEGO© as a therapeutic medium for improving social competence. *Journal of Autism and Developmental Disorders, 34,* 557–571.

Lerman, P., Apgar, D. H., & Jordan, T. (2005). Longitudinal changes in adaptive behaviors of movers and stayers: Findings from a controlled research design. *Mental Retardation, 43,* 25–42.

Levitas, A. S., & Reid, C. S. (1998). Rubinstein-Taybi syndrome and psychiatric disorders. *Journal of Intellectual Disability Research, 42,* 284–292.

Linuma, K., Minami, P., Cho, K., Kajii, N., & Pachi, N. (1998). Long-term effects of zonifamide in the treatment of epilepsy in children with intellectual disability. *Journal of Intellectual Disability Research, 42,* 68–73.

Liss, M., Fein, D., Bullard, S., & Robins, D. (2000). Cognitive estimation in individuals with Pervasive Developmental Disorders. *Journal of Autism and Developmental Disorders, 30,* 613–618.

Liss, M., Harel, B., Fein, D., Allen, D., Dunn, M., Feinstein, C., et al. (2001). Predictors and correlates of adaptive functioning in children and developmental disorders. *Journal of Autism and Developmental Disorders, 31,* 219–230.

Lord, C., Pickles, A., McLennan, J., Rutter, M., Bregman, J., Folstein, S., et al. (1997). Diagnosing autism: Analyses of data from the Autism Diagnostic Interview. *Journal of Autism and Developmental Disorders, 27,* 501–517.

Lowe, K., Felce, D., & Blackman, D. (1996). Challenging behaviour: The effectiveness of specialist support teams. *Journal of Intellectual Disability Research, 40,* 336–347.

Lowe, K., Felce, D., Perry, J., Baxter, H., & Jones, E. (1998). The characteristics and residential situations of people with severe intellectual disability and the most severe challenging behaviour in Wales. *Journal of Intellectual Disability Research, 42,* 375–389.

Luckasson, R., Borthwick-Duffy, S., Buntix, W. H. E., Coulter, D. L., Craig, E. M., Reeve, A., et al. (2002). Mental Retardation: Definition, Classification, and Systems of Supports (10th ed.). Washington, DC: American Association on Mental Retardation.

Luiselli, J. K., Campbell, S., Cannon, B., DiPietro, E., Ellis, J. T., Taras, M., et al. (2001). Assessment instruments used in the education and treatment of persons with autism: Brief report of a survey of national service centers. *Research in Developmental Disabilities, 22,* 389–398.

Luscre, D. M., & Center, D. B. (1996). Procedures for reducing dental fear in children with autism. *Journal of Autism and Developmental Disorders, 26,* 547–556.

Maaskant, M. A., van den Akker, M., Kessels, A. G. H., Haveman, M. J., van Schrojenstein Lantman-de Valk, H. M. J., et al. (1996). Care dependence and activities of daily living in relation to ageing: Results of a longitudinal study. *Journal of Intellectual Disability Research, 40,* 533–543.

Mansell, J., Ashman, B., Macdonald, S., & Beadle-Brown, J. (2002). Residential care in the community for adults with intellectual disability: Needs, characteristics and services. *Journal of Intellectual Disability Research, 46,* 625–633.

Mansell, J., Beadle-Brown, J., MacDonald, S., & Ashman, B. (2003). Functional grouping in residential homes for people with intellectual disabilities. *Research in Developmental Disabilities, 24,* 170–182.

Mansell, J., Elliott, T., Beadle-Brown, J., Ashman, B., & Macdonald, S. (2002). Engagement for meaningful activity and "active support" of people with intellectual disabilities in residential care. *Research in Developmental Disabilities, 23,* 342–352.

Matson, J. L. (1995). Matson evaluation of social skills for individuals with severe retardation. Baton Rouge, LA: Scientific Publishers.

Matson, J. L., Bielecki, J., Mayville, E. A., Smalls, Y., Bamburg, J. W., & Baglio, C. S. (1999). The development of a reinforcer choice assessment scale for persons with severe and profound mental retardation. *Research in Developmental Disabilities, 20,* 379–384.

Matson, J. L., Carlisle, C. B., & Bamburg, J. W. (1998). The convergent validity of the Matson Evaluation of Social Skills for Individuals with Severe Retardation (MESSIER). *Research in Developmental Disabilities, 19,* 493–500.

Matson, J. L., Dixon, D. R., Matson, M. L., & Logan, J. R. (2005). Classifying mental retardation and specific strength and deficit areas in severe and profoundly mentally retarded persons with the MESSIER. *Research in Developmental Disabilities, 26,* 41–45.

Matson, J. L., Mayville, S. B., & Laud, R. B. (2003). A system of assessment for adaptive behavior, social skills, behavioral function, medication side-effects, and psychiatric disorders. *Research in Developmental Disabilities, 24,* 75–81.

Matson, J. L., Rush, K. S., Hamilton, M., Anderson, S. J., Bamburg, J. W., & Baglio, C. S. (1999). Characteristics of depression as assessed by the Diagnostic Assessment for the Severely Handicapped-II (DASH-II). *Research in Developmental Disabilities, 20,* 305–313.

Matson, J. L., & Smiroldo, B. B. (1997). Validity of the mania subscale of the Diagnostic Assessment for the Severely Handicapped-II (DASH-II). *Research in Developmental Disabilities, 18,* 221–225.

Mazzocco, M. M. M., Baumgardner, T., Freund, L. S., & Reiss, A. L. (1998). Social functioning among girls with Fragile X or Turner syndrome and their sisters. *Journal of Autism and Developmental Disorders, 28,* 509–517.

McCarron, M., Gill, M., Lawlor, B., & Beagly, C. (2002). A pilot study of the reliability and validity of the Caregiver Activity Survey – Intellectual Disability (CAS-ID). *Journal of Intellectual Disability Research, 46,* 605–612.

McCarthy, J., & Boyd, J. (2001). Psychopathology and young people with Down's syndrome: Childhood predictors and adult outcome of disorder. *Journal of Intellectual Disability Research, 45,* 99–105.

McCarthy, J., & Boyd, J. (2002). Mental health services and young people with intellectual disability: Is it time to do better? *Journal of Intellectual Disability Research, 46,* 250–256.

McDermott, S., Martin, M., Weinrich, M., & Kelly, M. (1999). Program evaluation of a sex education curriculum for women with mental retardation. *Research in Developmental Disabilities, 20,* 93–106.

McIntyre, L. L., Blacher, J., & Baker, B. L. (2002). Behaviour/mental health problems in young adults with intellectual disability: The impact on families. *Journal of Intellectual Disability Research, 46,* 239–249.

Mervis, S. B., Klein-Tasman, B. P., & Mastin, M. E. (2001). Adaptive behavior of 4-through 8-year-old children with Williams syndrome. *American Journal on Mental Retardation, 106,* 82–93.

Miller, M. L., Fee, V. E., & Netterville, A. K. (2004). Psychometric properties of ADHD rating scales among children with mental retardation I: Reliability. *Research in Developmental Disabilities, 25,* 459–476.

Miltiades, H. B., & Pruchno, R. (2001). Mothers of adults with developmental disability: Change over time. *American Journal on Mental Retardation, 106,* 548–561.

Moss, J., Oliver, C., Hall, S., Arron, K., Sloneem, J., & Petty, J. (2005). The association between environmental events and self-injurious behaviour in Cornelia de Lange syndrome. *Journal of Intellectual Disability Research, 49,* 269–277.

Moss, S., & Patel, P. (1997). Dementia in older people with intellectual disability: Symptoms of physical and mental illness, and levels of adaptive behavior. *Journal of Intellectual Disability Research, 41,* 60–69.

Moss, S., Prosser, H., Costello, H., Simpson, N., Patel, P., Rowe, S., et al. (1998). Reliability and validity of the PAS-ADD Checklist for detecting psychiatric disorders in adults with intellectual disability. *Journal of Intellectual Disability Research, 42,* 173–183.

Mount, R. H., Charman, T., Hastings, R. P., Reilly, S., & Cass, H. (2003). Features of autism in Rett syndrome and severe mental retardation. *Journal of Autism and Developmental Disorders, 33,* 435–442.

Mudford, O. C., Cross, B. A., Breen, S., Cullen, C., Reeves, D., Gould, J., et al. (2000). Auditory integration training for children with autism: No behavioral benefits detected. *American Journal on Mental Retardation, 105,* 118–129.

Murphy, G., Hall, S., Oliver, C., & Kissi-Debra, R. (1999). Identification of early self-injurious behavior in young children with intellectual disability. *Journal of Intellectual Disability Research, 43,* 149–163.

Nachshen, J. S., Woodford, L., & Minnes, P. (2003). The Family Stress and Coping Interview for families of individuals with developmental disabilities: A lifespan perspective on family adjustment. *Journal of Intellectual Disability Research, 47,* 285–290.

Niccols, A., Atkinson, L., & Pepler, D. (2003). Mastery motivation in young children with Down's syndrome: Relations with cognitive and adaptive competence. *Journal of Intellectual Disability Research, 47,* 121–133.

Nihira, K., Leland, H., & Lambert, N. (1993). AAMR Adaptive Behavior Scale –Residential and Community Version (2nd ed.). Austin, TX: Pro-Ed.

Njardvik, U., Matson, J. L., & Cherry, K. E. (1999). A comparison of social skills in adults with autistic disorder, pervasive developmental disorder not otherwise specified, and mental retardation. *Journal of Autism and Developmental Disorders, 29,* 287–295.

Oliver, C., Crayton, L., Holland, A., & Hall, S. (2000). Cognitive deterioration in adults with Down syndrome: Effects on the individual, caregivers, and service use. *American Journal on Mental Retardation, 105,* 455–465.

Oliver, C., Demetriades, L., & Hall, S. (2002). Effects of environmental events on smiling and laughing behavior in Angelman syndrome. *American Journal on Mental Retardation, 107,* 194–200.

Oliver, C., Hall, S., & Murphy, G. (2005). The early development of self-injurious behaviour: Evaluating the role of social reinforcement. *Journal of Intellectual Disability Research, 49,* 591–599.

Oliver, C., Holland, T., Hall, S., & Crayton, L. (2005). Effects of increasing task load on memory impairment in adults with Down syndrome. *American Journal on Mental Retardation, 110,* 339–345.

Oliver, C., Murphy, G., Hall, S., Arron, K., & Leggett, J. (2003). Phenomenology of self-restraint. *American Journal on Mental Retardation, 108,* 71–81.

O'Reilly, M. F., & Lancioni, G. E. (2001). Treating food refusal in a child with Williams syndrome using the parent as therapist in the home setting. *Journal of Intellectual Disability Research, 45,* 41–46.

O'Reilly, M., Sigafoos, J., Lancioni, G., Edrisinha, C., & Andrews, A. (2005). An examination of the effects of a classroom activity schedule on levels of self-injury and engagement for a child with severe autism. *Journal of Autism and Developmental Disorders, 35,* 305–311.

Orsmond, G. I., Seltzer, M. M., Kraus, M. W., & Hong, J. (2003). Behavior problems in adults with mental retardation and maternal well-being: Examination of the direction of effects. *American Journal on Mental Retardation, 108,* 257–271.

Owen, D. M., Hastings, R. P., Noone, S. J., Chinn, J., Harman, K., Roberts, J., et al. (2004). Life events as correlates of problem behavior and mental health in a residential population of adults with developmental disabilities. *Research in Developmental Disabilities, 25,* 309–320.

Ozonoff, S., Cook, I., Coon, H., Dawson, G., Joseph, R. M., Klin, A., et al. (2004). Performance on Cambridge Neuropsychological Test Automated Battery subtests sensitive to frontal lobe function in people with Autistic Disorder: Evidence from the Collaborative Programs of Excellence in Autism network. *Journal of Autism and Developmental Disorders, 34,* 139–150.

Panerai, S., Ferrante, L., & Zingale, M. (2002). Benefits of the Treatment and Education of Autistic and Communication Handicapped Children (TEACCH) programme as compared with a non-specific approach. *Journal of Intellectual Disability Research, 46,* 318–327.

Paul, R., Augustyn, A., Klin, A., & Volkmar, F. R. (2005). Perception and production of prosody by speakers with Autism Spectrum Disorders. *Journal of Autism and Developmental Disorders, 35,* 205–220.

Paul, R., Miles, S., Cicchetti, D., Sparrow, S., Klin, A., Volkmar, F., et al. (2004). Adaptive behavior in autism and pervasive developmental disorder-not otherwise specified: Microanalysis of scores on the Vineland Adaptive Behavior Scales. *Journal of Autism and Developmental Disorders, 34,* 223–228.

Paul, R., Shriberg, L. D., McSweeny, J., Cicchetti, D., Klin, A., & Volkmar, F. (2005). Relations between prosodic performance and communication and socialization ratings in high functioning speakers with Autism Spectrum Disorders. *Journal of Autism and Developmental Disorders, 35,* 861–869.

Perry, A., Condillac, R. A., Freeman, N. L., Dunn-Geier, J., & Belair, J. (2005). Multi-site study of the Childhood Autism Rating Scale (CARS) in five clinical groups of young children. *Journal of Autism and Developmental Disorders, 35,* 625–634.

Perry, J., & Felce, D. (2005a). Correlation between subjective and objective measures of outcome in staffed community housing. *Journal of Intellectual Disability Research, 49,* 278–287.

Perry, J., & Felce, D. (2005b). Factors associated with outcome in community group homes. *American Journal on Mental Retardation, 110,* 121–135.

Pogson, D. (1997). Issues for consideration in dihydropteridine reductase (DHPR) deficiency: A variant form of hyperphenylaninaemia. *Journal of Intellectual Disability Research, 41,* 208–214.

Pollingue, A. (1987). Adaptive behavior and low incidence handicaps: Use of adaptive behavior instruments for persons with physical handicaps. *The Journal of Special Education, 21,* 117–125.

Prasher, V. P., Chung, M. C., & Haque, M. S. (1998). Longitudinal changes in adaptive behavior in adults with Down syndrome: Interim findings from a longitudinal study. *American Journal on Mental Retardation, 103,* 40–46.

Prasher, V. P., Chowdhury, T. A., Rowe, B. R., & Bain, S. C. (1997). ApoE genotype and Alzheimer's disease in adults with Down syndrome: Meta-analysis. *American Journal on Mental Retardation, 102,* 103–110.

Prasher, V., Farooq, A., & Holder, R. (2004). The Adaptive Behaviour Dementia Questionnaire (ABDQ): Screening questionnaire for dementia in Alzheimer's disease in adults with Down syndrome. *Research in Developmental Disabilities, 25,* 385–397.

Prasher, V. P., & Hall, W. (1996). Short-term prognosis of depression in adults with Down's syndrome: Association with thyroid status and effects on adaptive behaviour. *Journal of Intellectual Disability Research, 40,* 32–38.

Prosser, H., Moss, S., Costello, H., Simpson, N., Patel, P., & Rowe, S. (1998). Reliability and validity of the Mini PAS-ADD for assessing psychiatric disorders in adults with intellectual disabilities. *Journal of Intellectual Disability Research, 42,* 264–272.

Pruchno, R. A., & McMullen, W. F. (2004). Patterns of service utilization by adults with a developmental disability: Type of service makes a difference. *American Journal on Mental Retardation, 109,* 362–378.

Reschly, D. J., Myers, T. G., & Hartel, C. R. (2002). Mental Retardation: Determining Eligibility for Social Security Benefits. Washington, D.C.: National Academy Press.

Rellini, E., Tortolani, D., Trillo, S., Carbone, S., & Montecchi, F. (2004). Childhood Autism Rating Scale (CARS) and Autism Behavior Checklist (ABC) correspondence and conflicts with DSM-IV criteria in diagnosis of autism. *Journal of Autism and Developmental Disorders, 34,* 703–708.

Ricci, L. A., & Hodapp, R. M. (2003). Fathers of children with Down's syndrome versus other types of intellectual disability: Perceptions, stress and involvement. *Journal of Intellectual Disability Research, 47,* 273–284.

Richards, D. F., Williams, W. L., & Follette, W. C. (2002). Two new empirically derived reasons to use the Assessment of Basic Learning Abilities. *American Journal on Mental Retardation, 107,* 329–339.

Roberts, J. E., Mirrett, P., & Burchinal, M. (2001). Receptive and expressive communication development of young males with Fragile X syndrome. *American Journal on Mental Retardation, 106,* 216–230.

Robertson, J., Emerson, E., Gregory, N., Hatton, C., Kessissoglou, S., & Hallam, A. (2000). Receipt of psychotropic medication by people with intellectual disability in residential settings. *Journal of Intellectual Disability Research, 44,* 666–676.

Robertson, J., Emerson, E., Pinkney, L., Caesar, E., Felce, D., Meek, A., et al. (2004). Quality and costs of community-based residential supports for people with mental retardation and challenging behavior. *American Journal on Mental Retardation, 109,* 332–344.

Robertson, J., Emerson, E., Pinkney, L., Caesar, E., Felce, D., Meek, A., et al. (2005). Treatment and management of challenging behaviours in congregate and noncongregate community-based supported accommodation. *Journal of Intellectual Disability Research, 49,* 63–72.

Rogers, S. J., Hepburn, S., & Wehner, E. (2003). Parent reports of sensory symptoms in toddlers with autism and those with other developmental disorders. *Journal of Autism and Developmental Disorders, 33,* 631–642.

Rogers, T., Kalaydjieva, L., Hallmayer, J., Petersen, P. B., Nicholas, P., Pingree, C., et al. (1999). Exclusion of linkage to the HLA region in ninety multiplex sibships with autism. *Journal of Autism and Developmental Disorders, 29,* 195–201.

Rojahn, J. (1986). Self-injurious behavior and stereotypic behavior in non-institutionalized mentally retarded people. *American Journal of Mental Deficiency, 91,* 268–276.

Romski, M. A., Sevcik, R. A., & Adamson, L. B. (1999). Communication patterns of youth with mental retardation with and without their speech-output communication devices. *American Journal on Mental Retardation, 104,* 249–259.

Romski, M. A., Sevcik, R. A., Adamson, L. B., & Bakeman, R. A. (2005). Communication patterns of individuals with moderate or severe cognitive disabilities: Interactions with unfamiliar partners. *American Journal on Mental Retardation, 110,* 226–238.

Rose, J., Jones, F., & Fletcher, B. (1998). Investigating the relationship between stress and worker behaviour. *Journal of Intellectual Disability Research, 42,* 163–172.

Ross, D. E., & Greer, R. D. (2003). Generalized imitation and the mand: Inducing first instances of speech in young children with autism. *Research in Developmental Disabilities, 24,* 58–74.

Rousey, A. M., Wild, M., & Blacher, J. (2002). Stability of measures of the home environment for families of children with severe disabilities. *Research in Developmental Disabilities, 23,* 17–35.

Sallows, G. O., & Graupner, T. D. (2005). Intensive behavioral treatment for children with autism: Four-year outcome and predictors. *American Journal on Mental Retardation, 110,* 417–438.

Saloviita, T., Itälinna, M., & Leinonen, E. (2003). Explaining the parental stress of fathers and mothers caring for a child with intellectual disability: A Double ABCX Model. *Journal of Intellectual Disability Research, 47,* 300–312.

Schwartz, C., & Rabinovitz, S. (2003). Life satisfaction of people with intellectual disability living in community residences: Perceptions of the residents, their parents and staff members. *Journal of Intellectual Disability Research, 47,* 75–84.

Schupf, N., Zigman, W., Kapell, D., Lee, J. H., Kline, J., & Levin, B. (1997). Early menopause in women with Down's syndrome. *Journal of Intellectual Disability Research, 41,* 264–267.

Seal, B. C., & Bonvillian, J. D. (1997). Sign language and motor functioning in students with autistic disorder. *Journal of Autism and Developmental Disorders, 27,* 437–466.

Sicotte, C., & Stemberger, R. M. T. (1999). Do children with PDDNOS have a theory of mind? *Journal of Autism and Developmental Disorders, 29,* 225–233.

Silverman, W., Schupf, N., Zigman, W., Devenny, D., Miezejeski, C., Schubert, R., et al. (2004). Dementia in adults with mental retardation: Assessment at a single point in time. *American Journal on Mental Retardation, 109,* 111–125.

Simon, E. W., Rosen, M., & Ponpipom, A. (1996). Age and IQ as predictors of emotion identification in adults with mental retardation. *Research in Developmental Disabilities, 17,* 383–389.

Simpson, N. (2003). Delirium in adults with intellectual disabilities and DC-LD. *Journal of Intellectual Disability Research, 47,* 38–42.

Skinner, D. G., Correa, V., Skinner, M., & Bailey, D. B. Jr. (2001). Role of religion in the lives of latino families of young children with developmental delays. *American Journal on Mental Retardation, 106,* 297–313.

Smith, C., Felce, D., Ahmed, Z., Fraser, W. I., Kerr, M., Kiernan, C., et al. (2002). Sedation effects on responsiveness: Evaluating the reduction of antipsychotic medication in people with intellectual disability using a conditional probability approach. *Journal of Intellectual Disability Research, 46,* 464–471.

Smith, C., Felce, D., Jones, E., & Lowe, K. (2002). Responsiveness to staff support: Evaluating the impact of individual characteristics on the effectiveness of active support training using a conditional probability approach. *Journal of Intellectual Disability Research, 46,* 594–604.

Smith, E. A., & Van Houten, R. (1996). A comparison of the characteristics of self-stimulatory behaviors in "normal" children and children with developmental delays. *Research in Developmental Disabilities, 17,* 253–268.

Smith, T., Eikeseth, S., Klevstrand, M., & Lovaas, O. I. (1997). Intensive behavioral treatment of preschoolers with severe mental retardation and pervasive developmental disorder. *American Journal on Mental Retardation, 102,* 238–249.

Smith, T., Groen, A. D., & Wynn, J. W. (2000). Randomized trial of intensive early intervention for children with Pervasive Developmental Disorder. *American Journal on Mental Retardation, 105,* 269–285.

South, M., Williams, B. J., McMahon, W. M., Owley, T., Filipek, P. A., Shernoff, E., et al. (2002). Utility of the Gilliam Autism Rating Scale in research and clinical populations. *Journal of Autism and Developmental Disorders, 32,* 593–599.

Sparrow, S. S., Balla, D. A., & Cicchetti, D. V. (1984). Vineland Adaptive Behavior Scales. Circle Pines, MN: American Guidance Service.

Sparrow, S. S., Cicchetti, D. V., & Balla, D. A. (2005). Vineland Adaptive Behavior Scales (2nd ed.). Circle Pines, MN: American Guidance Service.

Spreat, S. (1999). Psychometric standards for adaptive behavior assessment. In Schalock R.L. (Ed.), Adaptive Behavior and Its Measurement: Implications for the Field of Mental Retardation. Washington, DC: AAMR.

Spreat, S., & Conroy, J. (2002). The impact on deinstitutionalization on family contact. *Research in Developmental Disabilities, 23,* 202–210.

Spreat, S., Conroy, J., & Fullerton, A. (2005). A cost–benefit analysis of community and institutional placements for persons with mental retardation in Oklahoma. *Research in Developmental Disabilities, 26,* 17–31.

Spreat, S., Conroy, J., & Rice, D. M. (1998). Improve quality in nursing homes or institute community placement? Implementation of OBRA for individuals with mental retardation. *Research in Developmental Disabilities, 19,* 507–518.

Stancliffe, R. J., Abery, B. H., & Smith, J. (2000). Personal control and the ecology of community living settings: Beyond living-unit size and type. *American Journal on Mental Retardation, 105,* 431–454.

Stancliffe, R. J., & Hayden, M. F. (1998). Longitudinal study of institutional downsizing: Effects on individuals who remain in the institution. *American Journal on Mental Retardation, 102,* 500–510.

Stancliffe, R. J., Hayden, M. F., Larson, S. A., & Lakin, K. C. (2002). Longitudinal study on the adaptive and challenging behaviors of deinstitutionalized adults with mental retardation. *American Journal on Mental Retardation, 107,* 302–320.

Stancliffe, R. J., & Lakin, K. C. (1998). Analysis of expenditures and outcomes of residential alternatives for persons with developmental disabilities. *American Journal on Mental Retardation, 102,* 552–568.

Starr, E., Szatmari, P., Bryson, S., & Zwaigenbaum, L. (2003). Stability and change among high-functioning children with Pervasive Developmental Disorders: A 2-year outcome study. *Journal of Autism and Developmental Disorders, 33,* 15–22.

Stella, J., Mundy, P., & Tuchman, R. (1999). Social and nonsocial factors in the Childhood Autism Rating Scale. *Journal of Autism and Developmental Disorders, 29,* 307–317.

Stephens, D. L., Collins, M. D., & Dodder, R. A. (2005). A longitudinal study of employment and skill acquisition among individuals with developmental disabilities. *Research in Developmental Disabilities, 26,* 469–486.

Stone, W. L., Ousley, O. Y., Hepburn, S. L., Hogan, K. L., & Brown, C. S. (1999). Patterns of adaptive behavior in very young children with autism. *American Journal on Mental Retardation, 104,* 187–199.

Sudhalter, V., & Belser, R. C. (2001). Conversational characteristics of children with Fragile X syndrome: Tangential language. *American Journal on Mental Retardation, 106,* 389–400.

Szatmari, P., Archer, L., Fisman, S., & Streiner, D. L. (1994). Parent and teacher agreement in the assessment of pervasive developmental disorders. *Journal of Autism and Developmental Disorders, 24,* 703–717.

Taubman, M., Brierley, S., Wishner, J., Baker, D., McEachin, J., & Leaf, R. B. (2001). The effectiveness of a group discrete trial instructional approach for preschoolers with developmental disabilities. *Research in Developmental Disabilities, 22,* 205–219.

Temple, V., Jozsvai, E., Konstantareas, M. M., & Hewitt, T. A. (2001). Alzheimer dementia in Down's syndrome: The relevance of cognitive ability. *Journal of Intellectual Disability Research, 45,* 47–55.

Thompson, J. R., McGrew, K. S., & Bruininks, R. H. (1999). Adaptive and maladaptive behavior: Functional and structural characteristics. In R. L. Schalock (Ed.), Adaptive Behavior and Its Measurement: Implications for the Field of Mental Retardation. Washington, DC: American Association on Mental Retardation.

Thompson, R. J., & Bolton, P. F. (2003). Angelman syndrome in an individual with a small SMC(15) and paternal uniparental disomy: A case report with reference to the assessment of cognitive functioning and autistic symptomatology. *Journal of Autism and Developmental Disorders, 33,* 171–176.

Tombokan-Runtukahu, J., & Nitko, A. J. (1992). Translation, cultural adjustment, and validation of a measure of adaptive behavior. *Research in Developmental Disabilities, 13,* 481–501.

Tsatsanis, K. D., Dartnall, N., Cicchetti, D., Sparrow, S. S., Klin, A., & Volkmar, F. R. (2003). Concurrent validity and classification accuracy of the Leiter and Leiter-R in low-functioning children with autism. *Journal of Autism and Developmental Disorders, 33,* 23–30.

Turk, J., & Cornish, K. (1998). Face recognition and emotion perception in boys with fragile-X syndrome. *Journal of Intellectual Disability Research, 42,* 490–499.

Turner, W. D., Realon, R. E., Irvin, D., & Robinson, E. (1996). The effects of implementing program consequences with a group of individuals who engaged in sensory maintained hand mouthing. *Research in Developmental Disabilities, 17,* 311–330.

Udwin, O., Howlin, P., Davies, M., & Mannion, E. (1998). Community care for adults with Williams syndrome: How families cope and the availability of support networks. *Journal of Intellectual Disability Research, 42,* 238–245.

Urv, T. K., Zigman, W. B., & Silverman, W. (2003). Maladaptive behaviors related to adaptive decline in aging adults with mental retardation. *American Journal on Mental Retardation, 108,* 327–339.

Van Bourgondien, M. E., Reichle, N. C., Campbell, D. G., & Mesibov, G. B. (1998). The Environmental Rating Scale (ERS): A measure of the quality of the residential environment for adults with autism. *Research in Developmental Disabilities, 19,* 391–394.

Van Bourgondien, M. E., Reichle, N. C., & Schopler, E. (2003). Effects of a model treatment approach on adults with autism. *Journal of Autism and Developmental Disorders, 33,* 131–140.

VanMeter, L., Fein, D., Morris, R., Waterhouse, L., & Allen, D. (1997). Delay versus deviance in autistic social behavior. *Journal of Autism and Developmental Disorders, 27,* 557–569.

Veltman, M. W. M., Thompson, R. J., Craig, E. E., Dennis, N. R., Roberts, S. E., Moore, V., Browne, J. A., & Bolton, P. F. (2005). A paternally inherited duplication in the Prader-Willi/Angelman syndrome critical region: A case and family study. *Journal of Autism and Developmental Disorders, 35,* 117–127.

Verri, A., Uggetti, C., Vallero, E., Ceroni, M., & Federico, A. (2000). Oral self-mutilation in a patient with rhombencephalosynapsys. *Journal of Intellectual Disability Research, 44,* 86–90.

Voelker, S., Shore, D., Hakim-Larson, J., & Bruner, D. (1997). Discrepancies in parent and teacher ratings of adaptive behavior of children with multiple disabilities. *Mental Retardation, 35,* 10–17.

Wall, M. E., & Gast, D. L. (1999). Acquisition of incidental information during instruction for a response-chain skill. *Research in Developmental Disabilities, 20,* 31–50.

Wallace, R. A., Schluter, P. J., & Webb, P. M. (2004). Effects of Helicobacter pylori eradication among adults with intellectual disability. *Journal of Intellectual Disability Research, 48,* 646–654.

Wallace, R. A., Webb, P. M., & Schluter, P. J. (2002). Environmental, medical, behavioural and disability factors associated with Helicobacter pylori infection in adults with intellectual disability. *Journal of Intellectual Disability Research, 46,* 51–60.

Walsh, K. K., & Shenouda, N. (1999). Correlations among the Reiss Screen, the Adaptive Behavior Scale Part II, and the Aberrant Behavior Checklist. *American Journal on Mental Retardation, 104,* 236–248.

Waterhouse, L., Morris, R., Allen, D., Dunn, M., Fein, D., Feinstein, C., et al. (1996). Diagnosis and classification in autism. *Journal of Autism and Developmental Disorders, 26,* 59–86.

Weber, A. M., Egelhoff, J. C., McKellop, J. M., & Franz, D. N. (2000). Autism and the cerebellum: Evidence from tuberous sclerosis. *Journal of Autism and Developmental Disorders, 30,* 511–517.

Weiss, J., Diamond, T., Demark, J., & Lovald, B. (2003). Involvement in Special Olympics and its relations to self-concept and actual competency in participants with developmental disabilities. *Research in Developmental Disabilities, 24,* 281–305.

Werner, E., Dawson, G., Munson, J., & Osterling, J. (2005). Variation in early developmental course in autism and its relation with behavioral outcome at 3–4 years of age. *Journal of Autism and Developmental Disorders, 35,* 337–350.

Werner, E., Dawson, G., Osterling, J., & Dinno, N. (2000). Recognition of Autism Spectrum Disorder before one year of age: A retrospective study based on home videotapes. *Journal of Autism and Developmental Disorders, 30,* 157–162.

Wetherby, A. M., Woods, J., Allen, L., Cleary, J., Dickinson, H., & Lord, C. (2004). Early indicators of Autism Spectrum Disorders in the second year of life. *Journal of Autism and Developmental Disorders, 34,* 473–493.

Williams, K. C. (1996). Piagetian principles: Simple and effective application. *Journal of Intellectual Disability Research, 40,* 110–119.

Williams, K. R., Wishart, J. G., Pitcairn, T. K., & Willis, D. S. (2005). Emotion recognition by children With Down syndrome: Investigation of specific impairments and error patterns. *American Journal on Mental Retardation, 110,* 378–392.

Wilson, C., Seaman, L., & Nettlebeck, T. (1996). Vulnerability to criminal exploitation: Influence of interpersonal competence differences among people with mental retardation. *Journal of Intellectual Disability Research, 40,* 8–16.

Yalon-Chamovitz, S., & Greenspan, S. (2005). Ability to identify, explain and solve problems in everyday tasks: Preliminary validation of a direct video measure of practical intelligence. *Research in Developmental Disabilities, 26,* 219–230.

Young, L., & Ashman, A. F. (2004). Deinstitutionalization for older adults with severe mental retardation: Results from Australia. *American Journal on Mental Retardation, 109,* 397–412.

Zanolli, K., Daggett, J., & Adams, T. (1996). Teaching preschool age autistic children to make spontaneous initiations to peers using priming. *Journal of Autism and Developmental Disorders, 26,* 407–422.

Zappella, M., Gillberg, C., & Ehlers, S. (1998). The preserved speech variant: A subgroup of the Rett complex: A clinical report of 30 cases. *Journal of Autism and Developmental Disorders, 28,* 519–526.

Zarcone, J. R., Crosland, K., Fisher, W. W., Worsdell, A. S., & Herman, K. (1999). A brief method for conducting a negative-reinforcement assessment. *Research in Developmental Disabilities, 20,* 107–124.

Zarcone, J. R., Hellings, J. A., Crandall, K., Reese, R. M., Marquis, J., & Fleming, K. (2001). Effects of risperidone on aberrant behavior of persons with developmental disabilities: I. A double-blind crossover study using multiple measures. *American Journal on Mental Retardation, 106,* 525–538.

Zigman, W. B., Schupf, N., Devenny, D. A., Miezejeski, C., Ryan, R., Urv, T. K., et al. (2004). Incidence and prevalence of dementia in elderly adults with mental retardation without Down syndrome. *American Journal on Mental Retardation, 109,* 126–141.

Zigman, W. B., Schupf, N., Urv, T., Zigman, A., & Silverman, W. (2002). Incidence and temporal patterns of adaptive behavior change in adults with mental retardation. *American Journal on Mental Retardation, 107,* 161–174.

Zwaigenbaum, L., Sonnenberg, L. K., Heshka, T., Eastwood, S., & Xu, J. (2005). A girl with Pervasive Developmental Disorder and complex chromosome rearrangement involving 8p and 10p. *Journal of Autism and Developmental Disorders, 35,* 393–399.

Zwaigenbaum, L., Szatmari, P., Mahoney, W., Bryson, S., Bartolucci, G., & MacLean, J. (2000). High functioning autism and Childhood Disintegrative Disorder in half brothers. *Journal of Autism and Developmental Disorders, 30,* 121–126.

Educational Assessment

MARK F. O'REILLY

DEPARTMENT OF SPECIAL EDUCATION, THE UNIVERSITY OF TEXAS AT AUSTIN, AUSTIN, TEXAS

BONNIE O'REILLY

GULLETT ELEMENTARY SCHOOL, AUSTIN INDEPENDENT SCHOOL DISTRICT, AUSTIN, TEXAS

JEFF SIGAFOOS AND VANESSA GREEN

DEPARTMENT OF EDUCATION, UNIVERSITY OF TASMANIA, HOBART TASMANIA, AUSTRALIA

GIULIO LANCIONI

DEPARTMENT OF PSYCHOLOGY, UNIVERSITY OF BARI, BARI, ITALY

WENDY MACHALICEK

DEPARTMENT OF SPECIAL EDUCATION, THE UNIVERSITY OF TEXAS AT AUSTIN AUSTIN, TEXAS

I. INTRODUCTION

Educational assessment is a vital component of the educational process for students with intellectual disabilities. Assessment is used when making decisions regarding educational placement, developing curriculum content, and

INTERNATIONAL REVIEW OF RESEARCH IN MENTAL RETARDATION, Vol. 34
0074-7750/07 $35.00

DOI: 10.1016/S0074-7750(07)34004-4

choosing instructional strategies. Students' progress through the curriculum, the student's quality of life, and the overall quality of the educational program are also subject to assessment.

Educational assessment may take several different forms depending on the purpose of the assessment. For example, a child may be assessed to diagnose a possible condition and to recommend an appropriate educational placement. Professionals such as psychologists or speech therapists conduct such assessments and will use the results of a combination of norm-referenced and criterion-referenced tests to make a recommendation. Norm-referenced instruments such as IQ tests can be used to assess the child's level of intellectual functioning. Some popular tests of intellectual functioning include the Bayley Scales of Infant Development II (Bayley, 1993) and the Stanford Binet Intelligence Scales (fifth edition) (Roid, 2003). Criterion-referenced tests such as the Adaptive Behavior Scale-School (second edition) (Lambert, Nihira, & Leland, 1993) and the Vineland Adaptive Behavior Scales (Sparrow, Balla, & Cicchetti, 1984) compare the student's levels of adaptive behavior (e.g., communication, social skills, daily living skills) to a predetermined level of mastery for a particular chronological age. Norm-referenced and criterion-referenced tests are described in great detail in Chapters 2 and 3 of this text and will not be discussed further in the current chapter.

The other major purpose of educational assessment revolves around the development and evaluation of a student's curriculum. This type of educational assessment is usually called an *informal* or *functional* assessment. A functional assessment is coordinated by the student's teacher(s). Information is gathered in a systematic manner from relevant others such as parents, previous teachers, and from other professionals such as occupational therapists, speech therapists, and psychologists. The student is also observed in relevant school environments (e.g., in the resource classroom, in the regular classroom, during lunch, and in community settings such as the grocery store). This systematic yet informal information-gathering process is used to identify functional age-appropriate skills that can be translated into a curriculum. The skills identified for teaching should be objective and measurable which allows for ongoing assessment of student progress throughout the academic year.

In this chapter we will focus on the process of conducting an informal or functional assessment of the student's environment in order to develop a curriculum that is amenable to ongoing evaluation.

II. LEGISLATION AND EDUCATIONAL ASSESSMENT

Educational assessment in public schools is profoundly influenced by legal requirements that have been enacted in legislation. The Individuals with Disabilities Education Act (IDEA, 1990; IDEA Amendments, 1997;

IDEA Improvement Act, 2004), formally entitled Public Law 94–142 (1975), protects the rights of students with disabilities to receive a free and appropriate public education (FAPE) that is created with their specific needs in mind, and provides specific guidelines for the assessment of students with intellectual disabilities. These IDEA-driven guidelines address many of the issues educators encounter when assessing students with intellectual disabilities, including: (a) the assessment process itself; (b) interdisciplinary team meetings; (c) educational goals and objectives; (d) the functional assessment of challenging behavior; (e) the determination of a student's least restrictive educational environment; (f) access to the general education curriculum; and (g) student involvement in the creation of the individualized education plan (IEP). Of specific interest are the guidelines that IDEA provides with regard to the development and evaluation of curricula for these students.

If tests of IQ or adaptive behavior scales are used they must not be discriminatory on a racial or cultural basis. Additionally, tests must be administered in the child's native language or primary mode of communication unless this is not feasible. The tests used must be valid and administered according to instructions by a trained professional. A variety of assessment tools must be used to determine appropriate educational placement and content of the student's curriculum. Educational placement decisions cannot be made on the basis of a single test.

Students with disabilities are entitled to an individualized education plan (IEP). This means that the educational goals for a student must be developed on an individual basis and must reflect the unique educational needs of the student. The IEP is developed by a team of individuals including parents and educational professionals. Parents should play a central role in the IEP process. Other key individuals involved in the process include the special educator, regular educator, and other disciplines that will be involved in the monitoring and delivery of the program. As the student gets older the makeup of this IEP team will change with the changing educational needs of the student. For example, transition specialists or vocational rehabilitation specialists will become involved once the student reaches 16 years. At this point the student should begin to prepare for adult life including work.

Educational goals of the IEP should be objective and measurable on an ongoing basis in order to determine whether the student is meeting these goals. Educators are required to use tools and strategies to assist in determining whether the student's educational needs are being satisfied. Hence, the IEP goals must be amenable to continuous assessment. In fact IDEA specifically requires that ongoing data be generated in the classroom and that this data should inform decision-making of the educational team. The student's educational goals are typically evaluated on an annual basis by the team, including the parents. At this annual meeting new educational goals are determined and earlier goals may be revised if they have not been achieved. Parents do have the right to call an IEP meeting at any period during the academic year to discuss their child's progress and possibly revise the IEP. The student's educational placement must be reevaluated at least every 3 years or earlier if there is some change in the student's performance (e.g., there might be a dramatic improvement or deterioration in the student's health).

Student themselves should be involved as much as possible in the IEP process. Involvement should not be limited to students who are higher functioning but may be extended to all students irrespective of disability. Given relatively recent developments in person-centered approaches to assessment (O'Brien, O'Brien, & Mount, 1997), effective and efficient strategies to assess choice and preference (Cannella, O'Reilly, & Lancioni, 2005), and a current emphasis on self-determination (Wehmeyer & Sands, 1998) students with severe and multiple disabilities should have some level of involvement in their own assessment process. We will discus these assessment strategies in detail in later sections of the chapter.

IDEA stipulates that the student's education should occur in the least restrictive environment. This means that to the maximum extent possible, a student should be educated with nondisabled peers. The law further stipulates that removal from the regular classroom should only occur when students cannot succeed in the regular classroom even with additional aids and support services. Furthermore, IDEA also requires that students participate to some degree in the general curriculum and that statewide assessments are adapted to assess performance on this curriculum. Access to the general curriculum by students with intellectual disabilities is also reflected in the No Child Left Behind Act (2001). These legislative requirements again set parameters with regard to IEP objectives and assessment strategies. Efforts must be made to adapt educational goals from the regular curriculum in meaningful ways for students with intellectual disabilities. Additionally, statewide assessment strategies must be adapted to incorporate regular educational goals within ecological or functional assessments.

Finally, IDEA identifies procedures for the assessment and support of students with intellectual disabilities who engage in challenging behavior. As many as 20% of individuals with intellectual disabilities engage in behaviors such as property destruction, self-injury, and aggression (Sigafoos, Arthur, & O'Reilly, 2003). Schools are required to conduct a functional behavioral assessment of the student's challenging behavior and implement a behavioral support plan based on the results of this assessment. It is important to note here that functional assessment has a very specific meaning when it comes to dealing with challenging behavior. Functional assessment of challenging behavior describes a series of assessment protocols that are designed to identify what may be influencing a student's challenging behavior. We use the term functional or informal assessment in a much broader sense in this chapter to describe an assessment process that is designed to identify and monitor a curriculum for a student. Assessment protocols used with challenging behavior are described in detail in Chapter 10.

This brief review of the IDEA legislation is by no means exhaustive. But it should give the reader an understanding of the legal parameters that school teachers, parents, and other professionals are working within when developing and conducting assessments with students with intellectual disabilities. In the remaining sections of this chapter we outline a process of functional assessment that is congruent with the assessment parameters laid down by this current legislation.

III. THE PROCESS OF ASSESSMENT

As mentioned previously, informal or functional assessment is conducted for two major reasons. First, such assessments are used to identify educational goals for the student for the upcoming academic year. In other words the student's curriculum is determined via this assessment. Second, student performance is continuously assessed during the academic year to ensure he or she is making adequate progress toward these educational goals. The major steps of educational assessment are outlined in the following sections.

A. Determining the Student's Current Strengths

The first step of any educational assessment is to get an accurate and comprehensive picture of the student's current levels of performance. For students with intellectual disabilities it is important to ascertain their skills within academic, leisure, domestic, and community domains. The first port of call for this information is to interview the previous teacher and to review the student's IEP from the previous year. The IEP will outline the previous educational goals and instructional objectives. It is usually instructive to review what educational goals were targeted in the IEP, what goals were met, and what instructional objectives remain to be achieved. We are by no means saying that educational goals from a previous IEP should be automatically transferred to a current IEP. However, it may be worthwhile discussing previous IEP goals with parents and previous teachers to determine whether they might be continued in the current IEP. It can also be helpful to review formal assessment results (i.e., IQ and adaptive behavior assessments) to get an overall view of the student's intellectual and adaptive functioning. This information can be helpful in determining the student's social skills, levels of receptive and expressive communication, the presence of challenging behavior, and so on. It is also worthwhile to interview the previous teacher to ascertain a picture of the student's typical school day the previous year. How much time did the student spend in inclusive settings or resource settings? What types of adaptations were made to the regular curriculum/instruction during inclusion activities? What types of additional supports were available in terms of personnel or assistive technology?

B. Interviewing Parents

It is a legal requirement that parents be involved in developing the IEP for their son or daughter. Specifically, parents should be present at an annual IEP meeting to provide input about educational goals and to approve the content of the IEP. This process can sometimes be daunting for parents. They may feel uncomfortable expressing their opinions among a group of professionals. It is important that interviewers place the parents at ease. Their input to the assessment process is invaluable. Also, instructional programming for students should span school, community, and family environments. Instructional gains made within a school environment may ultimately prove futile if parents are not working on these same goals with their child (Snell & Brown, 2006). Westling and Fox (2004) offer a set of guidelines for interviewing parents (see Fig. 1). These guidelines should enhance a respectful and productive interaction with most families.

The purpose of this initial interview(s) is to determine the parents' wishes in terms of educational goals for their child. It may be helpful for the teacher to meet individually with the parents prior to the IEP meeting in order to establish a trusting relationship and to inform parents of their central role in the educational planning process. Parents can be prepared to come to the subsequent IEP meeting with a list of educational goals that they wish to be addressed for the upcoming academic year.

Several strategies for planning the educational goals of students with intellectual disabilities have been proposed during the last two decades [Westling and Fox (2004) for a detailed review of these protocols]. Collectively, these strategies are typically called Person-Centered Plans. Some of the more popular person-centered planning approaches include Personal Futures Planning (Mount & Zwernik, 1988); the McGill Action Planning System (Vandercook, York, & Forest, 1989); and Choosing Options and Accommodations for Children (Giangreco, Cloninger, & Iverson, 1998).

While each of these person-centered planning approaches is different among a number of dimensions, they have a number of core common characteristics. The person with intellectual disabilities is central, in the sense that

1. Make an appointment with the parents at a time that is convenient for them and at a location of their choice, usually the school or their home.
2. Try to determine the familial and cultural values that exist within the family and show respect for them.
3. Attempt to build a relationship of trust, honesty, and openness with the family.
4. In order to facilitate the parent's opportunity to participate, if they wish, try to arrange child care for their child or children during the time of the meeting.
5. Avoid using professional jargon and displaying an air of arrogance. Show respect for the parents and be very open to their thoughts and opinions. Listen more than talk.
6. Arrive on time for scheduled meetings and only stay for a reasonable amount of time, usually no more than an hour.

Source: Westling and Fox (2004), Figure 6–1.

FIG. 1. Suggestions for interviewing parents.

they are actively involved, in all planning meetings. If the person with disabilities is unable to communicate for himself, a friend or relative who is able to interpret the person's wants and needs will facilitate communication during the meetings. A series of meetings and not a single meeting is required by the group to develop an initial person-centered plan. In addition to those who are typically required to attend IEP meetings the individual's circle of friends should also be present. This circle of friends includes individuals such as fellow students, additional family members such as grandparents, and other individuals who have personal and ongoing involvement with the student. The meetings then revolve around who the individual is (i.e., their place in the family, the classroom, among peers, in the community). Each person's dreams or goals for the individual are shared. The barriers to achieving these goals are discussed. Strategies for overcoming these barriers for achieving dreams or goals are then identified by the group.

A person-centered planning approach promotes the active involvement of family and friends in the IEP process. It facilitates consensus building in terms of developing educational goals. These educational goals can be more socially valid due to the active participation of the student and his or her circle of friends. Research has shown that parents are more positive about IEP conferences and participate more in these conferences when a person-centered approach is used. Unfortunately, the person-centered approach is not used very often in educational practice according to some preliminary research (Siegel & Allinder, 2005). This lack of widespread uptake of person-centered planning might be because it is a time-consuming process.

C. Incorporating Student Preference and Choice

Actively involving students with intellectual disabilities in the assessment, instructional, and evaluation process of their own education is an important agenda both in current educational legislation and in the special education professional literature (Snell & Brown, 2006; Wehmeyer & Sands, 1998). In fact, the person-centered planning process outlined in the previous section places the student at center stage when determining IEP goals. If educators are to involve students in determining their own IEP goals and in monitoring their own progress then strategies for acknowledging student preferences and incorporating student choice making must be included in the curriculum. It is important to clarify what is meant by choice and preference. Choice is the activity or behavior of engaging with an item, activity, or setting. Preference is said to be present when someone consistently chooses an item, activity, or setting. Choice and preference are therefore inextricably linked. Choice is the vehicle through which preferences are expressed.

While many students with intellectual disabilities are capable of voicing their own choices, other students with more severe disabilities may have very limited communication skills. This condition should not preclude these students from active involvement in the assessment process. In fact, there is a wealth of empirical literature that has documented a variety of effective assessment strategies for determining choice and preference for students with severe disabilities (Cannella, O'Reilly, & Lancioni, 2005; Lancioni, O'Reilly, & Emerson, 1996). Teachers should be familiar with and incorporate such assessment protocols to help determine IEP goals and select optimum instructional strategies. Choice and preference assessments should be incorporated on an ongoing basis throughout the academic year with these students to give them continuous opportunities to make new choices and identify new preferred items or activities. Additionally, persons with the most profound multiple disabilities are capable of making choices once the appropriate assistive technology is made available to them (Lancioni, Singh, O'Reilly, & Oliva, 2003; Lancioni, Singh, O'Reilly, Oliva, & Basili, 2005). It is therefore very important that schools and services make the appropriate assistive technology available to students with multiple disabilities in order to give them the opportunity to exercise choice.

Aside from the philosophical and legislative imperatives to actively involve students in their own assessment the research on choice and preference has demonstrated that such protocol can have many positive effects with students with severe disabilities (Cannella et al., 2005). Persons with the most severe multiple disabilities appear happier when they have the opportunities to make choices and engage in preferred activities or with preferred items (Lancioni, O'Reilly, Compodonico, & Mantini, 1998; Lancioni, O'Reilly, & Oliva, 2002). Challenging behavior can be reduced when students are given opportunities to make choices and engage in preferred activities (Cannella et al., 2005). Finally, active student involvement and student motivation seem to increase when students have the opportunity to choose between preferred activities (e.g., Hughes, Pitkin, & Lorden, 1998).

A number of choice assessment strategies are presented below. Prior to selecting any of these strategies the teacher should have a clear understanding of how the student indicates choice versus avoidance and positive versus negative emotions. This information can be obtained by observing the student over an extended period of time and/or interviewing parents and significant others. Approach responses can include such behaviors as moving toward an item, looking at the item consistently, touching the item, and so on. Avoidance responses may include such behaviors as not paying attention to the item, actively pushing the item away, moving away from the item, and so on. Positive affect might include such responses as smiling, giggling, and positive noises (as reported by significant others). Negative affect might include crying, screaming, moaning, or negative noises (as reported by significant others). Items that are consistently approached and are associated with positive affect may be considered preferred items. These behaviors can be assessed systematically across different settings or activities to gain a comprehensive picture of the items, settings, and tasks that are preferred by the student. Additionally, assessments need to be conducted in natural classroom or community settings (i.e., where the student will learn during the academic year) and the stimuli or activities to be assessed should be age-appropriate and reflect appropriate educational objectives.

Probably the simplest and most efficient assessment protocol to identify preferred items for students with severe disabilities is the brief stimulus preference assessment developed by Roane, Vollmer, Ringdahl, and Marcus, 1998. First, a series of items ($\sim$10 items) are identified that are hypothesized as preferred via interviews with parents, previous teachers, and significant others.

It is also important to periodically include one or two new items that the student has had no or little interaction with previously. This gives the student the opportunity to expand their horizons with opportunities to interact with and possibly express preference for novel items. Second, the student is given the opportunity to briefly interact with each of the items. Each item should be handed to the student and the teacher can help the student to operate the item (e.g., a vibrator and a tape recorder). This allows the student to have exposure to all the items individually prior to the preference assessment. The preference assessment itself then consists of simply placing all of the items on a table within access of the student. The student then has the opportunity to manipulate the items as she or he so wishes for 5 min. Every 10 sec during the 5-min period, the teacher should record what items the student is manipulating. The most preferred items would be the top three or four most manipulated items during the assessment. This simple assessment can be used to identify items that are preferred at the IEP planning stage. Additionally, this type of assessment could be used on a weekly basis during the school year to identify changes in student preferences.

To assess preference for activities or settings it is necessary to place the student in a setting or engage the student in the task and then systematically observe their levels of engagement and indices of happiness. Winking, O'Reilly, and Moon (1993) assessed preference for supported employment opportunities with four transition-aged students with autism and severe intellectual disabilities (janitorial, house keeping, dish washing) in a hotel. Prior to the assessment the authors identified how each of the participants expressed positive and negative affect by interviewing parents and teachers and by observing each of the students when they were engaged in pleasurable leisure activities (which presumably would be associated with expressions of positive affect). Each of the students was observed on a number of occasions as they performed each of the three jobs. Student preference for each of the jobs was determined by measuring their levels of positive (e.g., smiling, positive noises) and negative (e.g., hand biting, crying) affect as they performed each of the jobs. Each of the three students demonstrated idiosyncratic preferences. Such systematic assessments could also be conducted for classrooms tasks (academic, leisure) or instructional formats (individual versus group instruction).

When evaluating the results of preference assessments or completion of tasks, the teacher should consider possible setting events that may have temporarily altered the student's performance. For instance, if a student has been placed on a higher dose of seizure medication a couple of days before the preference assessment, the student may be more lethargic than usual and could have dampened, or unusual responses.

D. Incorporating Adaptive Behavior Scales and Curriculum Activity Guides into the IEP Planning Process

Earlier in the chapter we differentiated between assessment instruments that are primarily used in making educational placement decisions (IQ and adaptive behavior tests) from informal assessment procedures that are used primarily to develop and monitor curriculum content. An assessment of adaptive behavior must be completed for every student with intellectual disabilities. Adaptive behavior scales are typically administered by a professional such as an educational psychologist or behavioral diagnostician. The teacher will have the opportunity to access the results of such assessments from the student's file. The educational psychologist will be able to introduce the teacher to the adaptive behavior assessment and explain the results.

Adaptive behavior scales are designed to provide a general picture of the student's levels of performance in many major areas of daily life. Some of the areas that are typically assessed using adaptive behavior scales include daily living skills, social skills, motor skills, and communication skills. All adaptive behavior scales can give a general impression of a student's level of performance (relative to nondisabled students of his or her own age). This can be help guide discussion of IEP objectives. For example, a student may perform well on communication skills but may possess very poor social skills. There may therefore be a need to place more emphasis on selecting social skills goals for instruction over communication skills goals for the upcoming academic year.

Some adaptive behavior scales such as the Vineland Adaptive Behavior Scales (Sparrow et al., 1984) are very specific in terms of identifying behaviors that the student can and cannot do in the various domains of functioning (e.g., daily living, communication, and social skills). It may be possible to suggest specific skills for instruction within each of the performance domains based on a review of the student's performance on the Vineland Adaptive Behavior Scales. On the other hand, adaptive behavior scales may not be very helpful in terms of identifying instructional objectives with students with profound multiple disabilities. These students may be functioning at such low levels that these scales may pick up very little in terms of their functioning—resulting in a flat performance profile across all performance domains.

There are a variety of commercially available curriculum or functional skills guides that may be worthwhile consulting when developing IEP objectives. Similar to our discussion of the adaptive behavior scales above, these guides might be helpful in prompting the team, including parents, teachers, and other members to select functional age-appropriate goals for the student. For example, Wilcox and Bellamy (1987) published an activities catalog for high school students with severe disabilities. This catalog describes global activity goals in personal, daily activity, and work domains. The authors note that this catalog was composed in order to help teachers and parents to focus on inclusive and outcome-oriented goals instead of isolated skill clusters. The authors also emphasize that educational objectives for students with severe disabilities do not require an end goal of independent performance. Students with severe disabilities may productively participate in complex activities such as competitive employment with proper supports. These curriculum guides can help the IEP team to look beyond the disability to plan for age-appropriate functional goals for students with severe and multiple disabilities.

E. Conducting an Ecological Assessment

One of the most popular and enduring forms of functional assessment is that of the ecological inventory. This process of assessment was proposed in a seminal paper by Brown et al. (1979) and continues to be widely promoted as a method of informal assessment for students with intellectual disabilities (Snell & Brown, 2006; Westling & Fox, 2004). Ecological assessment basically involves the identification of the major environments in which the student will function in the upcoming academic year. The skills that the student will be required to perform in those environments are identified and prioritized. The tasks that are prioritized are then included as IEP goals for the upcoming academic year. This assessment process ensures that functional skills are selected for instruction. The reason for this is that the assessment process begins with identifying real world environments and then clarifies what skills the student needs to independently function in such environments. Of course all students (especially those with more severe disabilities) will not be able to independently function in many of these environments. This assessment process does identify functional and age-appropriate skills in which such students can participate with proper support.

In the last section we suggested that curriculum-based inventories and adaptive behavior scales might serve a similar purpose as the ecological inventory (i.e., identification of functional and age-appropriate goals). A significant advantage of the ecological inventory over lists of skills and activities is that it actually involves systematically observing the student in each of the targeted environments to develop an individualized inventory of that student's strengths and needs in each particular setting. In this respect the ecological inventory is more flexible than, for example, an activity catalog (Wilcox & Bellamy, 1987), which outlines a predetermined set of performance expectancies in each environment (i.e., work, leisure, community, and so on).

Furthermore, the model of skill building promoted by the ecological inventory is a top-down process. In other words, the ecological inventory is geared to identify functional and age-appropriate skills. Adaptive behavior instruments such as the Vineland Adaptive Behavior Scales approach assessment from a developmental perspective. Adaptive behavior assessments start with skills performed by infants and track skill development as it progresses developmentally. Using such a developmentally oriented assessment may produce educational goals that are nonfunctional and not age-appropriate. Therefore, curriculum-based inventories and adaptive behavior scales should be seen as supplements to an ecological inventory.

An ecological inventory begins with identifying a number of domains of functioning for the student. These domains should include critical environments in which the student currently functions or will function in the upcoming academic year. These domains usually include school, leisure, domestic, and vocational. There is some flexibility with regard to the domains chosen for assessment. For example, the vocational domain would not be relevant for a young child. Once domains are selected for a student, the assessment then involves a process of teasing out critical environments in those domains, the critical activities within these environments and the skills required to perform those activities. The assessment involves a five-step process:

1. Identify the core performance domains
2. Identify the environments in each of the domains
3. Divide the environments into subenvironments
4. Identify the critical activities within each subenvironment
5. Assess student performance on each of the critical skills

These five steps of an ecological assessment are outlined in the following sections. An example of using the ecological assessment for a student with severe disabilities is incorporated to help clarify the process.

Step 1: Identify the core domains. The core domains include the major activities and/or environments in which a person functions. As mentioned earlier, not all domains may be as relevant to a student at a given point in time in their lives. At any point in time in a person's life some domains may be more important than others. Prior to an ecological assessment it is vital to come to an agreement as to what domains should be included in an ecological assessment and what domains may have priority. This task of identifying, selecting, and prioritizing life domains can be completed as part of the person-centered planning process.

Example: *Shane is a 10-year-old boy with severe disabilities. He is currently attending fifth grade at a regular elementary school in a large urban area in the southwest United States. He is ambulatory but is confined to a wheelchair for some of the day due to congenital hip disorder. He has four words and is learning to use an AAC device to enhance his communication skills. He is not toilet trained and does not dress independently. He is learning to use a fork and spoon to eat independently. He drinks independently from an adapted cup. For a portion of the school day he attends a special classroom with students who have similar levels of disability. He is included in regular class with same-age peers for art, music, physical education, science, social studies, lunch, and recess (~70% of the school day). A person-centered plan was developed with Shane for the upcoming academic year. Some of the major educational priorities arising from the person-centered planning process included enhancing Shane's communication skills and increasing his overall skills/participation during leisure activities. The domains selected for ecological assessment for Shane for the upcoming academic year included Leisure/recreation, School, Community, and Domestic.*

Step 2: Identify the environments within each domain. The next step of the ecological assessment is to identify the environments within each domain in which the student learns, plays, and lives. This should not be an exhaustive search of all environments in each domain. Again, the student, teachers, and family should agree on core environments within each domain. This will allow for a clearer focus on instructional needs and supports that the student will require later in the process within each domain.

Example: The environments within each domain are outlined in Table I for Shane. There are more environments included under the Leisure/recreation domain than in the other domains. This emphasis on leisure skills instruction reflects the agenda of the previous person-centered plan for Shane. There is also overlap, with some environments included in several domains. When environments overlap across domains it means that these are priorities in terms of skill instruction and support for the student. These environments should have a particular emphasis when developing IEP goals and objectives.

TABLE I
CORE DOMAINS AND ENVIRONMENTS WITHIN EACH DOMAIN FOR SHANE

Core domains	Leisure/recreation	School	Domestic	Community
Environments	Joe's restaurant	Ridge River Elementary School	Home	Grocery store
	YMCA		Grandmother's home	YMCA
	Louie's go-carts, pizza and more			Church
	Home			Joe's restaurant
	Ridge River Elementary School			Louie's go-carts, pizza and more

TABLE II
SUBENVIRONMENTS OF EACH OF THE LEISURE ENVIRONMENTS FOR SHANE

Leisure environments	Joe's restaurant	YMCA	Louie's go-carts, pizza, and more	Home	Ridge River Elementary School
Subenvironments	Waiting area	Changing area	Go-cart track	Bedroom	Gym
	Table	Pool	Snack area	Playroom	Playground
	Bathroom	Shower	Video arcade	Backyard	
		Bathroom	Bathroom		

Step 3: Divide the environments into subenvironments. The next step then is to take each environment identified and break it into subenvironments. Each subenvironment will reflect a particular set of skills or activities needed by the student to participate or function independently.

Example: The subenvironments for each of the leisure environments are identified in Table II for Shane. For example, Shane goes to Joe's restaurant once a week with his dad and a friend from school. The major subenvironments in which Shane engages in activities at Joe's restaurant are at the table, in the bathroom, and in the waiting area. He goes to the YMCA with his sister and mother each week to swim. The main subenvironments in which he engages in activities at the YMCA include the changing area, pool, shower, and bathroom. The other leisure environments are broken down into key subenvironments using the same logic.

Step 4: Identify critical activities within each subenvironment. The next step is to list all of the activities that are required by the student within each subenvironment. These activities should be skills that the typical same-aged peer would be able to perform in that subenvironment. When conducting an assessment of the activities within each environment it is recommended that communication, choice, and social skills should be included as activities. Traditionally, ecological assessments have not included social and communication skills within the assessment process. More recent research has demonstrated the importance of teaching communication skills as part of ongoing natural routines (Sigafoos, Arthur-Kelly, & Butterfield, 2006). Additionally, it is important to include opportunities for choice as part of ongoing activities (Cannella et al., 2005). Therefore, the activities selected within this example of an ecological assessment reflect this emphasis on enhancing choice and communication skills for these students.

Example: The critical activities in each subenvironment are listed for Joe's Restaurant in Table III. There are a variety of activities within each subenvironment. Some activities differ across each subenvironment but others are common. Common activities and common environments should indicate that these environments

TABLE III

ACTIVITIES FOR EACH SUBENVIRONMENT WITHIN JOE'S RESTAURANT

Subenvironments	Waiting area	Table	Bathroom
Activities	Greeting others Waiting appropriately	Choosing/ordering items from menu Eating food with fork Drinking from cup Wiping mouth General Social/communication skills Waiting appropriately	Toileting Handwashing

and activities should have priority when it comes to developing instructional goals for the upcoming academic year. It is also important to note that there is a meld of social (e.g., greeting people), choice (e.g., selecting from the menu), communication (e.g., ordering food), and self-help (e.g., appropriately using a fork and cup) skills for Shane.

Step 5: Assess student performance on each of the critical skills. In the final step of the ecological assessment the teacher must describe or operationalize student behavior for each activity in such a manner that it can be measured. This step involves describing, in overt terms, what a student needs to do in order to perform each activity appropriately. Once this step is completed the teacher can obtain a clear picture of the student's performance levels on each of the activities. In other words, the teacher can now observe the student perform these behaviors in the targeted environments and subenvironments. This assessment can therefore allow the IEP team to pinpoint areas of strength (e.g., the student possesses many of the behaviors to perform a targeted activity) and weakness (e.g., the student may have few of the skills to perform a targeted activity). Areas of strength may need minimal instructional input, whereas the student will need ongoing instruction for other activities. The teacher is again able to prioritize instructional goals using this level of the assessment for the upcoming academic year.

Skills identified in each subenvironment can typically be broken into discrete behaviors or complex chains of behavior. A discrete behavior might include a communication or social skill. For example, the student may learn to greet the teacher ("Good morning, Ms. Shea!") when he/she arrives in the morning. In this example, greeting is a single oral response that occurs within a very specific context (when the student first arrives in the morning). Other skills may include complex chains of behavior. For example, the skill of hand washing may include turning on the faucet, wetting the hands, lathering the hands with soap, rubbing the hands together until dirt is removed, rinsing the hands, drying the hands, and so on. Student performance on each step of this skill should be assessed.

The assessment is usually conducted by observing the student perform the targeted skills in each subenvironment. The teacher should record whether or not each of the skills are performed correctly. It is advisable to observe the student perform the skills on at least two occasions. This assessment will give the IEP team a picture of the student's performance levels on each of the skills prior to instruction. It will also inform the teacher as to what types of instructional strategies might be best suited to teach different skills. A discussion of matching instructional strategies to targeted skills is beyond the scope of this chapter (see Snell & Brown, 2006).

Example: Two of the critical skills, choosing/ordering from the menu and eating with a fork, are presented in Tables IV and V, respectively. Shane has two preferred breakfast options on his AAC device (a picture of pancakes versus a picture of bacon and eggs). When the server greets him and asks for his order, Shane must choose from one of these breakfast options. He then chooses between milk and orange juice in a similar fashion (see Table IV). When the meal is served, Shane's dad cuts the food into bite-sized pieces. Shane then uses his fork to eat the food. He is learning to use a fork appropriately. Fork use is broken into a chain of responses. His performance has been assessed on these behaviors on two occasions. On both occasions he ordered his breakfast appropriately (see Table IV). He is experiencing some difficulties with fork use, especially holding the fork appropriately (see *Table V*).

IV. ONGOING ASSESSMENT

Up until this point in the chapter we have discussed a set of strategies that can be used to identify and prioritize meaningful and measurable educational goals for students with intellectual disabilities. Equally important is to establish a method of ongoing assessment of educational goals during the academic year. It is important to assess educational objectives on an ongoing

TABLE IV

CHECKLIST FOR USING AAC DEVICE TO ORDER BREAKFAST

	4/1	4/8
Makes meal choice at appropriate time	+	+
Makes drink choice at appropriate time	+	+

The "+" sign indicates that the skill was performed correctly.

TABLE V
TASK ANALYSIS FOR USING A FORK TO EAT FOOD

Step	Date 4/01	Date 4/08
Pick up fork with proper grip in right hand	+	+
Spear food with fork tines until food is secured on fork	–	–
Pick up fork with food attached	–	–
Bring fork to open mouth	+	+
Put fork in mouth	+	+
Close lips around food	+	+
Remove fork, leaving food in mouth	+	+
Bring fork down and places on plate	+	+
Chew and swallow food completely	+	+
Repeat steps 1–9 as necessary	–	–

The "+" sign indicates that the step was performed correctly while the "–" sign indicates that the step was performed incorrectly.

basis for a number of reasons. First, it is required by the IDEA legislation that ongoing assessment of student performance be conducted. Second, ongoing assessment allows for data-based documentation of student progress on the identified educational goals throughout the academic year. It is very important to have a clear overall picture of where the student is making progress and where he or she may be experiencing difficulties in learning. For example, a student may achieve some educational objectives quickly. In such circumstances new educational goals should be selected. In other instances the student may not be making adequate progress on educational goals. This may indicate that the goals were not appropriate (e.g., too complex) or perhaps the instructional strategies were not adequate. In such circumstances alternative educational goals may be selected, the current educational goals may be subdivided into more manageable educational goals, or alternative instructional strategies may be evaluated. Second, ongoing assessment provides stakeholders (e.g., parents) with frequent feedback as to the student's performance. For example, the student's performance might be summarized weekly by the teacher and provided to the family in written form.

The strategies identified for selecting educational goals can also be used to provide an ongoing assessment of student progress during the academic year. For example, the process of ecological assessment results in a series of objectively defined discrete behaviors (e.g., communication and social skills) and complex chains of behaviors (e.g., domestic, vocational, and community skills). The end result of an ecological assessment (e.g., task analyses of targeted skill clusters) allows the teacher to objectively measure performance of these skills on an ongoing basis. We also mentioned earlier in the chapter the importance of recognizing student choice and preference when developing educational goals. Students need to have ongoing opportunities to express choice and preference. Choice and preference can be incorporated within daily activities. In our example above, Shane was given opportunities to select between favorite meals and drinks during his weekly outing to Joe's Restaurant. Everyone's preferences change over time and so it is important to regularly assess changes in preference. Several simple and efficient strategies for assessing preference were described earlier in the chapter. These preference assessments can be incorporated regularly to assess for changes in preference. Finally, it is important to assess skills that have previously been mastered during the year and assess for maintenance of these skills. It is often the case that skills may not maintain at criterion performance and may need further instruction.

V. SUMMARY

Educational assessment is a very important process for students with intellectual disabilities. Assessment is used to determine student placement, to create an appropriate curriculum for the student, and to monitor student progress during the academic year. Much of the educational assessment process is mandated by legislation. In this chapter we focused on the informal or functional assessment process that is used to determine a functional and age-appropriate curriculum for a student. Several key features of informal assessment were highlighted. For example, it is important to involve parents and the student in an active and meaningful way in the planning process. A person-centered planning model of curriculum development is particularly helpful in this respect. Strategies for assessing student preference and choice should also be used in the curriculum development and ongoing assessment process. Educational goals stemming from the person-centered planning process should then be translated into observable skills and prioritized for instruction using an ecological assessment process. Finally, the skills identified during the ecological assessment should be measured on an ongoing basis during the academic year to assess student progress and make changes in the educational goals as needed.

REFERENCES

Bayley, N. (1993). *Bayley Scales of Infant Development II*. San Antonio, TX: Psychological Corporation.

Brown, L., Branston, M., Harme-Nietupski, S., Pumpian, I., Certo, N., & Gruenewald, L. (1979). A strategy for developing chronological-age-appropriate and functional curricular content for severely handicapped adolescents and young adults. *Journal of Special Education, 13,* 81–90.

Cannella, H., O'Reilly, M., & Lancioni, G. (2005). Choice and preference assessment research with people with severe to profound developmental disabilities: A review of the literature. *Research in Developmental Disabilities, 26,* 1–15.

Giangreco, M., Cloninger, C., & Iverson, V. (1998). *C.O.A.C.H.: Choosing outcomes and accommodations for children* (2nd ed.). Baltimore: Paul H. Brookes.

Hughes, C., Pitkin, S., & Lorden, S. (1998). Assessing preferences and choices of persons with severe and profound mental retardation. *Education and Training in Mental Retardation and Developmental Disabilities, 33,* 299–316.

Lambert, N., Nihira, K., & Leland, H. (1993). *Adaptive Behavior Scale-School.* Austin, TX: PRO-ED.

Lancioni, G., O'Reilly, M., Compodonico, F., & Mantini, M. (1998). Task variation versus task repetition for people with profound developmental disabilities: An assessment of preferences. *Research in Developmental Disabilities, 19,* 189–199.

Lancioni, G., O'Reilly, M., & Emerson, E. (1996). A review of choice research with people with severe and profound developmental disabilities. *Research in Developmental Disabilities, 17,* 391–411.

Lancioni, G., O'Reilly, M., & Oliva, D. (2002). Engagement in cooperative and individual task: Assessing the performance and preferences of persons with multiple disabilities. *Journal of Visual Impairment and Blindness, 96,* 50–53.

Lancioni, G., Singh, N., O'Reilly, M., & Oliva, D. (2003). Some recent research efforts on microswitches for persons with multiple disabilities. *Journal of Child and Family Studies, 12,* 251–256.

Lancioni, G., Singh, N., O'Reilly, M., Oliva, D., & Basili, G. (2005). An overview of research on increasing indices of happiness of people with severe/profound intellectual and multiple disabilities. *Disability and Rehabilitation, 27,* 83–93.

Mount, B., & Zwernik, K. (1988). *It's never too early, it's never too late: A booklet about personal futures planning.* St Paul, MN: St. Paul Metropolitan Council.

No Child left Behind Act of 2001. Pub. L. No. 107–110, § 101, 115 Stat. 1425 (2002).

O'Brien, J., O'Brien, C., & Mount, B. (1997). Person-centered planning has arrived...or has it? *Mental Retardation, 35,* 480–488.

Public Law 94–142 (1975). *Federal Register, 42,* 42474–42518.

Roane, H., Vollmer, T., Ringdahl, J., & Marcus, B. (1998). Evaluation of a brief stimulus preference assessment. *Journal of Applied Behavior Analysis, 31,* 605–620.

Snell, M., & Brown, F. (2006). *Instruction of students with severe disabilities* (6th ed.). Columbus Ohio: Pearson, Merrill, Prentice Hall.

Roid, G. H. (2003). *Stanford-Binet intelligence scales* (5th ed.). Chicago: Riverside.

Siegel, E., & Allinder, R. (2005). Review of assessment procedures for students with moderate and severe disabilities. *Education and Training in Developmental Disabilities, 40,* 343–351.

Sigafoos, J., Arthur-Kelly, M., & Butterfield, N. (2006). *Enhancing everyday communication for children with disabilities.* Baltimore: Paul H. Brookes.

Sigafoos, J., Arthur, M., & O'Reilly, M. (2003). *Challenging behavior and developmental disability.* London: Whurr Publishers.

Sparrow, S. S., Balla, D. A., & Cicchetti, D. V. (1984). *Vineland adaptive behavior scales: Interview edition.* Circle Pines MN: American Guidance Service.

The Individuals with Disabilities Education Improvement Act of 2004, Pub. L. No. 108–446, § 101, 118 Stat. 2647 (2004).

The Individuals with Disabilities Act Amendments of 1997, Pub. L. No. 17–105, § 101, 111 Stat. 37 (1997).

The Individuals with Disabilities Education Act of 1990, 20 U.S.C. §§ 1400 *et seq.*

Vandercook, T., York, J., & Forest, M. (1989). The McGill action planning system (MAPS): A strategy for building the vision. *Journal of the Association for Persons with Severe Handicaps, 14,* 205–215.

Wehmeyer, M. L. & Sands, D. (Eds.) (1998). *Making it happen: Student involvement in education planning, decision making, and instruction.* Baltimore: Paul H. Brookes.

Westling, D. L., & Fox, L. (2004). *Teaching students with severe disabilities* (3rd ed., p. 125). Columbus, Ohio: Pearson, Merrill, Prentice Hall.

Wilcox, B., & Bellamy, T. (1987). The activities catalog: An alternative curriculum for youth and adults with severe disabilities. Baltimore: Paul H. Brookes.

Winking, D., O'Reilly, B., & Moon, S. (1993). Assessing student preference for job tasks in a supported employment setting. *Journal of Vocational Rehabilitation, 10,* 85–93.

Autism and Pervasive Developmental Disorders

BART M. SEVIN, CHERYL L. KNIGHT, AND SCOTT A. BRAUD

UNIVERSITY CENTER FOR EXCELLENCE IN AUTISM, HUMAN DEVELOPMENT CENTER, LOUISIANA STATE UNIVERSITY HEALTH SCIENCES CENTER
NEW ORLEANS, LOUISIANA

I. INTRODUCTION

In 1943, Leo Kanner published the seminal paper, *Autistic Disturbances of Affective Contact*, in which he described the clinical presentation of 11 children whose common behavioral characteristics comprised what he deemed was a unique, previously unreported syndrome. The expression of the purported syndrome varied from case to case in terms of degree of impairment, specific attributes displayed, developmental course, and family background, although Kanner identified a number of common features that emerged as consistent themes across all the children he discussed. Defining features of this syndrome included an inability to develop relationships with others from birth, profound deficits in language development, particularly in the use of speech to convey meaning to others (i.e., for those who were not mute), and monotonous motor and vocal behavior accompanied by an "anxiously obsessive desire for the maintenance of sameness" (Kanner, 1943, p. 245). The diagnostic criteria (and other topics in autism, such as theories on pathogenesis) have undergone a number of permutations over the years; however, the defining symptomatology of autism captured in Kanner's original clinical depictions more than 60 years ago has proven remarkably consistent with the currently accepted definitions of autism contained in the American Psychiatric Association's (APA's) 4th edition of the *Diagnostic and Statistical Manual of Mental Disorders* (*DSM-IV*, 1994) and the 10th edition of the *International Classification of Diseases* [*ICD-10*; World Health Organization (WHO), 1993].

INTERNATIONAL REVIEW OF RESEARCH IN MENTAL RETARDATION, Vol. 34
0074-7750/07 $35.00

DOI: 10.1016/S0074-7750(07)34005-6

The terms "autism" and "Autistic Disorder" will be used interchangeably. As defined in the DSM-IV, Autistic Disorder is characterized by the symptoms most closely aligned with Kanner's original description (1943) of the syndrome: (1) qualitative impairments in social interaction, (2) qualitative impairments in communication, and (3) restrictive and repetitive patterns of behaviors. The terms Pervasive Developmental Disorders (PDDs) and Autistic Spectrum Disorders (ASDs) will be used synonymously to refer to all diagnoses in this category, including Autistic Disorder. The specific diagnostic entities comprising the PDDs are Autistic Disorder, Pervasive Developmental Disorder Not Otherwise Specified (PDD-NOS), Asperger's Disorder, Childhood Disintegrative Disorder, and Rett's Disorder (APA, 1994). The behavioral manifestation of the PDDs varies considerably across individuals falling on the autism spectrum (possibly to a lesser extent with individuals diagnosed with Rett's disorder) with respect to the specific symptom complex, symptom severity, age of onset, developmental course, and co-occurrence of associated disorders (e.g., intellectual disabilities, seizure disorders). Despite the well-documented heterogeneity in phenotypic expression, the core features recognized as common across and central to the PDDs are deficits in social interaction, vocal (e.g., in formal production and meaningful use of speech) and nonvocal (e.g., gesturing) communication, and excesses in repetitive, stereotyped motor, and/or vocal behavior.

Research over the last decade has indicated that autism and related PDDs are now more prevalent than other common pediatric disorders, such as cancer, diabetes, and Down syndrome (Filipek et al., 1999). Early prevalence estimates cited autism as occurring in ~1 per 2000 individuals (Lotter, 1966), although current epidemiological studies have reported prevalence for Autistic Disorder to be as high as 1 in 250–333 children (Baird et al., 2000; Bertrand et al., 2001). For the entire range of PDDs, prevalence has been reported to be as high as 1 in 150–170 people (Baird et al., 2000; Bertrand et al., 2001; Chakrabarti & Fombonne, 2001; Fombonne, 2003). Although Fombonne (2003) recommended more conservative estimates for autism and all the PDDs combined of ~1 per 1000 and 1 per 360, respectively. The conservative estimate of 1 per 1000 is perhaps only slightly less staggering considering the weighty economic impact related to provision of care over the lifetime of each affected individual, particularly in the absence of effective early intervention (Jacobson, Mulick, & Green, 1998; Järbrink, Fombonne, & Knapp, 2003; Järbrink & Knapp, 2001; cf. Marcus, Rubin, & Rubin, 2000).

There is a substantial accumulation of data demonstrating that children with a host of developmental disabilities have an increased chance for improved outcomes when interventions showing certain quality features are initiated early in life (Guralnick, 1998). With respect to individuals showing autism, scientific research over the last 20 years has documented the effectiveness of intensive early intervention based on the principles of Applied Behavior Analysis in improving outcomes (Eikeseth, Smith, Jahr, & Eldevik, 2002; Howard, Sparkman, Cohen, Green, & Stanislaw, 2005; Lovaas, 1987; McEachin, Smith, & Lovaas, 1993). This emphasis on early intervention for children with developmental disabilities, including autism, is supported by research on neural plasticity and the concept of critical periods of development (Huttenlocher, 1994, 2002). Plasticity, which is considered greater in children (Thomas, 2003), refers to the central nervous system's adaptive and corrective response to changes in the environment outside (e.g., through one or more of the sensory systems) and/or inside (e.g., via physical insult to the system) the skin. It then follows that the earlier evidence-based interventions begin, the greater the chances of improving the developmental trajectories of individuals with neurobiological characteristics that tend to manifest behaviorally as PDD. Therefore, early identification, referral for appropriate services, and introduction of validated intervention strategies are of primary importance for persons diagnosed with PDD. The first step in this process, which will be the focus of this chapter, is identification, via careful surveillance, screening, and diagnosis.

The diagnostic parameters of Autistic Disorder are well-defined, and consensus in the professional community, both within the United States and abroad, has greatly facilitated research and development of increasingly more sophisticated diagnostic instruments and broader methodologies (e.g., developmental surveillance) needed for early and accurate diagnosis. In recent years, several practice guidelines for the screening and diagnosis of PDDs have been outlined and endorsed by national organizations, such as the American Academy of Neurology and the Child Neurology Society (Filipek et al., 2000) and the American Academy of Child and Adolescent Psychiatry (Volkmar, Cook, Pomeroy, Realmuto, & Tanguay, 1999), as well as state organizations such as the New York State Department of Health (NYSDH, 1999). The convergence of information noted in the various practice guidelines suggests the professional community is actively working toward consensus on evidence-based practices indicated in identifying and thoroughly assessing individuals with PDD. Many guidelines target younger populations (Dua, 2003; NYSDH, 1999), although other guidelines provide recommendations for individuals of all ages (Volkmar et al., 1999). The present chapter was developed to provide the reader with an overview of recommended practice guidelines for the screening and diagnosis of autism and other PDDs in children. At present, very little work has been done regarding the diagnosis of adults with PDD, particularly when compared to the growing body of literature concerning identification and diagnosis of autism in infancy and early childhood (Baron-Cohen, Allen, & Gillberg, 1992). Therefore, information provided in the current work focuses on the assessment of autism and related PDDs in children. It should also be noted that a comprehensive review of psychometric properties for various screening and diagnostic instruments is beyond the scope of this chapter [Coonrod and Stone (2005) and Dumont-Mathieu and Fein (2005) for a detailed review of screening instruments; Lord and Corsello (2005) for a detailed review of diagnostic instruments for PDDs], although currently available instruments showing adequate psychometric properties will be discussed.

II. DIAGNOSTIC CRITERIA AND CLINICAL PRESENTATION OF THE PERVASIVE DEVELOPMENTAL DISORDERS

A. Autistic Disorder

Clinicians and researchers generally agree that autism and related conditions are disorders of neurobiological origin, although biological markers have not been identified (Zimmerman & Gordon, 2000). Diagnosis, therefore, is made on the basis of behavioral observation (Gomez & Baird, 2005). According to Diagnostic and Statistical Manual of Mental Disorders (DSM-IV) American Psychiatric Association (APA, 1994), a diagnosis of Autistic Disorder is indicated when a minimum of six behavioral symptoms are present, including a minimum of two in the area of social impairment, and one each in the areas of communication impairment and restricted repertoire of activities and interests. In addition, the onset of disturbances must begin within the first 3 years of life.

It has been suggested that perhaps the core feature of Autistic Disorder, consistent with Kanner's description (1943), is a qualitative disturbance in reciprocal social interactions or social relatedness (Volkmar, Cohen, Bregman, Hooks, & Stevenson, 1989; Walters, Barrett, & Feinstein, 1990). As Filipek et al. (1999) point out the social impairment (and communicative dysfunction) is qualitative in nature and not characterized by a complete lack of social behaviors. Many infants and/or young children with autism do not alter their posture prior to being held, and may become rigid when held. Children with autism also typically show marked deficits in the use of nonverbal behaviors, such as eye contact and gesturing. A developing body of literature has focused a great deal of attention on deficits in joint attention in individuals with autism. Joint attention has been defined in the cognitive-developmental literature as gesturing and making eye contact to direct another's attention for the purpose of sharing an experience involving an object or event (Mundy, Sigman, & Kasari, 1990; cf. Dube, MacDonald, & Mansfield, 2004). Joint attention repertoires may also include gaze shifting between stimuli in the environment and a nearby person, and may also involve pointing (MacDonald, Anderson, & Dube, 2006). Children with

Autistic Disorder have been found to show deficits in responding to joint initiation attempts (e.g., following an adult's pointing or gaze; Leekam, Hunnisett, & Moore, 1998; Leekam, Lopez, & Moore, 2000) and also in initiating joint attention via shifting gaze between items in the environment (e.g., toys) and adults in the room (Charman et al., 1997).

In childhood, persons with Autistic Disorder may demonstrate little to no interest in developing friendships with peers; if relationships are established, they may fail to behave in accordance with common social conventions governing such relationships (APA, 1994). Another consistent finding is a lack of emotional reciprocity, in which a child with autism fails to participate in social play with peers and/or adults and even may prefer to play alone. When others are incorporated into play activities, they may only be involved as helpers in the context of repetitive play routines (e.g., arranging toy cars in a certain way). Children with autism also typically show deficits in perspective taking (Charlop-Christy & Daneshvar, 2003) and difficulties recognizing expressions of emotion (e.g., sadness, anger) in others (Hobson, 1986).

Qualitative impairments in communication typically vary in severity, ranging from mutism to verbal fluency, and persist throughout life, impacting both vocal and nonvocal communicative functioning (APA, 1994). Language deficits tend to be complex and include abnormal production of sound (Wetherby, Yonclas, & Bryan, 1989) and vocal quality (e.g., pitch, intonation, cadence; APA, 1994; Sheinkopf, Mundy, Oller, & Steffens, 2000) errors in semantic (meaning) and pragmatic (functional communication) usage, and deficits in comprehension (Filipek et al., 1999). Many individuals who fail to develop speech may also demonstrate deficits in nonverbal communication such as gesturing and facial expressions. Parents commonly report that children with autism grab their hands/arms and lead them to items of interest, placing their hands on items rather than pointing or requesting using more developmentally appropriate methods of communicating. The DSM-IV criteria specify that for individuals who have developed speech, deficits in the ability to initiate, maintain, and terminate conversations are commonly present (APA, 1994).

Children and other individuals with Autistic Disorder also commonly display stereotyped and repetitive use of spoken language, such as immediate or delayed echolalia, which is repeating words, phrases, or sentences articulated by someone else recently or at some earlier point in time. In many cases, verbiage reproduced during delayed echolalia is taken from movies, television, or other similar mediums. Aberrant displays of echolalia generally occur and persist after ~24 months of age, although echolalia in children younger than 2 years represents an important aspect of typical language development (Filipek et al., 1999). Pronoun reversal, characterized by using second or third person pronouns to refer to oneself, is also fairly common in individuals with autism.

Many children with autism also fail to demonstrate variability in play (i.e., play behavior tends to be repetitive), and do not interact with toys and other items in a developmentally appropriate manner (APA, 1994). For example, a child may repeatedly arrange toy cars in a particular way or spin the wheels rather than roll the car on the floor "pretending" to drive (or if the car is rolled, it may be rolled in a repetitive, stereotyped manner). At times, although play may appear appropriate, certain behaviors may actually be routinized and consist of imitation of previously observed play behavior in others.

Individuals with Autistic Disorder display a number of behavioral excesses characterized as patterns of restricted, repetitive, and stereotypic behaviors, interests, and activities (APA, 1994). Many children diagnosed with autism engage in highly repetitive motor and/or verbal stereotypies such as hand-flapping, rocking, or toe-walking. Children and others with autism may also show a pathological interest or preoccupation with certain items, objects, or topics such as Thomas the Tank Engine®. Variability in play behavior is also deficient, in that play tends to be restricted in scope and repetitive [e.g., stacking blocks, knocking them over, restacking; New York State Department of Health (NYSDH), 1999]. Play observed in children with autism may also involve overselective attention to or focus on parts or irrelevant features of items and activities (Lovaas, Koegel, & Schreibman, 1979). Other children may demonstrate highly ritualistic or routinized patterns of responding, and may engage in problem behavior when adherence to these patterns is violated. For example, a child with autism may scream and aggress toward a family member when the route for a daily walk is altered. This general category of repetitive and restricted patterns of responding described by Kanner (1943) as an insistence on sameness is one of the quintessential features of autistic disorder.

There are a number of other features associated with Autistic Disorder that are not included in the DSM-IV (APA, 1994) diagnostic criteria. One of the most common diagnoses linked with autism is Mental Retardation, which co-occurs at some level in ~75% of all individuals diagnosed with autism (APA, 1994). Fombonne (2003) corroborated these figures, showing that 30% of participants functioned in the normal range of intellectual functioning, with another 30% falling in the mild to moderate range and 40% in the severe range. Another characteristic that tends to be associated with autism and is commonly reported by families is challenging behavior, which may include (but is not limited to) self-injurious behavior, aggression, property destruction, pica (Matson, Benavidez, Compton, Paclawskyj, & Baglio, 1996), and food refusal (Ahearn, Castine, Nault, & Green, 2001). Finally, individuals with Autistic Disorder may demonstrate atypical responses when presented with different types of sensory stimulation (NYSDH, 1999).

The unusual pattern of responding may range from a complete absence of any response to loud, sudden noises, to exhibiting extreme hypersensitivity and behavioral displays of distress (e.g., screaming, crying, covering ears) in response to fairly innocuous stimuli (e.g., vacuum cleaner; Koegel, Openden, & Koegel, 2004).

B. Rett's Disorder

According to DSM-IV (APA, 1994), Rett's Disorder is restricted to females and characterized by a period of seemingly typical development and functioning after birth, followed by a period of developmental regression. Prenatal and perinatal periods, psychomotor development through the fifth month of life, and head circumference all fall within normal limits. A period of developmental stagnation typically follows from approximately ages 6–18 months, in which development slows or even comes to a halt. Developmental regression then follows this period of arrested development. Specific deficits noted during developmental regression include a slowing or deceleration of head growth, loss of previously demonstrated purposeful hand skills, poorly coordinated motor movements (e.g., gait abnormalities), emergence of stereotypical hand movements, loss of social engagement, and severe disturbances in receptive and expressive communication and cognitive abilities. While regression is considered the hallmark of Rett's Disorder (Glaze, 2004), research has demonstrated that subtle delays, such as hypotonia (e.g., parents may report poor head control; Nomura & Segawa, 2005), or more obvious delays, such as motor problems, may occur earlier in development than previously suggested (Charman et al., 2002; Kerr, 1995). Many individuals initially may be misdiagnosed with Autistic Disorder due to overlap in the respective diagnostic criteria (Percy, Gillberg, Hagberg, & Witt-Engerstrom, 1990; Percy, Zoghbi, Lewis, & Jankovic, 1988). Other features associated with Rett's Disorder include epilepsy, sleep disturbances, scoliosis, breathing abnormalities (e.g., hyperventilation and breath holding), and chronic constipation (Glaze, 2004; Nomura, 2005). It should be noted that inclusion of Rett's Disorder on the PDD continuum is not without opposition (Gillberg, 1994), although Filipek et al. (1999) note that placing Rett's together with the PDDs may prove beneficial in preventing misdiagnosis of Rett's as Autistic Disorder.

C. Childhood Disintegrative Disorder

Childhood Disintegrative Disorder (CDD), also referred to as *Heller's Syndrome* (Filipek et al., 1999; Heller, 1930), is characterized by a period of marked developmental regression across multiple domains of functioning (e.g., communication, social relatedness, adaptive behavior) following a minimum of 2 years of apparently typical developmental progress (APA, 1994). The current DSM-IV nosology indicates a phenotypic expression identical to Autistic Disorder (Malhotra & Gupta, 1999). A closer look at available research, however, suggests several points of departure regarding the clinical course of the respective diagnoses. For example, it has been noted that deterioration of speech skills is striking (i.e., an almost total loss of speech) and occurs without exception in CDD (Volkmar, Koenig, & State, 2005). In contrast, regression is estimated to occur in ~10% to over 50% of cases of Autistic Disorder (Tuchman & Rapin, 1997), with only 20–40% of cases showing a complete loss of expressive language skills (Rutter & Lord, 1987). As mentioned, developmental regression has been reported in Autistic Disorder, although onset typically occurs prior to the second year of life (Tuchman & Rapin, 1997). While clinical presentation and core deficits are the same for Autistic Disorder and CDD, the severity of autistic symptoms is usually greater for CDD than for Autistic Disorder, despite the earlier onset of Autistic Disorder (Volkmar & Rutter, 1995). At present, the relationship between Autistic Disorder and CDD is not well understood, and additional research will be required to advance the current state of knowledge (Malhotra & Gupta, 1999).

D. Asperger's Disorder

Hans Asperger (1991/1944) first described a constellation of clinical features in a group of children which included impairments in social functioning and essentially typical intellectual functioning and communicative abilities. Now considered a variant of autism, Asperger's Disorder (AD) was classified in DSM-IV as one of the PDDs (APA, 1994). Behavioral characteristics of AD include qualitative deficits in social functioning, restricted and stereotyped behavior patterns and a narrow range of interests, and relatively intact language skills (e.g., functional use of single words by age 2 and phrases by age 3). This latter feature and average cognitive and adaptive functioning represent something of a departure from the large percentage of individuals with Autistic Disorder showing some level of Mental Retardation (incorporating deficits in intellectual ability and adaptive behavior, with onset before age 21; APA, 1994). While preservation of formal language is necessary for a diagnosis of AD, Klin and Shepard (1994) point out that communication abnormalities may discriminate between AD and Autistic Disorder in a number of ways. First, while prosody is usually aberrant in both autism and AD, atypical inflection and voice quality tend to be more prominent in the latter (Ghaziuddin & Gerstein, 1996). For example, a person with AD may use only a few inflection patterns, but fail to alter those patterns appropriately when asking a question versus making a statement (Volkmar & Klin, 2000). Another unique feature of speech in AD is the tendency for conversations to be weighted in favor of topics in which only the person with AD is interested (e.g., superheroes). Reciprocity and other common rules governing such exchanges are generally not followed, with the individual with AD often dominating the conversation with repeated intrusions, and a tendency to "talk over" others. Accompanying these features is also an inclination for verbosity, although affected individuals may fail to engage in interactive communication or adhere to basic rules governing appropriate conversation (Volkmar & Klin, 2000).

The status of AD as a diagnostic category distinct from what has been referred to as high-functioning autism (HFA; i.e., individuals with autism functioning in the average range of intelligence) remains a topic of debate and is in need of additional research (Volkmar et al., 1996). In some intervention outcome studies evaluating the effects of an intervention (e.g., a social skills curriculum) with both groups of individuals, significant differences between the groups in response to intervention have not been reported (Solomon, Goodlin-Jones, & Anders, 2004). Similarly, in some descriptive studies investigating whether certain core behavioral features (e.g., repetitive behaviors) reliably differentiated individuals with AD and HFA, results failed to substantiate the external validity of the two categories with respect to the behavioral symptoms studied (South, Ozonoff, & McMahon, 2005). Whether AD simply represents a milder variant of Autistic Disorder or stands the test of time as a distinct diagnostic category within the PDD's will be determined as a function of the results of research on associated behavioral and neurobiological (e.g., neuroimaging) symptomatology, treatment outcome, and other topics relevant to determining the validity and borders of AD as a diagnostic concept (Volkmar & Klin, 2000).

E. Pervasive Developmental Disorder not Otherwise Specified (Including Atypical Autism)

A diagnosis of PDD-NOS is given when marked impairments in the core features of autism are present, including deficits in social relatedness and verbal and/or nonverbal communication, and excesses in repetitive, stereotyped patterns of behavior, interests, or activities, but criteria for one of the PDDs are not fully met (APA, 1994). For example, the number of features present may not be sufficient for a diagnosis of Autistic Disorder (i.e., less than six in total), age of onset may be after the third year of life, and/or symptoms may be atypical or unusual (APA, 1994). The diagnosis of PDD-NOS is not a diagnostic category with accompanying criteria as is the case with the other PDDs; instead this label is often used when inadequate information is available or perhaps when clinicians are reluctant to make a formal diagnosis of autism or some other PDD (Filipek et al., 1999). Attaching a *not otherwise specified/NOS* designation to diagnoses included in the DSM-IV (APA) is common (e.g., Communication Disorder—NOS, Disruptive Behavior Disorder—NOS, Tic Disorder—NOS), although such nomenclature are not considered to be distinct clinical entities in their own right.

III. EARLY AUTISM IDENTIFICATION AND POTENTIAL BARRIERS

Early identification of PDD and other development disabilities has become a public health priority for a number of reasons (National Research Council & Institute of Medicine, 2000; Pinto-Martin, Dunkle, Earls, Fliedner, & Landes, 2005). As mentioned above, the economic impacts of providing special education services and long-term care for individuals with autism and related disorders are considerable (Jacobson et al., 1998; Järbrink & Knapp, 2001; Järbrink et al., 2003) and are surely exacerbated when identification and subsequent referral to appropriate services is unnecessarily delayed (Pinto-Martin et al., 2005). Furthermore, there is an increasingly large body of research suggesting that evidence-based interventions (see NYSDH, 1999 for an example of an evidence-based practice guideline) can produce improved outcomes (in some cases substantial) for individuals with autism (Eikeseth et al., 2002; Lovaas, 1987; McEachin et al., 1993). Data from these outcome studies and recognized developmental principles (Huttenlocher, 2002) undoubtedly have contributed to the widely accepted concept and endorsement of early intervention, particularly with respect to its application to young children with autism (Dawson & Osterling, 1997; National Research Council, 2001; NYSDH, 1999).

Fortunately, children with autism are being diagnosed earlier. Research indicates more diagnoses are being made around 3.5 to 4 years of age (Howlin & Moore, 1997; Smith, Chung, & Vostanis, 1994), which is younger than previous reports of between 4 and 5 years of age (Howlin & Asgharian, 1999). While this progress is encouraging, some authors report a formal diagnosis may be possible as early as 18–24 months of age (Baron-Cohen et al., 1992, 1996; Cox et al., 1999a; Lord, 1995; Siegel, 1996; Stone et al., 1999). However, additional research is needed to evaluate the stability of symptom expression over time. A handful of studies has demonstrated that the pattern of autism core features displayed in children 2 years of age does not necessarily correspond to that seen in a children 4 or 5 years of age (Cox et al., 1999b; Moore & Goodson, 2003; Rogers, 2001; Stone et al., 1999).

In a study by Charman et al. (2005), scores obtained via standardized psychometric tests and assessments of symptom severity, such as the Autism Diagnostic Interview-Revised (Lord, Rutter, & LeCouteur, 1994), at age 2 were not predictive of scores obtained at age 7, although scores taken at age 3 did predict later outcomes. Therefore, the authors recommended caution when interpreting standardized psychometric and other relevant data gathered during assessments of 2-year-olds. Such findings call into question whether an accurate diagnosis of autism can be made in children under 3 years of age (Charman et al., 2005).

Nevertheless, diagnoses typically occur sometime midway through the third year and into the fourth year of life as mentioned above. The frustration and potentially negative implications of delayed identification are compounded when considered in light of the fact that developmental delays in most children with autism are first detected by their parents during their second year of life, usually between 16 and 17 months of age (DeGiacomo & Fombonne, 1998; Rogers & DiLalla, 1990; Siegel, Pliner, Eschler, & Elliott, 1988; Smith et al., 1994). Available research shows that parent concerns about language delays are generally more prominent than reports of delays in social development (DeGiacomo & Fombonne, 1998; Siegel et al., 1988; Smith et al., 1994), particularly when open-ended questions are used to solicit information (Coonrod & Stone, 2005). However, when questionnaires containing specific queries about social functioning are used, parents do in fact report deficits in social development, vocabulary (expressive), and use of communicative gestures (Coonrod & Stone, 2005). Parental concerns about developmental delays in children require serious consideration and immediately should serve as a catalyst for more intensive screening and diagnostic activities, given that parent reports have been shown to be fairly accurate indicators of their children's overall developmental status (Glascoe, 1994, 1997a, 1998, 2000; Glascoe & Dworkin, 1995; Glascoe & Sandler, 1995). While parent concerns are not likely to pinpoint symptom constellations that map neatly onto diagnostic criteria for different developmental disorders, when parents tell health care or other professionals that there is a problem with their child's development, *almost always* some facet of development is aberrant (Filipek et al., 1999).

Parents generally bring their concerns to professionals' attention within a few months of noticing delays (Coonrod & Stone, 2005; DeGiacomo and Fombonne, 1998), although a number of factors likely converge at this point to delay and interfere with formal identification. First, making accurate diagnoses requires adequate professional preparation in recognizing the manifestation of positive (e.g., motor stereotypes, such as hand-flapping) and negative symptoms (e.g., absence of imitation and gesturing) evident at different age ranges (and possibly at differing levels of severity of the disorder).

Most healthcare professionals who encounter children with autism and their families have little to no training in these areas (Pinto-Martin et al., 2005). It has been documented that about only one-fifth of practitioners actually use standardized screening instruments in their clinical work, with the most common being the Denver II (Dobos, Dworkin, & Bernstein, 1994; Dworkin, 1992; Sand et al., 2006), which has been shown to have inadequate sensitivity and specificity (see below for definitions of these terms) regarding identification of children with developmental delays (Filipek et al., 1999; Glascoe et al., 1992). A lack of adequate time to conduct individual child well-visits combined with insufficient reimbursement for screening activities during those visits also contribute to poor identification. Additionally, many providers feel uncomfortable making a diagnosis and delivering upsetting news to families, seemingly more so for younger children (Pinto-Martin et al., 2005). Such reluctance stands in stark contrast to recommended practice guidelines for early identification and parent education (National Research Council, 2001; NYSDH, 1999). Some professionals have commented that also they may be hesitant to mention the word "autism" because they realize that if a diagnosis is made, appropriate services are not readily available to families or they can be obtained only at considerable personal expense (e.g., in-home consultants), which many families cannot afford. The result of the confluence of these factors is missed diagnoses, misdiagnoses, or simply misinformation (e.g., parents being told not to worry or to wait and return if problems persisted; Howlin & Moore, 1997; Smith et al., 1994), despite the fact that parents generally prefer to be told as soon as possible about developmental problems in their children (Midence & O'Neill, 1999; Piper & Howlin, 1992).

Landmark events have taken place in recent years resulting in development and adoption by many professional organizations of evidence-based practices in the surveillance, screening, and diagnosis of ASDs (for a full account of events, see Bristol-Power & Spinella, 1999). One practice parameter produced as a consequence of this series of events represents a comprehensive rubric, based on available scientific research, for practitioners to guide identification of individuals with autism (Filipek et al., 1999, 2000). The sections below provide an overview of guideline recommendations for the identification process, which includes developmental surveillance, screening, diagnosis, and related evaluations. The practice parameter (Filipek et al., 2000), the accompanying publication (Filipek et al., 1999), other relevant studies, practice guidelines (NYSDH, 1999), and policy statements, such as the "algorithm" for developmental surveillance and screening for young children with developmental disorders published by the American Academy of Pediatrics (AAP, 2006), served as the basis for the information presented below. General coverage of specific instruments showing adequate psychometric properties also will be included.

IV. DEVELOPMENTAL SURVEILLANCE, SCREENING, AND DIAGNOSIS

The terms *developmental surveillance* and *developmental screening* refer to different although highly related processes that are best used to compliment one another. Dworkin (1993) provided the following definition of *developmental surveillance*:

> a flexible, continuous process whereby knowledgeable professionals perform skilled observations of children during the provision of health care. The components of developmental surveillance include eliciting and attending to parental concerns, obtaining a relevant developmental history, making accurate and informative observations of children, and sharing opinions and concerns with other relevant professionals (p. 533).

The emphasis in surveillance is placed not on administering standardized assessment measures as in screening (see below), but instead refers to a broader process involving all activities related to identification of developmental delays, including collaborative input from health care practitioners, parents, and others involved with children suspected of having a developmental disability (Dworkin, 1989). Developmental surveillance as a concept is characterized by a partnership between parents and professionals that involves repeated data collection over time to identify developmental and behavioral problems that correspond to developmental disorders or diseases (Baird et al., 2000). Information may be gathered on developmental milestones (NYSDH, 1999), for example, through the use of a developmental checklist during preventive care appointments (AAP, 2001).

Developmental screening has been described in the following way (Dworkin, 1989):

> the process of testing whole populations of children at various set ages to detect those at high risk for significant unsuspected deviations from normal. The emphasis is on distinguishing between children at high and low risk for developmental problems, rather than diagnosing such conditions, and typically involves the application of rapidly administered tests, examinations, or other procedures (p. 1001).

Screening involves the use of relatively brief assessments (compared to comprehensive diagnostic evaluation methods) intended to identify children who warrant additional, in-depth diagnostic evaluations (Meisels & Provence, 1989). Research and practice guidelines recommend implementation of screening methods within the context of the overall surveillance process (AAP, 2006; Charman, 2003; Filipek et al., 2000; NYSDH, 1999) to supplement information provided by parents, particularly when there are heightened developmental concerns reported during ongoing surveillance activities. Generally speaking, results of screening measures can then facilitate decision making about further screening (or rescreening), parent education, referrals for more intensive diagnostic and developmental assessments, and possibly early intervention or other appropriate services.

There are a number of specific recommendations regarding features of developmental surveillance and the overall process that are generally endorsed by available practice guidelines. First, developmental surveillance should be conducted by adequately trained and qualified practitioners as part of a routine process that begins at birth and is ongoing (AAP, 2006; Filipek et al., 2000; NYSDH, 1999). According to the AAP (2006), developmental surveillance involves the following five components: (1) eliciting and attending to parents' concerns about their children's developmental status, (2) tracking and documenting a developmental history, (3) conducting accurate and informed observations of children, (4) identifying existing risks and protective factors, and (5) maintaining accurate records, including documentation of the process and data collected (cf. NYSDH, 1999). These surveillance activities are recommended as part of every well-child or preventive care health examination, which are typically scheduled at 9, 18, 24, and 30 months of age. At these visits, attainment of developmental milestones should be evaluated via probe question professionals pose directly to parents. Examples of developmental probes include "Does he/she..." or "Is there..." questions targeting behaviors, such as pointing, showing things to others, smiling when others smile, leading an adult by the hand, and so on (Filipek et al., 2000). The AAP (2006) algorithm recommends using standardized general screening instruments at all preventive care visits, such as the Ages & Stages Questionnaire (ASQ; Squires, Potter, & Bricker, 1999), and also an autism-specific screening instrument, such as the Checklist for Autism in Toddlers (CHAT; Baron-Cohen et al., 1992) at the 18-month appointment.

The practice parameter produced by the Quality Standards Subcommittee of the American Academy of Neurology and the Child Neurology Society (Filipek et al., 2000), which was later endorsed by the AAP in October, 2003, describes two levels of investigation that provide different types of information. Level 1 screening is recommended for all children and refers to routine developmental surveillance and nonspecific screening, or identifying children in the general population who are at risk for any abnormalities in development, used in conjunction with screening specifically for autism. Level 2 assessment consists of more intensive evaluation of children already shown to be at risk for developmental problems and is conducted by professionals with training and experience in distinguishing autism from other types of developmental disorders. Level 2 evaluation involves extensive diagnostic and related testing, resulting in a wealth of information needed for making a definitive diagnosis and determining areas of relative strengths and deficits that can be used in treatment planning.

A. Level 1 Investigation

Level 1 investigation consists of routine developmental surveillance combined with general or nonspecific and specific screening methods to differentiate children with any developmental delay and children with autism, respectively, from the general population of children who follow a normal developmental progression. Nonspecific screening measures cast a broad net, identifying children who are at risk for a range of developmental problems, including but not limited to autism. Autism-specific screening instruments target the constellation of symptoms that differentiate autism from other developmental disabilities (Coonrod & Stone, 2005). Specific autism screening may be used in conjunction with nonspecific screening or after a child fails a nonspecific screen to gain additional information. Screening measures generally are distinguished from diagnostic instruments in that they are less intensive in terms of administration time and training and/or expertise required for use. In addition, data generated by screening instruments are not used to make diagnoses, but rather provide information about the degree of risk for developmental disability (Coonrod & Stone, 2005). If a child fails a screening, then it may be appropriate to schedule a rescreening using the same or possibly a different screening instrument (e.g., if the first general screening identified the child as being at risk for disability, perhaps an autism-specific screening would then be conducted), or perhaps a full developmental and diagnostic work-up.

It is imperative that professionals implementing Level 1 screening practices learn what questions to ask parents and how to translate information into data-based decision making regarding the appropriate course of action. Common concerns reported by parents at routine well-child visits, for which practitioners should be prepared to respond, are (1) speech and language delays, (2) delays in social development with or without problems with communication, and (3) developmental status of a younger sibling of a child suspected of or diagnosed with autism (Filipek et al., 1999). Any of these concerns should be taken seriously, and further probing should be performed to assess for the presence of concomitant behavior problems, or the presence of several simultaneously co-occurring concerns. A number of parent concerns that should be regarded as red flags for autism were outlined by Filipek et al. (1999) in the areas of communication, social development, and behavior, with an accompanying list of indicators requiring immediate attention and further evaluation. In the area of communication, items included failure to respond to his/her name, inability to tell what he/she wants, appears deaf, and lack of pointing or waving bye. Under social concerns, items included lack of social smiling, poor eye contact, lives in his/her own world, and lack of interest in other children. Behavioral concerns included tantrums, being uncooperative or oppositional, lack of appropriate play skills, toe walking, an unusual attachment to objects, failure to imitate other's actions, and oversensitivity to certain types of stimulation. Parent concerns suggesting the immediate need for more intensive evaluations included no babbling or gesturing by 12 months of age, the absence of single words by 16 months and two-word spontaneous phrases (apart from echolalia) by 24 months, and any loss of any language or social skills at any age (for a complete list of red flags, see Filipek et al., 1999 and NYSDH, 1999).

As mentioned in the example above, if at any given point during Level 1 screening parents' concerns about development are identified via developmental probes or general screening measures, then autism-specific screening should be conducted as soon as possible (Coonrod & Stone, 2005). It is also recommended that children with any type of developmental delay, particularly when deficits in social interactions and communication are present, participate in a formal audiological hearing evaluation regardless of results of prior neonatal hearing screening (Filipek et al., 1999). Audiological assessment should be carried out by an audiologist (preferably a pediatric audiologist) with expertise in testing younger children and populations considered difficult to test, and who has access to necessary technologies and assessment methods. Behavioral and electrophysiological evaluation methods appropriate to the individual being tested should be considered to determine the contributions of hearing loss to social and communication deficits (Filipek et al., 1999; NYSDH, 1999).

Practitioners should also probe parents of children with (or suspected of) developmental delays for information about the occurrence of a form of self-injurious behavior, *pica*, which is the ingestion of inedible substances. Children suspected of having autism or other developmental delays who engage in pica are at an increased risk for repeated exposure to lead or other toxic matter (Shannon & Graef, 1997), and should be referred immediately for periodic and ongoing lead screenings and also for behavioral treatment of pica behavior (Piazza et al., 1998). Lead screenings should continue until pica has decreased to zero levels to evaluate whether exposure is continuing to occur, particularly given that pica may manifest as a covert behavior, making it difficult to observe and monitor.

1. SCREENING MEASURES

Screening measures are used as an aid in gathering information during the Level 1 screening process, and represent an initial step in an overall process that may suggest rescreening, screening using different instruments, and referral to Level 2 investigation. Screening measures are generally designed to either differentiate children at risk for disability from the general population or distinguish children at risk for autism from those at risk for other developmental problems (Coonrod & Stone, 2005). The features or dimensions along which screening instruments can vary include administration format (e.g., verbal report, direct observation, interactive) and length of time, degree of experience and training required, and level of familiarity with the targeted child. The psychometric properties relevant in designing and evaluating the adequacy of screening instruments are sensitivity, specificity, and positive predictive value (PPV) and negative predictive value (NPV). Sensitivity refers to the percentage of children who actually have developmental problems that are identified correctly by a screening test (i.e., they fail the screen or test positive). Recommended standards for sensitivity are at least 70–80% of children with disabilities identified during a single administration (Glascoe, 2005). Specificity is the percentage of children showing no developmental disabilities that are identified correctly by the screening measure (i.e., they pass the screen or test negative). The recommended cutoff for acceptable specificity is closer to 80% given the larger proportion of children without disabilities than with those having disabilities (Glascoe, 2005).

PPV refers to the accuracy with which a failed screen predicts the presence of an actual developmental problem, and is measured as the percentage of children testing positive who are later diagnosed with a disability (Glascoe, 2005). NPV refers to the accuracy with which a passed screen predicts the absence of any developmental problem, and is measured as the percentage of children testing negative who are not diagnosed with a disability (Aylward, 1997; Coonrod & Stone, 2005). Values of PPV and NPV for screening measures will be influenced strongly by the prevalence of the disorder, with PPV showing a positive relationship and NPV a negative relationship with prevalence (Coonrod & Stone, 2005; Reigelman & Hirsch, 1989). For purposes of this chapter, nonspecific and autism-specific screening measures generally showing adequate psychometric properties and recommended by the Filipek et al. (2000) practice parameter will be described. In addition, brief treatment of several other popular screening instruments developed since the publication of the practice parameter will be provided.

2. GENERAL OR NONSPECIFIC SCREENING INSTRUMENTS

The Ages and Stages Questionnaire, 2nd edition (ASQ; Bricker & Squires, 1999; Squires, Bricker, & Potter, 1997) was designed as a parent report measure for use during well-child appointments with children 0 to 3 years of age. The number of items varies slightly depending on the specific age of the child and administration time is between 10 and 15 minutes. Scoring is pass/fail in each of five developmental domains and was described by Filipek et al. (1999) as a useful prescreening tool due in part to its brevity. The Brigance Screens-II (Glascoe, 2002) uses a direct observation and elicitation-based format for children ranging in age from 0 to 90 months.

Administration time is about 10–15 minutes and assesses different developmental domains, including language, fine and gross motor, and preacademic and academic skills. The Brigance has availability in both English and Spanish. The Childhood Development Inventories (CDIs; Ireton, 1992; Ireton & Glascoe, 1995) were designed as parent report measures and require about 10–15 minutes to complete. The CDIs are appropriate for children ranging in age from 18 to 72 months, and tap into language, motor, cognitive, behavior, and other developmental areas. Results are presented as age equivalents in each domain. The CDIs are available in both English and Spanish. The Parents' Evaluation of Developmental Status (PEDS; Glascoe, 1997b, 1998) was developed to aid professionals in eliciting parental concerns about their child's development, and takes about 15–20 minutes to administer. Parents are required to answer 10 questions, which can be done while waiting for a well-child visit to begin, and scoring can be completed in ~2 minutes. Results yield probabilities for delays that are linked to different parent concerns, and an algorithm is provided that guides practitioners through decision points regarding ongoing surveillance, additional screening, and referrals. The PEDS is available in 14 different languages.

3. AUTISM-SPECIFIC SCREENING INSTRUMENTS

The CHAT (Baird et al., 2000; Baron-Cohen et al., 1992) is probably the most well-researched screening instrument of its kind. The CHAT was designed to differentiate children at risk for autism at 18 months of age from the general population during preventive child care visits. The instrument consists of 14 total items, with parent report required to complete the first 9 items and direct observation for the last 5 items. Research has showed that failing five key criterion items on the CHAT when administered two times, with each administration occurring 1 month apart, was highly predictive for receiving a formal diagnosis of autism at 20 and 42 months of age (Baron-Cohen et al., 1992, 1996; Charman et al., 1998; Cox et al., 1999b). While specificity was reported to be high for the CHAT, sensitivity was found to be poor, with as many as 80% of children (depending on the criteria used) later diagnosed with autism missed during the screen. In addition, the CHAT has been found to be less sensitive to milder variants on the autism spectrum such as Asperger's Disorder. The CHAT is considered to be a useful tool, although it is not recommended as the sole means of screening given that many children at risk do not routinely fail the CHAT.

The Modified Checklist for Autism in Toddlers (M-CHAT; Robins, Fein, Barton, & Green, 2001) expands on the CHAT by adding an additional 14 parent report items to the 9 parent report items in the CHAT, for a total of 23 total items. Administration time is between 5 and 10 minutes, and the age at which screening was conducted moved from 18 months as reported with the CHAT to 24 months. However, the M-CHAT is appropriate for use with children 16–30 months of age. The M-CHAT was designed to identify children on the spectrum rather than just children with Autistic Disorder. Two different criteria were used to generate a pass/fail score, the first being failure of any 3 of the total 23 items and the second being failure of 2 of the 6 critical (i.e., red flag) items. Initial reports about the psychometric properties of the M-CHAT have been encouraging, showing a notable improvement in sensitivity, although more research on this instrument is warranted (Coonrod & Stone, 2005).

A further permutation of the CHAT was reported by Wong et al. (2004), titled the CHAT-23, which was designed as a screening tool for Chinese children. The CHAT-23 consists of a translation of the 23 M-CHAT items into Chinese, combined with the 5 observation-based items from the original CHAT. Psychometric properties were acceptable and the authors suggested a two-part process beginning with the 23 M-CHAT items followed by the observation section for those failing 2 of 7 critical items or 6 of 23 total items. Children included in the sample ranged in age from 16–86 months, with known mental ages of 18–24 months.

The Pervasive Developmental Disorders Screening Test-II (PDDST-II; Siegel, 2004) involves 3 different assessment stages intended for use across 3 different settings, primary care settings, developmental clinics, and autism clinics for Stages 1, 2, and 3, respectively, with children under 72 months of age. Stage 1 was developed to identify children in need of additional evaluation to rule out a diagnosis on the PDD continuum. Data are collected via a parent report questionnaire, and administration takes about 5 minutes. Psychometric properties for Stage 1 are promising, although research on the PDDST-Stage 1 using a population-based sample has yet to be conducted. Stage 2 was designed to distinguish children needing extensive evaluations emphasizing an ASD from those requiring a general developmental assessment. Stage 3 was intended for use once children have been referred to autism clinics. While psychometric data for Stage 1 were encouraging, sensitivity and specificity for the latter two stages were not as good, and additional research in a nonreferred sample is needed to determine the utility of these instruments (Coonrod & Stone, 2005).

The Screening Tool for Autism in two-year-olds (STAT; Stone, Coonrod, & Ousley, 2000; Stone, Coonrod, & Turner, 2004) was designed to distinguish children between the ages of 24 and 35 months with autism from children with other developmental disorders. Administration takes 20 minutes and occurs in the context of interactive play with items scored as pass/fail. Initial data are encouraging, with sensitivity and specificity in the acceptable ranges, although additional research with larger samples is required to further evaluate the value of this measure.

B. Level 2 Investigation

Level 2 investigation involves the use of comprehensive diagnostic and the other evaluative measures to accomplish comprehensive diagnostic assessment and other relevant testing that are indicated once a child has screened positive during Level 1 investigation. At this point, an important question arises regarding who is qualified to make a diagnosis of autism. The Filipek et al. paper (1999) and accompanying practice parameter (2000) state that Level 2 testing should be conducted by professionals with specialized expertise in evaluating and treating autism, although disciplines potentially fitting these criteria are not specified. The NYSDH (1999) practice guideline points out that practice regulations vary on a state-by-state basis and provide guidance about credentials and licensing requirements outlining professionals who are qualified to make certain psychiatric diagnoses, such as autism. In New York State, for example, practice acts indicate that only licensed psychologists and physicians are adequately prepared and approved to make a diagnosis of autism. Information about who should and should not make formal diagnoses of autism and related developmental disabilities is relevant for parent education purposes, because while many disciplines have training and experience in recognizing the core features of autism, all individuals showing positive screenings for autism will not necessarily warrant a DSM-IV (APA, 1994) diagnosis of autism or a related PDD. The other side of the coin in terms of delayed diagnosis or hesitance in using the word "autism" with parents, is the tendency for professionals (who may or may not be qualified to give a diagnosis of autism) and others who come in contact with young children at risk for showing developmental delays to make a premature "armchair diagnosis" within minutes of meeting a family. While individuals who work with young children and their families (e.g., day care workers, preschool teachers, pediatricians) should certainly refer children presenting with developmental concerns for appropriate screening and evaluation, it may be prudent to ensure that such referrals are based on appropriate data, such as validated developmental milestone checklists and information received during parent probes acquired during routine developmental surveillance and/or screening activities.

As mentioned earlier in this chapter, a diagnosis of autism is made on the basis of a child's behavior. Practitioners conducting Level 2 diagnostic assessments generally accumulate the necessary information regarding behavioral symptoms via parent report, including an extensive family and developmental history, and direct observations of child behavior (NYSDH, 1999). In the absence of biological markers for autism, diagnosticians rely on their expertise, clinical judgment, the diagnostic framework provided by DSM-IV (APA, 1994) and/or the *International Classification of Diseases*, 10th edition (ICD-10; WHO,

1993), and results of currently available diagnostic instruments such as standardized parent interviews, rating scales, and checklists (Filipek et al., 1999). The diagnostic assessment may serve as the focal point of the Level 2 evaluative process, however, individuals with autism and related developmental disabilities commonly present with comorbid disorders and other health concerns that are not necessarily specific to the PDDs (although some may occur more commonly with PDDs), such as cognitive impairments and seizure disorders. As such, the diagnostic assessment should be considered as one piece of the overall Level 2 assessment process, conducted alongside relevant developmental and health and medical evaluations (Filipek et al., 1999; NYSDH, 1999). It is recommended that the overall evaluation process involve a team of interdisciplinary collaborators (e.g., psychologists, neurologists, speech pathologists, audiologists, pediatricians) who work closely with parents to identify an individualized profile of strengths and weaknesses for use in determining appropriate referrals for services and treatment planning (Filipek et al., 1999). Exhaustive reviews of health and medical evaluations and developmental assessment methods are beyond the scope of the present chapter. A brief overview of general recommendations for these evaluation processes is offered below, although readers are directed to the Filipek et al. (1999, 2000) publications for more extensive treatment of these topic areas. Coverage of Level 2 investigation in the present chapter will focus primarily on describing the basic features of diagnostic instruments demonstrating adequate psychometric properties (see below).

1. HEALTH AND MEDICAL EVALUATION

Health and medical evaluation is an important component of Level 2 testing, although methods included in this assessment category do not produce findings useful in diagnosing autism per se. Information gleaned from parent interview and behavioral observations serve as the primary basis for diagnosis. Nevertheless, health and medical evaluations for children with autism are productive in (1) determining the overall health status of children with or suspected of having developmental problems (recommended for this population of children), (2) identifying and/or ruling out medical conditions (e.g., hearing loss) often misdiagnosed as autism, and (3) determining the presence of medical or neurological conditions and genetic syndromes not included in the DSM-IV (APA, 1994) diagnostic criteria that may be more common in persons with autism (NYSDH, 1999). As might be expected, there is a large array of medical, laboratory, and related tests that are available for use during the health and medical evaluation. However, only a fraction of these tests are recommended during assessment of children with or suspected of having autism, as indicated by the presence of certain clinical features. Many available assessments are based on controversial theories about etiology and treatment options that have not been empirically validated, and are therefore not recommended at this time during routine health and medical evaluation.

Practitioners conducting health and medical evaluations are encouraged to actively assess for the co-occurrence of certain health conditions reported to have higher rates of comorbidity with autism, including neurological disorders such as tuberous sclerosis and seizure disorders (see NYSDH, 1999 for a list of conditions). First, as mentioned above, a hearing evaluation is always recommended as part of a health and medical evaluation for children at risk for or diagnosed with autism. Given that language delay is often an indication of developmental delay, possibly autism, hearing status must be evaluated via comprehensive audiological evaluation. Genetic testing for Fragile X and related chromosomal studies may be indicated in the presence of a family history of the disorder or possibly dysmorphic features, although the likelihood of testing positive is unlikely in individuals showing average or above average intellectual functioning (Filipek et al., 1999; NYSDH, 1999). Practitioners should always counsel parents about the increased risk, which is ~50 fold (Bolton et al., 1994; Szatmari et al., 1993), of subsequent children developing autism. Neurological evaluations should include a skin evaluation to look for signs of neurocutaneous disorders, such as neurofibromatosis or tuberous sclerosis complex, the latter of which shows a strong association with autism and comorbid epilepsy (Dykens & Volkmar, 1997). Sleep electroencephalogram (EEG) studies are currently recommended only when the clinical history indicates seizure activity, associated neurological abnormalities, regression (at any age but particularly in younger children), and when there is strong clinical suspicion of epilepsy (Filipek et al., 1999; NYSDH, 1999). Recommendations for neuroimaging studies generally follow customary practice guidelines that apply to any population, and use of functional imaging technologies are restricted at this time solely to research activities involving autism (Filipek et al., 1999; NYSDH, 1999). Testing linked with popularized conceptualizations about etiology and treatment, that is not recommended, and for which there is currently inadequate empirical support includes: (1) hair analysis for trace elements, (2) Celiac antibodies, (3) allergy testing (e.g., gluten, casein), (4) immunologic status and neurochemical abnormalities, (5) micronutrients (e.g., vitamin levels), (6) intestinal permeability studies, (7) stool analysis, and (8) urinary peptides (see Filipek et al., 1999 and NYSDH, 1999 for more in-depth reviews).

2. DEVELOPMENTAL EVALUATION

Children with autism and related disabilities tend to display highly idiosyncratic patterns of strengths and weaknesses across different developmental and skills domains. Developmental evaluations are typically conducted to

(1) objectively ascertain individualized profiles of strengths and weaknesses that highlight areas potentially requiring further assessment, (2) assist in eligibility determination for available services, and (3) facilitate treatment planning (NYSDH, 1999). Professionals conducting Level 2 evaluations are encouraged to conceptualize developmental testing as a periodic, ongoing process rather than an isolate, one-time event. Areas of functioning targeted during developmental evaluations typically include communication, cognitive/intellectual abilities, adaptive behavior, social skills, and behavioral excesses and deficits (e.g., aggression, self-injurious behavior, stereotypic behavior, unusual responses to sensory stimuli). Another component of developmental evaluation is assessment of pre-academic (e.g., imitation, compliance) and academic skills, the results of which are critical in developing curricula for subsequent evidence-based interventions (for more comprehensive coverage of various assessment methods conducted during the developmental evaluation, see Tyenda & Barrett, Dixon, and O'Reilly, this volume).

Evaluators also will need to allocate sufficient time and energy for assessing relevant aspects of family functioning and identifying available resources. Caring for a family member, or in some cases members, with autism or a related PDD can take a devastating toll on families and lead to considerable family stress, financial hardship, and other related challenges. Families' preparedness to accept the diagnosis and manage aspects of treatment and service coordination will likely vary as much as their respective children's profiles of strengths and weaknesses. Facilitating parent education regarding diagnoses, the progressively expanding maze of available "treatments," characteristics of evidence-based practices, and linkages to community resources related to intervention and other supports (e.g., family support groups) may represent the tip of the iceberg in terms of professionals' roles in working with families during and beyond the assessment process. Evaluators should recognize the extent and breadth of needs that families will have, and the impact overall family functioning is likely to have on child outcomes (National Research Council, 2001; NYSDH, 1999).

3. DIAGNOSTIC MEASURES

An array of standardized rating and observation scales and diagnostic interviews has been developed to assist practitioners in determining whether an individual is likely to have autism, in making autism diagnoses, and in evaluating the severity of autistic symptoms. The adequacy of measures implemented during the course of Level 2 evaluations is determined in part by the psychometric properties shown by each test. *Validity* has been defined as "the degree to which other evidence supports inferences drawn from the scores yielded by the diagnostic instrument" (Lord & Corsello, 2005, p. 740).

Validity is an overarching category that is typically divided into different subcategories of evidence, content, construct, and criterion-related validities. *Reliability* refers to "the degree to which a score or decision is free from errors of measurement" (Lord & Corsello, 2005, p. 736) and is determined on the basis of results from a number of related but different assessments (e.g., tests of internal consistency, interrater reliability). The following sections provide a general overview of commonly used autism diagnostic instruments generally showing acceptable psychometric properties (although not all measures covered are recommended at this point), although readers are directed to Lord and Corsello (2005) for more comprehensive coverage of diagnostic instruments and their respective psychometric data.

4. DIRECT OBSERVATION AND RATING SCALES

The Autism Behavior Checklist (ABC; Krug, Arick, & Almond, 1980a, 1980b) is composed of a list of questions about behavioral features of autism, with items categorized as sensory, relating, body and object use, language, and social and self-help skills. The actual content of the 57 items was developed on the basis of symptoms contained in other instruments and sources available at the time it was constructed, such as Kanner's early depiction (1943). The ABC was designed to differentiate school-age children with autism from those with other severe disabilities, although it has not been evaluated with children under 3 years of age. Administration takes about 10–20 minutes and is accomplished by parents or teachers or other caregivers knowledgeable about the child. Items are scored present/absent by assigning severity scores that are weighted, with higher scores indicating more severe symptomatology. Scoring and interpretation are then completed by a trained professional, and cutoffs of 67 or higher, 53–67, and below 53 characterized as highly probably, questionable, and unlikely autism, respectively (NYSDH, 1999). Sensitivity and specificity of the ABC was considered relatively low, and the absence of research with younger populations suggests the ABC may best be used when assessing older children and possibly adults (Coonrod & Stone, 2005).

The Childhood Autism Rating Scale (CARS; Schopler, Reichler, & Rochen-Renner, 1988) was developed as a direct observation measure to differentiate children with autism from those with other developmental disorders. The CARS has the reputation as being the most widely used, well-researched (DiLalla & Rogers, 1994; Sevin, Matson, Coe, Fee, & Sevin, 1991; Sturmey, Matson, & Sevin, 1992), and psychometrically sound rating scales available for diagnostic purposes (Lord & Corsello, 2005). The CARS is composed of 15 items and requires very relatively little training for use and administration, which may take ~20–30 minutes. The CARS also yields a severity rating, which may be useful in tracking outcomes in children diagnosed over time. While the

CARS has not been extensively researched with children under 3 years of age, it is a strong clinical instrument showing good psychometric properties, is very practical, and is highly recommended for use during Level 2 investigation.

The Gilliam Autism Rating Scale (GARS; Gilliam, 1995) is a 56-item behavioral checklist completed by parents to assess the presence and severity of autism symptoms in individuals 2–22 years of age. Items are grouped according to four subtests, including social interaction, stereotyped behaviors, communication, and developmental status. Reports describing psychometric properties for this instrument have been mixed, although a pending revision of the instrument is supposedly in development to address concerns. Discussion of the GARS was included in this section because the instrument has been used as a diagnostic tool by some researchers (Schreck & Mulick, 2000). However, the GARS is not recommended for independent use as diagnostic instrument at this point, and available research (South, Williams, & McMahon, 2002) does not support use of the GARS as a screening tool for preschool or school-age children.

The Autism Diagnostic Observation Schedule (ADOS; Lord, Rutter, DiLavore, & Risi, 1999; Lord et al., 2000) uses a standardized protocol to assess social and communicative skills in children suspected of having autism. The current ADOS represents a merger of the original ADOS (i.e., the ADOS-Generic) with the Pre-linguistic Autism Diagnostic Observation Schedule (PL-ADOS), plus the addition of two new modules (four total modules). The revision has greatly improved some previous problems with sensitivity and specificity, although the ADOS continues to under- and over-include children depending on the characteristic of the individuals assessed (Lord & Corsello, 2005). Nevertheless, the ADOS, along with the Autism Diagnostic Interview-Revised (ADI-R; Lord & Corsello, 2005; see below) continue to be regarded as the gold standard instruments of choice for research protocols involving diagnosis of autism (Filipek et al., 1999).

5. DIAGNOSTIC INTERVIEWS

The ADI-R (LeCouteur et al., 1989; Lord et al., 1994) is a semistructured clinical interview designed to be administered by a trained professional to parents of children suspected of having a diagnosis on the autism spectrum. The ADI-R was developed as a clinical diagnostic measure, and was based on the original ADI which served primarily as a research tool. Administration time for the ADI-R may be as long as 1.5–2 hours, and the instrument can be used with persons as young as 2 years of age (mental age of 18 months) through adulthood. The ADI-R is closely tied to DSM-IV (APA, 1994) diagnostic criteria and provides structure for gathering relevant parent information needed to make a diagnosis, although appropriate use of the ADI-R requires extensive and costly training. The ADI-R has strong psychometric properties and, as mentioned above, is regarded as the standard for comparison regarding autism diagnosis, particularly with respect to research protocols.

The Parent Interview for Autism (PIA; Stone & Hogan, 1993) is a structured interview designed to obtain diagnostic information from parents of young children with suspected autism. The instrument takes about 45 minutes to administer and contains 118 items phrased as questions that require parents to make judgments about frequencies of specific behaviors associated with autism. The one study found on the PIA reported strong psychometric properties, with social responses, communicative behavior, and play skills dimensions differentiating children with autism from children with mental retardation. Initial data on the PIA are supportive, although additional research is warranted.

V. SUMMARY

The development of and similarities between a number of practice parameters produced in recent years represents a confluence of scientific research and international priorities regarding the importance of early identification and intervention for individuals with PDDs and their families. Where differences between guideline recommendations do exist, discrepancies are relatively minor and are due in part to variations in the scopes of respective guidelines (Filipek et al., 1999). Perhaps, the most notable research activity during recent years is the explosion of new autism-specific screening measures, such as the M-CHAT and the PDDST-II, available for use during routine developmental surveillance. These instruments are designed to enhance recognition of children at risk for autism either in the general population or in groups of children already identified as being at risk for developmental disabilities. In the absence of biological markers, which many hope will eventually allow identification at birth or possibly *in utero*, researchers have been forced to focus efforts on discovering clinical symptoms of autism that at best allow differentiation and at minimum serve as red flags during the first year of life (Baranek, 1999; Mars, Mauk, & Dowrick, 1998; Osterling & Dawson, 1994). This line of research has paved the way for subsequent development of screening tests, some of which are recommended for use and some of which are in development. As stated above, there are differing views regarding the accuracy of diagnoses made in children younger than 3 years of age (Baron-Cohen et al., 1996; Charman et al., 2005). Nevertheless, what remains problematic with respect to lowering the age (e.g., closer to the beginning of the third year of life) at which diagnoses actually tend to occur is the shortage of professionals who are both well-placed to make contact with young children at risk for autism (e.g., day care staff, pediatricians) and who also are adequately prepared to respond in the presence of red flag clinical symptoms. Training and outreach models, such as Project First STEP (Screening, Training, Education Project) developed by Koegel et al. (2005), are desperately needed to transfer available surveillance and screening technologies into clinical practice. Such endeavors are likely to produce a cascade of effects, including increasing referrals of children at risk and lowering the age at which referrals are made, which may result in lowering the age at which evidence-based early intervention begins, and most importantly, maximizing developmental trajectories of children with autism.

REFERENCES

Ahearn, W. H., Castine, T., Nault, K., & Green, G. (2001). An assessment of food acceptance in children with autism or pervasive developmental disorder—not otherwise specified. *Journal of Autism and Developmental Disorders, 31,* 505–512.

American Academy of Pediatrics, Committee on Children With Disabilities (2001). Developmental surveillance and screening of infants and young children. *Pediatrics, 108,* 192–195.

American Academy of Pediatrics, Council on Children With Disabilities Section on Developmental Behavioral Pediatrics, Bright Futures Steering Committee and Medical Home Initiatives for Children With Special Needs Project Advisory Committee (2006). Identifying infants and young children with developmental disorders in the medical home: An algorithm for developmental surveillance and screening. *Pediatrics, 118*(1), 405–420.

American Psychiatric Association (1994). *Diagnostic and statistical manual of mental disorders* (4th ed.). Washington, DC: American Psychiatric Association.

Asperger, H. (1991). "Autistic psychopathy" in childhood. U. Frith (Ed. & Trans.), *Autism and Asperger Syndrome* (pp. 37–92). New York: Cambridge University Press. (Original work published 1944).

Aylward, G. P. (1997). Conceptual issues in developmental screening and assessment. *Journal of Developmental and Behavioural Pediatrics, 18,* 340–349.

Baird, G., Charman, T., Baron-Cohen, S., Cox, A., Swettenham, J., Wheelwright, S., et al. (2000). A screening instrument for autism at 18 months of age: A six year follow-up study. *Journal of the American Academy of Child and Adolescent Psychiatry, 39,* 694–702.

Baranek, G. T. (1999). Autism during infancy: A retrospective video analysis of sensory-motor and social behaviors at 9–12 months of age. *Journal of Autism and Developmental Disorders, 29,* 213–224.

Baron-Cohen, S., Allen, J., & Gillberg, C. (1992). Can autism be detected at 18 months? The needle, the haystack, and the CHAT. *British Journal of Psychiatry, 161,* 839–843.

Baron-Cohen, S., Cox, A., Baird, G., Swettenham, J., Nightingale, N., Morgan, K., et al. (1996). Psychological markers in the detection of autism in infancy in a large population. *British Journal of Psychiatry, 168,* 158–163.

Bertrand, J., Mars, A., Boyle, C., Bove, F., Yeargin-Allsop, M., & Decoufle, P. (2001). Prevalence of autism in a United States population: The Brick Township, New Jersey, investigation. *Pediatrics, 108,* 1155–1161.

Bolton, P., Macdonald, H., Pickles, A., Rios, P., Goode, S., Crowson, M., et al. (1994). A case-control family history study of autism. *Journal of Child Psychology and Psychiatry, and allied disciplines, 35,* 877–900.

Bricker, D., & Squires, J. (1999). *Ages and stages questionnaire* (2nd ed.). Baltimore: Paul H. Brookes.

Bristol-Power, M. M., & Spinella, G. (1999). Research on screening and diagnosis in autism: A work in progress. *Journal of Autism and Developmental Disorders, 29,* 435–438.

Chakrabarti, S., & Fombonne, E. (2001). Pervasive developmental disorders in preschool children. *Journal of the American Medical Association, 285,* 3093–3099.

Charlop-Christy, M. H., & Daneshvar, S. (2003). Using video modeling to teach perspective taking to children with autism. *Journal of Positive Behavioral Interventions, 5,* 12–21.

Charman, T. (2003). Screening and surveillance for autism spectrum disorder in research and practice. *Early Child Development and Care, 173,* 363–374.

Charman, T., Cass, H., Owen, L., Wigram, T., Slonims, V., Weeks, L., et al. (2002). Regression in individuals with Rett syndrome. *Brain & Development, 24,* 281–283.

Charman, T., Swettenham, J., Baron-Cohen, S., Cox, A., Baird, G., & Drew, A. (1997). Infants with autism: An investigation of empathy, pretend play, joint attention, and imitation. *Developmental Psychology, 33,* 781–789.

Charman, T., Swettenham, J., Baron-Cohen, S., Cox, A., Baird, G., & Drew, A. (1998). An experimental investigation of socialcognitive abilities in infants with autism: Clinical implications. *Infant Mental Health Journal, 19,* 260–275.

Charman, T., Taylor, E., Drew, A., Cockerill, H., Brown, J., & Baird, G. (2005). Outcome at 7 years of children diagnosed with autism at age 2: Predictive validity of assessment conducted at 2 and 3 years of age and pattern of symptom change over time. *Journal of Child Psychology and Psychiatry, and allied disciplines, 46,* 500–513.

Coonrod, E. E., & Stone, W. L. (2005). Screening for autism in young children. In F. R. Volkmar, R. Paul, A. Klin, & D. Cohen (Eds.), *Handbook of autism and pervasive developmental disorders* (pp. 707–729). Hoboken, NJ: John Wiley & Sons, Inc.

Cox, A., Klein, K., Charman, T., Baird, G., Baron-Cohen, S., Swettenham, J., et al. (1999a). The early diagnosis of autism spectrum disorders: Use of the autism diagnostic interview-revised at 20 months and 42 months of age. *Journal of Child Psychology and Psychiatry, and allied disciplines, 40,* 705–718.

Cox, A., Klein, K., Charman, T., Baird, G., Baron-Cohen, S., Swettenham, J., et al. (1999b). Autism spectrum disorders at 20 and 42 months of age: Stability of clinical and ADI-R diagnosis. *Journal of Child Psychology and Psychiatry, and allied disciplines, 40,* 719–732.

Dawson, G., & Osterling, J. (1997). Early intervention in autism: Effectiveness and common elements of current approaches. In M. J. Guralnick (Ed.), *The effectiveness of early intervention: Second generation research* (pp. 307–326). Baltimore: Brookes.

DeGiacomo, A., & Fombonne, E. (1998). Parental recognition of developmental abnormalities in autism. *European Child & Adolescent Psychiatry, 7,* 131–136.

DiLalla, D. L., & Rogers, S. J. (1994). Domains of the Childhood Autism Rating Scale: Relevance for diagnosis and treatment. *Journal of Autism and Developmental Disorders, 24,* 115–128.

Dobos, A. E., Dworkin, P. H., & Bernstein, B. (1994). Pediatricians' approaches to developmental problems: 15 years later. *American Journal of Diseases of Children, 2,* 34–38.

Dua, V. (2003). Standards and guidelines for the assessment and diagnosis of young children with autism spectrum disorder in British Columbia: An evidence-based report prepared for the British Columbia ministry of health planning. Retrieved June 1, 2006, from http://www.health.gov.bc.ca/cpa/publications/asd_standards_0318.pdf.

Dube, W. V., MacDonald, R. P. F., & Mansfield, R. C. (2004). Toward a behavioral analysis of joint attention. *Behavior Analyst, 27,* 197–207.

Dumont-Mathieu, T., & Fein, D. (2005). Screening for autism in young children: The modified checklist for Autism in toddlers (M-CHAT) and other measures. *Mental Retardation and Developmental Disabilities Research Reviews, 11,* 253–262.

Dworkin, P. H. (1989). British and American recommendations for developmental monitoring: The role of surveillance. *Pediatrics, 84,* 1000–1010.

Dworkin, P. H. (1992). Developmental screening: (Still) expecting the impossible? *Pediatrics, 89,* 1253–1255.

Dworkin, P. H. (1993). Detection of behavioral, developmental, and psychosocial problems in pediatric primary care practice. *Current Opinion in Pediatrics, 5,* 531–536.

Dykens, E. M., & Volkmar, F. R. (1997). Medical conditions associated with autism. In D. J. Cohen & F. R. Volkmar (Eds.), *Handbook of autism and pervasive developmental disorders* (2nd ed., pp. 388–410). New York: Wiley.

Eikeseth, S., Smith, T., Jahr, E., & Eldevik, S. (2002). Intensive behavioral treatment at school for 4–7-year-old children with autism. *Behavior Modification, 26,* 49–68.

Filipek, P. A., Accardo, P. J., Ashwal, S., Baranek, G. T., Cook, E. H., Jr., Dawson, G., et al. (2000). Practice parameter: Screening and diagnosis of autism. Report of the quality standards committee of the American Academy of Neurology and the Child Neurology Society. *Neurology, 55,* 468–479.

Filipek, P. A., Accardo, P. J., Baranek, G. T., Cook, E. H., Jr., Dawson, G., Gordon, B., et al. (1999). The screening and diagnosis of autistic spectrum disorders. *Journal of Autism and Developmental Disorders, 29,* 439–484.

Fombonne, E. (2003). Epidemiological surveys of autism and other pervasive developmental disorders: An update. *Journal of Autism and Developmental Disorders, 33,* 365–382.

Ghaziuddin, M., & Gerstein, L. (1996). Pedantic speaking style differentiates Asperger syndrome from high-functioning autism. *Journal of Autism and Developmental Disorders, 26,* 585–595.

Gillberg, C. (1994). Debate and argument: Having Rett syndrome in the ICD-10 PDD category does not make sense. *Journal of Child Psychology and Psychiatry, and Allied Disciplines, 35,* 377–378.

Gilliam, J. E. (1995). *Gilliam Autism Rating Scale (GARS)*. Austin, TX: Pro-Ed.

Glascoe, F. P. (1994). It's not what it seems. The relationship between parents' concerns and children with global delays. *Clinical Pediatrics, 33,* 292–296.

Glascoe, F. P. (1997a). Parents' concerns about children's development: Prescreening technique or screening test? *Pediatrics, 99,* 522–528.

Glascoe, F. P. (1997b). *Parents' evaluation of developmental status (PEDS)*. Nashville, TN: Ellsworth & Vandermeer.

Glascoe, F. P. (1998). *Collaborating with parents: Using parents' evaluation of developmental status to detect and address developmental and behavioral problems.* Nashville, TN: Ellsworth and Vandermeer.

Glascoe, F. P. (2000). Detecting and addressing developmental and behavioural problems in primary care. *Pediatric Nursing, 26*(3), 251–266.

Glascoe, F. P. (2002). The Brigance infant and toddler screen: Standardization and validation. *Journal of Developmental & Behavioral Pediatrics, 23,* 145–150.

Glascoe, F. P. (2005). Screening for developmental and behavioral problems. *Mental Retardation and Developmental Disabilities Research Reviews, 11,* 173–179.

Glascoe, F. P., Byrne, K. E., Ashford, L. G., Johnson, K. L., Chang, B., & Strickland, B. (1992). Accuracy of the Denver-II in developmental screening. *Pediatrics, 89,* 1221–1225.

Glascoe, F. P., & Dworkin, P. H. (1995). The role of parents in the detection of developmental and behavioral problems. *Pediatrics, 95,* 829–836.

Glascoe, F. P., & Sandler, H. (1995). Value of parents' estimates of children's developmental ages. *Journal of Pediatrics, 127,* 831–835.

Glaze, D. G. (2004). Rett syndrome: Of girls and mice-lessons for regression in autism. *Mental Retardation and Developmental Disabilities Research Reviews, 10,* 154–158.

Gomez, C. R., & Baird, S. (2005). Identifying early indicators for autism in self-regulation difficulties. *Focus on Autism and Other Developmental Disabilities, 2,* 106–116.

Guralnick, M. J. (1998). The effectiveness of early intervention for vulnerable children: A developmental perspective. *American Journal on Mental Retardation, 102,* 319–345.

Heller, T. (1930). Über Dementia infantilis. *Zeitschrift für Kinderforschnung, 37,* 661–667.

Hobson, R. P. (1986). The autistic child's appraisal of expressions of emotion. *Journal of Child Psychology and Psychiatry, and Allied Disciplines, 27,* 321–342.

Howard, J. S., Sparkman, C. R., Cohen, H. G., Green, G., & Stanislaw, H. (2005). A comparison of intensive behavior analytic and eclectic treatments for young children with autism. *Research in Developmental Disabilities, 26,* 359–383.

Howlin, P., & Asgharian, A. (1999). The diagnosis of autism and Asperger syndrome: Findings from a survey of 770 families. *Developmental Medicine & Child Neurology, 41,* 834–839.

Howlin, P., & Moore, A. (1997). Diagnosis of autism. A survey of over 1200 patients in the UK. *Autism, 1,* 135–162.

Huttenlocher, P. R. (1994). Synaptogenesis in the human cerebral cortex. In G. Dawson & K. W. Fischer (Eds.), *Human behavior and the developing brain* (pp. 137–152). New York: Guilford Press.

Huttenlocher, P. R. (2002). Neural plasticity: The effects of environment on the development of the cerebral cortex. In S. M. Kosslyn (Ed.), *Perspectives in cognitive neuroscience* Cambridge, MA: Harvard University Press.

Ireton, H. (1992). *Child development inventories.* Minneapolis, MN: Behavior Science Systems.

Ireton, H., & Glascoe, F. P. (1995). Assessing children's development using parents' reports. The child development inventory. *Clinical Pediatrics, 34,* 248–255.

Jacobson, J. W., Mulick, J. A., & Green, G. (1998). Cost benefit estimates for early intensive behavioral intervention for young children with autism-general model and single state case. *Behavioral Interventions, 13,* 201–226.

Järbrink, K., Fombonne, E., & Knapp, M. (2003). Measuring the parental service and costs of autistic spectrum disorder: A pilot study. *Journal of Autism and Developmental Disorders, 33,* 395–402.

Järbrink, K., & Knapp, M. (2001). The economic impact of autism in Britain. *Autism, 5,* 7–22.

Kanner, L. (1943). Autistic disturbances of affective contact. *Nervous Child, 2,* 217–250.

Kerr, A. M. (1995). Early clinical signs in the Rett disorder. *Neuropediatrics, 26,* 67–71.

Klin, A., & Shepard, B. (1994). Psychological assessment of autistic children. *Child and Adolescent Psychiatric Clinics of North America, 3,* 53–69.

Koegel, L. K., Koegel, R. L., Nefdt, N., Fredeen, R., Klein, E. F., & Bruinsma, Y. E. M. (2005). First S.T.E.P: A model for the early identification of children with autism spectrum disorders. *Journal of Positive Behavior Interventions, 7,* 247–252.

Koegel, R. L., Openden, D., & Koegel, L. K. (2004). A systematic desensitization paradigm to treat hypersensitivity to auditory stimuli in children with autism in family contexts. *Research & Practice for Person with Severe Disabilities, 29,* 122–134.

Krug, D. A., Arick, J. R., & Almond, P. J. (1980a). *Autism screening instrument for educational planning.* Portland, OR: ASIEP Education.

Krug, D. A., Arick, J. R., & Almond, P. J. (1980b). Behavior checklist for identifying severely handicapped individuals with high levels of autistic behavior. *Journal of Child Psychology and Psychiatry, and Allied Disciplines, 21,* 221–229.

LeCouteur, A., Rutter, M., Lord, C., Rios, P., Robertson, S., Holdgrafer, M., et al. (1989). Autism Diagnostic Interview: A standardized investigator-based instrument. *Journal of Autism and Developmental Disorders, 19,* 363–387.

Leekam, S. R., Hunnisett, E., & Moore, C. (1998). Targets and cues: Gaze following in children with autism. *Journal of Child Psychology and Psychiatry, and Allied Disciplines, 39,* 951–962.

Leekam, S. R., Lopez, B., & Moore, C. (2000). Attention and joint attention in preschool children with autism. *Developmental Psychology, 36,* 261–273.

Lord, C. (1995). Follow-up of two-year-olds referred for possible autism. *Journal of Child Psychology and Psychiatry, and Allied Disciplines, 36,* 1365–1382.

Lord, C., & Corsello, C. (2005). Diagnostic instruments in autism spectrum disorders. In F. R. Volkmar, R. Paul, A. Klin, & D. Cohen (Eds.), *Handbook of autism and pervasive developmental disorders* (3rd ed., pp. 730–771). Hoboken, NJ: John Wiley & Sons, Inc.

Lord, C., Risi, S., Lambrecht, L., Cook, E. H., Jr., Leventhal, B. L., DiLavore, P. C., et al. (2000). The Autism Diagnostic Observation Schedule—Generic: A standard measure of social and communication deficits associated with the spectrum of autism. *Journal of Autism and Developmental Disorders, 30,* 205–223.

Lord, C., Rutter, M., DiLavore, P. C., & Risi, S. (1999). *Autism diagnostic observation schedule-WPS.* (WPS ed.). Los Angeles: Western Psychological Services.

Lord, C., Rutter, M., & LeCouteur, A. (1994). Autism Diagnostic Interview-Revised: A revised version of a diagnostic interview for caregivers of individuals with possible pervasive developmental disorders. *Journal of Autism and Developmental Disorders, 24,* 659–685.

Lotter, V. (1966). Epidemiology of autistic conditions in young children, I. Prevalence. *Social Psychiatry, 1,* 124–137.

Lovaas, O. I. (1987). Behavioral treatment and normal educational and intellectual functioning in young autistic children. *Journal of Consulting and Clinical Psychology, 55,* 3–9.

Lovaas, O. I., Koegel, R. L., & Schreibman, L. (1979). Stimulus overselectivity in autism: A review of research. *Psychological Bulletin, 86,* 1236–1254.

MacDonald, R., Anderson, J., & Dube, W. V. (2006). Behavioral assessment of joint attention: A methodological report. *Research in Developmental Disabilities, 27,* 138–150.

Malhotra, S., & Gupta, N. (1999). Childhood disintegrative disorder. *Journal of Autism and Developmental Disorders, 29,* 491–498.

Marcus, L. M., Rubin, J. S., & Rubin, M. A. (2000). Benefit–cost analysis and autism services: A response to Jacobson and Mulick. *Journal of Autism and Developmental Disorders, 30,* 595–598.

Mars, A. E., Mauk, J. E., & Dowrick, P. (1998). Symptoms of pervasive developmental disorders as observed in prediagnostic home videos of infants and toddlers. *Journal of Pediatrics, 132,* 500–504.

Matson, J. L., Benavidez, D. A., Compton, L. S., Paclawskyj, T., & Baglio, C. (1996). Behavioral treatment of autistic persons: A review of research from 1980 to the present. *Research in Developmental Disabilities, 17,* 433–465.

McEachin, J. J., Smith, T., & Lovaas, O. I. (1993). Long-term outcome for children with autism who received early intensive behavioral treatment. *American Journal of Mental Retardation, 97,* 359–372.

Meisels, S. J., & Provence, S. (1989). Screening and assessment. *Guidelines for identifying young disabled and developmentally vulnerable children and their families.* Washington, DC: National Center for Clinical Infant Programs.

Midence, K., & O'Neill, M. (1999). The experience of parents in the diagnosis of autism. *Autism, 3,* 273–283.

Moore, V., & Goodson, S. (2003). How well does early diagnosis of autism stand the test of time? Follow-up study of children assessed for autism at age 2 and development of an early diagnostic service. *Autism, 7,* 47–63.

Mundy, P., Sigman, M., & Kasari, C. (1990). A longitudinal study of joint attention and language development in autistic children. *Journal of Autism and Developmental Disorders, 20,* 115–128.

National Research Council (2001). Educating children with autism. Committee on Educational Interventions for Children with Autism. In C. Lord & J. P. McGee (Eds.) *Division of behavioral and social sciences and education.* Washington, DC: National Academy Press.

National Research Council and Institute of Medicine (2000). *From neurons to neighborhoods: The science of early childhood development.* Committee on Integrating the Science of Early Childhood Development. In J. P. Shonkoff & D. A. Phillips (Eds.), *Board on Children, Youth, and Families, Commission on Behavioral and Social Sciences and Education.* Washington, DC: National Academy Press.

New York State Department of Health (1999). *Clinical practice guideline: The guideline technical report. Autism/pervasive developmental disorders, assessment and intervention for young children (0–3 Years).* Albany, NY: New York State Department of Health, Early Intervention Program.

Nomura, Y. (2005). Early behavior characteristics and sleep disturbance in Rett syndrome. *Brain & Development, 27,* S35–S42.

Nomura, Y., & Segawa, M. (2005). Natural history of Rett syndrome. *Journal of Child Neuroslogy, 20,* 764–768.

Osterling, J., & Dawson, G. (1994). Early recognition of children with autism: A study of first birthday home videotapes. *Journal of Autism and Developmental Disorders, 24,* 247–257.

Percy, A., Gillberg, C., Hagberg, B., & Witt-Engerstrom, I. (1990). Rett syndrome and the autistic disorders. *Neurologic Clinics, 8,* 659–676.

Percy, A. K., Zoghbi, H. Y., Lewis, K. R., & Jankovic, K. (1988). Rett syndrome: Qualitative and quantitative differentiation from autism. *Journal of Child Neurology, 3,* 65–67.

Piazza, C. C., Fisher, W. W., Hanley, G. P., LeBlanc, L. A., Worsdell, A. S., Lindauer, S. E., et al. (1998). Treatment of pica through multiple analyses of its reinforcing functions. *Journal of Applied Behavior Analysis, 31,* 165–189.

Pinto-Martin, J. A., Dunkle, M., Earls, M., Fliedner, D., & Landes, C. (2005). Developmental stages of developmental screening: Steps to implementation of a successful program. *American Journal of Public Health, 95,* 1928–1932.

Piper, E., & Howlin, P. (1992). Assessing and diagnosing developmental disorders that are not evident at birth: Parental evaluations of intake procedures. *Child: Care, Health and Development, 18,* 35–55.

Reigelman, R. K., & Hirsch, R. P. (1989). *Studying a study and testing a test. How to read the medical literature* (2nd ed.). Boston: Little, Brown and Co.

Robins, D. L., Fein, D., Barton, M. L., & Green, J. A. (2001). The Modified Checklist for Autism in Toddlers: An initial study investigating the early detection of autism and pervasive developmental disorders. *Journal of Autism and Developmental Disorders, 31,* 131–144.

Rogers, S. J. (2001). Diagnosis of autism before the age of 3. *International Review of Research in Mental Retardation, 23,* 1–31.

Rogers, S. J., & DiLalla, D. L. (1990). Age of symptom onset in young children with pervasive developmental disorders. *Journal of the American Academy of Child and Adolescent Psychiatry, 29,* 863–872.

Rutter, M., & Lord, C. (1987). Language disorders associated with psychiatric disturbance. In W. Rule & M. Rutter (Eds.), *Language development and disorders* (pp. 206–233). Philadelphia: J.B. Lippincott.

Sand, N., Silverstein, M., Glascoe, F. P., Gupta, V. B., Tonniges, T. P., & O'Connor, K. G. (2006). Pediatricians' reported practices regarding developmental screening: Do guidelines work? Do they help? *Journal of the American Academy of Child & Adolescent Psychiatry, 45,* 7–7.

Schopler, E., Reichler, R., & Rochen-Renner, B. (1988). *The Childhood Autism Rating Scale (CARS)*. Los Angeles, CA: Western Psychological Services.

Schreck, K. A., & Mulick, J. A. (2000). Parental report of sleep problems in children with autism. *Journal of Autism and Developmental Disorders, 30,* 127–135.

Sevin, J. A., Matson, J. L., Coe, D. A., Fee, V. E., & Sevin, B. M. (1991). A comparison and evaluation of three commonly used autism scales. *Journal of Autism and Developmental Disorders, 21,* 417–432.

Shannon, M., & Graef, J. W. (1997). Lead intoxication in children with pervasive developmental disorders. *Journal of Toxicology - Clinical Toxicology, 34,* 177–182.

Sheinkopf, S., Mundy, P., Oller, K., & Steffens, M. (2000). Atypical vocal development in young children with autism. *Journal of Autism and Related Disorders, 30,* 345–354.

Siegel, B. (1996). *The world of the autistic child: Understanding and treating autistic spectrum disorders*. New York, NY: Oxford University Press.

Siegel, B. (2004). *Pervasive Developmental Disorders Screening Test-II (PDDST-II): Early childhood screeners for autistic spectrum disorders*. San Antonio, TX: Harcourt Assessment, Inc.

Siegel, B., Pliner, C., Eschler, J., & Elliott, G. R. (1988). How children with autism are diagnosed: Difficulties in identification of children with multiple developmental delays. *Journal of Developmental and Behavioral Pediatrics, 9*(4), 199–204.

Smith, B., Chung, M. C., & Vostanis, P. (1994). The path to care in autism: Is it better now? *Journal of Autism and Developmental Disorders, 24,* 551–563.

Solomon, M., Goodlin-Jones, B., & Anders, T. (2004). A social adjustment for high functioning autism, Asperger's syndrome, and pervasive developmental disorder NOS. *Journal of Autism and Developmental Disorders, 34,* 649–668.

South, M., Ozonoff, S., & McMahon, W. M. (2005). Repetitive behavior profiles in Asperger syndrome and high-functioning autism. *Journal of Autism and Developmental Disorders, 35,* 145–158.

South, M., Williams, B. J., & McMahon, W. M. (2002). Utility of the Gilliam Autism Rating Scale in research and clinical populations. *Journal of Autism and Developmental Disorders, 32,* 593–599.

Squires, J., Bricker, D., & Potter, L. (1997). Revision of a parent-completed developmental screening tool: Ages and stages questionnaires. *Journal of Pediatric Psychology, 22,* 313–328.

Squires, J., Potter, L., & Bricker, D. (1999). *The ASQ user's guide for the Ages & Stages Questionnaires: A parent-completed, child-monitoring system* (2nd ed.). Baltimore: Paul Brookes.

Stone, W. L., Coonrod, E. E., & Ousley, O. Y. (2000). Screening tool for autism in two-year-olds (STAT): Development and preliminary data [Brief report]. *Journal of Autism and Developmental Disorders, 30,* 607–612.

Stone, W. L., Coonrod, E. E., & Turner, L. M. (2004). Psychometric properties of the STAT for early autism screening. *Journal of Autism and Developmental Disorders, 34,* 691–701.

Stone, W. L., & Hogan, K. L. (1993). A structured parent interview for identifying young children with autism. *Journal of Autism and Developmental Disorders, 23,* 639–652.

Stone, W. L., Lee, E. B., Ashford, L., Brissie, J., Hepburn, S. L., Coonrod, E. E., et al. (1999). Can autism be diagnosed accurately in children under three years? *Journal of Child Psychology and Psychiatry, and Allied Disciplines, 40,* 219–226.

Sturmey, P., Matson, J. L., & Sevin, J. A. (1992). Analysis of the internal consistency of three autism scales. *Journal of Autism and Developmental Disorders, 22,* 321–328.

Szatmari, P., Jones, M. B., Tuff, L., Bartolucci, G., Fisman, S., & Mahoney, W. (1993). Lack of cognitive impairment in first-degree relatives of children with pervasive developmental disorders. *Journal of the American Academy of Child and Adolescent Psychiatry, 32,* 1264–1273.

Thomas, M. C. S. (2003). Limits on Plasticity. *Journal of Cognition and Development, 4,* 99–125.

Tuchman, R. F., & Rapin, I. (1997). Regression in pervasive developmental disorders: Seizures and epileptiform electroencephalogram correlates. *Pediatrics, 99,* 560–566.

Volkmar, F. R., Cohen, D. J., Bregman, J. D., Hooks, M. Y., & Stevenson, J. M. (1989). An examination of social typologies in autism. *Journal of the American Academy of Child and Adolescent Psychiatry, 28,* 82–86.

Volkmar, F. R., Cook, E. H. J., Pomeroy, J., Realmuto, G., & Tanguay, P. (1999). Practice parameters for autism and pervasive developmental disorders. *Journal of the American Academy of Child and Adolescent Psychiatry, 38,* 32S–54S.

Volkmar, F. R., & Klin, A. (2000). Pervasive developmental disorders. In B. J. Sadock & V. A. Sadock (Eds.), *Kaplan and Sadock's comprehensive textbook of psychiatry* (7th ed., pp. 2659–2678). Philadelphia, PA: Lippincott Williams & Wilkins.

Volkmar, F. R., Klin, A., Schultz, R., Bronen, R., Marans, W. D., Sparrow, S., et al. (1996). Asperger's syndrome [Clinical conference]. *Journal of the American Academy of Child and Adolescent Psychiatry, 35,* 118–123.

Volkmar, F., Koenig, K., & State, M. (2005). Childhood disintegrative disorder. In F. R. Volkmar, R. Paul, A. Klin, & D. Cohen (Eds.), *Handbook of autism and pervasive developmental disorders* (3rd ed., pp. 730–771). Hoboken, NJ: John Wiley & Sons, Inc.

Volkmar, F. R., & Rutter, M. (1995). Childhood disintegrative disorder: Results of the DSM-IV autism field trial. *Journal of the American Academy of Child and Adolescent Psychiatry, 34,* 1092–1095.

Walters, A. S., Barrett, R. P., & Feinstein, C. (1990). Social relatedness and autism: Current research, issues, directions. *Research in Developmental Disabilities, 11,* 303–326.

Wetherby, A. M., Yonclas, D. G., & Bryan, A. A. (1989). Communicative profiles of preschool children with handicaps: Implications for early identification. *Journal of Speech and Hearing Disorders, 54,* 148–158.

Wong, V., Hui, L. H., Lee, W. C., Leung, L. S., Ho, P. K., Lau, W. L., et al. (2004). A modified screening tool for autism (Checklist for Autism in Toddlers [CHAT-23]) for Chinese children. *Pediatrics, 114,* 166–176.

World Health Organization (1993). *The ICD-10 classification of mental and behavioural disorders: Diagnostic criteria for research.* Geneva: World Health Organization.

Zimmerman, A. W., & Gordon, B. (2000). Neural mechanisms in autism. In P. J. Accardo, C. Magnusen, & A. J. Capute (Eds.), *Autism: Clinical and research issues* (pp. 659–721). Timonium: York Press.

Psychopathology: Depression, Anxiety, and Related Disorders

PETER STURMEY

DEPARTMENT OF PSYCHOLOGY, QUEENS COLLEGE AND THE GRADUATE CENTER, CITY UNIVERSITY OF NEW YORK, NEW YORK

I. INTRODUCTION

Mood and anxiety disorders are the most common forms of psychopathology: if a person has psychopathology, the chances are it is a mood or anxiety disorder. The two most comprehensive epidemiological surveys provide strong evidence for this assertion. The Epidemiologic Catchment Survey (ECS) estimated that 3.7% of the general population has some affective disorder, 2.7% has a major depressive episode and ~1% has experiences bipolar disorder in the previous 12 months. The lifetime prevalence of any affective disorder was 7.8% (Weissman et al., 1996). The National Comorbidity Survey (NCS) estimated 12-month prevalnces of 11.3% and a lifetime prevalence of 19.3% for any affective disorder (Kessler et al., 1994). Similarly high figures have also been reported for anxiety disorders. The ECS estimated that the 12-month prevalence of any anxiety disorder was 13% and the NCS estimated 19%. In contrast, these surveys estimated that prevalence of psychotic disorders to be one order of magnitude less prevalent, that is, ~1%. Thus, these surveys support the notion that mood and anxiety are indeed the most common psychiatric disorders; hence assessment of mood and anxiety disorders is likely to be a common and important clinical activity that practitioners should perform competently.

Mood and anxiety disorders are also relatively common in people with intellectual disabilities (ID). For example, depressive disorders in people with ID have received extensive interest over the last 30 years (Dosen & Menalascino, 1990; Matson, 1983; Sturmey, 2005a). Many authors have suggested that people with ID are at high risk for these disorders because of increased vulnerabilities, such as poor social skills, social strain, poor

INTERNATIONAL REVIEW OF RESEARCH IN MENTAL RETARDATION, Vol. 34
0074-7750/07 $35.00

DOI: 10.1016/S0074-7750(07)34006-8

problem-solving skills, social isolation, and stigmatization. Rojahn and Ebensen's (2005) careful review of the epidemiological literature indeed confirmed high prevalences reported in some studies. However, the generally poor quality of the diagnosis, case finding, sampling, and population definition precluded confidence in such a conclusion. Nevertheless, depressive sisorders remain an important aspect of mental health in people with ID, because they are so common. Depressive disorders are associated with preventable disability, human suffering, and financial and personal costs to many people. Anxiety disorders may also be common in people with ID. For example, Dekker and Koot (2003a,b) surveyed 474 Dutch children with ID aged 7 to 20 years in Dutch special education settings. Using a standardized assessment they found that 22% of children met DSM-IV criteria for an anxiety disorder. Again, as with studies of depression, these high figures should be considered cautiously, as issues of sampling and correspondence between psychometric measures and actual diagnosis are often suspect. Thus, as in the general population, there is evidence that depression and anxiety disorders are relatively common in people with ID. Hence, we should expect the assessment and treatment of mood and anxiety disorders in people with ID to be a common area of concern.

This chapter reviews the diagnosis and assessment of mood, anxiety, and related disorders in people with ID. It is important to note that assessment takes place for several different reasons, including determining eligibility for services, explaining behavior, facilitating communication among practitioners and scientists, guiding treatment, and making a prognosis. For each of these groups of disorders, I first review the *Diagnostic and Statistical Manual,* Fourth Edition, Text Revision (DSM-IV-TR) (American Psychiatric Association, 2000) criteria and their application to people with ID and related developmental disabilities. Then, I review the available interview protocols and psychometric instruments to aid diagnosis. Finally, I consider the role of assessment using functional assessment and analysis, both in understanding the nature of such behavior and in guiding behavior analytic-based treatment.

II. DEPRESSIVE DISORDERS

A. Diagnosis

DSM-IV-TR (American Psychiatric Association, 2000) distinguishes four disorders related to depressed mood: major depressive disorder, single episode; major depressive disorder, recurrent; dysthymic disorder; and depressive mood disorder not otherwise specified (NOS). These disorders are defined by the presence or absence of various mood episodes, such as major depressive episode, manic episode, mixed episode, and hypomanic episode, combined with other criteria related to length and severity of the problem and various rule out criteria.

A major depressive episode is diagnosed when five or more of nine depressive symptoms are found; when the criteria for a mixed episode is not met; when there is clinically significant distress or impairment; and when other causes, such as drugs, a general medical condition and normal bereavement are absent. The nine symptoms include: depressed mood, loss of pleasure and interest, change in weight, sleep disturbance, psychomotor agitation or retardation, fatigue of loss of energy, feelings of worthlessness and guilt, problems thinking or concentrating, and recurrent thoughts of death and/or suicidal ideas, plans, or attempts. A manic episode is diagnosed when there is a period of "abnormally and persistently elevated, expansive, or irritable mood lasting at least one week" (p. 332), at least three or more of seven manic symptoms, the person does not meet the criteria for a mixed episode, involve significant impairment and the effects are not due to drugs of abuse or a general medical condition. The seven manic symptoms include inflated self esteem or grandiosity, reduced sleeping, increased talking or pressured speech, flights or ideas or experiencing racing thoughts, increased goal-directed activities, and engagement in pleasurable activities that are potentially dangerous. A mixed episode is diagnosed when the person meets the criteria for both manic and depressed episode, but for only one week, there is marked impairment and drugs and medical conditions are not the cause of the presenting problem. A hypomanic episode is defined as a period of at least 4 days of elevated, expansive, or irritable mood, the person had three or more manic symptoms, the episode is a clear change in the person's behavior and observable to others, but is not severe enough to cause marked impairment in functioning, and is not due to drugs or general medical conditions. A mixed episode is defined as when the criteria for both a manic and a major depressed episode are met nearly every day for at least one week, that there is marked impairment in functioning and that the symptoms are not due to substance abuse or a general medical condition. A hypomanic episode is defined as "a distinct period of persistently elevated, expansive, or irritable mood, lasting through at least 4 days, that is clearly different from the usual non-depressed mood" (p. 338). The person should have at least three manic symptoms or at least four manic symptoms if only irritability is present. Additionally, the episode should be a clear change in functioning, the changes should be observable to others, and it does *not* cause marked impairment in functioning result in hospitalization, there are no psychotic features, and is not due to drugs or general medical conditions.

DSM-IV-TR goes on to define the various mood disorders in terms of the mood episodes and other criteria. Hence, a major depressive disorder, single episode, is defined as one major depressive episodes, not accounted for by psychotic disorders, with no manic episode. A major depressive disorder, recurrent, is defined the same as a major depressive disorder, except that there are at least two major depressive episodes. Dysthymic disorder is defined as two or more years of the presence of depressed mood recognized wither subjectively by the patient or by others, two or more of six depressed symptoms, persistence of the symptoms during the 2-year period, and no manic or psychotic disorder, drugs or general medical disorders as the cause and clinically significant distress or impairment. DSM-IV-TR also includes other mood disorders that may include symptoms of depression, including mood disorder due to a general medical condition, substance-induced mood disorder, and mood disorder NOS (American Psychiatric Association, 2000).

B. Application to People with ID

Charlot (2005) reviewed 11 empirical papers that reported the symptoms of depression in people with ID. She reported that the most commonly observed symptoms of depression were depressed or sad, anhedonia irritable mood, and sleep problems. Other symptoms such as agitation, motor retardation, fatigue, and decreased concentration were reported less frequently and with greater variability from study to study. Other symptoms, such as guilt, delusions, and hallucinations, were reported relatively infrequently (Charlot, 2005: Table 2.1). As might be expected the type of depressed symptom observed may be related to the degree of ID. People with mild ID are more likely to report cognitive and other private events than people with greater degrees of ID. For example, Tsiouris, Mann, Patti, and Sturmey (2003) reported that loss of interest, sleep disturbance, social isolation, and self-reproach were more like in adults with mild ID with depression than adult with ID alone. In contrast, depressed affect, diurnal mood variation, psychomotor retardation, loss of appetite, and social isolation were more common depressed symptoms in people with severe or profound ID and depression from people with severe/profound ID alone.

Application of unmodified DSM-IV-TR and other standardized diagnostic criteria for mood depressive disorders has received extensive attention. Standardized diagnostic criteria have formed the basis of a variety of screening instruments that have included scales to assess or screen for depressive disorders (Matson, 1988, 1995, 1998; Matson & Smiroldo, 1997; Moss, 2002; Moss et al., 1993, 1997; Prosser et al., 1998). Researchers have also evaluated scales based on standardized diagnostic criteria designed for the general population, such as the Beck Depression Inventory (BDI) (Lindsay & Lees, 2003), the Zung Depression Inventory (Matson, Kazdin, & Senatore, 1984; Lindsay, Howells, & Pithcaithly, 1993), the Child Depression Inventory (Helsel & Matson, 1988), and the Minnesota Multiphasic Personality Inventory (MMPI) (McDaniel & Gregory, 2005.) Despite the common use of standard diagnostic criteria, many have noted considerable potential limitation in their application to people with ID. Concerns include problems comprehending and using of metaphorical language, response acquiescence, nay saying, and other response sets. Standard diagnostic criteria also require that the client discriminates and reports private events such as depressed mood, diminished pleasure, fatigue, thinking and concentration problems, lack of energy, and suicidal ideation and thoughts of death. Although some people with mild ID may be able to report such private events, some may not and many people with moderate ID may have such problems also. Because most people with severe or profound ID have very limited or no expressive language, standardized diagnostic criteria cannot be used.

These concerns have prompted three responses: screening participants, the modification of standard diagnostic criteria, and the use of behavioral equivalents for mood disorders. Kazdin et al. (1983) screened participants for response acquiescence, and other response sets in their study of depression in people with ID. As an example of the second strategy, the Royal College of Psychiatrists (2001) proposed modified diagnostic criteria for depression, including adding increases in maladaptive behavior and onset or increase in somatic complaints as symptoms of depression. They also suggested that some depressive symptoms such as lack of interest might expressed as loss of self-help skills, lack of cooperation, and reduction in communication and that lack of confidence might be expressed as increased reassurance seeking or fear. In a manner similar to diagnosis of depression in children, some have suggested that irritability be used as an alternative to depressed mood (Charlot, 2005). The third response to this problem has been to suggest that certain maladaptive behaviors, such as self-injury, aggression, and crying, might be observable signs of depression (Clark & Gomez, 1999; Marston, Perry, & Roy, 1997). However, empirical studies have found little support for such speculation. For example, Reiss and Rojahn (1993) observed a very modest relationship between aggression and depression in adults with ID, and, although others have found high rates of aggression in inpatients with ID and depression, such associations may not be specific to depression. Tsiouris, Mann et al. (2003) used Marston et al.'s (1997) checklist of symptoms of depression and potential behavioral equivalents in adults with ID and found little or no relationship between International Classification of Diseases (ICD) symptoms of depression and possible behavioral equivalents. Thus, at this time there is little evidence to support any general relationship between depression and maladaptive behaviors, although idiosyncratic relationships might exist there is no evidence yet that questionnaires can measure such relationships.

C. Diagnostic Interviews

Deb and Iyer (2005) reviewed psychiatric interviewing strategies with people with ID and mood disorders. They made recommendations concerning the content of interviews as the best interviewing strategies that interviewers should use. In terms of content, interviewers should cover two broad areas: history and mental status. The history should include the family history of ID, psychiatric illness, and any other potential family variables, including possible genetic predisposition, aberrant family dynamics, and family relationships. The history should also include personal and developmental history, including the cause and development of ID, the family's reaction to and management of ID, education, and day placement and employment. One of the goals of the personal history is to ascertain the person's premorbid functioning and personality. The history also includes a medical history, especially for physical illness that may present as, mask or influence the course of a mood disorder, such as epilepsy and thyroid functioning. The history also includes a psychiatric history, including previous diagnoses and episodes of psychiatric disorders. A social history is taken to discover information about social circumstances, employment, and living arrangements. A history of legal and illicit drug use as well as forensic history should also be taken. The final and key part of the history includes a history of the presenting problem, including biological, psychological, and social factors that predisposed the individual to a mood disorder. The mental status exam (Sturmey, in press) includes six sections: appearance and behavior, speech, though processes, perceptual abnormalities, cognitive assessment, and rapport with the interviewer and client insight. They also recommend a physical examination to rule out any physical medical problems that might have gone unreported or undetected.

Deb and Iyer note that interviewing people with ID requires some careful adaptation of typical interviewing strategies. These include careful evaluation of the information reported by third party information that is often crucial when interviewing people with ID. This should include careful consideration of how well and how long the third party has known the client, how much of the client's life the informant knows about and their ability and motivation to report accurately and completely. They note that third part information may be crucial in determining the history of the presenting complaint and whether or not this complaint represents a change in client functioning. Considerable attention has also been given to client factors in psychiatric interviews. These include consideration of whether the client finds the interview threatening or otherwise aversive; problems in comprehension, expression, recall, and ability to report private events, such as mood and cognition; response sets, such as acquiescence, nay saying, and responding to the first or last of two alternatives; and social desirability. They note that many interviews consist of a triangle of client, informant, who may be a family member or staff person, and the interviewer. Managing this triangle to ensure that the interviewer gathers all the relevant information and that all parties have an opportunity to participate and are treated respectfully can be challenging.

Deb and Iyer conclude by making good practice guidelines for psychiatric interviews with people with ID and mood disorders. These include ensuring that there is sufficient time for interviews, that the time is scheduled appropriately, and that consideration is given as to the best location for the interview is given. They recommend several questioning strategies, including giving the client a clear framework as to the purpose of the interview, modifying questions to minimize responses sets, for example by refraining from leading questions, use of open-ended question early in the interview, and use of either/or questions. The interviewer should also use simplified language and use pictures and symbols to facilitate communication as appropriate. Interviewers should also use strategies, such as clarifying, summarizing, and recapping to check for the accuracy and completeness of information. They recommend using anchoring events, such as vacations or birth, to enhance the accuracy of a client's history (Prosser & Bromley, 1998).

Although many people with mild and some people with moderate ID can answer questions with adequate accuracy during interviews, the difficulties encountered should not be underestimated. Consider Charlot's transcript an interview with a person with mild ID.

> "Dr. C: Hi, M. I just wanted to ask you a few questions. Is that OK with you?
> Mr. M.: You are a handsome woman, I like you.
> Dr. C: You are very kind. I like you, too. I was wondering how you have been feeling lately.
> Mr. M.: I really do like you. Did you see my menu?
> Dr. C.: Yes, I did. It looks good. So, I want to ask you: Have you been feeling happy lately?
> Mr. M.: Yes! (*Mr. M smiles broadly.*)
> Dr. C.: Have you been feeling sad lately?
> Mr. M.: Yes (*Mr. M smiles broadly.*)" (Charlot, 2005, p. 19.).

Thus, although Charlot did follow several of Deb and Iyer's guidelines, including relatively simple language and use of positive and negative questions, she was unable to get any accurate information about mood because of the clients response acquiescence, but more importantly, because of the client not following the social convention of the psychiatric interview.

D. Psychometric Instruments

Fifteen yours ago there were relatively few psychometric instruments to assess psychopathology in people with ID and most were general screens of psychopathology that did not focus on depressive disorders and screening instruments for maladaptive behaviors (Aman, 1991; Sturmey, Reed, &

Corbett, 1991). Now there are many such instruments, including a variety of instruments specifically designed for assessment of depressive disorders (see Finlay [2005] for a heroic review of all available instruments at this time.)

A recent, potentially useful measure of mood and anxiety disorders in people with ID comes from Esbensen, Rojahn, Aman, and Ruedrich (2003). They developed a measure of anxiety, depression, and mood, for people with ID known as the ADAMS. A preliminary pool of 131 items was put together from existing measures, assessment of individuals with ID, and consultation with service providers and then reduced to 55 items by eliminating duplicated and overlapping items. This 55-item scale was then administered to 641 people with borderline through profound ID divided into three samples for statistical analysis. Using these data, items were eliminated if they had poor inter-rater reliability or lacked variability, leaving 49 items for further analysis. Ebensen et al. then conduced exploratory and confirmatory factor analyses. They adopted a five-factor solution using 28 items. They named the five factors manic/hyperactivity (4 items), depressed mood (7 items), social avoidance (7 items), general anxiety (7 items), and compulsive behavior (3 items). Cronbach alphas for the scales were all reasonably good, ranging from .75 to .83, test-retest reliabilitics were also good, ranging from .72 to .83, but inter-rater reliability was poor to middling, ranging from .37 to .62. In a validity study, Esbensen et al. (2003) compared ADAMS scores of five groups of people with ID and DSM diagnoses that corresponded to the five ADAMS scales with a large group of people with ID and no DSM diagnoses. They found good evidence of criterion groups validity. Hence, the ADAMS is a promising measure to screen for a variety of mood disorders in people with ID, but required further work to assure its inter-rater reliability. The authors suggested that the low inter-rater reliability might reflect the use of raters from different settings who may thus be exposed to different samples of client behavior.

Psychometric measures can also be used to track change, including response to treatment. For example, several researchers have used the BDI as a measure of change during therapy with people with mild ID (Lindsay, Stenfert Kroses, & Drew, 2005) and with Asperger syndrome (Hare, 1991). Thus, the BDI might be considered as a measure of change during treatment with some clients with mild ID.

E. Assessment of Mood-Related Cognitions

There has been increasing interest in cognitive behavior therapy with people with ID over the last 10 years (Dagnan & Lindsay, 2004; Dagnan, Chadwick, & Proudlove, 2000; Stenfert Kroese, Dagnan, & Loumidis, 1997), including work on depression-related cognitions. Researchers have attempted to assess mood, attributions, schemata, negative automatic thoughts, and self-esteem in people with mild ID. They have also gone on to assess more complicated aspects of cognitions, such as stating the connections between negative automatic thoughts, emotions, and actions (Lindsay et al., 2005).

One of Lindsay et al.'s (2005) case studies nicely illustrate this. Joanne was a 28-year-old woman with mild ID living independently referred for assessment and treatment of depression following withdrawal from work, college, and some legal problems. She completed a BDI which indicated suicidal thoughts, feelings of worthlessness, and guilt. Clinical interviews conducted over 2–3 sessions indicated anxiety, sensitivity to criticism, beliefs about stigmatization, and that other people talked about her negatively. Lindsay also used role play, drawing, and simplified diaries that are structured so that clients can report beliefs and actions. Lindsay et al. concluded that her core depression-related schema was "people are dreadful and they don't like me." They also isolated negative self-statements, such as "I don't go out 'cause people are watching me and they don't like me."

Clearly, some of the assessment methods associated with cognitive therapy can be used with some people with mild ID. However, many studies in this area are quite limited. For example, they neither define the population of interest nor do they randomly sample from some population. Additionally, participation in cognitive therapy does not merely require that the client can report mood, but rather can report many private events, such as mood, negative automatic thoughts, *and* the connection between negative automatic thoughts, emotions, and behavior (Sturmey, 2006a,b). So far we have little data on what proportion of people with ID can perform *all* the tasks necessary for participation in cognitive therapy. Thus, there are no good data on what proportion of people with ID can participate in cognitive therapy. There remains considerable disagreement between practitioners and researcher on this question (Emerson, 2006; Lindsay, 2006; Sturmey, 2004, 2006a,b,c; Taylor, 2005).

F. Functional Assessment and Analysis

Behaviorism, the philosophy of science that underpins both the experimental analysis of behavior and applied behavior analysis (ABA) (Chiesa, 1994), has long been interested in psychopathology (Skinner, 1953, 1971; Sturmey, 2007), including mood disorders (Ferster, 1973; Hopko, Hopko, & LeJuez, 2007; Lewinsohn, 1974; Matson, 1982.) radical behavioral approaches to problems generally eschew theoretical concepts and hypothetico-deductive science in favor of inductive approaches that remain close to the data. Hence, behavioral approaches pay a great deal of attention to the behavior of individual organisms over time, the variation in behavior, and the relationship between this variation in behavior and environmental events that can be manipulated. This is done in order to determine functional relationships between environmental variables that can be manipulated to control and predict behavior (Baer, Wolf, & Risley, 1968; Skinner, 1953; Sturmey, Ward-Horner, Marroquin, & Doran, 2007). Radical behaviorism addresses thoughts and feelings, but unlike nonbehavioral approaches, such private events are seen as the behavior to be explained, not the explanation of behavior, which ultimately lies outside the organism in the environment (Skinner, 1953).

Some of the earliest work on treatment of depressive disorders included various behavioral activation strategies (Lewinsohn, 1974). Although the rise of cognitive behavior therapy and cognitive therapy eclipsed behavioral approaches to the treatment of mood disorders for many years, behavioral activation remained an area of interest for some. Subsequently, a component analysis of cognitive behavioral strategies has revealed that the behavioral activation component alone was as effective as the combined cognitive behavior therapy package, strongly suggesting that behavioral activation is the effective component of the package (Jacobson et al., 1996). Further, a manualized version of this approach, brief behavioral activation treatment for depression (LeJuez, Hopko, & Hopko, 2003) has shown considerable promise in several randomized controlled trials (Hopko et al., 2007). Although contemporary behavioral approaches have been influenced by the ideas of functional assessment and analysis, there has been less explicit adoption of the technology and conceptual framework of ABA to conduct pre-intervention functional assessments and analyses as the basis for subsequent individualized treatments that match the function of the presenting problems (Hopko et al., 2007). Nevertheless, this work has led to a rejuvenation of behavioral accounts of depression.

Esbensen and Rojahn (2005) reviewed a variety of theoretical approaches to mood disorders in people with ID, including genetic, neuroendocrine, interpersonal, behavioral, and cognitive theories. Although there was support for several theoretical approaches they noted that there is insufficient data at this point to offer strong support for any one theoretical construction of depression over another. There is also relatively little controlled outcome research on treatment of depression in people with ID (Beail & Newman, 2005; Lindsay et al., 2005; Stigler, Posey, & McDougle, 2005; Sturmey, 2005b; Sturmey & Ghaziuddin, 2005,). Hence, the question of which theoretical framework to use is open to debate and behavioral approaches remain one of several promising options.

Behavior analytic approaches to assessment of mood and depression in people with ID have used two strategies. First, some studies have attempted to observe if there is a functional relationship between mood or depression and ongoing activities. Second, some studies have attempted to use mood induction procedures, using activities to induce positive mood, in order to reduce mood-related behavior problems. One example comes from Green and Reid (1996) who operationalized behavioral indices of happiness and unhappiness in adults with profound ID. Happiness was defined as "any facial expression or vocalization typically considered to be an indicator of happiness among people without disabilities, including smiling, laughing, and yelling while smiling" (p. 69). Unhappiness was defined as "frowning, grimacing, crying and yelling without smiling" (p. 69). Green and Reid reported high interobserver agreement on behavioral indices of mood. More interestingly, when they observed the functional relationship between mood behaviors and the presence of preferred or nonpreferred objects, they found that happy behavior was much more likely in the presence of preferred stimuli for two of four participants and that unhappy behavior was much more likely in the presence of nonpreferred stimuli. In their second study, they reported good convergent validity between mood ratings by both unfamiliar and familiar persons and observable behavior. This assessment of mood was then used as the basis of an intervention procedure to increase participants' happiness. During baseline the usual ongoing activities occurred, such as teaching, interaction, and usual activities. Intervention consisted of three components. First, staff briefly conducted stimulus preference assessment to determine preferred items empirically, rather than rely on staff reports. Second, staff interacted with the participants in the manner that they believed was preferred by the client. Third, the experimenters told the staff the definitions of unhappy and happy behavior; staff were instructed to immediately stop any ongoing activity associated with unhappy behavior and to change items after 1 min if the client showed no happy behavior. The experimenter provided feedback after each session on staff performance and client happy behavior relative to baseline. Using a multiple baseline design across three participants, Green and Reid showed that happy behavior systematically increased following the intervention. Subsequent studies have validated this assessment approach as one that is effective in promting client happiness (Green, Gardner, & Reid, 1997; Green & Reid, 1999; Green, Reid, Rollyson, & Passante, 2005). These studies are clearly promising, but are limited in that they did not select clients with clinical depression.

Lindauer, DeLeon, and Fisher (1999) reported assessment and treatment of depression-related self-injury in a 23-year-old woman with severe ID and major depression. Negative affect was defined as frowning, crying, whining, and saying "I am sad" and positive affect was defined as smiling, giggling, and laughing. Although her depression was treated with carbamazepine throughout the study, she continued to show negative affect and also self-injury associated with negative affect, especially when she was left alone.

Lindauer et al. (1999) conducted a stimulus preference assessment to identify the woman's preferred items which were subsequently used in an environmental enrichment program. In the baseline condition, the woman was left alone in an observation room. The environmental enrichment condition consisted of placing all 12 preferred items in the room. A hands down procedure was used throughout the study to prevent self-injury. Lindauer et al. showed that negative affect was much more common during baseline conditions and positive affect was more likely during environmental enrichment. Further, self-injury occurred almost exclusively during baseline conditions and was correlated with negative affect. Thus, this study demonstrated a functional relationship between the presence and absence of preferred items and both mood behavior and self-injury related to negative affect in a person with severe ID and depression.

Carr, McLaughlin, Giacobbe-Grieco, and Smith (2003) used a broadly similar approach using mood induction as a treatment for mood-related severe problem behavior. They first selected clients whom staff rated as having mood fluctuations associated with severe behavior problems. Second, they then conducted mood ratings in the natural environment, in which they rated mood on a 6-point scale. They found good interobserver agreement on mood ratings. During these observations they also systematically presented demands or no demands probes. In demand conditions the client was presented with tasks that staff reported were associated with severe behavior problem, such as making a sandwich. The experiments terminated almost all demand sessions during negative mood due to client safety but terminated few other sessions. Subsequently, Carr et al. (2003) used mood induction procedures, similar to those used by Green and Reid, to promote positive mood in three adults. They observed that when preferred activities and preferred patterns of interaction were scheduled that clients showed greater positive mood and were very unlikely to show severe behavior problems when staff presented demands.

G. Summary

Mood can be reliably observed in people with the full range of ID, including some with a diagnosis of a depressive disorder. Further, mood behavior is a function of the presence of preferred and nonpreferred activities as assessed by stimulus preference assessments. For some people, observational assessments show that severe behavior problems may be related to negative mood. These functional assessments and analyses have great treatment utility in that they direct practitioners to objectively measure mood and its relationship to the environment. These environment-behavior relationships can be the basis for highly effective interventions plans that are based on the results of preintervention assessments and that can be used to train staff to promote positive client mood. Future research should extend this research to the assessment and treatment of mood and related severe behavior problems in people with ID and clinically diagnosed mood disorders that are resistant to typical treatment or that may be treated before psychotropic medications and other restrictive procedures are used. Future research could also extend these methods by teaching self-control strategies to people with ID, so that they appropriately identify and select their own preferred stimuli to manage their own mood (Skinner, 1953, 1971).

III. BIPOLAR DISORDERS

DSM-IV-TR (American Psychiatric Association, 2000) distinguishes bipolar disorders I and II and cyclothymic disorders. Bipolar I disorders are characterized by single or recurrent manic and/or cyclothymic episodes without any major depressive episodes. Bipolar II disorders are characterized by both major depressive and hypomanic episodes without a manic episode. A cyclothymic disorder is characterized by at least 2 years of numerous hypomanic and depressive symptoms that did not meet the criteria for a major depressive disorder. (The reader is referred back to the section earlier for definitions of mood episodes.)

A. Application to People with ID

Researchers have studied bipolar disorders much less than depressive disorders in people with ID. Presumably, this reflects much lower prevalence of manic than depressive disorders. For example, there are fewer assessment measures, and no information was found on assessment of manic cognitions. Assessment of bipolar disorders in people with ID is complicated by the presence of other unusual behavior that may or may not be symptoms of a bipolar disorder. For example, unusual high levels of motor activity may be observed in some people with ID, but may be typical of the person, and hence not represent a change in functioning, may be a symptom of another psychiatric disorder, such as attention deficit hyperactivity disorder, may be medication side effects, such as tardive akathisia, excessive caffeine consumption, or may be simple operant behavior. Likewise, excessive and inappropriate sexual behavior might be taken as a symptom of a bipolar disorder, although it might also represent simple lack of social graces, lack of alternate sources of reinforcement in the person's life, or, again, simple operant behavior. The cyclic nature of the disorder may also be difficult to determine for a number of reasons. First, it may be difficult to obtain an accurate history of the presenting problem. Second, Pary, Levitas, and Hurley (1999) noted a number of other factors that could account for the presenting problem waxing and waning, including changes in staffing patterns, seasonal allergies, cluster headaches, and so on.

Cain et al. (2003) conducted a retrospective chart review of people with ID with bipolar disorders and other psychiatric disorders. They found that clients with bipolar disorder were more likely to present with mood symptoms, more nonmood symptoms, and greater functional impairment when compared to people with ID and other psychiatric disorders. Sovner and Hurley's (1982a,b) and Vanstraelen and Tyrer's (1999) reviews of published case reports of bipolar disorders in people with ID found that irritable mood, labile affect, overactivity, and decreased sleep were common although cognitive symptoms of bipolar disorders, such as grandiosity and inflated self-esteem were reported less frequently.

Several studies have considered the issue of behavioral equivalents of mania. Charlot's (2005) review noted that several earlier studies had used increased rate of speech and increased voice volume, increased signs of distractibility, aggression, self-injurious behavior, disruptive behavior (Lowry & Sovner, 1992), and agitation. The Royal College of Psychiatrists (2001) diagnostic criteria for phychiatric disorders for use with adults with learning disabilities (DC-LD) criteria included pressured speech, 1 hour less sleep than usual, increased vocalizations, loss of social inhibitions, and reckless or dangerous behavior. It is notable here that several of the proposed behavioral equivalents of bipolar disorders, such as self-injury, have also been proposed as behavioral equivalents of depressive disorders. Unfortunately, we have no guidance and no reliability trials as to when these behaviors are signs of depressive disorders, bipolar disorders, other disorders, or learned behaviors.

B. Screening Questionnaires

Several screening questionnaires, such as the phychiatric assessment schedules for adults with developmental disabilities (PAS-ADD) (Moss et al., 1993) and the diagnostic assessment for the severely handicapped II (DASH II) (Matson, 1998), contain items and scales to screen for bipolar disorders that may be useful (Finlay, 2005). Matson and Smiroldo (1997) assessed the internal consistency and validity of the DASH II mania scales in people with severe or profound ID. They found the mania scale to be reasonably internally consistent and the mania scale total score did distinguish people with mania from controls. As noted before, these scales are screens to identify people who need further assessment and not themselves equivalent to an actual psychiatric diagnosis.

C. Interviewing

Only one interview schedule specifically for bipolar disorders was identified. The Mini PAS-ADD interview (Prosser et al., 1998) contained symptom items and a mania scale. It also has some preliminary psychometric data, suggesting that it may be adequate for screening for bipolar disorders. The reader is referred to the earlier section on interviews and depressive disorders for general guidelines.

D. Functional Assessment and Analysis

Bipolar disorders have received little attention from behavior analysis (Sturmey, in press), indeed, no empirical studies were identified for this chapter.

IV. ANXIETY DISORDERS

A. Diagnosis

DSM-IV-TR (American Psychiatric Association, 2000) distinguishes many forms of anxiety disorders, including panic disorder with and without agoraphobia, agoraphobia with history of panic disorder, specific and social phobias, obsessive-compulsive disorder (OCD), posttraumatic and acute stress disorders, generalized anxiety disorder (GAD), anxiety disorder due to a medical condition, substance-induced anxiety disorder, and anxiety disorder NOS. Many anxiety disorders are characterized by excessive autonomic arousal, such as physical tension, sweating, rapid heart rate, nausea, abdominal distress, dizziness, chills and hot flushes, and so on. Avoidance characterizes many anxiety disorders including avoiding coming in contact with a provocative situations, such as a housebound person with agoraphobia, or terminating a fearful situation early by removing oneself from the provocative situation, undoing rituals, as in hand washing and checking in people with OCD, and abuse of anxiolytic substances, such as alcohol and prescribed medications to blunt the severity of anxiety symptoms. There are also many unusual and troubling cognitive features of anxiety disorders, such as excess worry, rumination, and cognitive rituals to undo anxiety. The extensive literature on cognitive therapy and anxiety lists numerous putative cognitive problems that people with anxiety disorders report, such as misattributions of fearful events or normal variation in one's own physiological state.

There is insufficient space in one chapter to review all the diagnostic criteria for all the DSM anxiety disorders in detail. However, it is worth noting several general differences among them. Some disorders, such as panic disorder without agoraphobia and panic disorder with agoraphobia, are characterized by the presence of a panic attack. A panic attack is characterized as "a discrete period of intense fear or discomfort, in which four (or more) of the following [anxiety] symptoms develop abruptly and reached a peak within 10 minutes .... Palpitations ... fear of losing control or going crazy ... fear of dying ...." (p. 395). Anxiety disorders also vary as to their breadth of focus. Thus, specific phobia may be focused on one animal or event and OCD may focus on fear of contamination from ultraviolet radiation leading to skin cancer, whereas GAD is characterized by excessive anxiety, fear, and worry concerning many aspects of life.

B. Applications to People with ID

Some anxiety disorders have been studied in people with ID (Poindexter, 1996), especially the behavioral assessment and treatment specific phobias and to a lesser extent OCD. Other anxiety disorders, such as panic disorder, agoraphobia without history of panic disorder, and GAD have received less attention. This may reflect the relative ease of detecting and treating specific phobia in people with ID through various forms of respondent extinction and the relative under-recognition and greater difficulty or treatment of less focused anxiety disorders in people with mild ID.

Some aspects of anxiety disorders are public and readily observable. These include certain symptoms, such as sweating, muscle tension, hyperventilating, and motor rituals, and various forms of avoidance, such as turning and running away. When these behaviors are observed in the presence of specific stimuli, such as animals, dental, or medical procedures, and they cause distress for the person and others around them, then an anxiety disorder is likely to be readily recognized. Other aspects of anxiety disorders, such as worry, mild physical tension, physical symptoms, embarrassment, and so forth, may not be readily observable, unless the person himself reports them.

Bailey and Andrews (2003) reviewed the issue of behavioral equivalents of anxiety disorders in people with ID as part of the development of DC-LD. They concluded that although some studies have evidence suggesting the usefulness of behavioral equivalents such as self-injury for anxiety disorders (Tsiouris, Cohen, Patti, & Koros, 2003), this issues remains open to further well-controlled studies (Bailey & Andrews, 2003).

C. Screening Questionnaires

There are many psychometric measures available to assess anxiety disorders in people with ID. These include use and modification of measures developed with the general population, general screening instruments to assess psychopathology in people with ID, that include items and scales for anxiety generally and some particular anxiety disorders and measures of anxiety disorders developed specifically for use with people with ID.

1. MEASURES FROM THE GENERAL POPULATION

Several instruments commonly used with children and adults have been used with people with ID, sometimes with adaptations. Various fear survey schedules used with children and adolescents of average intelligence have been used with children and adolescents with ID (Blomberg, Rosander, & Andersson, 2005; Gullone, King, & Cummins, 1999; Sarphare & Aman, 1999). These fear surveys can have adequate to good reliability, although sometimes reliability is more modest than in typically developing children and adolescents (Gullone et al., 1999; Sarphare & Aman, 1999). There is also evidence that these measures discriminate between different groups of people, suggesting criterion groups validity (Blomberg et al., 2005; Gullone et al., 1999). Ramirez and Lukenbill (2007) reported the latest in a series of modification to these fear survey schedules specifically designed for adults with mild, moderate, and severe ID which included 73 fear-related items, 6 repeated items to check fro reliability, and 6 items to assess response acquiescence. The scale was highly internally consistent. However, concurrent validity with other anxiety measures was surprisingly modest with correlations with other anxiety scales being only .4 and .3.

Several studies on adults with ID have used the Beck Anxiety Inventory (BAI) and the Zung self-rating anxiety scale and found them to be generally usable and psychometrically adequate (Glenn, Bihm, & Lammers, 2003; Lindsay & Lees, 2003; Lindsay & Mitchie, 1988; Masi, Brovedani, Mucci, & Favilla, 2002). However, Lindsay, and Mitchie (1988) adapted the Zung self-assessment of anxiety scale by rephrasing items and using a simplified rating to indicate the presence or absence of an item, rather than a Likert rating. McDaniel and colleagues have conducted several studies using the MMPI with people with mild ID, including screening for possible anxiety disorders, and found this to be an adequate for some clinical purposes, such as tracking change in client symptoms, but have also reported problems in concurrent validity with other measures of psychopathology (McDaniel, 1997; McDaniel & Gregory, 2005; McDaniel & Harris, 1999; McDaniel, Passmore, & Sewell, 2003).

2. GENERAL SCREENS FOR PSYCHOPATHOLOGY FOR PEOPLE WITH ID

There are several general screens of psychopathology and behavior disorders in people with ID include items and scales for anxiety disorders. These include the Psychopathology Inventory for Mentally Retarded Adults (PIMRA) (Balboni, Battagliese, & Pedrabissi, 2000), the ADD (Matson &

Bamberg, 1988) the DASH-II (Hill & Furniss, 2005; Matson, Smiroldo, Hamilton, & Baglio, 1997), the PAS-ADD (Holden & Gitlesen, 2003), the Reiss Screen (1988), and the Developmental Behavior Checklist (Dekker, Nunn, Einfeld, Tonge, & Koot, 2002) to name a few. These measures may be a useful part of an initial screen for psychopathology in people with ID, including possible anxiety disorders. Since they are broad screens for psychopathology, there will be relatively few items that specifically address anxiety symptoms and, thus, although these measures may detect the presence of some form of psychopathology more readily, they may lack sensitivity and specificity to detect the presence of an anxiety disorder or a specific form of an anxiety disorder. Hence, clinicians could find them useful to detect a possible anxiety disorder if they use a low cutoff and follow-up at risk clients with more specific and detailed assessment procedures.

3. SPECIFIC SCREENS FOR ANXIETY

Several authors have developed psychometric measures specifically to measure anxiety disorders in people with ID. A series of studies by Bramston, Bostock, Fogarty, and colleagues has developed an inventory to measure stress in people with mild ID (Bramston & Bostock, 1994; Bramston & Fogarty, 1995; Fogarty, Bramston, & Cummins, 1997). This measure does not produce scales that correspond to DSM-IV diagnoses; however, it does produce scores on two empirically derived scales, named general Worry and Interpersonal Experiences which may be useful to screen for anxiety disorders. Mindham and Espie (2003) developed the Glasgow Anxiety Scale for People with Intellectual Disabilities (GAS-ID). After developing an initial item pool from various sources they administered the GAS-ID to 19 anxious and 16 no-anxious people with ID. They also obtained validity data by correlating the scale with the BAI and change in pulse rate. They found good evidence of test-retest reliability, internal consistency, and validity with the BAI and pulse rate change. The GAS-ID is relatively quick to administer and is psychometrically robust and can therefore be recommended as a screen for anxiety disorders in this population.

Vitiello, Spreat, and Behar (1989) developed a measure of OCD in people with profound ID. They distinguished between compulsions, stereotypes, and other repetitive behaviors, and found good inter-rater reliability on this classification ($\kappa = .82$) as well as good inter-rater reliabilities on individual items in a sample of 283 people with mild to profound ID. They noted that ratings were based on observable behavior and that the ego dystonic nature of obsessions, inner resistance, and subjective distress cold not be assessed. This measure seems to be an appropriate instrument to assess OCD in people with ID. Bodfish and colleagues have also developed a checklist of compulsions for use with people with ID (Bodfish et al., 1995; Powell, Bodfish, Crawford, Golden, & Lewis, 1996) which has proven useful in directing pharmacological treatment of compulsions (Lewis, Bodfish, Powell, Parker, & Golden, 1996).

D. Interviewing

Several authors have used structured interviews to assess the presence of anxiety symptoms in people with ID. For example, Krakovsky, Huth, Lin, and Levin (2007) conducted phone interviews with parents of children with multiple disabilities. Masi, Favilla, and Mucci (2000) used structured diagnostic interviews to assess GAD in 22 people with ID aged 11–25 years, and 60 children and adolescents without ID. They found good inter-rater reliability between self- and parent reports of GAD in adolescents with mild ID. They noted that adolescent with GAD and ID presented in a broadly similar way to people without ID and GAD.

E. Assessment of Anxiety-Related Cognitions

Several studies have assessed anxiety-related cognitions in people with mild ID. Glenn et al. (2003) administered a battery of anxiety and depression symptom and cognition checklists to 46 people with mild ID who had been nominated by the director of their community agency for the study. They screened all participants for response acquiescence and biases. The measures of cognition were the Automatic Thoughts Questionnaire (ATQ; Hollon, Kendall, & Lumry, 1986) and the Cognitions Checklist (CCL; Beck, Brown, Steer, Eidelson, & Riskind, 1987.) Both of these scales has high internal consistencies—αs were .97 and .94, respectively—indicating that they were reliable measures. However, Glenn et al. noted that measures of depression and anxiety symptoms were highly correlated ($r = .74, p < .001$) leading them to question whether these should be considered independent constructs. Likewise, when they correlated CCL measures of depression- and anxiety-related cognitions, they found that both were equally correlated with depression and anxiety. Further, when they conducted hierarchical multiple regression, they found little evidence for the specificity of cognitions. Thus, although this study showed that anxiety- and depression-related cognitions can be assessed in people with mild ID and that cognitions did predict depression and anxiety symptoms quite well, there was little evidence that they were specifically related to each disorder.

Assessment of anxiety-related cognitions in people with mild ID is currently at an early stage. Although psychometric measures of cognition developed for the general population can be used with people with mild ID who have been screened for response sets, this area needs further research.

F. Behavioral Assessment

Behavioral assessment of anxiety disorders is characterized by observation of fearful behaviors in the natural environment, such as avoidance, noncompliance due to anxiety, and appropriate replacement behaviors, such as assertiveness, compliance, and use of treatment procedures. Many of these studies are related to the use of behavioral interventions for anxiety disorders. For example, several intervention studies for specific phobias have developed tasks analyses of nonfearful behavior. Conyers et al. (2004) treated dental phobia in six adults with severe or profound ID. The participants' staff identified them as having excessive avoidance at the dentist, as shown by crying, yelling, and other behavior challenges, all of which had to be seated prior to dental treatment, and four participants had to be restrained during dental treatment. Conyers et al. (2004) developed an 18-step task analysis of participating in dental treatment. Examples of steps included the participant entering the dentist's room with a staff member, sitting in the dentists' chair with the drill on for 10 sec, and leaning back in the chair, wearing a bib, with the drill, suction sounds, and dentists light on for 10 sec. The researchers collected data in a simulated dentist's office. In baseline, no participants completed all steps of the tasks analysis, and three only emitted ~4 steps. When the experiments evaluated the use of video modeling in three participants, two of three participants continued to emit only ~4 steps and one, for whom the video modeling was considered effective, emitted all 18 steps. Conyers et al. (2004) treated the three remaining participants' dental phobia with *in vivo* exposure and after treatment all three participants emitted close to all 18 steps. Following treatment three of the participants had an actual dental appointment and staff reported that they were much more cooperative than in previous appointments. These data demonstrate the sensitivity of this measure as well as its utility in guiding treatment choice and treatment procedures. Luscre and Center (1996) reported similar behavioral assessment data to guide and evaluate treatment of dental phobias in three children with autism and dental phobias.

Hagopian, Crockett, and Keeney (2001) reported an interesting assessment procedure to evaluate and guide treatment of a blood-injury-injection phobia in a 19-year-old man with moderate ID. The problem had been present for 10 years and had been resistant to other treatments, including sedation and exposure, modeling and "applied tension," a procedure to strain physically in order to increase blood pressure to avoid fainting. This problem was very severe in that the man had destroyed a waiting room, medical staff could not monitor him for possible medical problems, and he could not receive psychotropic medications requiring blood monitoring. During any invasive of medical procedures he would show extreme panic-like behaviors including hitting, kicking, and punching. Hagopian et al. therefore decided that in order to expose him to stimuli associated with injections it would be necessary to retrain him in order to permit exposure to occur. Therefore, treatment consisted of gradual fading restraint in, gradual fading of stimuli associated with medical treatment and finally fading out of restraint, such that at the end of treatment he could receive injections without restraint, anxiety, or challenging behavior. Thus, the authors developed two hierarchies for restraint and medical fading. For example, the restraint fading hierarchy included 8 steps, such as sitting on the bed with no papoose board, placing himself in the papoose board with the straps tied loosely, and finally tolerating 60 sec of restraint with the straps tightened. During treatment Hagopian et al. first faded in restraints, then faded in medical stimuli, and finally faded out restraint. Behavioral assessment data were used to guide the pace of treatment as progress was contingent on success at each step of the fading procedure. At the end of treatment the participant could have his blood drawn while sitting in a chair and the number of psychotropic medications had been reduced from 5 to 3.

G. Functional Assessment and Analysis

Section III.F illustrates the application of behavioral assessment to fears. However, these papers do not meet the criteria of functional analysis because they did not conduct a pretreatment assessment, did not manipulate environmental variables to show experimental control of relevant behavior, and used that information to design an effective treatment based on that information (Baer et al., 1968.) Indeed, Friman (2007) identified only one such study in the behavioral analytic literature.

Jones and Friman (1999) conducted a functional analysis and treatment of an insect phobia in a 14-year-old boy. The boy reported that he had problems concentrating and completing academic work and was often teased about his insect phobia. The authors systematically compared three conditions. In the *Bugs* condition, three live crickets were placed in the room with him. In the *Say Bugs* condition the experimenter said "there are bugs somewhere in this room" and in the *No Bugs* condition the experimenter said "There are no bugs anywhere in the room." The dependent variable was the number of math calculations completed in a 4-min session. The pretreatment functional analysis showed that, in contrast to staff reports that peer's talking about bugs was the most provocative stimulus, completing math problems was slowest in the *Bugs* condition. The initial treatment was self-directed exposure which was ineffective at increasing math performance. Only when self-directed exposure was supplemented with reinforcement of completing math problems did the boy's nonfearful behavior improve to an educationally significant degree.

This study makes an interesting contrast to the assessment of fears in many behavior therapy interventions for fear. First, the dependent variable was publicly observable, reliable behavior which was a measure of adaptive functioning, rather than subjective self-reports (Wolpe, 1986). Second, the experiments used the preassessment functional analysis to identify the controlling stimuli. Third, the experiments used observational data to evaluate treatment and, when it was ineffective, used that data to evaluate the second treatment.

H. Future Directions

Future research should address two issues. First, research should attend to expanding the application of behavioral assessment to more nebulous anxiety disorders, such as social phobia, agoraphobia (with and without panic attack), and GAD. Second, research is needed into identifying the functions of fearful behavior. It is tempting to assume that all such behavior is negatively reinforced by removal of the fear-provoking stimuli. However, the exact nature of such stimuli is not always readily apparent (Jones & Friman, 1999; Wolpe, 1986) and should be demonstrated rather than assumed. Further, the possibility of other consequences, such as attention, or access to medication, should also be evaluated.

V. ADJUSTMENT, ACUTE STRESS, POSTTRAUMATIC STRESS DISORDERS (PTSD)

DSM-IV describes three stress-related disorders. An adjustment disorder is characterized by behavioral symptoms (which DSM-IV does not specify) which involve either excessive distress or clinically significant impairment, and do not represent bereavement, another DSM-IV diagnosis. A specifier is added to describe the presenting symptoms, such as "with depressed mood" or "with disturbance of conduct." An acute stress disorder occurs in someone who experienced or has been exposed to a threatened or actual life-threatening event or serious injury, and experiences intense fear, helplessness, or horror. In addition, the person experiences three or more dissociative symptoms, such as subjective numbing or depersonalization, the traumatic event is reexperienced, for example through flashbacks, there is avoidance of trauma-related stimuli, and marked anxiety or arousal. Finally, the disturbance must be clinically significant, lasts for at least 2 days to 4 weeks, occurs within 4 weeks of the traumatic event, and is not better accounted for drugs, medication, a physical illness, or other DSM-IV diagnosis. PTSD is distinguished from acute stress disorder in that it also involves persistent symptoms of arousal such as sleep disturbance, irritability or anger, concentration problems, hypervigilence or exaggerated startle response and lasts for at least 1 month. Hence, DSM-IV distinguishes these three disorders from one another in terms of the duration, nature of the symptoms, and the presence of symptoms of increased arousal.

People with ID may experience many forms of stressful life events and trauma which may precipitate one of these three disorders in some cases. Some people have speculated that people with ID may be more vulnerable to adjustment disorders, because of poor social, problem solving and coping skills, lack of resources, and lack of social support. Like other people, people with ID experience more severe traumatic events, such as natural disaster and war, but are also at risk for physical and sexual abuse from family members, staff, and strangers (Mansell & Sobsey, 2001). In some cases these traumatic events may be related to adjustment, acute stress disorders, and PTSD, although such a relationship should not be assumed. For example, Harper and Wadsworth (1993) conducted direct structured interviews with 43 adults with ID and 100 staff concerning bereavement. They found that adults with moderate to severe ID showed bereavement in a manner similar to everyone else and only 10–15% also showed challenging behaviors, such as self-injury. It is necessary to carefully review the DSM-IV diagnostic criteria, especially those related to the nature of the trauma, and the presence of symptoms of reexperiencing the event and hypervigilence before these diagnoses are made (e.g., I have observed clinicians routinely assume that people who lived in institutions in the past and now present with challenging behaviors must have PTSD from the presumed trauma institutionalization without demonstrating that a life-threatening event occurred). Ryan (1996) describes two case studies of PTSD in people with ID, one adult woman who had been involved in satanic rituals and physically traumatized and another boy whose mother had attempted to kill him three times.

VI. CONCLUDING REMARKS

Thirty years ago the emotional life of people with ID was largely ignored. Researchers could still ask whether or not people with ID experienced various forms of mental health problems and there were few assessment instruments and procedures available. This chapter shows that some aspects of this problem have been addressed—perhaps more than it should be! There is now a plethora—if not excess—of psychometric instruments available to assess anxiety and depression in people with ID. There have also been recent developments in the areas of cognitive assessment and functional assessment and, to a lesser extent, functional analysis, of depression and anxiety in people with ID. These approaches to assessment are welcome as they are clearly treatment-oriented and may perhaps guide the selection of the most effective treatment for each individual client. Perhaps this point should be the last point of this chapter. What is the most important purpose of all this assessment? Assessment serves other functions, yet, surely the most important one is to guide the selection of the most effective treatment for each individual client. Future research should build on these decades of research on better assessment of depression and anxiety disorders in people with ID and use that information to ensure that they receive the most effective treatment for these problems.

REFERENCES

Aman, M. G. (1991). *Assessing psychopathology and behavior problems in persons with mental retardation:. A review of available instruments.* (DHSS Publication No. ADM 91–1712). Rockville, MD: US Department of Health and Human Services.

American Psychiatric Association (2000). *Diagnostic and Statistical Manual of Mental Disorders Fourth edition (Text Revision)*. Washington, DC: Author.

Baer, D. M., Wolf, M. M., & Risley, T. R. (1968). Some current dimensions of applied behavior analysis. *Journal of Applied Behavior Analysis, 1,* 91–97.

Bailey, N. M., & Andrews, T. M. (2003). Diagnostic Criteria for psychiatric disorders for use with adults with learning disabilities, (DC-LD) and the diagnosis of anxiety disorders: A review. *Journal of Intellectual Disability Research, 47*(Suppl. 1), 50–61.

Balboni, G., Battagliese, G., & Pedrabissi, L. (2000). The Psychopathology Inventory for Mentally Retarded Adults: Factor structure and comparisons between subjects with or without dual diagnosis. *Research in Developmental Disabilities, 21,* 311–321.

Beail, N., & Newman, D. (2005). Psychodynamic counseling and psychotherapy for mood disorders. In P. Sturmey (Ed.), *Mood Disorders in People with Mental Retardation* (pp. 273–292). Kingston, NY: NADD Press.

Beck, A. T., Brown, G., Steer, R. A., Eidelson, J. I., & Riskind, J. H. (1987). Differentiating anxiety and depression: A test of the cognitive specificity hypothesis. *Journal of Abnormal Psychology, 96,* 179–182.

Blomberg, S., Rosander, M., & Andersson, G. (2005). Fears, hyperacusis and musicality in Williams syndrome. *Research in Developmental Disabilities, 27,* 668–680.

Bodfish, J. W., Crawford, T. W., Powell, S. B., Parker, D. E., Golden, R. N., & Lewis, M. H. (1995). Compulsions in adults with mental retardation: Prevalence, phenomenology, and comorbidity with stereotypy and self-injury. *American Journal on Mental Retardation, 100,* 183–192.

Bramston, P., & Bostock, J. (1994). Measuring perceived stress in people with intellectual disabilities: The development of a new scale. *Australia and New Zealand Journal of Developmental Disabilities, 19,* 149–157.

Bramston, P., & Fogarty, G. (1995). Measuring stress in the mildly intellectually handicapped: The factorial structure of the Subjective Stress Scale. *Research in Developmental Disabilities, 16,* 117–131.

Cain, N. N., Davidson, P. W., Burham, A. M., Andolsek, M. E., Baxter, J. T., Sullivan, L., et al. (2003). Identifying bipolar disorders in individuals with intellectual disability. *Journal of Intellectual Disability Research, 47,* 31–38.

Carr, E. G., McLaughlin, D. M., Giacobbe-Grieco, T., & Smith, C. E. (2003). Using mood ratings and mood induction in assessment intervention for severe problem behaviors. *American Journal on Mental Retardation, 108,* 32–55.

Charlot, L. (2005). Use of behavioral equivalents for symptoms of mood disorders. In P. Sturmey (Ed.), *Mood Disorders in People with Mental Retardation* (pp. 17–46). Kingston, NY: NADD Press.

Chiesa, M. (1994). *Radical behaviorism: The philosophy of the science.* Sarasota, FL: Authors Cooperative.

Clark, D., & Gomez, G. A. (1999). Utility of the DCR*ICD-10 criteria in the diagnosis of depression associated with intellectual disability. *Journal of Intellectual Disability Research, 43,* 412–420.

Conyers, C., Miltenberger, R. G., Peterson, B., Gubin, A., Jurgens, M., Selders, A., et al. (2004). An evaluation of *in vivo* desensitization and video modeling to increase compliance with dental procedures in persons with mental retardation. *Journal of Applied Behavior Analysis, 37,* 233–238.

Dagnan, D., Chadwick, P., & Proudlove, L. (2000). Toward an assessment of suitability of people with mental retardation for cognitive therapy. *Cognitive Therapy and Research, 24,* 627–636.

Dagnan, D., & Lindsay, W. R. (2004). Research issues in cognitive therapy. In E. Emerson, C. Hatton, T. Thompson, & T. Parmenter (Eds.), *Handbook of Applied Research in Intellectual Disabilities* (pp. 517–530). UK: Wiley.

Deb, S., & Iyer, A. (2005). Clinical interviews. In P. Sturmey (Ed.), *Mood Disorders in People with Mental Retardation* (pp. 156–174). Kingston, NY: NADD Press.

Dekker, M. C., & Koot, H. M. (2003a). DSM-IV disorders in children with borderline to moderate intellectual disability. I. Prevalence and impact. *Journal of the American Academy of Child and Adolescent Psychiatry, 42,* 915–922.

Dekker, M. C., & Koot, H. M. (2003b). DSM-IV disorders in children with borderline to moderate intellectual disability. I: Child and family predictors. *Journal of the American Academy of Child and Adolescent Psychiatry, 42,* 923–931.

Dekker, M. C., Nunn, R. J., Einfeld, S. E., Tonge, B. J., & Koot, H. M. (2002). Assessing emotional and behavioral problems in children with intellectual disability: Revising the factor structure of the Developmental Checklist. *Journal of Autism and Developmental Disorders, 32,* 601–610.

Dosen, A., & Menalascino, F. J. (1990). *Depression in mentally retarded children and adults.* Leiden, NL: Logon Publications.

Emerson, E. (2006). The need for credible evidence. Comments on 'On some recent claims for the efficacy of cognitive therapy for people with intellectual disabilities. *Journal of Applied Research in Intellectual Disabilities, 19,* 121–124.

Esbensen, A. J., & Rojahn, J. (2005). Causes of mood disorders in people with mental retardation. In P. Sturmey (Ed.), *Mood disorders in people with mental retardation* (pp. 89–112). Kingston, NY: NADD Press.

Esbensen, A. J., Rojahn, J., Aman, M. G., & Ruedrich, S. (2003). Reliability and validity of an assessment instrument for anxiety, depression, and mood among individuals with mental retardation. *Journal of Autism and Developmental Disorders, 33,* 617–629.

Ferster, C. B. (1973). A functional analysis of depression. *American Psychologist, 28,* 857–870.

Finlay, W. M. L. (2005). Psychometric assessment of mood disorders in people with intellectual disabilities. In P. Sturmey (Ed.), *Mood Disorders in People with Mental Retardation* (pp. 175–210). Kingston, NY: NADD Press.

Fogarty, G. J., Bramston, P., & Cummins, R. A. (1997). Validation of the lifestress Inventory for people with mild intellectual disability. *Research in Developmental Disabilities, 18,* 435–456.

Friman, P. C. (2007). The fear factor: A functional perspective on anxiety. In P. Sturmey (Ed.), *Functional Analysis in Clinical Treatment* (pp. 335–356). San Diego, CA: Elsevier.

Glenn, E., Bihm, E. M., & Lammers, W. J. (2003). Depression, anxiety and relevant cognitions in person with mental retardation. *Journal of Autism and Developmental Disorders, 33,* 69–76.

Green, C. W., Gardner, S. M., & Reid, D. H. (1997). Increasing indices of happiness among people with profound multiple disabilities: A program replication and component analysis. *Journal of Applied Behavior Analysis, 30,* 217–228.

Green, C. W., & Reid, D. H. (1996). Reducing indices of unhappiness among individuals with profound multiple disabilities. *Journal of Applied Behavior Analysis, 32,* 103–106.

Green, C. W., & Reid, D. H. (1999). Reducing indices of unhappiness among individuals with profound multiple disabilities during therapeutic exercise routines. *Journal of Applied Behavior Analysis, 32,* 137–147.

Green, C. W., Reid, D. H., Rollyson, J. H., & Passante, S. C. (2005). An enriched teaching program for reducing resistance and indices of unhappiness among individuals with profound multiple disabilities. *Journal of Applied Behavior Analysis, 38,* 221–233.

Gullone, E., King, N. J., & Cummins, R. A. (1999). Fear of youth with mental retardation. l: Psychometric evaluation of the fear survey schedule for children-II. (FSSC-II.). *Research in Developmental Disabilities, 17,* 269–284.

Hagopian, L. P., Crockett, J. L., & Keeney, K. M. (2001). Multicomponent treatment of blood-injury-injection phobia in a young man with mental retardation. *Research in Developmental Disabilities, 21,* 141–149.

Hare, D. J. (1991). The use of cognitive behavioural therapy with people with Asperger syndrome. *Autism, 1,* 215–225.

Harper, J. S., & Wadsworth, D. C. (1993). The social needs of adolescents with cerebral palsy. *Developmental Medicine and Child Neurology, 35,* 1019–1122.

Helsel, W. J., & Matson, J. L. (1988). The assessment of depression in children: The internal structure of the Child Depression Inventory (CDI). *Behaviour Research and Therapy, 22,* 289–298.

Hill, J., & Furniss, F. (2005). Patterns of emotional and behavioral disturbance associated with autistic traits in young people with severe intellectual disabilities and challenging behaviors. *Research in Developmental Disabilities, 27,* 517–528.

Holden, B., & Gitlesen, J. (2003). Prevalence of psychiatric symptoms in adults with mental retardation and challenging behavior. *Research in Developmental Disabilities, 24,* 323–332.

Hollon, S. D., Kendall, P. C., & Lumry, A. (1986). Specificity of depressotypic cognitions in clinical depression. *Journal of Abnormal Psychology, 95,* 52–59.

Hopko, D. R., Hopko, S. D., & Lejuez, C. W. (2007). Mood disorders. In P. Sturmey (Ed.), *Functional Analysis and Clinical Treatment* (pp. 307–334). San Diego, CA: Elsevier.

Jacobson, N. S., Dobson, K. S., Truax, P. A., Addis, M. E., Koerner, K., Gollan, J. K., et al. (1996). A component analysis of cognitive behavior treatment for depression. *Journal of Consulting and Clinical Psychology, 64,* 295–304.

Jones, K. M., & Friman, P. C. (1999). A case study of behavioral assessment and treatment of insect phobia. *Journal of Applied Behavior Analysis, 32,* 95–98.

Kazdin, A. E., Matson, J. L., & Senatore, V. (1983). Assessment of depression in mentally retarded adults. *American Journal of Psychiatry, 140,* 1040–1043.

Kessler, R. C., McGonagle, K. A., Zhao, S., Nelson, C. B., Highes, M., Eshelman, S., et al. (1994). Lifetime and 12-month prevalence of DSM-III-R psychiatric disorders in the United States: Results from the National Comorbidity Survey. *Archives of General Psychiatry, 51,* 8–19.

Krakovsky, G., Huth, M. M., Lin, L., & Levin, R. S. (2007). Functional changes in children and adolescents and young adults with cerebral palsy. *Research in Developmental Disabilities, 28,* 331–340.

LeJuez, C. W., Hopko, D. R., & Hopko, S. D. (2003). *The Brief Behavioral Activation Treatment of Depression (BATD): A comprehensive patient guide.* Boston, MA: Pearson.

Lewis, M. H., Bodfish, J. W., Powell, S. B., Parker, D. E., & Golden, R. N. (1996). Clomipramine treatment for self-injurious behavior of individuals with mental retardation: A double-blind comparison with placebo. *American Journal on Mental Retardation, 100,* 656–665.

Lewinsohn, P. M. (1974). A behavioral approach to depression. In R. M. Friedman & M. M. Katz (Eds.), *The psychology of depression: Contemporary theory and research* (pp. 157–185). New York, NY: Wiley.

Lindauer, S. E., DeLeon, I. G., & Fisher, W. W. (1999). Decreasing signs of negative and correlated self-injury mental retardation and mood disturbance. *Journal of Applied Behavior Analysis, 32,* 103–106.

Lindsay, W. I. (2006). That poor laddie cannae tell his thoughts fae his actions: A reply to Sturmey. *Journal of Applied Research in Intellectual Disabilities, 19,* 119–120.

Lindsay, W. I., Howells, L., & Pithcaithly, D. (1993). Cognitive therapy for depression with individuals with intellectual disability. *British Journal of Medical Psychology, 66,* 135–141.

Lindsay, W. R., & Lees, M. S. (2003). A comparison of anxiety and depression in sex offenders with intellectual disabilities and a control group with intellectual disability. *Sex Abuse, 15,* 339–345.

Lindsay, W. R., & Mitchie, A. M. (1988). Adaptation of the Zung self-rating anxiety scale for people with a mental handicap. *Journal of Mental Deficiency Research, 32,* 485–490.

Lindsay, W. R., Stenfert Kroses, B., & Drew, P. (2005). Cognitive-behavioral approaches to depression in people with learning disabilities. In P. Sturmey (Ed.), *Mood Disorders in People with Mental Retardation* (pp. 241–272). Kingston, NY: NADD Press.

Lowry, M. A., & Sovner, R. (1992). Severe behavior disorders associated with rapid cycling bipolar disorder in two adults with profound mental retardation. *Journal of Intellectual Disability Research, 36,* 269–281.

Luscre, D. M., & Center, D. B. (1996). Procedures for reducing dental fear in children with autism. *Journal of Autism and Developmental Disorders, 26,* 547–556.

Mansell, S., & Sobsey, D. (2001). *Counseling people with developmental disability who have been sexually abused.* Kingston, NY: NADD Press.

Marston, G. M., Perry, D. W., & Roy, A. (1997). Manifestations of depression in people with intellectual disability. *Journal of Intellectual Disability Research, 41,* 476–480.

Masi, G., Brovedani, P., Mucci, M., & Favilla, L. (2002). Assessment of anxiety and depression in adolescents with mental retardation. *Child Psychiatry and Human Development, 32,* 227–237.

Masi, G., Favilla, L., & Mucci, M. (2000). Generalized anxiety disorder in adolescents and adult with mild mental retardation. *Psychiatry, 6,* 54–64.

Matson, J. L. (1982). The treatment of behavioral characteristics of depression in the mentally retarded. *Behavior Therapy, 13,* 209–218.

Matson, J. L. (1983). Depression in the mentally retarded: Toward a conceptual analysis of diagnosis. *Progress in Behavior Modification, 15,* 57–79.

Matson, J. L. (1988). *The PIMRA manual.* Worthington, OH: IDS Publishing.

Matson, J. L. (1995). *Assessment of dual diagnosis.* Baton Rouge, LA: Scientific Publishers.

Matson, J. L. (1998). *Diagnostic assessment for the severely handicapped II*. Baton Rouge, LA: Scientific Publishers Incorporated.

Matson, J. L., & Bamberg, J. W. (1988). Reliability of the Assessment of Dual Diagnosis (ADD). *Research in Developmental Disabilities, 19,* 89–95.

Matson, J. L., Kazdin, A. E., & Senatore, V. (1984). Psychometric properties of the psychopathology instrument for mentally retarded adults. *Applied Research in Mental Retardation, 5,* 81–89.

Matson, J. L., & Smiroldo, B. B. (1997). Validity of the mania subscale of the Diagnostic assessment for the severely handicapped II (DASH-II). *Research in Developmental Disabilities, 18,* 221–225.

Matson, J. L., Smiroldo, B. B., Hamilton, M., & Baglio, C. S. (1997). Do anxiety disorders exist in persons with severe and profound mental retardation? *Research in Developmental Disabilities, 18,* 39–44.

McDaniel, W. F. (1997). Criterion-related diagnostic validity and test-retaest reliability of the MMPI-168 (L) in mentally retarded adolescents and adults. *Journal of Clinical Psychology, 53,* 724–732.

McDaniel, W. F., & Gregory, A. (2005). Diagnostic criteria for mood disorders and applications to people with mental retardation. In P. Sturmey (Ed.), *Mood Disorders in People with Mental Retardation* (pp. 3–16). Kingston, NY: NADD Press.

McDaniel, W. F., & Harris, D. W. (1999). Mental health outcomes in dually diagnosed individuals with mental retardation assessed with the MMPI-168(L): Case studies. *Journal of Clinical Psychiatry, 55,* 487–496.

McDaniel, W. E., Passmore, C. E., & Sewell, H. M. (2003). The MPI-168(L) and Add in assessing psychopathology in individuals with mental retardation between and within instrument associations. *Research in Developmental Disabilities, 24,* 19–32.

Mindham, J., & Espie, C. A. (2003). Glasgow Anxiety Scale for people with an intellectual disability (GAS-ID): Development and psychometric properties of a new measure for use with people with intellectual disabilities. *Journal of Intellectual Disability Research, 47,* 22–30.

Moss, S., Patel, P., Prosser, H., Goldberg, D., Simpson, N., Rowe, N., et al. (1993). Psychiatric morbidity in older people with moderate and severe learning disability. I: Development and reliability of the patient interview (PAS-ADD). *British Journal of Psychiatry, 163,* 471–480.

Moss, S., Ibbotson, B., Prosser, H., Goldberg, H., Patel, P., & Simpson, N. (1997). Validity of the PAS-ADD for detecting psychiatric symptoms in adult with learning disability (mental retardation). *Social Psychiatry and Psychiatric Epidemiology, 32,* 344–354.

Pary, R. J., Levitas, A. S., & Hurley, A. D. (1999). Diagnosis of bipolar disorder in persons with developmental disabilities. *Mental Health Aspects of Developmental Disabilities, 2,* 59–63.

Poindexter, A. (1996). *Assessment and Treatment of Anxiety Disorders in Person with Mental retardation*. Kingston, NY: NADD Press.

Prosser, H., & Bromley, J. (1998). Interviewing people with intellectual disabilities. In E. Emerson, C. Hatton, J. Bromley, & J. Craine (Eds.), *Clinical Psychology and people with intellectual disabilities* (pp. 99–113). Chichester: Wiley.

Prosser, H., Moss, S., Costello, H., Simpson, N., Patel, P., & Rowe, S. (1998). Reliability and validity of the Mini PAS-ADD for assessing psychiatric disorders in adults with intellectual disability. *Journal of Intellectual Disability Research, 42,* 264–272.

Powell, S. B., Bodfish, J. W., Crawford, T. W., Golden, R. N., & Lewis, M. H. (1996). Growth differences associated with compulsive and stereotyped behavior disorders in adults with mental retardation. *Anxiety, 2,* 90–94.

Ramirez, S. Z., & Lukenbill, J. F. (2007). Development of the fear survey schedule for adults with mental retardation. *Research in Developmental Disabilities, 28,* 225–237.

Reiss, S. (1988). *The Reiss screen for maladaptive behaviors test manual.* Worthington, OH: IDS Publishing.

Reiss, S., & Rojahn, J. (1993). Joint occurrence of depression and aggression in children and adults with mental retardation. *Journal of Intellectual Disability Research, 37,* 28–33.

Rojahn, J., & Ebensen, A. J. (2005). Epidemiology of mood disorders in people with mental retardation. In P. Sturmey (Ed.), *Mood Disorders in People with Mental Retardation* (pp. 67–88). Kingston, NY: NADD Press.

Royal College of Psychiatrists (2001). DC-LD: *Diagnostic Criteria for Psychiatric Disorders for use with Adults with Learning Disabilities/Mental Retardation.* Occasional Paper OP48. London: Gaskell Press.

Ryan, R. (1996). Post-traumatic stress disorder in persons with developmental disabilities. In A. Poindexter (Ed.), *Assessment and treatment of anxiety disorders in person with mental retardation* (pp. 41–52). Kingston, NY: NADD Press.

Sarphare, G., & Aman, M. G. (1999). Parent- and self-ratings of anxiety in children with mental retardation. Agreement levels and test-retest reliability. *Research in Developmental Disabilities, 17,* 27–39.

Skinner, B. F. (1953). *Science and human behavior.* New York, NY: McMillan.

Skinner, B. F. (1971). *Beyond freedom and dignity.* New York, NY: Knopf.

Sovner, R., & Hurley, A. D. (1982a). Diagnosing depression in the mentally retarded. *Psychiatric Aspects of Mental Retardation Newsletter, 1,* 1–3.

Sovner, R., & Hurley, A. D. (1982b). Diagnosing mania in the mentally retarded. *Psychiatric Aspects of Mental Retardation Newsletter, 1,* 9–11.

Stenfert Kroese, B., Dagnan, D., & Loumidis, K. (Kroese 1997). *Cognitive therapy for people with learning disabilities.* London: Routlege.

Stigler, K. A., Posey, D. J., & McDougle, C. J. (2005). Psychotropic medication for mood disorders in people wit mental retardation. In P. Sturmey (Ed.), *Mood disorders in people with mental retardation* (pp. 211–228). Kingston, NY: NADD Press.

Sturmey, P. (2004). Against psychotherapy with people with mental retardation. *Mental Retardation, 43,* 55–57.

Sturmey, P. (2005a). *Mood disorders in people with mental retardation.* Kingston, NY: NADD Press.

Sturmey, P. (2005b). Behavioral formulation and treatment of depression in people with mental retardation. In P. Sturmey (Ed.), *Mood disorders in people with mental retardation* (pp. 293–315). Kingston, NY: NADD Press.

Sturmey, P. (2006a). On some recent claims for the efficacy of cognitive therapy for people with intellectual disabilities. *Journal of Applied Research in Intellectual Disabilities, 19,* 109–118.

Sturmey, P. (2006b). In response to Lindsay and Emerson. *Journal of Applied Research in Intellectual Disabilities, 19,* 125–129.

Sturmey, P. (2006c). Against psychotherapy with people who have mental retardation: In response to the responses. *Mental Retardation, 44,* 71–74.

Sturmey, P. (in press). Psychosocial and Mental Status Assessment. In J. W. Jacobson, J. A. Mulick, & J. Rojahn (Eds.), *Handbook of Intellectual and Developmental Disabilities.* New York, NY: Kluwer.

Sturmey, P. (2007). *Functional analysis in clinical treatment.* San Diego, CA: Elsevier.

Sturmey, P., Reed, J., & Corbett, J. (1991). Assessment of psychiatric disorders in people with learning difficulties: A psychometric review of available measures. *Psychological Medicine, 21,* 143–155.

Sturmey, P., & Ghaziuddin, M. (2005). Other biological treatments. In P. Sturmey (Ed.), *Mood Disorders in People with Mental Retardation* (pp. 229–240). Kingston, NY: NADD Press.

Sturmey, P., Ward-Horner, J., Marroquin, M., & Doran, E. (2007). Structural and functional approaches to psychopathology and case formulation. In P. Sturmey (Ed.), *The Handbook of Functional Analysis and Clinical Psychology*. San Diego, CA: Elsevier.

Taylor, J. (2005). In support of psychotherapy for people with mental retardation. *Mental Retardation, 43,* 450–453.

Tsiouris, J. A., Cohen, I. L., Patti, P., & Koros, W. M. (2003). Treatment of previously undiagnosed psychiatric disorders in persons with developmental disabilities decreased or eliminated self-injurious behavior. *Journal of Clinical Psychiatry, 64,* 1081–1090.

Tsiouris, J. A., Mann, R., Patti, P., & Sturmey, P. (2003). Challenging behaviours should not be considered as depressive equivalents in individuals with intellectual disabilities. *Journal of Intellectual Disabilities Research, 47,* 14–21.

Vanstraelen, M., & Tyrer, S. P. (1999). Rapid cycling bipolar affective disorder in people with intellectual disability: A systematic review. *Journal of Intellectual Disability Research, 43,* 349–359.

Vitiello, B., Spreat, S., & Behar, D. (1989). Obsessive compulsive disorder in mentally retarded patients. *Journal of Nervous and Mental Disease, 177,* 232–236.

Weissman, M. M., Bland, R. C., Canino, G. J., Faravelli, K., Greenwald, S., Hwu, H. G., et al. (1996). Cross national epidemiology of major depression and bipolar disorder. *Journal of the American Medical Association, 276,* 293–299.

Wolpe, J. (1986). Individualization: The categorical imperative of behavior therapy practice. *Journal of Behavior Therapy and Experimental Psychiatry, 17,* 145–153.

Psychotropic Medication Effects and Side Effects

ERIK A. MAYVILLE

INSTITUTE FOR EDUCATIONAL PLANNING, CONNECTICUT CENTER FOR CHILD DEVELOPMENT, MILFORD, CONNECTICUT

I. INTRODUCTION

As information and technology has evolved to increase the standards of care for persons with developmental disabilities, the spectrum of phenomenon subject to assessment has broadened. Accordingly, a field of assessment of the intended and unintended effects of psychotropic medication in persons with developmental disabilities has developed, and an expanding body of literature on the subject is now available (Aman & Singh, 1988; DesNoyers Hurley et al., 1998; Kalachnik, 1999a,b; Schroeder, Rojahn, & Reese, 1997). However, the literature in this area has emerged at a relatively slow pace relative to the documented need since the mid-1970s for formal assessment practices and methodologies (Kalachnik, 1999a). Indeed, there has been a clearly justified and defined need to measure the effects of psychotropics with persons with developmental disabilities, stemming from the history of overuse and susceptibility of this population to adverse medication effects, among other reasons. Thus, the relatively recent arrival of published assessment instruments and literature to guide this effort is overdue.

The focus of this chapter is to provide a review of the extant conceptual and methodological issues in assessment of both therapeutic and side effects of psychotropic medications in persons with developmental disabilities. Because this chapter is the only one in this handbook relating to psychotropic medications, some attention will be devoted to the broader context in which the assessment methodologies in this field have evolved. Specifically, the history of psychotropic use, description of specific effects related to particular classes of medications, and prevalence rates of usage in persons with developmental disabilities. The reader is referred to Reiss and Aman (1998) for an extensive discussion of each of these topics.

INTERNATIONAL REVIEW OF RESEARCH IN MENTAL RETARDATION, Vol. 34
0074-7750/07 $35.00

DOI: 10.1016/S0074-7750(07)34007-X

Additionally, terminology referring to the subject matter of this assessment domain is relatively unique, and requires some clarification. The term "psychotropic" is used to describe medications that are prescribed specifically for modifying an individual's emotional state or behavior (Aman & Singh, 1988). In contrast, "psychoactive" refers to behavioral, cognitive, and/or emotional effects of a medication which may or may not have been intended by the prescribing physician. "Therapeutic effect" refers to the intended effect of a particular medication (indicated or "off-label"), whereas "side effect" means any unintended, usually harmful, effect of a medication. The terms "adverse drug reaction" and "adverse drug event" also describe negative and potentially harmful effects, with adverse drug events generally referring to more serious reactions (Kalachnik, 1999b). The term side effect will be used here to refer to all unwanted psychotropic medication effects. Though terminology varies somewhat throughout the literature in this area, the terms defined here have been selected because of their frequency of use and availability of consistent definition. For more extensive discussions of terminology, see Kalachnik (1999b) and Nebeker, Barach, and Samore (2004).

II. A HISTORICAL CONTEXT FOR ASSESSMENT OF MEDICATION EFFECTS

For nearly as long as their existence, psychotropic medications have been a common intervention agent for a wide variety of problematic behavior and psychiatric disturbance in individuals with developmental disabilities. Shortly after the introduction of chlorpromazine in 1952, Davies (1954) published an abstract of its efficacy for "mental deficiency," and widespread prescription of chlorpromazine for a variety of problems (Schroeder et al., 1998). Though little information was available to inform safe and efficacious administration and effect monitoring processes, by 1970, prevalence studies estimated that about half the population of individuals with mental retardation residing in institutions were receiving psychotropic medications (Lipman, 1970). While subsequent studies reflect less frequent prescribing practices, estimates continue to hover around 30–40%, with slightly higher rates in institutional settings compared to community-based environments (Hill, Balow, & Bruinicks, 1985; Nøttestad & Linaker, 2003; Rinck, 1998). These estimates are well in excess of rates of psychopathology in this population (Borthwick-Duffy, 1994), which, combined with other factors, has led to the impression that individuals with developmental disabilities represent an "overmedicated" population.

As psychotropic use became widespread, it became apparent that they were not without potentially serious iatrogenic effects. The risks associated with a wide variety of psychotropic medications are now well-documented, with side effects potentially affecting functioning within many bodily functioning systems (e.g., cardiovascular, hematologic, endocrine and metabolic; see Wilson, Lott, & Tsai, 1998, for an example). In some cases, such effects constitute irreversible, disfiguring, and even life-threatening conditions. Much attention has been devoted to the side effects of the antipsychotics given that they have historically been the most frequently used class of psychotropics for persons with developmental disabilities (Rinck, 1998). Antipsychotics, or "neuroleptics" as they are also referred to (see Baumeister, Sevin, & King, 1998, for a discussion of terminology), are commonly noted for their effects on the extrapyramidal motor system, which may result in neuromuscular movement disorders (see Wilson et al., 1998, for a review). They may also induce a potentially life-threatening condition known as neuroleptic malignant syndrome (NMS), which involves severe muscle rigidity, autonomic nervous system instability, and sudden onset of severe hyperthermia, among other symptoms (Wilson et al., 1998). Though older agents described as "typical" are thought to have a significantly greater potential for such effects relative to the newer, more commonly used "Atypical" antipsychotics (e.g., risperidone, ziprasidone, aripripizole; see Glazer, 2000 and Kane, 2001, for reviews), the atypical antipsychotics are not without similar potentially severely impairing side effects as well (Chakraborty & Johnston, 2004; Kane, 2001; Nielsen & Bruhn, 2005). Moreover, some have questioned the veracity of the literature establishing differences between the two types with respect to effectiveness and safety profile (Verhoeven, Van der Heijden, Wijers, & Tuinier, 2005).

As high prevalence rates would suggest, psychotropic pharmacotherapy practices were less than judicious as they emerged over the decades since their introduction. Central to this problem was the lack of theoretical rationale for therapeutic actions of psychotropics. As noted by Baumeister and Sevin (1990):

> Despite the widespread use of drugs in persons with mental retardation, research and clinical practice in this area seem to differ from other areas of biological psychiatry in that little consideration is given to the neural substrates that underlie either the conditions being treated or the actions of the drugs used. (p. 254)

In practice, psychotropics were often prescribed without sufficient investigation regarding the need for medication (i.e., psychiatric diagnosis), and were not properly monitored once they were started. This led to potentially dangerous practices such as frequent dose and drug changes, high doses of antipsychotics, intraclass polypharmacy, and contraindicated long-term use of particular medications (e.g., long-acting sedative hypnotics, benzodiazepines, anticholinergics), among others (Kalachnik et al., 1998). Further, the use of psychotropics for problem behavior treatment became increasingly troublesome as alternative, often less restrictive technologies evolved (see Iwata et al., 1997, for a comprehensive review). In the 1970s and 1980s, lawsuits and subsequent federal regulations and accreditation council statements help lay the groundwork for guidelines and standards supporting safer practice. To date, no fewer than 18 formal statements (e.g., class action lawsuits, accreditation council statements) have been issued that have influenced guidelines and standards of the use of psychotropics in the developmentally disabled (see Kalachnik, 1999a, for a review). Nonetheless, potentially dangerous practices continue in many cases, such as psychotropic use without proper research support for the prescribed purpose, insufficient investigation of less-restrictive alternatives, and implementation without baseline or efficacy measurement (Aman, Lamb, & Collier-Crespin, 2003; Holden & Gitleson, 2004; Matson et al., 2000). This is likely the result of a confluence of factors, including the often immediate suppression of target problem behavior as well as the effort and expense associated with alternative management methods (Holden & Gitleson, 2004; Matson, Bielecki, Mayville, & Matson, 2003).

As information emerged regarding psychotropic administration practices in persons with developmental disabilities, it became clear that the problem of high psychotropic usage was compounded by, if not stemming from, insufficient and deficient research. Indeed, the history of this field is commonly associated with inglorious medication efficacy research practices (Baumeister, Todd, & Sevin, 1993; Matson et al., 2000; Sprague & Werry, 1971). Several comprehensive reviews have detailed these practices, the most notable of which include inadequate experimental design (i.e., absence of placebo control, random assignment of subjects, use of double blind subjects), and absence of objective dependent variable measures. Thus, the field of psychopharmacology in persons with developmental disabilities did not evolve inductively from sound research. Moreover, medical professionals attempting research-based practice were left without sound literature to guide their endeavors. While the field is not completely devoid of sound research (Research Units on Pediatric Psychopharmacology Network, 2005), in many cases, the aforementioned problems persist (Matson et al., 2000; Singh, Matson, Cooper, Dixon, & Sturmey, 2005).

In summary, research and practice with psychotropic medications in persons with developmental disabilities have historically been fraught with problems. Guidelines and standards now exist that outline indicated practice, of which proper assessment of therapeutic and side effects is a significant part.

III. CONCEPTUALIZATIONS OF ASSESSMENT OF MEDICATION EFFECTS

Similar to other branches of medical practice, psychiatric practices emerged from a model of traditional biomedicine, or a medical model (Engel, 1977). The medical model emphasized an exclusively biomedical approach, characterized by reductionism (i.e., molecular biology can ultimately explain the complexities of all biological events), mind-body dualism (separate conceptualizations of mental and physical states), and exclusionism (discounting any phenomenon not explainable through molecular biology). Engel observed that illness was not fully accounted for through biomedicine, and offered several points broadening the scope of this approach. He noted that illness resulted from the interaction of diverse causal factors, that psychosocial variables could be integral in determining susceptibility to and severity of an illness, and that illness could be observed in the absence of biochemical disturbance, among other points (Borrell-Carrio, Suchman, & Epstein, as cited in Biderman, Yeheskel, & Herman, 2005). These ideas, among others, formed the framework of the "biopsychosocial" model, a conceptualization of illness and treatment that integrated biomedical and social science approaches.

It is not likely that the biopsychosocial model was initially adopted by many practitioners prescribing psychotropic medications to the developmentally disabled, and that this contributed to less than ideal assessment practices. Indeed, some have argued that widespread proliferation of this approach has yet to occur, citing practical and economic limitations (Biderman et al., 2005). Nonetheless, this model is readily endorsed by experts of varied backgrounds in this field, and is considered a "unifying concept" in contemporary approaches to monitoring psychotropic medications (Kalachnik et al., 1998). Perhaps the most critical aspect of its utility is that it emphasizes addressing problems within a context of integrated treatment modalities (Kalachnik et al., 1998), thereby utilizing the expertise of professionals from diverse training backgrounds to incrementally construct a comprehensive evaluation of the role and efficacy of psychotropic medications. The "interdisciplinary team" model is a primary example of the implementation of the biopsychosocial model, in that professionals from medicine, psychology, education, rehabilitation, and social work are a standard part of assessment and interpretation regarding psychotropic medication use (Davis et al., 1998). This model followed the 1972 Wyatt v. Stickney decision in which inappropriate psychotropic use was a central tenet, and was subsequently incorporated into accreditation council statements

(Accreditation Council for Services for Mentally Retarded and Other Developmentally Disabled Persons, 1980). Properly functioning interdisciplinary teams have been associated with reductions in psychotropic medication usage, increases in judicious prescription and assessment practices, and increased successful multidisciplinary treatment efforts (Glaser & Morreau, 1986; Schalock, Foley, Toulouse, & Stark, 1985).

Assessment of psychotropic medication effects within a biopsychosocial approach, then, includes data collected from various theoretical viewpoints, so long as the data is objective, verifiable, and interpretable. Perhaps the clearest example of the influence of a social science discipline has been the application of behavior analytic assessment and evaluation methodologies. Several authors have noted that behavior analysis, a discipline derived from a natural science approach that emphasizes the contextual nature of behavior, is particularly well suited for assessment and analysis of psychotropic medication effects (Poling & Cleary, 1986; Poling & Ehrhardt, 1999; Singh & Beale, 1986). Indeed, it has become common to assess therapeutic and side effects, historically defined as biomedical phenomenon, within a behavioral conceptualization (Kalachnik, 1999a). Within behavioral assessment, medication effects are specifically and objectively defined according to their topography, and can be recorded with respect to occurrence (e.g., frequency, permanent products) as well as time (e.g., interval, duration, latency recording).

While behavior assessment methodologies have become increasingly common in psychotropic medication effect monitoring, application of additional aspects of behavior analytic technology has been slow to occur. A behavior analytic evaluation of medication effects involves more than just behavior recording procedures; single-subject research methodologies, graphic analysis (i.e., visual inspection) of data, repeated measurement of the dependent variable, and isolation of extraneous variables in analyzing variable data have been identified as relevant procedures (Poling & Ehrhardt, 1999). Moreover, behavior analysis advances a "contextual stance" (Foxall, 2004), or analysis of the relationship between behavior, consequences, and other contextual stimuli. This position is demonstrated in several recent studies evaluating the effects of the antipsychotic risperidone on particular functional relations (Crossland et al., 2003; Zarcone et al., 2004). For example, Crossland et al. evaluated the effect of risperidone on destructive behavior in different functional relation conditions in two individuals with autism. Destructive behavior occurred during some contrived antecedent and consequence conditions but not others. Subsequent treatment with risperidone produced selective reductions across functional relation conditions. That is, destructive behavior would reduce following risperidone in some situations (e.g., when asked to comply with tasks) but not others (e.g., when preferred items were taken from the participant). Similar studies have been conducted in persons with mental retardation with the opioid-antagonist medication naltrexone (Garcia & Smith, 1999), in which this medication was found to have function-specific and topographic-specific effects on self-injurious behavior. While studies of this sort are few, they offer a relatively unique analysis of the effects of psychotropic medications, making use of the technology and conceptualization that has evolved over a half-century of research within the science of human behavior. Additional examples of behavior analytic conceptualizations of medication effect assessment are offered throughout this chapter.

Thus, conceptualization of effects of psychotropic medications for persons with developmental disabilities was borne out of a traditional, biomedical model, but has since expanded to diverse domains outside the realm of medicine. In light of recent research in behavior analysis, further expansion of a conceptualization within the science of human behavior is likely.

IV. PSYCHOTROPIC MEDICATION EFFECT ASSESSMENT IN PERSONS WITH DEVELOPMENTAL DISABILITIES

Assessment processes are the foundation on which competent and ethical pharmacotherapy with persons with developmental disabilities rests. Assessment practices within psychology and psychiatry have historically varied with respect to definitions of subject matter and objectivity of methodology (Groth-Marnat, 1999). The particular issues inherent in assessment of how medication effects behavior in persons with developmental disabilities necessitate objectivity as a primary characteristic in assessment methodologies. Self-report of effects, an often standard means of determining if a psychotropic medication is having intended or unintended effects, is often compromised or not possible given the communication and cognitive difficulties this population often experiences. Moreover, objective measurement is likely a superior assessment methodology for persons with developmental disabilities even in cases where self-report is viable (Sovner & Hurley, 1987). Objectivity here refers to the source of information regarding behavior (i.e., self-report vs third-party report), as well as to the means by which descriptions of behavior are recorded and interpreted (i.e., quantification and physical recording of behavior, clinician opinion vs structured interpretation guidelines). Though objective assessment may be composed of subjective interpretation to some degree (see Hagopian et al., 1997, for a discussion), interpretation is limited to a relatively narrow range relative to data. However, data is often derived from reports of direct observation by caregivers and/or family members, which, in turn, necessitates valid observational tools and methodologies. Using assessment techniques with established reliability and validity properties has been identified as a tenet of best practice in this field (Kalachnik et al., 1998; Sprague & Werry, 1971).

A. Assessing Medication Therapeutic Effects

The assessment of medication therapeutic effects is central to understanding the role of a psychotropic medication in an individual's treatment regimen. Expert consensus is that in nearly all cases, psychotropic medication should be a treatment component to reduce symptomotology of a validly assessed mental health disorder, or in accordance with a specific behavioral-pharmacologic hypothesis (Baumeister & Sevin, 1990; Kalachnik et al., 1998). However, identification of mental health symptomotology is often a difficult task for several reasons. First, there is a general lack of recognition that persons with developmental disabilities suffer from such conditions, though prevalence rates are higher in this population than in typically developing individuals. Symptoms can be misinterpreted as a manifestation of mental retardation, referred to as "diagnostic overshadowing" (Reiss, Levitan, & Szysko, 1982). Second, persons with developmental disabilities often are not able to report their experience of such symptoms to aid in the assessment process, leaving the investigative work exclusively to others in many cases. Compounding the problem is that individuals with advanced knowledge of identifying symptoms may come into contact with the individual only sporadically, leaving the symptom identification to likely untrained individuals (e.g., direct care staff, family members). Third, those who are capable of self-reporting symptomatology may attempt to hide mental health difficulties, or may be embarrassed to ask for clarification on interviewer language they may not understand (Reiss, 1994). Thus, to adequately assess mental health symptomatology, clinicians must be familiar with how such phenomenon present in this population and the complications associated with it, as well as population-specific assessment tools and systems (Matson, Mayville, & Laud, 2003). The reader is referred to Rush, Bowman, Eidman, Toole, and Mortenson (2004), for a more comprehensive discussion of these issues.

A key assessment component, then, is the identification of "index behaviors," or particular behaviors that are associated with the condition the medication was prescribed for, as well as subsequent measurement of such behaviors prior to and throughout the medication trial. Consensus panels have emphasized the use of the particular term "index" over "target," in keeping with the point that psychotropics should generally not be used to reduce behavior outside of the psychiatric disorder or behavioral-pharmacologic hypothesis contexts (Kalachnik et al., 1998). Index behaviors can be defined on an individual basis or can be derived from existing assessments of mental health disorders designed for persons with developmental disabilities, such as the Diagnostic Assessment for the Severely Handicapped (Matson, Gardner, Coe, & Sovner, 1991) or the Reiss Screen for Maladaptive Behavior (Reiss, 1988). Monitoring can be achieved in this case either through direct observation of individual behavior(s) described in the scale, or through monitoring of subscale scores over time (e.g., mania, mood). Direct observation of index behaviors can be achieved through methodologies developed within the field of applied behavior analysis, and include event, duration, and interval recording, as well as momentary time sampling (see Mayville & Mayville, 2005, for a review). The reader is referred to Pyles, Muniz, Cade, and Silva (1997) for a description of how rating scale and direct observation data can be integrated within a multidisciplinary treatment evaluation paradigm to assess medication therapeutic effects.

It should be noted that rating scales will only be viable in cases where they are used in the context for which they were intended. For example, instruments used to identify core behaviors of mental health disorders may be less effective in measuring the effect of medications on "nonspecific" problem behaviors (e.g., aggression and self-injury; cf. Valdovinos, Zarcone, Hellings, Kim, & Schroeder, 2004). Thus, it is important for the clinician to be familiar with the investigated efficacy of instruments for particular medication effect monitoring purposes, in addition to other relevant psychometric properties of that scale. Table I contains a brief description of relevant instruments encompassing the domain of therapeutic effects, including the related areas of quality of life and social validity, to be discussed below.

B. Quality of Life

In addition to reducing and increasing particular index behaviors, psychotropic medications can also be related to global positive or negative effects on an individual's life (i.e., collateral behaviors). As previously alluded to, this equates to an increased likelihood that an individual will contact contingencies that produce beneficial outcomes in many domains as a result of the medication. Improvements and deterioration in index and collateral behaviors are related to the construct of "quality of life" (QOL), which encompasses objective assessments of conditions of a person's life, as well as a person's subjective satisfaction with life (Perry & Felce, 1995). QOL has been the focus of much investigation over the past few decades in a number of clinical populations, with researchers attempting to balance the need for standardization in a valid assessment process with the subjectivity inherent in such a construct (Perry & Felce, 1995). For persons with developmental disabilities, several models have been offered and a number

TABLE I
SELECT LIST OF VIABLE RATING SCALES AND CHECKLISTS FOR THE EVALUATION OF PSYCHOTROPIC MEDICATION THERAPEUTIC EFFECTS AND RELATED DOMAINS

Scale	Scale type	Citation	Research as medication evaluation. Tool in DD population?
Vineland Adaptive Behavior Scale	Adaptive behavior	Sparrow, Balla, & Cicchetti, 1984	Yes (e.g., Williams et al., 2006)
Motivation Assessment Scale	Behavior function	Durand & Crimmins, 1988	No
Questions About Behavior Function Scale	Behavior function	Matson & Vollmer, 1995	No
Aberrant Behavior Checklist	Problem behavior	Aman & Singh, 1986	Yes (e.g., Aman, Singh, Stewart, & Field, 1985)
Behavior Problems Inventory	Problem behavior	Rojahn, Matson, Lott, Esbensen, & Smalls, 2001	Yes (e.g., Sturmey, Fink, & Sevin, 1993)
Assessment for Dual Diagnosis	Psychiatric	Matson, 1997	No
Diagnostic Assessment for the Severely Handicapped Scale-II	Psychiatric	Matson, Gardner, Coe, & Sovner, 1991	Yes – for problem behavior (e.g., Valdovinos et al., 2004)
Reiss Screen for Maladaptive Behavior	Psychiatric	Reiss, 1988	Yes (e.g., Branford, 1996)
Evaluation of Quality of Life Instrument	Quality of life	Nota et al., 2006	No
Matson Evaluation of Social Skills in Persons with Severe Retardation	Social skills	Matson, 1995	No
The Abbreviated Acceptability Rating Profile	Social validity	Tarnowski & Simonian, 1992	No
Treatment Evaluation Inventory	Social validity	Kazdin, 1980	Yes (e.g., Lindeman et al., 1992)

of objective assessments have been employed to measure QOL (see Hughs, Hwang, Kim, Eisenman, & Killian, 1995, and Perry & Felce, 1995, for reviews), though few specific QOL measures have been created. Perry and Felce (1995), Felce and Perry (1996) have generated a model in which QOL is composed of five subdomains: physical, material, social, and emotional wellbeing, as well as development and activity. Assessments of QOL have been conducted with this model in persons with profound multiple disabilities (Petry, Maes, & Vlaskamp, 2004), with results supporting this conceptualization. In their comprehensive review of assessments that have measured QOL in empirical studies, Hughs et al. (1995) identified 15 different dimensions after reviewing 87 studies, and stated that numerous empirical measures supported their model of QOL, though the measures were not necessarily created primarily for that purpose. At least one instrument has been specifically devised to measure QOL, the Evaluation of Quality of Life Instrument (Nota, Soresi, & Perry, 2006), with initial investigations of psychometric properties suggesting that this instrument is reliable and valid. Additionally, assessments designed to measure specific domains such as community integration (e.g., Index of Community Involvement; Raynes, Sumpton, & Pettipher, 1989), and social interaction (e.g., Matson Evaluation of Social Skills in Persons with Severe Retardation; Matson, 1995), as well as multiple construct measures (i.e., communication, socialization, and daily living skills; Sparrow, Ciccetti, & Balla, 2005) are among those that could be potentially useful in measuring QOL within a psychotropic medication context. Such measures are useful in measuring the degree to which an individual's QOL has been affected by a psychotropic, including detecting a decline in aspects of an individual's life despite improvement in index behavior (Kalachnik et al., 1998).

The degree to which persons with developmental disabilities appear happy has been considered a component of a QOL assessment (Perry & Felce, 1995), and is an area of increasing research focus in persons with severe and profound disabilities (see Lancioni, Singh, O'Reilly, Oliva, & Basili, 2005, for a review). The term "indices of happiness" has come to refer to the means by which behaviors typically associated with this emotion (e.g., smiling, laughing, yelling while smiling) can be measured and subsequently increased in this population (Favell, Realon, & Sutton, 1996; Green & Reid, 1996). Means of measuring how such persons express feelings of happiness have implications for assessing the indirect effects of a psychotropic medication, though few, if any studies have used happiness as an objectively defined dependent measure in a medication evaluation. Though medication was not an independent variable, Jordan, Singh, and Repp (1989) describe how indices happiness can be used to evaluate the collateral effects of a multicomponent procedure designed to reduce problem behavior. Happiness was measured through counting episodes of smiling (identified as a component of "bonding" behavior in the study) and was reliably observed occurring following administration of the treatment plan which contained a punishment procedure. Objective assessment of happiness would be particularly relevant as a QOL measure in developmentally disabled persons with limited communication skills.

C. Social Validity

Social validity relates to the social significance of target behaviors (or index behaviors, in this case), the appropriateness of procedures, and the perceived importance of results of an intervention (McMahon & Forehand, 1983; Poling & LeSage, 1995; Wolf, 1978). The notion that these characteristics are important in evaluating the overall import of a behavior change intervention emerged from the field of applied behavior analysis (Wolf, 1978), and has since become a common characteristic of interventions of this type. Though researchers have pointed out the relevance of this assessment domain to psychotropic medication interventions for persons with developmental disabilities (Aman & Singh, 1988, Poling & LeSage, 1995), few studies have included such measures (Aman & Wolford, 1995; Lindeman, Miltenberger, & Lennox, 1992; McAdam, Zarcone, Hellings, Napolitano, & Schroeder, 2002). It is also likely that such measures are rarely employed in clinical practice.

Assessing social validity entails having caregivers complete a survey indicating the degree to which they believed the intervention was satisfying and useful to the individual and his/her family, as well as whether or not they would participate in the study again (Aman & Wolford, 1995). Additionally, raters naïve to the study may be asked to view samples of behavior via videotape, then they are asked to answer questions indicating the segment (e.g., placebo or treatment) in which they believed the participant appeared to exhibit particular desired or undesired behaviors, as well as side effects (McAdam et al., 2002). While such efforts are not a substitute for medication efficacy data, they provide a greater understanding of how psychotropics may have impacted a client and his/her support network. As pointed out by Poling and LeSage (1995), social validity data require relative little additional effort to collect, but can potentially provide a broader, richer context in which to evaluate effects, positive or negative, of psychotropic medications. Social validity could encompass the domains of quality of life and indices of happiness; that is, interventions could be rated as socially significant, appropriate, and important, because of increases in quality of life and increased behaviors related to happiness.

D. Behavior Analysis and Therapeutic Effects

Within a behavior analytic conceptualization, a therapeutic effect of a psychotropic medication should serve as an establishing operation (EO) for positive reinforcers (Keller & Schoenfeld, 1950; Michael, 1982, 1993); that is, a stimulus condition that increases the effectiveness of a positive reinforcer, resulting in a subsequent increase in the behaviors preceding that reinforcer.

Thus, within a therapeutic effect context, items, activities, and other stimuli that have been known reinforcers (i.e., when presented following behavior, result in an increase in that behavior) are now particularly reinforcing (or once again reinforcing) as a result of a medication trial. In the previous example, the reinforcing value of social contact from others would be increased as a result of antidepressant medication, resulting in an increase in speech in social contexts. In this context, the reinforcers and behavior are tied directly to the purpose for which the medication was described, though this may not be the case in every instance. In a study with children diagnosed with Attention-Deficit/Hyperactivity Disorder (ADHD), Northup, Fusilier, Swanson, Roane, and Borrero (1997) indicated that the stimulant medication methylphenidate could have acted as an EO for "common" classroom reinforcers such as edible items and leisure activities.

A psychotropic therapeutic effect could also serve as what is known as an abolishing operation, or a stimulus condition that results in reduction in the effectiveness of stimuli as reinforcers. This is relevant for stimuli that serve as negative reinforcers (i.e., stimuli that result in increases in behavior contingent on their termination). For example, in an examination of the effect of risperidone on various functional relations of destructive behavior and its consequences, Crossland et al. (2003) hypothesized that risperidone may have served to reduce the negative reinforcing value of escape behavior, thereby reducing aberrant behavior to achieve this end. However, one might argue that this would only be a desired effect if indeed specific to this particular context. That is, such an effect may have been related to sedation, defined in part by concurrent suppression of other desired behaviors. Therapeutic effects conceptualized as establishing and abolishing operations (collectively referred to as motivating operations; Laraway, Snycerski, Michael, & Poling, 2003; Michael, 1982) can assist the clinician in understanding medication effects on index and collateral behavior at an individual level.

E. Assessing Medication Side Effects

Side-effects can range in impact on the individual, and may not always appear to be of clinical significance on first look, if even detectable. However, within the context of the multiple levels of difficulties this population often faces in social, emotional, and physical realms, side-effects constitute another complication, at the least, and prohibitive obstacle, at worst, to habilitation efforts. Side effects can affect all major body and organ systems, and are associated with all psychotropics, though severity profiles tend to vary between and within medication class. Estimates place as many as 20% of persons with developmental disabilities demonstrating adverse reactions to psychotropics (Aman & Singh, 1988), with some side effects likely manifesting more severely in this population relative to typically developing individuals. For example, NMS appears to be fatal in persons with developmental disabilities at rates twice those described in the general population (Boyd, 1993).

There are particular side effects than can be especially impacting and should receive special consideration in assessment efforts. For example, reduced learning capabilities (Aman & Singh, 1988; Evans & Gualtieri, 1985) either through direct cognitive effect or through secondary means (e.g., distraction and agitation) are of particular concern for the developmentally disabled for obvious reasons. Additionally, given that antipsychotics are the most commonly prescribed psychotropic in this population, and are associated with potentially irreversible central nervous system damage, careful monitoring of symptoms related to particular CNS effects (e.g., extrapyramidal symptoms) should be a specific goal of any psychotropic side effect assessment program. Unfortunately, there is a relative paucity of studies regarding the frequency and aspects of severity of psychotropic side effects specific to this population (Kalachnik, 1999b), leaving the clinician to extrapolate from literature generated primarily from other populations when investigating side effect manifestation, impact, and so forth. Examples of common psychotropic side effects are presented in Table II, which presents sample items from the Matson Evaluation of Drug Side Effects (MEDS; Matson & Baglio, 1998), a comprehensive assessment of side effects designed for persons with developmental disabilities.

1. ASSESSMENT METHODOLOGIES

Side effect assessment methodologies for the developmentally disabled population have been discussed in great detail within several professional publications (e.g., Kalachnik 1999a,b) as well as within an international expert consensus handbook (Wilson et al., 1998). Kalachnik (1999b) describes assessment models from three different perspectives: organizational, clinical research, and applied individual. Organizational models are those adopted for use within mental and physical health care settings, and are composed of four primary methods: retrospective chart review, laboratory methods, "alerting order" methods screen, and spontaneous volunteer reporting methods. Clinical research approaches side effect assessment from a "protocol assessment" model, which generally consists of five basic methods: Rating scales and checklists, electrophysiological methods, physical and neurological examination, laboratory methods, and various cognitive and electronic devices. Applied individual methods include those previously identified in the therapeutic effects section (i.e., event, duration, and interval recording, momentary time sampling). Rating scales could be employed in

TABLE II
SAMPLE ITEMS FROM THE MATSON EVALUATION OF DRUG SIDE EFFECTS

Cardiovascular and hematologic effects	Gastrointestinal effects	Endocrine and genitourinary effects
A sudden loss of strength or fainting	Nausea, vomiting	Lactation or other breast discharge
Trouble breathing or shortness of breath	Diarrhea	Excessive hair growth (hirsutism)
Rapid breathing (tachypnea)	Irregular stools (loose or bloody)	Excessive hair loss
Chest pain	Constipation	Passing of urine without control (enuresis)
Irregularity of the heartbeat	Abdominal pain	Urinary hesitancy or retention
Eyes, ears, nose and throat effects	**Skin, allergies, and temp.**	**CNS: General**
Rapid involuntary eye movements (nystagmus)	Dry skin	Seizures
Increased visual sensitivity to light (photophobia)	Rashes	Headache
Sinus congestion or nasal stuffiness	Excessively oily skin (seborrhea)	Slurred speech
Nose bleeds	Easy bruising or hemorrhaging	Change in sleep patterns
Excessive salivation or drooling	Respiratory allergies or frequent sneezing	Drowsiness or sedation
CNS: Dystonia	**CNS: Parkinsonism/ Dyskinesia**	**CNS: Behavioral/Akathesia**
Prolonged contractions of tongue or face (client may describe tongue as "thick")	Tremor of the hands or feet	Motor restlessness or agitation
Acute spasms of tongue, jaw, and neck	Pill rolling (of thumb and fingers at rest)	Pacing or inability to sit still
Other facial tics	Rapid eye blinks	Weight shifting while standing or sitting (rocking or swaying)
Abnormal tightness and positioning of the head or neck (opisthotonos, torticollis)	Abnormal oral movements (lip smacking, puckering, cheek bulging)	Hyperactive or disorganized behavior
Eyes locked upward (oculogyric crisis)	Abnormal tongue movement	Anxiety or nervousness

either of the first two models, or within an individual clinical assessment context. While a number of formal methodologies exist, there is some evidence to suggest that professionals likely continue to rely on informal assessment of side effects (e.g., brief unstructured interview of the client and/or caregivers), particularly general practitioners as opposed to psychiatrists (Holden & Gitleson, 2004).

2. RATING SCALES

Similar to therapeutic effects, the most commonly used formal methodologies for measuring side effects are likely behavioral observation and rating scales, the latter of which may be based on the former or on third-party observation. Rating scales are usually organized by one of three types: medication specific, side-effect specific, or comprehensive assessments (Kalachnik, 1999b). Because standardized medication-specific scales are rare, with almost none available that have been developed for persons with developmental disabilities, it is the likely that most medication-specific scales are adapted from standard pharmaceutical information sources (e.g., Physician's Desk Reference, 2006). An example of a medication-specific subscale for persons with developmental disabilities is the scale for the evaluation and identification of seizures, epilepsy, and anticonvulsant side effects (SEIZES B; Matson, 2000). A third-party completed checklist, scores for the SEIZES B are derived in 15 different areas representative of known antiepileptic medication side effects. Examples include hematological disturbance, electrolyte disturbance, weight disturbance, respiratory disturbance, sedation, affect disturbance, cognitive disturbance, and drug-related dizziness (Matson, 2000).

Standardized side-effect specific scales provide a detailed assessment of a limited range of a particular effect or family of effects (e.g., tardive dyskinesia). Such measures are likely most commonly used for persons with developmental disabilities in the assessment of extrapyramidal effects, such as tardive dyskinesia (e.g., Dyskinesia Identification System Condensed User Scale (DISCUS; Sprague & Kalachnik, 1991) and akathisia (e.g., Barnes Akathesia Rating Scale (BARS; Barnes, 1989). Such scales tend to have good psychometric properties (Kalachnik, 1999b), as well as detailed training protocols, though few evaluations specific to developmentally disabled populations have been conducted (Sprague & Kalachnik, 1991).

Comprehensive rating scales consist of multiple side effects corresponding to effects seen within a variety of bodily functioning systems, as well as across medication classes. An obvious advantage of this type of scale is the breadth of effects assessed. Such measures are useful in conducting screens for possible effects across a variety of medications, particularly for those known for multisystem effects. A disadvantage, however, is that particular effects may not be described in sufficient detail, or may be particularly difficult to assess in developmentally disabled populations (e.g., "blurred or double vision"; "disturbed sexual function"; from the MEDS, Matson & Baglio, 1998).

The majority of rating scales typically described in publications do not have established psychometric properties or norms within developmentally disabled populations, though some such assessments do exist. Assessment measures of side effects should contain valid representations of biological and behaviorally based side effects that are readily objectifiable, and, to the degree as can be ascertained from research, described as they might manifest in persons with developmental disabilities.

A number of rating scales are commercially available, though a relative few have been evaluated with developmentally disabled populations. Kalachnik (1999b) and Wilson and colleagues have provided detailed reviews of most relevant scales. Table III contains instruments relevant to side effect assessment in persons with developmental disabilities, with references to relevant research supporting the scales.

3. IMPLEMENTATION OBSTACLES

The fact that side effects should be carefully monitored and mitigated whenever possible has been articulated in numerous legal statements (Kalachnik et al., 1998). While this may appear a common sense issue federal investigations related to state-funded programs' failures to implement such measures, among other reasons, continue. Indeed, programmatic assessment can be difficult to achieve; limitations in resources for training staff and implementing programs, as well as the availability of knowledgeable staff, are common barriers (Kalachnik, 1999b; Matson et al., 2003).

Aside from practical implementation issues, assessment of side effects can be a challenging process for persons with developmental disabilities for several reasons. First, individual variation in medication response appears greater in this population, making side effects less predictable and possibly more difficult to detect (Wilson et al., 1998). Second, such reactions may be topographically similar to other disorders common to this population, or may in fact be the same condition stemming from nonmedication-related causes. Examples include stereotypic movement disorder (Shay et al., 1993), language impairment (Aman, Paxton, Field, & Foote, 1986), and behavioral disturbance. Moreover, behaviors such as physical aggression may be manifestations of side effects but not recognized as such, resulting in misdirected treatment (e.g., Kalachnik, Hanzel, Sevenich, & Harder, 2003; Valdovinos, Caruso, Roberts, Kim, & Kennedy, 2005). Last, the problem of diminished ability to report internal experiences applies to side effects as well as therapeutic effects, particularly in cases where side effects negatively influence cognitive functioning.

4. BEHAVIOR ANALYSIS AND SIDE EFFECTS

As with therapeutic effects, side effects can be conceptualized within a behavior analytic framework. With an understanding of known principles of learning, the clinician is able to form a more sophisticated formulation

TABLE III
SELECT LIST OF VIABLE RATING SCALES AND CHECKLISTS FOR THE EVALUATION OF PSYCHOTROPIC MEDICATION SIDE EFFECTS

Scale	Scale type	Citation	Research as medication evaluation. Tool in DD population?
Liverpool University Neuroleptic Side Effects Rating Scale (LUNSERS)	Medication specific	Day, Wood, Dewey, & Bentall, 1995	No
Naltrexone Side Effects Scale	Medication specific	Sandman et al. 1998	Yes (e.g., Kolmen, Feldman, Handen, & Janosky, 1995)
Stimulant Drug Side Effects Scale	Medication specific	Barkley, McMurray, Edelbrock, & Robbins, 1990	No
Abnormal Involuntary Movement Scale	Side-effect specific	NIMH, 1985a	Ellis et al. (1996)
Akathisia Ratings of Movement Scale	Side-effect specific	Bodfish, Newell, Sprague, & Harper, 1997	Yes (e.g., Bodfish et al., 1997)
Dyskinesia Identification System Condensed User Scale	Side-effect specific	Sprague & Kalachnik, 1991	Yes (e.g., Sprague & Kalachnik, 1991)
Barnes Akathisia Rating Scale	Side-effect specific	Barnes, 1989	No
Dosage Record and Treatment Emergent Symptom Scale	Comprehensive	NIMH, 1985b	No
Matson Evaluation of Drug Side Effects	Comprehensive	Matson & Baglio, 1998	Yes (e.g., Matson et al., 1998)
Monitoring of Side Effects Scale	Comprehensive	Kalachnik, 1999b	No

of how side effects of psychotropics impact the behavior of the client. Valdovinos and Kennedy (2004) offered such an analysis, describing how psychotropic side effects can be interpreted within the concepts of stimulus control, response-reinforcer relations, and the motivating operation. Likely of particular interest to the clinician is how side effects can serve as motivating operations (MO), or stimulus conditions that alter the effectiveness of reinforcers and punishers, resulting in a subsequent increase or decrease in the behaviors preceding these consequences (Laraway et al., 2003). Valdovinos and Kennedy (2004) point out that side effects can have either establishing or abolishing effects on positive and negative reinforcers. As an example of an establishing effect on a positive reinforcer, a side effect of increased hunger can increase the reinforcing value of food, which could subsequently increase behaviors associated with obtaining food (e.g., asking others, traveling to and using a vending machine, physical aggression). In the case of establishing effects on negative reinforcers, photosensitivity may lead to an increase in avoiding situations where relatively bright light is encountered (e.g., out of doors, in brightly lit social areas). Abolishing effects on positive and negative reinforcers include the examples of reduction of appetite as reducing the reinforcing effects of food, and a reduction in social anxiety leading to decreased avoidance of social situations, respectively. As identified by Valdovinos and Kennedy (2004), side effects may not necessarily negatively impact the individual, as could be explicated by an analysis of motivating operations, stimulus control, and response-reinforcer relations.

V. CONCLUSION

Assessment of the effects of psychotropic medications is a necessary component of ensuring safe and ethical pharmacotherapy practices for persons with developmental disabilities. The conceptualization and philosophies underlying assessment processes have, over time, shifted from an exclusive biomedical tradition to those of diverse origins, including the science of human behavior. While tools to achieve objective assessments are readily available, population-specific technology is still in its infancy. Additionally, there is a paucity of research that will help guide assessment efforts specific to this population (e.g., studies regarding the frequency, manifestation, and aspects of severity of psychotropic side effects in persons with developmental disabilities). Continued advancement of this field is paramount to better understand the role of psychotropics as mental health treatment components, and to reduce adverse effects to individuals for whom additional obstacles are particularly unwelcome.

REFERENCES

Accreditation Council for Services for Mentally Retarded and Other Developmentally Disabled Persons (1980). *Standards for services for developmentally disabled individuals.* Washington, DC: Author.

Aman, M. G., Lamb, K. S. L., & Collier-Crespin, A. (2003). Prevalence and patterns of use of psychoactive medications among individuals with autism in the Autism Society of Ohio. *Journal of Autism and Developmental Disorders, 33,* 527–534.

Aman, M. G., Paxton, J. W., Field, C. J., & Foote, S. E. (1986). Prevalence of toxic anticonvulsant drug concentration in mentally retarded persons with epilepsy. *American Journal of Mental Deficiency, 90,* 643–650.

Aman, M. G., & Singh, N. N. (1986). *Aberrant Behavior Checklist: Manual.* East Aurora, NY: Slosson Educational Publications.

Aman, M. G., & Singh, N. N. (1988). *Psychopharmacology of the developmental disabilities.* New York: Springer-Verlag.

Aman, M. G., Singh, N. N., Stewart, A. W., & Field, C. J. (1985). The aberrant behavior checklist: A behavior rating scale for the assessment of treatment effects. *American Journal of Mental Deficiency, 89,* 485–491.

Aman, M. G., & Wolford, P. L. (1995). Consumer satisfaction with involvement in drug research: A social validity study. *Journal of the American Academy of Child and Adolescent Psychiatry, 34,* 940–945.

Barkley, R. A., McMurray, M. B., Edelbrock, C. S., & Robbins, K. (1990). Side effects of methylphenidate in children with attention deficit hyperactivity disorder: A systematic, placebo-controlled evaluation. *Pediatrics, 86,* 184–192.

Barnes, T. R. E. (1989). A rating scale for drug induced akathisia. *British Journal of Psychiatry, 154,* 672–676.

Baumeister, A. A., & Sevin, J. A. (1990). Pharmacologic control of aberrant behavior in the mentally retarded: Toward a more rational approach. *Neuroscience and Biobehavioral Reviews, 14,* 253–262.

Baumeister, A. A., Sevin, J. A., & King, B. H. (1998). Neuroleptics. In S. Reiss & M. G. Aman (Eds.), *Psychotropic medication and developmental disabilities: The international consensus handbook* (pp. 133–150). Columbus, OH: The Ohio State University Nisonger Center.

Baumeister, A. A., Todd, M. E., & Sevin, J. A. (1993). Efficacy and specificity of pharmacological therapies for behavior disorders in persons with mental retardation. *Clinical Neuropharmacology, 16,* 271–294.

Biderman, A., Yeheskel, A., & Herman, J. (2005). The biopsychosocial model-have we made any progress since 1977? *Families, Systems, & Health, 23,* 379–386.

Bodfish, J. W., Newell, K. M., Sprague, R. L., & Harper, V. N. (1997). Akathisia in adults with mental retardation: Development of the Akathisia Ratings of Movement Scale (ARMS). *American Journal of Mental Retardation, 101,* 413–423.

Borthwick-Duffy, S. A. (1994). Epidemiology and prevalence of psychopathology in people with mental retardation. *Journal of Consulting and Clinical Psychology, 62,* 17–27.

Boyd, R. D. (1993). Neuroleptic malignant syndrome and mental retardation: Review and analysis of 29 cases. *American Journal of Mental Retardation, 98,* 143–155.

Branford, D. (1996). Factors associated with the successful or unsuccessful withdrawal of antipsychotic drug therapy prescribed for people with learning disabilities. *Journal of Intellectual Disability Research, 40,* 358–368.

Chakraborty, N., & Johnston, T. (2004). Aripripizole and neuroleptic malignant syndrome. *International Clinical Psychopharmacology, 19,* 351–353.

Crossland, K. A., Zarcone, J. R., Lindauer, S. E., Valdovinos, M. G., Zarcone, T. J., Hellings, J. A., et al. (2003). Use of functional analysis methodology in the evaluation of medication effects. *Journal of Autism and Developmental Disorders, 33,* 271–279.

Davies, T. S. (1954). Chlorpromazine in mental deficiency. *The Lancet, 264,* 819.

Davis, S., Wehmeyer, M. L., Board, Jr., J.P., Fox, S., Maher, F., & Roberts, B. (1998). Interdisciplinary teams. In S. Reiss & M. G. Aman (Eds.), *Psychotropic medication and developmental disabilities: The international consensus handbook* (pp. 73–84). Columbus, OH: The Ohio State University Nisonger Center.

Day, J. C., Wood, G., Dewey, M., & Bentall, R. P. (1995). A self-rating scale for measuring neuroleptic side effects. Validation in a group of schizophrenic patients. *The British Journal of Psychiatry, 166,* 650–653.

DesNoyers Hurley, A., Reiss, S., Aman, M. G., Salvador-Carulla, L., Demb, H., Loschen, E., et al. (1998). Instruments for assessing effects of psychotropic medication. In S. Reiss & M. G. Aman (Eds.), *Psychotropic medication and developmental disabilities: The international consensus handbook* (pp. 85–94).

Durand, V. M., & Crimmins, D. B. (1988). Identifying the variables maintaining self-injurious behavior. *Journal of Autism and Developmental Disorders, 18,* 99–117.

Ellis, C. R., Carmanico, S. J., Ricketts, R. W., Chambers, S., Singh, Y. N., & Singh, N. N. (1996). Reliability and validity of three rating scales for assessing tardive dyskinesia in individuals with developmental disabilities. *Journal of Developmental and Physical Disabilities, 8,* 391–406.

Engel, G. (1977). The need for a new medical model: A challenge for biomedicine. *Science, 196,* 129–136.

Evans, R. W., & Gualtieri, C. T. (1985). Carbamazepine neurophysiological and psychiatric profile. *Clinical Neuropharmacology, 8,* 221–241.

Favell, J. E., Realon, R. E., & Sutton, K. A. (1996). Measuring and increasing the happiness of people with profound mental retardation and physical handicaps. *Behavioral Interventions, 11,* 47–58.

Felce, D., & Perry, J. (1996). Assessment of quality of life. In R. L. Schalock (Ed.), *Quality of life: Conceptualization and measurement* (Vol. I, pp. 63–72). Washington, DC: American Association on Mental Retardation.

Foxall, G. R. (2004). *Context and cognition: Interpreting complex behavior.* Reno, NV: Context Press.

Garcia, D., & Smith, R. G. (1999). Using analog baselines to assess the effects of naltrexone on self-injurious behavior. *Research in Developmental Disabilities, 20,* 1–21.

Glazer, W. H. (2000). Extrapyramidal side effects, tardive dyskinesia, and the concept of atypicality. *Journal of Clinical Psychiatry, 61*(Suppl. 3), 16–21.

Glaser, B. A., & Morreau, L. E. (1986). Effects of interdisciplinary team review on the use of antipsychotic agents with severely and profoundly mentally retarded persons. *American Journal of Mental Retardation, 90,* 371–379.

Green, C. W., & Reid, D. H. (1996). Defining, validating, and increasing indices of happiness among people with profound multiple disabilities. *Journal of Applied Behavior Analysis, 29,* 67–78.

Groth-Marnat, G. (1999). *Handbook of psychological assessment* (3rd ed.). New York: John Wiley & Sons, Inc.

Hagopian, L. P., Fisher, W. W., Thompson, R. H., Owen-DeSchryver, J., Iwata, B. A., & Wacker, D. P. (1997). Toward the development of structured criteria for interpretation of functional analysis data. *Journal of Applied Behavior Analysis, 30,* 313–326.

Hill, B. K., Balow, E. A., & Bruinicks, R. M. (1985). A national study of prescribed drugs in institutions and community residential facilities for mentally retarded people. *Psychopharmacology Bulletin, 21,* 279–284.

Holden, B., & Gitleson, J. P. (2004). Psychotropic medication in adults with mental retardation: Prevalence, and prescription practices. *Research in Developmental Disabilities, 25,* 509–521.

Hughs, C., Hwang, B., Kim, J. H., Eisenman, L., & Killian, D. J. (1995). Quality of life in applied research: A review and analysis of empirical measures. *American Journal of Mental Retardation, 99,* 623–641.

Iwata, B. A., Bailey, J. S., Neef, N. A., Wacker, D. P., Repp, A. C., & Shook, G. L. (Eds.) (1997). *Behavior Analysis in Developmental Disabilities, 1968–1995* (3rd ed.). Lawrence, KS: Society for the Experimental Analysis of Behavior.

Jordan, J., Singh, N. N., & Repp, A. C. (1989). An evaluation of gentle teaching and visual screening in the reduction of stereotypy. *Journal of Applied Behavior Analysis, 22,* 9–22.

Kalachnik, J. E. (1999a). Monitoring psychotropic medication. In N. A. Weiseler & R. H. Hanson (Eds.), *Challenging behavior of persons with mental health disorders and severe developmental disabilities* (pp. 151–203). Washington DC: AAMR.

Kalachnik, J. E. (1999b). Measuring side effects of psychopharmacologic medication in individuals with mental retardation and developmental disabilities. *Mental Retardation and Developmental Disabilities Research Reviews, 5,* 348–359.

Kalachnik, J. E., Hanzel, T. E., Sevenich, R., & Harder, S. R. (2003). Clonazepam behavioral side effects with an individual with mental retardation. *Journal of Autism and Developmental Disorders, 33,* 349–354.

Kalachnik, J. E., Leventhal, B. L., James, D. H., Sovner, R., Kastner, T. A., Walsh, K., et al. (1998). Guidelines for the use of psychotropic medication. In S. Reiss & M. G. Aman (Eds.), *Psychotropic medication and developmental disabilities: The international consensus handbook* (pp. 45–72). Columbus, OH: The Ohio State University Nisonger Center.

Kane, J. M. (2001). Extrapyramidal side effects are unacceptable. *European Neuropsychopharmacology, 11*(Suppl. 4), 59–75.

Kazdin, A. E. (1980). Acceptability of altemative treatments for deviant child behavior. *Journal of Applied Bihavior Analysis, 13,* 259–273.

Keller, F. S., & Schoenfeld, W. N. (1950). *Principles of psychology*. New York: Appleton-Century-Crofts.

Kolmen, B. K., Feldman, H. M., Handen, B. L., & Janosky, J. E. (1995). Naltrexone in young autistic children: A double-blind, placebo-controlled crossover study. *Journal of the American Academy of Child and Adolescent Psychiatry, 34,* 223–231.

Lancioni, G. E., Singh, N. N., O'Reilly, M. F., Oliva, D., & Basili, G. (2005). An overview of research on increasing indices of happiness of people with severe/profound intellectual and multiple disabilities. *Disability and Rehabilitation, 27,* 83–93.

Laraway, S., Snycerski, S., Michael, J., & Poling, A. (2003). Motivating operations and terms to describe them: Some further refinements. *Journal of Applied Behavior Analysis, 36,* 407–414.

Lindeman, D. P., Miltenberger, R. G., & Lennox, D. B. (1992). Acceptability of behavioral interventions: Perceptions of superintendents of residential facilities. *Behavioral Residential Treatment, 7,* 35–44.

Lipman, R. S. (1970). The use of psychopharmacological agents in residential facilities for the retarded. In F. J. Menolascino (Ed.), *Psychiatric approaches to mental retardation* (pp. 387–398). New York: Basic Books.

Matson, J. L. (1995). *The matson evaluation of social skills in persons with severe retardation (MESSIER)*. Baton Rouge, LA: Disability Consultants, LLC.

Matson, J. L. (1997). *The assessment for dual diagnosis: Manual.* Baton Rouge, LA: Disability Consultants, LLC.

Matson, J. L. (2000). *Manual for the scale for the evaluation and identification of seizures, epilepsy, and anticonvulsant side effects.* Baton Rouge, LA: Disability Consultants, LLC.

Matson, J. L., & Baglio, C. S. (1998). *The matson evaluation of drug side effects.* Baton Rouge, LA: Disability Consultants, LLC.

Matson, J. L., Bamburg, J. W., Mayville, E. A., Pinkston, J., Bielecki, J., Kuhn, D., et al. (2000). Psychopharmacology and mental retardation: A ten-year review (1990–1999). *Research in Developmental Disabilities, 21,* 263–296.

Matson, J. L., Bielecki, J., Mayville, S. B., & Matson, M. L. (2003). Psychopharmacology research for individuals with mental retardation: Methodological issues and suggestions. *Research in Developmental Disabilities, 24,* 149–157.

Matson, J. L., Gardner, W. I., Coe, D. A., & Sovner, R. (1991). A scale for evaluating emotional disorders in severely and profoundly mentally retarded persons. *British Journal of Psychiatry, 159,* 404–409.

Matson, J. L., Mayville, E. A., Bielecki, J., Barnes, W. H., Bamburg, J. W., & Baglio, C. (1998). Reliability of the Matson Evaluation of Drug Side Effects Scale (MEDS). *Research in Developmental Disabilities, 19,* 501–506.

Matson, J. L., Mayville, S. B., & Laud, R. B. (2003). A system of assessment for adaptive behavior, social skills, behavioral function, medication side-effects, and psychiatric disorders. *Research in Developmental Disabilities, 24,* 75–81.

Matson, J. L., & Vollmer, T. (1995). *Questions about behavior function.* Baton Rouge, LA: Disability Consultants, LLC.

Mayville, E. A., & Mayville, S. B. (2005). Data collection and observation systems. In J. L. Matson, R. B. Laud, & M. L. Matson (Eds.), *Behavior modification for persons with developmental disabilities: Empirically supported treatments* (Vol. 1, pp. 130–159). Kingston, NY: NADD Press.

McAdam, D. B., Zarcone, J. R., Hellings, J., Napolitano, D. A., & Schroeder, S. R. (2002). Effects of risperidone on aberrant behavior in persons with developmental disabilities: II. Social validity measures. *American Journal of Mental Retardation, 107,* 261–269.

McMahon, R. J., & Forehand, R. L. (1983). Consumer satisfaction in behavioral treatment of children: Types, issues, and recommendations. *Behavior Therapy, 14,* 209–225.

Michael, J. (1982). Distinguishing between discriminative and motivational functions of stimuli. *Journal of the Experimental Analysis of Behavior, 37,* 149–155.

Michael, J. (1993). Establishing operations. *The Behavior Analyst, 16,* 191–206.

National Institute of Mental Health (1985a). AIMS (Abnormal involuntary movement scale). *Psychopharmacology Bulletin, 21,* 1077–1079.

National Institute of Mental Health (1985b). DOTES (Dosage record and treatment emergent symptom scale). *Psychopharmacology Bulletin, 21,* 1067–1068.

Nebeker, J. R., Barach, P., & Samore, M. H. (2004). Clarifying adverse drug events: A clinician's guide to terminology, documentation, and reporting. *Annals of Internal Medicine, 140,* 795–801.

Nielsen, J., & Bruhn, A. M. (2005). A typical neuroleptic malignant syndrome caused by olanzapine. *Acta Psychiatrica Scandinavica, 112,* 238–240.

Northup, J., Fusilier, I., Swanson, V., Roane, H., & Borrero, J. (1997). An evaluation of methylphenidate as a potential establishing operation for some common classroom reinforcers. *Journal of Applied Behavior Analysis, 30,* 615–625.

Nota, L., Soresi, S., & Perry, J. (2006). Quality of life in adults with an intellectual disability: The Evaluation of Quality of Life Instrument. *Journal of Intellectual Disability Research, 50,* 371–385.

Nøttestad, J. Aa., & Linaker, O. M. (2003). Psychotropic drug use among people with intellectual disability before and after deinstitutionalization. *Journal of Intellectual Disability Research, 47,* 464–471.

Perry, J., & Felce, D. (1995). Objective assessments of quality of life: How much do they agree with each other? *Journal of Community and Applied Social Psychology, 5,* 1–19.

Petry, K., Maes, B., & Vlaskamp, C. (2004). Domains of quality of life of people with rofound multiple disabilities: The perspective of parents and direct support staff. *Journal of Applied Research in Intellectual Disabilities 2005, 18,* 35–46.

Physicians Desk Reference 60th Edition (2006). Montvale, NJ: Thomson Healthcare.

Poling, A., & Cleary, J. (1986). The role of applied behavior analysis in evaluating medication effects. In A. Poling & R. W. Fuqua (Eds.), *Research methods in applied behavior analysis: issues and advances* (pp. 299–312). New York: Plenum Press.

Poling, A., & Ehrhardt, K. (1999). Applied behavior analysis, social validation, and the psychopharmacology of mental retardation. *Mental Retardation and Developmental Disabilities Research Reviews, 5,* 342–347.

Poling, A., & LeSage, M. (1995). Evaluating psychotropic drugs in people with mental retardation: Where are the social validity data? *American Journal of Mental Retardation, 100,* 193–200.

Pyles, D. A. M., Muniz, K., Cade, A., & Silva, R. (1997). A behavioral diagnostic paradigm for integrating behavior-analytic and psychopharmacological interventions for people with a dual diagnosis. *Research in Developmental Disabilities, 18,* 185–214.

Raynes, N. V., Sumpton, R. C., & Pettipher, C. (1989). *The index of community involvement.* Manchester, England: The University Department of Social Policy and Social Work.

Reiss, S. (1988). *Test manual for the reiss screen for maladaptive behavior.* Worthington, OH: IDS Publishing Corporation.

Reiss, S. (1994). *Handbook of challenging behavior: Mental health aspects of mental retardation.* Worthington, OH: IDS Publishing Corporation.

Reiss, S., & Aman, M. G. (1998). *Psychotropic medication and developmental disabilities: The international consensus handbook.* Columbus, OH: The Ohio State University Nisonger Center.

Reiss, S., Levitan, G. W., & Szysko, J. (1982). Emotional disturbance and mental retardation: Diagnostic overshadowing. *American Journal of Mental Deficiency, 86,* 567–574.

Research Units on Pediatric Psychopharmacology Network (2005). Risperidone treatment of autistic disorder: Longer-term benefits and blinded discontinuation after 6 months. *American Journal of Psychiatry, 162,* 1361–1369.

Rinck, C. (1998). Epidemiology and psychoactive medication. In S. Reiss & M. G. Aman (Eds.), *Psychotropic medication and developmental disabilities: The international consensus handbook* (pp. 31–44). Columbus, OH: The Ohio State University Nisonger Center.

Rojahn, J., Matson, J. L., Lott, D., Esbensen, A. J., & Smalls, Y. (2001). The Behavior Problems Inventory: An instrument for the assessment of self-injury, stereotyped behavior, and aggression/destruction in individuals with developmental disabilities. *Journal of Autism and Developmental Disorders, 31,* 577–588.

Rush, K. S., Bowman, L. C., Eidman, S. L., Toole, L. M., & Mortenson, B. P. (2004). Assessing psychopathology in individuals with developmental disabilities. *Behavior Modification, 28,* 621–637.

Sandman, C. A., Thompson, T., Barrett, R. P., Verhoeven, W. M. A., McCubbin, J. A., Schroeder, S. R., et al. (1998). Opiate blockers. In S. Reiss & M. G. Aman (Eds.), *Psychotropic medication and developmental disabilities: The international consensus handbook* (pp. 291–302). Columbus, OH: The Ohio State University Nisonger Center.

Schalock, R. L., Foley, J. W., Toulouse, A., & Stark, J. A. (1985). Medication and programming in controlling the behavior of mentally retarded individuals in community settings. *American Journal of Mental Deficiency, 89,* 503–509.

Schroeder, S. R., Bouras, N., Ellis, C. R., Reid, A. H., Sandman, C., Werry, J. S., et al. (1998). Past research on psychopharmacology of people with mental retardation and developmental disabilities. In S. Reiss & M. G. Aman (Eds.), *Psychotropic medication and developmental disabilities: The international consensus handbook* (pp. 19–30). Columbus, OH: The Ohio State University Nisonger Center.

Schroeder, S. R., Rojahn, J., & Reese, R. M. (1997). Brief report: Reliability and validity of instruments for assessing psychotropic medication effects of self-injurious behavior in mental retardation. *Journal of Autism and Developmental Disorders, 27,* 89–102.

Shay, J., Sanchez, L. E., Cueva, J. E., Armenteros, J. L., Overall, J. E., & Campbell, M. (1993). Neuroleptic-related dyskinesia and stereotypies in autistic children: Videotaped ratings. *Psychopharmacology Bulletin, 29,* 359–363.

Singh, N. N., & Beale, I. L. (1986). Behavioral assessment of pharmacotherapy. *Behaviour Change, 3,* 34–40.

Singh, A. N., Matson, J. L., Cooper, C. L., Dixon, D., & Sturmey, P. (2005). The use of risperidone among individuals with mental retardation: Clinically supported or not? *Research in Developmental Disabilities, 26,* 203–218.

Sovner, R., & Hurley, A. D. (1987). Objective behavioral monitoring of psychotropic drug therapy. *Psychiatric Aspects of Mental Retardation Reviews, 6,* 47–51.

Sparrow, S. S., Balla, D. A., & Cicchetti, D. V. (1984). *Vineland Adaptive Behavior Scales: Interview edition survey form.* Circle Pines, MN: American Guidance Service.

Sparrow, S. S., Ciccetti, D. V., & Balla, D. A. (2005). *Vineland Adaptive Behavior Scales, second edition: Survey forms manual.* Circle Pines, MN: American Guidance Service.

Sprague, R. L., & Kalachnik, J. E. (1991). Reliability, validity, and a total score cut-off for the Dyskinesia Identification System Condensed User Scale (DISCUS) with mentally ill and mentally retarded populations. *Psychopharmacology Bulletin, 27,* 51–58.

Sprague, R. L., & Werry, J. S. (1971). Methodology of psychopharmocological studies with the retarded. In N. R. Ellis (Ed.), *International review of research in mental retardation* (Vol. 5, pp. 147–219). New York: Academic Press.

Sturmey, P., Fink, C., & Sevin, J. A. (1993). The Behavior Problems Inventory: A replication and extension of its psychometric properties. *Journal of Developmental and Physical Disabilities, 5,* 327–336.

Tarnowski, K. J., & Simonian, S. J. (1992). Accepting treatment acceptance: The abbreviated acceptability rating profile. *Journal of Behavior Therapy and Experimental Psychiatry, 23,* 101–106.

Valdovinos, M. G., Caruso, M., Roberts, C., Kim, G., & Kennedy, C. H. (2005). Medical and behavioral symptoms as potential medication side effects in adults with developmental disabilities. *American Journal of Mental Retardation, 110,* 164–170.

Valdovinos, M. G., & Kennedy, C. H. (2004). A behavior analytic conceptualization of the side effects of psychotropic medication. *The Behavior Analyst, 27,* 231–238.

Valdovinos, M. G., Zarcone, J. R., Hellings, J. A., Kim, G., & Schroeder, S. R. (2004). Using the Diagnostic Assessment of the Severely Handicapped-II (DASH-II) to measure the therapeutic effects of risperidone. *Journal of Intellectual Disability Research, 48,* 53–59.

Verhoeven, W. M. A., Van der Heijden, F. M. M. A., Wijers, F. W. H. M., & Tuinier, S. (2005). Novel antipsychotics: Facts and fictions. *Clinical Neuropsychiatry: Journal of Treatment Evaluation, 2,* 212–222.

Williams, S. K., Scahill, L., Vitello, B., Aman, M. G., Arnold, L. E., McDougle, C. J., et al. (2006). Risperidone and adaptive behavior in children with autism. *Journal of the American Academy of Child and Adolescent Psychiatry, 45,* 431–439.

Wilson, J. G., Lott, R. S., & Tsai, L. (1998). Side effects: Recognition and management. In S. Reiss & M. G. Aman (Eds.), *Psychotropic medication and developmental disabilities: The international consensus handbook* (pp. 95–114). Columbus, OH: The Ohio State University Nisonger Center.

Wolf, M. M. (1978). The case for subjective measurement, or how behavior analysis is finding its heart. *Journal of Applied Behavior Analysis, 11,* 203–214.

Zarcone, J. R., Lindauer, S. E., Morse, P. S., Crosland, K. A., Valdovinos, M. G., McKerchar, T. L., et al. (2004). Effects of risperidone on destructive behavior of persons with developmental disabilities: III. Functional analysis. *American Journal of Mental Retardation, 109,* 310–321.

Memory Disorders

HEATHER ANNE STEWART AND HOLLY GARCIE-MERRITT

DEPARTMENT OF PSYCHOLOGY, LOUISIANA STATE UNIVERSITY
BATON ROUGE, LOUISIANA

I. INTRODUCTION

Development of dementia is now one of the most prevalent health concerns for older individuals and is the eighth leading cause of death (US DHH, CDCP, National Center for Health Statistics, 2007). This chapter is intended to provide clinicians with the information necessary to conduct the best possible evidence assessments of dementia when serving individuals with intellectual disabilities (ID). Dementia is an organic illness characterized by memory loss and a disturbance of cognition, behavior, or motor functioning. It profoundly damages the mind of the affected individual, and imparts immense cognitive and emotional stress on the individuals, their family members, and their caregivers. The chapter will discuss memory disorders, with particular attention toward dementia, as presented in individuals with ID. The chapter will also discuss the various types of dementias, differential diagnosis, diagnostic criteria, guidelines for assessment, and brief discussions of the most common measures that are used to assist in the diagnosis of dementia in individuals with ID.

II. PROJECTED RATES AND IMPORTANCE OF EARLY IDENTIFICATION OF DEMENTIA

Due to improvements in public healthcare and medical technologies within the last few decades, the expected lifespan of individuals with and without ID have dramatically increased. Since the early 1900s, the average life expectancy has increased from 47 to 77 years of age, giving rise to numerous health concerns in the oldest generations (US DHH, CDCP, National Center for Health Statistics, 2007). People are living longer, including those with seriously disabling medical conditions. Historically, individuals with ID have

INTERNATIONAL REVIEW OF RESEARCH IN
MENTAL RETARDATION, Vol. 34
0074-7750/07 $35.00

DOI: 10.1016/S0074-7750(07)34008-1

typically had significantly shorter life spans than those without. However, the differences in expected life span between these two groups are diminishing, particularly for individuals with mild ID (Patja, Iivanainen, Vesala, Oksanen, & Ruoppila, 2000). The increasing lifespan of individuals with ID is at least partially due to improvements in the public's interest in understanding and supporting individuals with ID, and in helping them to live longer and more fulfilling lives. As a result of this increased interest, research institutions and public healthcare facilities have improved medical and behavioral technologies and services specific to individuals with ID. These improvements have contributed to individuals with ID living longer and projections indicate that this trend will continue (Janicki, 1996; Silverman, Zigman, Kim, Krinsky-McHale, & Wisniewski, 1998; Strauss & Eyman, 1996). However, while the improving life expectancies of individuals with ID are encouraging, individuals with more severe levels of ID continue to have shorter life expectancies than those without ID (Patja et al., 2000). This emphasizes the importance of continued efforts toward improving methods of assessing, diagnosing, and treating the various disorders that are often present in aging individuals with ID.

As any individual grows older, the likelihood of developing medical problems increases. This is especially true for neurological disorders, and particularly the dementias. Projections of future prevalence rates indicate that the prevalence of Alzheimer's disorder (AD) alone will increase from the 1997 rates of 2.32 million to 8.64 million by the year 2047 (Brookmeyer, Gray, & Kawas, 1998). Early identification of the onset of dementia has a number of advantages. Early detection of memory disorders increases the potential for interventions to be put in place that may help individuals maintain higher levels of independence, and therefore better quality of life, for longer durations. For example, if the onset of dementia is detected in its earlier stages, medications can be introduced to the person's treatment regimen, which have been shown to slow the progression of disease and potentially prolong the individual's independence (Boustani, Peterson, Hanson, Harris, & Lohr, 2003; Post, 1999). Dementia disorders are often present with co-occurring psychiatric problems. Early identification of dementia increases the likelihood that such issues will be identified and treated (Boustani et al., 2003; Lyketsos et al., 2002).

Early identification of dementia also increases the likelihood that behavioral training programs will be introduced, and that caregivers will have opportunities to seek higher quality educational and supportive services. Such programs have the potential to improve the quality of life of individuals with dementia, as well as the quality of life of their caregivers (Haupt, Karger, & Jänner, 2000; Moore, Sandman, McGrady, & Kesslak, 2001; Oliver, Crayton, Holland, & Hall, 2000). Early identification also provides individuals, their caregivers, and their treatment teams with opportunities to develop plans for future safety precaution, housing modification, financial management, and legal rights needs and protections (Boustani et al., 2003).

Early identification of dementia among individuals with and without ID may also reduce the burden of costs associated with the disorder on the individuals themselves, as well as family members, other caregivers, and society in general. The cost of providing appropriate care to individuals with AD is significant. As the population of individuals with these disorders grows, related costs will grow as well. Researchers examining the financial effects of delaying the onset of AD have shown that just a 1-year delay of AD would equate to about 770,000 fewer persons with AD after 50 years. The same researchers also showed that simply a 5-year delay of AD onset would reduce projected prevalence rates of AD by about 1.15 million after 10 years and by about 4.04 million after 50 years (Brookmeyer et al., 1998). When considering the number of individuals with AD and other forms of dementia, the importance of prevention and early identification of the onset of dementia is undeniable.

Early identification of memory loss enables treatment teams to provide optimal supportive interventions. Such interventions may include medications, which can slow the progression of dementia and potentially delay the onset of the more disabling stages of the respective disorder. Some forms of memory loss are not necessarily progressive and identification of such cases increases the likelihood that potentially rehabilitative interventions may be put in place. Finally, some forms of memory loss may actually be reversible. Hypothyroidism, vitamin deficiency (e.g., vitamins B_1, B_{12}, and A), normal pressure hydrocephalus, and tumor may result in memory loss and be reversible. Gedye (1998), for example, described cases of medication-induced dementia, which were eventually reversed when the medications were withdrawn. Identification of these conditions allows the treatment team to pursue interventions that may reverse the condition and subsequent symptoms, thus improving the individual's quality of life, independence, and life span (Table I).

TABLE I

EXAMPLES OF POTENTIALLY REVERSIBLE CAUSES OF DEMENTIA

Depressive pseudodementia
Hypothyroidism
Vitamin B_{12} deficiency
Vitamin A deficiency
Normal pressure hydrocephalus
Tumor induced
Vascular induced
Toxic induced
Metabolic induced
Immunological

III. DIAGNOSTIC CAVEATS

While the assessment and identification of dementia disorders are extremely important, current approaches to do so are far from perfect. Even with increased awareness and improved technologies, many individuals with dementia remain undiagnosed and therefore untreated. This is particularly true for individuals in the earlier stages of dementia. Current estimates indicate that up to 50% of individuals older than 85 years of age have a dementia disorder. Researchers in one study, however, found that among primary care patients older than 65 years of age who had a clearly diagnosable dementia disorder, ~50% had not yet received a dementia diagnosis (Boustani et al., 2003).

The underdiagnosis of co-occuring disorders, such as dementia, in individuals with ID is considered diagnostic overshadowing (DO) and is not a new problem (Reiss, Levitan, & Szyszko, 1982). Essentially, clinicians often fail to accurately attribute symptomatology, such as impaired memory, to a co-occuring disorder, such as dementia, and would rather attribute observed cognitive deficits to the ID in general (Levitan & Reiss, 1983; Reiss & Szyszko, 1983; Reiss, Levitan, & McNally, 1982). The problem of DO underscores the importance of continued efforts toward improving our assessment of memory disorders, as well as our overall understanding of memory disorders, in individuals with ID. The reader is directed to Jopp and Keys (2001) for an excellent review of DO.

In addition to being a symptom of dementia, cognitive decline is also a normal part of the aging experience. While remaining aware of the potential for diagnostic overshadowing, clinicians must strive to ensure that they are not attributing cognitive decline, which may actually be due to normal aging, to dementia. Because aging is associated with increasing deficits in memory, a diagnosis of dementia should be considered only when the cognitive impairment is determined to be greater than that expected in normal aging. The clinician should also be aware that cognitive decline may also be a symptom of psychological disorders unrelated to dementia, further complicating the diagnostic process. When the individual with ID is being assessed, the clinician must also ensure that cognitive impairment is greater than that expected for individuals with similar disabilities.

Assessments of multiple areas of functioning, such as intellectual, memory, and adaptive functioning, using methodologies specifically designed for individuals with ID are a practical and valuable means of detecting problems related to the onset of dementia. *The American Journal on Mental Retardation's Expert Consensus Guidelines* (Rush & Frances, 2000) for the assessment of psychiatric and behavioral problems in individuals with ID indicated that the preferred means of evaluation include: (1) interview with caregivers/family members; (2) direct observation; (3) medical history and physical examination; (4) functional assessment of behavior; (5) evaluation of medication and related side effects; and, if the individual's level of ID is mild or moderate, (6) an unstructured diagnostic interview. The same guidelines also recommended, including standardized rating scales, laboratory tests, and standardized testing, when possible.

Assessments that include the above stated components reduce the likelihood that the diagnosis of dementia may be overshadowed by other factors such as preexisting impairments in functioning. Assessing memory and related areas of functioning is not an easy task, however, because some of the most common impairments in aging adults with ID already involve longstanding, preexisting, and progressive impairments in memory. Therefore, assessments tailored to the particular presentation of each individual with ID will allow the clinician to measure individualized strengths and weaknesses, as well as measurements of specific and uniquely presenting problems (Burt & Aylward, 2000). Such assessments also provide the clinician with opportunities to increase the accuracy of predicted trends and rates of progression. These improvements decrease the likelihood that onset of dementia will go unnoticed and therefore untreated.

IV. LEVEL OF ID AND DEMENTIA

Studies of the relationship between level of ID and dementia have yielded mixed results. Researchers who have found that more profound levels of ID were associated with greater likelihoods of developing dementia have often cited the cognitive reserve hypothesis as an explanation for their findings. The cognitive reserve hypothesis proposes that neuronal loss will not significantly impact a person's cognitive functioning when the person continues to possess sufficient reserves of cognitive capacity. However, when a certain threshold of neuronal loss is reached, a person's ability to compensate for such losses will no longer be sufficient, and the initial stages of dementia will proceed. Researchers have shown that increased cognitive capacity and neuronal reserves are associated with greater participation in activities that foster social, cognitive, and physical development, such as education (Bäckman et al., 2004). Individuals with ID often have histories of limited educational experience and otherwise limited exposure to stimulating environments. According to the cognitive reserve hypothesis, these limitations, combined with already impaired cognitive functioning related to their ID, reduce the number of opportunities for individuals with ID to increase their cognitive reserves, and therefore to retain sufficient cognitive functioning once such neural loss begins (Whalley et al., 2000).

Researchers examining the differences in prevalence rates, however, have not shown a clear positive relationship between the level of ID and the likelihood of developing dementia. However, they did find a positive relationship between the level of ID and dementias that involved frontal lobe impairment (Holland, Hon, Huppert, Stevens, & Watson, 1998). Zigman et al. (2004); however, they found that individuals with ID, but without Down syndrome (DS), were either as likely or slightly less likely to develop dementia than those without ID or DS. Because researchers have not yet identified a clear relationship between an individual's level of ID and the likelihood of developing dementia, one way or another, assessments of memory and related functioning should be conducted for individuals with all levels of ID.

V. TYPES OF DEMENTIA

Common factors often present in dementia disorders, regardless of the etiology, include initial short-term memory loss, as well as disturbances in attention, language, and problem solving. Dementia can also affect a number of other factors, including motor skills, reaction speed, personality, behavioral, and psychiatric symptoms such as delusional thinking. In the *Diagnostic and Statistical Manual of Mental Disorders*, 4th Edition, Text Revision (DSM-IV-TR), the American Psychological Association (APA, 2000) defines dementia as a clinical disorder characterized by the development of multiple cognitive impairments, including memory impairment and one of the following: aphasia, agnosia, apraxia, or disturbance in executive functioning. In addition, the acquired deficits (1) must be severe enough to cause impairment in occupational or social functioning, (2) must not occur exclusively during the course of a delirium, and (3) must not be better accounted for by another Axis I disorder. Symptoms of dementia are also often classified along two axes, from reversible to irreversible and from static to progressive. Most forms of dementia, however, are irreversible and progressive.

According to the DSM-IV-TR, a dementia is characterized by multiple cognitive deficits that include impairment in memory (APA, 2000). The 10th edition of the *International Classification of Diseases* (ICD-10) (Table II) and the DSM-IV-TR list the various dementias according to their presumed etiologies. For example, the DSM-IV-TR lists dementias as the following: dementia of the Alzheimer's type, vascular dementia, dementia due to other general medical conditions, substance-induced persisting dementia, dementia due to multiple etiologies, and dementia not otherwise specified (Table III). Two of the more common medical conditions that cause dementia, other than AD, include Lewy bodies disease and frontotemporal disease. Both of these

TABLE II
TYPES OF DEMENTIA LISTED BY THE ICD-10[a]

F00 Dementia in Alzheimer's disease
- F00.0 Dementia in Alzheimer's disease with early onset
  - Alzheimer's disease, type 2
  - Presenile dementia, Alzheimer's type
  - Primary degenerative dementia of the Alzheimer's type, presenile onset
- F00.1 Dementia in Alzheimer's disease with late onset
  - Alzheimer's disease, type 1
  - Primary degenerative dementia of the Alzheimer's type, senile onset
  - Senile dementia, Alzheimer's type
- F00.2 Dementia in Alzheimer's disease, atypical or mixed type
  - Atypical dementia, Alzheimer's type
- F00.9 Dementia in Alzheimer's disease, unspecified

F01 Vascular dementia
- F01.0 Vascular dementia of acute onset
- F01.01 Multi-infarct dementia
- F01.2 Subcortical vascular dementia
- F01.3 Mixed cortical and subcortical vascular dementia
- F01.8 Other vascular dementia
- F01.9 Vascular dementia, unspecified

F02 Dementia in other diseases classified elsewhere
- F02.0 Dementia in Pick's disease
- F02.1 Dementia in Creutzfeldt–Jakob disease
- F02.2 Dementia in Huntington's disease
- Huntington's chorea
- F02.3 Dementia in Parkinson's disease
  - Paralysis agitans
  - Parkinsonism
- F02.4 Dementia in human immunodeficiency virus (HIV) disease
- F02.8 Dementia in other specified diseases classified elsewhere
  - Cerebral lipidosis
  - Epilepsy
  - Hepatolenticular degeneration
  - Hypercalcaemia
  - Hypothyroidism
  - Intoxications
  - Multiple sclerosis
  - Neurosyphilis
  - Niacin deficiency (pellagra)
  - Polyarteritis nodosa
  - Systemic lupus erythematosus
  - Trypanosomiasis
  - Vitamin B_{12} deficiency

F03 Unspecified dementia
  - Presenile dementia NOS
  - Presenile psychosis NOS
  - Primary degenerative dementia NOS
  - Senile dementia NOS
  - Senile dementia depressed or paranoid type
  - Senile psychosis NOS

[a]World Health Organization (2006).

TABLE III
Types of Dementia Listed by the DSM-IV-TR

Dementia of the Alzheimer's type (294.1*x*)
- With early onset
- With late onset
  - Without behavioral disturbance (294.10)
  - With behavioral disturbance (294.11)

Dementia due to other general medical conditions (294.1*x*)
- Without behavioral disturbance (294.10)
- With behavioral disturbance (294.11)
  - HIV disease
  - Head trauma
  - Parkinson's disease
  - Huntington's disease
  - Pick's disease
  - Creutzfeldt–Jakob disease
  - Other medical conditions

Vascular dementia (290.4*x*)
- With delirium (290.41)
- With delusions (290.42)
- With depressed mood (290.43)
- Uncomplicated (290.40)
- With behavioral disturbance

Substance-induced persisting dementia
- Alcohol (291.2)
- Inhalant (292.82)
- Sedative, hypnotic, or anxiolytic (292.82)
- Other (or unknown) substance (292.82)

will be discussed briefly. Some of the less common forms of dementia include dementia due to Parkinson's disease, Huntington's disease, *Human immunodeficiency virus* and acquired immune deficiency syndrome, Creutzfeldt–Jakob disease, and head trauma. Other than AD, there is very little research on the various forms of dementia as presented in individuals with ID.

A. Dementia of the Alzheimer's Type

Alzheimer's disease is the most common cause of dementia (Snyder & Nussbaum, 1998) and is frequently observed in individuals who are diagnosed with DS. Individuals with DS are more likely to develop AD than any other group (Devenny, Krinsky-McHale, Sersen, & Silverman, 2000; Devenny et al., 1996; Prasher, 1995; Pulsifer, 1996; Zigman et al., 1997, 2004). Cognitive decline after 30 years of age is often attributed to the onset of AD in persons with DS (Bush & Beail, 2004). Researchers have shown that

Alzheimer's-type neuropathology is more likely to occur in adults with DS than in adults without DS (Visser et al., 1997). Some researchers have described the likelihood of neuropathological signs of AD as being universally present in DS (Deb et al., 1992; Mann, 1988). However, the frequency of diagnosis of dementia within a DS population is much less than would be expected if such neuropathology were indeed present. The discrepancy between the actual rate of AD diagnosis and the expected rate of diagnosis, given the frequently identified neuropathological signs of dementia, underscores the importance of assessing memory functioning with measures specific to individuals with ID (Aylward, Burt, Thorpe, Lai, & Dalton, 1997).

Dementia of the Alzheimer's Type is a degenerative and progressive cortical dementia in which the pathology of the disease involves the presence of amyloid plaques, neurofibrillary tangles, and neuronal loss, occurring primarily in the hippocampus, medial temporal lobe, and association areas of the neocortex (Castellon, Hinkin, & Satz, 2001; Raskind & Peskind, 2001; Welsh-Bohmer & Warren, 2006). The physiological changes seen in AD are typically progressive, and present with subsequent changes in multiple areas of functioning. In the past, confirmation of an AD diagnosis has only been possible on autopsy or biopsy. Although diagnostic accuracy is improving, an actual diagnosis of AD is not given unless there are autopsy or biopsy results to support the diagnosis. Without autopsy or biopsy results supporting the presence of the physiological markers of AD, clinicians should limit their diagnostic certainty to probable AD.

According to the National Institute of Neurological and Communicative Diseases–Alzheimer's Disease and Related Disorders Association (NINCDS–ADRDA) (McKhann et al., 1984), the criteria for clinical diagnosis of probable AD must include: documented dementia by examination and confirmation by neuropsychological tests, deficits in two or more areas of cognition, progressive deterioration of memory and other cognitive functions, lack of disturbance of consciousness, onset between 40 and 90 years of age, and the absence of other disorders that could account for such deficits. Progressive deterioration of multiple functions such as activities of daily living, altered behavior, language, motor skills, and perception support the diagnosis of probable AD.

The initial onset of AD is insidious, with deficits first measurable in recent memory and spontaneous speech production (Castellon et al., 2001). Earlier stages of AD are also remarkable for visuospatial deficits and impaired executive functioning (Baudic et al., 2005). As AD progresses, symptoms of aphasia increase, and apraxia and agnosia often emerge. Also in the later stages of the disease, changes in personality, emotions, and emotional stability, and social functioning begin to occur. These can be accompanied by delusions and hallucinations (APA, 2000; Boustani et al., 2003).

Behavioral problems, such as disturbances in sleeping and eating, urinary incontinence, wandering, aggression, excessive vocalization, paranoia, and inappropriate sexual behavior also develop in the later stages of the disease (Barrick, 2006; Eustace et al., 2002; Greenwood, Tam, & Chan, 2005; Lyketsos et al., 2002). Long-term memory remains relatively intact until the final stages of the disease (Sagar, Cohen, Sullivan, Corkin, & Growden, 1988). The typical duration of AD and other dementias is ~10 years, though it can be much shorter, with the deterioration eventually leading to death (Wolfson et al., 2001).

The onset of dementia in individuals with DS presents with a number of commonly observed factors. Some of the more common factors, beyond general memory loss, include impairments in expressive, semantic, and language fluency, as well as impairments in complex fine-motor learning tasks, psychomotor functioning, dyspraxia, and adaptive functioning (Burt et al., 2005; Devenny et al., 1996; Hawkins, Eklund, James, & Foose, 2003; Prasher & Chung, 1996). In a review of the relationship between DS, AD, and seizure activity, Menéndez (2005) described research that linked reductions in estrogen after menopause to the development of AD (Schupf et al., 2003). Menéndez described studies showing that middle-aged women with DS will develop a more severe form of AD and at an earlier age than others (Raghavan et al., 1994). Menéndez (2005) also found that visual memory loss was a primary clinical sign of AD and was frequently followed by impaired learning capacity, decreased adaptive behavior, seizures, urinary incontinence, and deterioration of gait and speech functions. It should be emphasized, however, that the sequence of skill loss is quite variable across individuals (Evenhuis, 1990; Holland et al., 1998). Menéndez (2005) reviewed a study that showed that adults over the age of 45 with DS and a history of seizures were more likely to develop AD than those who were younger than 45 (Puri, Ho, & Singh, 2001). The same study also showed that up to 84% of the individuals in their study with dementia and DS would also later develop seizures. Another study showed that about 8% of individuals with DS also had a seizure disorder (Pueschel, Louis, & McKnight, 1991).

Intellectual and adaptive functioning of individuals with DS declines in general as these individuals age (Collacott, 1992), thus complicating the diagnostic process and potentially resulting in underdiagnosis of AD. These impairments in functioning commonly preexist levels of impairment significant enough to warrant a diagnosis of dementia. These age-related, rather than dementia-related, cognitive declines in persons with DS are specific in nature, and tend to follow patterns similar to aging in the non-ID and non-DS population (Devenny et al., 1996; Hawkins et al., 2003).

B. Dementia Due to Non-AD Causes

By far the majority of research examining dementia in individuals with ID has focused on AD. Much less is known about dementia as presented in individuals with ID who do not have diagnoses of DS and/or do not have diagnoses of AD. Dementias due to conditions other than Alzheimer's type pathologies are etiologically distinctive. Accurate diagnoses of these conditions are obtained based on the individual's medical history and the symptoms present in their clinical profile. Zigman et al. (2004) found that the age-specific prevalence rates of individuals with ID, but without DS, were equal to or slightly less than those found in the general population. This finding potentially provides evidence against the cognitive reserve hypothesis.

Diagnosis of dementias due to etiologies other than AD requires the same set of generalized symptoms. That is, acquired memory impairment must be evident, as well as disturbance in aphasia, agnosia, apraxia, or executive functioning. The deficits must be severe enough to cause impairment in occupational or social functioning, and must not occur exclusively during the course of a delirium. Furthermore, the disturbances must not be better accounted for by another Axis I disorder. Diagnosis of dementia due to other etiologies requires evidence from the person's history, physical examination, or laboratory findings that the dementia is the direct consequence of the respective medical condition.

1. DEMENTIA DUE TO VASCULAR DISEASE

Vascular disease (VaD) is generally considered the second most common cause of dementia. Unsurprisingly, considering the complicated nature of this disease, there is a need for improved understanding of VaD as it is presented among individuals with ID. The complexity of VaD is due to the varying neurological factors involved, including the type of vascular disease present (e.g., hypertension and stroke), the location of the insult (e.g., diffuse or focal), and the severity of the insult (Román, 2002). Dementia due to vascular disease actually encompasses a number of subtypes of vascular disorders, including multi-infarct vascular disease, single-infarct vascular disease, hemorrhagic lesions, and small-vessel disease.

A diagnosis of probable vascular dementia according to the NINDS-AIREN criteria (Román et al., 1993) requires the demonstrated decline of memory functioning, as well as two or more of the following: orientation, attention, language functioning, motor functioning, praxis, visuospatial functioning, and executive functioning. These deficits should be confirmed by neuropsychological evaluation, should be severe enough to interfere with activities of daily living, and not due to the effects of stroke alone. However, cerebrovascular disease must be documented in evaluation. The relationship between cerebrovascular disease and dementia must be demonstrated by the onset of dementia within 3 months of stroke. Abrupt deterioration of cognitive functioning or a stepwise progression of cognitive deficits must be observed. As with the other dementias, other disorders that could account for the onset of such deficits must be ruled out.

Cognitive deficits frequently observed in individuals with VaD include impairments in verbal fluency, processing speed, executive functioning, and language. As with any other form of dementia, the onset of these disturbances must cause significant impairment in the individual's social or occupational functioning, and the deficits must not occur exclusively during the course of a delirium. Unique to the diagnosis of vascular dementia, however, the clinician must identify focal neurological signs and symptoms. If such evidence is not possible or available, then laboratory evidence that is indicative of cerebrovascular disease must be present.

Despite the different pathological processes involved in AD and VaD, the behavioral presentations and functional decline observed in individuals with the two disorders can be more similar than not often rendering the two disorders indistinguishable. As with other forms of dementia, however, it is possible that an individual could have pathological symptoms supporting mixed AD and VaD. Indeed, the two disorders often co-occur (Welsh-Bohmer & Warren, 2006). Research has shown that vascular risk factors are often involved in the development of AD, and neurodegenerative factors involved in AD are frequently involved in the development of VaD (Bäckman et al., 2004; Kalaria & Ballard, 1999).

Distinguishing features of VaD, compared to changes seen in AD, include cognitive changes that are often abrupt or stepwise. In addition, the cognitive changes often vary according to the type and location of insult. VaD can also be distinguished from AD by the effect of prompting. Prompting on memory tests often improves the performance of individuals with VaD, but not the performance of individuals with AD (Welsh-Bohmer & Warren, 2006).

2. DEMENTIA DUE TO LEWY BODIES DISEASE

Dementia due to Lewy bodies disease (DLB) is a progressive disorder with features that typically involve deficits of attention, abnormal perceptions (e.g., visual hallucinations), mild parkinsonism, frequent falls, nighttime agitation, sleep behavior disorders, and mild depression (Baskys, 2004; Kalra, Bergeron, & Lang, 1996; McKeith et al., 1996). Two of the following core features of the disorder must be present for a diagnosis of probable DLB: fluctuating levels of attention and alertness, recurrent visual hallucinations, and the spontaneous motor features of parkinsonism. Memory impairment may not be obvious in the earlier stages of the disorder but will eventually progress to significant levels. Diagnostic criteria include a progressive decline in functioning that interferes with normal social or occupational functioning (McKeith et al., 1996).

Commonly observed features of the disorder include rapidly fluctuating levels of cognitive functioning, syncope, repeated falls, transient loss of consciousness, agitation, crying, neuroleptic sensitivity, delusions, and hallucinations (McKeith et al., 1996). In general, hallucinations, delusions, and depression help differentiate DLB from AD. Some researchers have shown that hallucinations and depression occur more frequently in individuals with DLB than in those with AD. In addition, delusions are more frequent among individuals with DLB and AD than among individuals with pervasive developmental disorder (PDD). The clinician should remain aware of the likelihood that symptoms such as varying levels of attention, concentration, and memory ability may also occur in other types of dementia and should ensure to the best possible extent that alternative explanations for the onset of such deficits have been sufficiently excluded.

3. FRONTOTEMPORAL DEMENTIA

The Lund and Manchester Groups (1994) proposed core diagnostic features that include slow and insidious changes in behavior, affective symptoms, speech, and physical functioning, which support the diagnosis of frontotemporal dementia (FTD). Behavioral and cognitive signs of the disorder include early loss of personal and social awareness, as well as an early loss of insight into the relationship between changes in functioning and the onset of the disorder. Other behavioral and cognitive changes include early signs of disinhibition, distractibility, mental inflexibility, perseveration, hyperorality, and stereotyped behavior. Affective symptoms of FTD include depression, suicidality, sentimentality, anxiety, and delusions. Hypochondriasis is common as well as bizarre preoccupations with somatic functioning. At times, individuals with this disorder may present as emotionally unconcerned, with lack of empathy and sympathy, and emotional indifference. Commonly observed changes in speech include the progressive reduction of speech leading to mutism, stereotypy of speech, echolalia, and verbal perseveration. Physical signs of the disorder include blood pressure that is low and fluctuating, early primitive reflexes, and the early loss of continence. Akinesia, rigidity, and tremor typically develop in the later stages of the disorder. Individuals with FTD typically have normal electroencephalogram (EEG) and brain imaging studies. Onset of the disorder typically occurs before the individual is 65 years of age, and such individuals frequently have family members with similar histories.

VI. DIFFERENTIAL DIAGNOSIS

Differential diagnosis between the various types of dementias is difficult. Add to the clinical profile other factors that may be responsible for memory impairment, such as depression, psychosis, substance abuse, delirium, and normal aging, and the task of assessment becomes extremely challenging. For instance, the diagnosis of AD, DLB, and PDD are complicated by the fact that each of these disorders involves movement disorders and depression (Kalra et al., 1996). It is also important to remember that such diagnoses may be of exclusion and are provided only after the clinician has determined that the presenting cognitive impairments are not substance-induced and are not due to another medical diagnosis. As discussed in the sections above, there are some features of dementia that can differentiate between different types of dementia. Considering the impairments often present among individuals with ID such as limited insight into cognitive functioning and limited communication skills, the differential diagnoses between these disorders in a population of individuals with ID become even more challenging.

A. Delirium and Amnestic Disorder

In addition to a change in cognitive functioning that develops over a short time, the diagnostic criteria for delirium listed by the DSM-IV-TR require a disturbance of consciousness with reduced ability to focus, sustain, or shift attention (APA, 2000). As with the dementia disorders, the DSM-IV-TR lists the types of delirium according to the following etiologies: delirium due to a general medical condition, substance-induced delirium, delirium due to multiple etiologies, and delirium not otherwise specified. Common causes of delirium include medications, infections, sleep deprivation, nutritional changes, and dehydration. Just as with the co-occurrence of depression and dementia, individuals may also be diagnosed with co-occurring delirium and dementia. Therefore, a diagnosis of delirium does not necessarily rule out the possible co-occurrence of a dementia disorder. Delirium can be distinguished from dementia by its presenting symptoms and course. Signs that presenting changes in functioning may be due to delirium rather than due to the onset of a dementia include the individual with delirium presenting with a reduced ability to maintain and shift attention, symptoms that fluctuate throughout the course of the illness, and symptoms that fluctuate throughout the course of the day. As with the other forms of memory disorders, the assessment of an individual's medication regimen is crucial. This factor is especially important when considering delirium because several pharmaceuticals agents can produce cognitive and psychiatric symptoms that are similar to those of dementia and can be easily mistaken for dementia.

Amnestic disorders are differentiated from the other memory disorders in that the memory impairment is present in the absence of other cognitive deficits (APA, 2000). With these disorders, the memory impairment must be directly due to the physiological effects of a medical condition, or must be due to the persisting effects of a substance. Of course, the memory impairment must cause impairment in social or occupational functioning and must represent a significant decline from previous functioning. Again, the DSM-IV-TR lists the amnestic disorders according to the following etiologies: amnestic disorder due to a general medical condition, substance-induced persisting amnestic disorder, and amnestic disorder not otherwise specified.

B. Mild Cognitive Impairment and Age-Related Cognitive Decline

A diagnosis of mild cognitive impairment requires the subjective perception of memory impairment, abnormal memory for the individual's age, normal activities of daily living functioning, normal general cognitive functioning, and the lack of a diagnosis of dementia (Petersen et al., 1999). A diagnosis of age-related cognitive decline must demonstrate a decline in cognitive or memory functioning, which is attributable to the aging process, and within normal limits for the individual's age (APA, 2000).

C. Depression

An appropriate evaluation of dementia is not complete without the additional consideration of symptoms of depression and the role those symptoms may play in any observed changes in functioning (Kaszniak & Christenson, 1994). Affective symptoms exhibited by an individual with dementia increases the levels of distress experienced by the individual, as well as distress experienced by the person's caregivers. It is important to recognize that cognitive impairments subsequent to the onset of dementia do not always occur in isolation. Symptoms of depression and dementia disorders frequently co-occur, and the prevalence rates of depression are often quite high among individuals in the early stages of AD. Depressive symptoms have been reported in 10–70% of individuals with dementia (Lyketsos et al., 2002; Pearlson et al., 1990; Reifler, Larson, Teri, & Poulsen, 1986). Some researchers have shown that depression is more likely to be experienced by individuals with AD than those without (Migliorelli et al., 1995).

The cognitive deficits of dementia are typically unaffected by deficits that occur as a result of depression such as lack of interest and difficulties concentrating. Possible explanations for the absence of additional cognitive deficits in individuals with depression and dementia include the possibility that cognitive impairments in depression are already accounted for by the dementia. That is, many of the symptoms of depression are cognitively loaded to begin with (Bäckman, Hill, & Forsell, 1996).

Differential diagnosis should include a review of medical records, family history, premorbid conditions, illness onset, course, temporal sequencing of depressive and cognitive symptoms, and treatment response. Such a review assists in highlighting typical differences found between the two conditions. An indicator that the change in functioning may be due to depression rather than dementia include an abrupt decline in functioning, rather than a premorbid history of gradually declining cognitive functioning.

VII. ASSESSMENT OF DEMENTIA

There is currently no gold standard for the diagnosis of dementia in adults with ID (Aylward et al., 1997; Deb & Braganza, 1999; Strydom & Hassiotis, 2003). Beyond psychological assessment, the methods of evaluating possible dementia include imaging techniques, such as magnetic resonance imaging (MRI) and EEGs. Each of these methods has their advantages, but each method also has difficulties specific to the method. Neuroimaging techniques, such as MRI, are often useful for identifying conditions such as normal pressure hydrocephalus and stroke, which may be responsible for memory deficits. In addition, neuroimaging techniques have documented anatomical and structural abnormalities specific to the onset of dementia within intellectually disabled as well as nonintellectually disabled adults. Examples of these include generalized cerebral atrophy and reduction in total brain volume, enlargement of the lateral ventricles, and atrophy of the temporal lobes (Prasher et al., 2003).

Techniques such as MRIs and EEGs, however, provide only a snapshot of a person's functioning and do not demonstrate a person's strengths and weaknesses as they function in their day-to-day life. In addition, these methods require that an individual remain still for relatively long periods. Individuals who have difficulty remaining still for long periods in unusual environments often require sedation to obtain adequate measurements. Individuals with more severe IDs are often even less likely to cooperate with such procedures, thus increasing the likelihood that they will require sedation to obtain an accurate assessment. Prasher et al. (2003) described a study in which only 21% of their participants were compliant with MRI procedures without sedation. An adequate MRI scan was obtained for only 63% of their participants, including those individuals who required sedation. It is important to remember that sedation can be dangerous and ethically problematic.

In fact, the study by Prasher et al. was terminated early primarily due to complications related to sedation of their study participants. The need for sedation to complete neuroimaging scans for individuals with more severe IDs underscores the difficulties frequently inherent in such procedures.

Difficulties arise in the assessment of dementia in individuals with ID using nonimaging techniques as well. Standard neuropsychological tests typically require at least minimal language skills, vision, and hearing. Individuals with ID, particularly those with more severe and profound levels of disability, often have limited expressive and receptive communication skills, motor impairments, poor cooperation, and limited insight of the possible onset of worsening cognitive impairments (McDaniel, Edland, Heyman, & the CERAD Clinical Investigators, 1995). In addition, cognitive impairments in such individuals have been present throughout their lifetime, and impairments measured at the time of evaluation cannot necessarily be attributed to the onset of a dementia (Menéndez, 2005). However, psychological evaluations have the advantage of flexibility. The ability to modify assessment procedures as needed for evaluation specific to the needs of individuals with ID allows clinicians and researchers alike to compare individual performances with norms that are more representative of the population.

The general consensus regarding the assessment of dementia for individuals with ID requires the demonstration of a decline in functioning above and beyond that attributable to normal aging. The American Association on Mental Retardation–International Association for the Scientific Study of Intellectual Disability (AAMR–IASSID) task force on the establishment of criteria for the diagnosis of dementia in individuals with ID have provided guidelines for the diagnosis of dementia in individuals with ID (Aylward et al., 1997; Burt & Aylward, 2000). The assessment of a perceived decline in functioning should be accomplished by comparing sequential assessments to a person's baseline functioning (Aylward et al., 1997; Deb & Braganza, 1999; Prasher, Krishnan, Clarke, & Corbett, 1994). The assessments should incorporate informant-based measures as well as direct measurement of functioning, both cognitively and adaptively (Aylward & Burt, 1998; Burt & Aylward, 2000; Burt et al., 1999; Deb & Braganza, 1999; Devenny et al., 1996; Strydom & Hassiotis, 2003).

Longitudinal assessments of changes in cognitive functioning are preferable, particularly when assessing potentially progressive disorders, and clinicians should remain cautious when using only a single measure of functioning (Strydom & Hassiotis, 2003). Researchers have identified cognitive deficits, above and beyond those deficits found in normal aging, which are present long before the onset of deficits severe enough to warrant a diagnosis of dementia. These cognitive deficits often follow an initial period of slow changes in functioning, followed by a rapid decline in cognitive functioning just before the diagnosis of dementia (Bäckman et al., 2004). The identification of early cognitive deficits, combined with other information such as genetic history, adaptive functioning, and health status, increases the likelihood of early detection of dementia disorders. In a review of measures of dementia in an ID population, Strydom and Hassiotis (2003) identified several instruments that measured cognitive impairment, were relatively easy to use, and that had been utilized in the assessment of memory impairment in people with ID.

A. Direct Assessments

Direct measures of cognitive functioning are an important part of the psychological assessment of cognitive functioning. The Test for Severe Impairment (TSI; Albert & Cohen, 1992; Cosgrave et al., 1998) was designed for use with adults with more severe forms of ID. The TSI is composed of 24 items that assess a broad range of cognitive functioning, including motor performance, language production, language comprehension, memory, conceptualization, and general knowledge. The TSI is particularly useful for assessing individuals with limited verbal skills because only one-third of the points on the measure requires a verbal answer (Cosgrave, Tyrrell, McCarron, Gill, & Lawlor, 1999). The TSI is also most useful for assessing individuals with moderate and severe ID (Cosgrave, Tyrrell, McCarron, Gill, & Lawlor, 2000). The administration time of the TSI is ~10 min and test materials are small and easily available. Albert and Cohen (1992) showed that the TSI significantly correlated with the Mini-Mental State Exam (MMSE; Folstein, Folstein, & McHugh, 1975). In addition, test–retest reliability was high and internal reliability was good. Cosgrave et al. (1998) showed that the TSI has satisfactory levels of convergent validity and levels of concurrent validity equivalent to other measures of dementia specific to individuals with DS. Chronbach's α-coefficient, interrater reliability, and test–retest reliability were excellent.

Researchers have not studied the Severe Impairment Battery (SIB; Saxton, McGonigle, Swihart, & Boller, 1993) as much as the TSI to date. The TSI is composed of 39 items that measure social interaction, memory, orientation, language, attention, and praxis. The SIB has been shown to have adequate test–retest reliability and criterion validity when compared with the Vineland Adaptive Behavior Scales (Witts & Elders, 1998). Discriminant validity has also been demonstrated (McKenzie et al., 2002), which shows promise for this measure.

The MMSE (Folstein et al., 1975) is the most widely used test of global cognitive ability used to screen for dementia in a non-ID population. Bäckman et al. (2004) showed that the MMSE was a particularly good measure for the identification of individuals without dementia in particular.

When used with individuals who do not have an ID, a MMSE score of less than 24 suggests the possible onset of dementia. However, the use of the MMSE to screen for dementia among individuals with ID is discouraged (Menéndez, 2005) because of its poor specificity to individuals with limited communication and educational backgrounds. That is, most individuals with limited communication and educational backgrounds will score within the significantly impaired range of the MMSE, suggesting the onset of a dementia disorder when, in fact, such a disorder may not actually be present. Sturmey, Reed, and Corbett (1991) showed that the use of the MMSE is inappropriate with individuals with moderate or greater levels of ID.

B. Indirect Assessments

Informant-based measures of changes in cognitive and adaptive skills functioning have also been developed for adults with ID. Due to the nature of informant-based assessments, the clinician must ensure that the informant providing information about the individual being evaluated is very familiar with them. Ideally, such an informant would be a family member, spouse, or caregiver who has worked closely with the individual for many years. When such an informant cannot be identified, the results of such assessments will have questionable validity. However, when used with proper informants, the results of indirect (i.e., informant-based) assessments have been shown to be an important and often integral component of the assessment of cognitive functioning in individuals with ID.

The Early Signs of Dementia Checklist (ESDC; Visser et al., 1997) is one such informant-based measure of functioning. The ESDC is composed of a list of 37 binary scored questions that measures the early signs of mental deterioration. The ESDC was developed for use with adults with DS who reside within institutionalized settings and its internal consistency and interrater reliability have been shown to be quite good.

The Dementia Questionnaire for Persons with Mental Retardation (DMR; Evenhuis, 1992, 1996) is an informant-based standardized interview that is used to screen cognitive and adaptive skills functioning in older persons with ID. The DMR was also developed to assist in the identification of early onset of dementia and changes in physical and psychiatric status. The DMR takes $\sim$20 min to administer and is composed of 50 items with responses that a particular behavior never, sometimes, or always occurs. The DMR provides a sum of cognitive scores (SCS) and a sum of social scores (SOS). The SCS are composed of items measuring short-term memory, long-term memory, and spatial and temporal orientation. The SOS are composed of items that measure speech, practical skills, mood, activity and interest, and behavior disturbance. One of the advantages of the DMR is that the cutoff scores suggestive of dementia vary according to the individual's level of ID

(Evenhuis, 1996; Prasher, 1997). The DMR should be completed by interviewing caregivers, and does not require direct patient participation. Most of the research examining the psychometric properties of the DMR has shown that the measure is most applicable to people with DS, and is one of the most promising informant-based screening measures (Strydom & Hassiotis, 2003). However, false positive results are more likely when the DMR is administered to nondemented individuals with challenging behaviors (Prasher, 1997), and the sensitivity and specificity of the DMR in relation to expert opinion have been questionable (Hoekman & Maaskant, 2002).

The Dementia Scale for Down Syndrome (DSDS, Gedye, 1995) is an informant-based measure that can screen for cognitive changes over time suggestive of dementia. The DSDS is composed of 60 items that are divided according to three categories of dementia (i.e., early, middle, and late). Respondents indicate whether a particular behavior is present, absent, not applicable, or typical of the individual. The DSDS assesses changes in cognitive functioning over time particularly for individuals with severe to profound ranges of ID who live within the community. One of the advantages of the DSDS is that it contains items that help the clinician to differentiate between AD with depression, hypothyroidism, visual impairment, and hearing impairment (Deb & Braganza, 1999). Particular scores combine to suggest early, middle, or late stage dementia. The DSDS does not require direct patient participation and should ideally be administered by interviewing two informants who know the individual well. Huxley, Prasher, and Haque (2000) found a high correlation between the DSDS and the diagnosis of AD, particularly in the middle- or later-stages of the disorder. When DMR was compared with the DSDS in a population-based sample of adults with DS, the overall scores of the two measures were shown to highly correlate with each other, particularly within the more advanced stages of dementia (Deb & Braganza, 1999).

C. Adaptive Behavior

The severity of impairments in individuals with memory disorders significantly impacts the individual's overall adaptive behavior, such as daily living skills and social skills (Galasko et al., 2005). Loss of adaptive skills reduces the level of independence an individual maintains, resulting in increased need for assistance and supervision (Wimo, Winblad, Stoffler, Wirth, & Mobius, 2003). Measurement of adaptive skills functioning, therefore, is another integral part of a thorough assessment of possible memory impairment. However, researchers have found that, in practice, the formal assessment of adaptive behavior is missing in many clinicians' batteries (Dammers et al., 1995). Two adaptive behavior scales that are used to assess the functioning of individuals with ID include the American Association on Mental

Deficiency (AAMD) Adaptive Behavior Scale (ABS) and the Vineland Adaptive Behavior Scales.

Prasher et al. (1994) showed that serial assessments of adaptive behavior using the AAMD ABS (Nihira, Foster, Shellhaas, & Leland, 1974) improved the accuracy of diagnoses of dementia, particularly in individuals with severe to profound levels of ID. They showed that for individuals with DS who were over the age of 30 years, dementia led to a loss of skills in all domains of adaptive functioning, with strengths and weaknesses that remained essentially the same as at baseline.

The VABS is a semistructured interview that allows the clinician to assess the primary domains of adaptive functioning, which include communication, daily living skills, socialization, motor skills, and maladaptive behaviors. The communication domain comprises three subdomains of receptive, expressive, and written communication skills. The daily living skills domain comprises three subdomains of personal skills, domestic skills, and community skills. The socialization domain comprises the subdomains of interpersonal relationships, play and leisure time, and coping skills. The Interview Expanded and Interview Survey forms of the VABS provide norms for the assessment of individuals with ID (Sparrow, Balla, & Cicchetti, 1984) and should be administered by interviewing a person who knows the individual well. In addition to standardized scores for each of the domains of the VABS, an overall adaptive behavior composite can be obtained, which provides a broader measure of overall adaptive functioning. Items on the VABS are rated as "no or never," equal to zero points; "sometimes or partially," equal to one point; and "yes or usually," equal to two points. Items in which an individual has no opportunity to engage in specific behaviors are rated as "N" for "No Opportunity," and items in which the rater does not know about a specific behavior are rated as "DK" for "Don't Know." Each of these responses is equal to one point. The assessment of maladaptive behaviors is a useful component of the VABS because increases in some types of such behaviors have been shown to be potential indicators of the onset of dementia (Urv, Zigman, & Silverman, 2003). The manuals of each of the VABS forms provide details regarding reliability and validity. Specifically, the VABS have been shown to have good test–retest reliability, interrater reliability, subscale intercorrelations, construct validity, and criterion validity.

VIII. CONCLUSIONS

Memory disorders have received increased attention over the last few decades, leading to a number of advances and refinements in their assessment and identification. As awareness of the nature of memory disorders has grown, the assessment of memory impairment and diagnosis of dementia have been occurring at increasingly earlier stages in the disease. These welcome advances have provided caregivers and treating professionals with more opportunities to implement better and more appropriate interventions and strategies for care. The result is that individuals who have developed the onset of dementia are provided with better care at an earlier stage in their disease than has typically occurred in the past. These individuals therefore have greater opportunities to seek and receive care that may slow the progression of their disease, as well as greater opportunities to maintain their independence and quality of life. As with other areas of functioning such as psychiatric and general healthcare, most of the advances in assessment and treatment of memory disorders have been developed for and applied to individuals who are free of significant ID. Despite this disparity, there have also been advances in these areas for individuals with ID, though to a lesser extent. The result is that, just as within the population of individuals without ID, there continues to be a need for improved understanding of memory disorders, assessment strategies, diagnostic guidelines, and treatment options that are specific to individuals with ID.

REFERENCES

Albert, M., & Cohen, C. (1992). The test for severe impairment: An instrument for the assessment of patients with severe cognitive dysfunction. *Journal of the American Geriatric Society, 40,* 449–453.

American Psychiatric Association (APA) (2000). *Diagnostic and statistical manual of men disorders* (4th ed., text revision). Washington, DC: American Psychiatric Press.

Aylward, E. H., & Burt, D. B. (1998). *Test battery for the diagnosis of dementia in individuals with intellectual disability.* Report of the Working Group for the establishment of criteria for the diagnosis of dementia in individuals with ID. Washington, DC: American Association on Mental Retardation.

Aylward, E. H., Burt, D. B., Thorpe, L. U., Lai, F., & Dalton, A. (1997). Diagnosis of dementia in individuals with intellectual disability. *Journal of Intellectual Disability Research, 41,* 152–164.

Bäckman, L., Hill, R. D., & Forsell, Y. (1996). The influence of depressive symptomotology on episodic memory functioning in nondepressed older adults. *Journal of Abnormal Psychology, 105,* 97–105.

Bäckman, L., Wahlin, Å., Small, B. J., Herlitz, A., Winblad, B., & Fratiglioni, L. (2004). Cognitive functioning in aging and dementia: The Kungsholmen Project. *Aging Neuropsychology and Cognition, 11,* 212–244.

Barrick, A. L. (2006). Behavioral treatment of impaired functioning and behavioral symptoms. In D. K. Attix & K. A. Welsh-Bohmer (Eds.), *Geriatric neuropsychology: Assessment and intervention* (pp. 333–345). New York: The Guilford Press.

Baskys, A. (2004). Lewy body dementia: The litmus test for neuroleptic sensitivity and extrapyramidal symptoms. *Journal of Clinical Psychiatry, 65,* 16–22.

Baudic, S., Gianfranco, D. B., Thibaudet, M. C., Smagghe, A., Remy, P., & Traykov, L. (2005). Executive function deficits in early Alzheimer's disease and their relations with episodic memory. *Archives of Clinical Neuropsychology, 21,* 15–21.

Boustani, M., Peterson, B., Hanson, L., Harris, R., & Lohr, K. N. (2003). Screening for dementia in primary care: A summary of the evidence for the U.S. Preventive Services Task Force. *Annals of Internal Medicine, 138,* 927–937.

Brookmeyer, R., Gray, S., & Kawas, C. (1998). Projections of Alzheimer's disease in the United States and the public health impact of delaying disease onset. *American Journal of Public Health, 88,* 1337–1342.

Burt, D. B., & Aylward, E. H. (2000). Test battery for the diagnosis of dementia in individuals with ID. Working Group for the establishment of criteria for the diagnosis of dementia in individuals with ID. *Journal of Intellectual Disability Research, 44,* 175–180.

Burt, D. B., Primeaux-Hart, S., Loveland, K. A., Cleveland, L. A., Lewis, K. R., Lesser, J., et al. (2005). Aging in adults with intellectual disabilities. *American Journal of Mental Retardation, 110,* 268–284.

Burt, D. B., Primeaux-Hart, S., Phillips, N. B., Greene, T., Loveland, K. A., Cummings, E., et al. (1999). Assessment of orientation: Relationship between informant report and direct measures. *Mental Retardation, 37,* 364–370.

Bush, A., & Beail, N. (2004). Risk factors for dementia in people with Down syndrome: Issues in assessment and diagnosis. *American Journal of Mental Retardation, 109,* 83–97.

Castellon, S., Hinkin, C., & Satz, P. (2001). Behavioral disorders associated with central nervous system dysfunction. In P. Sutker & H. Adams (Eds.), *Comprehensive handbook of psychopathology.* New York: Plenum Publishers.

Collacott, R. A. (1992). The effect of age and residential placement on adaptive behaviour of adults with Down's syndrome. *British Journal of Psychiatry, 161,* 675–679.

Cosgrave, M. P., McCarron, M., Anderson, M., Tyrrell, J., Gill, M., & Lawlor, B. (1998). Cognitive decline in Down syndrome: A validity/reliability study of the test for severe impairment. *American Journal on Mental Retardation, 103,* 193–197.

Cosgrave, M. P., Tyrrell, J., McCarron, M., Gill, M., & Lawlor, B. A. (1999). Determinants of aggression, and adaptive and maladaptive behaviour in older people with Down's syndrome with and without dementia. *Journal of Intellectual Disabilities Research, 43,* 393–399.

Cosgrave, M. P., Tyrrell, J., McCarron, M., Gill, M., & Lawlor, B. A. (2000). A five-year follow-up study of dementia in persons with Down's syndrome: Early symptoms and patterns of deterioration. *Irish Journal of Psychological Medicine, 17,* 5–11.

Dammers, P. M., Bolter, J. F., Todd, M. E., Gouvier, W. D., Batiansila, B., & Adams, S. G. (1995). How important is adaptive functioning in the diagnosis of dementia? A survey of practicing clinical psychologists. *The Clinical Neuropsychologist, 9,* 27–31.

Deb, S., & Braganza, J. (1999). Comparison of rating scales for the diagnosis of dementia in adults with Down's syndrome. *Journal of Intellectual Disability Research, 43,* 400–407.

Deb, S., de Silva, P. N., Gemmell, H. G., Besson, J., Ebmeier, K. P., & Smith, S. (1992). Alzheimer's disease in adults with Down's syndrome: The relationship between regional cerebral blood flow deficits and dementia. *Acta Psychiatrica Scandinavica, 86,* 340–345.

Devenny, D. A., Krinsky-McHale, S. J., Sersen, G., & Silverman, W. P. (2000). Sequence of cognitive decline in dementia in adults with Down's syndrome. *Journal of Intellectual Disability Research, 44,* 654–665.

Devenny, D. A., Silverman, W. P., Hill, A. L., Jenkins, E., Sersen, E. A., & Wisniewski, K. E. (1996). Normal ageing in adults with Down's syndrome: A longitudinal study. *Journal of Intellectual Disability Research, 40,* 208–221.

Eustace, A., Coen, R., Walsh, C., Cunningham, C. J., Walsh, J. B., Coakley, D., et al. (2002). A longitudinal evaluation of behavioural and psychological symptoms of probable Alzheimer's disease. *International Journal of Geriatric Psychiatry, 17,* 968–973.

Evenhuis, H. M. (1990). The natural history of dementia in Down's syndrome. *Archives of Neurology, 47,* 263–267.

Evenhuis, H. M. (1992). Evaluation of a screening instrument for dementia in ageing mentally retarded persons. *Journal of Intellectual Disability Research, 36,* 337–347.

Evenhuis, H. M. (1996). Further evaluation of the Dementia Questionnaire for Persons with Mental Retardation (DMR). *Journal of Intellectual Disability Research, 40,* 369–373.

Folstein, M. F., Folstein, S. E., & McHugh, P. R. (1975). Mini-mental state. A practical method for grading the cognitive state of patients for the clinician. *Journal of Psychiatric Research, 12,* 189–198.

Galasko, D., Schmitt, F., Thomas, R., Jin, S., Bennett, D., & Ferris, S. (2005). Detailed assessment of activities of daily living in moderate to severe Alzheimer's disease. *Journal of the International Neuropsychological Society, 11,* 446–453.

Gedye, A. (1995). *Dementia Scale for Down Syndrome.* Vancouver: Gedye.

Gedye, A. (1998). Neuroleptic induced dementia documented in four adults with mental retardation. *Mental Retardation, 36,* 182–185.

Greenwood, C. E., Tam, C., & Chan, M. (2005). Behavioral disturbances, not cognitive deterioration, are associated with altered food selection in seniors with Alzheimer's disease. *Journals of Gerontology, Series A: Biological Sciences and Medical Sciences, 60A,* 499–505.

Haupt, M., Karger, A., & Jänner, M. (2000). Improvement of agitation and anxiety in demented patients after psychoeducative group intervention with their caregivers. *International Journal of Geriatric Psychiatry, 15,* 1125–1129.

Hawkins, B. A., Eklund, S. J., James, D. R., & Foose, A. K. (2003). Adaptive behavior and cognitive function of adults with Down syndrome: Modeling change with age. *Mental Retardation, 41,* 7–28.

Hoekman, J., & Maaskant, M. A. (2002). Comparison of instruments for the diagnosis of dementia in individuals with intellectual disability. *Journal of Intellectual and Developmental Disability, 27,* 296–309.

Holland, A. J., Hon, J., Huppert, F. A., Stevens, F., & Watson, P. (1998). Population-based study of the prevalence and presentation of dementia in adults with Down's syndrome. *British Journal of Psychiatry, 172,* 493–498.

Huxley, A., Prasher, V. P., & Haque, M. S. (2000). The dementia scale for Down's syndrome. *Journal of Intellectual Disability Research, 44,* 697–698.

Janicki, M. P. (1996). Longevity increasing among older adults with an intellectual disability. *Aging, Health, & Society, 2,* 2.

Jopp, D. A., & Keys, C. B. (2001). Diagnostic overshadowing reviewed and reconsidered. *American Journal on Mental Retardation, 106,* 416–433.

Kalaria, R. N., & Ballard, C. (1999). Overlap between pathology of Alzheimer disease and vascular dementia. *Alzheimer Disease and Associated Disorders, 13,* 115–123.

Kalra, S., Bergeron, C., & Lang, A. E. (1996). Lewy body disease and dementia: A review. *Archives of Internal Medicine, 156,* 487–493.

Kaszniak, A., & Christenson, G. (1994). Differential diagnosis of dementia and depression. In M. Storandt & G. VandenBos (Eds.), *Neuropsychological assessment of dementia and depression* (pp. 81–118). Washington, DC: American Psychological Association.

Levitan, G., & Reiss, S. (1983). Generality of diagnostic overshadowing across disciplines. *Applied Research in Mental Retardation, 4,* 59–64.

Lund and Manchester Groups (1994). Clinical and neuropathological criteria for frontotemporal dementia. *Journal of Neurology, Neurosurgery, and Psychiatry, 57,* 416–418.

Lyketsos, C. G., Lopez, O., Jones, B., Fitzpatrick, A. L., Breitner, J., & DeKosky, S. (2002). Prevalence of neuropsychiatric symptoms in dementia and mild cognitive impairments: Results from the cardiovascular health study. *Journal of the American Medical Association, 288,* 1475–1483.

Mann, D. M. A. (1988). Alzheimer's disease and Down's syndrome. *Histopathology, 13,* 125–137.

McDaniel, K. D., Edland, S. D., Heyman, A., & the CERAD Clinical Investigators (1995). Relationship between level of insight and severity of dementia in Alzheimer disease. *Alzheimer Disease and Associated Disorders, 9,* 101–104.

McKeith, I. G., Galasko, D., Kosaka, K., Perry, E. K., Dickson, D. W., Hansen, L. A., et al. (1996). Consensus guidelines for the clinical and pathologic diagnosis of dementia with Lewy bodies (DLB). Report of the consortium on DLB international workshop. *Neurology, 47,* 1113–1124.

McKenzie, K., Harte, C., Sinclair, E., Matheson, E., Patrick, S., & Murray, G. C. (2002). An examination of the Severe Impairment Battery as a measure of cognitive decline in clients with Down's syndrome. *Journal of Learning Disabilities, 6,* 89–96.

McKhann, G., Drachman, D., Folstein, M., Katzman, R., Price, D., & Stadlan, E. M. (1984). Clinical diagnosis of Alzheimer's disease. Report of the NINCDS-ADRDA Work Group under the auspices of Department of Health and Human Services Task Force on Alzheimer's Disease. *Neurology, 34,* 939–944.

Menéndez, M. (2005). Down syndrome, Alzheimer's disease and seizures. *Brain and Development, 27,* 246–252.

Migliorelli, R., Tesón, A., Sabe, L., Petracci, M., Leiguarda, R., & Starkstein, S. E. (1995). Prevalence and correlates of dysthymia and major depression among patients with Alzheimer's disease. *American Journal of Psychiatry, 152,* 37–44.

Moore, S., Sandman, C. A., McGrady, K., & Kesslak, J. P. (2001). Memory training Improves cognitive ability in patients with dementia. *Neuropsychological Rehabilitation, 11,* 245–261.

Nihira, K., Foster, R., Shellhaas, M., & Leland, H. (1974). *AAMD Adaptive Behavior Scale* (Revision). Washington, DC: American Association on Mental Deficiency.

Oliver, C., Crayton, L., Holland, A., & Hall, S. (2000). Cognitive deterioration in adults with Down syndrome: Effects on the individual, caregivers, and service use. *American Journal on Mental Retardation, 105,* 455–465.

Patja, K., Iivanainen, M., Vesala, H., Oksanen, H., & Ruoppila, I. (2000). Life expectancy of people with ID: A 35-year follow-up study. *Journal of Intellectual Disability Research, 44,* 591–599.

Pearlson, G. D., Ross, C. A., Lohr, W. D., Rovner, B. W., Chase, G. A., & Folstein, M. G. (1990). Association between family history of affective disorder and the depressive syndrome of Alzheimer's disease. *American Journal of Psychiatry, 147,* 452–456.

Petersen, R. C., Smith, G. E., Waring, S. C., Ivnik, R. J., Tangalos, E. G., & Kikmen, E. (1999). Mild cognitive impairment: Clinical characterization and outcome. *Archives of Neurology, 56,* 303–308.

Post, S. G. (1999). Future scenarios for the prevention and delay of Alzheimer disease onset in high-risk groups. An ethical perspective. *American Journal of Preventive Medicine, 16,* 105–110.

Prasher, V., Cumella, S., Natarajan, K., Rolfe, E., Shah, S., & Haque, M. S. (2003). Magnetic resonance imaging, Down's syndrome and Alzheimer's disease: Research and clinical implications. *Journal of Intellectual Disability Research, 47,* 90–100.

Prasher, V. P. (1995). Age-specific prevalence, thyroid dysfunction and depressive symptomotology in adults with Down syndrome and dementia. *International Journal of Geriatric Psychiatry, 10,* 25–31.

Prasher, V. P. (1997). Dementia Questionnaire for persons with Mental Retardation (DMR): Modified criteria for adults with Down's syndrome. *Journal of Applied Research in Intellectual Disabilities, 10,* 54–60.

Prasher, V. P., & Chung, M. C. (1996). Causes of age related decline in adaptive behavior of adults with Down syndrome: Differential diagnosis of dementia. *American Journal on Mental Retardation, 101,* 175–183.

Prasher, V. P., Krishnan, V. H. R., Clarke, D. J., & Corbett, J. A. (1994). The assessment of dementia in people with Down syndrome: Changes in adaptive behaviour. *The British Journal of Developmental Disabilities, XL*(Part 2), 120–130.

Pueschel, S. M., Louis, S., & McKnight, P. (1991). Seizure disorders in Down syndrome. *Archives of Neurology, 48,* 318–320.

Pulsifer, M. B. (1996). The neuropsychology of mental retardation. *Journal of the International Neuropsychological Society, 2,* 159–176.

Puri, B. K., Ho, K. W., & Singh, I. (2001). Age of seizure onset in adults with Down's syndrome. *International Journal of Clinical Practice, 55,* 442–444.

Raghavan, R., Khin-Nu, C., Brown, A. G., Day, K. A., Tyrer, S. P., Ince, P. G., et al. (1994). Gender differences in the phenotypic expression of Alzheimer's disease in Down's syndrome (trisomy 21). *Neuroreport, 5,* 1393–1396.

Raskind, M. A., & Peskind, E. R. (2001). Alzheimer's disease and related disorders. *Medical Clinics of North America, 85,* 803–817.

Reifler, B. V., Larson, E., Teri, L., & Poulsen, M. (1986). Dementia of the Alzheimer's type and depression. *Journal of the American Geriatric Society, 34,* 855–859.

Reiss, S., Levitan, G., & McNally, R. (1982). Emotionally disturbed mentally retarded people: An underserved population. *American Psychologist, 37,* 361–367.

Reiss, S., Levitan, G., & Szyszko, J. (1982). Emotional disturbance and mental retardation diagnostic overshadowing. *American Journal of Mental Deficiency, 86,* 567–574.

Reiss, S., & Szyszko, J. (1983). Diagnostic overshadowing and professional experience with mentally retarded persons. *American Journal of Mental Deficiency, 87,* 396–402.

Román, G. C. (2002). Vascular dementia revisited: Diagnosis, pathogenesis, treatment, and prevention. *Medical Clinics of North America, 86,* 477–499.

Román, G. C., Tatemichi, T. K., Erkinjuntti, T., Cummings, J. L., Masdeu, J. C., Garcia, J. H., et al. (1993). Vascular dementia: Diagnostic criteria for research studies. Report of the NINDS-AIREN International Workshop. *Neurology, 43,* 250–260.

Rush, A. J., & Frances, A. (2000). Expert Consensus Guideline Series. Treatment of psychiatric and behavioral problems in mental retardation. Guideline 1: Diagnosis and assessment. *American Journal on Mental Retardation, 105,* 165–168.

Sagar, H. J., Cohen, N. J., Sullivan, E. G., Corkin, S., & Growden, J. H. (1988). Remote memory function in Alzheimer's disease and Parkinson's disease. *Brain, 111,* 185–206.

Saxton, J., McGonigle, K. L., Swihart, A. A., & Boller, F. (1993). *The Severe Impairment Battery*. London: Thames Valley Test Company.

Schupf, N., Pang, D., Patel, B. N., Silverman, W., Schubert, R., Lai, F., et al. (2003). Onset of dementia is associated with age at menopause in women with Down's syndrome. *Annals of Neurology, 54,* 433–438.

Silverman, W., Zigman, W., Kim, H., Krinsky-McHale, S., & Wisniewski, H. (1998). Aging and dementia among adults with mental retardation and Down syndrome. *Topics in Geriatric Rehabilitation, 13,* 29–64.

Snyder, J. J., & Nussbaum, P. D. (1998). *Clinical neuropsychology: A pocket handbook for assessment* (pp. 211–239). Washington, DC: American Psychological Association.

Sparrow, S. S., Balla, D. A., & Cicchetti, D. V. (1984). *Vineland Adaptive Behavior Scales: Survey form manual.* Circle Pines, MN: American Guidance Service.

Strauss, D., & Eyman, R. K. (1996). Mortality of people with mental retardation in California with and without Down syndrome, 1986–1991. *American Journal on Mental Retardation, 100,* 643–653.

Strydom, A., & Hassiotis, A. (2003). Diagnostic instruments for dementia in older people with ID in clinical practice. *Aging & Mental Health, 7,* 431–437.

Sturmey, P., Reed, J., & Corbett, J. (1991). Psychometric assessment of psychiatric disorders in people with learning difficulties (mental handicap): A review of measures. *Psychological Medicine, 21,* 143–155.

Urv, T. K., Zigman, W. B., & Silverman, W. (2003). Maladaptive behaviors related to adaptive decline in aging adults with mental retardation. *American Journal on Mental Retardation, 108,* 327–339.

US DHH, CDCP, National Center for Health Statistics (2007). Trends in health and aging: Life expectancy. http://209.217.72.34/aging/Report/Folders/ReportFolders.aspx?If_ActivePath Name=P/Life%20 Expectancy/.

Visser, F., Aldenkamp, A., van Huffelen, A., Kuilman, M., Overweg, J., & van Wijk, J. (1997). Prospective study of the prevalence of Alzheimer-type dementia in institutionalized individuals with Down syndrome. *American Journal on Mental Retardation, 101,* 400–412.

Welsh-Bohmer, K. A., & Warren, L. H. (2006). Neurodegenerative dementias. In D. K. Attix & K. A. Welsh-Bohmer (Eds.), *Geriatric neuropsychology: Assessment and intervention* (pp. 56–88). New York: The Guilford Press.

Whalley, L. J., Starr, J. M., Athawes, R., Hunter, D., Pattie, A., & Deary, I. J. (2000). Childhood mental ability and dementia. *Neurology, 55,* 1455–1459.

Wimo, A., Winblad, B., Stoffler, A., Wirth, Y., & Mobius, H. (2003). Resource utilization and cost analysis of mematine in patients with moderate to severe Alzheimer's disease. *Pharmacoeconomics, 21,* 327–340.

Witts, P., & Elders, S. (1998). The Severe Impairment Battery: Assessing cognitive ability in adults with Down syndrome. *British Journal of Clinical Psychology, 37,* 213–216.

Wolfson, C., Wolfson, D. B., Asgharian, M., M'Lan, C. E., Østbye, T., Rockwood, K., et al. (2001). A reevaluation of the duration of survival after the onset of dementia. *The New England Journal of Medicine, 344,* 1111–1116.

World Health Organization (2006). *International statistical classification of diseases and related health problems.* (10th Revision Version for 2006). http://www.who.int/classifications/apps/icd/icd10online/.

Zigman, W. B., Schupf, N., Devenny, D. A., Miezejeski, C., Ryan, R., Urv, T. K., et al. (2004). Incidence and prevalence of dementia in elderly adults with mental retardation without Down syndrome. *American Journal on Mental Retardation, 109,* 126–141.

Zigman, W. B., Schupf, N., Haveman, M. J., Anderson, D., Babula, M., Collacott, R., et al. (1997). Epidemiology of Alzheimer disease in mental retardation: Results and recommendations from an international conference. *Journal of Intellectual Disability Research, 41,* 76–80.

Assessment of Self-Injurious and Aggressive Behavior

JOHANNES ROJAHN AND KATIE WHITTAKER

CENTER FOR BEHAVIORAL AND COGNITIVE DEVELOPMENT
DEPARTMENT OF PSYCHOLOGY, GEORGE MASON UNIVERSITY, VIRGINIA

THEODORE A. HOCH

NORTHERN VIRGINIA TRAINING CENTER
AND GEORGE MASON UNIVERSITY, VIRGINIA

MELISSA L. GONZÁLEZ

DEPARTMENT OF PSYCHOLOGY
LOUISIANA STATE UNIVERSITY, LOUISIANA

I. DEFINITION AND EPIDEMIOLOGY

Self-injurious and aggressive behaviors are common problems in children and adults with intellectual disabilities (Adams & Allen, 2001; Allen, 2000; Rojahn, Borthwick-Duffy, & Jacobson, 1993; Rojahn, Matson, Lott, Esbensen, & Smalls, 2001). The severe types of challenging behavior can be extremely dangerous and present major challenges that cannot be ignored. Their management requires clinical expertise and experience, and absorbs a tremendous amount of resources. Not only do self-injurious behavior (SIB) and aggressive outbursts cause physical harm, they also tend to cause parental and caregiver stress (Baker et al., 2003; Wanless & Jahoda, 2002). As a result, behavior problems undermine personal development, diminish the opportunities for learning adaptive behavior, and ultimately impinge on the person's quality of life. Although we have learned a great deal about behavior problems in the past few decades, continued research is needed to give us an even better understanding of the causes and factors maintaining problem behaviors and for the improvement of treatment and prevention.

0074-7750/07 $35.00

DOI: 10.1016/S0074-7750(07)34009-3

The success of such research will depend on the quality of our assessment technology. While there is a need for the improvement of treatment and prevention of SIB and aggressive behavior, the focus of this chapter is on the assessment technology that enables accurate identification and effective treatment of these challenging behaviors.

Although aggressive behavior and SIB have been defined in many different ways by different investigators and in standardized assessment instruments, there is no universally accepted definition of these two groups of behaviors. Within the context of intellectual disabilities, aggressive behavior typically refers to physical (and sometimes also verbal) assaults directed at other people. Whether these acts are premeditated or spontaneous might be an important distinction for the understanding of the behavioral function, but since this cannot be observed this feature is typically excluded from a behavioral definition. For SIB, the behavioral literature strives to use operational behavior definitions for the sake of objectivity, avoiding implicit references to motives and intentions or to social value judgment. For instance, Tate and Baroff (1966) defined SIB as repetitive acts directed toward a person's own body, which result in physical harm or tissue damage. But even this "stripped-down" definition implies social undesirability (*harm*, *damage*), which justifies intervention (Schroeder, Mulick, & Rojahn, 1980).

While we know that self-injurious and aggressive behaviors are common in individuals with intellectual disabilities, exact prevalence rates continue to elude us. Epidemiological estimates vary widely, in part due to the lack of a standardized survey methodology, including behavioral definitions and severity thresholds, sampling methods, and reference populations.[1] Lowe et al. (in press) reported prevalence rates of 4.5% for aggressive behavior and 3.2% for SIB in a sample of 1700 children and adults with intellectual disabilities in the United Kingdom. Holden and Gitlesen (2006) published the results of a total population study in a county in Norway screening 822 individuals with all levels of intellectual disability. They found that 6.4% had aggressive behavior (attacking others) and 4.4% showed SIB. In contrast, in one of the largest surveys from the United States, Rojahn et al. (1993) reported that among individuals up to age 45 years across all levels of intellectual disability who received public services in California and New York, 12.1% had *severe* aggressive behavior and 8.5% had *severe* SIB. Regardless of the relatively varying prevalence rate estimates, the problems these behaviors cause are real and substantial. What is interesting is that the prevalence ratio between aggressive behavior and SIB was roughly 1.4:1 in all three of these reports.

[1]For critical reviews of the epidemiological literature, the reader is referred to Allen (2000) for aggressive behavior and Rojahn and Esbensen (2002) for SIB.

The severity of intellectual disability is positively correlated with the presence of SIB and aggressive behavior (Allen, 2000; McClintock, Hall, & Oliver, 2003; Rojahn et al., 1993). The relationship between age and SIB and aggressive behavior is more complicated. Allen (2000) reported that severity of aggressive behavior seems to peak during late adolescence in disabled populations. On the other hand, Chadwick, Piroth, Walker, Bernard, and Taylor (2000) found that younger children with intellectual disability were more likely to have severe behavioral problems compared to older children. In a meta-analytic review, McClintock et al. (2003) found that self-injury was more common in persons and with deficits in expressive and/or receptive communication, including disorders such as Autism.

Individuals with certain genetic syndromes, especially Lesch-Nyhan syndrome, but also Cornelia de Lange, Prader–Willi, and Smith–Magenis syndrome have an increased risk to develop SIB (Schroeder, Oster-Granite, & Thompson, 2002). The association between aggressive behavior directed at others and genetic syndromes is not as distinct.

II. STRUCTURAL ASSESSMENT METHODS

Behavioral assessment includes several different steps and serves a number of different interrelated purposes. It includes (1) the identification of critical parameters of target behaviors, replacement behaviors, and unintended behavioral side effects of an intervention; (2) the detection of the functions that serve to maintain the behavior; and finally, (3) monitoring and evaluating the effects of treatment. The first purpose can be described as the assessment of topographical or structural characteristics of behavior such as the form, frequency, severity, and kinetic characteristics or the impact. This can be done for both behaviors that are to be weakened/eliminated or strengthened. The second purpose is referred to as functional assessment and analysis, which is vital in developing effective and individualized treatment programs. The third purpose includes assessment methods of the first and includes methods that are generally known as single-subject experimental design. This chapter will focus on the first two components of behavioral assessment of SIB and aggression. For more detail about single-subject experimentation, the reader is referred to Bailey and Burch (2002), Kazdin (1982), or Hersen and Barlow (1976).

A. Direct Behavior Assessment

1. SYSTEMATIC BEHAVIOR OBSERVATION

The hallmark of applied behavior analysis is direct assessment of behavioral parameters (such as frequency and duration, intensity, response latency and interresponse time, sequential intrabehavioral response patterns and interresponse sequences) through direct and systematic *in vivo* observation. Traditionally, behavior observation in behavior analytic research involved observers who, during predefined observation periods, recorded some parameter of one or two behaviors guided by operational definitions. Direct behavior observation is a scientific methodology, however, and cannot possibly be discussed here in full detail. The interested reader is again referred to other sources (Bailey & Burch, 2002; Cooper, Heron, & Heward, 2007; Rojahn & Schroeder, 1991; Thompson, Felce, & Symons, 2000). Rapid advances in affordable electronic equipment from multichannel data input devices, video-recording and repeat display options, digitization, analysis techniques, and data analysis computer software have revolutionized the observational technology.

A precursor of this development was a standardized observation system called the *Ecobehavioral Assessment Instrument* (Schroeder, Rojahn, & Mulick, 1978). This system was designed to capture the occurrence not only of a target behavior (such as SIB and aggressive behavior) but also of collateral behavior of the person, as well as social interactive behavior, contingent and noncontingent behavior of others directed toward the person with the problem behavior, and contextual events (number of staff and peers present, medication types and dosage, scheduled activities, and so on). Ecobehavioral observation was successfully implemented in a number of SIB intervention studies (Mulick, Barbour, Schroeder, & Rojahn, 1980; Mulick, Hoyt, Rojahn, & Schroeder, 1978; Rojahn, Mulick, McCoy, & Schroeder, 1978; Schroeder & Gualtieri, 1985; Schroeder et al., 1978). As an assessment technology it was limited at the time by the low-tech interval recording method. However, the basic assumptions underlying this approach, namely the recognition of the importance of contextualized behavior analysis which required more than the recording of a single target behavior, is still relevant. Thus, the concurrent assessment of relevant contextual events can provide rich information on a behaviors functions. It is also assumed that the manipulation of hypothesized controlling variables in combination with the assessment of molar and molecular behavior–antecedent contingent events would reveal behavioral dynamics in the natural environment. In that sense, the *Ecobehavioral Assessment Instrument* can be seen as a forerunner of functional and structural analyses and assessment, which will be discussed in detail in a later section of this chapter.

2. Behavioral Kinematic Analyses

Concerned with more basic research issues, Newell and Bodfish (2002) analyzed the temporal and force dynamics of SIB. The assessment of *temporal dynamics* involved real-time coding of SIB to generate short-term (occurrence within a bout and within observation sessions) and long-term time series (across days, weeks, and so on). Thanks to readily available computer software data can be readily analyzed with linear (e.g., autocorrelations, ARIMA models, spectral analysis) and nonlinear (e.g., approximate entropy) statistical procedures. *Force dynamics* analysis, on the other hand, relies on classical mechanics and involves kinematics (describing the motions of the torso and limbs) and kinetics (characterizing the force produced over time). Kinematic analyses have been increasingly used to study stereotyped behavior and SIB (Newell, Sprague, Pain, Deutsch, & Meinhold, 1999; Sprague & Newell, 1996). Newell et al. (1999), for instance, discovered that the head-banging of an 8-year-old girl with profound intellectual disabilities and an autistic disorder had a qualitatively highly consistent dynamic. In addition, the impact forces of her SIB were similar to the low end of forces generated in boxing blows and karate hits.

3. ASSESSMENT OF SIB TARGET SITES AND TRAUMA SEVERITY

Especially with dangerous SIB, inflicted trauma can be a type of behavioral outcome that could be of clinical and research interest. While two examples of SIB-produced trauma measures will be briefly introduced, no such behavior–product measures have come to the attention of the authors for aggressive behavior among individuals with intellectual disabilities.

a. Self-Injury Trauma Scale. To classify and quantify surface tissue damage caused by SIB, Iwata, Pace, Kissel, Nau, and Farber (1990) developed the Self-Injury Trauma (SIT) Scale. This instrument was modeled after several injury measurement instruments common in emergency and trauma medicine. The SIT Scale classifies trauma by the type of injury (abrasions/lacerations and contusions), by the number of inflicted wounds (1 = one wound; 2 = two to four; 3 = five or more), and by severity, which can occur on 21 specific body sites on the head, the upper and lower torso, and the extremities. Two types of injury severity are rated on 3-point scales: Severity of abrasions or lacerations (1 = area is red or irritated, with only spotted breaks in the skin; 2 = break in the skin is distinct but superficial, no avulsions; 3 = break in the skin is deep or extensive or avulsions present) and severity of contusions (1 = local swelling only or discoloration without swelling; 2 = extensive swelling; 3 = disfigurement or tissue rupture). In addition to summary data for the number and severity of wounds, SIT also provides an algorithm to estimate the current risk that is based on the location and the severity of the trauma. Interrater reliability was found to be very high when analyzed in a sample of 35 individuals with SIB across 4 raters. The authors insist that the SIT is not an alternative to behavioral data or medical screenings. Instead, it is a more systematic method to determine the extent of SIB-inflicted trauma. The SIT Scale has been used by several researchers, including by McDonough et al. (2000) who utilized the SIT to assess treatment progress in seven adults with intellectual disabilities and severe SIB who were participating in medication trials.

b. SIB Site Preference Charts. In an effort to identify injury sites relative to analgesia sites of the body, Symons and Thompson (1997) developed a booklet with 14 schematic figures of body parts and the entire the human body with superimposed grids. Staff shade the squares on the gird that corresponded to the SIB-targeted site. A detailed system of interrater agreement indices was developed based on the records of 29 participants with daily SIB occurrences, teaching staff agreed on 71% of the body areas toward which SIB was directed. This analysis revealed that SIB injury sites were disproportionately associated with acupuncture analgesia sites (Fig. 1). Thompson and Caruso (2002) used the same body picture assessment technology to demonstrate differences in SIB injury sites between individuals with Prader–Willi syndrome and those with other forms of intellectual disability.

B. Standardized Clinical Interviews

Most clinical assessment procedures start with interviews with parents, teachers, or care takers, and many clinicians follow their own script. For research purposes, however, interviews need to be standardized in order to ensure consistency across participants and the ability to replicate methods across studies. Two such standardized interview protocols specifically geared to problem behavior research in intellectual disabilities will be described below.

1. CHALLENGING BEHAVIOUR INTERVIEW

The Challenging Behaviour Interview (CBI) was developed by Oliver et al. (2003) in the United Kingdom as an assessment instrument for behavior problems, including SIB and aggressive behavior. It consists of two parts. Part I identifies the occurrence of concrete forms of behavior problems during the past month, including SIB, physical and verbal aggressive behavior, as well as disruption and destruction of property or the environment, and stereotyped behavior. Operational definitions are provided for the informant that characterize these behavior categories and distinguish them from one another. Part II assesses the seriousness of the problems. Fourteen scales measure the frequency and duration of the episodes, the effects the behavior had on the person and others, and the management strategies used by staff.

Preliminary psychometric properties have been reported by the authors. For Part I, mean interrater reliability kappa was .67 (range: .50–.80) and mean test–retest reliability kappa was .86 (range: .70–.91). In Part II, Pearson correlation mean interrater reliability was .48 (range: .02–.77) and mean

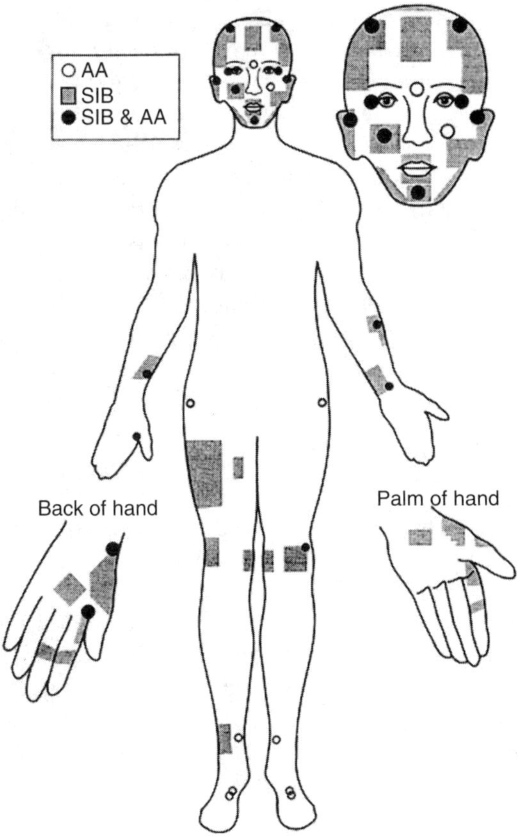

FIG. 1. SIB Site Preference Charts locating SIB injury sites (SIB) relative to acupuncture analgesia sites (AA) of the body (Symons & Thompson, 1997).

test–retest reliability .76 (range: .66–.85). Concurrent validity was assessed by Pearson correlations with the Aberrant Behavior Checklist (ABC) (see further below) and varied between .19 and .68. Content validity was assessed by comparing scores for each behavior on specific items relative to the aspects of severity that would be expected depending on the behavior category.

To assess physical aggression and other behavior problems among a group of children with intellectual disabilities, Adams and Allen (2001) used a combined questionnaire and interview method. The questionnaire asked caregivers about 22 different types of aggression. When a caregiver affirmed that a certain type of aggression occurred, the following were asked in a structured-interview format: targets of the behavior, frequency of the behavior, severity of resulting injuries, management problems, intrusiveness of caregiver response, and efficacy of response. Davidson et al. (1999) used both observational data and one-on-one interviews with patients and caregivers to assess frequency, severity, and duration of problem behaviors such as aggression and SIB.

Using interviews to assess aggression and SIB in persons with intellectual disabilities may have some limitations that other methods do not. Frequently, nonstandardized interviews are utilized, which creates problems in reliability and validity. Interviewers ask parents or caregivers to assess the presence and severity of challenging behaviors, and thus rely heavily on the caregiver's memory and subjective interpretations of behavior (Nottestad & Linkaer, 2002).

2. CHALLENGING BEHAVIOUR SURVEY: INDIVIDUAL SCHEDULE

The Challenging Behaviour Survey: Individual Schedule (CBS:IS), a comprehensive semistructured interview, was developed for a total population survey by Alborz, Bromley, Emerson, Kiernan, and Qureshi (1994). The interview has three major sections. The first section collects information on personal characteristics, such as age, gender, ethnic origin, residence, residential history, day service history and employment, education, and history of detention. In addition, several questions are clustered around broad areas of adaptive functioning such as level of physical functioning, self-care and domestic skills, communication skills, social skills, and stereotyped behaviors. The second section explores aggressive, self-injurious, and other serious disruptive or socially unacceptable behavior. The specific form of the behavior, frequency, circumstances or functional properties, and the interventions required to deal with it are noted. Items are topographic descriptions of physical attacks on other people (8 items), SIB (15 items), and stereotyped behaviors (5 items). These items are either identical or slightly modified versions of a precursor of the (then unpublished) BPI-01 (Rojahn et al., 2001). Items are scored on a categorical rating scale (1 = one of this person's most serious challenging behaviors; 2 = previously or potentially a challenge, but controlled in the setting; 3 = present, but a lesser challenge; 4 = not characteristic of person). In addition to the ratings of the topographic items, a number of detailed follow-up questions are provided to create a more comprehensive clinical picture. The third section of the CBS:IS deals with more general aspects of challenging behaviors such as stress and the demands placed on staff, overall behavior consequences to the setting, required services, and treatments. No psychometric properties have been published for the CBS:IS.

C. Specialized Structural Behavior Rating Scales

While interviews can be invaluable for qualitative information about behavior problems, their utility in research is limited due to a general lack of objectivity and unknown reliability and validity. The following will present three behavior rating scales in alphabetical order that were developed with a narrow focus on the structural aspects of behavior disturbances such as SIB and aggressive behavior.

1. BEHAVIOR PROBLEMS INVENTORY (BPI-01)[2]

The BPI-01 is a 49-item behavior rating instrument with 14 specific SIB, 24 stereotypic behavior, and 11 aggressive/destructive behavior items. Each of the three problem behavior groups is preceded by a generic definition that applies to all items within the group. Item are scored on a 5-point frequency scale (0 = never, 1 = monthly, 2 = weekly, 3 = daily, and 4 = hourly) and a 4-point degree-of-the-problem or severity scale (0 = no problem, 1 = a slight problem, 2 = a moderate problem, 3 = a severe problem). Only behaviors that have occurred at least once during the past 2 months are scored. For clinically significant behaviors that are not captured by the 49 items, "other" categories are provided for each of the 3 behavior groups.

The most comprehensive psychometric study of the BPI-01 was published by Rojahn et al. (2001) involving 432 individuals with intellectual disabilities who lived in a developmental center. Four clinical psychology graduate students administered the BPI-01 via semistructured interviews with direct care staff. The frequency and severity scales correlated highly with one another (full-scale $r = .90$, SIB subscale .93, aggressive behavior/destruction subscale .87). Factor validity was established by confirmatory and exploratory factor analyses and by item total correlations within and across subscales. These analyses indicated good psychometric properties. As for internal consistency (frequency scale), Cronbach's α for SIB, stereotyped behavior, aggressive/destructive behavior subscales were .61, .79, and .82, respectively. In a different study, Sturmey, Sevin, and Williams (1995) also reported relatively high internal consistency with Cronbach's α for the SIB scale ($\alpha = .71$) and for the aggressive behavior/destruction scale ($\alpha = .77$). Sturmey, Fink, and Sevin (1993) found good interrater and test–retest reliability. Test–retest reliability for the frequency scale as well as for dichotomous scores (each item scored as occurring or not) was calculated by Pearson's correlation. The BPI-01 full-scale reliability for the frequency scale was $r = .76$ while the SIB subscale had a frequency scale test–retest reliability of .71 and the aggressive

[2]A PDF copy of the BPI-01 is available through the author at jrojahn@gmu.edu.

behavior/destruction subscale had a reliability of .64. Test–retest reliabilities for the dichotomous data were similar: the BPI-01 full-scale reliability was $r = .77$; the SIB subscale $r = .72$, and the aggressive behavior/destruction $r = .64$. Criterion-related validity was explored in two other studies. Bodfish, Symons, and Lewis (1999) compared the SIB and the stereotypy scales of the *Repetitive Behavior Scale* (RBS, as describe in more detail below) and the BPI-01 with 64 adults with intellectual disabilities, establishing criterion-oriented validity. The SIB scales correlated at $r = .77$, and the stereotypy scales correlated at $r = .68$. In another study, Rojahn, Aman, Matson, and Mayville (2003) compared the BPI-01 with the *ABC*. The two instruments cross-validated one another such that they converged where expected, and they diverged for subscales thought to have little relationship. In summary, criterion validity of the BPI-01 was promising. Further, the BPI-01 aggressive/destructive subscale was found to be sensitive to drug effects in two studies of risperidone with children with subaverage cognitive functioning (Aman, DeSmedt, Derivan, Lyons, & Findling, 2002a,b; Snyder et al., 2002).

The BPI-01 may be particularly useful for epidemiological research, administrative databases, and perhaps repeated measurement of behavior problems. Preliminary data are indicative that the BPI-01 was sensitive to certain medication effects. The instrument may also prove useful for longitudinal assessments for people who are at risk for behavior problems, as it permits monitoring changes in the frequency or intensity of existing behavior problems, the emergence of new behaviors, and the remission of others.

2. REPETITIVE BEHAVIOR SCALE-REVISED

The Repetitive Behavior Scale-Revised (RBS-R) is an empirically derived behavior rating instrument that was designed for the assessment of the presence and severity of abnormal, repetitive behaviors in persons with a variety of conditions, including intellectual disabilities, psychiatric, neurological, and behavioral disorders. The 43 items were assigned by clinical staff to 1 of 6 dimensions or subscales of repetitive behavior: (1) *stereotyped behavior* (6 items), (2) *SIB* (8 items), (3) *compulsive behavior* (8 items), (4) *ritualistic behavior* (6 items), (5) *sameness behavior* (11 items), and (6) *restricted behavior* (4 items) (Bodfish et al., 1999; Bodfish, Symons, Parker, & Lewis, 2000). The first version of the instrument, the RSB, consisted only of the first three subscales (Bodfish et al., 1995) and the other three were later added. The scale was developed by compiling items from several existing behavior rating scales that measured repetitive behaviors (Campbell, 1985; Gedye, 1992; Goodman et al., 1989a,b; Maurice & Trudel, 1982). Items are evaluated on a 4-point Likert scale (from 0 = behavior does not occur to 3 = behavior occurs and is a severe problem). The scale has been used to measure repetitive behavior in people with intellectual disabilities and autism spectrum disorders.

Preliminary data as reported by the authors (Bodfish et al., 1999) suggest very good psychometric properties in general and for the SIB subscale in particular. Interrater agreement of the severity scores was examined with a group of 114 adults with intellectual disabilities and/or autism. Overall interrater agreement for the overall RSB score was $r = .82$ and for the SIB subscale $r = .93$. Test–retest stability in a sample of 30 adults with intellectual disabilities was $r = .71$ for the RSB overall score, and .69 for the SIB subscale. Diagnostic precision was estimated by comparing the RSB SIB outcome with the target behaviors identified by clinicians. This finding was based on a sample of 210 adults with severe/profound intellectual disabilities. Diagnostic precision was found to be high, with only 1.9% false positive rate of SIB cases identified by the RSB as compared to the clinicians (i.e., proportion of cases identified by the RSB but not the clinicians).

The authors also examined the extent to which the RSB subscales concurred with structured direct observations of behavior in samples of adults with severe/profound intellectual disabilities and repetitive behaviors. The resulting percentage agreement for SIB was 90.2% ($n = 41$). As mentioned earlier, Bodfish et al. (1999) established criterion-oriented validity by correlating the RBS and BPI-01 self-injury subscales in adults with intellectual disabilities ($r = .77$).

3. SELF-INJURIOUS BEHAVIOR QUESTIONNAIRE

Gualtieri and Schroeder (1989) developed a 25-item rating instrument with a 5-point frequency rating scale (ranging from 0 = not a problem to 4 = severe problem) intended for clinical research to evaluate the effect of psychotropic medication on problem behaviors. The items were grouped a priori into four areas. The first five items refer to a generic SIB category (SIB severity, SIB frequency, whether restraints were used, whether self-inflicted bruises were present, whether tissue damage or wounds were present). Items 6 through 14 assess common antisocial behavior problems (physical aggression, difficulty sleeping, stereotyped behavior, yelling, screaming, destruction, eating problems [pica], tantrums, and peculiar behavior). Items 15 through 18 are concerned with attention and conduct problems. Finally, items 19 through 25 address emotional and mood problems. Schroeder, Rojahn, and Reese (1997) conducted a Self-Injurious Behavior Questionnaire (SIBQ) reliability study for SIB and antisocial behavior problems and reported Pearson r interrater of .63 and .57, test–retest .78 and .58, and internal consistency Cronbach's α .94 and .71, respectively. No information is available on the validity of the SIBQ to date (e.g., factor structure, concurrent).

D. Psychopathology Assessment Instruments

Several broad-spectrum psychopathology instruments have been developed for individuals with intellectual disabilities. Given that SIB and aggressive behavior comprise only a small portion of behavioral manifestations of psychopathology, such instruments contain only small number of items. By implication that means low reliability. Therefore, while broad-spectrum instruments may not be the instruments of choice for fine grained analyses of specific types of behavior problems, select items may function as screens for the occurrence of SIB or aggressive behavior. The instruments will be introduced in alphabetical order. Space limitation allows us to discuss only the most relevant aspect of such rating instruments as far as aggressive behavior and SIB are concerned. For a more comprehensive and critical discussion of rating scales, see Lecavalier and Aman (2003).

1. ABERRANT BEHAVIOR CHECKLIST

The *ABC* is one of the most researched and psychometrically sound instruments in the developmental disabilities literature. It is an informant-oriented problem behavior rating scale that was empirically derived by factor analysis based on a large sample in New Zealand (Aman, Singh, Stewart, & Field, 1985). It consists of 58 items, each scored on a 4-point scale (0 = not a problem through 3 = problem is severe in degree). The items divide into five subscales: (1) *irritability, agitation, crying*; (2) *lethargy, social withdrawal*; (3) *stereotypic behavior*; (4) *hyperactivity, noncompliance*; and (5) *inappropriate speech*. Norms are available for adults and for children and adolescents (Aman & Singh, 1994; Aman et al., 1985a; Brown, Aman, & Havercamp, 2002; Marshburn & Aman, 1992). The factor structure of the ABC has been found to be stable across the age span (Brown et al., 2002; Marshburn & Aman, 1992; Rojahn & Helsel, 1991) and a number of psychometric studies have confirmed that the *ABC* is a reliable and valid behavior rating instrument (Aman et al., 1985; Aman, Singh, & Turbott, 1987; Bihm & Pointdexter, 1991; Paclawskyj, Matson, & Bamburg, 1997; see Aman, 2003 for summary). The ABC was primarily designed as an outcome measure for treatment evaluation (e.g., psychotropic medication; Aman, 1991), but has been more often employed as a general assessment tool. The ABC has also consistently been found to be sensitive to meaningful pharmacological and subject comparisons (Aman, 2003). Three nonspecific SIB and three aggressive/tantrum behavior items are part of the *irritability, agitation, crying* subscale.

2. ASSESSMENT OF DUAL DIAGNOSIS

The Assessment of Dual Diagnosis (ADD) (Matson, 1997) was designed as a psychopathology screening tool for adults with mild and moderate intellectual disabilities. It contains 79 items that were assigned to 1 of 13 subscales that reflect DSM-IV symptoms. The subscales are: (1) *mania*, (2) *depression*, (3) *anxiety*, (4) *posttraumatic stress disorder*, (5) *substance abuse*, (6) *somatoform disorder*, (7) *dementia*, (8) *conduct disorder*, (9) *pervasive developmental disorder (PDD)*, (10) *schizophrenia*, (11) *personality disorders*, (12) *eating disorders*, and (13) *sexual disorders*. Items are scored on a 3-point Likert scale for the last month in terms of frequency (0 = not at all through 2 = more than 10 times), duration (0 = less than 1 month through 2 = over 12 months), and severity (0 = no disruptions or damage through 2 = caused property damage or injury). The ADD was standardized and validated by having trained interviewers score the responses of direct care staff. Available data suggest that the ADD has good reliability. Matson and Bamburg (1998) examined the ratings obtained on a sample of 101 adults with intellectual disabilities. Internal consistency for the 13 subscales ranged from .77 to .95; interrater reliability for the 13 subscales, based on Spearman ranked correlations, ranged between .82 and 1.00, and test–retest reliability calculated with Pearson's product moment correlations for the 13 subscales after a 2-week interval ranged from .82 to 1.00. Three aggressive behavior items are part of the conduct disorder subscale (sexual assault, starting fights, and having used weapon to inure another), while one generic SIB item contributes to the PDD subscale.

3. DEVELOPMENTAL BEHAVIOUR CHECKLIST

The Developmental Behaviour Checklist (DBC) is a standardized and normed assessment instrument completed by nonprofessional informants to assess emotional and behavioral problems in children and adolescents with intellectual disabilities (Einfeld & Tonge, 1992, 2002). The DBC comes in a parent and teacher version. Raters use 3-point scales that range from 0 (not true) to 2 (very true or often true). Total 96 (parent version) and 93 items (teacher version—3 sleep disturbance items were removed from the teacher version) were assigned to 1 of 5 subscales: (1) *disruptive/antisocial*, (2) *self-absorbed*, (3) *communication disturbance*, (4) *anxiety*, and (5) *social relating*. The DBC has good psychometric properties. Three SIB items (bangs head, hits or bites self, scratches or picks skin) and three aggressive behavior items (bites others, abusive, kicks others) are imbedded in the disruptive/antisocial subscale.

4. DIAGNOSTIC ASSESSMENT FOR THE SEVERELY HANDICAPPED

The Diagnostic Assessment for the Severely Handicapped-II (DASH-II) (Matson, 1995) is a multidimensional behavior rating instrument that was designed as a psychopathology screening tool for individuals with severe and profound intellectual disabilities. Items and subscales were generated to reflect major DSM categories that are assumed to be most prevalent in this population. It is an informant-based instrument administered by interview. Forty-eight items are scored on three 3-point scales to capture the frequency (0 = not at all; 1 = 1- to 10-times; 2 = more than 10 time), the duration (0 = less than 1 month; 1 = 1–12 months; 2 = over 12 months), and the severity (0 = no disruption or damage; 1 = no injury or damage but interrupted others; 2 = property damage or injury). The DASH-II has 13 a priori subscales. Eight subscales represent major psychiatric conditions and five scales reflect behavior problems common for individuals with intellectual disabilities. The eight psychiatric conditions subscales are (1) *anxiety*, (2) *depression*, (3) *mania*, (4) *PDD/autism*, (5) *schizophrenia*, (6) *stereotypies/tics*, (7) *organic syndromes*, and (8) *impulse control and miscellaneous behavior problems*. The five additional scales are: *self-injurious behavior* (5), *elimination disorders* (2), *eating disorders* (6), *sleep disorders* (5), and *sexual disorders* (3). Subsequent factor analysis yielded six factors that were labeled *emotional lability*, *aggressive behavior/conduct disorder*, *language disorder/verbal aggressive behavior*, *social withdrawal/stereotypy*, *eating disorder*, and *sleep disorder*. Psychometric studies have produced adequate levels of test–retest, interrater reliability, and internal consistency (Matson, 1998; Matson, Coe, Gardner, & Sovner, 1991; Sevin, Matson, Williams, & Kirkpatrick-Sanchez, 1995), and validity (Matson, 1989; Matson, Kiely, & Bamburg, 1997; Matson, Smiroldo, & Bamburg, 1998; Matson, Smiroldo, & Hastings, 1998; Matson, Smiroldo, Hamilton, & Baglio, 1997). Physically aggressive behavior is assessed by two items that are part of the impulse subscale ("hits, kicks, pinches other people," "bites other people"), while SIB is not assessed via a subscale, but is recorded in a generically as one of several "other behavior problems."

5. NISONGER CHILD BEHAVIOR RATING FORM

The Nisonger Child Behavior Rating Form (Nisonger CBRF) is an informant-based rating scale for children and adolescents (Aman, Tassé, Rojahn, & Hammer, 1996; Tassé, Aman, Hammer, & Rojahn, 1996). The scale was adapted form of the CBRF (Edelbrock, 1985) by altering the instructions and adding new behavior problem items. The Nisonger CBRF has a teacher and a parent version with identical items. Both consist of a Social Competence and a Problem Behaviors section. The Social Competence section contains 10 items describing general adaptive/prosocial behaviors such as "Shared with or helped others," which are rated on a 4-point Likert scale ranging from 0 (=not true) to 3 (=completely or always true). Factor analysis produced two subscales that were labeled as Compliant/Calm and Adaptive Social. The 66-item Problem Behaviors section contains 66 items that are rated on a 4-point Likert scale reflecting a combination of rate and severity of the behavior. It ranges from 0 (=did not occur or was not a problem) to 3 (=occurred a lot or was a severe problem). Items are assigned to six subscales, (1) *conduct problem*, (2) *insecure/anxious*, (3) *hyperactive*, (4) *self-injury/stereotypic*, (5) *self-isolated/ritualistic*, and (6) *overly sensitive*. The Nisonger CBRF was found to be psychometrically sound with regard to factor structure (Lecavalier, Aman, & Hammer, 2004; Lecavalier, Aman, Hammer, Stoica, & Mathews, 2004), test–retest reliability (Girouard, Morin, & Tassé, 1998), and interrater reliability and useful in assessing emotional and behavioral problems in children and adolescents with intellectual disabilities (Tassé & Lecavalier, 2000). It has also been shown to be sensitive to the effects of psychotropic medication in children with Autism and in low functioning children with comorbid conduct disorder (Aman et al., 2002; Cohen, 2003; Snyder et al., 2002). The NCBRF has age- and gender-based norms on a restricted sample of 369 children and adolescents between the ages of 3 and 16 years (Tassé et al., 1996). The NCBRF contains two generic aggressive behavior items in the conduct problem subscale ("Physically attacks other people" and "Threatens others") and six specific SIB items in the self-injury/stereotypic subscale (e.g., hits, slaps own head, neck, hand, or other body parts; harms self by scratching skin or pulling hair; gouges self, puts things in ears, nose, and so on or eats inedible things; and repeatedly bites self hard enough to leave tooth marks or break skin).

6. PDD BEHAVIOR INVENTORY

The PDD Behavior Inventory (PDDBI) is an informant-based rating scale designed to assess children with a PDD (Cohen, 2003; Cohen, Schmidt-Lackner, Romanczyk, & Sudhalter, 2003). It has both a teacher and parent form. The parent form consists of a priori defined subscales, 10 for the parent form and 8 for the teacher form. Both versions assess behavior along a maladaptive–adaptive continuum focusing on specific behaviors commonly associated with PDD. The maladaptive behavior subscales consist of (1) *sensory/perceptual approach behaviors*, (2) *specific fears*, (3) *arousal problems*, (4) *aggressiveness/behavior problems* (assesses both self- and other-directed aggression, (5) *social pragmatic problems*, and (6) *semantic pragmatic problems*. The criterion-related validity of each subscale and the construct validity of the PDDBI have been demonstrated through regression and factor analytic techniques. It is important to note that the PDDBI is intended for use solely with persons with autism spectrum disorders, and was not designed to be used for persons of intellectual disability with a different diagnosis (e.g., intellectual disabilities).

7. REISS SCREEN FOR MALADAPTIVE BEHAVIOR

The Reiss Screen for Maladaptive Behavior (RSMB) is another screening instrument to facilitate the identification of concurrent psychopathology in adults with intellectual disabilities (Reiss, 1988). Thirty-eight items are scored on a 3-point scale (0 = "no problem," 1 = "problem," 2 = "major problem") that were assigned to eight subscales: (1) *aggressive behavior*, (2) *autism*, (3) *psychosis*, (4) *paranoia*, (5) *depression—behavioral signs*, (6) *depression—physical signs*, (7) *dependent personality disorder*, and (8) *avoidant personality disorder*. Reiss (1988) reported a Pearson *r* interrater reliability for the 5-item aggressive behavior scale ranging from .73 to .75, and internal consistency of .84 (Cronbach α, $n = 306$). As for SIB, the RSMB has only one item, namely "self-injury," which is defined in the RSMB as "Repeatedly injures body on purpose. Examples: bites arm, hits self repeatedly, repeated hand-banging." The RSMB may be a useful screening tool for aggressive behavior; however, it is probably not particularly useful for the assessment of SIB.

E. Standardized Adaptive Behavior Scales

Standardized adaptive behavior scales play an important role in the diagnosis of intellectual disability and they can serve to establish training and rehabilitation goals for individuals. Most adaptive behavior scales also contain a section on maladaptive behavior, which typically include SIB and aggressive behavior.

1. ADAPTIVE BEHAVIOR SCALES

The AAMR Adaptive Behavior Scale Second Edition-School (ABS-S:2; Lambert, Nihira, & Leland, 1993) was designed to measure personal independence and social skills in children as young as three years up to adulthood. Internal consistency and validity measures were high (exceeding .8), but the lack of test-retest and inter-rater reliabilities can be a concern for instruments that may be completed by different raters (i.e., teachers, parents, guardians) and possibly repeated several times over the course of a few years. Two types of validity data are presented in the manual: (1) data on the relationship between adaptive behavior ratings and intelligence test performance; and (2) data on the predictive power of the ABS for accurately classifying normal and mentally retarded children. Seven maladaptive behavior domains are assessed by the ABS-S:2: including one for "Self-Abusive Behavior" and one for "Disturbing Interpersonal Behavior." The AAMR Adaptive Behavior Scales-Residential and Community (ABS-RC:2; Nihira, Leland, & Lambert, 1993) was standardized for older individuals and has similar psychometric properties.

2. SCALES OF INDEPENDENT BEHAVIOR-REVISED (SIB-R)

The SIB-R was developed for children and adults with developmental disabilities and other populations with needs for special assistance (Bruininks, Woodcock, Weatherman, & Hill, 1996) and was designed to determine the type and amount of special assistance that people with disabilities may need. Existing SIB-R norms were established on a sample of 2182 individuals in

15 US states, with ages ranging from 3 months to over 80 years. It contains four clusters of independence behavior (i.e., motor skills, social interaction and communication skills, personal living skills, and community living skills) and three clusters of problem behaviors (i.e., internalized, externalized, and asocial). The SIB-R can be administered either as a questionnaire or as a structured interview. The SIB-R contains one SIB item, "Hurtful to Self" [Does (name) injure his/her own body—e.g., by hitting self, banging head, scratching, cutting or puncturing, biting, rubbing skin, pulling out hair, picking on skin, biting nails, or pinching self?] If the answer is yes, raters are asked to estimate the frequency (1 = "less than once a month" to 5 = "one or more times an hour") and the severity of SIB on a 5-point scale (0 = "not serious, not a problem" to 4 = "extremely serious, a critical problem").

3. VINELAND ADAPTIVE BEHAVIOR SCALES, SECOND EDITION

The Vineland Adaptive Behavior Scales, Second Edition (VABS) is a measure of personal and social skills designed for individuals intellectual disabilities, autism spectrum disorders, attention deficit/hyperactivity disorder, posttraumatic brain injury, hearing impairment, and dementia/ Alzheimer's disease (Sparrow, Cicchetti, & Balla, 2005a,b). It is the new edition of one of the most widely used standardized assessment instruments for adaptive and maladaptive behavior. Four different VABS forms exist, the *Survey Interview Form*, the *Parent/Caregiver Rating Form*, the *Expanded Interview Form*, and the *Teacher Rating Form*. The first three forms, which cover the ages from birth through 90, include an optional maladaptive behavior section. Maladaptive behaviors, which are rated on a 3-point frequency scale (0 = never; 1 = sometimes; 2 = often) and a 2-point severity scale (S = severe; M = moderate), include 10 internalizing behaviors, 10 externalizing behaviors, 15 "other" behavior problems, and 14 "critical" items. Physically aggressive behavior is one of the externalizing behaviors ["Is physically aggressive (e.g., hits, kicks, bites)"]. One of the "critical items" is reserved for SIB (displays behaviors that cause injury to self e.g., bangs head, hits or bites self, tears skin). Given that the Vineland-II only has only one generic item for SIB and aggressive behavior, it may lend itself as a screening tool for the presence of SIB; however, no sensitivity and specificity data are available for the of these two items at this point.

III. FUNCTIONAL ASSESSMENT AND ANALYSIS

Functional assessment and consequent functional analysis aim to identify motivating operations, antecedents, and contingent events that contribute to the maintenance of a problem behavior. Depending on the outcome interventions may consist of manipulating antecedents, eliminating reinforcers, teaching functionally equivalent behavior to replace problem behavior, or a combination of all of them. Interventions developed on the basis of functional assessment and analysis are called function-relevant treatment procedures, which have been considered best practice applied behavior analysis since at least the mid-1980s.

In contrast, procedures implemented without regard to the factors maintaining the behavior but instead based on behavioral topography, intended effect, or organizational policy are called default procedures (Iwata, Dorsey, Slifer, Bauman, & Richman, 1982, 1994). Default procedures were characteristic of much of applied behavior analysis prior to the mid-1980s. Many instances of default procedures were effective in suppressing SIB and other problem behaviors. The default procedure most often reported as effective was punishment (Iwata et al., 1982, 1994). However, since the advent of functional analysis and functional assessment procedures, there has been an inverse relationship in the frequency with which functional analysis or assessment procedures and punishment procedures for SIB are published in the behavior analytic literature (Hanley, Iwata, & McCord, 2003; Kahng, Iwata, & Lewin, 2002; Pelios, Morren, Tesch, & Axelrod, 1999).

The purpose common to functional assessment and analysis is to generate hypotheses about the maintaining variables of behavioral disturbances. In the literature, a common distinction is made between the two insofar as functional assessment relies on information obtained through behavioral observation, interviews, rating scales, and other methods, whereas functional analysis refers to procedures that involve the experimental manipulation of contingencies of reinforcement of the target behavior.

A. Functional Assessment

The most common functional assessment methods are structured behavioral interviews, rating scales, descriptive ABC recording charts and checklists, and scatter plots. Each one will be briefly described.

1. STRUCTURED BEHAVIORAL INTERVIEWS

Structured behavioral interviews with individuals who have frequent contact with the person exhibiting the problem behavior such as relatives, teachers, and staff members are particularly useful sources of information about behavior's functional properties, especially in the initial assessment of potential events that are relevant for an individual's target behavior at hand (Lalli, Browder, Mace, & Brown, 1993; O'Neill et al., 1997). In a survey of staff responsible for the treatment of behavior challenges in agencies serving persons with intellectual disabilities, Ellingson, Miltenberger, and Long (1999) found that behavioral interviews are used more often than any other functional assessment method. Information obtained through interviews can than be systematically corroborated by other assessment techniques such as rating scales, checklists, direct observations in the natural environment, or by experimental manipulations of critical variables that are potentially influencing the occurrence of the behavior. While structured interviews are a rich source of information, the objectivity, reliability, and validity of the obtained information are rarely explored and must be considered with caution.

2. RATING SCALES

Several behavior rating scales have been introduced in the literature in recent years that are designed to systematically explore to what extent the functional property subtypes are relevant for a given person's behavior problem. They typically consist of four or five subscales that correspond with the most common behavioral functions known to be associated with SIB and aggressive behavior.

a. Functional Analysis Screening Tool. The Functional Analysis Screening Tool (FAST) is a 27-item informant-based rating scale developed on the basis of general rules of scale construction (Iwata & DeLeon, 1995). The items were assigned into three sections or subscales: (1) *social influences on behavior*, (2) *social reinforcement*, and (3) *nonsocial (automatic) reinforcement.* Iwata (personal communication, 2002), reported that the FAST interrater agreement was found to be only modest (around 67%).

b. Functional Assessment for Multiple Causality Tool. Many individuals show more than one behavior problem with their distinct functional profiles (Derby et al., 1994) The Functional Assessment for Multiple Causality Tool (FACT) was empirically developed by Matson et al. (2003) to generate information that would allow prioritizing of rational, function-relevant intervention strategies for behavior problems that are concurrently maintained by more than one function. It is an informant-based, forced-choice measure that consists of 35 items that are assigned to 5 subscales that were derived and confirmed by factor analysis: (1) *physical*, (2) *tangible*, (3) *attention*, (4) *self-stimulation*, (5) *escape*. The FACT subscales have excellent internal consistency (KR-20 coefficients ranging from .94–.95). The scale shows great promise but more data on validity and reliability (interrater agreement and test–retest) will show its true potential.

c. Motivation Assessment Scale. The Motivation Assessment Scale (MAS), one of the earliest functional assessment scales, is an informant-based behavior rating scale that consists of 16 questions assigned to 4 subscales (Durand & Crimmins, 1988): (1) *attention*, (2) *escape*, (3) *sensory*, (4) *tangible*. It is perhaps the most widely used and extensively examined functional behavior rating scale (Sturmey, 1994). Items are rated on a 7-point Likert-type scale (0 = never, 1 = almost never, 2 = seldom, 3 = half the time, 4 = usually,

5 = almost always, 6 = always). Durand and Crimmins (1988) reported strong reliability and validity. Later studies, however, have failed to replicate the optimistic psychometric findings of the developers (Duker & Sigafoos, 1998; Sigafoos, Kerr, & Roberts, 1994; Zarcone, Rodgers, Iwata, Rourke, & Dorsey, 1991).

d. Questions About Behavioral Function. The Questions About Behavioral Function (QABF) is another informant-based behavior rating scale created by Matson and his collaborators (Matson & Vollmer, 1995), which consists of 25 items. Each item is rated on a 4-point Likert-type scale (X = does not apply, 0 = never, 1 = rarely, 2 = some, 3 = often). The items were developed to probe five different functional properties, which are reflected by five subscales: (1) *attention*, (2) *escape*, (3) *tangible*, (4) *nonsocial*, and (5) *physical*. The QABF was developed by Paclawskyj, Matson, Rush, Smalls, and Vollmer (2000) who reported promising interrater and test–retest reliability, and they also conducted a factor analysis that revealed five factors that were consistent with the a priori subscales.

Figure 2 shows the mean QABF behavioral functions of six topographies across individuals: three SIB topgoraphies, and three aggressive behavior topographies. Figure 3 presents the mean aggregate scores for SIB and aggressive behavior. Six trained graduate interviewed direct-care staff, who had known the participant for a minimum of 6 months. The QABF was administered for problem behaviors that were rated as "severe" on the BPI-01 (Rojahn et al., 2001). If there were no topographies rated as "severe" on the BPI, information was gathered on the topographies with the next highest ratings of severity. BPI and QABF were administered to the same staff person. Seventy-two participants had a total of 161 behaviors rated as a "moderate" or "severe" problem showing 27 different topographies. The six most frequently occurring topographies accounted for 60.9% of the behaviors rated as a "moderate" or "severe" problem. The behavioral function for each behavior on the QABF was determined based on the highest total subscale score. When two topographies in a person had two or more equally high QABF function scores, both were noted. If more than two behavioral functions were rated equally high, the function of that behavior was noted as undifferentiated. A MANOVA with the two aggregate topographies as the independent variable and the QABF scores as the multivariate dependent variable showed an overall statistically significant differences between the topographies (Wilks' $\lambda = .84$, $F = 3.6$, [5, 92], $p < .05$). SIB had significantly higher scores on the *nonsocial* subscale than aggressive behavior [$F\,(1, 96) = 6.5$, $p < 0.5$]. No other subscale was statistically significant. The data, although not conclusive, indicate that there may be relationship between function and topography, but that this relationship is a weak one. This is consistent with other reports (Bienstein, Smith, Rojahn, & Matson, 2006;

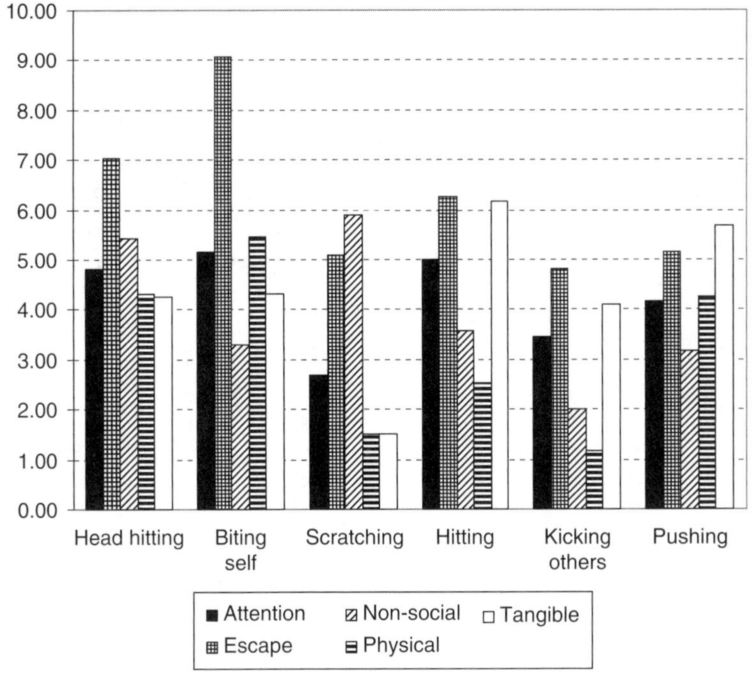

FIG. 2. Mean QABF scores [hitting head ($n = 33$); self-biting ($n = 13$); self-scratching ($n = 10$); hitting others ($n = 19$); kicking others ($n = 11$); pushing others ($n = 12$)].

Emerson & Bromley, 1995; Iwata et al., 1982) and supports the position held by behavior analysts that focuses exclusively on functional characteristics of the target behavior for the choice of behavioral interventions and that the behavior topography holds relatively little relevant clinical information.

Validity of the QABF and the MAS was examined by Paclawskyj, Matson, Rush, Smalls, and Vollmer (2001) by comparing the rating scale outcomes with the results produced by analogue functional analysis. The QABF agreement with the analogue functional analysis was 69.2%, while MAS agreed at 53.8% with the analogue functional analysis. Shogren and Rojahn (2003) compared MAS and the QABF on 20 adults with intellectual disabilities and problem behaviors (aggression, SIB, or property destruction). Test–retest reliability of the subscales in both scales was good to excellent (Cicchetti, 1994), and—except for one QABF subscale—internal consistency was good considering the small number of items and the purpose of the scale. Consistent with some earlier studies, interrater reliability was less satisfactory with both scales falling only into the *fair* to *good* range. Correlations between

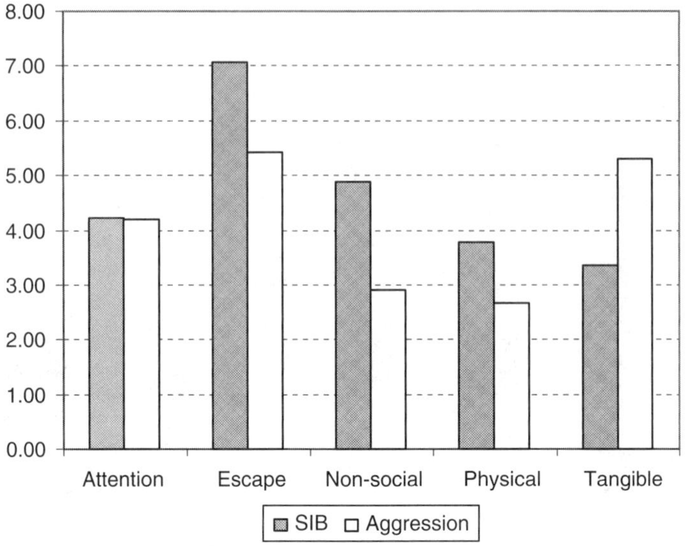

FIG. 3. Mean QABF scores for aggregate SIB ($n = 56$) and aggressive behavior ($n = 42$).

functionally equivalent subscales were statistically significant and were generally higher than correlations between nonequivalent subscales. The QABF and the MAS were found to be comparable in terms of the assessed reliabilities, and both instruments appear to be measuring very similar constructs.

Several other rating scales for functional properties of behavior problems have been constructed, including the *Setting Events Checklist* for aggressive behavior by Gardner, Cole, Davidson, and Karan (1986). Some studies explored to what extent the a priori (functional) subscales of those rating scales can be confirmed empirically by (structural) factor analysis. The results have been inconsistent (Bihm, Kienlen, & Ness, 1991; Duker & Sigafoos, 1998; Kearney, Cook, Chapman, & Bensaheb, 2006; Paclawskyj et al., 2001).

3. DESCRIPTIVE A-B-C RECORDING CHARTS AND CHECKLISTS

Other practical tools to identify critical information about the functional properties of a behavior problem are contingency observation records or checklists. They involve brief description of the antecedents (A), the behavior (B), and its consequences (C). These charts are completed whenever the targeted problem behavior occurs (for an example of a descriptive A-B-C

Contingencies observation chart

Name: ______________________________

Date: ______________________________

Time: ______________________________

Informant: ___________________________

General setting	Immediate antecedent event	Target behavior	Immediate consequence

FIG. 4. Example of a descriptive A-B-C recording chart.

recording chart see Fig. 4). Caretakers are instructed to indicate the day and time of the incident, provide a brief description of the general situation in which the incident occurred, the immediate antecedents, the specifics of the target behavior, and the immediate consequences. The assumption is that repeated contingency observation charts will provide frequency data and detailed information on the varied circumstances in which the behavior occurs. Thus, this information leads to a formulation of one or more functional hypotheses. The advantage is that such structured incidence reports do not rely on the memory of the informant, but are completed whenever the behavior occurs. Practical limitations may be encountered in cases when the target behaviors occur too frequently, or if the informant reports only nonfunctional aspects of the antecedents and consequences. A-B-C Recording

Checklists use categorized antecedent and consequent events that are checked by the observer rather then using free descriptions.

4. SCATTER PLOTS

Touchette, MacDonald, and Langer (1985) produced a simple but efficient method that combined data collection and visual data presentation, called a scatter plot. Such a scatter plot can identify responding patterns associated with events in the person's natural environment. It consists of a grid printed on a coding sheet, where the vertical segments refer to the time of the day broken down into time units as needed (e.g., 15 min or 1 h), and the horizontal segments of the grid represent successive days. Each cell in the grid represents a particular time unity on a given day. Blank cells represent zero rate of occurrence and filled cells indicate that the target behavior had occurred. This is an inexpensive and easy to use tool that can be used by participant observers such as teachers or direct care staff. Scatter plot data can contribute to the formulation of functional behavioral hypotheses.

B. Experimental Functional Analysis

Experimental functional analysis (EFA) involves the systematic manipulation of the antecedent events and the consequences of a target behavior for the purpose of empirically identifying the contingencies that maintain the behavior. Iwata et al. (1982, reprinted in 1994) provided the first published demonstration of pretreatment identification of maintaining contingencies for SIB. In this study, nine children with various severe self-injurious topographies were exposed to four different experimental conditions, twice daily. Conditions were described as follows: (1) The *Social Disapproval* condition designed to test the positive social reinforcement hypothesis. The experimenter[3] would first instruct the participant to interact with the leisure material and then appear to read a book or magazine. Contingent on each instance of SIB, the experimenter would give a disapproving statement (i.e., "don't do that"), but would otherwise not attend to the participants' behavior. (2) The *Academic Demand* condition was intended to test the negative reinforcement by demand termination. The experimenter made academic task instructions and praised instruction following. SIB produced a 30-sec no-instruction interval. (3) The *Alone* condition tested the automatic reinforcement model of SIB. The participant was left alone without leisure

[3]McCord and Neef (2005) and Ringdahl, Winborn, Andelman, and Kitsukawa (2002) pointed out that available leisure items (e.g., games, toys) can be problematic in functional analysis attention conditions as they may compete with attention maintained behavior.

materials. (4) A control condition was staged in the *Unstructured Play* condition where the experimenter and participant were present in the room with leisure items without instructions. The experimenter would praise the participant every 30 sec during which SIB had not occurred. This condition was intended to control for the presence of the experimenter, availability of potentially stimulating materials, absence of demands, and delivery of social interaction.

A review of 152 functional analyses of SIB conducted across an 11-year period featuring the original four conditions (Iwata et al., 1982) and variations thereof was conducted by Iwata, Pace, Dorsey et al. (1994). A summary of some of the results are presented in Table I. Only 5.3% of participants had multiple maintaining contingencies of their behaviors, and 4.6% seemed uncontrolled. Each participant subsequently received treatment determined by EFA outcome, and the authors report 84.2% treatment effectiveness when antecedent interventions (e.g., noncontingent reinforcement, task modification) were used, 86.8% effectiveness when extinction was used, 82.5% effectiveness for differential reinforcement, and 88.2% for punishment. Only 12.3% of all successful interventions involved punishment. Ellingson et al. (1999) reported that staff responsible for behavior plans in agencies serving people with intellectual disabilities rated functional analysis to be more useful and effective than behavioral interviews, rating scales, and checklists.

TABLE I

Outcome of 152 functional analyses of SIB by Iwata, Pace, Dorsey et al. (1994)

Negative reinforcement (socially medicated)	38.1%
Demand termination	35.4%
Social interaction termination	1.3%
Physical exam termination	0.7%
Ambient noise termination	0.7%
Positive social reinforcement (socially mediated)	26.3%
Attention	23.0%
Access to materials	2.0%
Access to food	1.3%
Automatic or sensory reinforcement (suspected)	25.7%
Sensory positive reinforcement	19.7%
Sensory negative reinforcement	1.3%
Undifferentiated high responding	4.6%
Multiple controlling variables	5.3%
Uncontrolled	4.6%

Given that EFA is an experimental procedure, many variables must be considered that can influence and potentially distort the outcome of the analysis. Some of them parameters have been addressed by empirical research.

1. NUMBER OF SESSIONS AND SESSION DURATION

Judging from a review of published studies, EFA involves between one and eight sessions per day (Iwata et al., 1982, 1994; Kahng & Iwata, 1999; Shore, Iwata, DeLeon, Kahng, & Smith, 1997; Smith & Churchill, 2002). However, most publications failed to mention this information. Reported session durations have ranged from 2 to 30 min, the most frequently reported duration being 10 min (Hanley et al., 2003). A comparison of functional analyses incorporating multielement designs with either 5-, 10-, or 15-min session durations showed perfect agreement between 10- and 15-min session durations, and only few disagreements when session duration was 5 min (Wallace & Iwata, 1999). This suggests that economy can be enhanced by using briefer session durations while maintaining the utility of the procedures. However, several studies have reported that different within-session response patterns can occur, or that shorter session durations may preclude acquisition of responding under session contingencies (Kahng & Iwata, 1999). Given this, briefer sessions may sometimes preclude development of responding patterns that may be of interest.

Total length of time required to conduct an EFA cannot be determined prior to the analysis. It depends on the rate at which differential response rates can be attained under differing conditions. Iwata et al. (1982) reported a mean number of thirty 15-min sessions (ranging from 24 to 53 sessions) and a mean of 7.5 h of in-session time (ranging from 6.0 to 13.25 h). In their 152 functional analyses, Iwata et al. (1994) reported that the number of sessions required ranged from 8 to 66, and total in-session time ranged from 2 to 16.5 h. Certainly, length of time needed to conduct an EFA could be influenced by session length, intersession interval length, number of sessions conducted per day, and number of days during which sessions are conducted per week.

Northup et al. (1991) described a brief EFA procedure, which could potentially have the utility of a full EFA while maximizing economy. Only a single exposure to each condition was used with sessions of 2–5 min, and intersession intervals between 1 and 2 min. Subsequent brief EFA-derived treatment produced reductions in problem behaviors for all three participants. Nevertheless, there are instances when brief functional analyses do not produce the desired differential responding between the conditions (Kahng & Iwata, 1999).

2. SELECTION OF EXPERIMENTAL CONDITIONS

Many published functional analyses have included attention, tangible, demand, alone, and play/leisure conditions. These conditions permit assessment of maintenance by various types of positive, negative, or automatic reinforcement contingencies. Further, motivating establishing (or abolishing) operation effects, such as attention or tangible satiation or deprivation, may also be assessed, should presession or intersession interval procedures be arrange for this purpose. A number of studies have additionally assessed effects of participant-specific variables, such as response to medication (Crosland et al., 2003; Mace, Blum, Sierp, Delaney, & Mauk, 2001), menses (Carr, Smith, Giacin, Whelan, & Pancari, 2003), otitis (O'Reilly, 1997), varying levels of sleep deprivation in people with sleep disturbances (O'Reilly & Lancioni, 2000), and having been in respite care versus having been at home (O'Reilly, 1996). EFA test conditions need not include all standard test conditions (English & Anderson, 2004). Participant–specific conditions have been developed and conducted on the basis of pre-EFA interview, observation, or other information gathering (Fisher et al., 1998; Harding et al., 2005; McCord, Thompson, & Iwata, 2001).

3. INTERSESSION INTERVAL LENGTH AND ACTIVITIES

Intersession intervals are typically between 5 and 15 min (Zarcone et al., 1993, 1994), but they are rarely reported in published papers. McGonigle, Rojahn, Dixon, and Strain (1987) discovered that intersession interval lengths can be critical because intervals that are too short may cause confounding "spillover" effects from the previous to the subsequent EFA condition. Other studies have shown that activities that take place between the EFA conditions can also have an effect on the performance within the EFA conditions (Fisher et al., 2004; Kurtz et al., 2003). The extent to which intersession interval conditions can affect EFA outcomes has not been fully explored, but it seems important for researchers and practitioners to be cognizant of the possible confounding effects of intersession activities. Given those findings, providing explicit information about intersession length and activities should become standard requirement for publication of EFA-based research.

4. SETTING, STIMULUS DISCRIMINATION, AND GENERALIZATION

To accelerate differential response rates between conditions, some researchers introduced discriminative stimuli (S^Ds) to EFA conditions. For instance, McGonigle et al. (1987) paired different auditory (e.g., a low-tone buzzer or classical music) or tactile (e.g., a handheld vibrator or a handheld flashlight) stimuli with different experimental conditions. Connors et al. (2000), Roscoe et al. (1998), and Wordsell et al. (2000) conducted each type of EFA condition in its own room and with a different experimenter. Added S^Ds may not only facilitate discriminative stimulus control over the participant's responding, but may also assist in preventing response "spillover" to subsequent EFA conditions. Conversely, it maybe in the interest of the experimenter to facilitate stimulus generalization. Iwata et al. (1982), for example, rotated different therapists to prevent development of therapist related confounds.

The extent to which associating various extraexperimental stimuli with EFA conditions affects EFA outcome (other than by enhancing the rapidity with which condition-relevant responding is acquired under each condition) has not been adequately examined. Whether experimenters should strengthen stimulus discrimination or generalization across EFA conditions depends on a variety of issues related to the individual at hand. This issue may be relevant in the choice of settings in which EFA is conducted. Many functional analyses are conducted in specially designed and padded rooms to ensure the participant's safety (Iwata et al., 1982) and some have raised the concern that this may produce results with poor setting generality (Anderson, Freeman, & Scotti, 1999). It seems, however, that many service provider agencies conduct EFAs in the persons' natural settings rather than in controlled, analogue environments (Anderson et al., 1999; Ellingson et al., 1999; Harding et al., 2005).

5. MULTIPLE TARGET BEHAVIORS AND BEHAVIOR CHAINS

Many individuals exhibit more than one problem topography (McClintock et al., 2003). When this is the case, it is essential to conduct separate analyses for all problem topographies as they may have different functional properties and therefore require potentially separate intervention strategies (Derby et al., 1994). Problem behaviors so, however, sometimes occur in a predictable *behavior chain* sequence in which the preceding behavior links are reinforced by occurrence of the succeeding behavior links and ultimately by the same final reinforcer. For instance, behavior chains can sometimes be observed in learned behavior escalations that may start with growling and irritable pacing, yelling, throwing objects, to finally lashing out. In the case of behavior chains, the treatment of the earlier behavior links in the chain is likely to result in a reduction of subsequent behavior as well (Lalli, Mace, Wohn, & Liverzy, 1995; Smith & Churchill, 2002).

6. LOW-RATE RESPONDING

EFA is complicated when the behavior of concern occurs only sporadically. When days to weeks may pass between bouts of a behavior, should EFA sessions be conducted during that time, most or all sessions would produce undifferentiated, low-rate responding (O'Reilly, 1996, 1997). Tarbox, Wallace, Tarbox, Landaburu, and Williams (2004) conducted EFA sessions only following occurrence of sporadic SIB of three adults with intellectual disabilities, in what they termed a low-rate EFA. Their low-rate EFA outcomes, when compared with standard EFA (conducted irrespective of prior occurrence of sporadic SIB), revealed clearly differentiated response patterns, and so demonstrations of maintaining contingencies, for all three participants.

7. RISKS, LIMITATIONS, AND CONCERNS

Limitation of EFAs, especially in controlled analogue settings, are that they are labor intensive, necessitate highly trained staff, and often require special settings. In other words, they are expensive. However, there can also be some risks involved, which raise ethical concerns. Given that conducting an EFA implies that the potentially dangerous behavior is permitted to occur, steps need to be taken to ensure the immediate safety of the participant and the therapists/experimenters who are conducting the procedures. Especially with dangerous behavior, termination criteria need to be developed (Iwata et al., 1982, 1994). In addition to the immediate threat of physical injury, one also needs to be concerned about potential protracted effects. Exposing an individual's target behavior to new contingencies could provide an inadvertent opportunity for exacerbate the problem. For instance, a person's head banging may be under primary control of some automatic internal reinforcer. If that same behavior under an EFA condition produces continuous social reinforcement which it had not produced in the past (in addition to the internal reinforcement) over several sessions, a potentially dangerous learning process may be set in motion. Lovaas and Simmons' (1969) early and starling discovery during their careful EFA of "Gregg's" SIB should be a warning.

C. Functional Diagnostics and Multimodal Functional Analyses

Variations of the EFA described by Iwata et al. (1982) are functional diagnostics (Crosland et al., 2003; Mace et al., 2001) and *multimodal functional analyses* (Gardner & Sovner, 1994). They expand the scope from the contingency based antecedent–behavior consequence to include variables with indirect effects in the contingencies of reinforcement. Functional diagnostics refers to functional analyses in the context of psychoactive drug trials, which allows for simultaneous examination of pharmacological versus contingency-based intervention across both behavioral function and behavioral topography. Multimodal functional analysis, on the other hand, incorporates biomedical, psychological (trait and state), and environmental factors that are presumed to influence a person's problem behavior.

IV. SUMMARY AND CONCLUSIONS

This chapter described structural (or topographical) and functional assessment methodologies that may be relevant for SIB and aggressive behavior in individuals with intellectual disability, with a focus on procedures described in the behavioral research literature. Structural and functional assessment techniques are not mutually exclusive and can complement each other. Each one has important functions, depending on the assessment task at hand. While functional assessment and analysis are designed to identify critical variables that maintain a given problem behavior in order to derive a rational strategy, structural assessment instruments are required for single-subject experimentation, treatment outcome evaluations, survey research and other group studies, and screening. While we were able to touch on only the most relevant features of assessment, we hope that we made it apparent that a variety of approaches and methods exist to obtain relevant information about SIB and aggressive behavior, ranging from simple and inexpensive techniques to sophisticated and expensive high-tech methods.

Research into assessment technologies has already produced a considerable number of promising instruments and offers the researcher and clinician many options from which to choose. However, many of the available assessment instruments have limited evidence of their psychometric properties and need more research to highlight their strengths and correct their weaknesses. Some of the psychometric weaknesses are, in part, inherent in the nature of problem behavior in persons with intellectual disabilities and, therefore, probably do not have a quick fix. For instance, behavior problems tend to be of low incidence (10% prevalence or less) and are not normally distributed in the population. Typically, they are positively skewed, which means that only a (relatively) small number of individuals exists with high frequency and highly severe problems, often with multiple behavior topographies, while the majority of individuals does not exhibit any behavior challenges at all. Low-incidence skewed-distribution phenomena unfortunately create technical challenges for the construction of assessment instruments and for statistical data analysis. For instance, it is an axiom of classical test theory that scales with fewer items have lower reliability than scales with more items. Rare but clinically important behaviors such as SIB and aggressive behavior are typically represented by only one item in a scale, which consequently makes it all but impossible to measure them reliably. This problem has been encountered again and again in specialized rating scales, psychopathology scales, and in standardized maladaptive behavior scales. In addition, inferential statistics require normal distribution of variables, an assumption that tend to get violated in group based on such instruments.

There is an ongoing debate over the best, most accurate, and feasible strategy to identify functional properties of target behaviors. While indirect measures such as functional interviews and informant rating scales and checklists are much less expensive and avoid some of the problems of EFA, their critics point out that they suffer from the drawbacks common to all indirect behavior assessments, namely, that they tend to be subjective and often unreliable. Some functional assessment tools fare better than others as far as their reliability and validity are concerned, and additional research is needed to provide more detailed and comprehensive information about the psychometric properties of indirect methods. This is especially true for behavioral interviews, which are relatively inexpensive, flexible, and seem to be favored by staff (Ellingson et al., 1999). This is also true for many of the existing functional assessment rating scales which, compared with EFA, have great advantages as far as cost and risk containment are concerned. EFA, on the other hand, which was found to be effective and useful by many behavior specialists (Ellingson et al., 1999), is still often considered the gold standard and criterion against which functional assessment instruments must be compared for the documentation of their validity. However, the precision, cost, and potential risk of an EFA must be carefully weighted against the lessened immediate risk and cost, but potential imprecision of an indirect assessment.

REFERENCES

Adams, D., & Allen, D. (2001). Assessing the need for reactive behaviour management strategies in children with intellectual disability and severe challenging behaviour. *Journal of Intellectual Disability Research, 45,* 335–343.

Alborz, A., Bromley, J., Emerson, E., Kiernan, C., & Qureshi, H. (1994). *Challenging Behaviour Survey: Individual Schedule.* Manchester: Hester Adrian Research Centre: University of Manchester.

Allen, D. (2000). Recent research on physical aggression in persons with intellectual disability: An overview. *Journal of Intellectual & Developmental Disability, 25,* 41–57.

Aman, M. G. (1991). Review and evaluation of instruments for assessing emotional and behavioral disorders. *Australia and New Zealand Journal of Developmental Disabilities, 17,* 127–145.

Aman, M. G. (2003). *Annotated Bibliography on the Aberrant Behavior Checklist (June 2003 update).* Columbus, OH: Ohio State University.

Aman, M. G., De Smedt, G., Derivan, A., Lyons, B., Findling, R. L., & The Risperidone Disruptive Behavior Study Group (2002). Risperidone treatment of children with disruptive behavior disorders and subaverage IQ: A double-blind, placebo-controlled study. *American Journal of Psychiatry, 159,* 1337–1346.

Aman, M. G., DeSmedt, G., Derivan, A., Lyons, B., Findling, R. L., & The Risperidone Conduct Study Group (2002). Double-blind, placebo-controlled study of risperidone for the treatment of disruptive behaviors in children with subaverage intelligence. *American Journal of Psychiatry, 159,* 1337–1346.

Aman, M. G., & Singh, N. N. (1994). *Aberrant Behavior Checklist - Community. Supplementary Manual.* East Aurora, NY: Slosson Educational Publications.

Aman, M. G., Singh, N. N., Stewart, A. W., & Field, C. J. (1985). Psychometric characteristics of the Aberrant Behavior Checklist. *American Journal on Mental Deficiency, 89,* 492–502.

Aman, M. G., Singh, N. N., & Turbott, S. H. (1987). Reliability of the Aberrant Behavior Checklist and the effect of variations in instructions. *American Journal on Mental Retardation, 92,* 237–240.

Aman, M. G., Tassé, M. J., Rojahn, J., & Hammer, D. (1996). The Nisonger CBRF: A child behavior rating form for children with developmental disabilities. *Research in Developmental Disabilities, 17,* 41–57.

Anderson, C. M., Freeman, K. A., & Scotti, J. R. (1999). Evaluation of the generalizability (reliability and validity) of analog functional assessment methodology. *Behavior Therapy, 30,* 31–50.

Bailey, J. S., & Burch, M. (2002). *Research methods in applied behavior analysis.* Thousand Oaks, CA: Sage Publication.

Baker, B. L., McIntyre, L. L., Blacher, J., Crnic, K., Edelbrok, C., & Low, C. (2003). Pre-school children with and without developmental delay: Behaviour problems and parenting over time. *Journal of Intellectual Disabilities Research, 47,* 217–230.

Bienstein, P., Smith, K., Rojahn, J., & Matson, J. L. (2006). Differential functional properties profiles of chronic behavior problems in adults with severe and profound mental retardation. Poster presented at the Annual Meeting of the American Psychological Association, New Orleans, August 10.

Bihm, E. M., Kienlen, T. L., & Ness, M. E. (1991). Factor structure of the Motivation Assessment Scale for persons with mental retardation. *Psychological Reports, 68,* 1235–1238.

Bihm, E. M., & Poindexter, A. R. (1991). Cross-validation of the factor structure of the Aberrant Behavior Checklist for persons with mental retardation. *American Journal on Mental Retardation, 96,* 209–211.

Bodfish, J. W., Crawford, T. W., Powell, S. B., Parker, D. E., Golden, R. N., & Lewis, M. H. (1995). Compulsions in adults with mental retardation: Prevalence, phenomenology, and co-morbidity with stereotypy and self-injury. *American Journal on Mental Retardation, 100,* 183–192.

Bodfish, J. W., Symons, F. J., & Lewis, M. H. (1999). *Repetitive Behavior Scales.* Western Carolina Center Research Reports.

Bodfish, J. W., Symons, F. J., Parker, D. E., & Lewis, M. H. (2000). Varieties in repetitive behavior in autism: Comparisons to mental retardation. *Journal of Autism and Developmental Disorders, 30,* 237–243.

Brown, E. C., Aman, M. G., & Havercamp, S. M. (2002). Factor analysis and norms for parent ratings on the Aberrant Behavior Checklist-Community for young people in special education. *Research in Developmental Disabilities, 23,* 45–60.

Bruininks, R. H., Woodcock, R. W., Weatherman, R. F., & Hill, B. K. (1996). *Scales of Independent Behavior – Revised.* Chicago, IL: Riverside.

Campbell, M. (1985). Timed stereotypies rating scale. *Psychopharmacology Bulletin, 21,* 1082–1085.

Carr, E. G., Smith, C. E., Giacin, T. A., Whelan, B. M., & Pancari, J. (2003). Menstrual discomfort as a biological setting event for severe problem behavior: Assessment and intervention. *American Journal on Mental Retardation, 108,* 117–133.

Chadwick, O., Piroth, N., Walker, J., Bernard, S., & Taylor, E. (2000). Factors affecting the risk of behaviour problems in children with severe intellectual disability. *Journal of Intellectual Disability Research, 44,* 108–123.

Cicchetti, D. V. (1994). Guidelines, criteria, and rules of thumb for evaluating normed and standardized assessment instruments in psychology. *Psychological Assessment, 6,* 284–290.

Cohen, I. L. (2003). Criterion-related validity of the PDD Behavior Inventory. *Journal of Autism and Developmental Disorders, 33,* 47–53.

Cohen, I. L., Schmidt-Lackner, S., Romanczyk, R., & Sudhalter, V. (2003). The PDD Behavior Inventory: A rating scale for assessing response to intervention in children with pervasive developmental disorder. *Journal of Autism and Developmental Disorders, 33,* 31–45.

Connors, J., Iwata, B. A., Kahng, S. W., Hanley, G. P., Wordsell, A. S., & Thompson, R. H. (2000). Differential responding in the presence and absence of discriminative stimuli during multielement functional analyses. *Journal of Applied Behavior Analysis, 33*(3), 299–308.

Cooper, J. O., Heron, T. E., & Heward, W. L. (2007). *Applied behavior analysis* (2nd ed.). Columbus, OH: Merrill.

Crosland, K. A., Zarcone, J. R., Lindauer, S. E., Valdovinos, M. G., Zarcone, T. J., Hellings, J. A., & Schroeder, S. R. (2003). Use of functional analysis methodology in the evaluation of medication effects. *Journal of Autism and Developmental Disorders, 33,* 271–279.

Davidson, P. D., Houser, K. D., Cain, N. N., Sloane-Reeves, J., Quijano, L., Matons, L., Giesow, V., & Ladrigan, P. M. (1999). Characteristics of older adults with intellectual disabilities referred for crisis intervention. *Journal of Intellectual Disability Research, 43,* 38–46.

Derby, K. M., Wacker, D. P., Peck, S., Sasso, G., DeRaad, A., Berg, W., Asmus, J., & Ulrich, S. (1994). Functional analysis of separate topographies of aberrant behavior. *Journal of Applied Behavior Analysis, 27,* 267–278.

Duker, P. C., & Sigafoos, J. (1998). The Motivation Assessment Scale: Reliability and construct validity. *Research in Developmental Disabilities, 19,* 131–141.

Durand, V. M., & Crimmins, D. B. (1988). Identifying the variables maintaining self-injurious behavior. *Journal of Autism and Developmental Disorders, 18,* 99–117.

Edelbrock, C. S. (1985). Child Behavior Rating Form. *Psychopharmacology Bulletin, 21,* 835–837.

Einfeld, S. L., & Tonge, B. J. (1992). *Manual for the Developmental Behaviour Checklist.* Clayton, Malbourne, and Sydney: Monash University Center for Developmental Psychiatry and School of Psychiatry, University of New South Wales.

Einfeld, S. L., & Tonge, B. J. (2002). *Manual for the Developmental Behaviour Checklist (Second Edition).* Clayton, Malbourne, and Sydney: Monash University Center for Developmental Psychiatry and School of Psychiatry, University of New South Wales.

Ellingson, S. A., Miltenberger, R. G., & Long, E. S. (1999). A survey of the use of functional assessment procedures in agencies serving individuals with developmental disabilities. *Behavioral Interventions, 14,* 187–198.

Emerson, E., & Bromley, J. (1995). The form and function of challenging behaviors. *Journal of Intellectual Disability Research, 39,* 388–398.

English, C. L., & Anderson, C. M. (2004). Effects of familiar versus unfamiliar therapists on responding in the analog functional analysis. *Research in Developmental Disabilities, 25,* 39–55.

Fisher, W. W., Bowman, L. G., Thompson, R. H., Contrucci, S. A., Burd, L., & Alon, G. (1998). Reductions in self-injury produced by transcutaneous electrical nerve stimulation. *Journal of Applied Behavior Analysis, 31,* 493–496.

Fisher, W. W., DeLeon, I. G., Rodrigues-Carter, V., & Keeney, K. M. (2004). Enhancing effects of extinction on attention-maintained behavior through noncontingent delivery of attention or stimuli identified via a competing stimulus assessment. *Journal of Applied Behavior Analysis, 37,* 171–184.

Gardner, W. I., Cole, C. L., Davidson, D. P., & Karan, O. C. (1986). Reducing aggression in individuals with developmental disabilities: An expanded stimulus control, assessment, and intervention model. *Education and Training in Mental Retardation, 21,* 3–12.

Gardner, W. I., & Sovner, R. (1994). *Self-injurious behaviors.* Willow Street, PA: VIDA Publishing Co.

Gedye, A. (1992). Recognizing obsessive-compulsive disorder in clients with developmental disabilities. *The Habilitative Mentalhealthcare Newsletter, 11,* 73–77.

Girouard, N., Morin, I. N., & Tassé, M. J. (1998). Étude de fidelité test-retest et accord interjuges de la Grille d'évaluation comprtementale pour enfants Nisonger (GÉCEN). [Test–retest and interrater reliability of the French version of the Nisonger Child Behavior Rating Form.]. *Revue Francophone de la Déficience Intellectuelle, 9,* 127–136.

Goodman, W. K., Price, L. H., & Rasmussen, S. A. (1989a). The Yale-Brown Obsessive Compulsive Scale: I. Development, use, and reliability. *Archives of General Psychiatry, 46,* 1006–1011.

Goodman, W. K., Price, L. H., & Rasmussen, S. A. (1989b). The Yale-Brown Obsessive Compulsive Scale: II. Validity. *Archives of General Psychiatry, 46,* 1012–1016.

Gualtieri, C. T., & Schroeder, S. R. (1989). Pharmacotherapy of self-injurious behavior: Preliminary tests of the D-l hypothesis. *Psychopharmacology Bulletin, 25,* 364–371.

Hanley, G. P., Iwata, B. A., & McCord, B. E. (2003). Functional analysis of problem behavior: A review. *Journal of Applied Behavior Analysis, 36,* 147–185.

Harding, J., Wacker, D. P., Berg, W. K., Barretto, A., & Ringdahl, J. (2005). Evaluation of relations between specific antecedent stimuli and self-injury during functional analysis conditions. *American Journal on Mental Retardation, 110,* 205–215.

Hersen, M., & Barlow, D. H. (1976). *Single-case experimental designs: Strategies for studying behavior change.* New York: Pergamon.

Holden, B., & Gitlesen, J. P. (2006). A total population study od challenging behaviour in the county of Hedmark, Norway: Prevalence and risk markers. *Research in Developmental Disabilities, 27,* 456–465.

Iwata, B. A., & DeLeon, I. G. (1995). *The functional analysis screening tool* (FAST). Unpublished manuscript, Gainesville: University of Florida.

Iwata, B. A., Dorsey, M. F., Slifer, K. J., Bauman, K. E., & Richman, G. S. (1982). Toward a functional analysis of self-injury. *Analysis and Intervention in Developmental Disabilities, 2,* 3–20.

Iwata, B. A., Dorsey, M. F., Slifer, K. J., Bauman, K. E., & Richman, G. S. (1994). Toward a functional analysis of self-injury. *Journal of Applied Behavior Analysis, 27*(2), 197–209.

Iwata, B. A., Pace, G. M., Dorsey, M. F., Zarcone, J. R., Vollmer, T. R., Smith, R. G., et al. (1994). The functions of self-injurious behavior: An experimental-epidemiological analysis. *Journal of Applied Behavior Analysis, 27,* 215–240.

Iwata, B. A., Pace, G. M., Kissel, R. C., Nau, P. A., & Farber, J. M. (1990). The self-injury trauma (SIT) scale: A method for quantifying surface tissue damage caused by self-injurious behavior. *Journal of Applied Behavior Analysis, 23,* 99–110.

Kahng, S., & Iwata, B. A. (1999). Correspondence between outcomes of brief and extended functional analyses. *Journal of Applied Behavior Analysis, 32,* 149–159.

Kahng, S. W., Iwata, B.A, & Lewin, A. B. (2002). Behavioral treatment of self-injury, 1964–2000. *American Journal on Mental Retardation, 107,* 212–221.

Kazdin, A. E. (1982). *Single-case research designs.* New York: Oxford University Press.

Kearney, C. A., Cook, L. C., Chapman, G., & Bensaheb, A. (2006). Exploratory and confirmatory factor analyses of the Motivation Assessment Scale and Resident Choice Assessment Scale. *Journal of Developmental and Physical Disabilities, 18,* 1–11.

Kurtz, P. F., Chin, M. D., Huete, J. M., Tarbox, R. S. F., O'Connor, J. T., Paclawskyj, T. R., et al. (2003). Functional analysis and treatment of self-injurious behavior in young children: A summary of 30 cases. *Journal of Applied Behavior Analysis, 36,* 205–219.

Lalli, J. S., Browder, D. M., Mace, F. C., & Brown, D. K. (1993). Teacher use of descriptive analysis data to implement interventions to decrease students' problem behaviors. *Journal of Applied Behavior Analysis, 26,* 227–238.

Lalli, J. S., Mace, F. C., Wohn, T., & Liverzy, K. (1995). Identification and modification of a response-class hierarchy. *Journal of Applied Behavior Analysis, 28,* 551–559.

Lambert, N., Nihira, K., & Leland, H. (1993). AAMR Adaptive Behavior Scales-School (ABS-S:2). Pro-Ed, Inc.

Lecavalier, L., & Aman, M. G. (2003). Rating instruments. In J. L. Matson, R. B. Laud, & M. L. Matson (Eds.), *Behavior modification for persons with developmental disabilities: Treatment and supports* (Vol. 1, pp. 160–189). Kingston, New York: National Association for the Dually Diagnosed.

Lecavalier, L., Aman, M. G., & Hammer, D. (2004). Factor Analysis of the Nisonger Child Behavior Rating Form in Children with Autism Spectrum Disorders. *Journal of Autism and Developmental Disorders, 34,* 709–721.

Lecavalier, L., Aman, M. A., Hammer, D., Stoica, W., & Mathews, G.L (2004). Factor analysis of the Nisonger Child Behavior Rating Form in children with autism spectrum disorders. *Journal of Autism and Developmental Disorders, 34,* 709–721.

Lovaas, O.I, & Simmons, J. Q. (1969). Manipulation of self-destruction in three retarded children. *Journal of Applied Behavior Analysis, 2,* 143–157.

Lowe, K., Allen, D., Jones, E., Brophy, Moore, K., James, W. (in press). Challenging behaviours: Prevalence and topographies. *Journal of Intellectual Disability Research.*

Mace, F. C., Blum, N. J., Sierp, B. J., Delaney, B. A., & Mauk, J. E. (2001). Differential response of operant self-injury to pharmacologic versus behavioral treatment. *Journal of Developmental and Behavioral Pediatrics, 22,* 85–91.

Marshburn, E. C., & Aman, M. G. (1992). Factor validity and norms for the Aberrant Behavior Checklist in a community sample of children with mental retardation. *Journal of Autism and Developmental Disorders, 22,* 357–373.

Matson, J. L. (1995). *The diagnostic assessment of the severely handicapped-revised* (DASH-II). Baton Rouge, LA: Disability Consultants, LLC.

Matson, J. L. (1997). *The assessment of dual diagnosis* (ADD). Baton Rouge, LA: Disability Consultants, LLC.

Matson, J. L. (1998). *Diagnostic Assessment for the Severely Handicapped II – Manual.* Baton Rouge, LA: Scientific Publishers Incorporated.

Matson, J. L., & Bamburg, J. W. (1998). Reliability of the assessment of dual diagnosis (ADD). *Research in Developmental Disabilities, 19,* 89–95.

Matson, J. L., Coe, D. A., Gardner, W. I., & Sovner, R. (1991). A factor analytic study of the Diagnostic Assessment for the Severely Handicapped (DASH) Scale. *The Journal of Nervous and Mental Disease, 179,* 553–557.

Matson, J. L., Kiely, S. L., & Bamburg, J. W. (1997). The effects of stereotypies on adaptive skills as assessed with the DASH-II and the Vineland Adaptive Behavior Scale. *Research in Developmental Disabilities, 18,* 471–476.

Matson, J. L., Kuhn, D. E., Dixon, D. R., Mayville, S. B., Laud, R. B., Cooper, C. L., et al. (2003). The development and factor structure of the Functional Assessment for Multiple Causality (FACT). *Research in Developmental Disabilities, 24,* 485–495.

Matson, J. L., Smiroldo, B. B., & Bamburg, J. W. (1998). The relationship of social skills to psychopathology for individuals with severe and profound mental retardation. *Journal of Intellectual Disabilities Research, 23,* 137–145.

Matson, J. L., Smiroldo, B. B., Hamilton, M., & Baglio, C. (1997). Do anxiety disorders exist in persons with severe and profound mental retardation? *Research in Developmental Disabilities, 18,* 39–44.

Matson, J. L., Smiroldo, B. B., & Hastings, T. (1998). Validity of the autism/PDD subscale of the DASH-II. *Journal of Autism and Developmental Disabilities, 28,* 77–81.

Matson, J. L., & Vollmer, T. (1995). *Questions About Behavioral Function* (QABF). Baton Rouge, LA: Disability Consultants, LLC.

McClintock, K., Hall, S., & Oliver, C. (2003). Risk markers associated with challenging behaviours in people with intellectual disabilities: A meta-analytic study. *Journal of Intellectual Disability Research, 47,* 405–416.

McCord, B. E., & Neef, N. A. (2005). Leisure items as controls in the attention condition of functional analyses. *Journal of Applied Behavior Analysis, 38,* 417–426.

McCord, B. E., Thompson, R. J., & Iwata, B. A. (2001). Functional analysis and treatment of self-injury associated with transitions. *Journal of Applied Behavior Analysis, 34,* 195–210.

McDonough, M., Hillery, J., & Kennedy, N. (2000). Olanzapine for chronic, stereotypic self-injurious behavior: A pilot study in seven adults with intellectual disability. *Journal of Intellectual Disability Research, 44,* 677–684.

McGonigle, J. J., Rojahn, J., Dixon, J., & Strain, P. S. (1987). Multiple treatment interference in the alternating treatments design as a function of the intercomponent interval length. *Journal of Applied Behavior Analysis, 20,* 171–178.

Mulick, J. A., Barbour, R., Schroeder, S. R., & Rojahn, J. (1980). Overcorrection of pica in two profoundly retarded adults: Analysis of setting effects, stimulus and response generalization. *Applied Research in Mental Retardation, 1,* 241–252.

Mulick, J. A., Hoyt, P., Rojahn, J., & Schroeder, S. R. (1978). Reduction of a "nervous habit" in a profoundly retarded youth by increasing toy play. *Journal of Behavior Therapy and Experimental Psychiatry, 9,* 381–385.

Newell, K. M., & Bodfish, J. W. (2002). Temporal and force dynamics of self-injury. In S. R. Schroeder, M. L. Oster-Granite, & T. Thompson (Eds.), *Self-injurious behavior: Gene-brain-behavior relationship* (pp. 235–247). Washington, DC: American Psychological Association.

Newell, K. M., Sprague, R. L., Pain, M. T., Deutsch, K. M., & Meinhold, P. (1999). Dynamics of self-injurious behavior. *American Journal on Mental Retardation, 104,* 11–21.

Northup, J., Wacker, D., Sasso, G., Steege, M., Cigrand, K., Cook, J., & DeRaad, A. (1991). A brief functional analysis of aggressive and alternative behavior in an outpatient clinic setting. *Journal of Applied Behavior Analysis, 24,* 509–522.

Nottestad, J. A., & Linkaer, O. M. (2002). Predictors for attacks on people after deinstitutionalization. *Journal of Intellectual Disability Research, 46,* 493–502.

Oliver, C., McClintock, K., Hall, S., Smith, M., Dagnan, D., & Stenfert-Kroese, B. (2003). Assessing the severity of challenging behaviour: Psychometric properties of the Challenging Behavior Interview. *Journal of Applied Research in Intellectual Disabilities, 16,* 53–61.

O'Neill, R. E., Horner, R. H., Albin, R. W., Sprague, J. R., Storey, K., & Newton, J. S. (1997). *Functional assessment and program development for problem behavior: A practical handbook.* New York, NY: Brooks / Cole.

O'Reilly, M. F. (1996). Assessment and treatment of episodic self-injury: A case study. *Research in Developmental Disabilities, 17,* 349–361.

O'Reilly, M. F. (1997). Functional analysis of episodic self-injury correlated with recurrent otitis media. *Journal of Applied Behavior Analysis, 30,* 165–167.

O'Reilly, M., & Lancioni, G. (2000). Response covariation of escape-maintained aberrant behavior correlated with sleep deprivation. *Research in Developmental Disabilities, 21,* 125–136.

Paclawskyj, T. R., Matson, J. L., & Bamburg, J. W. (1997). A comparison of the Diagnostic Assessment for the Severely Handicapped-II (DASH-II) and the Aberrant Behavior Checklist (ABC). *Research in Developmental Disabilities, 18,* 289–298.

Paclawskyj, T. R., Matson, J. L., Rush, K. S., Smalls, Y., & Vollmer, T. R. (2000). Questions About Behavioral Function (QABF): A behavioral checklist for functional assessment of aberrant behavior. *Research in Developmental Disabilities, 21,* 223–230.

Paclawskyj, T. R., Matson, J. L., Rush, K. S., Smalls, Y., & Vollmer, T. R. (2001). Assessment of the convergent validity of the Questions About Behavioral Function scale with analogue functional analysis and the Motivation Assessment Scale. *Journal of Intellectual Disability Research, 45*(6), 484–494.

Pelios, L., Morren, J., Tesch, D., & Axelrod, S. (1999). The impact of functional analysis methodology on treatment choice for self-injurious behavior and aggressive behavior. *Journal of Applied Behavior Analysis, 32,* 185–195.

Reiss, S. (1988). *The Reiss screen for maladaptive behavior.* Worthington, OH: International Diagnostic Systems.

Ringdahl, J. E., Winborn, L. C., Andelman, M. S., & Kitsukawa, K. (2002). The effects of noncontingently available altyernative stimuli on functional analysis outcomes. *Journal of Applied Behavior Analysis, 35,* 407–410.

Rojahn, J., Aman, M. G., Matson, J. L., & Mayville, E. (2003). The Aberrant Behavior Checklist and the behavior problems inventory: Convergent and divergent validity. *Research in Developmental Disabilities, 24,* 391–404.

Rojahn, J., Borthwick-Duffy, S., & Jacobson, J. (1993). The association between psychiatric diagnoses and severe behavior problems in mental retardation. *Annals of Clinical Psychiatry, 5,* 163–170.

Rojahn, J., & Esbensen, A. (2002). Epidemiology of self-injurious behavior in mental retardation. In S. Schroeder, M. L. Oster-Granite, & T. Thompson (Eds.), *Self-injurious behavior: Gene-brain-behavior relationships* (pp. 41–77). Washington, D.C.: APA Books.

Rojahn, J., Matson, J. L., Lott, D., Esbensen, A. J., & Smalls, Y. (2001). The behavior problem inventory: An instrument for the assessment of self-injury, stereotyped behavior and aggression/destruction in individuals with developmental disabilities. *Journal of Autism and Developmental Disorders, 31,* 577–588.

Rojahn, J., Mulick, J. A., McCoy, D., & Schroeder, S. R. (1978). Setting effects and the modification of head-banging and self-restraint in two profoundly retarded adults. *Behavioural Analysis and Modification, 2,* 185–196.

Rojahn, J., & Schroeder, S. R. (1991). Behavioral assessment. In J. L. Matson & J. A. Mulick (Eds.), *Handbook of mental retardation* (pp. 240–259) (2nd ed.). New York: Pergamon.

Roscoe, E. M., Iwata, B. A., & Goh, H. L. (1998). A comparison of noncontingent reinforcement and sensory extinction as treatments for self-injurious behavior. *Journal of Applied Behavior Analysis, 31,* 635–646.

Schroeder, S. R., & Gualtieri, C. T. (1985). Behavioral interactions induced by chronic neuroleptic therapy with persons with mental retardation. *Psychopharmacology Bulletin., 21,* 310–315.

Schroeder, S. R., Mulick, J. A., & Rojahn, J. (1980). The definition, taxonomy, epidemiology, and ecology of self-injurious behavior. *Journal of Autism and Developmental Disorders, 10,* 417–432.

Schroeder, S. R., Oster-Granite, M. L., & Thompson, T. (Eds.) (2002). *Self-injurious behavior: Gene-brain-behavior relationships.*Washington, DC : American Psychological Association Books.

Schroeder, S. R., Rojahn, J., & Mulick, J. A. (1978). Ecobehavioral organization of developmental day care for the chronically self-injurious. *Journal of Pediatric Psychology, 3,* 81–88.

Schroeder, S. R., Rojahn, J., & Reese, R. M. (1997). Reliability and validity of instruments for assessing psychotropic medication effects on self-injurious behavior in mental retardation. *Journal of Autism and Developmental Disorders, 27,* 89–102.

Sevin, J. A., Matson, J. L., Williams, D., & Kirkpatrick-Sanchez, S. (1995). Reliability of emotional problems with the diagnostic assessment for the severely handicapped (DASH). *British Journal of Clinical Psychology, 94,* 33–34.

Shogren, K. A., & Rojahn, J. (2003). Convergent reliability and validity of the Questions About Behavioral Function and the Motivational Assessment Scale: A replication study. *Journal of Developmental and Physical Disabilities, 15,* 367–375.

Shore, B. A., Iwata, B. A., DeLeon, I. G., Kahng, S., & Smith, R. G. (1997). An analysis of reinforcer substitutability using object manipulation and self-injury as competing responses. *Journal of Applied Behavior Analysis, 30,* 21–41.

Sigafoos, J., Kerr, M., & Roberts, D. (1994). Interrater reliability of the Motivation Assessment Scale: Failure to replicate with aggressive behavior. *Research in Developmental Disabilities, 15,* 333–342.

Smith, R. G., & Churchill, R. M. (2002). Identification of environmental determinants of behavior disorders through functional analysis of precursor behaviors. *Journal of Applied Behavior Analysis, 35,* 125–136.

Snyder, R., Turgay, A., Aman, M. G. M., Binder, C., Fisman, S., & The Risperidone Conduct Study Group (2002). Effects of risperidone on conduct and disruptive disorders in children with subaverage IQ's. *Journal of the American Academy of Child and Adolescent Psychiatry, 41,* 1026–1036.

Sprague, R. L., & Newell, K. M. (1996). *Stereotyped movements: Brain and behavior relationships.* Washington, DC: American Psychological Association.

Sturmey, P. (1994). Assessing the functions of aberrant behaviors: A review of psychometric instruments. *Journal of Autism and Developmental Disabilities, 24*(3), 293–304.

Sturmey, P., Fink, C., & Sevin, J. (1993). The Behavior Problems Inventory: A replication and extension of its psychometric properties. *Journal of Developmental and Physical Disabilities, 5,* 327–336.

Sturmey, P., Sevin, J., & Williams, D. E. (1995). The Behavior Problems Inventory: A further replication of its factor structure. *Journal of Intellectual Disability Research, 39,* 353–356.

Symons, F. J., & Thompson, T. (1997). Self-injurious behavior and body site preference. *Journal of Intellectual Disability Research, 41,* 456–468.

Tarbox, J., Wallace, M. D., Tarbox, R. S. F., Landaburu, H. J., & Williams, L. (2004). Functional analysis and treatment of low rate problem behavior in individuals with developmental disabilities. *Behavioral Interventions, 19,* 187–204.

Tassé, M. J., Aman, M. G., Hammer, D., & Rojahn, J. (1996). The Nisonger Child Behavior Rating Form: Age and gender effects and norms. *Research in Developmental Disabilities, 17,* 59–75.

Tassé, M. J., & Lecavalier, L. (2000). Comparing parent and teacher ratings of social competence and problem behavior. *American Journal on Mental Retardation, 105,* 252–259.

Tate, B. G., & Baroff, G. S. (1966). Aversive control of self-injurious behavior in a psychotic boy. *Behavior Research and Therapy, 4,* 281–287.

Thompson, T., & Caruso, M. (2002). Self-injurious behavior: Knowing what we're looking for. In S. R. Schroeder, M. L. Oster-Granite, & T. Thompson (Eds.), *Self-injurious behavior: Gene-brain-behavior relationships* (pp. 3–21). Washington, DC: American Psychological Association.

Thompson, T., Felce, D., & Symons, F. J. (2000). *Behavioral observation*. Baltimore: Brookes.

Touchette, P. E., MacDonald, R. F., & Langer, S. N. (1985). A scatter plot for identifying stimulus control of problem behavior. *Journal of Applied Behavior Analysis, 18,* 343–351.

Wallace, M. D., & Iwata, B. A. (1999). Effects of session duration on functional analysis outcome. *Journal of Applied Behavior Analysis, 32,* 175–183.

Wanless, L. K., & Jahoda, A. U. (2002). Responses of staff towards people with mild to moderate intellectual disability who behave aggressively: A cognitive emotional analysis. *Journal of Intellectual Disability Research, 46,* 507–516.

Wordsell, A. S., Iwata, B. A., Hanley, G. P., Thompson, R. H., & Kahng, S. W. (2000). Effects of continuous and intermittent reinforcement for problem behavior during functional communication training. *Journal of Applied Behavior Analysis, 33,* 167–179.

Zarcone, J. R., Iwata, B. A., Hughes, C. E., & Vollmer, T. R. (1993). Momentum versus extinction effects in the treatment of self-injurious escape behavior. *Journal of Applied Behavior Analysis, 26,* 135–136.

Zarcone, J. R., Iwata, B. A., Mazaleski, J. L., & Smith, R. G. (1994). Momentum and extinction effects on self-injurious behavior and noncompliance. *Journal of Applied Behavior analysis, 27,* 649–658.

Zarcone, J. R., Rodgers, T. A., Iwata, B. A., Rourke, D. A., & Dorsey, M. F. (1991). Reliability analysis of the Motivation Assessment Scale: A failure to replicate. *Research in Developmental Disabilities, 12,* 349–360.

Social Skills

JONATHAN WILKINS AND JOHNNY L. MATSON

DEPARTMENT OF PSYCHOLOGY, LOUISIANA STATE UNIVERSITY
BATON ROUGE, LOUISIANA

I. SOCIAL SKILLS

The importance of social norms, the ability to adapt to the environment, and social skills have been discussed within the field of intellectual disability (ID) since the beginning of the twentieth century (Givens, 1978; Lambert, Wilcox, & Gleason, 1974). Treatment of social skill deficits and excesses has helped drive the development of both definitions and specific assessment techniques in the fields of mental health and education (Matson & Wilkins, 2007). However, it was only 30 years ago that the American Association on Mental Retardation (AAMR) issued a directive requiring deficits in adaptive behavior to be a core requirement in the definition of ID (Grossman, 1973). Level of social skill is a more specific component of adaptive functioning, making it an important part of the diagnostic criteria for ID (AAMR, 1992; APA, 1994).

One of the earliest studies specifically looking at social skills was a paper by McFall and Marston (1970), which dealt with helping shy male college students develop "appropriate assertiveness" as a means of getting dates. The strategies described in this study were later modified and applied to clinical populations, specifically adults with schizophrenia and major depression (Hersen & Bellack, 1976a). Such applications were soon extended to persons with intellectual disabilities (Matson & Senatore, 1981; Matson, Kazdin, & Esveldt-Dawson, 1980) and those with visual impairments (Matson, Heinze, Helsel, Kapperman, & Rotatori, 1986; Van Hasselt, Hersen, & Kazdin, 1985).

It is well known then, that individuals with ID exhibit more social skill deficits than the general population. Social skill deficits in such persons can be the result of a lack of opportunities, knowledge, practice, feedback, and/or reinforcement, as well as other problems (Elliott & Gresham, 1993).

INTERNATIONAL REVIEW OF RESEARCH IN MENTAL RETARDATION, Vol. 34
0074-7750/07 $35.00

DOI: 10.1016/S0074-7750(07)34010-X

Inappropriate social behaviors displayed by persons with ID are often characterized as either social deficits (e.g., failure to make eye contact when interacting with others) or social excesses (e.g., constantly seeking reassurance from a caregiver; Kuhn, Matson, Mayville, & Matson, 2001). The social skill deficits seen with this population become further exacerbated by limitations in the ability to communicate. Many people with severe ID are nonverbal or have problems with speech and hearing. These deficiencies are also associated with increases in challenging behaviors.

Because it is generally conceded that changes in the environment make individuals with ID more vulnerable to a wide range of disorders, social skills are of particular importance in providing such persons with the tools necessary to cope with the unpredictable flux of daily life (Parkes, 1975). To better prepare persons with ID for independent living, an increase in adaptive and social functioning must be achieved (Matson, Carlisle, & Bamburg, 1998). Although intelligence level cannot usually be increased, levels of adaptive functioning and social skills can be improved through social skills training (Hazinski & Matson, 1985). Another means of achieving increased independence is to decrease maladaptive behaviors and psychiatric symptomology, which can also be achieved through increases in social and adaptive behaviors (Helsel & Matson, 1988; Matson & Barrett, 1993). Therefore, assessment of social skills is of utmost importance with this population.

II. DEFINING SOCIAL SKILLS

Because social skills constitute such a large and heterogeneous area of study, there do not appear to be any agreed-on definitions that apply to all interpersonal situations. Some early definitions by Argyris (1965, 1968, 1969) describe social skills in terms of behaviors that enhance a person's contribution to the larger network of which he or she is a part. Hersen and Bellack (1977) stress the importance of an individual having the ability to express both positive and negative feelings in interpersonal situations without losing social reinforcement. Similarly, social skills can be seen as the ability to behave in ways that elicit positive and negative reinforcement as well as the ability to refrain from behaving in ways that elicit extinction or punishment (Libet & Lewinsohn, 1973). Hops (1983) views social skills as specific, identifiable skills that result in socially competent behavior.

As a construct, social skills generally refer to behaviors that enable an individual to interact effectively with other people and avoid socially unacceptable behavior (Gresham & Elliott, 1984). Social skills not only enable an individual to adjust and respond to environmental cues but can also assist with coping in stress-inducing situations and avoiding interpersonal conflict

(Matson & Swiezy, 1994). Such skills also enable the person to obtain social interactions and relationships that are necessary for healthy emotional functioning and psychological adjustment (Guralnick, 1986). Still, no general consensus has been reached on a blanketing definition for social skills. Other have described social behaviors in the context of orientation and communication (Stella, Mundy, & Tuchman, 1999); framed social skills in terms of interactions, play, and communication (Wing, Leekam, Libby, Gould, & Larcombe, 2002); and provided discrete operational definitions such as asking for objects, getting the attention of another person, and waiting for his or her turn (Laushey & Heflin, 2000).

Although many of these definitions were not formulated specifically with regards to individuals with ID, their common theme should apply to all populations. Christoff and Kelly (1983) define social skillfulness functionally, in terms of effectiveness. In any situation, a response can be termed skillful if it, in turn, elicits a desired response from the environment. Determining the effectiveness of a particular skill varies across different situations and contexts. However, effective social behavior always involves the coordination of appropriate verbal and nonverbal responses.

Since different behavioral responses may be necessary components of skillful behavior in different situations, the remainder of this section will be devoted to the discussion of several social skills that can be seen as especially relevant to individuals with ID. Specific skills to be discussed include: self-care skills, conversational skills, assertiveness skills, social problem-solving skills, employment-related skills, and heterosocial skills. The focus in discussing such skills will be on behavioral rather than traditional assessment procedures since behavioral procedures have more heuristic value with this population in that they contribute directly to the development of viable treatment programs (Hersen & Bellack, 1976b).

III. SELF-CARE SKILLS

Although social skills training and assessment frequently focus on verbal and cognitive skills for individuals without ID, those with ID often require attention to more basic elements of physical appearance, such as grooming, dressing, and other self-care skills, before receiving training in the more complex skills necessary for social interaction (Christoff & Kelly, 1983). First impressions have the tendency to affect future interactions and are ultimately important for social acceptance. A job interview is one situation where making a good first impression can be especially crucial. For institutionalized persons with ID, achieving independence in these skills is oftentimes the first step toward gaining access to less restrictive environments and eventually community placement (Konarski & Diorio, 1985).

Obviously, it is important to first establish the baseline capabilities of the person being assessed and trained. In severe and profoundly disabled individuals, the exact behaviors the person is capable of emitting should be determined. Generating a list of such behaviors can easily be facilitated with the utilization of one of the rating scales described later in this chapter such as the Matson Evaluation of Social Skills for Individuals with Severe Retardation (MESSIER) or Vineland. Is the individual able to take care of him/herself (i.e., dress, bathe, eat independently)? What behaviors does the person require assistance to complete? Task analyses of such behaviors have been delineated elsewhere (Matson, DiLorenzo, & Esveldt-Dawson, 1981; Martin, Kehoe, Bird, Jansen, & Darbyshire, 1971; Matson et al., 1980; Treffrey, Martin, Samuels, & Watson, 1970). The steps outlined can then be used as a checklist to determine the individual's exact proficiency in completing the behavior. Caretakers can also be interviewed if time is limited.

It should never be assumed that the ability to perform appropriate self-care skills is not already contained in an individual's repertoire simply because the behaviors are not occurring spontaneously (Kazdin et al., 1981). An individual with ID may not be evincing a certain behavior simply because he or she has never been reinforced for it and/or because he or she has been reinforced for evincing other incompatible behaviors. Someone may not be bathing, grooming, or dressing properly simply because others have always done it for him or her—not because the person is incapable of performing the behavior. The setting where the person lives must also be considered. For example, expectations of what skills a person can perform independently may vary across settings, and as a result, acquisition of independence in these areas is more likely to occur in group homes than in an institution (Felce, de Kock, Thomas, & Saxby, 1986). Assessment must take these notions into account so that it can be determined whether the skills actually need to be trained, if reinforcers for incompatible behaviors (i.e., helplessness) should be withdrawn, or both.

IV. CONVERSATIONAL SKILLS

Conversational skills simply refer to the ability to initiate and maintain informal conversations with others (Kelly, 1982). Such skills are essential for facilitating acceptance in short-term interactions and provide the basic components necessary for establishing longer-term relationships such as employment, friendships, and making dates. Individuals with ID have long been described as having deficits in effective communication skills

(Longhurst, 1974; McClure, 1968; Rychtarik & Bornstein, 1979), which can result in negative perceptions from those in the community and even isolation and segregation (Sipperstein & Gottlieb, 1977; Wildman, Wildman, & Kelly, 1986). Appropriate conversation skills are particularly limited in individuals with autism spectrum disorders (ASD) of which deficits in language is one of the primary diagnostic criteria (APA, 1994). Such individuals have particular difficulties in both the production (Baltaxe, 1977; Baltaxe & D'Angiola, 1992; Stone & Caro-Martinez, 1990; Tager-Flusberg & Anderson, 1991) and comprehension of pragmatic language (Hewitt, 1998; Paul & Cohen, 1985). In addition, institutionalized or formerly institutionalized persons who lack conversation skills are sometimes perceived as peculiar, dull, and even threatening (Bellack & Hersen, 1978; Kelly, 1982; Kelly, Urey, & Patterson, 1980; Kelly, Wildman, Urey, & Thurman, 1979; Urey, Laughlin, & Kelly, 1979). Having the ability to converse in a cooperative manner can therefore serve to facilitate social acceptance of persons with ID (Chennault, 1967; Rucker & Vincenzo, 1970).

As is the case with any of the social skills discussed in this chapter, adequate assessment of conversational skills should address not only the environment in which the individual normally functions but also any other environments to which the person might reasonably aspire (Christoff & Kelly, 1983). Persons with ID who reside in institutional settings may be able to adequately communicate their wants and needs in that environment. However, the communication strategies employed here may not be effective outside of the institution. Such people oftentimes have the benefit of direct care staff who have known them for many years. Staff members in these cases can understand an individual with ID's unique methods of communication that someone outside of the institution may not. Certain gestures or vocalizations that an individual utilizes in the institution would most likely not achieve the same ends (i.e., fulfillment of needs/wants) if employed while in the community. Lack of formal communication strategies may ultimately hinder an individual with ID's integration into a community placement. Conversational skills should generally be assessed with respect to how closely they approximate that of same age persons without intellectual impairment. In the case of nonverbal individuals, formal communications strategies, such as sign language or the use of a picture board, should be trained. General questions to be considered during assessment may include: What communication strategies does the individual utilize to express wants and desires? Are these strategies effective and appropriate? How does he or she interact with others and what play/leisure skills does he or she possess?

Formal assessment of these skills usually focuses on evaluating the presence (or absence) of the behavioral components contained within the individual with ID's conversational repertoire. Different skills reported in the literature as essential components of appropriate conversational behavior include: conversational questions, self-disclosing statements, reinforcing or acknowledging comments, speech duration and latency, eye contact, appropriate smiling, appropriate affect, voice intonation, vocal fluency, posture, gesturing, and appropriate conversational content (Bradlyn et al., 1983; Kelly, 1982; Kelly, Furman, Phillips, Hathorn, & Wilson, 1979; Kelly, Wildman, et al., 1979; Minkin et al., 1976; Stalonas & Johnson, 1979; Urey et al., 1979; Wildman et al., 1986). The first step therefore in an assessment of conversational skills would be operationally defining the different components in terms that apply to the individual being assessed.

The behavioral assessment of conversational skills has typically consisted of an audio- or videotaped structured interaction with a confederate or therapist. This interaction is later rated for the frequencies of some or all of the specific behaviors listed above. Examples of these interactions are contained as a series of scenes in such instruments as the Interpersonal Behavior Role-Playing Test (Goldsmith & McFall, 1975) or the revised Behavioral Assertiveness Test (BAT-R; Eisler, Hersen, Miller, & Blanchard, 1975). However, it has been demonstrated that the behavior elicited in structured role-play scenarios does not necessarily correspond to behavior in the natural environment (Bellack, Hersen, & Lamparski, 1979; Bellack, Hersen, & Turner, 1978, 1979; Christoff & Edelstein, 1981). A more natural, semistructured interaction would seem intuitively to be a better gauge of the client's general conversational abilities than a standard role-play assessment. For example, a less-structured alternative would be to simply ask the individual being assessed to interact with another person (a peer with ID or a confederate without ID) and to "get to know each other better" (Bradlyn et al., 1983; Kelly, 1982; Kelly, Wildman, & Berler, 1980; Urey et al., 1979; Wildman et al., 1986). Wildman et al. (1986) also assessed social validity by recruiting volunteers from the community to rate the participants' conversational abilities. Volunteers listened to recorded conversations and rated each subject on five questions based on a 7-point Likert-type scale. Examples of the questions asked included: "How much would you like to meet this person?" and "How well do you think this person would fit into the average apartment complex, church, or other social community?"

During the initial assessments, it is critical to attend to all skill components in order to get a complete picture of the individual's potential deficits and excesses as well as those areas that do not require further training. In later assessments then, the focus should be on the specific behaviors that had been observed earlier to be deficient or excessive and targeted as areas needing training. It should be noted that many researchers have demonstrated improved conversational skills in persons with ID of all age-groups following training (Bornstein et al., 1980; Bradlyn et al., 1983; Gibson et al., 1976;

Kelly, Furman et al., 1979; Kelly, Wildman et al., 1980; Longhurst, 1972; McClure, 1968; Nelson, Gibson, & Cutting, 1973; Rychtarik & Bornstein, 1979; Wildman et al., 1986). In each of these studies, training was predicated on an objective assessment of baseline skill levels of component behaviors. A more detailed description of the most commonly referenced conversational components detailed in these studies follows.

A. Conversational Questions

Conversational questions are any questions asked of the conversational partner and basically function to elicit information from that person. Asking questions during a conversation not only allows for more extended interactions but lets the conversational partner know that the other person is interested in what he or she has to say. Effective communication requires both the production and response to conversational questions. Assessment of this component involves simply counting the number of questions asked by the client over the course of the assessment interaction or counting the number of times the client provides responses to conversational questions made by the partner. Individuals with ASD have particular difficulty in responding to conversational questions that are either lengthy and/or requiring the person to draw inferences in order to respond (Hewitt, 1998). This should be taken into consideration when assessing the conversational skills of such individuals.

B. Self-Disclosing Statements

Self-disclosing statements are expressions that convey appropriate information about oneself to the conversational partner. Describing one's thoughts, feelings, likes, hobbies, or background during conversation allows the partner to get to know the speaker better and possibly establish common interests or ideas that may foster more lasting interpersonal relationships (Kelly, Furman et al., 1979; Urey et al., 1979). Individuals with ID often have difficulty discerning when self-disclosure is appropriate as well as what information is appropriate to disclose. During assessment these statements can be rated in terms of frequency and content.

C. Reinforcing or Acknowledging Comments

Reinforcing or acknowledging comments are statements that serve to keep the partner talking by providing reinforcement for whatever he or she is saying. These also include direct compliments made to the partner. Some examples include one-word acknowledgments like "Yeah" or "Right!," as well as more extended comments such as "I see what you're saying,"

"That must have been a good experience for you," or "I've really enjoyed talking with you." Such reinforcing or acknowledging statements, by definition, facilitate more extended interaction by keeping the conversational partner talking (Bradlyn et al., 1983). Once again, a typical assessment of these comments would involve rating the frequency of occurrence.

D. Speech Duration and Latency

Speech duration and latency are both time-based measures that have been associated with conversational competence. Specifically, a longer duration of total speaking time and a shorter latency from the time the conversational partner stops speaking to the time the client begins to talk have generally been deemed more skillful (Christoff & Kelly, 1983). Both excesses and/or deficiencies in these areas can be targeted for training. Speech duration is typically measured by using a stopwatch to time the periods the client is speaking during the assessment interaction. If the individual frequently makes long pauses during speech, timing can be terminated until he or she begins speaking again (Hersen, Bellack, & Turner, 1978). The duration of each individual verbalization or the cumulative length the client was speaking over the entire conversation can be reported. Conversely, speech latency is typically measured by activating the stopwatch when the partner stops speaking and then stopping it when the client begins to talk. These numbers are then reported as a mean for all latencies during the entire conversation.

E. Eye Contact

Eye contact can simply be defined as the amount of time the client looks directly at the partner's face during the interaction. It can be reported as total duration for the entire conversation as measured cumulatively with a stopwatch, as a percentage of the total conversation time, as separate percentages for both the times when the client is speaking and times when the partner is talking, on an occurrence or nonoccurrence basis, or as a subjective rating of appropriateness (Christoff & Kelly, 1983). It can also be reported as a ratio of the total duration of eye contact to the total duration of speech (Hersen et al., 1978).

F. Affect and Tone

Appropriate affect is the extent to which a person's nonverbal behaviors, tone of voice, and posture are congruent with the topic of conversation and present situation. A client's affect can be rated on a 7-point Likert-type scale with a score of 1 representing an extremely inappropriate affect and a score of 7 representing an extremely appropriate affect. Affect during a conversation can also be rated on a scale anchored with negative one representing negative affect, zero representing neutral affect, and positive one representing positive affect (Christoff & Kelly, 1983). Appropriate intonation can be rated in terms of emotionality on a 5-point scale with a score of one representing a very flat, unemotional tone of voice and a score of 5 representing a full lively intonation (Hersen et al., 1978).

G. Conversational Content

Individuals with ID appear to experience difficulty in selecting and talking about topics that would be of interest to those without ID. Such individuals often have restricted areas of interest and may not know when it is appropriate to switch to a different topic of conversation. While many studies have demonstrated successful training of persons with ID in the conversational components discussed above, relatively little attention seems to have been directed toward assessing and training appropriate conversational topics or content. This behavior represents an area requiring further study and would greatly facilitate the social acceptance of persons with ID who lack this skill.

V. ASSERTIVENESS SKILLS

The term assertiveness generally refers to a person's ability to express thoughts, feelings, beliefs, or opinions in an effective and comfortable manner. Assertiveness skills can be viewed as a specialized group of social skills that facilitate the attainment of specific objectives. Assertiveness oftentimes pertains to how an individual acts in anger-arousing situations (i.e., does the person behave and communicate assertively as opposed to aggressively?; Nezu, Nezu, & Arean, 1991). It has also been suggested that the expression of appropriate assertive behavior is determined by situation rather than being a unitary trait (Eisler et al., 1975). Assessment of assertiveness skills, therefore, should occur across a variety of situations and persons. Components of assertive behavior to be assessed include voice intensity (loud vs soft), latency of response (impulsive vs appropriate), duration of response (focused vs lengthy), eye contact (focused vs unfocused), voice quality (angry vs assertive), body language (threatening vs appropriate), and listening ability (listening to the other person vs talking constantly; Nezu et al., 1991). Three different types of assertiveness will be discussed here: refusal, request, and commendatory. The attainment of successful interpersonal outcomes depends on the effective utilization of all three of these forms of assertion (Kelly, Frederiksen, Fitts, & Phillips, 1978).

The assessment of assertiveness usually occurs during role-play situations with the therapist or confederate. Assessment of children can also occur within the context of a game situation (e.g., a card game or ball game; McGee, Krantz, & McClannahan, 1984). The Role-Play Test (RPT) of anger-arousing situations is one formal measure that can be used in the assessment of assertiveness in those with ID (Benson, Rice, & Miranti, 1986). The RPT consists of five potentially anger-evoking situations (e.g., being teased, receiving criticism) that are acted out in a role-play with a confederate. Role-play scenarios are videotaped and raters independently code the client's responses to these situations along a 7-point scale of appropriateness (1 = very inappropriate; 7 = very appropriate). Percentage agreement between raters for the RPT has been found to range between 0.87 and 0.94.

Although mentioned in the section on conversational skills, the Revised Behavioral Assertiveness Test (BAT-R) is an instrument containing different role-play situations that specifically targets the expression of appropriate assertiveness (Eisler et al., 1975). The BAT-R contains 32 situations requiring both positive and negative assertion and interaction with partners of different sexes and varying familiarity. It is important that role-plays of assertive behavior include variability across these areas because as mentioned above an individual is likely to express different levels of assertiveness in different situations.

A. Refusal Assertiveness

Refusal or negative assertions involve refusing an inappropriate request or interfering statement made by another person. In these situations, the individual may also be required to request that the other person change or discontinue his or her behavior to ensure that it does not happen again. This type of assertiveness is labeled request assertiveness and described in more detail below. Situations requiring refusal assertiveness usually arise within the context of a disagreement or dispute with another person. The ability to utilize effective refusal assertions serves to maintain not only an individual's current level of reinforcement (when it might otherwise be diminished) but also prevents the loss of self-esteem (Kelly et al., 1978). Refusal assertiveness has received a large amount of attention in the social skills training literature (Kelly, 1982). This type of assertiveness may be of particular importance to individuals with ID who may be at a higher risk for being taken advantage of by peers without ID. Persons with mental illness are noted to be at an increased risk for being coerced into having unprotected sex

(Carey, Carey, Weinhardt, & Gordon, 1997; Kelly et al., 1998) and using illegal drugs (Rusch, Hall, & Griffin, 1986), and it would seem that these deficits in refusal assertiveness would be evident in those with ID as well. Whenever applicable, role-play assessment should target these situations.

In one investigation of refusal assertiveness, Zisfein and Rosen (1974) found that 25 institutionalized persons with ID all signed what was referred to as a "legal" document containing several blank spaces after being given no explanation as to why they were being requested to do so. Sixty-two percent of this sample also gave the experimenter a small amount of money when asked. These things occurred even though most of participants reported earlier that they did not sign things or give money away indiscriminately. Deficits in refusal assertiveness skills can be inferred from a client's self-reports of passivity, staff or family member's observations of nonassertive behavior, or indications that the client has previously been exploited by others (Christoff & Kelly, 1983). However, as described in the study mentioned above, self-reports of adequate refusal assertiveness skills may be inaccurate since clients who reported that they did not give away money or sign documents did do these things when confronted with the actual situations.

Assessment of refusal assertiveness skills usually involves the client participating in role-play scenarios where he or she is presented with an unreasonable request from the therapist or confederate. In addition to the components of assertiveness listed above, the individual's behavioral responses are rated in terms of compliance (i.e., did the person actually resist the inappropriate request) and requests (i.e., did the person actually show evidence that he or she wanted the partner's behavior to stop or change; Hersen et al., 1978). Skillful examples of refusal assertion include longer replies, a quick response, greater affect, less compliance, and making greater demands of the other person (Eisler, Miller, & Hersen, 1973). If the client does not provide appropriate responses in structured role-play situations, it can probably be assumed that training is needed on whatever components are observed to be deficient. It should not be assumed, however, that demonstrations of skillful behavior in these structured role-play scenarios are clear indications that the client will actually respond appropriately in real-life situations. Therefore, the individual should also be observed in the natural environment (e.g., a residential facility dayroom, a group home living room, a day-program classroom, or sheltered workshop) to see how the person actually handles conflict in these situations. If instances of ineffective assertion skills are observed, the components that are deficient or lacking should be identified so that they can be targeted for intervention. Another aspect of refusal assertiveness skills that should be assessed is whether an individual can discriminate situations where refusal is appropriate, such as when asked to sign something or give away possessions or money, and situations where refusal is inappropriate, such as when asked to perform a job-related task by one's employer (Christoff & Kelly, 1983). Requiring clients to role-play a variety of situations, some in which refusal assertiveness is appropriate and others in which it is not, can facilitate assessment of a client's ability to make these discriminations and elucidate any need for training in this area.

B. Request Assertiveness

Asking for help and making requests of others is a form of assertion that is oftentimes necessary in order to facilitate the fulfillment of one's needs or the attainment of one's goals. As mentioned earlier, such requests oftentimes occur in conjunction with assertions of refusal, in which the individual turns down someone's unreasonable behavior and asks that he or she does not act in such a manner in the future. A request can also exist by itself as a means to achieving a specific goal, such as asking another person for directions, what time it is, or for help in completing a particular task. Since helplessness, withdrawal from social interaction, and passivity have frequently been attributed to persons with ID, particularly those with a history of institutionalization (Bates, 1980; Bornstein et al., 1980; Brody & Stoneman, 1977; Geller, Wildman, Kelly, & Laughlin, 1980; Zisfein & Rosen, 1974), assessment and training of request assertionsare warranted with this population.

As has previously been discussed with respect to other skills, adequate assessment of request assertiveness should take into account whether the individual is actually capable of performing the targeted behaviors and if and when the client actually uses them in the natural environment. Assessment should also determine whether the individual possesses the ability to discriminate situations in which the behaviors would be appropriate and the persons to whom requests should be directed toward. Again, reports of skill deficits can be obtained from the client directly, from significant others or direct-care staff, or from direct observation of the client's behavior in the natural environment and/or structured role-play situations. Bates (1980) assessed the assertion skill of "asking for help" by giving participants money and instructing them to purchase a particular item that was hidden from view in a store by prior arrangement with the store management. However, orchestrating such scenarios in the natural environment may not always be feasible, and in these cases structured role-plays approximating such types of interactions may be the most realistic mode of assessment.

C. Commendatory Assertiveness

Commendatory or positive assertiveness simply refers to expressions of positive feelings, such as praise, appreciation, approval, encouragement, and admiration, toward another person that can be seen as facilitative of positive interpersonal relationships (Hersen et al., 1978; Kelly, 1982). The use of effective commendatory assertions can serve to increase the social reinforcement value of an individual with ID by making interactions with that person more reinforcing, which in turn increases the chances of the person receiving positive responses from others (Kelly et al., 1978). While deficits in commendatory assertiveness are certainly not limited to persons with ID, this population stands to benefit maximally from training in these skills. While it is normally the case that deficits in assertiveness skills are relatively situation-specific, persons with ID seem to exhibit deficiencies in these skills across a wide range of situations. The situations determined to be most problematic for the individual should be made priorities for training in future treatment planning.

Skillful commendatory assertions are composed of many of the same components as refusals and requests (e.g., eye contact, appropriate affect, speech loudness, and duration). The content of a commendatory statement, however, will differ in its specific inclusion of approval or praise (Geller et al., 1980; Kelly et al., 1978), in its inclusion of explicit statements conveying positive feelings resulting from the other person's positive behavior (Schinke, Gilchrist, Smith, & Wong, 1979), and in its inclusion of an offer to reciprocate a positive act to the other person sometime in the future (Geller et al., 1980; Kelly et al., 1978; Skillings, Hersen, Bellack, & Becker, 1978). Demonstrated deficits in any of these components will imply the need for training, either training in how to perform the behavior, instructions in situations for which it is appropriate, or both.

VI. SOCIAL PROBLEM-SOLVING SKILLS

Effective social behavior requires an individual to process information about the environment, make inferences regarding available courses of action and the consequences of each, and then use this information to decide on the best course of action (Trower, Bryant, & Argyle, 1978). Problem-solving in general can be defined as a cognitive-behavioral process that consists of generating a number of alternative responses that might be effective in dealing with a particular stressful or problematic situation (D'Zurilla & Goldfried, 1971; Nezu, Nezu, & Perri, 1989). In particular, individuals with ID have marked difficulties in coming up with alternative strategies for solving problems (Smith, 1986; Wehmeyer & Kelchner, 1994). This group also tends to rely most often on simple requests (e.g., "Can I?," "Please") in achieving interpersonal goals (Weiss & Weinstein, 1967). Individuals with ID usually persist in this approach even when it does not produce desired outcomes, whereas age-matched peers of normal intelligence are likely to switch to a different tactic when an initial request fails to provide the desired outcome (Chan, Smith, & Reid, 1977; Smith, 1986). Even though individuals with ID generally lack problem-solving skills and tend to exhibit avoidance behaviors and passivity when confronted with problematic situations, effective problem solving can be trained (Ross, 1969; Ross & Ross, 1973, 1978). Providing intellectually disabled persons with a repertoire of possible responses that can be utilized in dealing with problematic social situations will ultimately facilitate interpersonal competence.

Social problem-solving skills can be broken down into five problem-solving processes: (1) problem orientation (understanding that problems are a normal part of everyday life and can be handled effectively), (2) problem definition (correctly identifying the nature of the problem and setting realistic goals), (3) generation of alternative solutions (brainstorming a list of possible alternative solutions), (4) decision making (reviewing the consequences of each solution and selecting ones that are optimal given the specific problem), and (5) solution implementation (carrying out the solution and assessing the outcome to determine one's success in resolving the problem; D'Zurilla & Goldfried, 1971; Nezu et al., 1989). This model can be adapted for use with the intellectually disabled by presenting instructions in a concrete manner and modeling and practicing the problem-solving processes through videotaped role-play situations showing the person "thinking out loud" (Nezu et al., 1991). Since deficits in social problem-solving may result from the inability to perform any, all, or any combination of these steps, each step should be assessed. While problem-solving training will be useful to any client who is ineffective in handling a wide range of problematic situations, the training should ultimately focus on the specific difficulties and deficits exhibited by the client. In addition, it may be useful to assess whether the individual is able to identify antecedent stimuli that necessitate particular social responses and then select the appropriate response to use (Brody & Stoneman, 1977). Deficits in this area represent another potential target for training.

Formal methods for assessing social problem-solving skills are available. The Problem Solving Task (PST) is a behavioral measure designed specifically for those with ID (Nezu et al., 1991). The PST consists of five problematic interpersonal situations commonly encountered by individuals with ID (e.g., making new friends and conflict resolution with another person). These situations are read to the client, who is then required to respond verbally to four questions concerning means of resolving the problem (e.g., "What is the actual problem?," "Think of as many ideas to solve the problem as you can," "What are the positive and negative consequences of each idea?," and "Which idea do you think will solve the problem?"). Responses are rated on a 5-point scale (1 = low quality, 5 = high quality). Psychometric properties of the PST are good (0.83 for interrater and 0.79 for test–retest reliability). A total score can then be derived by summing the person's response to each of the four questions in each of the five situations. Measures such as this can be useful in assessing a client's abilities in different areas of social problem-solving. Before using such measures, however, one needs to consider whether the particular client being assessed can actually use these skills to solve the problems that arise in his or her own daily life.

VII. EMPLOYMENT-RELATED SKILLS

Some employment-related skills, such as job finding, job interviewing, and employer–employee relationship skills, are interpersonal in nature and therefore can be classified as social skills (Christoff & Kelly, 1983). Vocational training has historically been an important component of treatment programs for people with ID, but it was only relatively recently that treatment planning for persons with ID has included the training of employment-related interpersonal skills. Researchers have demonstrated that although persons with ID may be more than capable of performing the work expected of them in community employment settings, they often experience major problems adjusting to these types of work environments due to the interpersonal interactions required of them (Bullis & Foss, 1986; Foss & Bostwick, 1981; Greenspan & Shoultz, 1981). Appropriate social behavior may also contribute directly to successful job performance (Schalock & Harper, 1978). In addition, problems in getting along with supervisors and coworkers oftentimes interferes with adequate work functioning and leads to job termination (La Greca, Stone, & Bell, 1982). Therefore, it is important to include the training of job-finding, interview, and interpersonal skills in any treatment program aimed at increasing employment-related social skills. A discussion of each of these three main categories of employment-related skills follows.

A. Job-Finding Skills

Individuals with ID who possess adequate job performance skills, but who, for one reason or another, are unable to obtain gainful employment may be deficient in either job-finding or interviewing skills. In these cases, assessment of possible deficits in employment-related skills is most certainly warranted. Because it is been reported that up to two-thirds of job leads come from friends and relatives, individuals with ID may be at a disadvantage due to deficits in other interpersonal skills (Jones & Azrin, 1973). Component skills reported in the literature as particularly important to obtaining employment include: locating and using information about potential jobs, asking others to serve as references or write letters of recommendation, knowing the right people to ask for references and letters of recommendation, initiating telephone and personal contacts with potential employers, and completing job application forms (Azrin, Flores, & Kaplan, 1975; Christoff & Kelly, 1983; Clark, Boyd, & Macrae, 1975; Jones & Azrin, 1973; Perrin, 1977). Formal assessment of these skills can be conducted via structured role-play scenarios as well as by listening to the client actually make such a request of a friend, relative, or former employer on the telephone. The client can also be assessed making telephone calls to potential employers and any noted skill deficits can be targeted for training.

B. Interviewing Skills

A good interview can oftentimes be the deciding factor in whether someone gets a job. The assessment of job interview skills typically involves conducting a role-play interview with the client and noting the presence, frequency, and/or appropriateness of component skills (Christoff & Kelly, 1983). Component behaviors of job interview skills are similar to those described in the previous discussions of conversational and assertiveness skills and include: eye contact; appropriate affect; and loudness, clarity, and fluency of speech (Hollandsworth, Dressel, & Stevens, 1977; Hollandsworth, Glazeski, & Dressel, 1978; Pinto, 1979). Additional skills more specific to the job interview setting include: providing concise, direct answers to an interviewer's questions (Barbee & Keil, 1973; Hollandsworth et al., 1978); job-relevant questions asked by the client to the interviewer (Barbee & Keil, 1973; Hollandsworth et al., 1978; Kelly, Laughlin, Claiborne, & Patterson, 1979); positive self-statements regarding past education, training, or work experience (Barbee & Keil, 1973; Furman, Geller, Simon, & Kelly, 1979; Kelly et al., 1979); positive self-statements regarding interests, hobbies, or activities (Kelly et al., 1980); and expressions of enthusiasm and interest in the prospective position (Furman et al., 1979; Kelly et al., 1980).

A typical job interview role-play scenario involves a therapist acting as a potential employer and asking the individual a series of predetermined questions similar to those that the person would be likely to encounter in an actual interview for a job he or she might apply. The client should be prepared to respond to queries regarding past work experience, including why the client may have left his or her last job or if he or she was fired. Skillful responses should not disclose any information that may potentially hurt a person's chance of getting hired, however, if such questions are posed, the best response seems to be an honest summary of the past problems followed by an elaboration of reasons why the client is now able to work, is responsible, and would be an asset to the employer (Kelly, 1982). Some researchers have gone so far as to assess a client's job interviewing skills in probe interviews with potential employers at the actual job site (Hall, Sheldon-Wildgen, & Sherman, 1980; Kelly et al., 1980). In both of these studies, the interviewing employers were asked by the researchers to conduct the interviews as they would for any job interview. Presumably, client behaviors observed in these kinds of assessments will closely approximate the person's actual *in vivo* behavior. As with all targeted social skills, the more closely the assessment situation approximates the real-life situations in which the client will be required to perform, the more likely it is that client performance during assessment will reflect his or her behavior in the natural environment. Assessment situations should, therefore, always be structured with this in mind.

C. Employment-Related Interpersonal Skills

On the other hand, if a client has demonstrated ability to obtain employment but has a history of problematic relations with supervisors or coworkers, or has previously been fired, his or her skills in getting along with others should also be assessed. The skills required to successfully interact with others in the workplace are a specialized subset of the relationship building, interpersonal, and conversational skills that have been previously discussed. Role-plays to approximate job site interactions can be constructed to represent the situations the client has previously had difficulty with and could include scenarios involving commendatory assertiveness toward coworkers and supervisors, refusals of unreasonable requests, requesting assistance or time-off, handling criticism, and the general ability to carry on appropriate conversations with others in the job setting (Christoff & Kelly, 1983).

Standardized measures of interpersonal competence in vocational settings are also available. The Test of Interpersonal Competence for Employment (TICE) is a measure designed to specifically assess the knowledge of interpersonal skills in the employment setting of individuals with mild ID (Bullis & Foss, 1986). This instrument contains questions pertaining to potentially problematic interpersonal situations relating to two domains (supervisor and coworker). Questions are presented in a knowledge-based three-option multiple choice format that can be administered orally individually or to small groups. For example, a typical question on the TICE would be: "If another worker refuses to share a tool with you, you should: (1) ask another worker to help get the tool, (2) ask why he will not share, (3) take the tool from the worker." Content of questions on the TICE was derived by asking both individuals with ID and employers of problematic interpersonal situations commonly encountered in the workplace. Test–retest data for the TICE is good with a coefficient of 0.78 for the supervisor subtest and a coefficient of 0.84 for the coworker subtest.

The Vocational Problem Behavior Inventory (VPBI) is a checklist consisting of 48 interpersonal problem behaviors commonly exhibited by individuals with ID in vocational settings (La Greca et al., 1982). Raters asses the frequency of each behavior on a 4-point scale (1 = never, 2 = sometimes, 3 = frequently, 4 = always) and seriousness of each behavior on a 5-point scale (1 = not at all serious, 5 = very serious). The 48 problem behaviors are categorized into six domains: (1) inappropriate interpersonal behavior (with coworkers and supervisors, both verbal and nonverbal, e.g. panhandling, distracting coworkers by clowning around); (2) aggressive interpersonal behaviors (with coworkers and supervisors, both physical and verbal, e.g., hitting or pushing coworkers, using nasty language to coworkers); (3) inappropriate reaction to frustration or anger (both aggressive and nonaggressive, e.g., throwing things when angry, crying when upset or frustrated); (4) attention/memory problems (e.g., daydreaming); (5) inappropriate personal habits, mannerisms (e.g., making noises while working); and (6) inappropriate work habits (e.g., working slowly). The psychometric properties of the VPBI are acceptable in terms of reliability (interrater and test–retest) and validity (convergent and divergent). Scores on the VPBI are also predictive of actual job performance, as assessed by number of days worked. The VPBI can be used to obtain information necessary for creating employment-related interpersonal skills training programs with the ultimate goal of preparing individuals with ID for community employment.

The Vocational Assessment and Curriculum Guide (VACG) is a behavior rating scale that contains eight domains, some of which tap into employment-related social behavior (e.g., communication, social skills, self-help skills; Menchetti & Rusch, 1988). Any noted deficits on the VACG can then be targeted for further training. The VACG has good psychometric properties with a mean internal coefficiency α of 0.76 across the eight domains and a mean test–retest coefficient of 0.79. Domain scores on the VACG have also been shown to differentiate between individuals in different vocational programs and with different employment histories.

VIII. HETEROSOCIAL SKILLS

Heterosocial skills consist of the behaviors involved in initiating and maintaining conversations with persons of the opposite sex as well as affectionate motor behavior such as holding hands or touching (Christoff & Kelly, 1983). Specific examples of heterosocial skills such as date initiation are specialized examples of conversational skills directed at reaching a specific goal. The goal in this case then, is establishing an intimate sexual and/or social relationship with another person. To achieve this goal, an individual must meet prospective dates, converse with them, and arrange for further social contacts. Date initiation is a skill that occurs within the context of heterosocial conversation and refers specifically to the behavior of asking another person to accompany the requester in some prearranged social activity.

Individuals with ID have been recognized as deficient in dating and other heterosocial skills. These problems in heterosocial interactions have been attributed, in part, to institutional living as well as difficulties in community adjustment, emotional adjustment, appropriate expression of sexuality, and vulnerability to sexual abuse (Smith, Valenti-Hein, & Heller, 1985; Zisfein & Rosen, 1974). In the not-too-distant past, nearly all intellectually disabled persons resided in institutional settings and were expected to remain in these settings for life. Institutional settings often limit the opportunities of its residents to observe and engage in age-appropriate date initiation, dating, and/or other heterosocial skills. The expectations that these residents would remain in the same setting indefinitely may have led to an implicit denial that these skills are necessary for individuals with ID (Christoff & Kelly, 1983). However, the continuing emphasis on deinstitutionalization for persons with ID has provided these individuals with increased opportunities to observe the heterosocial behavior of others in the community which may lead them to express interest in engaging in such behaviors themselves. All people have sexual desires and needs, and persons with ID are no exception. We believe that they should be provided with the training necessary to fulfill these needs, including birth control counseling, as well as heterosocial training. These issues should be dealt with when the individual expresses an interest or it becomes apparent to someone in the environment that these issues should be addressed, and as with all social skills, heterosocial behavior should be assessed with respect to the degree it approximates that of peers without ID.

Since the majority of heterosocial skills require the ability to converse effectively, many of the components are the same as the conversational skills discussed previously. These behaviors include eye contact (Bander, Steinke, Allen, & Mosher, 1975; Heimberg, Madsen, Montgomery, & McNabb, 1980; Valenti-Hein, Yarnold, & Mueser, 1994), interpersonal distance (Valenti-Hein et al., 1994), appropriate affect (Bander et al., 1975; Heimberg et al., 1980), conversational questions (Heimberg et al., 1980), speech duration (Martinez-Diaz & Edelstein, 1979, 1980; Ziechner, Wright, & Herman, 1977), complementary remarks (Curran, 1975; Farrell, Mariotto, Conger, Curran, & Wallender, 1979; Wessberg, Mariotto, Conger, Farrell, & Conger, 1979), requests for dates (Curran, 1975; Curran, Gilbert, & Little, 1976), and follow-up/acknowledgment statements that indicate interest, attentiveness, or a reaction to what the partner is saying (Heimberg et al., 1980; Kupke, Hobbs, & Cheney, 1979). The assessment of heterosocial skills usually focuses on the presence or absence of these components within the form of role-play scenarios, direct observation, or written tests of knowledge. Any of these components found to be deficient can then be targeted for training. Observed deficiencies in other areas beyond those mentioned above such as stereotypic behavior, strange mannerisms, speech dysfluencies, long silences, or inappropriate self-disclosures may also be targeted for treatment if they appear to be problematic for the individual.

Heterosocial skill assessments should always aim to approximate the actual settings in which these behaviors are likely to occur; this makes it more likely that the observed behaviors will be an accurate reflection of the client's *in vivo* behavior. The partner in these assessments should be someone the client perceives as a reasonable person to ask on a date and the setting should be described as one in which the client might actually have the opportunity to meet someone of the opposite sex, such as a workshop breakroom, or in the hall or cafeteria at school (Christoff & Kelly, 1983). The individual should also be assessed for knowledge of appropriate dating activities as well as other behaviors required for actually carrying out a date, such as arranging a meeting time and place, dressing appropriately for the planned activity, arranging to pay for activities during the date, and planning transportation to and from the activity. The individual's performance should also be assessed for active listening, which can be defined as when a subject is involved in conversation via nonverbal cues such as head nodding or eye contact (Valenti-Hein et al., 1994). Deficiencies or lack of knowledge in any of these areas are also potential training targets and should be assessed in any person with ID who functions relatively independently and has expressed a desire to go on dates.

Role-play assessment of heterosocial skills can occur within a semistructured or unstructured interaction with a person of the opposite sex across a range of social/sexual situations that the individual has the potential of encountering. Such interactions can be as simple as instructing the client "to get to know the partner and ask him or her on a date" (Christoff & Kelly, 1983). More structured role-play assessment can focus on common interpersonal problem situations such as initiating, maintaining, and ending conversations; listening, understanding, and expressing emotions; finding similarities between oneself and others; giving and receiving compliments; asking for a date; dealing with rejection; compromising; resisting persuasion; and sexual functioning and birth control (Valenti-Hein & Mueser, 1990). The assessor can rate the client's performance as it occurs or record the interaction and make formal ratings later. Ratings can be made on a Likert-type scale. The client can also be asked to generate alternatives for solving particular heterosocial problems, and these can be rated in a similar fashion as described in the section on social problem-solving skills.

The Stacking the Deck Procedure (STD) is a test that can be used to assess an individual with ID's current level of knowledge concerning dating (Foxx, McMorrow, Storey, & Rogers, 1984). The STD contains a series of questions involving social/sexual situations presented in the context of a board game. Scores regarding the correctness of responses can be recorded and used as a baseline measure of social/sexual knowledge.

IX. SOCIAL SKILLS AND PSYCHOPATHOLOGY

Psychopathology and problem behaviors are closely related to deficits and excesses in social skills. Deficits in social skills may contribute to the etiology of both psychiatric disorders and behavioral problems (Borthwick-Duffy & Eyeman, 1990; Matson & Sevin, 1994). Individuals who exhibit varying profiles of psychopathology and challenging behavior, with respect to frequency, intensity, and duration, are thus likely to demonstrate different profiles of social skills impairment. Different levels of ID are also likely to produce distinctive patterns of deficits in social skills. Social skills rating scales are useful to present a picture of such profiles. Service options designed for individuals with ID may be less suitable for adults with ASD, although upward of 70% of this group also have ID (Matson & Nebel-Schwalm, 2006; Van Bourgondien & Elgar, 1990). Mapping out the differences in social skill deficits between these groups can be helpful in creating different service options and treatment plans for such individuals (Matson, 2007).

A positive correlation has been found between severity of ID and social impairment (Wing & Gould, 1979). Individuals with severe and profound ID are therefore more likely to have greater social skill deficits than those with mild or moderate impairment. In persons with autism, these deficits appear to be even more pronounced than in people with other developmental disorders (Njardvik, Matson, & Cherry, 1999). Children with autism appear to display greater deficits in social behaviors than nonautistic, developmentally delayed children of similar age and intelligence (Volkmar et al., 1987; Volkmar, Carter, Sparrow, & Cicchetti, 1993). In addition to having deficits in appropriate social skills, persons with ASD also exhibit high levels of inappropriate social behaviors (Matson, Stabinsky-Compton, & Sevin, 1991). Although communication deficits are among the defining features of ASD, the deficits of greatest importance seem to be in adaptive social skills rather than communication skills (Volkmar et al., 1993). ASD children also have greater difficulty in discriminating social and emotional cues than children with ID of the same age (Hobson, 1986a,b). In a study by

Jacobson and Ackerman (1990), children with ASD displayed more developed adaptive skills than children with ID matched by age and intelligence. However, the opposite trend was observed when comparing adults in these two groups. Njardvik et al. (1999) found similar results in that adults with ID showed significantly more adaptive social skills than adults with ASD.

Social skill deficits seem to have a similar positive correlation with severity of autism. In fact, individuals with Pervasive Developmental Disorder-Not Otherwise Specified (PDD-NOS), which can be viewed as a less severe form of autism, were shown to exhibit better positive nonverbal social skills than a group with autism (Njardvik et al., 1999). However, no significant difference was found in social skill deficits with the PDD-NOS group and a group of adults with ID (Njardvik et al., 1999). Children with PDD-NOS have also been shown to display better communicative and cognitive skills than those with autism (Cohen, Paul, & Volkmar, 1986), as well as less severe disturbances in social relatedness (Mayes, Volkmar, Hooks, & Cicchetti, 1993). It could be inferred that people with Asperger's syndrome, who are usually higher functioning than people with autism, would also show less deficits in social skills than people with autism. One characteristic of Asperger's is normal to highly developed language skills so there is likely to be marked differences in these skills. Overall, the results of these studies indicate that children and adults with ASD may be in greater need of social skills training than those with ID. The specific skills addressed in such training would also most likely differ.

Along with more pronounced deficits in social skills, a higher percentage of individuals with ID have some form of mental illness compared with persons of normal intellectual functioning (Dorsen, 1993; Rojahn & Tasse, 1996). According to various learning theories of depression in the literature, persons with ID are more likely to exhibit depressive symptomology (Lewinsohn, 1975; Seligman, Klein, & Miller, 1976). Depressed persons receive less social reinforcement from others, interact with less people, evince fewer positive reactions to others, and have a longer action latency than nondepressed people (Libet & Lewinsohn, 1973). Without functional social skills, such people's depressive-like characteristics may become the only available means likely to result in the reduction of demands and increased compliance from others, thus reinforcing the depressive behavior (Schloss, 1982). Measures of social skills have been shown to correlate with measures of depression in those with ID (Helsel & Matson, 1988). In addition, the lack of social support, social skills, and opportunities to learn adaptive ways of coping with stress in individuals with ID may make them increasingly vulnerable to depression and other mental illnesses (Nezu et al., 1991).

Higher levels of psychopathology were also found to manifest lower levels of positive social behavior (e.g., appropriate social skills and communication) and higher levels of maladaptive behavior (e.g., inappropriate assertion and sociopathic behavior) in adults with mild and moderate ID (Matson, Anderson, & Bamburg, 2000). Matson, Smiroldo, and Bamburg (1998) found that increases in symptoms of psychopathology among adults with severe and profound ID corresponded with increases in negative behavior. However, they found no relationship between symptoms of psychopathology and positive behaviors in this group. Therefore, it appears that social skill profiles of persons with and without dual diagnosis also differ by level of ID (Matson et al., 2000). Because of these increased deficits, individuals with dual diagnosis require a greater need for skill acquisition and support protocols that target both deficits in social functioning as well as symptoms of psychopathology.

The function of problem behaviors may also be related to different social skill profiles. Individuals for whom problem behaviors are automatically reinforcing tend to be generally more nonsocial than individuals with similar demographic characteristics but for whom an identifiable function of problem behavior can be recognized (Matson, Mayville, & Lott, 2002). It was also found that social behavior did not vary with different behavior motivation when the behavior was maintained by external contingencies (Matson et al., 2002). With severe and profoundly impaired individuals, levels of social skills may be so low that often the individual may resort to extreme forms of maladaptive behaviors to gain reinforcement or escape from environments or situations that they find unpleasant (Cipani & Spooner, 1997).

Duncan, Matson, Bamburg, Cherry, and Buckley (1999) demonstrated that persons with ID who display maladaptive behaviors, such as self-injury and aggression, exhibit a restricted range of social behaviors compared to controls. Individuals with ID exhibiting rumination have also been shown to possess significantly less positive social behaviors than those with ID who do not ruminate (Kuhn et al., 2001). Individuals who engage in stereotypies also display significantly lower levels of general positive and positive nonverbal social skills than controls (Matson, Smiroldo et al., 1998). It is possible that the existence of such aberrant behaviors (e.g., rumination and stereotypies) may have emerged to compensate for inadequacies in social skills (Kuhn et al., 2001). Such problem behaviors may also co-occur with some emotional disturbance or other psychiatric condition. It is not entirely clear, however, if the presence of such maladaptive behaviors results in social skill deficits or if the social skill inadequacies are responsible for the maladaptive behaviors (Duncan et al., 1999). Problem behaviors may also be exacerbated by the individual's social skill deficits, and more specifically, inabilities to adequately communicate (Sovner, 1986). Because of the interrelationship between social skill deficits and maladaptive behaviors, the presence of such behaviors may be detrimental to the development of appropriate social skills

(Duncan et al., 1999). It also appears that it is more difficult to train appropriate skills to such individuals because of the presence of problem behaviors (Coe, Matson, Craigie, & Gossen, 1991). Therefore, increasing social skills in individuals evincing significant challenging behaviors is of utmost importance since it can serve these two important functions (i.e., increasing social skills and decreasing problem behavior). It can also decrease an individual's vulnerability to abuse in that aggression, self-injurious behavior, and deficits in social skills are characteristics that differentiate abused persons with ID from nonabused persons (Rusch, Hall, & Griffin, 1986).

Social skills training that is derived from a thorough assessment should be an essential component in treatment protocols that are utilized to manage high-intensity maladaptive behaviors such as aggression and self-injury (Marchetti & Campbell, 1990). Such training is important because many times it affords the individual with a means of communicating the function that the maladaptive behavior was previously serving (Duncan et al., 1999). Developing appropriate social skills is also imperative for community-based moves that have become a large part of the normalization process for persons with severe and profound ID (Matson, LeBlanc, Weinheimer, & Cherry, 1999). Most community providers are looking for individuals who possess a higher number of social skills and a lower number of maladaptive behaviors as potential tenants of their apartments and group homes (Duncan et al., 1999). Treatment protocols that train social skills and help decrease the frequency of problem behaviors, thus, serve to increase the community readiness of individuals with ID and increase the number of such individuals who are prepared for community placement (White, Conroy, & Smith, 1993).

X. METHODS OF ASSESSING SOCIAL SKILLS

Identification of specific social skill deficits and excesses is an integral component in the assessment and treatment planning for persons with ID. Skills necessary for community integration can be targeted and trained to these individuals so that they can achieve more independence in their daily lives and be better prepared for living outside of residential facilities. Measures of social skills are obviously only a single component of a comprehensive assessment for those with ID. Such an assessment battery should also include information related to adaptive functioning, behavior problems and/or psychiatric disorders, and medication side effects (Matson, Mayville, & Laud, 2003). A variety of methods exist for the identification of deficits in social skills including, sociometric techniques, direct observation, behavioral interviews, and ratings made by teachers, parents, and self (Lyon, Albertus, Birkinbine, & Naibi, 1996).

XI. RATINGS SCALES

Ratings scales have proven to be the most popular assessment technique for assessing social skills in people with ID because of their efficient administration and interpretation (Marchetti & Campbell, 1990). Administering rating scales to caregivers can save time and financial resources as well as provide a reliable and valid means of assessment (Matson et al., 2003). Measures are available for children and adults and cover the entire spectrum of ID. Such scales have proven to be more objective, reliable, and efficient than other frequently used methods for assessing social skills (Marchetti & Campbell, 1990).

A. MESSIER

The Matson Evaluation of Social Skills for Individuals with Server Retardation (MESSIER) is an 85-item questionnaire designed to assess social strengths and weaknesses in individuals with severe and profound ID (Matson, 1995). Items on the MESSIER were compiled from items on the communication and socialization domains of the Vineland Adaptive Behavior Scales (VABS), the Matson Evaluation of Social Skills for Youngsters (MESSY), and nomination by experts. The scale consists of six clinically derived dimensions: positive nonverbal (e.g., distinguishes caregiver from others); positive verbal (e.g., thanks or compliments others); general positive (e.g., responds appropriately when introduced to strangers); negative nonverbal (e.g., isolates self); negative verbal (e.g., makes embarrassing comments); and general negative (e.g., has trouble waiting for needs to be met). The frequency of each item is rated using a 4-point Likert scale: never (0), rarely (1), sometimes (2), and often (3). A typical MESSIER interview is conducted by a trained examiner with a direct care staff serving as the informant, who has worked with the individual in question for at least 6 months. The interview usually lasts about 20 minutes. Endorsed items are transcribed onto a scoring profile under their respective subscales. This method of scoring allows the clinician to examine which subscale(s) have the most items endorsed. For example, numerous endorsements in the positive domain compared to few endorsements in the negative domain can indicate a good foundation of social skills, whereas the reverse pattern may indicate social skill deficits and specific training needs (Paclawskyj, Rush, Matson, & Cherry, 1999). Like most social skill measures, factor analysis of the items on the MESSIER yielded two dimensions: one factor describing positive social behaviors and another describing negative social behaviors (Paclawskyj et al., 1999).

The MESSIER has also been shown to successfully classify level of ID at the severe and profound levels (Matson, Dixon, Matson, & Logan, 2005). This is advantageous since standardized IQ tests are of minimal value in distinguishing strengths and weaknesses for treatment planning in this population (Matson, 1990). Adaptive behavior scales also tend to fall short in describing possible treatment goals and are geared primarily to persons with mild or moderate ID (Matson et al., 2005).

The MESSIER can also be used to differentiate individuals with ID presenting with psychopathology from those without psychopathology (Matson et al., 1998). Researchers have demonstrated that individuals displaying such problem behaviors as rumination and stereotypies evince significantly less general positive behaviors on the MESSIER than controls (Kuhn et al. 2001; Matson et al., 1998). Profiles of scores on the MESSIER have also been shown to consistently place individuals into appropriate maladaptive behavior groups (aggression, self-injury, or both; Duncan et al., 1999).

Reliability ratings for the MESSIER have been demonstrated to be quite high (Matson et al., 1999). Internal reliability is very high (0.94), and consistency for the six individually derived subscales is also high, which supports the notion that each set of items represents different constructs that account for a significant portion of the variance in their respective scores. Test–retest reliability following a period of 2–3 weeks was also quite high (0.86). Inter-rater reliability was good for the total MESSIER score (0.73), for all positive (0.79), and for all negative MESSIER items (0.71).

Convergent validity of the MESSIER was determined by comparing the MESSIER subscales to equivalent subdomains from the VABS (Matson et al., 1998). Significant positive correlations ($p < 0.01$) were found between the general positive subscale of the MESSIER and the interpersonal relationships subdomain of the VABS (0.84); the positive verbal subscale of the MESSIER and the coping skills subdomain of the VABS (0.52); the nonverbal subscale of the MESSIER and the play and leisure time subdomain of the VABS (0.71); and finally the total positive score from the MESSIER and the socialization domain from the VABS (0.77). Convergent validity of the MESSIER was also demonstrated to be high when compared with sociometric ranking (0.79; LeBlanc, Matson, Cherry, & Bamburg, 1999). This pattern suggests that the ratings on the MESSIER accurately reflect a person's social status with higher scores indicative of better social functioning (LeBlanc et al., 1999).

The MESSIER appears to be a valuable and versatile tool in the assessment of individuals with severe and profound ID. The original clinical profile can be used for determining individualized treatment goals, and with repeated assessment, the clinical profile can then be used for the evaluation of such training (Paclawskyj et al., 1999). The specificity of the MESSIER is also important because it contains social skill deficits that should be core components of individualized treatment packages (Matson et al., 1998).

B. SPSS

The Social Performance Survey Schedule (SPSS) is a scale consisting of 100 items measuring positive and negative social behaviors (Lowe & Cautella, 1978). The items on the SPSS are divided into two categories: positive and negative behavior. Ratings are made on a 5-point Likert-type scale: not at all, a little, a fair amount, much, and very much. Typical items on the SPSS include such things as: has eye contact, shows enthusiasm for other's good fortune, interrupts others, threatens others verbally and physically, and knows how to leave people alone.

The SPSS was originally developed for adults of normal intelligence and could be used as a self-report or significant-other rating scale; it has also been shown to be reliable and valid as an other-report measure with individuals with mild and moderate ID (Matson, Helsel, Bellack, & Senatore, 1983). The results of this study were used to create a modified 57-item version of the SPSS with roughly equivalent numbers of positive and negative social behaviors. The average interrater reliability for these items was 0.57, and not surprisingly, the items assessing overtly observable social behaviors were found to be most reliable.

A factor analysis of these items was conducted in which four separate factors emerged: appropriate social skills, poor communication skills, inappropriate assertion, and sociopathic behavior (Matson et al., 1983). The first factor, appropriate social skills, reflects appropriate social behaviors and refers to the individual in question's ability to exhibit socially acceptable behavior requiring him or her to evince support for others or verbalize a desired behavior. The other three factors reflect inappropriate social behaviors. The first of these negative factors, poor communication skills, includes a wide range of interpersonal responses frequently seen in adults with ID. Inappropriate assertion includes a number of behaviors that imply intent to harm others for the individual's personal benefit. The final negative factor, sociopathic behavior, includes items such as tries to manipulate others to do what (s)he wants and deceives others for personal gain. A self-report form of the SPSS has also been developed with the same items but without pronouns. The SPSS has been correlated to measures of depression (Beck Depression Inventory-Revised for Mentally Retarded Adults and Zung Self-Rating Depression Scale-Revised for Mentally Retarded Adults) and psychopathology (Psychology Instrument for Mentally Retarded Adults; Helsel & Matson, 1988).

C. MESSY

The MESSY is a 64-item inventory of social behaviors (Matson, 1989). The scale is in wide use and has been translated into Japanese, Chinese, Turkish, Spanish, and Dutch. The items are rated on a Likert scale ranging from 1 to 5, with 1 being "not at all" and 5 being "very much." There are two versions of the MESSY, a teacher-report form and a self-report form. The teacher-report form yields two factors: (1) inappropriate assertiveness/impulsiveness and (2) appropriate social skills. The inappropriate assertiveness/impulsiveness subscale contains items such as "threatens people or acts like a bully" and "becomes angry easily." The appropriate social skills subscale contains items such as "helps a friend who is hurt" and "walks up to people and starts a conversation." Factor scores are considered "problematic" if they fall one standard deviation below the normative mean, while scores are considered "very problematic" if they fall two or more standard deviations below the mean. Both factors have demonstrated excellent split-half reliability (0.94 for factor 1 and 0.98 for factor 2; Matson, Rotatori, & Helsel, 1983). Good internal reliability in assessment of the hearing impaired was also demonstrated (0.88; Matson, Macklin, & Helsel, 1985). Internal reliability was also found to be good in a sample of visually handicapped children: for inter-item reliability, it was 0.93 for the teacher-report form and 0.80 for the self-report form; and for split-half reliability, it was 0.88 for teacher report and 0.78 for self report (Matson et al., 1986).

The MESSY has been demonstrated to be effective in measuring social skill deficits in autistic children (Matson et al., 1991), the hearing impaired (Matson et al., 1985), and the visually handicapped (Matson et al., 1986). In the study, with hearing impaired children, the MESSY was shown to correlate with intelligence level as well as the A-M-L Behavior Rating Scale (AML), which is a measure of emotional behavior (Matson et al., 1985). Specifically, factor 1 was highly correlated with total AML score, while factor 2 was negatively correlated with total AML score and positively correlated with intellectual level. The MESSY norms are currently in the process of being updated.

D. SSRS

The Social Skills Rating System (SSRS) is a norm-referenced rating scale that is composed of three separate rating forms, one for teachers, parents, and students (Gresham & Elliott, 1990). The length of these forms varies depending on the person making the ratings and the grade level of the student being assessed. The number of items across all three forms ranges from 34 to 55 with the student form possessing the smallest number of items.

The SRSS has been normed for use with students in preschool (ages 3–5), elementary school (grades K-6), and secondary school (grades 7–12). All responses are completed on a 3-point Likert-type scale. Raters make two judgments about each item: (1) "how often" a social behavior occurs (never, sometimes, very often) and (2) "importance" for classroom success (not important, important, critical). The SSRS contains three main scales: social skills (teacher, parent, and student forms), problem behaviors (teacher and parent forms), and academic competence (teacher form only). The problem behavior scale samples three domains of behaviors: externalizing (aggression, temper problems, and arguing), internalizing (anxiety, loneliness, and poor self-esteem), and hyperactivity. On the academic competence scale, items are rated on a 5-point scale corresponding to percentage clusters (1 = lowest 10%, 5 = highest 10%) of all the students in the class.

The SSRS also includes norms for elementary students with disabilities. In general, disabled school children score between one and two standard deviations below their nondisabled peers (Gresham & Elliott, 1990). This difference has been demonstrated in disabled preschoolers as well (Lyon et al., 1996). In that study, disabled preschoolers were rated as significantly less skilled on all three domains of the teacher form, suggesting pervasive rather than isolated deficits, which is predictive of poor outcomes in adolescence and adulthood (Lyon et al., 1996). The SSRS has been shown to discriminate between broad groups of handicapped and nonhandicapped students but failed to distinguish between more specific groups such as learning disabled, mild ID, and behaviorally disordered (Bramlett, Smith, & Edmonds, 1994; Gresham, Elliott, & Black, 1987). However, students classified as ID were more likely than learning disabled students to score within "at risk" levels on teacher ratings of social skills and problem behaviors (Bramlett et al., 1994). The teacher form has also been shown to effectively discriminate between a group of children with behavior disorders and a group of emotionally disturbed children—the emotionally disturbed group was rated to have more positive social skills (Stinnett, Oehler-Stinnett, & Stout, 1989).

The SRSS is based on a social validity model of social skills and therefore attempts to assess whether specific social skills are mastered that are predictive of important social outcomes such as acceptance of the child by peers and adults (Lyon et al., 1996). Reliability for the total score of the teacher form is excellent (internal consistency ranged from 0.93 to 0.95, and test–retest reliability ranged from 0.84 to 0.93; Gresham & Elliott, 1990). The parent form has adequate internal consistency and excellent test–retest reliability for the social skills scale but limited reliability for the problem behavior scale (Demaray et al., 1995). The total score of the student or self-report form has good internal consistency (0.86; DiPerna & Volpe, 2005), while the test–retest reliability for the social skills scale is limited (Demaray et al., 1995). Interrater reliability for the teacher and student forms was low for the total score (0.22) and even lower across the subscales (DiPerna & Volpe, 2005).

The total score of the SSRS teacher form has a moderately strong correlation with both the socialization domain of the VABS (0.79) and the teacher questionnaire (0.87; Lyon et al., 1996). Moderate to strong correlations regarding developmental changes have also been found with the SSRS teacher form and the Walker–McConnell Scale of Social Competence and School Adjustment as well as with the MESSY (Demaray et al., 1995). Convergent validity of the student form has not been as encouraging: low to moderate correlations with the Youth Self-Report Form of the Child Behavior Checklist; low to moderate correlations with the Piers–Harris Children's Self-Concept Scale; and a moderate correlation (0.34 for the teacher ratings of academic skills scale and 0.40 for the Academic Enablers scale) with the Academic Competence Evaluation Scales (ACES; DiPerna & Volpe, 2005). In a comprehensive review of six scales designed to measure social skills in preschool and school-aged children, the SSRS was determined to be the most comprehensive and was recommended for use by the authors of the review (Demaray et al., 1995).

E. VABS

The VABS was one of the first standardized checklists used for assessing the social behavior of persons with ID (Sparrow, Balla, & Cicchetti, 1984). This measure consists of five domains (communication, daily living skills, socialization, motor skills, and maladaptive behavior) that provide a useful means of assessing adaptive behavior. In addition to providing information that can be compared to peers of similar demographic characteristics, the VABS also provides information useful for determining skill level for training. Each item can receive a score of 2 (yes, usually), 1 (sometimes or partially), 0 (no, never), N (no opportunity), or DK (do not know). Reliability coefficients for internal consistency are high averaging in the 0.80s and 0.90s. The Vineland contains norms for both ambulatory and nonambulatory adults with ID as well as those who live in residential and nonresidential facilities. The socialization domain contains general questions about social skills which are listed in the order they should be developmentally achieved. This domain has 58 items and has proven to be very reliable and valid. It contains three subdomains: (1) interpersonal relationships, (2) play and leisure time, and (3) coping skills. Tests of internal consistency on this domain resulted in coefficients above 0.80, whereas measures of construct validity resulted in coefficients above 0.70.

XII. OBSERVATION TECHNIQUES

Another common social skills assessment method is direct observation. Assessment using observation techniques can be conducted in either naturalistic or analogue conditions. Naturalistic observations usually occur in settings that the individual being assessed commonly spends time in and can include observations made by several raters based on target behaviors identified before the observation (Marchetti & Campbell, 1990). An analogue observation, on the other hand, would occur in an artificial environment and involves the manipulation of situational variables to evaluate a person's overall repertoire of social behaviors (Castles & Glass, 1986). Although such techniques can be very useful in certain situations, variables such as differences in conversational skills, preestablished operations, and situational specificity often limit their reliability, external validity, and predictive abilities (Van Hasselt, Hersen, & Bellack, 1981).

XIII. ROLE-PLAY

One of the most widely used means of assessing social skills in children has been the use of role-play scenes (Matson, Esveldt-Dawson, & Kazdin, 1983). We have already discussed specific role-play scenarios with regards to different social skills. Typical role-play scenes consist of both positive situations (e.g., giving complements, giving help, sharing) and negative social interactions (e.g., response to threats or provocation from peers). Responses are typically evaluated for the presence or absence of 4–6 operationally defined target behaviors (Kazdin, Esveldt-Dawson, & Matson, 1983; Matson et al., 1983). Although a client's behavior will undoubtedly contain elements of many more social skills, reliable assessment of more than 4–6 in any given assessment is unlikely (Matson & Wilkins, 2007). Social skills displayed during assessment can be rated individually and overall performance can be assessed as well. An advantage of role-play is that the client's behavior can be observed directly rather than inferred from the responses on checklists which are often completed by a second party. However, it is not clear that performance in these role-play scenes predicts how well the individual actual behaves *in vivo*, which is why we have previously advocated arranging these situations to be as close to real-life as possible. In the study by Matson et al. (1983), behavioral role-play performance was shown to not be consistently correlated with peer nominations, the MESSY, and a structured interview with the child being assessed. Other studies have found test–retest reliability and validity of these role-assessment approaches to be low (Van Hasselt et al., 1981), and that positive experiences immediately preceding the assessment could radically affect performance (Kazdin, Esveldt-Dawson, & Matson, 1982).

The Social Skills Test for Children is one example of a standardized role-play measure (Williamson, Moody, Granberry, Lethermon, & Blouin, 1983). This measure consists of 30 scenes with topics such as giving and accepting help, giving and accepting praise, and assertiveness. These scenarios are presented and the predetermined targeted behaviors can be observed, recorded, and rated.

Standard role-play assessments can also be supplemented by other measures. A study by Kazdin, Matson, and Esveldt-Dawson (1984) augmented the typical role-play assessment with a knowledge questionnaire. Such a questionnaire is useful in that social skill deficits can oftentimes be traced back to a lack of information. This questionnaire consisted of 10 items each corresponding to one of the role-play scenes presented to the participants. Each question was presented along with three possible answers and the child was to pick the best one. These researchers also had the participants complete a self-efficacy measure that asked questions regarding their own assessment of whether they could complete the role-play scenarios appropriately. Finally, the children rated their own skills on the child report of the MESSY.

XIV. CONCLUSIONS

Over the past two decades, it has become apparent that treatment programs for the intellectually disabled should contain provisions for the training of appropriate social skills. The ultimate goal of such programs has shifted to facilitating the development of effective interpersonal functioning in settings outside of the institution so that these individuals can move into community-based living situations. This change in direction can be traced back to both the movement to "deinstitutionalize" individuals with ID and the AAMR required focus on adaptive behavior. It has also become common for many severe and profoundly impaired individuals to make such transfers into the community now that the necessary supports are more readily available. The successful integration of persons with ID into community settings is largely dependent on the training of appropriate social and interpersonal behavior. In addition to increasing social skills, such training can also help decrease the frequency of maladaptive behaviors, which is especially important in that most community providers are looking for individuals who possess a higher number of social skills and a lower number of maladaptive behaviors to move into apartments and group homes (Duncan et al., 1999). Increasing social skills and decreasing maladaptive behaviors can also make such individuals less vulnerable to abuse (Rusch et al., 1986).

Since the effectiveness of any treatment program relies heavily on the adequacy of the assessment on which it is based, the accurate assessment of social skills excesses and deficits is of critical importance (Christoff & Kelly, 1983). The development of social skills rating scales, such as the MESSIER, SPSS, MESSY, and SSRS, has been very beneficial in facilitating quick and efficient assessments. The results of such assessments can illuminate specific areas in which the individual is deficient and that can be targeted in future training programs. Social skill rating scales are just one component of a larger assessment of an individual's current global functioning. Measures of adaptive behavior, psychopathology, medication side effects, and functional assessments of problem behaviors should also be included (Matson et al., 2003).

In this chapter, we have reviewed social skills required of all people in their everyday lives and described various methods of assessing these behaviors. We have suggested that the assessment of social skills occur in the natural environment whenever possible. Performance *in vivo* can be compared to more structured interactions in the laboratory or office. These interactions can be audio- or videotaped and analyzed further. Social skill checklists should be completed by third-party raters across the different settings requiring the targeted skills (e.g., teachers, direct-care staff) as well as the clients themselves whenever possible. The accurate assessment of social skills is often the very crucial first step preceding training to facilitate the attainment of the client's goals, and in the case of individuals with ID, this can make an incredible difference as it can ultimately allow these persons to function independently in the community.

REFERENCES

American Association on Mental Retardation (AAMR) (1992). *Mental retardation: Definition, classification, and systems of supports* (9th ed). Washington, DC: AAMR.

American Psychiatric Association (APA) (1994). *Diagnostic and statistical manual of mental disorders* (4th ed). Washington, DC: APA.

Argyris, C. (1965). Explorations in interpersonal competence–I. *Journal of Applied Behavioral Science, 1,* 58–63.

Argyris, C. (1968). Conditions for competence acquisition and therapy. *Journal of Applied Behavioral Science, 4,* 147–177.

Argyris, C. (1969). The incompleteness of social-psychological theory: Examples from small group cognitive consistency, and attribution research. *The American Psychologist, 24,* 893–908.

Azrin, N. H., Flores, T., & Kaplan, S. J. (1975). Job-finding club: A group assisted program for obtaining employment. *Behavior Research and Therapy, 13,* 17–27.

Baltaxe, C. (1977). Pragmatic deficits in the language of autistic adolescents. *Journal of Pediatric Psychology, 2,* 176–180.

Baltaxe, C., & D'Angiola, N. (1992). Cohesion in the discourse interaction of autistic, specifically language-impaired, and normal children. *Journal of Autism and Developmental Disorders, 22,* 1–17.

Bander, K. W., Steinke, G. V., Allen, G. J., & Mosher, D. L. (1975). Evaluation of three dating-specific treatment approaches for heterosexual dating anxiety. *Journal of Consulting and Clinical Psychology, 43,* 259–265.

Barbee, J. R., & Keil, E. C. (1973). Experimental techniques of job interview training for the disadvantaged: Videotape feedback, behavior modification, and microcounseling. *The Journal of Applied Psychology, 58,* 209–213.

Bates, P. (1980). The effectiveness of interpersonal skills training on the social skill acquisition of moderately and mildly retarded adults. *Journal of Applied Behavior Analysis, 13,* 237–248.

Bellack, A. S., & Hersen, M. (1978). Chronic psychiatric patients: Social skills training. In M. Hersen, & A. S. Bellack (Eds.), *Behavior therapy in the psychiatric setting.* Baltimore: Williams & Wilkins.

Bellack, A. S., Hersen, M., & Lamparski, D. (1979). Role play tests for assessing social skills: Are they valid? Are they useful? *Journal of Consulting and Clinical Psychology, 47,* 335–342.

Bellack, A. S., Hersen, M., & Turner, S. M. (1978). Role play tests for assessing social skills: Are they valid? *Behavior Therapy, 9,* 448–461.

Bellack, A. S., Hersen, M., & Turner, S. M. (1979). The relationship of role playing and knowledge of appropriate behavior to assertion in the natural environment. *Journal of Consulting and Clinical Psychology, 47,* 670–678.

Benson, B. A., Rice, C. J., & Miranti, S. V. (1986). Effects of anger management training with mentally retarded adults in group treatment. *Journal of Consulting and Clinical Psychology, 54,* 728–729.

Bornstein, P. H., Bach, P. J., McFall, M. E., Friman, P. C., & Lyons, P. D. (1980). Application of a social skills training program in the modification of interpersonal deficits among retarded adults: A clinical replication. *Journal of Applied Behavior Analysis, 13,* 171–176.

Borthwick-Duffy, S. A., & Eyeman, R. K. (1990). Who are the dually diagnosed? *American Journal of Mental Retardation, 94,* 586–595.

Bradlyn, A. S., Himadi, W. G., Crimmins, D. B., Christoff, K. A., Graves, K. G., & Kelly, J. A. (1983). Conversational skills training for retarded adolescents. *Behavior Therapy, 14,* 314–325.

Bramlett, R. K., Smith, B. L., & Edmonds, J. (1994). A comparison of nonrefferred, learning-disabled, and mildly mentally retarded students utilizing the social skills rating system. *Psychology in the Schools, 31,* 13–19.

Brody, G. H., & Stoneman, A. (1977). Social Competencies in the developmentally disabled. *Mental Retardation, 15,* 314–325.

Bullis, M., & Foss, G. (1986). Assessing the employment-related interpersonal competence of mildly mentally retarded workers. *American Journal of Mental Deficiency, 91*(1), 43–50.

Carey, M. P., Carey, K. B., Weinhardt, L. S., & Gordon, C. M. (1997). Behavioral risk for HIV infection among adults with a severe and persistent mental illness: Patterns and psychological antecedents. *Community Mental Health Journal, 33*(2), 133–142.

Castles, E. E., & Glass, C. R. (1986). Training in social and interpersonal problems solving skills for mildly and moderately retarded adults. *American Journal of Mental Deficiency, 91,* 35–42.

Chan, K. S., Smith, D. C., & Reid, H. (1977). *Interpersonal tactics of mentally retarded and normally achieving children.* Seattle: Paper presented at the meeting of the Western Psychological Association.

Chennault, M. (1967). Improving the social acceptance of unpopular educable mentally retarded pupils in special class. *American Journal of Mental Deficiency, 72,* 455–485.

Christoff, K. A., & Edelstein, B. A. (1981). *Functional aspects of assertive and aggressive behavior: Laboratory and in vivo observations.* Toronto: Paper presented at the meeting of the Association for Advancement of Behavior Therapy.

Christoff, K. A., & Kelly, J. A. (1983). Social skills. In J. L. Matson, & S. E. Beuning (Eds.), *Assessing the mentally retarded.* New York: Grune and Stratton.

Cipani, E., & Spooner, F. (1997). Treating problem behaviors maintained by negative reinforcement. *Research in Developmental Disabilities, 18,* 329–342.

Clark, H. B., Boyd, S. B., & Macrae, J. W. (1975). A classroom program teaching disadvantaged youths to write biographic information. *Journal of Applied Behavior Analysis, 8,* 67–75.

Coe, D., Matson, J., Craigie, C., & Gossen, M. (1991). Play skills of autistic children: Assessment and instruction. *Child and Family Behavior Therapy, 13,* 13–40.

Cohen, D. J., Paul, R., & Volkmar, F. R. (1986). Issues in the classification of pervasive developmental disorders: Toward DSM-IV. *Journal of the American Academy of Child and Adolescent Psychiatry, 25,* 213–220.

Curran, J. P. (1975). An evaluation of a skills training program and a systematic desensitization program in reducing dating anxiety. *Behaviour Research and Therapy, 13,* 65–68.

Curran, J. P., Gilbert, F. S., & Little, L. M. (1976). A comparison between replication training and sensitivity training approaches to heterosocial dating anxiety. *Journal of Counseling Psychology, 23,* 190–196.

Demaray, M. K., Ruffalo, S. L., Carlson, J., Busse, R. T., Olson, A. E., McManus, S. M., et al. (1995). Social skills assessment: A comparative evaluation of six published rating scales. *School Psychology Review, 24*(4), 648–671.

DiPerna, J. C., & Volpe, R. J. (2005). Self-report on the social skills rating system: Analysis of reliability and validity for an elementary sample. *Psychology in the Schools, 42*(4), 345–354.

Dorsen, A. (1993). Diagnosis and treatment of psychiatric and behavioural disorders inmentally retarded individuals: The state of the art. *Journal of Intellectual Disability Research, 37,* S1–S7.

Duncan, D., Matson, J. L., Bamburg, J. W., Cherry, K. E., & Buckley, T. (1999). The relationship of self-injurious behavior and aggression to social skills in persons with severe and profound learning disability. *Research in Developmental Disabilities, 20*(6), 441–448.

D'Zurilla, T. J., & Goldfried, M. R. (1971). Problem solving and behavior modification. *Journal of Abnormal Psychology, 78,* 107–126.

Eisler, R. M., Hersen, M., Miller, P. M., & Blanchard, E. B. (1975). Situational determinants of assertive behaviors. *Journal of Consulting and Clinical Psychology, 43,* 330–340.

Eisler, R. M., Miller, P. M., & Hersen, M. (1973). Components of assertive behavior. *Journal of Clinical Psychology, 29,* 295–299.

Elliott, S. N., & Gresham, F. M. (1993). Social skills interventions for children. *Behavior Modification, 17,* 287–313.

Farrell, A. D., Mariotto, M. J., Conger, A. J., Curran, J. P., & Wallender, J. L. (1979). Self-ratings and judges' ratings of heterosexual social anxiety and skill: A generalizability study. *Journal of Consulting and Clinical Psychology, 47,* 164–175.

Felce, D., de Kock, U., Thomas, M., & Saxby, H. (1986). Changes in adaptive behaviour of severely and profoundly mentally handicapped adults in different residential settings. *The British Journal of Psychology, 77*(4), 489–501.

Foss, G., & Bostwick, D. (1981). Problems of mentally retarded adults: A study of rehabilitation service consumers and providers. *Rehabilitation Counseling Bulletin, 25,* 66–73.

Foxx, R. M., McMorrow, M. J., Storey, K., & Rogers, B. M. (1984). Teaching social/sexual skills to mentally retarded adults. *American Journal of Mental Deficiency, 89,* 9–15.

Furman, W., Geller, M., Simon, S. J., & Kelly, J. A. (1979). The use of a behavior rehearsal procedure for teaching job-interviewing skills to psychiatric patients. *Behavior Therapy, 10,* 157–167.

Geller, M. M., Wildman, H. E., Kelly, J. A., & Laughlin, C. S. (1980). Teaching assertive and commendatory social skills to an interpersonally-deficient retarded adolescent. *Journal of Clinical Child Psychology, 9,* 17–21.

Gibson, F. W., Jr., Lawrence, P. S., & Nelson, R. O. (1976). Comparison of three training procedures for teaching social responses to developmentally disabled adults. *American Journal of Mental Deficiency, 81,* 379–387.

Givens, T. (1978). The current status of three major techniques for the assessment of social competence in the diagnosis of the potentially retarded child. *Southern Journal of Educational Research, 12,* 75–84.

Goldsmith, J. B., & McFall, R. M. (1975). Development and evaluation of an interpersonal skill-training program for psychiatric inpatients. *Journal of Abnormal Psychology, 84,* 51–58.

Greenspan, S., & Shoultz, B. (1981). Why mentally retarded workers lose their jobs: Social competence as a factor of work adjustment. *Applied Research in Mental Retardation, 2,* 32–38.

Gresham, F. M., & Elliott, S. N. (1984). Assessment and classification of children's social skills. A review of methods and issues. *School Psychology Review, 13,* 292–301.

Gresham, F. M., & Elliott, S. N. (1990). *Social skills rating system.* Circle Pines, MN: American Guidance Service.

Gresham, F. M., Elliott, S. N., & Black, F. (1987). Teacher-rated social skills of mainstreamed mildly retarded and nonhandicapped children. *School Psychology Review, 17,* 78–88.

Grossman, H. J. (1973). *Manual on terminology and classification in mental retardation.* Washington, DC: American Association on Mental Deficiency.

Guralnick, M. J. (1986). *Children's social behavior: Development, assessment, and modification.* Orlando, FL: Academic Press.

Hall, C., Sheldon-Wildgen, J., & Sherman, J. A. (1980). Teaching job interview skills to retarded clients. *Journal of Applied Behavior Analysis, 13,* 433–442.

Hazinski, L., & Matson, J. L. (1985). A comparison of social skills training and direct reinforcement methods with mentally retarded adults. *Scandinavian Journal of Behavior Therapy, 14,* 23–31.

Heimberg, R. G., Madsen, C. H., Montgomery, D., & McNabb, C. E. (1980). Behavioral treatments for heterosocial problems: Effects on daily self-monitored and role played interactions. *Behavior Modification, 4,* 147–172.

Helsel, W. J., & Matson, J. L. (1988). The relationship of depression to social skills and intellectual functioning in mentally retarded adults. *Journal of Mental Deficiency Research, 32,* 411–418.

Hersen, M., & Bellack, A. S. (1976a). A multiple-baseline analysis of social-skills training in chronic schizophrenics. *Journal of Applied Behavior Analysis, 9,* 239–245.

Hersen, M., & Bellack, A. S. (1976b). *Behavioral assessment: A practical handbook.* Oxford: Pergamon Press.

Hersen, M., & Bellack, A. S. (1977). Assessment of social skills. In A. R. Ciminero, K. S. Calhoun, & H. E. Adams (Eds.), *Handbook for behavioral assessment.* New York: Wiley.

Hersen, M. L., Bellack, A. S., & Turner, S. M. (1978). Assessment of assertiveness in female psychiatric patients: Motor and autonomic measures. *Journal of Behavior Therapy and Experimental Psychiatry, 9,* 11–16.

Hewitt, L. E. (1998). Influence of question type on response adequacy in young adults with autism. *Journal of Communication Disorders, 31,* 135–152.

Hobson, R. P. (1986a). The autistic child's appraisal of expressions of emotions. *Journal of Child Psychology and Psychiatry, 27,* 321–327.

Hobson, R. P. (1986b). The autistic child's appraisal of expressions of emotions: A further study. *Journal of Child Psychology and Psychiatry, 27,* 671–680.

Hollandsworth, J. G., Dressel, M. E., & Stevens, J. (1977). Use of behavioral versus traditional procedures for increasing job interview skills. *Journal of Counseling Psychology, 24,* 503–510.

Hollandsworth, J. G., Jr., Glazeski, R. C., & Dressel, M. E. (1978). Use of social-skills training in the treatment of extreme anxiety and deficient verbal skills in the job-interview setting. *Journal of Applied Behavior Analysis, 11,* 249–269.

Hops, H. (1983). Children's social competence and skill: Current research practices and future directions. *Behavior Therapy, 14*(1), 3–18.

Jacobson, J. W., & Ackerman, L. J. (1990). Difference in adaptive functioning among people with autism or mental retardation. *Journal of Autism and Developmental Disabilities, 20,* 205–219.

Jones, R. J., & Azrin, N. H. (1973). An experimental application of a social reinforcement approach to the problem of job-finding. *Journal of Applied Behavior Analysis, 6,* 345–353.

Kazdin, A. E., Matson, J. L., & Esveldt-Dawson, K. (1981). Social skill performance among normal and psychiatric inpatient children as a function of assessment conditions. *Behaviour Research and Therapy, 19,* 145–152.

Kazdin, A. E., Esveldt-Dawson, K., & Matson, J. L. (1982). Changes in children's social skills performance as a function of preassessment experiences. *Journal of Clinical Child Psychology, 11,* 243–248.

Kazdin, A. E., Esveldt-Dawson, K., & Matson, J. L. (1983). The effects of instructional set on social skills performance among psychiatric inpatient children. *Behavior Therapy, 14,* 413–423.

Kazdin, A. E., Matson, J. L., & Esveldt-Dawson, K. (1984). The relationship of role-play assessment of children's social skills to multiple measures of social competence. *Behaviour Research and Therapy, 22,* 129–140.

Kelly, J. A. (1982). *Social skills training: A practical guide for interventions.* New York: Springer.

Kelly, J. A., Frederiksen, L. W., Fitts, H., & Phillips, J. (1978). Training and generalization of commendatory assertiveness: A controlled single subject experiment. *Journal of Behavior Therapy and Experimental Psychiatry, 9,* 17–21.

Kelly, J. A., Furman, W., Phillips, J., Hathorn, S., & Wilson, T. (1979). Teaching conversational skills to retarded adolescents. *Child Behavior Therapy, 1,* 85–97.

Kelly, J. A., Laughlin, C., Claiborne, M., & Patterson, J. (1979). A group procedure for teaching job interviewing skills to formerly hospitalized psychiatric patients. *Behavior Therapy, 10,* 299–307.

Kelly, J. A., McAuliffe, T. L., Gudmundson, J. L., Murphy, D. A., Sikkema, K. J., & Hackl, K. L. (1998). Role play assessments of sexual assertiveness skills: Relationship with HIV/AIDS sexual risk behavior practices. *AIDS and Behavior, 2*(4), 319–328.

Kelly, J. A., Urey, J. R., & Patterson, J. (1980). Improving heterosocial conversational skills of male psychiatric patients through a small group training procedure. *Behavior Therapy, 11,* 179–188.

Kelly, J. A., Wildman, B. G., & Berler, E. S. (1980). Small group behavioral training to improve the job interview skills repertoire of mildly retarded adolescents. *Journal of Applied Behavior Analysis, 13,* 461–471.

Kelly, J. A., Wildman, B. G., Urey, J. R., & Thurman, C. (1979). Group skills training to increase the conversational repertoire of retarded adolescents. *Child Behavior Therapy, 1,* 323–336.

Konarski, E. A., & Diorio, M. S. (1985). A quantitative review of self-help research with the severely and profoundly mentally retarded. *Applied Research in Mental Retardation, 6,* 229–245.

Kuhn, D. E., Matson, J. L., Mayville, E. A., & Matson, M. L. (2001). The relationship of social skills as measured by the MESSIER to rumination in persons with profound mental retardation. *Research in Developmental Disabilities, 22,* 503–510.

Kupke, T. E., Hobbs, S. A., & Cheney, T. H. (1979). Selection of heterosocial skills: I. Criterion-related validity. *Behavior Therapy, 10,* 327–335.

La Greca, A. M., Stone, W. L., & Bell, III, C. R. (1982). Assessing the problematic interpersonal skills of mentally retarded individuals in a vocational setting. *Applied Research in Mental Retardation, 3,* 37–53.

Lambert, N. M., Wilcox, M. R., & Gleason, W. P. (1974). *The educationally retarded child.* New York: Grune & Stratton.

Laushey, K. M., & Heflin, L. J. (2000). Enhancing social skills of kindergarten children with autism through the training of multiple peers as tutors. *Journal of Autism and Developmental Disorders, 30*(3), 183–193.

LeBlanc, L. A., Matson, J. L., Cherry, K. E., & Bamburg, J. W. (1999). An examination of the convergent validity of the Matson evaluation of social skills for individuals with severe retardation (MESSIER) with sociometric rating. *The British Journal of Developmental Disabilities, 45,* 85–91.

Lewinsohn, P. M. (1975). The behavioral study and treatment of depression. In M. Hersen, R. M. Eisler, & P. M. Miller (Eds.), *Progress in behavior modification* (Vol. 1, pp. 19–64). New York: Academic Press.

Libet, J., & Lewinsohn, P. M. (1973). Concept of social skill with special reference to the behavior of depressed persons. *Journal of Consulting and Clinical Psychology, 40,* 304–312.

Longhurst, T. M. (1972). Assessing and increasing descriptive communication skills in retarded children. *Mental Retardation, 10,* 42–45.

Longhurst, T. M. (1974). Communication in retarded adolescents: Sex and intelligence level. *American Journal of Mental Deficiency, 78,* 607–618.

Lowe, M. R., & Cautella, J. R. (1978). A self-report measure of social skills. *Behavior Therapy, 9,* 535–544.

Lyon, M. A., Albertus, C., Birkinbine, J., & Naibi, J. (1996). A validity study of the social skills rating system-teacher version with disabled and nondisabled preschool children. *Perceptual and Motor Skills, 83,* 307–316.

Marchetti, A., & Campbell, V. (1990). Social skills. In J. L. Matson (Ed.), *Handbook of behavior modification with the mentally retarded* (2nd ed., pp. 333–355). New York: Plenum Press.

Martin, G. L., Kehoe, B., Bird, E., Jansen, V., & Darbyshire, M. (1971). Operant conditioning in dressing behavior of severely retarded girls. *Mental Retardation, 9,* 27–31.

Martinez-Diaz, J. A., & Edelstein, B. A. (1979). Multivariate analysis of demand characteristics on the analogue of competence. *Journal of Applied Behavior Analysis, 12,* 679–689.

Martinez-Diaz, J. A., & Edelstein, B. A. (1980). Heterosocial competence: Predictive and construct validity. *Behavior Modification, 4,* 115–129.

Matson, J. L. (1989). *The Matson evaluation of social skills with youngsters: Manual.* Orland Park, IL: International Diagnostics Systems, Incorporated.

Matson, J. L. (1990). *Handbook of behavior modification with the mentally retarded* (2nd ed). New York: Plenum Press.

Matson, J. L. (1995). *The Matson evaluation of social skills for individuals with severe retardation.* Baton Rouge, LA: Scientific Publishers, Inc.

Matson, J. L. (2007). Current status of differential diagnosis for children with autism spectrum disorders. *Research in Developmental Disabilities, 28*(2), 109–118.

Matson, J. L., & Barrett, R. P. (Eds.) (1993). *Psychopathology in the mentally retarded* (2nd ed.). Boston: Allyn and Bacon.

Matson, J. L., & Nebel-Schwalm, M. S. (2006). Comorbid psychopathology with autism spectrum disorders in children: An overview. *Research in Developmental Disabilities, doi:10.1016/j.ridd.2005.12.004.*

Matson, J. L., & Senatore, V. (1981). A comparison of traditional psychotherapy and social skills training for improving interpersonal functioning of mentally retarded adults. *Behavior Therapy, 12,* 369–382.

Matson, J. L., & Sevin, J. A. (1994). Theories of dual diagnosis in mental retardation. *Journal of Consulting and Clinical Psychology, 62,* 6–16.

Matson, J. L., & Swiezy, N. (1994). Social skills training with autistic children. In J. Matson (Ed.), *Autism in children and adults.* Pacific Grove, CA: Brooks Cole.

Matson, J. L., & Wilkins, J. (2007). A critical review of assessment targets and methods for social skills excesses and deficits in children with autism spectrum disorders. *Research in Autism Spectrum Disorders, 1,* 28–37.

Matson, J. L., Anderson, S. J., & Bamburg, J. W. (2000). The relationship of social skills to psychopathology for individuals with mild and moderate mental retardation. *The British Journal of Developmental Disabilities, 46,* 15–22.

Matson, J. L., Carlisle, C. B., & Bamburg, J. W. (1998). The convergent validity of the Matson evaluation of social skills in persons with severe retardation (MESSIER). *Research in Developmental Disabilities, 19,* 493–500.

Matson, J. L., DiLorenzo, T. M., & Esveldt-Dawson, K. (1981). Independence training as a method of enhancing self-help skills acquisition of the mentally retarded. *Behaviour Research and Therapy, 19,* 399–405.

Matson, J. L., Dixon, D. R., Matson, M. L., & Logan, J. L. (2005). Classifying mental retardation and specific strength and deficit areas in severe and profoundly mentally retarded persons with the MESSIER. *Research in Developmental Disabilities, 26,* 41–45.

Matson, J. L., Esveldt-Dawson, K., & Kazdin, A. E. (1983). Validation of methods for assessing social skills in children. *Journal of Clinical Child Psychology, 12*(2), 174–180.

Matson, J. L., Heinze, A., Helsel, W. J., Kapperman, G., & Rotatori, A. F. (1986). Assessing social behaviors in the visually handicapped: The Matson evaluation of social skills with youngsters (MESSY). *Journal of Clinical Child Psychology, 15*(1), 78–87.

Matson, J. L., Helsel, W. J., Bellack, A. S., & Senatore, V. (1983). Development of a rating scale to assess social skill deficits in mentally retarded adults. *Applied Research in Mental Retardation, 4,* 399–407.

Matson, J. L., Kazdin, A. E., & Esveldt-Dawson, K. (1980). Training interpersonal skills among mentally retarded and socially dysfunctional children. *Behaviour Research and Therapy, 18,* 419–427.

Matson, J. L., LeBlanc, L. A., Weinheimer, B., & Cherry, K. E. (1999). Reliability of the Matson evaluation of social skills for individuals with severe retardation (MESSIER). *Behavior Modification, 23*(4), 647–661.

Matson, J. L., Macklin, G. F., & Helsel, W. J. (1985). Psychometric properties of the Matson evaluation of social skills with youngsters (MESSY) with emotional problems and self concept in deaf children. *Journal of Behavior Therapy and Experimental Psychiatry, 16*(2), 117–123.

Matson, J. L., Marchetti, A., & Adkins, J. A. (1980). Comparison of operant- and independence-training procedures for mentally retarded adults. *American Journal of Mental Deficiency, 84,* 487–494.

Matson, J. L., Mayville, E. A., & Lott, J. D. (2002). The relationship between behaviour motivation and social functioning in persons with intellectual impairment. *The. British Journal of Clinical Psychology, 41,* 175–184.

Matson, J. L., Mayville, S. B., & Laud, R. B. (2003). A system of assessment for adaptive behavior, social skills, behavioral function, medication side-effects, and psychiatric disorders. *Research in Developmental Disabilities, 24,* 75–81.

Matson, J. L., Rotatori, A., & Helsel, W. J. (1983). Development of a rating scale to measure social skills in children: The Matson evaluation of social skills with youngsters (MESSY). *Behavior Research and Therapy, 21,* 335–340.

Matson, J. L., Smiroldo, B. B., & Bamburg, J. W. (1998). The relationship of psychopathology to social skills in persons with severe and profound mental retardation. *Journal of Intellectual Disability Research, 23,* 137–145.

Matson, J. L., Stabinsky-Compton, L., & Sevin, J. A. (1991). Comparison and item analysis of the MESSY for autistic and normal children. *Research in Developmental Disabilities, 12,* 361–369.

Mayes, L., Volkmar, F., Hooks, M., & Cicchetti, D. (1993). Differentiating pervasive developmental disorder not otherwise specified from autism and language disorders. *Journal of Autism and Developmental Disorders, 23,* 79–90.

McClure, R. F. (1968). Reinforcement of verbal social behavior in moderately retarded children. *Psychological Reports, 23,* 317–376.

McFall, R. M., & Marston, A. R. (1970). An experimental investigation of behavior rehearsal in assertive training. *Journal of Abnormal Psychology, 76*(2), 295–303.

McGee, G. G., Krantz, P. J., & McClannahan, L. E. (1984). Conversational skills for autistic adolescents: Teaching assertiveness in naturalistic game settings. *Journal of Autism and Developmental Disorders, 14*(3), 319–330.

Menchetti, B. M., & Rusch, F. R. (1988). Reliability and validity of the vocational assessment and curriculum guide. *American Journal on Mental Retardation, 93*(3), 283–289.

Minkin, N., Braukmann, C. J., Minkin, B. L., Timbers, G. D., Timbers, B. J., Fixsen, D. F., et al. (1976). The social validation and training of conversational skills. *Journal of Applied Behavior Analysis, 9,* 127–139.

Nelson, R. O., Gibson, F., Jr., & Cutting, D. S. (1973). Video taped modeling: The development of three appropriate social responses in a mildly retarded child. *Mental Retardation, 11,* 24–28.

Nezu, C. M., Nezu, A. M., & Arean, P. (1991). Assertiveness and problem-solving training for mildly mentally retarded persons with dual diagnoses. *Research in Developmental Disabilities, 12,* 371–386.

Nezu, A. M., Nezu, C. M., & Perri, M. G. (1989). *Problem-solving therapy for depression: Theory, research, and clinical guidelines*. New York: Wiley.

Njardvik, U., Matson, J. L., & Cherry, K. E. (1999). A comparison of social skill in adults with autistic disorder, pervasive developmental disorder not otherwise specified, and mental retardation. *Journal of Autism and Developmental Disorders, 29*(4), 287–295.

Paclawskyj, T. R., Rush, K. R., Matson, J. L., & Cherry, K. E. (1999). Factor structure of the Matson evaluation of social skills for individuals with severe retardation (MESSIER). *British Journal of Clinical Psychology, 38,* 289–293.

Parkes, M. (1975). Psycho-social transitions: A field for study. *Social Sciences and Medicine, 5,* 101–115.

Paul, R., & Cohen, D. J. (1985). Comprehension of indirect requests in adults with autistic disorder and mental retardation. *Journal of Speech and Hearing Research, 28,* 475–479.

Perrin, T. O. (1977). Job seeking training for adult retarded clients. *Journal of Applied Rehabilitation Counseling, 8,* 181–188.

Pinto, R. P. (1979). An evaluation of job-interview training in the rehabilitation setting. *Journal of Rehabilitation Medicine, 45,* 71–76.

Rojahn, J., & Tasse, M. J. (1996). Psychopathology in mental retardation. In J. W. Jacobson, & J. A. Mulick (Eds.), *Manual of diagnosis and professional practice in mental retardation* (pp. 147–156). Washington, DC: American Psychological Association.

Ross, S. A. (1969). Effects of intentional training in social behavior on retarded children. *American Journal of Mental Deficiency, 73,* 912–919.

Ross, D. M., & Ross, S. A. (1973). Cognitive training for the EMR child: Situational problem solving and planning. *American Journal of Mental Deficiency, 78,* 20–26.

Ross, D. M., & Ross, S. A. (1978). Cognitive training for EMR children: Choosing the best alternative. *American Journal of Mental Deficiency, 82,* 598–601.

Rucker, C. N., & Vincenzo, F. M. (1970). Maintaining social acceptance gains made by mentally retarded children. *Exceptional Children, 36,* 679–680.

Rusch, R. G., Hall, J. C., & Griffin, H. C. (1986). Abuse-provoking characteristics of institutionalized mentally retarded individuals. *American Journal of Mental Deficiency, 90*(6), 618–624.

Rychtarik, R. G., & Bornstein, P. H. (1979). Training conversational skills in mentally retarded adults: A multiple baseline analysis. *Mental Retardation, 17,* 289–293.

Schalock, R. L., & Harper, R. S. (1978). Placement from community-based mental retardation programs: How well do clients do? *American Journal of Mental Deficiency, 83*(3), 240–247.

Schinke, S. P., Gilchrist, L. D., Smith, T. E., & Wong, S. E. (1979). Group interpersonal skills training in a natural setting: An experimental study. *Behaviour Research and Therapy, 17,* 149–154.

Schloss, P. J. (1982). Verbal interaction patterns of depressed and non-depressed institutionalized mentally retarded adults. *Applied Research in Mental Retardation, 3,* 1–12.

Seligman, M. E. P., Klein, D. C., & Miller, W. R. (1976). Depression. In H. Leitenberg (Ed.), *Handbook of behavior modification and behavior therapy.* Englewood Cliffs, NJ: Prentice Hall.

Sipperstein, G. N., & Gottlieb, J. (1977). Physical stigma and academic performance as actors affecting children's first impressions of handicapped persons. *American Journal of Mental Deficiency, 8,* 455–462.

Skillings, R. E., Hersen, M., Bellack, A. S., & Becker, M. P. (1978). Relationship of specific and global measures of assertion in college females. *Journal of Clinical Psychology, 34,* 346–353.

Smith, D. C. (1986). Interpersonal problem-solving skills of retarded and nonretarded children. *Applied Research in Mental Retardation, 7,* 431–442.

Smith, D., Valenti-Hein, D., & Heller, T. (1985). Interpersonal competencies and community adjustment of retarded adults: Implications for social, vocational, and sexual adjustment. In M. Sigman (Ed.), *Children with dual diagnosis: Mental retardation and mental illness.* Orlando, FL: Grune & Stratton.

Sovner, R. (1986). Limiting factors in the use of DSM-III criteria with mentally ill/mentally retarded persons. *Psychopharmacology Bulletin, 22,* 1055–1059.

Sparrow, S. S., Balla, D. A., & Cicchetti, D. V. (1984). *Vineland Adaptive Scales I: A revision of the Vineland Social Maturity Scale by Edgar A. Doll Survey Form.* Circle Pines, MN: American Guidance Service.

Stalonas, P. M., & Johnson, W. G. (1979). Conversation skills trainings for obsessive speech using an aversive-cueing procedure. *Journal of Behavior Therapy and Experimental Psychiatry, 10,* 61–63.

Stella, J., Mundy, P., & Tuchman, R. (1999). Social and nonsocial factors in the Childhood autism scale. *Journal of Autism and Developmental Disorders, 29*(4), 307–317.

Stinnett, T. A., Oehler-Stinnett, J., & Stout, L. J. (1989). Ability of the social skills rating system-teacher version to discriminate behavior disordered, emotionally disturbed and nonhandicapped students. *School Psychology Review, 18*(4), 526–535.

Stone, W., & Caro-Martinez, L. (1990). Naturalistic observation of spontaneous communication in autistic children. *Journal of Autism and Developmental Disorders, 20,* 437–453.

Tager-Flusberg, H., & Anderson, M. (1991). The development of contingent discourse ability in autistic children. *Journal of Child Psychiatry, 32,* 1123–1134.

Treffrey, D., Martin, G., Samuels, J., & Watson, C. (1970). Operant conditioning of grooming behavior of severely retarded girls. *Mental Retardation, 8,* 29–33.

Trower, P., Bryant, B., & Argyle, M. (1978). *Social skills and mental health.* Pittsburgh: University of Pittsburgh Press.

Urey, J. R., Laughlin, C. S., & Kelly, J. A. (1979). Teaching heterosocial conversational skills to male psychiatric patients. *Journal of Behavior Therapy and Experimental Psychiatry, 10,* 323–328.

Valenti-Hein, D., & Mueser, K. (1990). *The dating skills program: Teaching social-sexual skills to adults with mental retardation.* Orlando Park, IL: International Diagnostic Systems.

Valenti-Hein, D. C., Yarnold, P. R., & Mueser, K. T. (1994). Evaluation of the dating skills program for improving heterosocial interactions in people with mental retardation. *Behavior Modification, 18*(1), 32–46.

Van Bourgondien, M. E., & Elgar, S. (1990). The relationship between existing residential services and the needs of autistic adults. *Journal of Autism and Developmental Disorders, 20,* 299–308.

Van Hasselt, V., Hersen, M., & Bellack, A. S. (1981). The validity of role play tests for assessing social skills in children. *Behavior Therapy, 12,* 202–216.

Van Hasselt, V. B., Hersen, M., & Kazdin, A. E. (1985). Assessment of social skills in visually-handicapped adolescents. *Behavior Research and Therapy, 23*(1), 53–63.

Volkmar, F. R., Carter, A., Sparrow, S. S., & Cicchetti, D. V. (1993). Quantifying social development in autism. *Journal of the American Academy of Child and Adolescent Psychiatry, 32,* 627–632.

Volkmar, F. R., Sparrow, S. S., Goudreau, D., Cicchetti, D. V., Paul, R., & Cohen, D. (1987). Social deficits in autism: An operational approach using the Vineland Adaptive Behavior Scales. *Journal of the American Academy of Child and Adolescent Psychiatry, 26,* 156–161.

Wehmeyer, M. L., & Kelchner, K. (1994). Interpersonal cognitive problem-solving skills of individuals with mental retardation. *Education & Training in Mental Retardation and Developmental Disabilities, 29*(4), 265–278.

Weiss, D., & Weinstein, E. (1967). Interpersonal tactics among mental retardates. *American Journal of Mental Deficiency, 72,* 653–661.

Wessberg, H. W., Mariotto, M. J., Conger, A. J., Farrell, A. D., & Conger, J. C. (1979). Ecological validity of role plays for assessing heterosocial anxiety and skill of male college students. *Journal of Consulting and Clinical Psychology, 47,* 525–535.

White, J. A., Conroy, J., & Smith, D. M. (1993). Following the course of change: A study of adaptive and maladaptive behaviors in young adults living in the community. *Education and Training in Mental Retardation, 28,* 149–154.

Wildman, B. G., Wildman, H. E., & Kelly, J. (1986). Group conversational-skills training and social validation with mentally retarded adults. *Applied Research in Mental Retardation, 7,* 443–458.

Williamson, D. A., Moody, S. C., Granberry, S. W., Lethermon, V. R., & Blouin, D. C. (1983). Criterion-related validity of a role-play social skill test for children. *Behavior Therapy, 14,* 466–481.

Wing, L., & Gould, J. (1979). Severe impairments of social interaction and associated abnormalities in children: Epidemiology and classification. *Journal of Autism and Developmental Disorders, 9,* 11–29.

Wing, L., Leekam, S. R., Libby, S. J., Gould, J., & Larcombe, L. (2002). The diagnostic interview for social and communication disorders: Background, inter-rater reliability and clinical use. *Journal of Child Psychology and Psychiatry, 43*(3), 307–325.

Ziechner, A., Wright, J. C., & Herman, S. (1977). Effects of situation on dating and assertive behavior. *Psychological Reports, 40,* 375–381.

Zisfein, L., & Rosen, M. (1974). Effects of a personal adjustment training group consulting program. *Mental Retardation, 12,* 50–53.

Self-Care Skills

REBECCA L. MANDAL

RESOURCE CENTER FOR PSYCHIATRIC AND BEHAVIORAL SUPPORTS
HAMMOND, LOUISIANA

BRANDI SMIROLDO AND JOANN HAYNES-POWELL

HAMMOND DEVELOPMENTAL CENTER, HAMMOND, LOUISIANA

I. INTRODUCTION

One of the basic diagnostic criteria of mental retardation is deficits in adaptive behavior which includes conceptual, social, and practical skills, such as dressing, self-feeding, toileting, personal hygiene, social, and vocational skills [American Association on Mental Retardation (AAMR), 2002; American Psychiatric Association (APA), 2000]. However, with the continued increase in community integration for people with mental retardation, it is becoming increasingly imperative for this population of people to posses self-care skills. By having the knowledge and ability to use self-care skills, people with mental retardation increase their own autonomy and decrease their dependence on others to care for them, thus creating more self-reliance (Hagner & Davies, 2002; Matson, Smalls, Hampff, Smiroldo, & Anderson, 1998; Reid & Parsons, 2002) and adding to their quality of life (Shogren, Faggella-Luby, Bae, & Wehmeyer, 2004). Having self-care skills also reduces the likelihood that the person with mental retardation will develop behavioral challenges (Reid & Parsons, 2002; Shogren et al., 2004), medical complications, or socially offensive behavior (Lockwood & Williams, 1994) and provides them with opportunities to control their environment by achieving or avoiding objects, sensory input, activities, or people (Griffiths, 1999). Furthermore, when a person who has mental retardation possesses self-care skills, the opportunity for them to engage in productive activities increases since less time will be spent having someone else complete self-care skills for them (Christian & Luce, 1985). There has been documented success of people

INTERNATIONAL REVIEW OF RESEARCH IN
MENTAL RETARDATION, Vol. 34
0074-7750/07 $35.00

DOI: 10.1016/S0074-7750(07)34011-1

with varying severity levels of mental retardation learning and using self-care skills such as functional communication (Koegel, Koegel, Kellegrew, & Mullen, 1996; Shogren et al., 2004), hand washing and operating a television (Matson et al., 1998), personal hygiene after bowel movements (Stokes, Cameron, Dorsey & Fleming, 2004), food preparation and mealtime skills (Bat-Haee, 2001; Lancioni & O'Reily, 2002; Luiselli, 1993), grooming (Bat-Haee, 2001; Saloviita & Tuulkari, 2000), household chores (Snell, 1982), dressing (Bat-Haee, 2001; Sewell, Collins, Hemmetter, & Schuster, 1998; Sisson, Kilwein, & Van Hasselt, 1988); toileting (Bat-Haee, 2001; Saloviita, 2000; Tarnowski & Drabman, 1987), and managing money (Browder & Grasso, 1999). The goal in teaching self-care skills is to provide people with mental retardation functional skills that are age appropriate and that will allow them to care for themselves in the pursuit of greater independence. The training programs should be designed to help the person learn a functional skill in a practical way so that it can be generalized to a variety of settings such as home, work, school, and community (Christian & Luce, 1985). Determining what self-care skills to teach someone with mental retardation involves a multimethod approach of standardized assessment, observations, data collection, rating scales, and clinical judgment (AAMR, 2002; Christian & Luce, 1985; Reid & Parsons, 2002). In addition, it is important to involve the people responsible for teaching the self-care skills to be part of the assessment process and have them receive training on how to teach these skills. Given that the eventual goal of assessment and teaching self-care skills is that the person will generalize and maintain the self-care skills across different settings and people, it is imperative to evaluate ways of improving generalization and maintenance of skills during the assessment process so that barriers may be addressed prior to the beginning of training.

II. ASSESSING SELF-CARE SKILLS

The most recent AAMR definition of mental retardation identifies multiple domains of adaptive behavior: conceptual, social, and practical. The individual must have deficits of at least two standard deviations below the mean on any one of the three domain areas or on an overall score on a standardized assessment tool (AAMR, 2002). Self-care skills are just one of the areas listed in all three domains. For example, according to the AAMR text (2002) that discusses the new definition, self-direction and money concepts fall under the conceptual domain; interpersonal skills are found under the social domain; living and occupational skills are categorized under the practical domain.

Even among the skills in these domains, deficits are not necessarily consistent and are person specific. For instance, an individual may be able to toilet independently, but may struggle with some dressing skills that require more skillful motor coordination. In addition, there are often discrepancies about what self-care skills to teach individuals with mental retardation among those who provide services such as developmental centers, supported independent living programs (Rudrud & Vaudt, 1986), families, and caregivers. Thus, determining which self-care skills that may require focus for education and training needs to be based on a holistic assessment. The assessment should focus on which skills will be most beneficial or are of the most importance for that individual; assessing those areas in which the individual is having the most difficulty should follow (AAMR, 2002). This is necessary because the skills one individual may be learning may be very different from the skills that another individual may be learning but of equal importance to both people.

The evaluation of self-care skills should be undertaken within the context of a person-centered assessment process. A person-centered assessment begins with identifying what matters the most to the individual by focusing on the following areas: participating in community life, relationships, choices, their roles in the community, and personal competencies (Kincaid, 1996). Gahan, Dykstra, and Summers (2002) also stress that those involved in the person-centered planning group are "governed by the principles that include community integration, normalization, increasing competency, and empowerment" (p. 195). After these considerations, the team can begin to look at what skills might benefit the person in having the life that he would like and/or what obstacles exist that prevent achieving that life (Griffiths, 1999). This process will assist in prioritizing the focus on the self-care skills that will be most beneficial as well as provide a motivator for the individual to learn the skill. For example, the individual may wish to have a job to earn his own money but has poor hygiene skills. In this instance, hygiene may be the first place to start for self-care skills training. If the individual learns better hygiene skills, he not only becomes more independent, but he is also likely to get the job he wants resulting in greater independence and life satisfaction.

When the individual is unable to report his own life vision, the people who know him best should be included in assisting the support team in developing goals and related training objectives in the same manner (Kincaid, 1996). These people may be family members, teachers, direct support professionals, case managers, Qualified Mental Retardation Professional (QMRP), friends, and so on. However, the person who is assisting in reporting the wants and needs of the individual should be careful to use the substituted judgment methodology rather than the best interest approach (Dinerstein, 1999).

That is, the person should speak to what the individual's wishes are or they are believed to be in the individual's best interest or for his or her own good. When there is no one available to serve as the individual's advocate, the team of professionals and support staff must attempt to prioritize the wants and needs based on the best available information.

Some researchers provide guidelines for choosing skills to teach (Bosch & Fuqua, 2001; Griffiths, 1999; Reid & Parsons, 2002). Reid and Parsons (2002) discuss guidelines that should be used when making decisions about which self-care skills to teach someone. These guidelines can be most helpful when an individual is unable to assist in setting his/her own priorities. The first two guidelines specifically apply to teaching self-care skills, while the last guideline is a related consideration teaching skills to earn money. Although earning money is a self-care skill, it does not involve skills that are life sustaining (e.g., eating) or personal hygiene skills (e.g., dressing or tooth brushing).

The first guideline by Reid and Parsons (2002) is called the "longest-standing criterion for selecting functional skills" (p. 107). This pertains to the analysis and choosing of skills that are necessary for someone to function daily and that must be completed independently or, if unable, with dependence on another person. The emphasis here is in choosing those skills that, if learned, will move an individual toward greater independence which ultimately affects the person's overall lifestyle (Browder & Grasso, 1999; Stokes et al., 2004). If, for example, someone knew how to bath or brush his teeth, then he would not be dependent on the caregiver to do this for him. Thus, there is rich opportunity for creating more independence in individuals' lives by using this guideline as an indicator.

The second guideline in choosing which self-care skills to teach someone with mental retardation is based on the frequency with which the person will need to perform the skill (Reid & Parsons, 2002). For example, if someone were to learn tooth brushing, an event which is supposed to occur at least three times a day, then possessing that self-care skill would significantly decrease the amount of caregiver involvement and dependence. In addition, choosing to teach frequently performed self-care skills provides more opportunity for practice in learning the skills. Less performed skills should not be ignored obviously; however, in order of importance, those skills that are performed frequently should be taught to competence first. They should be considered the foundation on which to build additional frequently performed skills and less performed skills.

Third, self skills that will enable someone to earn money are functional and an important consideration when deciding on what self skills to teach (Browder & Grasso, 1999; Reid & Parsons, 2002). Earning money to buy things that are needed or desired has become the way of life in many cultures and has been instilled throughout generations. Learning how to earn, manage, and save money and how to use the banking system will help individuals with mental retardation reach their potential in self-sufficiency (Browder & Grasso, 1999). Though the challenges they face in achieving this may be different and greater than the general population, they too want to have enjoyable jobs that will allow them to earn money. Asking people what their likes and dislikes are (or observing them to determine such) and providing choices in job activities will foster success in meeting this objective. It will also decrease the likelihood that behavioral challenges will develop on the job site since they are engaging in activities they have chosen.

According to Reid and Parsons (2002), vocational programs should teach people with mental retardation job-related skills that will allow them to earn paid work now or in the immediate future. Materials that are used in the paid job should be available and used in teaching the skills to the person in order to improve generalization of the skill even before they enter the job site (if possible). Naturally, self skills to be used in the vocational setting should also be age appropriate (Christian & Luce, 1985; Luce, Anderson, Thibadeau, & Lipsker, 1984).

Finally, this last guideline by Reid and Parsons (2002) emphasizes teaching people with mental retardation skills that allow them to communicate in making choices, obtaining objects/needs or getting out of activities. Communication and choice-making skills assist people with mental retardation in getting what they want by controlling their environment without exhibiting challenging behavior (Felce & Emerson, 2001; Griffiths, 1999, Koegel et al., 1996; Shogren et al., 2004). Similarly, Griffiths (1999) suggest that when determining self-care skills, consideration should be given to what skills should be taught as a replacement for problem behaviors that may exist. For example, teaching someone how to ask for a break or for lunch or refreshment may help minimize the guess work in determining why someone sometimes acts aggressively.

The behavioral cusp criteria can also be used to select skills of most benefit (Bosch & Fuqua, 2001; Stokes et al., 2004). A cusp is "a behavior change that has consequences for the organism beyond the change itself, some of which may be considered important" (Rosales-Ruiz & Baer, 1997). This model sets five criteria for judging skill selection such that skills with the greatest likelihood for long-term benefit to the individual can be targeted first.

The first criterion in judging the skill is assessing if the skill will provide access to new reinforcers, contingencies, and environments (Bosch & Fuqua, 2001). Use of this criterion allows for consideration of the utility of learning a new skill as well as choice of reinforcers (motivation) in the learning process as compared to natural reinforcers following completion of the skill.

For example, learning how to make a sandwich will allow the person to become self-sufficient so that she may be able to eat any time she chooses rather than at a scheduled time. In addition, the person also will have choices over the amount of condiments she wants on the sandwich so that it is made to her own specifications. Thus, the sandwich may taste better and increase the motivation to make the sandwich again. Taking it a step further, learning how to make sandwiches may help train this person to work at a sandwich shop which would lead to more community inclusion and more potential to earn money. This exemplifies Griffiths (1999) suggestion that identifying skills that are relevant to the person's life may reinforce the person while also increasing integration with other people.

The second criterion considers if the skill is a prerequisite for or a part of other more complex skills (Bosch & Fuqua, 2001). For example, an individual must learn to distinguish between two coins before he is able to learn the value of each. Both of these tasks are necessary in making change and to manage one's own money. Depending on the individual's current skill level, training may need to be focused on smaller tasks. Rather than teaching an individual to make a meal, training may focus on stirring/mixing. A simpler task allows for quicker success and can generalize to a number of cooking tasks involved in making a meal. The individual's learning could then be expanded by learning other component tasks such as pouring and measuring.

The third criterion takes into account if the skill will compete with an inappropriate behavior (Bosch & Fuqua, 2001). Exhibition of inappropriate behaviors is more prevalent among individuals with developmental disabilities due to a number of factors including lack of communication and social skills and increased prevalence of medical and mental health difficulties (AAMR, 2002, Reid & Parsons, 2002). A full assessment of inappropriate behaviors should include completion of a functional assessment to determine the factors that trigger and/or maintain the inappropriate behaviors (Graziano, 2002; Reid & Parsons, 2002; Wacker, Peck, Derby, Berg, & Harding, 1996). Once these factors are determined, the process of choosing behaviors to replace the inappropriate behavior can begin and interventions can be implemented. A later section of this chapter discusses inappropriate behaviors and skills training in greater detail.

The fourth criterion considers if the skill will benefit other people from the required skill response (Bosch & Fuqua, 2001). In prioritizing skills for teaching, consideration should be given to those skills that impact other people beyond the individual. The previous example of teaching hygiene skills to a gentleman who wished to get a job illustrates this point. Not only will acquiring hygiene skills impact him and his work access, but it will also impact all people who interact with him most notably his family or direct support professionals who assist him in his current living situation.

The final criterion determines if the new response meets the demands of the social community (Bosch & Fuqua, 2001). Social validity is especially important given the greater focus today on community inclusion and behavioral autonomy. Using the hygiene example again, cleanliness may not only be a requirement at a particular job (i.e., work in a restaurant), but may also result in more acceptance from others both on and off the job. While the individual's family or support staff may have come to accept his poor hygiene, the larger social community typically will not. Thus, teaching hygiene skills also meets the social validity criterion.

Besides using the behavioral cusps to evaluate what self-care skills to teach, communication and choice-making skills are also important variables that should be considered when evaluating what self-care skills to teach. Often individuals with mental retardation communicate in a nontraditional manner; thus, direct support professionals or caregivers may often miss subtle attempts to communicate preferences and dislikes which can be linked to some self-care skills. For example, some individuals do not like to be touched too much. When assisting in completing self-care skills, caregivers may need to provide some physical contact. Knowing this dislike can allow for planned modifications to teach the procedure in a way that minimizes physical contact and makes the learning situation more successful. Providing individuals with the opportunity to choose when activities occur and incorporating some flexibility in routine can also, in many cases, set the stage for a more successful learning experience. Choice is often overlooked when it comes to self-care skills because most support staff or direct support professionals believe that self-care skills must be completed totally without negotiation; these ideas may originate from the way self-care skills plans are written and how they are explained to direct care professionals to carry out. While it may be true that we must brush our teeth everyday, exactly when during the day may be flexible.

Whether the individual chooses by themselves or with the help of the family/team what skills to be taught, the individual's abilities across a variety of self-care skills should be assessed as part of the person-centered assessment (AAMR, 2002; Reid & Parsons, 2002). There are a variety of methods for assessing skill levels including direct observations, interviews with the individual/family/support staff, data collection, rating scales, and broad adaptive behavior scales (AAMR, 2002; Baker & Brightman, 2004; Reid & Parsons, 2002). The most effective assessment uses multiple methods across multiple settings and people including the individual with mental retardation to determine skill ability as well as skill performance.

Observations and data collection about the person's behavior during the assessment process are vital because they allow the observer to actually watch the individual complete (or be assisted in completing) each skill,

Behavioral Descriptions	
Bad Descriptions	**Good Descriptions**
Mike is angry	Mike hit Bob in the face
Susie is sad	Susie is crying
Bill is happy	Bill is smiling and laughing
Mary got upset	Mary hit her head on the wall
Joe is disrespectful	Joe steals money from others

FIG. 1. Examples of good and bad behavioral descriptions.

see what factors may impede the learning of each self skill where applicable, objectively define the target behavior (e.g., handwashing, see Fig. 1), and see what techniques make a training session successful. Having the ability to examine if a certain time of day or particular setting or person is better for the individual during a training session is valuable information that can be used in future trainings. Additionally, information obtained from the individual, family, or other caregivers through interviews is important to the assessment process. However, it is important to understand that caregivers and direct care professionals have many duties and responsibilities that encompass the care of someone; because of these duties the ability of the caregiver to reliably remember may be compromised and biases may interfere with the objectiveness of the person's skills (Griffiths, 1999). In addition, observations and data collection allow one to collect baseline data on the target behavior (Christian & Luce, 1985), analyze the necessary steps in the target behavior in a task analysis (Griffiths, 1999), and facilitate program planning for teaching the skill. Collecting data at baseline and throughout the teaching process will help caregivers assess what steps the person is learning and what steps need improvement. Also when challenging behaviors exists, collecting data on the problem behaviors as well as the replacement behaviors may shed light on the effectiveness of the training program. There should be an inverse relationship between the challenging behaviors and self-care skills (Griffiths, 1999). Program planning can be modified based on this information to ensure that the person with mental retardation will effectively learn the self-care skills.

Rating scales can also be used to identify self-care skills. They provide only minimal information about developing teaching techniques or interventions (Christian & Luce, 1985); however, rating scales can be used over time to assess if there is an overall increase or decrease in self-care skills. Rating scales may be specific to a skill area or may be a broader-based standardized assessment for adaptive behavior (AAMR, 2002; Lawton & Brody, 1969). Most rating scales involve a listing of possible self-care skills to be rated on a Likert-type scale, while other ratings scales are based on frequency or consistency with which the task is completed without assistance. The score is derived from the rating and allows for comparison to other individuals in different age categories.

All rating scales have their limitations, but can be useful in tracking progress in some instances. They do not account for if the low frequency or failure to perform is due to a skill deficit or lack of motivation. It is important to note that more accurate information can be obtained from the rating scales when paired with interviews with the individual, family, and support staff. These interviews allow for the distinction between an actual skill problem (i.e., the person does not know how or is unable to complete the task) and a motivation or performance problem (i.e., the individual knows how to do the task, but chooses not to do so).

One rating scale that is used to assess social skills in people with developmental disabilities is the Matson Evaluation of Social Skills for Individuals with Severe Retardation (MESSIER). The MESSIER is an 85-item inventory covering a wide array of positive and negative verbal and nonverbal social behaviors (Matson, 1995). It was designed to be used with individuals with severe and profound mental retardation. The goals of the MESSIER are to delineate communication weaknesses and monitor treatment effectiveness for those areas that become targets of a behavior support plan (positive and negative behaviors). The MESSIER is a structured interview and the items are read to a caregiver who knows the individual well. This rating scale allows the interviewer to utilize a scoring form that can reveal the relative strengths and weaknesses regarding the six factors on the MESSIER: positive verbal, positive nonverbal, general positive, negative verbal, negative nonverbal, and general negative.

The Screening Tool of fEeding Problems (STEP) is another assessment tool used with individuals with mental retardation to identify feeding and meal time behavior problems (Matson & Kuhn, 2001). This assessment instrument divides feeding problems into five groups including behaviors that may place someone at risk of aspiration, behaviors linked with food selectivity, behavioral skill deficits and excesses, behaviors related to food refusal, and nutrition-related behavior problems.

The Functional Independence Measure (FIM) is designed for use with individuals who have sustained a brain injury. It allows for assessment of feeding, grooming, bathing, dressing, toileting, and swallowing on a seven-point scale from total assistance to complete independence (Hamilton, Granger, Sherwin, Zielezny, & Tashman, 1987). It is designed to track progress over time and can be used as a measure of current skill and treatment effectiveness. However, it may not be useful for individuals with significant cognitive and/or physical limitations because it captures the global skills areas. These individuals may only be able to, for example, do a portion of the dressing task such as pulling his pants up. Though this is his tasks of focus, progress on this one task would not be reflected in assessment of the broader dressing item.

With regards to broad standardized assessments, adaptive behavior assessment instruments are used to obtain information that can be used in a variety of ways ranging from diagnosis to planning supports for the person. Adaptive behavior assessment tools can be used as a means to collect information on what people individually can or cannot complete by themselves, their resistance to certain skills, and the estimated percentage of time they are able to complete the self-care skills. However, most of these assessments provide a more global measure of adaptive behavior beyond specific self-care skills. AAMR (2002) states that adaptive behavior measures "that provide enough detail to assist with programming may be too long to be useful for diagnostic testing, may lack standardization data, or may describe behaviors that do not usually distinguish individuals with from individuals without mental retardation" (p. 82).

One adaptive behavior measure that has been used with this population is the Vineland Adaptive Behavior Scales-II (VABS-II) written by Sparrow, Cicchetti, and Balla (2005). The VABS-II is an adaptive behavior measure that is administered individually for people between birth and 90 years of age. This measure assesses four domain areas: communication, daily living skills, socialization, and motor skills (for children ages 0–6 years). There is also a maladaptive behavior domain that can be used to assess problem behaviors. There are two forms of the VABS-II: Survey Interview Form and Parent/Caregiver Rating Form. There is also an Expanded Interview Form and Teacher Rating Form that can be used to assess adaptive behaviors, and in planning education, habilitation, and treatment programs. The VABS-II can be used to identify strengths and weakness as well as age-related declines in older people. Additional adaptive behavior measures that examine conceptual, social, and practical skills for people with developmental disabilities include AAMR Adaptive Behavior Scale-School: 2nd Edition (Lambert, Nihira, & Leland,1998), AAMR Adaptive Behavior Scales-Residential and Community: 2nd Edition (Nihira, Leland, & Lambert, 1993) and Scales of Independent Behavior-Revised (Bruininks, Woodcock, Weatherman, & Hill, 1996).

The MESSIER, mentioned earlier, has been researched as a possible adaptive behavior measure. This instrument can be used to assess strengths and weakness in the person so that treatment and placement decisions can be made. Matson, Dixon, Matson, and Logan (2005) conducted a study where they assessed the utility of the MESSIER using the adaptive behavior scoring method and comparing these results with the individuals' previous diagnosis of mental retardation by a Ph.D. level psychologist (Stanford-Binet, Vineland Adaptive Behavior Scale, behavioral observations, and input of the treatment team during an annual review of the individuals' intellectual status) (Matson et al., 2005). The results suggested that the MESSIER Adaptive Scale cutoff scores classified 86% of those with a previous diagnosis of severe mental retardation as having a severity level of severe with 14% misclassification as profound mental retardation. Seventy-three percent of those previously classified as profound mental retardation were classified correctly using the MESSIER Adaptive Scale cut-off scores, with a 27% misclassification as severe. Thus, the results suggest that the utility of the MESSIER for classifying the severity levels of mental retardation is possible, but needs further investigation.

In summary, a multi-method, multi-informant, multi-setting assessment is the ideal for prioritizing the types of self-care skills to teach a person with mental retardation. The assessment should cover what matters most to the individual as well as direct assessment of self-care skills abilities and performances. With this information self-care skills can be prioritized for training in a manner that has the greatest benefit for the individual as based on a person-centered planning approach. Using multiple methods of assessment over time allows for evaluation of effectiveness of any training program both on the skill acquisition itself, as well as on skill performance and related quality of life benefits.

III. GENERALIZATION AND MAINTENANCE PLANNING FOR SELF-CARE SKILLS WITH INDIVIDUALS WITH MENTAL RETARDATION

In addition to assessment of self-care skills and training programs, it is necessary to include generalization and maintenance planning in the forefront so barriers that might impede the generalization of skills may be addressed prior to training. After the skill is taught, it is necessary to assess and monitor if the person is continuing to maintain, regress, or improve in the use of their self-care skills; thus, continual assessment of the skills is necessary. Additionally, continual assessment of someone's self-care skills over time allows those teaching the skills to determine if any modification needs to be made to the program. Orelove and Sobsey (1996) suggest that when trying to assess for generalization and maintenance, it is important to consider how the individual with mental retardation will be able to discriminate when to use the skills across appropriate and inappropriate settings and people. For example, washing a delicate piece of clothing in the bathroom or kitchen sink is appropriate for that setting; however, it would be inappropriate for the individual to wash the clothing item in the bathroom sink at the gas station. Griffiths (1999) also suggests setting up multiple situations in which the skill might be used in order to assess if the individual has decision-making/problem-solving skills in determining when/where to use skills.

After a skill is taught, it may be necessary for ongoing assessment as the person comes into contact with various situations in the community. General case instruction has been utilized when considering generalization programming after the individual has learned the self-care skill (Stokes et al., 2004). This procedure involves the trainer assessing and using in teaching samples objects that the person may come into contact with in the natural environment. Of course in order to know what items to assess and use in this approach of teaching skills, it is necessary to know the individual's experiences across people and settings. After the trainer is able to assess what items or objects are needed, they provide instruction on the different items so that the individual's repertoire of items to use for the self-care skills increases. For example, it is possible to put jelly on toast with a variety of utensils, yet some trainers would only teach using a knife. Using the general case instruction procedure to increase generalization, the trainer would use metal and plastic knives, spoons, and rubber spatulas. Thus, the individual will learn all the possibilities that may exist when in different settings or situations (e.g., restaurant, breakfast at a friend's house, breakfast at home).

Throughout the self-care skills literature, generalization and maintenance of the skill must be considered and planned for during the initial assessment process. An individual's ability to discriminate between different stimuli is a necessary component to consider when teaching self-care skills. In addition, an ongoing assessment of use of skills needs to be planned for and addressed during the assessment process so that potential barriers will not be stumbling blocks during the training process.

IV. CONSIDERATION OF CAREGIVER/TRAINER VARIABLES

Given the importance of teaching self-care skills to individuals with developmental disabilities/mental retardation, it is necessary that the people closest to them know how to teach and assess the progress of these skills (Koegel et al., 1996). Family members or other care providers (friends and direct support professionals) are often the people who have the most contact with the person and need clear instructions on how to teach self-care skills and collect data to assess if the person's skills are progressing or regressing. In addition, there is evidence that increasing the caregiver's performance with teaching self-care skills will often lead to a decrease in inappropriate behavior and an increase in adaptive behavior skills (Burgio, Whitman, & Reid, 1983). It is necessary while assessing what self-care skills to teach to the individual that the caregivers be involved in the assessment process. Determining the caregiver's ability, time, and involvement in teaching the skills should be discussed before any training begins. For example, if elderly parents must assist in teaching bathing skills to their adult child, but the parents cannot lift the adult into the bath tub, then it is not reasonable to expect that they will be available to help teach these skills without some assistance themselves. Thus, appropriate supports may need to be put into place so that the bathing skills may be taught (i.e., direct care professional may teach this skill). In addition, the caregivers should be instructed on how to assess and monitor the progression or regression of skills.

V. INITIAL AND ONGOING TRAININGS FOR CAREGIVERS

According to Reid and Parsons (2002) and AAMR (2002), all trainings on self-care skills should be competency- and performance-based for the caregiver. Initial and ongoing in-service training (at least every three months) that focuses on these topics is necessary to ensure that proper delivery of quality service is being provided to those individuals (Reid & Parsons, 2002). The following section describes ways of assessing and teaching caregiver skills prior to and during the training period.

Competency-based training means that the trainee (e.g., direct care professional) is expected to learn the targeted self-care skills prior to the actual training. Oral and written descriptions that focus on the rational, procedure, and process needed in training someone on the self-care skills are necessary so that the person conducting the training can learn all aspects of the self-care skills. In addition, defining caregiver behaviors in observable and measurable terms is also necessary so that they are aware of the type of behavior they should be demonstrating when the trainer (e.g., direct care professional's supervisor) assesses competency and performance skills. It is also important that the trainee learn about the data collection that will be utilized for tracking self-care skill progress. If the trainee is unable to read and if the following is possible, a drawing of each component of the skill should be made. An oral or written test should be administered so that an assessment of the caregiver's understanding of the oral and written components of the self-skill training can be obtained. If the student is unable to pass the test with at least 80% criterion (Reid & Parsons, 2002), it is an indicator that more training on the competency-based part of the training is necessary. Feedback and discussion about answers that are incorrect may help the trainee better understand what the correct answer is and why.

Performance-based staff training identifies what trainees are expected to do as demonstrated by trainers and, consequently, those procedures that will be demonstrated by the trainees. The trainers should use various techniques to assist the people being trained in learning the training program, such as instruction and modeling (Burch, Reiss, & Bailey, 1987), feedback (Reid & Parsons, 2002), and self-monitoring procedures (Richman, Riordan, Reiss, Pyles, & Bailey, 1988). All people in contact with the person being taught (family members, caregivers, direct support staff, supervisors, and so on) must meet a criterion of at least 80% or higher on both competency- and performance-based trainings (Reid & Parsons, 2002). The trainer should demonstrate the self-care skill while explaining the need for that component (e.g., "Place his left hand on the toothbrush because he is left-handed."). Observations, praise, and corrective feedback should be provided to the trainees on their performance on teaching each skill. Trainer demonstration, observation of caregivers performing the skill, and feedback to the caregiver should be repeated until the caregiver demonstrates 80% proficiency in performing the self-care skill.

In addition to the training sequence above, Reid and Parsons (2002) and AAMR (2002) also suggest monitoring the training session with the caregiver or direct care professional by using one of the following: evaluation of the course or training, pre- and/or post-written tests, return demonstration, application of skills as indicated on the employee's yearly evaluation, and treatment integrity observations (three each quarter). As a side note, any of these recommendations may be utilized better in a work environment, such as with direct care professionals, teachers, and multidisciplinary teams, as some of these may be offensive to families (e.g., giving families a written test on the way that they instruct their son or daughter in tying his or her shoes). Even in the workplace, training skills can be implemented in creative ways. Conducting treatment integrity (the percentage of time the plan is being followed consistently as written) observations with the caregivers followed by corrective feedback is such an instance. Graphing the treatment integrity and behavioral data on the same graph can be an effective teaching tool in showing how behavior increases or decreases when the skill is taught with high treatment integrity.

VI. BEHAVIORAL CHALLENGES

On some occasions, problem behaviors impede the assessment or teaching of self-care skills. Thus, positive behavioral support has been developed to create and sustain learning environments that improve lifestyle results (personal, health, social, family, work, recreational, and so on) for both youth and adults by making problem behavior less effective, less efficient, and less relevant while making desired behavior more functional due to reinforcement (Carr et al., 2002). Haring and De Vault (1996) suggest that positive behavioral supports are composed of: (a) "interventions that consider the contexts within which the behavior occurs," (b) "interventions that address the functionality of the problem behavior," (c) "interventions that can be justified by the outcomes," and (d) "outcomes that are acceptable to the individual, the family, and the supportive community" (p. 116). Albin, Lucyshyn, Horner, and Flannery (1996) stress the importance of having a positive behavior plan that has "contextual" fit between the components of the plan and characteristics of the person who the plan was written for, who will implement the plan, and other environmental and programmatic factors.

The implementation of a positive behavioral support plan can vary greatly depending on the setting for which it is intended as well as the age of the individual and specifics related to the targeted behavior. Starting with the identification of the individual's long- and short-term goals followed by environmental manipulation/control (changing aspects of the setting where a behavior occurs), curriculum (teaching new skills/replacement behaviors), modification of behavior (teaching or changing behavior), and removing rewards that maintain problem behaviors while promoting replacement behaviors are all key components to an effective positive behavioral support plan. Griffiths (1999) states that:

> Unless new replacement behaviors are as effective as the inappropriate behavior in bringing about the desired positive or negative reinforcement, these behaviors may not be used. When the new behavior fails to achieve the same results at equal or greater the rate or intensity as the inappropriate behavior does, it is likely the person will use the problem behavior to gain the desired outcome (p. 200).

The goal of positive behavioral supports is to use information from functional assessments as a blueprint for the design of learning and teaching environments which train and sustain adaptive behaviors and decrease reinforcement or usefulness of nonadaptive, socially nonacceptable, or problematic behavior (Carr et al., 2002; Griffiths, 1999).

A functional assessment provides a systematic approach in ascertaining the environmental contingencies that mediate the occurrence of a target behavior. Function-based approaches to treatment have consistently proven to be effective. Once a challenging behavior is identified, an analysis of controlling variables is conducted to delineate those factors maintaining the behavior. Maintaining factors that have been empirically validated as having causal relationships to challenging behaviors in the people with developmental disabilities include attention, escape, tangibles, pain, and non-social reasons. Once a function is identified, a person can be taught specific replacement behaviors to have his or her needs met in more socially acceptable ways. The result is that the individual gains greater independence, autonomy, and choice making in his or her world. Two instruments that may be utilized during the functional assessment are described below.

The Questions About Behavioral Function (QABF) is designed to assess motivation behind each challenging behavior (Matson & Vollmer, 1994). If a person has multiple challenging behaviors then a separate analysis should be conducted for each behavioral difficulty. The QABF consists of 25 items that are rated on a scale of never (0) to often (3) and is administered with someone who knows the individual well (e.g., a caregiver or family member). On an accompanying score sheet, the items endorsed should be circled and graphed for visual analysis. A more fine-grained analysis of the function may be derived from the sum of the actual item ratings with higher totals indicating greater likelihood of function.

In addition to the QABF, the Functional Analysis Interview (FAI) can be utilized during the functional assessment (O'Neil et al., 1997). The FAI is a structured interview that allows for the systematic gathering of information related to challenging behaviors. It is not scored in any manner, but rather serves as an interview guide for obtaining information from those who know the individual best. It is designed to allow for the organization of information gathered into treatment hypothesis that can be translated into actual treatment steps.

In addition to the QABF and FAI, it is also necessary to consider setting event manipulations and the individual's ability to make their own choices (Horner & Carr, 1997). By identifying various setting events which make a challenging behavior more likely to occur, those events can be either eliminated when plausible or at least altered and neutralized so that behaviors are less likely to occur or less likely to interfere with teaching. With regard to self-care skills, setting events that should be examined include a particular family or staff member, lighting, room or weather temperature, noise level, pain, hunger, crowds, tiredness, or anxiety. To illustrate the importance of setting events, Wehmeyer, Baker, Blumberg, and Harrison (2004) explored how students/individuals could take a more active role in their functional assessments and thus the development of interventions. These authors showed a high rate of agreement between individuals and service providers in identification of problem behaviors. The individuals, however, often pointed to different setting events than service providers who knew these individuals the best. These results should be further explored and kept in mind when developing teaching strategies.

Finally, it is important to consider if the person has the ability to make their own choices in relation to their life when addressing noncompliance and behavioral challenges related to learning. On some occasions, the person is able to make decisions, but other environmental variables prevent this from happening such as, parental control. Many studies have illustrated that inclusion of choice and self-determination in people with developmental disabilities throughout their daily life has significant impacts on learning and compliance with training (Bambara, Koger, Katzer, & Davenport, 1995; Bannerman, Sheldon, Sherman, & Harchik, 1990; Cole & Levinson, 2002; Felce & Emerson, 2001; Shevin & Klein, 1984). Researchers have shown that choice reduces problem behaviors and thus increases learning through two different mechanisms: avoidance of aversive situations and access to larger rewards (Reid & Parsons, 1991). Often times when an individual is able to make a choice of not only what activity to do, but when to complete the task, less problem behaviors will be exhibited. Less reluctance or aversion toward a task means there will likely be less challenging behaviors encountered.

Shukla, Surratt, Horner, and Albin (1995) reported a case study whereby a woman was given the opportunity to initiate tasks as opposed to being instructed to complete tasks by staff during her morning routine. This was undertaken in response to challenging behaviors she exhibited during her morning routine that were shown (through functional analysis) to be related to escape from task demands placed on her by staff. The result of the case, a decrease in challenging behavior, shows that even small changes in staff training that teaches the direct care professionals to allow the individual to initiate and complete tasks with minimal instruction (along with the assistance of a picture schedule where applicable) may be quite imperative in reaching goals. Furthermore, though the case study specifically targeted the morning routine, the results generalized to daytime and evening routines whereby staff instructed the individual less and found her to initiate more tasks and demonstrate less behavioral challenges. These minor alterations have opened doors for individuals to increase their self-determination and autonomy. Increasing self-determination, involvement of the individual, and choice making are all crucial in the development and successfulness of curriculum and behavioral supports. With this in mind, it is important that professionals, support staff, and parents assess what barriers, if any, the individual has in regards to making choices and that options/choices are offered in daily activities and scheduling whenever possible.

VII. CONCLUSIONS

Learning self-care skills is important for individuals with developmental disabilities and mental retardation. Given the recent increases in community living in the developmental disabilities arena, more attention has been focused on self-care skills. These skills increase self-reliance and autonomy, and they prepare individuals for independent living. Moreover, teaching these adaptive skills gives individuals more choice and freedom in their personal lives and fosters the replacement of socially unacceptable or challenging behaviors for appropriate adaptive behaviors.

Assessing which self-care skills to teach individuals with mental retardation involves a person-centered approach. Additionally, assessment information that is multi-method, multi-setting, and multi-informant should be obtained. Clinicians and researchers have provided guidelines to use when determining what self-care skills are taught in order of importance. Observations, data collection, rating scales, and adaptive behavior measures are necessary to assess baseline skills and can also be utilized over time to monitor skill acquisition.

In addition to the training techniques, generalization and maintenance planning must be considered during the assessment process and incorporated into the self-care skills program for both the individuals with mental retardation as well as their caregivers. Ongoing assessment must occur so that one may determine if the person's skills are being maintained at an acceptable level or if there is a loss or gain of skills.

Besides generalization and maintenance planning, caregiver training is an essential component when teaching self-care skills to individuals with mental retardation. The caregivers are the closest people to the individual, have the most contact with the individual, and know the individual the best. Caregiver training must be competency- and performance-based so that the caregiver's skills needed to teach the self-care skills are instilled through various techniques. Competency-based trainings should include oral and written descriptions of procedures, objective definitions of behaviors, illustrations of data collection, and oral or written tests. In addition, the performance-based training should consist of demonstrations by the trainer, instructions, corrective feedback, and self-monitoring procedures. Some care should be given when working with families given the sensitive nature of working in their homes; incidental teaching is often a better alternative to the competency- and performance-based trainings.

Finally, challenging behaviors often impede the learning of self-care skills in some individuals with mental retardation. Often times, it is necessary to have a positive behavior support plan that is person-centered and consists of interventions based on functional behavioral assessments.

REFERENCES

Albin, R. W., Lucyshyn, J. M., Horner, R. H., & Flannery, K. B. (1996). In L. K. Koegel, R. L. Koegel, & G. Dunlap (Eds.), *Positive behavioral support: Including people with difficult behavior in the community* (pp. 81–98). Baltimore, MD: Paul H. Brookes Publishing Co.

American Association on Mental Retardation (AAMR) (2002). *Mental retardation: Definition, classification, and systems of supports* (10th ed.). Washington, DC: American Association on Mental Retardation.

American Psychiatric Association (APA) (2000). *Diagnostic and statistical manual of mental disorders IV-text revision.* Washington, DC: American Psychiatric Association.

Baker, B. L., & Brightman, A. J. (2004). *Steps to independence: Teaching everyday skills to children with special needs.* Baltimore, MD: Paul H. Brooks Publishing.

Bambara, L. M., Koger, F., Katzer, T., & Davenport, T. A. (1995). Embedding choice in the context of daily routines: An experimental case study. *Journal of the Association for Persons with Severe Handicaps, 20,* 185–195.

Bannerman, D. J., Sheldon, J. B., Sherman, J. A., & Harchik, A. E. (1990). Balancing the right to habilitation with the right to personal liberties: The rights of people with developmental disabilitities to eat too many doughnuts and take a nap. *Journal of Applied Behavior Analysis, 3,* 79–89.

Bat-Haee, M. A. (2001). A longitudinal study of active treatment of adaptive skills of individuals with profound mental retardation. *Psychological Reports, 89,* 345–354.

Bosch, S., & Fuqua, R. W. (2001). Behavioral cusps: A model for selecting target behaviors. *Journal of Applied Behavior Analysis, 34,* 123–125.

Browder, D. W., & Grasso, E. (1999). Teaching money skills to individuals with mental retardation. *Remedial and Special Education, 20,* 297–308.

Bruininks, R. H., Woodcock, R. W., Weatherman, R. F., & Hill, B. K. (1996). *Scales of independent behavior-revised.* Itasca, IL: Riverside.

Burch, M. R., Reiss, M. L., & Bailey, J. S. (1987). A competency-based "hands-on" training package for direct care staff. *Journal of the Association for Severe Handicaps, 12,* 67–71.

Burgio, L. D., Whitman, T. L., & Reid, D. H. (1983). A participative management approach for improving direct care staff performance in institutional setting. *Journal of Applied Behavior Analysis, 16,* 37–53.

Carr, E. G., Dunlap, G., Horner, R. H., Koegel, R. L., Turnbull, A. P., Sailor, W., et al. (2002). Positive behavior support: Evolution of an applied science. *Journal of Positive Behavior Interventions, 4,* 4–16.

Christian, W. P., & Luce, S. C. (1985). Behavioral self-help training for developmentally disabled individuals. *School Psychology Review, 14,* 177–181.

Cole, C. L., & Levinson, T. R. (2002). Effects of within-activity choices on the challenging behavior of children with severe developmental disabilities. *Journal of Positive Behavior Interventions, 4,* 29–37.

Dinerstein, R. D. (1999). Introduction. In R. D. Dinerstein, S. S. Herr, & J. L. O'Sullivan (Eds.), *A guide to consent.* Washington, DC: American Association on Mental Retardation.

Felce, D., & Emerson, E. (2001). Living with support in a home in the community: Predictors of behavioral development and household and community activity. *Mental Retardation and Developmental Disabilities Research Reviews, 7,* 75–83.

Gahan, S., Dykstra, L., & Summers, J. (2002). Person-centered approaches to services and supports. In D. M. Griffiths, C. Stavrakaki, & J. Summers (Eds.), *Dual diagnosis: An introduction to the mental health needs of persons with developmental disabilities.* Ontario, Canada: Habilitiative Mental Health Resource Network.

Graziano, A. M. (2002). *Developmental disabilities: Introduction to a diverse field.* Boston, MA: Allyn & Bacon.

Griffiths, D. M. (1999). Training procedures for teaching prosocial skills. In D. M. Griffiths, W. I. Garderner, & J. Nugent (Eds.), *Individual centered behavioral interventions: A multi-modal functional approach* (pp. 181–205). Kingston, NY: NADD Press.

Hagner, D., & Davies, T. (2002). "Doing my own thing": Supported self-employment for individuals with cognitive disabilities. *Journal of Vocational Rehabilitation, 17,* 65–74.

Hamilton, B. B., Granger, C. V., Sherwin, C. V., Zielezny, M., & Tashman, J. S. (1987). A uniform national data system for medical rehabilitation. In M. J. Fuhrer (Ed.), *Rehabilitation outcomes: Analysis and measurement* (pp. 137–147). Baltimore, MD: Paul H. Brookes Publishing.

Haring, N. G., & De Vault, G. (1996). Family issues and family support: Discussion. In L. K. Koegel, R. L. Koegel, & G. Dunlap (Eds.), *Positive behavioral support: Including people with difficult behavior in the community* (pp. 116–120). Baltimore, MD: Paul H. Brookes Publishing Co.

Horner, R. H., & Carr, E. G. (1997). Behavioral support for students with severe disabilities: Functional assessment and comprehensive intervention. *The Journal of Special Education, 31,* 84–104.

Kincaid, D. (1996). Person-centered planning. In L. K. Koegel, R. L. Koegel, & G. Dunlap (Eds.), *Positive behavioral support: Including people with difficult behavior in the community* (pp. 439–465). Baltimore, MD: Paul H. Brookes Publishing Co.

Koegel, L. K., Koegel, R. L., Kellegrew, D., & Mullen, K. (1996). Parent education for prevention and reduction of problem behaviors. In L. K. Koegel, R. L. Koegel, & G. Dunlap (Eds.), *Positive behavioral support: Including people with difficult behavior in the community* (pp. 116–120). Baltimore, MD: Paul H. Brookes Publishing Co.

Lambert, N., Nihira, K., & Leland, H. (1998). *AAMR Adaptive Behavior Scale-School* (2nd ed.). Austin, TX: Pro-Ed.

Lancioni, G. E., & O'Reily, M. F. (2002). Teaching food preparation skills to people with intellectual disabilities: A literature overview. *Journal of Applied Research in Intellectual Disabilities, 15,* 236–253.

Lawton, M. P., & Brody, E. M. (1969). Assessment of older people: Self-maintaining and instrumental activities of daily living. *The Gerontologist, 9,* 179–186.

Lockwood, K., & Williams, D. E. (1994). Treatment and extended follow-up of chronic hand mouthing. *Journal of Behavior Therapy and Experimental Psychiatry, 25,* 161–169.

Luce, S. C., Anderson, S. R., Thibadeau, S. F., & Lipsker, L. E. (1984). Preparing the client for transition to community-based living. In W. P. Christian, G. T. Hannah, & T. J. Glahn (Eds.), *Programming effective human services: Strategies for institutional change and client transition* (pp. 157–176). New York: Plenum Press.

Luiselli, J. K. (1993). Training self-feeding skills in children who are deaf and blind. *Behavior Modification, 17,* 457–473.

Matson, J. L. (1995). Manual for the Matson evaluation of social skills in individuals with severe retardation (MESSIER). Baton Rouge, Louisiana: Scientific Publishers Incorporated.

Matson, J. L., Dixon, D. R., Matson, M. L., & Logan, J. R. (2005). Classifying mental retardation and specific strength and deficit areas in severe and profoundly mentally retarded person with the MESSIER. *Research in Developmental Disabilities, 26*(1), 41–45.

Matson, J. L., & Kuhn, D. E. (2001). Identifying feeding problems in mentally retarded persons: development and reliability of the screening tool of feeding problems (STEP). *Research in Developmental Disabilities, 22,* 165–172.

Matson, J. L., Smalls, Y., Hampff, A., Smiroldo, B., & Anderson, S. (1998). A comparison of behavioral techniques to teach functional independent-living skills to individuals with severe and profound mental retardation. *Behavioral Modifications, 22,* 298–306.

Matson, J. L., & Vollmer, T. (1994). *Questions about behavioral function administrator's manual.* Baton Rouge, Louisiana: Disability Consultants, LLC.

Nihira, K., Leland, H., & Lambert, N. (1993). *AAMR Adaptive Behavior Scale-Residential and Community* (2nd ed.). Austin, TX: Pro-Ed.

O'Neil, R. E., Horner, R. H., Albin, R. W., Sprague, J. R., Storey, K., & Newton, J. S. (1997). *Functional assessment and program development for problem behavior.* New York: Brooks/Cole Publishing Company.

Orelove, F. P., & Sobsey, D. (1996). *Educating children with multiple disabilities: A transdisciplinary approach* (4th ed.). London: Paul H. Brooks Publishing Company.

Reid, D. H., & Parsons, M. B. (1991). Making choice a routine part of mealtimes for persons with profound mental retardation. *Behavioral Residential Treatment, 6,* 249–261.

Reid, D. H., & Parsons, M. B. (2002). *Working to overcome challenging behavior among people who have severe disabilities.* Morganton, NC: Habilitative Management Consultants, Inc.

Richman, G. S., Riordan, M. R., Reiss, M. L., Pyles, D. A., & Bailey, J. S. (1988). The effects of self-monitoring and supervisor feedback on staff performance in a residential setting. *Journal of Applied Behavior Analysis, 21,* 401–409.

Rosales-Ruiz, J., & Baer, D. M. (1997). Behavioral cusps: A developmental and pragmatic concept for behavior analysis. *Journal of Applied Behavior Analysis, 30,* 533–544.

Rudrud, E. H., & Vaudt, T. M. (1986). Prerequisite skills for semi-independent living services (SILS) placement. *Journal of the Association for Persons with Severe Handicaps, 11,* 182–187.

Saloviita, T. (2000). Generalized effects of dry bed training on day-time incontinence. *Behavioral Interventions, 15,* 79–81.

Saloviita, T. J., & Tuulkari, M. (2000). Cognitive-behavioural treatment package for teaching grooming skills to a man with an intellectual disability. *Scandinavian Journal of Behaviour Therapy, 29,* 140–147.

Sewell, T. J., Collins, B. C., Hemmetter, M. L., & Schuster, J. W. (1998). Using simultaneous prompting within an activity-based format to teach dressing skills to preschoolers with developmental delays. *Journal of Early Intervention, 21,* 132–145.

Shevin, M., & Klein, N. K. (1984). The importance of choice making skills for students with severe disabilities. *Journal of the Association for Persons with Severe Handicaps, 9,* 159–166.

Shogren, K. A., Faggella-Luby, M. N., Bae, S., & Wehmeyer, J. (2004). The effect of choice making as an intervention of problem behavior: A meta-analysis. *Journal of Positive Behavior Interventions, 6,* 228–237.

Shukla, S., Surratt, A. V., Horner, R. H., & Albin, R. W. (1995). Case study: Examining the relationship between self-initiations of an individual with disabilities and directive behavior of staff persons in a residential setting. *Behavioral Interventions, 10,* 101–110.

Sisson, L. A., Kilwein, M. L., & Van Hasselt, V. B. (1988). A graduated guidance procedure for teaching self-dressing skills to multi-handicapped children. *Research in Developmental Disabilities, 9,* 419–432.

Snell, M. E. (1982). Analysis of time delay procedures in teaching daily living skills to retarded adults. *Analysis and Intervention in Developmental Disabilities, 2,* 139–155.

Sparrow, S. S., Cicchetti, D. V., & Balla, D. A. (2005). *Vineland Adaptive Behavior Scales* (2nd ed.). Circle Pines, MN: AGS Publishing.

Stokes, J. V., Cameron, M. J., Dorsey, M. F., & Fleming, E. (2004). Task analysis, correspondence training, and general case instruction for teaching personal hygiene skills. *Behavioral Interventions, 19,* 121–135.

Tarnowski, K. J., & Drabman, R. S. (1987). Teaching intermittent self-catheterization skills to mentally retarded children. *Research in Developmental Disabilities, 8,* 521–529.

Wacker, D. P., Peck, S., Derby, K. M., Berg, W., & Harding, J. (1996). Deveolping long-term reciprocal interactions between parents and their young children with problematic behavior. In L. K. Koegel, R. L. Koegel, & G. Dunlap (Eds.), *Positive behavioral support: Including people with difficult behavior in the community* (pp. 51–80). Baltimore, MD: Paul H. Brookes Publishing Co.

Wehmeyer, M. L., Baker, D. J., Blumberg, R., & Harrison, R. (2004). Self-determination and student involvement in functional assessment: Innovative practices. *Journal of Positive Behavior Interventions, 6,* 29–35.

Feeding Disorders

DAVID E. KUHN, PETER A. GIROLAMI, AND CHARLES S. GULOTTA

DEPARTMENT OF BEHAVIORAL PSYCHOLOGY, KENNEDY KRIEGER INSTITUTE
JOHNS HOPKINS MEDICAL SCHOOL, BALTIMORE, MARYLAND

I. INTRODUCTION

Feeding is the process by which people accept and digest food in amounts adequate to meet their nutritional needs. What seems at first glance as a simple intuitive act is actually a complex process requiring successful caregiver interaction, adequate oral motor skills, and intact gastrointestinal motility and absorption. In order to understand feeding and swallowing disorders in individuals with intellectual disability, one must recognize that there are dynamically changing developmental skills and social abilities in this population. For typically developing individuals, progression through the normal stages of feeding (Table I) requires the attainment of physical abilities such as postural stability, oral motor coordination, and sensory awareness. In addition, factors such as emerging cognitive skills and socialization play an important role in an effective feeding interaction. When one or more of these variables are not intact, individuals with intellectual disability can develop a "feeding problem" or "feeding disorder."

Individuals with intellectual disability with severe feeding problems share one common characteristic: they do not eat enough by mouth to adequately meet their nutritional needs. However, after that similarity, the individuals often differ in the severity, topography, and etiology of their feeding problem. This chapter will provide information about various assessments that should be conducted prior to implementing treatment, as well as attempt to categorize feeding problems and discuss the variables associated with the onset and maintenance of pediatric feeding disorders.

INTERNATIONAL REVIEW OF RESEARCH IN MENTAL RETARDATION, Vol. 34
0074-7750/07 $35.00

DOI: 10.1016/S0074-7750(07)34012-3

TABLE I
PROVIDES THE TYPICAL CHRONOLOGICAL DEVELOPMENT OF APROPRIATE EATING BEHAVIORS

Age (month)	Stage
Birth–12	Suck/swallow liquids (breast or bottle)
4–6	Pureed solids by spoon (cereal, fruits, vegetables, meats)
8–9	Cup drinking liquids
	Ground or junior foods by spoon
	Finger feeding soft dissolvables
10–12	Soft table food
24	Self-feed with utensils

II. EPIDEMIOLOGY

Feeding disorders and related inappropriate mealtime behaviors represent significant problems that can have serious physiological and behavioral consequences. While these behaviors are also observed in the typically developing population, particularly among children, these problems appear to be more prevalent among the developmentally disabled. According to Borthwick-Duffy (1994) the prevalence of comorbid psychopathology among individuals diagnosed with intellectual disability is significantly greater than the general population. This appears to hold true when considering the comorbidity of feeding disorders and intellectual disability. Crist and Napier-Phillips (2001) reported that problems associated with feeding and meals were reported ~12–21% of typically developing children. Reports of feeding and mealtime behavior problems among individuals with developmental disabilities have generally been higher, including estimates of approximately one-third of children with developmental disabilities (Palmer, Thompson, & Linscheid, 1975) and as high as 80% among individuals with severe and profound intellectual disability (Perske, Clifton, McClean, & Stein, 1977). Gravestock (2000) suggested that overall these disorders are found at a higher rate in institutionalized settings (6–42%) as opposed to the community (19%).

Not surprisingly, in addition to setting, the prevalence of these disorders/problems varies across disorders and across functioning level. Crist and Napier-Phillips (2001) reported that food refusal and selectivity behaviors were reported in ~12–19% of a sample of typically developing children as compared to 30% reported by Thommessen, Heiberg, Kase, Larsen, and Riis (1991) among children with intellectual disability. Gravestock (2000) reported that both pica and rumination are more prevalent among individuals functioning in the severe to profound levels of intellectual disability.

In addition, these behaviors are more commonly observed among individuals residing in institutional settings when compared to community samples. Pica has been reported to occur in ~9–16% of individuals residing in institutional settings (Lofts, Schroeder, & Maier, 1990; McAlpine & Singh, 1986), and rumination in ~6–10% (Rogers, Stratton, Victor, Kennedy, & Andres, 1992).

Secondary to many of the problems stated above, significant health and medical complications are apparent. Pica has been associated with serious and even life-threatening consequences, including poisoning (Feldman, 1986) and intestinal blockages (Ausman, Ball, & Alexander, 1974). Similarly, rumination may result in weight loss, dehydration, and aspiration (Ellis, Parr, Singh, & Wechsler, 1997) among other problems. Stewart, Beange, and Mackerras (1994) found that in a sample of 142 adults with varying levels of intellectual disability ~14% of males and ~25% of females met criteria for being obese, while MacDonald, McConnell, Stephen, and Dunnigan (1989) found that ~43% of individuals with developmental disabilities were significantly underweight.

Additionally, as described in subsequent sections, often times a gastronomy tube is used to supplement or replace oral feedings for those individuals who cannot or do not take food by mouth. Strauss, Kastner, Ashwal, and White (1997) found that among individuals with severe developmental disabilities ranging in age from 2 to 14 years, tube-feedings significantly increased mortality rates. Furthermore, he suggests that this increase may be a function of the higher rates of pulmonary disease secondary to "overly vigorous nutritional maintenance and subsequent aspiration after tube placement."

An increased risk of feeding problems can be associated with certain conditions where intellectual disability is typically present. For example, Spender et al. (1996) found that oral motor functions of individuals with Down syndrome, specifically jaw and tongue function, were often impaired resulting in feeding difficulties. Similarly, Frazier and Friedman (1996) found a high prevalence of aspiration among individuals with Down syndrome. Riordan, Iwata, Finney, wohl, and Stanley (1984) suggested that developmentally disabled individuals are more likely to have oral motor dysfunction.

III. ETIOLOGY

The causes or maintaining factors of feeding problems can include medical conditions (Dellert, Hyams, Treem, & Geertsma, 1993) (e.g., gastroesophageal reflux), anatomical abnormalities (e.g., cleft-lip, palate), oral-motor delay or dysfunction subsequent to other conditions (e.g., cerebral palsy), physical disease (e.g., cystic fibrosis, food allergies), and behavioral mismanagement during feeding (Iwata et al., 1994).

A. Social

In discussing the etiology of feeding disorders it is important to consider that, similar to other problem behaviors (e.g., self-injurious behavior), the variables that occasion and maintain the behavior may shift over time. That is, the behavior may have first emerged in response to a medical condition [e.g., gastroesophageal reflux disease (GERD)], but may persist because of the social consequences the behavior produces (e.g., attention from caregivers). Conversely, the behavior (e.g., food refusal) may have been shaped by the consequences it produced (e.g., caregiver attention), but persists because the individual did not learn the oral-motor skills necessary to eat efficiently by mouth. Therefore, this section will discuss the social/environmental variables that may be associated with either the emergence of the feeding disorder and/or its maintenance.

In general, information regarding the etiology of feeding and mealtime behavior problems is limited (Piazza et al., 2003). Furthermore, the identification of functional relations between the behavior and social/environmental variables is generally not assessed until an organic etiology has been ruled out. Thus, only following an inconclusive interdisciplinary evaluation or insufficient medical treatment are residual feeding problems thoroughly assessed and treated behaviorally. Studies completed in recent years have begun to shed some light on the variables that occasion and the consequences that maintain problematic feeding and mealtime behavior.

Similar to other destructive behaviors (Iwata, Pace et al., 1994), feeding and mealtime behavior problems may be maintained by social reinforcement contingencies including positive and negative reinforcement. The contingency most commonly associated with mealtime behavior problems is negative reinforcement (Iwata, Pace et al., 1994). That is, the presentation of food may function as an aversive stimulus that occasions behavior(s) (e.g., problem behavior or noncompliance) to escape from or avoid the stimulus. For example, when presented with a bite of fruit, a client may push the food away or aggress against the caregiver in order to terminate or delay the food presentation. The aversiveness of the food is often a function of past experiences with food, where consumption was paired with pain or discomfort related to a medical problem (e.g., GERD). However, these behaviors often persist following treatment of the medical problem.

The other contingency sometimes associated with the maintenance of feeding and mealtime behavior problems is positive reinforcement. In this arrangement, the reinforcer typically takes the form of access to either social (e.g., caregiver attention) or tangible (e.g., preferred edibles or leisure items) stimuli. That is, the individual may continue to engage in problem behavior or noncompliance because doing so results in either access to more highly preferred foods, preferred leisure items or attention from caregivers. For example, an individual who is fussy at mealtimes may receive a great deal of attention from care givers, be given highly preferred (and not necessarily nutritious) foods, or be rewarded with favorite toys—all in the name of "getting them to eat *something*." This may be effective in the short term, but creates—in the long term—a pattern whereby the individual will not eat without these rewards, and may then receive them when fussy and refusing behaviors occur, thus maintaining these responses through positive reinforcement. Such operant paradigms can develop concurrent with organic/medical problems or persist long after their resolution; however, nearly 20% of feeding problems may be explained by environmental influences alone (Palmer & Horn, 1978; Sisson & Van Hasselt, 1989; see also Babbitt et al., 1994; Iwata et al., 1982; Kerwin, 1999; Linscheid et al., 1995; Riordan et al., 1984; Sanders, Patel, Le Grice, & Shepard, 1993; Sisson & Dixon, 1986a; Werle, Murphy, & Budd, 1993), and these behavior problems contribute to over 50% of the nutritional problems seen in children with developmental disabilities (Pesce, Wodarski, & Wang, 1989).

Using functional assessments (both indirect and experimental), several research groups have attempted to identify social functions of mealtime behavior problems. Girolami and Scotti (2001) found that these behaviors might be maintained by both negative and positive reinforcement (as described above). Across three participants, an escape function was evident; however, with one subject positive reinforcement in the forms of access to attention and toys were demonstrated to maintain the inappropriate behavior as well. Piazza et al. (2003) found that 10 of 15 participants demonstrated problematic mealtime behavior sensitive to social reinforcement. Of those 10, negative reinforcement was identified as a maintaining variable for 9 of them. Problem behaviors were also found to be sensitive to positive reinforcement in the forms of attention (53% of cases) and preferred tangible items (13% of cases).

On a larger scale, Matson et al. (2005) identified 125 adults with developmental disabilities who displayed one or more feeding problems categorized as either problem behaviors (e.g., aggression) during a meal, pica, rumination, food stealing, and food refusal, and assessed behavioral function using the Questions About Behavioral Function (QABF; Matson & Vollmer, 1995). Results from that study were consistent with the findings of both Girolami and Scotti (2001) and Piazza et al. (2003) in that mealtime problem behavior and food refusal behavior were found to be primarily maintained by negative reinforcement. In addition, positive reinforcement contingencies in the form of access to attention or preferred foods were most commonly associated with food stealing and food refusal behaviors. Lastly, behaviors most commonly hypothesized to maintain independent of social consequences included pica and rumination.

In summary, there appears to be strong evidence to suggest that mealtime behavior problems and food refusal behaviors are maintained in large part by negative reinforcement, and to a lesser extent positive reinforcement. In addition, both rumination and pica may persist predominantly because of the sensory consequences that the behavior itself produces. However, it is important to note that it remains unclear whether these reinforcement contingencies are responsible for the emergence of these behaviors or whether they are only involved in the maintenance. Regardless, based on the results of the assessments described in the following sections, treatment(s) should address the presenting problem and the variables that now maintain the behavior.

B. Medical

Biologically based problems can cause significant discomfort during mealtimes or after food consumption, making the process of eating aversive for the individual. The individual may then refuse to eat because of this discomfort, establishing an escape paradigm whereby refusal is negatively reinforced by the termination of caregiver demands to eat. Even after the organic conditions have been successfully treated and the discomfort associated with eating has decreased, continuation of this pattern of interactions can maintain refusal behaviors. Virtually any medical condition can set the stage for poor feeding. Anything that can be associated with the disruption of the normal eating process leading to a lack of exposure required to practice and develop the requisite skills to eat (Manikam & Perman, 2000; Rudolph & Link, 2002).

For example, GERD is a condition often associated with individuals with feeding disorders. GERD occurs when the lower esophageal sphincter (LES) does not close properly the liquid content of the stomach regurgitates (backs up, or refluxes) into the esophagus. When refluxed stomach acid touches the lining of the esophagus, it can cause a burning sensation in the chest or throat called heartburn. The fluid may even be tasted in the back of the mouth, and this is called acid indigestion. Often painful, this condition can provide "motivation" for someone to avoid food or drink that may be associated with its onset.

Dysphagia (swallowing dysfunction) is the term used to describe when someone has difficulty safely transporting food from the mouth, into the throat, and down into the esophagus into the stomach (Logemann, 1983). Swallowing is a complex act that involves the mouth, throat area, and esophagus (tube that transports food to the stomach). Many nerves and muscles affect the correct function of these parts. Part of the act of swallowing is under

TABLE II
LISTS COMMON DIAGNOSABLE MEDICAL CONDITIONS THAT ARE ASSOCIATED WITH THE PRESENCE OF FEEDING DISORDERS

Dysphagia	Cleft lip and/or palate
Aspiration pneumonia	Cerebral palsy
Constipation	Esophageal atresia
Celiac disease	Cricopharyngeal achalasia
Motility disorders	Tracheoesophageal fistula
Gastroeophageal reflux	Esophageal mass
Food allergies	Esophageal stricture
Malrotation	Chronic lung disease
Infectious gastrointestinal disorders	Gastric emptying syndrome
Malabsorbtive disorders	

conscious (voluntary) control. However, much of swallowing is involuntary. Problems at any point —from chewing food and moving it into the back of the mouth to moving the food into the stomach—can result in difficulty swallowing (Morris & Klein, 1987). Frequently, symptoms of chest pain, food stuck in the throat, heaviness or pressure in the neck or upper chest, are the result of swallowing difficulties (Tuchman, 1989). Table II lists a number of common medical/developmental diagnoses that are commonly associated with feeding problems.

IV. CLASSIFICATION OF FEEDING DISORDERS

A wide variety of different disorders, diagnoses, skill deficits, and excess behaviors fall under the term of "feeding disorders." These include: (a) failure to thrive (FTT), a term descriptive of children who have trouble gaining weight, often due to serious pediatric ailments (Hamill et al., 1979; Heffer & Kelly, 1994; Stickler, 1984); (b) feeding disorder of infancy or early childhood, a formal diagnostic category for children who persistently fail to eat adequately and gain weight [American Psychiatric Association (APA), 1994]; (c) rumination disorder, characterized by repeated regurgitation and rechewing of food (APA, 1994); and (d) pica, which is the persistent eating of non-nutritional substances (APA, 1994).

Beyond these formal diagnoses, feeding problems can be categorized by their topography (Linscheid, Budd, & Rasnake, 1995) and include clusters such as: (a) self-feeding deficits (e.g., acquisition and maintenance of independent self-feeding skills; Palmer & Horn, 1978; Sisson & Van Hasselt, 1989); (b) limited food intake (e.g., eating small quantities or being highly selective; Iwata, Riordan, Wohl, & Finney, 1982; Luiselli & Gleason, 1987); (c) coughing, gagging, and choking (i.e., exaggeration of normal defense mechanisms which can interfere with eating or lead to aspiration; Linscheid, 1992; Skuse, Pickles, Wolke, & Reilly, 1994); (d) improper pacing (i.e., self-feeding, but at a very fast or slow rate; Luiselli, 1989); (e) food refusal; and (f) vomiting and rumination (which must be distinguished from involuntary regurgitation; Luiselli, 1989; Singh, 1981). Finally, there is the category of mealtime behavior problems. These behaviors, exhibited during mealtime, include tantrumming (i.e., crying, screaming, and agitation), spitting out food, throwing utensils, aggression, and getting out of the seat (Luiselli, 1989; Wren & Tarbell, 1998). These types of mealtime behavior problems often co-occur with the other forms of feeding issues noted above, and can create a pattern of negative interactions between care giver and child (Luiselli, 1989; Sisson & Van Hasselt, 1989).

A single underlying cause for why children refuse to eat enough to sustain normal growth is rarely evident and therefore this problem presents a significant diagnostic and therapeutic challenge to clinicians and caregivers alike. Given the complexity of this challenge, numerous attempts at classifying feeding disorders have been attempted based on the apparent etiology, physical condition or associated behaviors (Burklow, Phelps, Schultz, McConnell, & Rudolph, 1998). Because most feeding disorders are the result of multiple factors (i.e., physical, motivational, skill, and parent/child relationships) a more functional classification has been developed that allows differentiation of patient types by symptoms rather than an arbitrary disease-based diagnostic approach (Table III).

Individuals with intellectual disability with food refusal that require any kind of enteral tube feed would be categorized as *food refusal—enteral tube dependent,* whereas an individual who drinks more than 80% of his/her calorie requirement would be considered *food refusal—liquid dependent*. Another feeding problem category is *food selective-type.* In this category individuals would eliminate 75% of the four basic food groups from his/her diet.

TABLE III

PROVIDES MEANINGFUL DIAGNOSTIC CATEGORIES THAT DESCRIBE THE NATURE OF THE FEEDING DISORDER

Food refusal-partial/total
Liquid dependent
Enteral tube dependent
Food selectivity
Texture
Type

Typically, a person with this categorization would have the skill to eat, but chooses to only eat one or two different foods and restricts all other foods. The individual may or may not be able to sustain normal growth or maintain a healthy body weight with this kind of diet. *Food selective-texture* would be when the individual does not eat an age appropriate texture of food due to lack of skill or oversensitivity to a particular food texture; for example, a 5-year-old child who only eats pureed foods when he should be able to handle regular textured food. Again the child may or may not sustain normal growth.

V. ASSESSMENT

An appropriate assessment of an individual's feeding disorder is a critical first step in initiating treatment. The management of complicated feeding disorders usually requires an interdisciplinary team devoted to establishing diagnosis, assessment of need and developing a thorough treatment plan. This team may include a variety of specialists, including physicians (e.g., family practitioner, developmental physician, gastroenterologists, allergists, and otolaryngologists), nurse practitioners, nutritionist, occupational therapists, speech therapists, psychologists, and social workers. The assembled team must begin its approach to diagnosis and therapy with complete history taking by all interested parties. These include a careful prenatal, birth, and neonatal history. Determining the nutritional and medical status of the individual must be accompanied by an appropriate psychological and developmental evaluation. Figure 1 provides a flow chart outlining an appropriate course of interdisciplinary assessment of individuals with intellectual disability presenting with food selectivity.

A. Physicians

An important goal of the physician history taking is to assess for any comorbid conditions that would require treatment prior to the implementation of a therapeutic treatment program for the food refusal (Table II for comorbid conditions). As part of the initial evaluation, an observation of a feeding session between the client and primary caregiver will often offer insight into the feeding problem, especially from an oral-motor/sensory and behavioral perspective. Clinical signs of oral-motor dysfunction, length of meals, and nature of the caregiver-client interaction are all noted. Observation of the muscle tone, posture and positioning, as well as special seating systems and feeding devices are routine as these can give insight into the individual's overall neurological functioning. Physical examination of the client includes a general survey examination for the determination of any

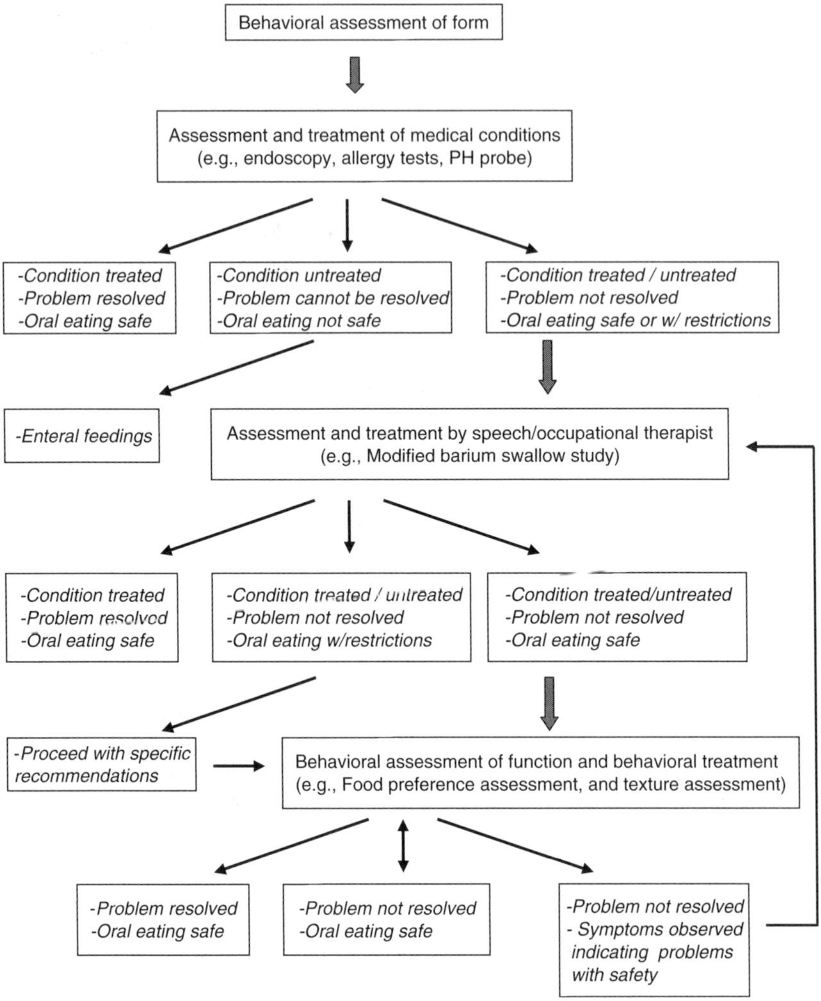

FIG. 1. Flow chart outlining an appropriate course of interdisciplinary assessment of individuals with food selectivity.

underlying medical disorders that may preclude safe feeding. These include evaluation of tongue and jaw movement, dentition, airway sounds, speech, and oral cavity assessment. Additionally, a complete physical examination including cardiac, pulmonary, and abdominal examinations are mandatory.

The goal of all therapy is directed toward allowing parents to safely feed their clients in a developmentally appropriate manner. The physician in the

TABLE IV
LISTS DIAGNOSTIC EVALUATIONS AND TESTS THAT MAY BE CONDUCTED IN THE ASSESSMENT OF FEEDING DISORDERS

Gastrointestinal (GI)
Upper gastrointestinal contrast radiography
Esophogram
Small bowel follow through
Gastric emptying study
pH monitoring
Esophagogastroduodenoscopy with biopsies
Antroduodenal manometry
Swallowing
Fiberoptic Endoscopic Evaluation of Swallowing (FEES)
Video-fluoroscopic swallow study
Allergy testing
RAST analysis for food allergies
Skin test for food allergies
Metabolic
CBC
Comprehensive metabolic panel
Thyroid function
Plasma amino acids
Urine organic acids
Karyotype

treatment team must ensure that all appropriate diagnostic studies have been performed to determine if an underlying medical condition has predisposed a client into developing an unusual feeding pattern. This includes appropriate utilization of consultants and diagnostic modalities (Table IV). Once these studies have been performed, the physician must coordinate all the resources and direct care so that feeding therapy may proceed with minimal risk to the client—keeping him/her safe from aspiration and other complications.

The initial and perhaps most important part of any therapeutic approach to introducing or increasing oral food intake is to establish the safety of eating as well as the types and textures of food the client can consume most efficiently. Approaches to therapy are often described as nutritive or non-nutritive. Non-nutritive oral stimulation is performed to reduce hypersensitivity, facilitate management of secretions, establish or retrain the swallowing mechanism, maintain coordination of breathing and swallowing, and develop oral movement for sound production and communication.

Objectives for a nutritive approach include increasing oral intake, advancing food texture, transitioning to utensil use, and improvement of self-feeding.

Oral motor techniques to improve muscle tone and postural control as a foundation for feeding and swallowing are largely based on a neurodevelopmental framework. The use of adaptive seating systems is a key component to feeding a client with physical disabilities that require external devices to provide head, neck, and trunk support. Attention must be paid to how positioning affects the feeding process, as a change in head and neck posture and how oral motor structures may affect oral motor control.

Once airway safety, positioning, and sensitivity have been controlled, a variety of treatment approaches have been suggested for individuals with feeding disorders. These range from individual psychotherapy to interactional therapy between the client and caregiver. However, the most widely employed and empirically validated treatments for feeding disorders are behavioral interventions usually included within an interdisciplinary team approach that also addresses physiology, oral motor functioning, caregiver-client interactions, and community or social support.

B. Diagnostic Testing

Diagnostic evaluations may be warranted to better assess swallowing and anatomy (Table IV). The modified barium swallow study (MBS) is the procedure of choice to assess oral, pharyngeal, and upper esophageal phases of swallowing. Seat positioning, food texture, and rate and amount of food presented can be manipulated during the performance of the modified barium swallow study to determine the safest and most efficient method of feeding. Clinical evaluation prior to the MBS is essential so that the food textures and liquid consistencies are ready at the time of the study. Changes in head and neck position, such as chin tuck, should be tried before the actual study to better correlate clinical and radiologic findings.

Additionally, a standard upper gastrointestinal contrast series utilizing barium is required for assessment of anatomy of the GI tract. Those individuals with repetitive vomiting or abdominal pain will need endoscopic evaluation, many of whom will also need colonoscopy to rule out the possibility of underlying inflammatory bowel disease. Some of the persons assessed will need cranial imaging such as computed tomography or magnetic resonance imaging to look for evidence of intracranial mass lesions, hydrocephaly or posterior fossa anomalies, such as the Chiari malformation. Fiberoptic endoscopic evaluation of swallowing (FEES) allows for direct visualization of the hypopharynx and larynx during swallowing by use of a flexible laryngoscope. This will allow evaluation of the valleculae and pyriform sinuses as well as the assessment of anatomy during swallowing and potential aspiration problems. This procedure, however, does not provide information on the oral phase of swallowing. FEES may also be combined with sensory testing (FEESST) to induce a laryngeal adductor response. Lastly, increasingly important is the need for allergy evaluation, including consultation by an allergist. Appropriate skin testing may be necessary as well as the appropriate RAST testing to look for response to food allergy.

C. Nutritionists

Nutritionists dedicated to the care of individuals with intellectual disability are also essential in the diagnostic team functioning. The role of the nutritionist in the assessment of the current nutritional status, anticipated growth, and recommended caloric intake that would be age and diagnosis appropriate is an essential part of the diagnostic and therapeutic team.

D. Speech Pathologists/Occupational Therapists

When it comes to feeding disorders, speech pathologists and occupational therapists often provide similar roles as "oral-motor" specialists by providing assessments of oral-motor skills and swallowing dysfunction. Not all speech and occupational therapy professionals receive specialized feeding training, but if they have, they can provide an important piece of the comprehensive assessment puzzle. By examining the child's jaw strength, chewing patterns, swallowing process, and reaction to new stimuli, speech pathologists and occupational therapists provide information about the persons "ability" to safely consume food/drink and can aid in the development of new skills. The speech pathologist and occupational therapist are also the individuals who would be responsible for carrying out any modified barium swallow study.

E. Social Workers

As the medical issues, behavioral needs and family psychodynamics play a central role in the development of the abnormal feeding patterns, a clinical social work evaluation is necessary for assessment and treatment of underlying familial interactions and support systems. These assessments and planning help to ensure continued success once the child has returned to the home environment.

F. Psychologists/Behavioral Therapists

Behavior therapists help to provide detailed observation and an analysis of variables that may be contributing toward inappropriate feeding and mealtime behaviors. As describe below, an integral part of the therapist's approach is performing an in-depth assessment of the individual's behavior patterns in regards to eating. The goal of an assessment is to help the therapist identify what behaviors have been shaped in regards to eating patterns, and furthermore, to help identify preferred items to help reinforce or shape new eating patterns. The behavior therapist then designs a treatment plan oriented toward shaping new appropriate behaviors, and ultimately, the therapist teaches the caregiver how to implement these strategies in the home environment.

There are many forms of behavioral assessment each of which has associated strengths and weaknesses. In general behavioral assessments typically serve one of two functions: (1) to identify the presence (or absence) of a problem/disorder and (2) to test hypotheses regarding the problem/disorder. In discussing the different behavioral assessments of feeding disorders, this section will initially separate the assessments into two broad categories: (1) the assessment of form, and (2) the assessment of function. Within these categories, each type of assessment will be further categorized according to the method of assessment (i.e., experimental, descriptive, and indirect).

1. ASSESSMENT OF FORM

Assessing the form of the behavior is a necessary step in the comprehensive assessment process. Often, the behavioral assessment of form may be necessary prior to an interdisciplinary evaluation. That is, before a treatment can be prescribed or an analysis initiated, the problem must first be identified. In addition to identifying the "occurrence/nonoccurrence" of feeding problems, some assessments may also be useful when administered repeatedly over time for the purpose of evaluating the stability of the problem and/or the effects of a treatment.

One modality of the assessment of form is indirect. This typically includes behavior-rating scales, which are characterized by an informant (i.e., a caregiver familiar with the client) responding to questions about client behaviors that he or she has observed. Caregiver interviews may also fit within this category; however, for the purpose of this review only empirically validated measures will be discussed. There are several indirect behavioral assessments that provide information regarding the presence of a feeding disorder. A few of the assessments described below focus exclusively of feeding, while others are more global assessments of either dual diagnosis or adaptive functioning.

The Vineland Adaptive Behavior Scales, Interview Survey Form (Sparrow, Balla, & Cicchetti, 1984) measures adaptive functioning across several domains including communication, socialization, and daily living skills, and has normative data for individuals with intellectual disability. A positive endorsement of an item (either a "1" or "2") would indicate that the behavior has been observed either usually or sometimes, respectively. However, if the behavior has not been observed, a "0" may be entered if the behavior has never occurred, or and "N" or "DK" if the informant had not had the opportunity to observe or did not know, respectively. Of interest to the current review is the daily living skills domain which contains 92 items and assesses an individual's ability to complete or participate in various hygiene and self-help behaviors as well as behaviors which would permit someone to live and function independently (e.g., holding a job and managing money). Many of the early items in this domain address skills associated with participation in eating, such as "opens mouth when spoon with food is presented," "eats solid foods," and "feeds self with spoon." The lack of positive endorsements on these items, and others, provides information regarding the identification of a problem.

The Reiss Screen for Maladaptive Behavior (SRMB; Reiss, 1988) is a behavior rating scale that assesses symptoms of psychopathology and maladaptive behavior in individuals with intellectual disability. This measure, like others described below, screen for a wide variety of symptoms, including psychosis, depression, and autism. This instrument is widely used and has been researched extensively. Adequate psychometrics have been found with this measure including test-retest and inter-rater reliability, and internal consistency (Sturmey, Burcham, & Perkins, 1995). One item on this scale (question 12) addresses weight gain or loss secondary to excessive or insufficient food intake. Again, a critical examination of the endorsements following administration of this measure can be helpful in the identification of a significant feeding problem.

Another instrument that has received a significant amount of attention is the Diagnostic Assessment for the Severely Handicapped-II (DASH-II; Matson, 1995). This assessment of psychopathology was developed for individuals functioning in the severe and profound levels of intellectual disability, and contains 84 items each of which is rated along three dimensions: frequency, duration, and severity. The items on the DASH-II comprise 13 subscales that represent different diagnostic categories such as anxiety, depression, autism, and eating disorders. Test-retest and inter-rater reliability coefficients were also good for this measure (Matson, 1995). There are six items on the DASH-II that focus on feeding and mealtime behaviors, specifically pica, vomiting, choking, food stealing, eating too fast, and eating an insufficient amount of food.

The Assessment of Dual Diagnosis (ADD; Matson & Bamburg, 1998) is similar to the DASH-II, but was developed to assess symptoms of psychopathology among individuals functioning in the mild and moderate ranges of intellectual disability. The ADD has very good psychometric properties including internal consistency, test-retest and inter-rater reliability (Matson & Bamburg, 1998) and consists of 79 items that make up 13 subscales (e.g., mania, depression, schizophrenia, and eating disorders). This measure also contains six items related to eating including a question about food refusal, pica, rumination, vomiting, eating too quickly, and a fear of gaining weight.

The Screening Tool of fEeding Problems (STEP; Kuhn & Matson, 2002; Matson & Kuhn, 2001) was designed for the purpose of identifying feeding and mealtime behavior problems displayed by individuals with intellectual disability. This tool allows for quick and efficient identification of specific feeding and mealtime behavior problems exhibited by persons with intellectual disability using a third-party informant procedure. The STEP consists of 23 items, each targeting a specific problem or deficit. These 23 items are grouped into five categories of feeding problems. These categories include aspiration risk, selectivity, feeding skills, food refusal-related behavior problems, and nutrition-related feeding problems. Items included in the aspiration category include items where food is repeatedly brought past the airway placing the individual at risk for aspirating. The selectivity category includes items addressing five different dimensions of selectivity, including selectivity by food type, food texture, food temperature, meal location, and selectivity by feeder. Items included in the feeding skills category address deficits in ability to chew or swallow, feed independently, regulate the rate of food ingestion, as well as identifying the need for adaptive equipment such as adaptive spoons or G-tubes. Items included in the food refusal-related behavior problems targets behaviors often associated with meal refusal or termination, such as physical aggression, self-injury, pushing the food away, or spitting the food out. Lastly, the nutrition-related behavior problems category includes items that may be associated with the individual consuming an insufficient amount of food and/or nutrients within their usual diet. Behaviors included in this category include, food stealing, pica, and eating too much or too little.

Similar to other measures discussed above, the STEP measures the target behaviors across two dimensions: frequency and severity. Informants are prompted to indicate how often the behavior has been observed in the last month (e.g., "between 1 and 10 times") and the extent to which the behaviors have adversely impacted the client. Test-retest reliability and inter-rater reliability were both found to be moderate (Matson & Kuhn, 2001).

Another instrument that focuses exclusively on eating and mealtime behavior is the Children's Eating Behavior Inventory (CEBI; Archer, Rosenbaum, & Streiner, 1991). The CEBI is parent-report instrument that contains 40 items addressing various eating and mealtime problems commonly described in the literature in this area and was designed to be used with individuals ranging in age and mental and developmental disabilities. The items are divided into two general domains: (1) those pertaining to the child, and (2) those pertaining to the parent and family system. The items in the first domain address such problems as compliance with the meal, vomiting or choking during the meal, food preferences, and developmental feeding skills. The second domain targets issues such as caregiver thoughts and perceptions about the meal. Items are scored across two dimensions. The frequency of the behavior is scored on a five-point Likert scale ranging from "Never" to "Always." Following a rating of the frequency, caregivers are prompted to indicate whether or not the corresponding behavior is a problem for him/her. Both internal consistency and test-retest reliability were completed for the CEBI and were found to be good (Archer, Rosenbaum, & Streiner, 1991). Furthermore, based on a comparison of the mean number of items identified to be problematic by caregivers between clinic and nonclinic samples, the authors indicate that the cutoff for identifying the presence of a feeding problem is 16% of items scores as problematic for caregivers.

The last indirect assessment that represents an effective instrument in the identification of problematic eating and mealtime behavior problems is the Behavioral Pediatric Feeding Assessment Scale (Crist & Napier-Phillips, 2001). This parent-report measure contains 35 items which, similar to the CEBI, is divided into two broad domains: (1) those items pertaining to the child, and (2) those items that pertain to the parent's feelings about or strategies used for dealing with the problem. Items in the first domain address problems such as food texture refusal (e.g., "eats only ground or soft foods") and food selectivity (e.g., "eats junky snack foods but will not eat at meals"). The frequency of occurrence of these items are also rated using a five-point Likert scale, as well as a rating of whether or not the corresponding behavior is a problem for caregivers. While internal consistency was reported as adequate (Crist & Napier-Phillips, 2001), it does not appear as though this measure has been evaluated with individuals with developmental disabilities, though its application may be useful.

In addition to the indirect methods of assessments to identify the form of the behavior problem, several experimental analyses have been used. One commonly used method is the paired-choice preference assessment (Fisher et al., 1992), which allows clinicians to identify a hierarchy of preferences. This procedure involves identifying a variety of items and presenting them two at a time until each item has been paired with every other item. Data are collected on the client's behavior when presented with the two items, specifically which item(s) was and was not approached, consumed, or avoided. This method has been and can be applied toward the identification of food preferences across type (Babbitt et al., 1994), texture, and size. That is, this approach allows clinicians to identify which foods an individual prefers and may be more likely to consume, and which foods he/she will not approach/consume or even avoid.

Munk and Repp (1994) designed an assessment to evaluate the effects of the type and texture of the presented food on the occurrence of problem behavior. This assessment critically evaluated the relative effects of the type and texture of foods on occasioning noncompliance and mealtime problem behavior. In doing so, Munk and Repp independently manipulate the type(s) of foods presented (e.g., fruits, vegetables, meats, and starches) as well as the texture of the food (e.g., pureed, ground, and chopped). The dependent variable in this assessment is whether or not the client accepted and expelled the food. These procedures yield information about the specific of conditions under which the problematic behavior(s) are likely to be observed, such as when certain foods are presented and or when foods at certain textures are presented. Recently, others have suggested that the observed problems may be a function of response effort (Kerwin, Ahearn, Eicher, & Burd, 1995; Patel, Piazza, Santana, & Volkert, 2002). That is, an individual may expel or refuse foods of a course texture because those foods require more effort (i.e., chewing and tongue control) than liquids or pureed foods.

2. ASSESSMENT OF FUNCTION

Assessing the function of the behavior can be a necessary step in the development of an effective intervention. It is important to note that an assessment of function cannot be initiated until an assessment of form has been completed. That is, before a functional assessment can be completed it is necessary to identify the problem. As stated earlier, it is possible or likely that the function of the presenting problem has shifted over time. An assessment of behavioral function would only yield information relevant to the current variables maintaining the behavior, but not necessarily provide information on why the problem first emerged. Functional assessment technologies have only recently been applied toward feeding and mealtime behavior problems. However, based on the results of the studies presented below, a case could be made to forgo the functional assessment of certain mealtime behaviors because of the probability of certain functions.

Similar to the assessment of form, there are different assessment modalities within functional assessment that have been applied to the assessment of feeding and mealtime behavior problems. The QABF (Matson & Vollmer, 1995) is a behavior rating scale, which consists of 25 questions about possible behavioral functions (e.g., "engages in the behavior to draw attention to him/herself"). A four-point Likert scale is used to estimate the frequency that the behavior seems to occur under the conditions described in the question, ranging from 0 (never) to 3 (often). Following a factor analysis, the questions on the QABF are divided into five different subscales, which match commonly discussed behavioral functions, including attention, escape, tangible, nonsocial, and physical. The subscale scores are subsequently summed and plotted. Visual inspection of the summed scores is used to interpret the data. The psychometric properties of the QABF have generally been good, including test-retest and inter-rater reliability (Paclawskyj, 1998). In addition, Paclawskyj, Matson, Rush, Smalls, and Vollmer (2001) reported low to moderate levels of convergent validity with analogue functional analyses using the procedures described by Iwata, Dorsey, Slifer, Bauman, and Richman (1982/1994). While much of the research conducted using the QABF (and other functional assessment rating scales) has focused on the assessment of other severe behavior problems, such as self-injurious behavior and aggression, a recent study by Matson et al. (2005) used the QABF to evaluate the behavioral functions of feeding and mealtime behavior problems as identified by the STEP (described above) in a sample over 100 individuals with intellectual disabilities.

Experimental analyses have also been used in the assessment of behavioral function as it applies to feeding and mealtime behavior problems. Girolami and Scotti (2001) published the first study using analog functional analyses to identify the variables maintaining food refusal and related mealtime behavior displayed by three participants. Procedures were similar to those described by Iwata, Dorsey et al. (1982/1994). Six experimental conditions were conducted, attention, tangible toy, tangible food, demand, alone, and control. These conditions corresponded to five hypotheses regarding the function of the problem behavior: (1) positive reinforcement in the form of access to attention, (2) positive reinforcement in the form of access to tangibles, (3) positive reinforcement in the form of access to preferred edibles, (4) negative reinforcement in the form of escape from bite/meal, and (5) nonsocial reinforcement. During all sessions, with the exception of an alone condition, a bite of nonpreferred food was presented every 20 sec. The occurrence of problem or refusal behaviors resulted in either caregiver attention, access to preferred toys, access to a preferred food, or no differential consequence. The different experimental conditions were compared using a multielement design. Good interobserver agreement coefficients were maintained across all participants. Consistent with Matson et al. (2005) and others, food refusal behavior was found to be maintained by escape from the meal for all three participants.

Piazza et al. (2003) used descriptive and analogue analyses to assess the function of inappropriate mealtime behaviors of 15 individuals, 9 of which had intellectual disability. The descriptive analysis involved observing caregivers feed the participant as he/she typically would. This type of assessment allows clinicians to generate hypotheses about behavioral function. Data were collected on caregiver response to inappropriate behavior, including whether or not attention, preferred foods, preferred drinks, or toys were delivered, or whether the caregiver permitted a break or escape from eating. Interobserver agreement coefficients were high for data collected on both participant and caregiver behavior.

Analogue functional analyses conducted by Piazza et al. (2003) were similar to those conducted by Girolami and Scotti (2001) with several significant differences. In the study by Girolami and Scotti, when either attention or tangibles (food or toys) were delivered following inappropriate behavior, the spoon of food was also temporarily removed. Conversely, the procedures used by Piazza and colleagues involved the continuous presentation of the food independent of the other social consequence (with the exception of the escape condition). Also, within these procedures experimental control was demonstrated using a series of reversals. In addition, the length of time in which each bite was presented differed slightly, and Piazza et al. did not conduct an alone condition. Again, interobserver agreement coefficients remained high for data collected on participant's behavior(s). Similar to results described above, for all but one of the participants for inappropriate behavior was observed, negative reinforcement was identified as a maintaining variable.

VI. CASE EXAMPLES

The following two case examples illustrate how the integration of various interdisciplinary assessments is necessary in the development of an appropriate and effective intervention.

Case Example 1: Amy

Amy was a 7-year-old female diagnosed with an unspecified level of intellectual disability admitted to an inpatient feeding program for chronic food refusal and feeding difficulties. Amy's medical/developmental history included prematurity, gastroesophageal reflux, and chronic lung disease requiring a tracheotomy. When she was 6 months, subsequent to a decrease in consumption, a gastronomy tube was placed to supplement oral feedings. Physicians also performed a Nissen fundoplication to decrease Amy's vomiting. To meet some of her nutritional needs, Amy was receiving Pediasure® formula through her tube several times a day (or gradually overnight). On admission, Amy' would eat small amounts of pureed solids and drink water but would refuse most foods with any texture.

Initially, a CEBI (Archer, Rosenbaum, & Streiner, 1991) was completed with Amy's caregiver. The results of the CEBI indicated that there was a significant feeding problem characterized by her refusing to eat food presented to her, thereby confirming that her referral to the inpatient program was appropriate. Examination of specific items provided helpful information about other variables that may impact her participation in meals. For example, Amy's caregiver reported that Amy often "brings toys or books to the table" and "watches TV during meals." A stimulus preference assessment (Fisher et al., 1992) was conducted to identify Amy's preferred and nonpreferred foods. To determine whether the texture of the food would impact her selections, two assessments were conducted using different textures (i.e., pureed/smooth and wet ground). During the assessment, each item was presented once with every other item, and Amy was asked to make a choice between the two. Amy's preference was evaluated among foods, on the basis of initial approach, consume, avoidance, and neutral responses. At both textures, Amy chose carrots more than any other food (Fig. 2).

Despite the limited food consumed in these assessments, the information provided about what foods Amy may be most likely to consume is important for several reasons. First, observing her consumption of carrots provides a potential "starting point" for further assessments/treatment. As discussed earlier, because Amy would not consume any food at a higher texture with any consistency, Amy's ability (due to suspected poor oral-motor skills) to consume high volumes of food at a higher texture had yet to be appropriately assessed. Her consumption of the carrots indicated that she "can" (without exhibiting refusal) eat *some* foods at a higher texture. If she had refused all

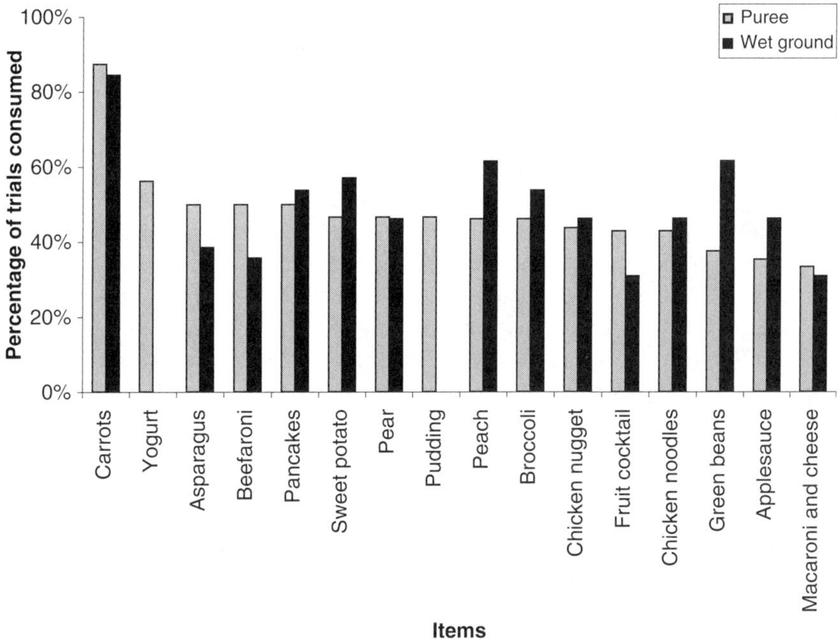

FIG. 2. Percentage of bites consumed during Amy's edible preference assessment.

the foods at higher texture, it would be difficult to tell if it was the stimulus properties of the texture or her inability to manipulate and swallow the food. With this knowledge, the team started presenting carrots at a higher texture in oral-motor sessions in order to observe her skills. The behavioral team also used that information when developing their treatment strategy. A "pre-ferred" food was used in simultaneous or sequential presentations (Piazza et al., 2002) as a reinforcer for the acceptance of other foods (Premack Principle).

At the end of the admission, Amy was accepting and swallowing over 80% of bites presented to her and her problem behavior was greatly decreased, and was taking all of her needs PO (by mouth).

Case Example 2: Sandy

Sandy was a 2-year 10-month-old female diagnosed with moderate intellectual disability admitted to a day treatment program for the treatment of food refusal and failure to thrive. Amy had interuterine growth retardation with birth weight of 4 lb 3 oz. Her medical history also includes hyperbilirubinemia, gastroesophageal reflux, failure to thrive, history of otitis media, and bronchitis. She had been receiving Prevacid® to manage her reflux and Lactulose® for constipation. At the time of the admission, she was meeting her nutritional needs by consuming 7 oz. of milk two times a day and a mixture of broth, avocado, milk, half and half,® and almonds.

Similar to the assessments completed with Amy, a CEBI (Archer, Rosenbaum, & Streiner, 1991) was initially completed with Sandy's caregiver. The results of the CEBI also indicated that there was a significant feeding problem characterized by her refusing to eat food presented to her, confirming an appropriate admission. Sandy's CEBI results assisted her team in addressing important family dynamics that may have been impacting the caregiver's behavior during meals. Sandy's mother reported that "relatives complain about my child's eating" very often and that this was a problem. Further investigation revealed that extended family (and friends) were repeatedly providing Sandy's mother with suggestions about what to do in meals. Additional comments by family/friends focused on the fact that it was something that Sandy's parents were doing that maintained the behavior. Sandy's mother reported that this behavior placed a lot of pressure on her and increased her stress levels. Different from the previous case example, when presented food in an edible preference assessment, Sandy refused all the food presented to her. Subsequently, another method of assessing texture was conducted whereby four textures [i.e., puree (PR), junior (JR), wet ground (WG), and chopped fine (CF) foods] were presented under treatment conditions (nonremoval of the spoon; Ahearn et al., 1996). In this assessment, four 5-bite sessions were conducted during mealtimes. Each session consisted of a different texture and the orders of textures were varied across each session (Fig. 3). Another way to conduct this session would be to have only one food presented during each mealtime. Sandy's acceptance and swallowing (i.e., mouth cleans) decreased from 100% to 0% as the texture

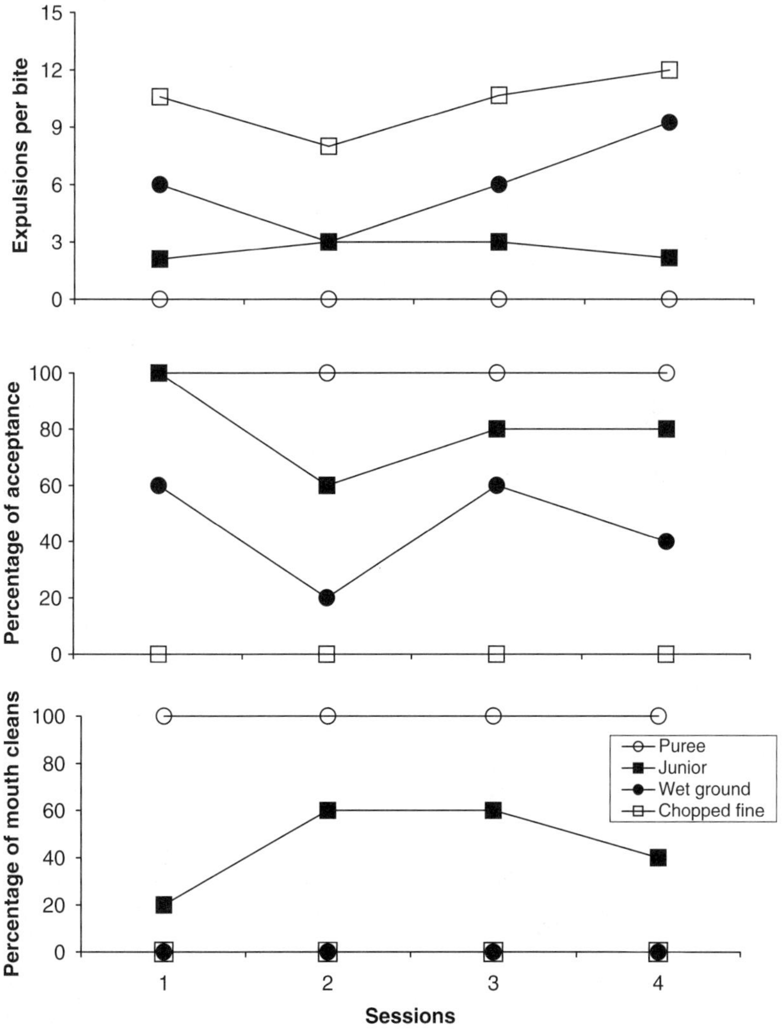

FIG. 3. Number of expulsions per bite (top panel), and percentage of acceptance (middle panel) and bites swallowed (bottom panel) within 30 sec during Sandy's texture assessment.

increased from puree to a chopped fine. The number of expelled bites increased with higher textures. This highlights that while treatment was successful, it was most effective with lower textures.

This case also highlights the importance of continuing to involve medical throughout the treatment of severe food refusal. After initial treatment gains, Sandy's acceptance decreased and problem behavior increased. Medical evaluation of Sandy demonstrated that she was suffering from a viral infection and was running a temperature along with having congestion. After several days and some medical management, Sandy's acceptance increased and problem behavior decreased and remained stable throughout the admission and after discharge.

At the end of the admission, Sandy was accepting and swallowing over 80% of bites presented to her and her problem behavior was greatly decreased, and was taking all of her needs at a wet ground texture PO (by mouth).

VII. CONCLUSIONS

The comorbidity of feeding and mealtime behavior problems among individuals with intellectual disability is estimated to be high, and the potential health-related complications associated with these problems are significant. Identification and treatment of these problems can be a difficult and daunting task because in some cases the behavior is maintained by social consequences while in other cases the presenting problem is secondary to a medical condition. Therefore, different from some other severe behavior problems such as aggression or property destruction, the assessment and ultimately the treatment of problems associated with feeding should be approached by an interdisciplinary team. Behavioral assessment may be a necessary first step in the identification of the "form" of the behavior; however, a medical assessment may be the appropriate next step to rule out the existence of an existing medical condition. According to the model presented in this chapter, subsequent behavioral assessment of function may not be necessary until other disciplines (e.g., medical, nutrition, and speech) have unsuccessfully assessed and/or treated the presenting problem. In recent years efforts have been made to use assessments to diagnose feeding and mealtime behavior problems displayed by children and individuals with intellectual disability. This chapter provides meaningful diagnostic groups based on a thorough assessment that can be helpful in prescribing treatment.

REFERENCES

Ahearn, W. H., Kerwin, M. E., Eicher, P. S., Shantz, J., & Sweringin, W. (1996). An alternating treatments comparison of two intensive interventions for food refusal. *Journal of Applied Behavior Analysis, 29,* 321–332.

American, Psychiatric Association (APA) (1994). *Diagnostic and statistical manual of mental disorders* (4th ed.). Washington, DC: American Psychiatric Association.

Archer, L. A., Rosenbaum, P. L., & Streiner, D. L. (1991). The children's eating behavior inventory: Reliability and validity results. *Journal of Pediatric Psychology, 16,* 629–642.

Ausman, J., Ball, T. S., & Alexander, D. (1974). Behavior therapy of pica with a profoundly retarded adolescent. *Mental Retardation, 12,* 16–18.

Babbitt, R. L., Hoch, T. A., Coe, D. A., Cataldo, M. F., Kelly, K. J., Stackhouse, C., et al. (1994). Behavioral assessment and treatment of pediatric feeding disorders. *Journal of Developmental and Behavioral Pediatrics, 15,* 278–291.

Borthwick-Duffy, S. A. (1994). Epidemiology and prevalence of psychopathology in people with mental retardation. *Journal of Consulting and Clinical Psychology, 62,* 17–27.

Burklow, K., Phelps, A., Schultz, J., McConnell, K., & Rudolph, C. (1998). Classifying complex pediatric feeding problems. *Journal of Pediatric Gastroenterology and Nutrition, 27,* 143–147.

Crist, W., & Napier-Phillips, A. (2001). Mealtime behaviors of young children: A comparison of normative and clinical data. *Journal of Developmental and Behavioral Pediatrics, 22*(5), 279–286.

Dellert, S. F., Hyams, J. S., Treem, W. R., & Geertsma, M. A. (1993). Feeding resistance and gastroesophageal reflux in infancy. *Journal of Pediatric Gastroenterology and Nutrition, 17*(1), 66–71.

Ellis, C. R., Parr, T. S., Singh, N. N., & Wechsler, H. A. (1997). Rumination. In N. Singh (Ed.), *Prevention and treatment of severe behavior problems: Models and methods in developmental disabilities* (pp. 237–252). Belmont, CA, US: Brooks/Cole Publishing Co.

Feldman, M. D. (1986). Pica: Current perspectives. *Psychosomatics, 27,* 519–523.

Fisher, W. W., Piazza, C. C., Bowman, L. G., Hagopian, L. P., Owens, J. C., & Slevin, I. (1992). A comparison of two approaches for identifying reinforcers for persons with severe and profound disabilities. *Journal of Applied Behavior Analysis, 25,* 491–498.

Frazier, J. B., & Friedman, B. (1996). Swallow function in children with Down syndrome: A retrospective study. *Developmental Medicine and Child Neurology, 38,* 695–703.

Girolami, P. A., & Scotti, J. R. (2001). Use of analog functional analysis in assessing the function of mealtime behavior problems. *Education and Training in Mental Retardation and Developmental Disabilities, 36,* 207–223.

Gravestock, S. (2000). Eating disorders in adults with intellectual disability. *Journal of Intellectual Disability Research, 44,* 625–637.

Hamill, P. V., Drizd, T. A., Johnson, C. L., Reed, R. B., Roche, A. F., & Moore, W. M. (1979). Physical growth: National Center for Health Statistics percentiles. *American Journal of Clinical Nutrition, 32,* 607–629.

Heffer, R. W., & Kelly, M. L. (1994). Nonorganic failure to thrive: Developmental outcomes and psychosocial assessment and intervention issues. *Research in Developmental Disabilities, 15,* 247–268.

Iwata, B. A., Dorsey, M. F., Slifer, K. J., Bauman, K. E., & Richman, G. S. (1994). Toward a functional analysis of self-injury. *Journal of Applied Behavior Analysis, 27,* 197–209. (Reprinted from *Analysis and Intervention in Developmental Disabilities, 2,* 3–20, 1982).

Iwata, B. A., Pace, G. M., Dorsey, M. F., Zarcone, J. R., Vollmer, T. R., Smith, R. G., et al. (1994). The functions of self-injurious behavior: An experimental-epidemiological analysis. *Journal of Applied Behavior Analysis, 27,* 215–240.

Iwata, B. A., Riordan, M. M., Wohl, M. K., & Finney, J. W. (1982). Pediatric feeding disorders: Behavioral analysis and treatment. In P. J. Accordo (Ed.), *Failure to thrive in infancy and early childhood: A multidisciplinary team approach* (pp. 297–329). Baltimore: University Park Press.

Kerwin, M. E. (1999). Empirically supported treatments in pediatric psychology: Severe feeding problems. *Journal of Pediatric Psychology, 24*(3), 193–214.

Kerwin, M. E., Ahearn, W. H., Eicher, P. S., & Burd, D. M. (1995). The costs of eating: A behavioral economic analysis of food refusal. *Journal of Applied Behavior Analysis, 28,* 245–260.

Kuhn, D. E., & Matson, J. L. (2002). A validity study of the Screening Tool of fEeding Problems (STEP). *Journal of Intellectual and Developmental Disability, 27,* 161–167.

Linscheid, T. R. (1992). Eating problems in children. In C. E. Walker & M. C. Roberts (Eds.), *Handbook of clinical child psychology* (2nd ed., pp. 451–473). Oxford, England: John Wiley & Sons.

Linscheid, T. R., Budd, K. S., & Rasnake, L. K. (1995). Pediatric feeding disorders. In M. C. Roberts (Ed.), *Handbook of pediatric psychology* (2nd ed., pp. 501–515). New York, NY: Guilford Press.

Lofts, R. H., Schroeder, S. R., & Maier, R. H. (1990). Effects of serum zinc supplementation on pica behavior of persons with mental retardation. *American Journal of Mental Retardation, 95,* 103–109.

Logemann, J. (1983). *Evaluation and treatment of swallowing disorders.* San Diego: College Hill Press.

Luiselli, J. K. (1989). Behavioral assessment and treatment of pediatric feeding disorders in developmental disabilities. In M. Hersen, R. M. Eisler, & P. M. Miner (Eds.), *Progress in Behavior Modification* (pp. 91–131). Newbury Park, CA: Sage.

Luiselli, J. K., & Gleason, D. J. (1987). Combining sensory reinforcement and texture fading procedures to overcome chronic food refusal. *Journal of Behavior Therapy and Experimental Psychiatry, 18,* 149–155.

MacDonald, N. J., McConnell, K. N., Stephen, M. R., & Dunnigan, M. G. (1989). Hypernatraemic dehydration in patients in a large hospital for the mentally handicapped. *British Medical Journal, 299,* 1426–1429.

Manikam, R., & Perman, J. (2000). Pediatric feeding disorders. *Journal of Clinical Gastroenterology, 30*(1), 34–45.

Matson, J. L. (1995). *The Diagnostic Assessment for the Severely Handicapped-II.* Baton Rouge, LA: Scientific Publishers, Inc.

Matson, J. L., & Bamburg, J. W. (1998). Reliability of the Assessment of Dual Diagnosis (ADD). *Research in Developmental Disabilities, 19,* 89–95.

Matson, J. L., & Kuhn, D. E. (2001). Identifying feeding problems in mentally retarded persons: Development and reliability of the Screening Tool of Feeding Problems (STEP). *Research in Developmental Disabilities, 22,* 165–172.

Matson, J. L., Mayville, S. B., Kuhn, D. E., Sturmey, P., Laud, R., & Cooper, C. (2005). The behavioral function of feeding problems as assessed by the Questions About Behavioral Function (QABF). *Research in Developmental Disabilities, 26,* 399–408.

Matson, J. L., & Vollmer, T. R. (1995). *User's guide: Questions About Behavioral Function (QABF).* Baton Rouge, LA: Scientific Publishers, Inc.

McAlpine, C., & Singh, N. N. (1986). Pica in institutionalized mentally retarded persons. *Journal of Mental Deficiency Research, 30,* 171–178.

Morris, S. E., & Klein, M. D. (1987). *Pre-feeding skills: A comprehensive resource for feeding development.* Tuscon, AZ: Therapy Skill Builders.

Munk, D. D., & Repp, A. C. (1994). Behavioral assessment of feeding problems of individuals with severe disabilities. *Journal of Applied Behavior Analysis, 27,* 241–250.

Paclawskyj, T. (1998). Questions about behavioral function (QABF): A behavioral checklist for functional assessment of aberrant behavior. Unpublished dissertation.

Paclawskyj, T., Matson, J. L., Rush, K. S., Smalls, Y., & Vollmer, T. R. (2001). Assessment of the convergent validity of the Questions About Behavioral Function (QABF) with analog functional analysis and the Motivation Assessment Scale (MAS). *Journal of Intellectual Disability Research, 45,* 484–494.

Palmer, S., & Horn, S. (1978). Feeding problems in children. In S. Palmer & S. Ekval (Eds.), *Pediatric Nutrition in Developmental Disorders.* Springfield, IL: Charles, C. Thomas.

Palmer, S., Thompson, R. J., & Linscheid, T. R. (1975). Applied behavior analysis in the treatment of childhood feeding problems. *Developmental Medicine and Child Neurology, 17,* 333–339.

Patel, M. R., Piazza, C. C., Santana, C. M., & Volkert, V. M. (2002). An evaluation of food type and texture in the treatment of a feeding problem. *Journal of Applied Behavior Analysis, 35,* 183–186.

Perske, R., Clifton, A., McClean, B. M., & Stein, J. I. (Eds.) (1977). *Mealtimes for severely and profoundly handicapped persons: New concepts and attitudes.* Baltimore, MD: University Park Press.

Pesce, K. A., Wodarski, L. A., & Wang, M. (1989). Nutritional status of institutionalized children and adolescents with developmental disabilities. *Research in Developmental Disabilities, 10,* 33–52.

Piazza, C. C., Fisher, W. W., Brown, K. A., Shore, B. A., Patel, M. R., Katz, R. M., et al. (2003). Functional analysis of inappropriate mealtime behaviors. *Journal of Applied Behavior Analysis, 36,* 187–204.

Piazza, C. C., Patel, M. R., Santana, C. M., Goh, H., Delia, M. D., & Lancaster, B. M. (2002). An evaluation of simultaneous and sequential presentation of preferred and nonpreferred food to treat food selectivity. *Journal of Applied Behavior Analysis, 35,* 259–270.

Reiss, S. (1988). *The Reiss Screen for Maladaptive Behavior.* Orlando Park, IL: International Diagnostic Systems.

Riordan, M. M., Iwata, B. A., Finney, J. W., Wohl, M. K., & Stanley, A. E. (1984). Behavioral assessment and treatment of chronic food refusal in handicapped children. *Journal of Applied Behavior Analysis, 17,* 327–341.

Rogers, B., Stratton, P., Victor, J., Kennedy, B., & Andres, M. (1992). Chronic regurgitation among persons with mental retardation: A need for combined medical and interdisciplinary strategies. *American Journal of Mental Retardation, 96,* 522–527.

Rudolph, C., & Link, D. (2002). Feeding disorders in infants and children. *Pediatric Clinics of North America, 49*(1), 97–112.

Sanders, M. R., Patel, R. K., le Grice, B., & Shepherd, R. W. (1993). Children with persistent feeding difficulties: An observational analysis of the feeding interactions of problem and non-problem eaters. *Health Psychology, 12*(1), 64–73.

Singh, N. N. (1981). Rumination. In N. R. Ellis (Ed.), *International Review of Research in Mental Retardation* (pp. 139–182). New York, NY: Academic Press.

Sisson, L. A., & Dixon, M. J. (1986). Improving mealtime behaviors through token reinforcement: A study with mentally retarded behaviorally disordered children. *Behavior Modification, 10*(3), 333–354.

Sisson, K. A., & Van Hasselt, V. B. (1989). Feeding disorders. In J. K. Luiselli (Ed.), *Behavioral medicine and developmental disabilities* (pp. 45–73). New York: Springer-Verlag.

Skuse, D. H., Pickles, A., Wolfe, D., & Reilly, S. (1994). Postnatal growth and mental development. Evidence for a sensitive period. *Journal of Child Psychology and Psychiatry, 35,* 521–545.

Sparrow, S. S., Balla, D. A., & Cicchetti, D. V. (1984). *Vineland Adaptive Behavior Scales I: A revision of the Vineland Social Maturity Scale by Edgar A. Doll. Survey Form.* Circle Pines, MN: American Guidance Service.

Spender, Q., Stein, A., Dennis, J., Reilly, S., Percy, E., & Cave, D. (1996). An exploration of feeding difficulties in children with Down syndrome. *Developmental Medicine and Child Neurology, 38,* 681–694.

Stewart, L., Beange, H., & Mackerras, D. (1994). A survey of dietary problems of adults with learning disabilities in the community. *Mental Handicap Research, 7,* 41–50.

Stickler, G. B. (1984). Failure to thrive or the failure to define. *Pediatrics, 74,* 559.

Strauss, D., Kastner, T., Ashwal, S., & White, J. (1997). Tubefeeding and mortality in children with severe disabilities and mental retardation. *Pediatrics, 99,* 358–362.

Sturmey, P., Burcham, K. J., & Perkins, T. S. (1995). The Reiss Screen for Maladaptive Behavior: Its reliability and internal consistencies. *Journal of Intellectual Disability Research, 39,* 191–195.

Thommessen, M., Heiberg, A., Kase, B. F., Larsen, S., & Riis, G. (1991). Feeding problems, height and weight in different groups of disabled children. *Acta Paediatrica Scandinavica, 80,* 527–533.

Tuchman, D. (1989). Dysfunctional swallowing in pediatric patients: Critical considerations. *Dysphasia, 2,* 203–208.

Werle, M. A., Murphy, T. B., & Budd, K. S. (1993). Treating chronic food refusal in young children: Home-based parent training. *Journal of Applied Behavior Analysis, 26,* 421–433.

Wren, F., & Tarnell, S. (1998). Feeding and growth disorders. In R. Ammerman & J. Campo (Eds.), *Handbook of Pediatric Psychology and Psychiatry* (pp. 133–165). Boston, MA: Allyn and Bacon.

Pain Assessment

FRANK ANDRASIK AND CARLA RIME

DEPARTMENT OF PSYCHOLOGY, UNIVERSITY OF WEST FLORIDA
PENSACOLA, FLORIDA

I. PAIN: THE BIG PICTURE

The International Association for the Study of Pain (1986) has defined pain as "an unpleasant sensory and emotional experience associated with actual and potential tissue damage, or described in terms of such damage." Elsewhere, the following is mentioned: "It is unquestionably a sensation in a part or parts of the body, but it is also always unpleasant and therefore also an emotional experience." A comprehensive review of available epidemiological studies yielded a median point prevalence of chronic benign pain of 15% in adults, with individual study values ranging from 2 to 40% (Verhaak, Kerssens, Dekker, Sorbi, & Bensing, 1998). Low-back pain, for example, is one of the most common forms of pain, taking the back seat only to the common cold in primary care settings. Its total cost is estimated to exceed $100 billion per year (Katz, 2006). (See Crombie, Croft, Linton, LeResche, & Von Korff, 1999, for more extended discussions of pain epidemiology.)

Recognition of the widespread occurrence and personal, social, and economic impact of pain led the Joint Commission on Accreditation of Healthcare Organizations in the summer of 1999 to mandate regular assessment of pain and establishment of policies and procedures that support the appropriate use of pain medication. Henceforth, pain has become known as the "fifth vital sign" (being added to the list that already includes heart rate, blood pressure, temperature, and respiration).

II. PAIN: BRIEF REVIEW OF MODELS

The prevailing model to account for all forms of chronic pain is best termed as the "biomedical model," and it is characterized as viewing pain as a direct transmission of impulses from the periphery to structures within

INTERNATIONAL REVIEW OF RESEARCH IN MENTAL RETARDATION, Vol. 34
0074-7750/07 $35.00

DOI: 10.1016/S0074-7750(07)34013-5

the central nervous system (Turk & Flor, 1999). This unidirectional model has led to a number of important insights into pathophysiological mechanisms and development of pharmacological treatments directed at modifying aberrant aspects. At the same time, this model has a number of limitations and has difficulty explaining the following: (1) pain that continues in the absence of identifiable pathology, (2) pathology that exists in the absence of pain, (3) the markedly varied individual responses to identical treatments, (4) the failure of potent medications to provide consistent pain relief, and (5) the absence of a strong relationship between pain, impairment, and disability. Some dismiss these limitations of the biomedical model, claiming these issues will be resolved in due time with appropriate advances in technology. Yet, a competing and more compelling viewpoint is that varied psychological factors are playing an important role in the genesis and maintenance of recurrent pain conditions, and a proper explication of these factors is needed for a complete understanding.

Early psychological models of pain were unidirectional, oversimplified (e.g., pain in the absence of identifiable pathology was judged either to be consciously motivated for secondary gain or was believed to be maintained because of reinforcement contingencies), and had minimal impact on the field. This view, like the biomedical model, also perpetuated an artificial dichotomy that pain was either somatogenic or psychogenic (Turk & Flor, 1999). A model that is more fruitful and heuristic is that which has been labeled the "biopsychosocial" or more simply the "biobehavioral" model (in the latter case, behavioral subsumes psychological and social factors). This model views pain (and any chronic illness, for that matter) as emanating from a complex interaction of biological, psychological, and social variables. From this perspective the diversity in illness expression (including severity, duration, and consequences to the individual) can be accounted for by the complex interrelationships among predispositional, biological, and psychological characteristics (e.g., genetics, prior learning history), biological changes, psychological status, and the social and cultural contexts that shape the individual's perceptions and response to illness. This model stands in sharp contrast to the traditional biomedical perspective that conceptualizes illness in terms of more narrowly defined physiochemical dimensions. This alternative model differs in other key ways, as it is dynamic and recognizes reciprocal multifactorial influences over time. Thus, there is much potentiality to be gained by application of this model, which, unfortunately, has not been fully exploited within the realm of developmental disabilities (DD).

III. PAIN: THE PICTURE AS IT APPLIES TO PERSONS WITH DEVELOPMENTAL DISABILITIES

Although pain is common and prevalent throughout the world and respects no demographic or intellectual borders, scant attention has been devoted to its occurrence among people who are experiencing intellectual or developmental disabilities. Reasons for this dearth of information are many, some of which consist of the following (Bottos & Chambers, 2006). Chief among the reasons for under-recognition of pain has been the erroneous assumption that such individuals are either indifferent to pain or are less sensitive to pain (have a heightened pain threshold). Recent controlled laboratory studies, monitoring pain behaviors of persons with disabilities and those without, help shed light on why such false perceptions have endured. For example, Hennequin, Morin, and Feine (2000) examined cold-pain thresholds among persons diagnosed with Down syndrome and controls. Briefly, an ice cube was directly applied to the skin while the experimenters noted the time lapse to the first verbal or behavioral reaction. Both groups showed similar reactions, but latencies to respond were much longer for persons having Down syndrome.

Compounding the problem is the fact that persons with developmental disabilities appear to express their pain in a manner different from those who do not have such disabilities. In an examination of typical everyday pains (bumps and bruises) experienced in a child care setting, children with developmental disabilities, in comparison to children without such a diagnosis, were less likely to cry or seek out help and more likely to be absent of any observable reaction (Gilbert-MacLeod, Craig, Rocha, & Mathias, 2000). However, an attenuated behavioral response is not the rule. Observations made during venipuncture with children with autism suggest they may have a heightened sensitivity to acute pain, as evinced by their intense facial expressions (Nader, Oberlander, Chambers, & Craig, 2004). Results from these and other studies refute the notion that persons with developmental disabilities are insensitive or indifferent to pain. It is more accurate to say that persons with developmental disabilities display pain behaviors that are different and that may be attenuated in certain circumstances.

Further, it is believed by some that pain may be much less frequent overall in people with developmental disabilities. Here, too, the limited available evidence suggests otherwise. In fact, one can make the case for just the opposite conclusion—that individuals with developmental disabilities may be at increased risk for pain conditions, for two chief reasons. First, persons with developmental disabilities are more likely to be exposed to surgical or medical procedures that are painful, such as corrective surgeries, treatment for irritations resulting from protheses, and intravenous needle placements. Second, the high presence of comorbid medical conditions can increment pain, such as spasticity in cerebral palsy (CP). Bottos and Chambers (2006) discuss these differences in depth. The next section provides a brief overview of the prevalence and types of pain in individuals with intellectual and developmental disabilities. Readers desiring a more extended coverage are referred to the excellent review by Bottos and Chambers (2006).

IV. PAIN PREVALENCE IN DD

Research conducted with children and adolescents experiencing intellectual disabilities reveals them to exhibit high levels of pain persistently. Over the course of a month, nearly 80% of the sample was noted by caregivers to experience at least one episode of pain; between one-third and one-half were reported as experiencing pain on a weekly basis (Breau, Camfield, McGrath, & Finley, 2003). Similar findings have been reported by Stallard, Williams, Lenton, and Velleman (2001) and Stallard, Williams, Velleman, Lenton, and McGrath (2002). Looking more closely at the causes of pain, pain from nonaccidental sources has been found to occur at a rate double that for pain resulting from accidents (Breau, Camfield, McGrath, & Finley, 2003) and the former type of pain is typically judged to be more severe in nature. These rates of pain exceed those for children absent of disabilities. Pain knows no boundaries within DD, being highly prevalent in persons with Down syndrome, autism, and CP (see review by Bottos & Chambers, 2006).

To aid in understanding the complexity and severity of pain in persons with DD, consider the person with CP. CP is a term that refers to a group of nonprogressive chronic conditions affecting body movements and muscle coordination. It results from damage to one or more specific areas of the brain, usually happening during fetal development, during or following birth, or during infancy. Depending on the extent of brain damage, one or more of the following may occur: muscle tightness or spasm; involuntary movement; disturbance in gait and mobility; abnormal sensation and perception; impairment of sight, hearing, or speech; and seizures. The motor impairments are diverse, including spasticity (muscular hypertonicity with increased tendon reflexes), rigidity (excessive muscle stiffness), dystonia (disordered tonicity of the muscles), athetosis (writhing movements that are slow and uncontrolled), and ataxia (generalized instability in movement). Treatments commonly include physiotherapy, orthopedic surgery, neurosurgery, and medication (Oberlander & Craig, 2003).

The plight of someone with CP and pain is no better illustrated than in the case of Tracy Latimer. Below is a brief verbatim synopsis from a Canadian Broadcast News report:

Robert Latimer, a farmer working a spread in Saskatchewan northwest of Saskatoon, killed his 12-year-old daughter Tracy on October 24, 1993. There has never been any doubt about this. Latimer told police he did it. He said he loved his daughter and could not bear to watch her suffer from a severe form of cerebral palsy. So he placed her in the cab of his Chevy pickup, ran a hose from the exhaust to the cab, climbed into the box of the truck, sat on a tire and watched her die. Tracy was a 40-pound quadriplegic, a 12-year-old who functioned at the level of a 3-month-old. She had been repeatedly operated on and at the time of her murder was due for more surgery, this time to remove a thighbone. She could not walk, talk, or feed herself, though she responded to affection and occasionally smiled. Tracy was in constant, excruciating pain yet, for reasons not entirely clear, could not be treated with a painkiller stronger than Tylenol.

Although this news account says it is unclear why strong analgesics were not administered, concerns elsewhere are expressed that such medications, in combination with her antiepileptic medication, would serve to further suppress her muscle reflexes and inhibit her respiration, rendering her comatose and in need of constant hospitalization and life support. Although postmortems of her situation and the years of ensuing legal battles have done little to suggest treatment alternatives, coverage of this case has done much to raise consciousness (at least in Canada) of the extent of suffering that is possible. Table I succinctly lists the array of conditions that can accompany CP and complicate its care.

V. PAIN AND SELF-INJURIOUS BEHAVIOR

The potential relationship between self-injurious behavior (SIB) and pain needs addressing. SIB is a serious, complex, and multidetermined behavior that can serve varied functions (attention, escape, nonsocial, physical, and tangible). We (Baldridge & Andrasik, in preparation) and others (Bosch, Van Dyke, Smith, & Poulton, 1997), however, have found instances where such behavior has been indicative of an underlying pain condition. DG,

TABLE I
OTHER CONDITIONS CONTRIBUTING TO PAIN IN PERSONS WITH CEREBRAL PALSY

Placement of gastric feeding devices	Gastroesophagel reflux
Release of muscular contractures	Constipation
Needle injections	Abdominal gas
Blood pressure tests	Muscle spasms
Surgeries	Joint problems
Medical examinations	Headaches
Enemas	Earaches
Dental procedures	Seizures
Dislocated hips	

a person seen at a developmental center, had a long-standing history of pounding and pulling on his ears (Baldridge & Andrasik, in preparation). This behavior resulted in sores on his ears that would not heal and, as a result, gave his ears a cauliflower appearance. At times, he would remain in bed in a fetal position, crying, and displaying a furrowed brow. At other times, he frequently moved about. Prior medical evaluations completed by his attending physician and an ENT consultation all proved to be negative. When a careful functional analysis performed by his treating psychologist was unable to identify controlling environmental factors, our thoughts turned to the possibility of an underlying pain condition (noticing his behavior being similar to that of a colicky infant). Following more in-depth interviews some direct care staff opined that DG simply did not look comfortable at the times when SIB was in evidence. Observation revealed him to have excessive flatus. A review of his medications indicated that he was receiving Lactulose, a medicine known to promote abdominal cramping and gas. The Lactulose was discontinued and changed to Miralax, a medication whose different mechanism of action lessens these particular side effects. After a few days, DG was noted as more comfortable, being now able to rest quietly absent of whining and the drawing up of his legs. A short time later his ears began to heal. A year later, staff reported his SIB as infrequent.

Isolated cases of ours and others reported in the literature (Bosch et al., 1997) do not inform us of the prevalence of pain and SIB. Rather, they serve to remind us of the importance of utilizing the multidisciplinary team approach when evaluating and treating persons suspected of having an underlying pain disorder. In cases where SIB is present, measures such as the Questions About Behavioral Function (Applegate, Matson, & Cherry, 1999; Paclawskyj, Matson, Rush, Smalls, & Vollmer, 2000) can be invaluable in guiding assessment and treatment efforts.

VI. ASSESSMENT APPROACHES

The "Initiative on Methods, Measurement, and Pain Assessment in Clinical Trials" (IMMPACT) grew out of a recognition that many patients with recurring pain conditions often do not obtain adequate relief and/or experience untoward side effects from extant treatments. They (Turk et al., 2003) recommended that all treatment trials consider incorporating measures for six key domains: (1) pain itself, (2) physical functioning, (3) emotional functioning, (4) participant evaluations of improvement and treatment satisfaction, (5) symptoms and adverse events, and (6) participant disposition. A more recent article from the IMMPACT group (Dworkin et al., 2005) offers more specificity regarding these core domains. These more specific recommendations may be found in Table II. These and subsequent guidelines that have emanated (Turk et al., 2006; von Baeyer & Spagrud, 2007) and will continue to be produced from this emphasis clearly layout the ideal or aspirational

TABLE II

Recommended Core Outcome Measures for Clinical Trials of Chronic Pain Treatment Efficacy and Effectiveness

Pain	
	11-point (0–10) numerical rating scale of pain intensity
	Usage of rescue analgesics
	Categorical rating of pain intensity (none, mild, moderate, & severe) in circumstances in which numerical ratings may be problematic
Physical functioning (either one of two measures)	
	Multidimensional Pain Inventory Interference Scale
	Brief Pain Inventory interference items
Emotional functioning (at least one of two measures)	
	Beck Depression Inventory
	Profile of Mood States
Participant ratings of global improvement and satisfaction with treatment	
	Patient Global Impression of Change
Symptoms and adverse events	
	Passive capture of spontaneously reported adverse events and symptoms and use of open-ended prompts
Participant disposition	
	Detailed information regarding participant recruitment, and progress through the trial, including all information specified in the CONSORT guidelines

Dworkin et al., 2005. Permission granted by the International Association for the Study of Pain.

approach, which is consistent with the biopsychosocial model reviewed in brief earlier. Unfortunately, the current state of affairs concerning pain assessment with DD is far from the ideal. In the sections that remain we summarize what little is known about pain assessment.

As already mentioned, the assessment of pain for individuals experiencing developmental disabilities poses a special challenge for health care professionals. The ability to comprehend and translate a pain sensation may be compromised for those with cognitive deficits. In cases where there are language deficits, nonverbal communication should be explored in relation to pain expression (Anand & Craig, 1996). Davies and Evans (2001) advise nurses to acknowledge and observe other modes of communication for those who are learning disabled. Here we review issues in utilizing self-report, proxy report, observational tools, and physiological responses, as these are the domains that have been focused on to date in individuals who are DD.

VII. SELF-REPORT

Self-report has been regarded as the "gold standard" in pain assessment (Anand & Craig, 1996; Bodfish, Harper, Deacon, Deacon, & Symons, 2006; Foley & McCutcheon, 2004). This method, however, is undermined when patients are unable to verbalize the characteristics of their pain. Even if an individual can signify the presence of pain, s/he may have trouble quantifying, (Cook, Niven, & Downs, 1999), specifying the location, or describing the pain experience (Foley & McCutcheon, 2004). The Colored Analogue Scale (CAS) (McGrath et al., 1996) and the Faces Pain Scale (FPS) (e.g., Bieri, Reeve, Champion, Addicoat, & Ziegler, 1990) were designed to aid young children in self-reporting the degree of their pain and may be appropriate for those who have mild cognitive impairment (see Fig.1 for an example).

FIG. 1. Wong and Baker (1988) Faces scale. • *Face 0* is very happy because he or she doesn't hurt at all. • *Face 1* hurts just a little bit. • *Face 2* hurts a little more. • *Face 3* hurts even more. • *Face 4* hurts a whole lot. • *Face 5* hurts as much as you can imagine, although you don't have to be crying to feel this bad.

The CAS is an alternative to the Visual Analogue Scale (VAS), which is a numerically anchored scale used with cognitively intact adults. The CAS is a vertical scale, much like a thermometer, with progressively darker shades of red moving upward on the scale to illustrate more pain intensity (McGrath et al., 1996). Children are instructed to move a marker on the scale where the gradation of color best reflects their pain intensity. The scale has numerical values on the back for clinicians to document the child's response. McGrath et al. found the CAS to be a simple, practical tool with preliminary validity to assess pain in those ages 5–16.

Although the CAS may facilitate the self-report for pain in children, it has some limitations for DD individuals. LaChapelle, Hadjistavropoulos, and Craig (1999) implemented the CAS for their study of adults ranging from borderline to severe mental retardation (mean IQ = 45, SD = 15.1). Participants who were able to provide a self-report of pain before and during an injection had unreliable CAS ratings. This could be due to difficulties in comprehending the CAS instructions, difficulties in self-reporting pain, or both.

The FPS is another tool intended to assist in the self-reporting of pain in children. There are several different versions of the FPS. One example is the FPS developed by Bieri et al. (1990) who recruited first and third graders to draw faces with assorted levels of pain. Seven faces with increasing pain levels were derived from the children's schematics. This initial FPS was found to have nearly equal intervals and appeared to be a valid measure of pain intensity for those ages 6–8, and for children as young as 3. The FPS was later revised from seven to six faces in order to translate the measure numerically into a 0–5 or 0–10 metric scale (FPS-R; Hicks, von Baeyer, Spafford, van Korlaar, & Goodenough, 2001). The FPS-R was found to be suitable for children who were at least 4 or 5 years old.

Various versions of the FPS may include three, five, six, or seven pain face intensities. Another feature that deviates for each FPS version is whether the first, "no pain" face is neutral or smiling, or whether tears are included in the higher intensity pain faces. The FPS (Bieri et al., 1990) and FPS-R (Hicks et al., 2001) have neutral "no pain" faces and there are no tears present. There has been some debate as to whether the different versions of the FPS measures pain intensity or pain distress. One study reported consistently higher pain ratings from both children and parents with FPS versions including smiling, "no pain" faces, even though children and parents preferred scales with "happy" and cartoon-like faces (Chambers, Giesbrecht, Craig, Bennett, & Huntsman, 1999). A subsequent study found that nurses also reported higher patient pain ratings for scales with a smiling, "no pain" face compared to a neutral, "no pain" face (Chambers, Hardial, Craig, Court, & Montgomery, 2005). These factors need to be taken into consideration when obtaining pain intensity ratings. Additionally, age and mental capabilities should also be taken into account with self-report measures.

Although the FPS-R was found to be appropriate for those who are at least 4 or 5 (Hicks et al., 2001), another study found that their sample of 3- to 6-year olds had trouble with this scale (Stanford, Chambers, & Craig, 2006). While the children who were 6 were able to use the FPS-R more accurately than the 5-year olds and the 5-year olds more accurately than the 4-year olds, and so forth, more than half of the 6-year olds in the study had trouble with this scale. Due to some of these inconsistent findings, Stinson, Kavanagh, Yamada, Gill, and Stevens (2006) have listed some guidelines for the use of self-report assessment tools with children. The authors propose the use of FPS-R with children ages 4–12, but that any self-report response for children ages 3–7 be supplemented with other observational measures. In some instances, clinicians may overestimate a child's ability to self-report and should also obtain proxy reports in addition to observational assessments (Breau, McGrath, & Zabalia, 2006).

Depending on the mental age of a DD individual, the CAS and a version of the FPS may be appropriate to aid self-reported pain. There are, however, some limitations of these tools such as comprehension of the instructions and reliability of the ratings. Despite some of the shortcomings with self-report measures, it is still worthwhile to attempt obtaining such reports from young children (Stanford, Chambers, & Craig, 2006) and DD individuals who posses appropriate understanding (Hadjistavropoulos, von Baeyer, & Craig, 2001). When self-reports are not an option or are suspected to be unreliable, health care professionals may turn to proxy reports of parents and other caregivers for pain details.

VIII. PROXY REPORT

Parents and other caregivers can corroborate self-reports and speak on behalf of those who cannot verbalize a self-report. According to a survey, physicians and nurses prefer self-report for children without cognitive impairments or children with mild impairments and proxy reports for children who have moderate or severe cognitive impairments (Fanurik et al., 1999). Parents and other caregivers who are familiar with a child's or DD adult's routine behaviors can provide valuable information.

Fanurik, Koh, Schmitz, Harrison, and Conrad (1999) divide pain expression of children with cognitive impairment into direct or indirect behaviors. Direct pain expression includes the child's effort to communicate the pain and its location, verbalizing the presence of pain without localization, and localization of pain with nonverbal behavior. In contrast, indirect pain expression includes inferred pain through behaviors such as crying, facial movements, physical or emotional changes, and self-injury behaviors. Sixty-six percent of parents with children who are mild to moderately impaired report an ability to determine pain in their child through direct expression, whereas 90% of parents with severe to profound impaired children infer the presence of pain through indirect pain expressions. If someone is unfamiliar with a child who has a cognitive impairment, such as a health care professional, pain behaviors may be misinterpreted.

Pain assessment is further complicated in that individuals with DD may display atypical pain patterns (McGrath, Rosmus, Canfield, Campbell, & Hennigar, 1998). Caregivers are in a position to distinguish unique behaviors that may be suggestive of the presence of pain. For instance, parents have reported that cries of a certain tone, laughing, seizures, self-abusive behaviors, particular postures, and changes in eating, sleeping, and socializing patterns may be indicative of pain (Carter, McArthur, & Cunliffe, 2002; Hadden & von Baeyer, 2002). These pain behaviors may not be obvious to someone other than the caregiver.

Fanurik, Koh, Schmitz, Harrison, and Conrad (1999) found that several parents of children with cognitive impairment believe that pain is often underestimated and undertreated in their child. Even parents (Chambers, Reid, Craig, McGrath, & Finley, 1998) and nurses (Romsing, Moller-Sonnergaard, Hertel, & Rasmussen, 1996) have been found to underestimate pain in children without any cognitive impairment. Overall, it appears as though pain intensity is miscalculated in children with or without cognitive impairment. Although parents may be able to detect subtle pain behaviors, there are factors that may influence the accuracy of their proxy report.

Breau et al. (2003) found that some caregivers have a preexisting belief that children with cognitive impairment are less sensitive to pain compared to nonimpaired children (see earlier discussion of this topic). The investigators of this study suggest that this belief may be due to health care professionals shaping parent's beliefs on their child's sensitivity to pain. Another explanation is that this belief may be protective because parents often have to witness their child undergoing a number of painful procedures. Regardless of how the belief was formed, it can lead to caregivers underestimating pain. This same study also found that caregivers had beliefs based on a child's cognitive level and reaction to pain. It was believed that children with mild or moderate impairment may over-react to pain compared to nonimpaired children. On the contrary, it was believed that an extreme reaction from children with severe or profound impairments was associated with a great amount of pain. The basis of these beliefs is unclear, but they can interfere with an accurate parental assessment of pain.

Nader, Oberlander, Chambers, and Craig (2004) investigated parent reports of venipuncture pain in children with autism and children who were unimpaired. The facial activity of the children in both groups was found to be similar during the venipuncture. Parent reports of pain for the nonimpaired children showed greater concordance with facial activity than the parental reports of pain for the autistic children. In fact, the children who were autistic had greater facial activity and were judged to be less sensitive and reactive by their parents. Again, it is unclear as to why the parents of autistic children underestimated their child's pain.

Caregivers are in a position to identify expressions and behaviors that can predict the presence of pain that would be otherwise undetectable to a person not familiar with the individual. Even so, caregiver beliefs and attitudes can affect the accuracy of such reports. While self-report and proxy reports are subjective in nature, observational methods are more objective. Caregivers, nurses, and physicians have assisted in the development of observational assessment tools.

IX. OBSERVATIONAL METHODS

As noted in the study of autistic and nonimpaired children, facial expressions are a nonverbal cue that can signify pain. The frequency and intensity of facial activity can convey an expression of pain. LaChapelle et al. (1999) found that the frequency of chin raises in addition to the intensity of brow lowering and chin raises is significant in indicating pain during a vaccination. Prkachin (2005) asserts that brow-lowering, eyelid tightening with raised cheeks, nose wrinkling, and eyes closing are facial movements commonly associated with pain. Facial expressions are frequently included in pain behavior assessment tools.

One of the first studies on common pain behaviors in those with CP was a list of pain behaviors observed by physicians (Giusiano, Jimeno, Collignon, & Chau, 1995). McGrath et al. (1998) enlisted caregivers to provide a list of pain behaviors. Common behaviors were organized into a 31-item checklist and this devise came to be known as the Non-Communicating Children's Pain Checklist (NCCPC). It consists of seven categories of behaviors: vocal, eating/sleeping, social/personality, facial expression of pain, activity, body and limbs, and physiological. The NCCPC has been demonstrated to be a valid and reliable tool in evaluating pain in nonverbal children (Breau, McGrath, Camfield, Rosmus, & Finley, 2000).

Breau, Camfield, McGrath, Rosmus, and Finley (2001) conducted an item analysis, excluding the eating/sleeping category, of the NCCPC and found that seven of the items are particularly reliable for pain compared to distress. Two of these items, cranky and seeks comfort, were from the social category. One item, change in eyes (squeezing eyes, eyes wide open, and eyes frown) was from the facial expression category. Another item, less active, was from the activity category. One item, gestures to body part that hurts, was from the body and limb category. The last two items, tears and sharp intake of breath or gasping, were from the physiological category. Although the entire checklist may offer an overall picture of pain, this subgroup of items could be utilized as an abbreviated assessment method.

A series of other studies have used modified versions of the NCCPC and, in doing so, have replicated its validity. Breau, Camfield et al. (2003) proposed a revised version (NCCPC-R) that is composed of 30 out of the original 31 items with a rating system of 0–3 assigned to each item. In order to document its validity, caregivers of children with severe cognitive impairments were instructed to record during 2-h observations for a duration when the child was in pain and a duration in which the child was without pain. The observers rated each item as follows: 0 for a behavior that did "not occur at all," 1 for a behavior that occurred "just a little," 2 for a behavior that occurred "fairly often," and a 3 for a behavior that occurred "very often." Possible scores on the checklist ranged from 0–90. A score of 7 or more suggested the presence of pain.

Breau, Finley, McGrath, and Camfield (2002) created another adaptation of the NCCPC, the postoperative version (NCCPC-PV), and investigated whether ratings from individuals unfamiliar with a cognitively impaired child would be consistent with the caregivers' ratings. The NCCPC-PV excludes the eating/sleeping category and each of the remaining 27 items is assigned a rating of 0–3 based on the frequency of the behavior, similar to that of the NCCPC-R. Good inter-rater reliability was established between the caregiver, a researcher, and a nurse. A score of 11 on the NCCPC-PV indicated moderate to severe pain. This study demonstrated that an individual other than the caregiver can reliably observe pain behaviors from the checklist. Hadden and von Baeyer (2005) utilized the NCCPC-PV for children with CP before, during, and after stretching exercises. They found that a significantly greater number of pain behaviors on the checklist occurred during the stretching compared to the time before and after the stretching.

Other research on common pain behaviors has been undertaken. Stallard, Willliams, Velleman, Lenton, and McGrath (2002) investigated behaviors associated with chronic pain. Caregivers of noncommunicating children were interviewed and a total of 203 pain cues were identified. The researchers categorized these behaviors into 11 categories: vocal, facial, physical, withdrawal, seeks comfort, physiological, agitation, tense, inconsolable, pain sites, and anger/irritability. Of these categories, vocal, facial, and inconsolable were determined to signify definite and severe pain. Six specific cues from five of the categories were deemed significant in denoting the presence of pain: cries, screams/yells, face screwed up, flinches from contact, appears tense, and unable to be comforted. In a subsequent study, Stallard et al. (2002) termed these six behaviors as the Pain Indicator for Communicatively Impaired Children (PICIC). The behavior of screwed up/distressed face was shown to be the strongest predictor of the presence of pain. The five other cues were also significant taken together, but it is more likely to indicate "possible pain."

Terstegen, Koot, de Boer, and Tibboel (2003) studied pain behaviors before and after surgery in children who had profound cognitive impairments. The frequency of 134 potential pain behaviors categorized as facial expressions, motor behaviors, social behaviors/mood, attitude toward sore body part, vocalization, and physiological were observed. It was found that 23 of these behaviors were distinct in signifying pain. Four of these items on the checklist that were not present before surgery but appeared after surgery were trembling chin, protecting sore body part, crying hard/loudly, and breath holding. Moreover, the behaviors "eyes squeezed" and "trembling chin" reflected pain intensity.

Zwakhalen, van Dongen, Hamers, and Abu-Saad (2004) surveyed nurses who work at institutions for profound intellectually disabled persons. Nurses were instructed to rate 158 pain indicators on a scale of 1–10 based on observations they use in assessing pain in their patients. More than half of the nurses deemed seven of the pain cues as important, which are as follows: moaning during manipulation, crying during manipulation, painful facial expression during manipulation, swelling, screaming during manipulation, not using the sore body part, and moving the body in a specific way.

It appears as though a number of common pain behaviors can be detected from the diverse population of cognitively impaired individuals. There is some overlap among the aforementioned checklists in terms of nonverbal vocalizations and facial expressions. Additionally, it seems as though a number of core pain cues can be derived from each assessment measure. There are, however, some internal contradictions. For instance, in the various versions of the NCCPC items such as "tense" and "floppy," "less active" and "jumping around," and "seeks comfort" and "inconsolable" are opposing behaviors. This suggests that in addition to common pain expressions, there are also behaviors that are distinctive for each individual. Even though a person may react differently to pain compared to another person, parents have reported that their children respond to pain in a predictable manner

(Carter et al., 2002). Observational methods coupled with proxy reports may provide a more accurate means of detecting pain.

An assessment tool involving observation and proxy reports is the Face Legs Activity Cry and Consolability (FLACC) (Malviya, Voepel-Lewis, Burke, Merkel, & Tait, 2006). The name of this method reflects the categories contained within. A rating of 0–2 is assigned to each of the five categories, where 0 is usual behavior, 1 is occasional pain behaviors associated with each category, and 3 is more intense pain behaviors (Table III). In addition to these general ratings, caregivers also give input about idiosyncratic pain behaviors expressed by the cognitively impaired child. This tool is an individualized approach to assessment, where both common and unique pain behaviors are observed and rated. We have found great utility with this measure at our work at a developmental center, modifying categories to track behaviors specific to individuals being treated.

Observational instruments can be of great assistance to caregivers, physicians, and nurses in assessing pain in cognitively impaired individuals. A majority of the research has focused on pain behaviors associated with acute pain, such as postoperative pain and needle injections (Stallard, Williams, Lenton, & Velleman, 2001). It is unclear whether the same behaviors for acute pain would apply to chronic pain or if the cues are more subtle and difficult to detect (Stallard, Williams, Velleman, Lenton, & McGrath, 2002).

TABLE III
FLACC

	Scoring		
Category	1	2	3
Face	No particular expression or smile	Occasional grimace or frown, withdrawn, disinterested	Frequent to constant quivering chin, clenched jaw
Legs	Normal position or relaxed	Uneasy, restless, tense	Kicking, or legs drawn up
Activity	Lying quietly, normal position, moves easily	Squirming, shifting back and forth, tense	Arched, rigid or jerking
Cry	No cry (awake or asleep)	Moans or whimpers; occasional complaint	Crying steadily, screams or sobs, frequent complaints
Consolability	Content, relaxed	Reassured by occasional touching, hugging or being talked to, distractible	Difficult to console or comfort

X. PHYSIOLOGICAL MEASURES

In the previously described survey conducted by Zwakhalen et al. (2004), nurses had rated physiological measures as a source for determining pain in their patients. These include turning red in the face, vomiting, gasping for breath, changes in respiration, an increase or decrease in heart, and breath holding. The various adaptations of the NCCPC consist of a physiological category with items such as shivering, change in color/pallor, sweating, tears, sharp intake of breath/gasping, and breath-holding (Breau, Finley et al., 2002; Breau, Camfield et al., 2003; McGrath et al., 1998). These cues are attributed to distress (Hadjistavropoulos et al., 2001) and possible symptoms of pain (Zwakhalen et al., 2004), rather than pain directly.

The Royal College of Paediatrics and Child Health (1997, as cited in Davies & Evans, 2001) contends that physiological responses to pain vary between children and adults, and between individuals who are cognitively impaired and individuals who are unimpaired. It has been suggested that there is a higher incidence of pain insensitivity and indifference in cognitively impaired individuals (Biersdorff, 1991) and that some of these individuals have higher pain thresholds (Biersdorff, 1994). In a study of a small sample of neurologically impaired adolescents, mean heart rate, and heart rate variability were not significantly different between the baseline measure and the vaccination measure (Oberlander, Gilbert, Chambers, O'Donnell, & Craig, 1999).

While some individuals who are cognitively impaired may have a reduced physiological response to pain, this does not generalize to all individuals with cognitive impairment. Defrin, Pick, Peretz, and Carmeli (2004) found that individuals with DD were actually more sensitive to pain than a nonimpaired comparison group, but that there was a delayed reaction to pain. It is not fully known how pain sensation, perception, and cognitive processes affect physiological responses. Due to these inconsistent findings, physiological measures in cognitively impaired individuals are not recommended as a sole pain assessment technique (Breau et al., 2006).

In summary, presumed insensitivity to pain in the DD may be a consequence of communication barriers. In a study on developmentally delayed children, the older children were found to respond to pain with more anger (Gilbert-MacLeod, Craig, Rocha, & Mathias, 2000). This may be a learned behavior for gaining attention to communicate the presence of pain. If an individual displays atypical pain behaviors and reacts differently to pain, it cannot be concluded that s/he is not experiencing pain. In order to understand the pain in the DD, the assessment tools of self-report, proxy report, observational methods, and physiological measures can be employed. Each of these methods has its advantages and disadvantages. A multidimensional approach in combining these evaluative tools would be more likely to reveal an overall, accurate picture of pain.

REFERENCES

Anand, K. J. S., & Craig, K. D. (1996). New perspectives on the definition of pain. *Pain, 67,* 3–6.

Applegate, H., Matson, J. L., & Cherry, K. E. (1999). An evaluation of functional variables affecting severe problem behaviors in adults with mental retardation by using the Questions about Behavioral Function Scale (QABF). *Research in Developmental Disabilities, 20,* 229–237.

Baldridge, K., & Andrasik, F. (in preparation). Barriers to effective pain management in people with mental retardation/developmental disabilities.

Biersdorff, K. K. (1991). Pain insensitivity and indifference: Alternative explanations for some medical catastrophes. *Mental Retardation, 29,* 359–362.

Biersdorff, K. K. (1994). Incidence of significantly altered pain experience among individuals with developmental disabilities. *American Journal on Mental Retardation, 98,* 619–631.

Bieri, D., Reeve, R. A., Champion, D., Addicoat, L., & Ziegler, J. B. (1990). The Faces Pain Scale for the self-assessment of the severity of pain experienced by children: Development, initial validation, and preliminary investigation for ratio scale properties. *Pain, 41,* 139–150.

Bodfish, J. W., Harper, V. N., Deacon, J. M., Deacon, J. R., & Symons, F. J. (2006). Issues in pain assessment for adults with severe to profound mental retardation. In T. F. Oberlander & F. J. Symons (Eds.), *Pain in children and adults with developmental disabilities* (pp. 173–192). Baltimore, MD: Paul H. Brookes Publishing.

Bosch, J., Van Dyke, D. C., Smith, S. M., & Poulton, S. (1997). Role of medical conditions in the exacerbation of self-injurious behavior: An exploratory study. *Mental Retardation, 35,* 124–130.

Bottos, S., & Chambers, C. T. (2006). The epidemiology of pain in developmental disabilities. In T. F. Oberlander & F. J. Symons (Eds.), *Pain in children and adults with developmental disabilities* (pp. 67–87). Baltimore: Paul H. Brookes Publishing.

Breau, L. M., Camfield, C. S., McGrath, P. J., & Finley, G. A. (2003). The incidence of pain in children with severe cognitive impairments. *Archives of Pediatric and Adolescent Medicine, 157,* 1219–1226.

Breau, L. M., Camfield, C., McGrath, P. J., Rosmus, C., & Finley, G. A. (2001). Measuring pain accurately in children with cognitive impairments: Refinement of a caregiver scale. *The Journal of Pediatrics, 138,* 721–727.

Breau, L. M., Finley, G. A., McGrath, P. J., & Camfield, C. S. (2002). Validation of the non-communicating children's pain checklist-postoperative version. *Anesthesiology, 96,* 528–535.

Breau, L. M., MacLaren, J., McGrath, P. J., Camfield, C. S., & Finley, A. F. (2003). Caregivers' beliefs regarding pain in children with cognitive impairment: Relation between pain sensation and reaction increases with severity of impairment. *The Clinical Journal of Pain, 19,* 335–344.

Breau, L. M., McGrath, P. J., Camfield, C., Rosmus, C., & Finley, G. A. (2000). Preliminary validation of an observational pain checklist for persons with cognitive impairments and inability to communicate verbally. *Developmental Medicine and Child Neurology, 42,* 609–616.

Breau, L. M., McGrath, P. J., & Zabalia, M. (2006). Assessing pediatric pain and developmental disabilities. In T. F. Oberlander & F. J. Symons (Eds.), *Pain in children and adults with developmental disabilities* (pp. 149–172). Baltimore, MD: Paul H. Brookes Publishing.

Carter, B., McArthur, E., & Cunliffe, M. (2002). Dealing with uncertainty: Parental assessment of pain in their children with profound special needs. *Journal of Advanced Nursing, 38,* 449–457.

Chambers, C. T., Giesbrecht, K., Craig, K. D., Bennett, S. M., & Huntsman, E. (1999). A comparison of faces scales for the measurement of pediatric pain: Children's and parents' ratings. *Pain, 83,* 25–35.

Chambers, C. T., Hardial, J., Craig, K. D., Court, C., & Montgomery, C. (2005). Faces scales for the measurement of postoperative pain intensity in children following minor surgery. *The Clinical Journal of Pain, 21,* 277–285.

Chambers, C. T., Reid, G. J., Craig, K. D., McGrath, P. J., & Finley, G. A. (1998). Agreement between child and parent reports of pain. *The Clinical Journal of Pain, 14,* 336–342.

Cook, A. K. R., Niven, C. A., & Downs, M. G. (1999). Assessing the pain of people with cognitive impairment. *International Journal of Geriatric Psychiatry, 14,* 421–425.

Crombie, I. K., Croft, P. R., Linton, S. J., LeResche, L., & Von Korff, M. (1999). *Epidemiology of pain.* Seattle: International Association for the Study of Pain.

Davies, D., & Evans, L. (2001). Assessing pain in people with profound learning disabilities. *British Journal of Nursing, 10,* 513–516.

Defrin, R., Pick, C. G., Peretz, C., & Carmeli, E. (2004). A quantitative somatosensory testing of pain threshold in individuals with mental retardation. *Pain, 108,* 58–66.

Dworkin, R. H., Turk, D. C., Farrar, J. T., Haythornthwaite, J. A., Jensen, M. P., Katz, N. P., et al. (2005). Core outcome measures for chronic pain clinical trials: IMMPACT recommendations. *Pain, 113,* 9–19.

Fanurik, D., Koh, J. L., Schmitz, M. L., Harrison, R. D., & Conrad, T. M. (1999). Children with cognitive impairment: Parent report of pain and coping. *Journal of Developmental and Behavioral Pediatrics, 20,* 228–234.

Fanurik, D., Koh, J. L., Schmitz, M. L., Harrison, R. D., Roberson, P. K., & Killebrew, P. (1999). Pain assessment and treatment in children with cognitive impairment: A survey of nurses' and physicians' beliefs. *The Clinical Journal of Pain, 15,* 304–312.

Foley, D. C., & McCutcheon, H. (2004). Detecting pain in people with an intellectual disability. *Accident and Emergency Nursing, 12,* 196–200.

Gilbert-MacLeod, C. A., Craig, K. D., Rocha, E. M., & Mathias, M. D. (2000). Everyday pain responses in children with and without developmental delays. *Journal of Pediatric Psychology, 25,* 301–308.

Giusiano, B., Jimeno, M. T., Collignon, P., & Chau, Y. (1995). Utilization of a neural network in the elaboration of an evaluation scale for pain in cerebral palsy. *Methods Information in Medicine, 34,* 498–502.

Hadden, K. L., & von Baeyer, C. L. (2002). Pain in children with cerebral palsy: Common triggers and expressive behaviors. *Pain, 99,* 281–288.

Hadden, K. L., & von Baeyer, C. L. (2005). Global and specific behavioral measures of pain in children with cerebral palsy. *The Clinical Journal of Pain, 21,* 140–146.

Hadjistavropoulos, T., von Baeyer, C., & Craig, K. D. (2001). Pain assessment in persons with limited ability to communicate. In D. C. Turk & R. Melzack (Eds.), *Handbook of pain assessment* (2nd ed., pp. 134–148). New York: Guilford Press.

Hennequin, M., Morin, C., & Feine, J. S. (2000). Pain expression and stimulus localization in individuals with Down's syndrome. *Lancet, 356,* 1882–1887.

Hicks, C. L., von Baeyer, C. L., Spafford, P. A., van Korlaar, I., & Goodenough, B. (2001). The Faces Pain Scale-Revised: Toward a common metric in pediatric pain measurement. *Pain, 93,* 173–183.

International Association for the Study of Pain (1986). Classification of chronic pain: Descriptions of chronic pain syndromes and definitions of pain terms. *Pain, 3*(Suppl. 3), S1–S225.

Katz, J. N. (2006). Lumbar disc disorders and low-back pain: Socioeconomic factors and consequences. *Journal of Bone and Joint Surgery, 88-A* (Suppl.), 225–226.

LaChapelle, D. L., Hadjistavropoulos, T., & Craig, K. D. (1999). Pain measurement in persons with intellectual disabilities. *The Clinical Journal of Pain, 15,* 13–23.

Malviya, S., Voepel-Lewis, T., Burke, C., Merkel, S., & Tait, A. R. (2006). The revised FLACC observational pain tool: Improved reliability and validity for pain assessment in children with cognitive impairment. *Pediatric Anesthesia, 16,* 258–265.

McGrath, P. A., Seifert, C. E., Speechley, K. N., Booth, J. C., Stitt, L., & Gibson, M. C. (1996). A new analogue scale for assessing children's pain: An initial validation study. *Pain, 64,* 435–443.

McGrath, P. J., Rosmus, C., Canfield, C., Campbell, M. A., & Hennigar, A. (1998). Behaviours caregivers use to determine pain in non-verbal, cognitively impaired individuals. *Developmental Medicine and Child Neurology, 40,* 340–343.

Nader, R., Oberlander, T. F., Chambers, C. T., & Craig, K. D. (2004). Expression of pain in children with autism. *The Clinical Journal of Pain, 20,* 88–97.

Oberlander, T. F., & Craig, K. D. (2003). Pain in children with developmental disabilities. In N. L. Schechter, C. B. Berde, & M. Yaster (Eds.), *Pain in infants, children, and adolescents* (pp. 599–619). Philadelphia, PA: Lippincott Williams & Wilkins.

Oberlander, T. F., Gilbert, C. A., Chambers, C. T., O'Donnell, M. E., & Craig, K. D. (1999). Biobehavioral responses to acute pain in adolescents with a significant neurologic impairment. *The Clinical Journal of Pain, 15,* 201–209.

Paclawskyj, T. R., Matson, J. L., Rush, K. S., Smalls, Y., & Vollmer, T. R. (2000). Questions about Behavioral Function (QABF): A behavioral checklist for functional assessment of aberrant behavior. *Research in Developmental Disabilities, 21,* 223–229.

Prkachin, K. M. (2005). The consistency of facial expressions of pain. In P. Ekman & E. L. Rosenberg (Eds.), *What the face reveals: Basic and applied studies of spontaneous expression using the Facial Action Coding System (FACS)* (2nd ed., pp. 181–197). New York: Oxford University Press.

Romsing, J., Moller-Sonnergaard, J., Hertel, S., & Rasmussen, M. (1996). Postoperative pain in children: Comparison between ratings of children and nurses. *Journal of Pain and Symptom Management, 11,* 42–46.

Stallard, P., Williams, L., Lenton, S., & Velleman, R. (2001). Pain in cognitively impaired, non-communicating children. *Archives of Disease in Childhood, 85,* 460–462.

Stallard, P., Williams, L., Velleman, R., Lenton, S., & McGrath, P. J. (2002). Brief report: Behaviors identified by caregivers to detect pain in noncommunicating children. *Journal of Pediatric Psychology, 27,* 209–214.

Stallard, P., Williams, L., Velleman, R., Lenton, S., McGrath, P. J., & Taylor, G. (2002). The development and evaluation of the pain indicator for communicatively impaired children (PICIC). *Pain, 98,* 145–149.

Stanford, E. A., Chambers, C. T., & Craig, K. D. (2006). The role of developmental factors in predicting young children's use of a self-report scale for pain. *Pain, 120,* 16–23.

Stinson, J. N., Kavanagh, T., Yamada, J., Gill, N., & Stevens, B. (2006). Systematic review of the psychometric properties, interpretability and feasibility of self-report pain intensity measures for use in clinical trials in children and adolescents. *Pain, 125*(1–2), 143–157.

Terstegen, C., Koot, H. M., de Boer, J. B., & Tibboel, D. (2003). Measuring pain in children with cognitive impairment: Pain response to surgical procedures. *Pain, 103,* 187–198.

Turk, D., & Flor, H. (1999). Chronic pain: A biobehavioral perspective. In R. J. Gatchel & D. C. Turk (Eds.), *Psychosocial factors in pain.* NY: Guilford Press.

Turk, D. C., Dworkin, R. H., Allen, R. R., Bellamy, N., Brandenburg, N., Carr, D. B., et al. (2003). Core outcome domains for chronic pain clinical trials: IMMPACT recommendations. *Pain, 106,* 337–345.

Turk, D. C., Dworkin, R. H., Burke, L. B., Gershon, R., Rothman, M., Scott, J., et al. (2006). Developing patient-reported outcome measures for pain clinical trials: IMMPACT recommendations. *Pain, 125,* 208–215.

Verhaak, P. F. M., Kerssens, J. J., Dekker, J., Sorbi, M. J., & Bensing, J. M. (1998). Prevalence of chronic benign pain disorder among adults: A review of the literature. *Pain, 77,* 231–239.

von Baeyer, C. L., & Spagrud, L. J. (2007). Systematic review of observational (behavioral) measures of pain for children and adolescents aged 3 to 18 years. *Pain, 127,* 140–150.

Wong, D., & Baker, C. (1988). Pain in children: Comparison of assessment scales. *Pediatric Nursing, 14,* 9–17.

Zwakhalen, S. M. G., van Dongen, K. A. J., Hamers, J. P. H., & Abu-Saad, H. H. (2004). Pain assessment in intellectually disabled people: Non-verbal indicators. *Journal of Advanced Nursing, 45,* 236–245.

Index

I

Q

R

S

T

Contents of Previous Volumes

Volume 3

Volume 4

Volume 5

Volume 6

Volume 7

Volume 8

Volume 12

Volume 13

Volume 14

Volume 15

Volume 16

Volume 17

Volume 18

Volume 19

Volume 20

Volume 21

Volume 22

Volume 23

Volume 24

Volume 25

Volume 26

Volume 27

Volume 28

Volume 29

Volume 30

Volume 31

Volume 32

Volume 33